BIOLOGICAL PSYCHOLOGY

THIRD EDITION

To my parents, Edward and Rachael Kalat
and my in-laws, David and Sara Pickard

About the Author

James W. Kalat (rhymes with ballot), born in
1946, received an A.B. degree summa cum laude
from Duke University in 1968 and a Ph.D. in
psychology in 1971 from the University of
Pennsylvania, where he worked with Paul Rozin.
He was a faculty member at Duke University
from 1971 to 1977 and has been at North
Carolina State University since 1977. He is also
the author of *Introduction to Psychology*,
published by Wadsworth in 1986.

BIOLOGICAL PSYCHOLOGY

THIRD EDITION

James W. Kalat
North Carolina State University

Wadsworth Publishing Company
Belmont, California
A Division of Wadsworth, Inc.

About the cover: Every cell of the nervous system is bounded by a membrane. Embedded in the membrane are receptors that respond to synaptic transmitters, which are chemical messengers released by other neurons. The receptor that responds to the transmitter substance GABA is shown here. Tranquilizers and several other chemicals influence behavior by attaching to sites on this complex and thereby modifying the responsiveness of the GABA receptor.

Psychology Editor: Kenneth King
Production: Del Mar Associates
Designer: Louis Neiheisel
Copy Editor: Jackie Estrada
Photo Researcher: Linda Rill
Illustrator: Linda McVay
Compositor: Thompson Type
Cover: John Odam

Printed in the United States of America
4 5 6 7 8 9 10—92 91 90

ISBN 0-534-08466-4

Library of Congress Cataloging-in-Publication Data
Kalat, James W.
   Biological psychology.

   Bibliography: p.
   Includes index.
   1. Neuropsychology. 2. Psychobiology. I. Title.
[DNLM: 1. Neurophysiology. 2. Psychophysiology.
WL 103 K14b]
QP360.K33 1987   612'.8   87-23137
ISBN 0-534-08466-4

Preface

Biological psychology is the most interesting topic in the world. I am sure every professor and every textbook author feels that way about his or her own topic. But the others are wrong; this really *is* the most interesting topic. It deals with the fundamental questions of what is the human mind, what is its relationship with the brain, how does it work, and why are we the way we are.

My primary goal in writing this text has been to engage the reader's interest. I have tried not to focus on biological mechanisms for their own sake but to concentrate on their relationship to some of the central phenomena of psychology—topics such as the mind-body problem, the evolution of behavior, the relationship of sleep to mood and work efficiency, eating disorders, alcoholism, language development, sexual behavior, psychosomatic illnesses, anxiety, aggressive behavior, amnesia, recovery from brain damage, depression, and schizophrenia. I hope that no reader who finishes the book will still be wondering what the study of the brain has to do with "real psychology."

In a field that progresses as rapidly as biological psychology has, no text can tell the reader everything that is important to know now, much less everything that will be important to know ten years from now. One important function of a text is to give the reader enough background to go to the library to read the latest professional books and journal articles. With that in mind, I have introduced a much expanded glossary, which includes a number of terms that a student might encounter in outside readings, even if the terms are not used in this text. I hope this will prove a useful reference source both during the course and afterward for many students.

The organization of the third edition is the same as the second, with these exceptions: (1) Chapter 1 has been extensively revised, with new sections on issues in the evolution of behavior and the ethics of animal experimentation. (2) The chapter on language and lateralization has been moved from Chapter 13 to Chapter 5. (3) The autonomic nervous system is now discussed in Chapter 4, and ulcers are discussed in the chapter on emotion. In the second edition, both were in Chapter 1.

The main change has been in bringing this text up-to-date. More than one-third of the references in this edition were published in the years 1983–1987. At least small revisions were made in almost every section, other than the Introduction. Two of the BioSketches are new. Many of the illustrations are new or revised, and color has been added throughout. New to this edition are two sections of full-color photos and illustrations.

Some of the new topics in this edition: ways a drug can affect synaptic transmission (Chapter 3), the relationship between brain size and body size (4), the history of prefrontal lobotomy (4), Geschwind's hypothesis on the determination of handedness (5), the controversy on "blindsight" (7), biological rhythms and three kinds of insomnia (9), biological predispositions toward alcohol abuse (10), puberty (11), biological predisposition to panic disorder (12), reference memory and working memory (13), infant amnesia and old-age loss of memory (13), test batteries to evaluate human brain damage (14), sensory neglect and sensory extinction (14), viral hypotheses of depression and schizophrenia (15 and 16), altered sleep patterns as an antidepressant (15), seasonal affective disorder and light therapy (15), and prediction or early diagnosis of schizophrenia (16). Among topics that have been expanded in light of current research are Parkinson's disease and Huntington's disease (8), and tranquilizers and GABA synapses (12).

Each chapter starts with a list of main ideas. Key words appear in boldface the first time they are used and defined. Most chapters include one or more BioSketches of key investigators and one or more Digressions that introduce peripheral but interesting information. Each chapter concludes with a summary, review questions, thought questions that challenge the student to go beyond the text, terms to remember, and suggestions for further reading. The text concludes with the glossary and a thorough subject index and name index. A study guide is available at an additional charge. A manual is also available for instructors who adopt the text.

I have received a great deal of mail from readers of the second edition, both students and faculty. A number of the changes I made were in response to their questions and suggestions. I would like to thank two of those students for their especially helpful comments, William Barto from Seton Hall University and Richard DeWald from the University of Texas. Mr. DeWald provided particularly insightful suggestions for the vision chapter, which led to new ways of presenting lateral inhibition and visual fields.

I thank the reviewers who made extensive and most helpful suggestions based on the second edition or earlier drafts of the third edition: Herbert Alpern, University of Colorado, Boulder; Kent Berridge, University of Michigan; Harry Carlisle, University of California, Santa Barbara; Gaylord Ellison, University of California, Los Angeles; Michael Gardner, Los Angeles Valley College; Joel E. Grace, Mansfield University; Elaine M. Hull, State University of New York, Buffalo; Lynn Nadel, University of Arizona; Peter H. Platenius, Queen's University; Paul R. Sanberg, University of Cincinnati; Roc Walley, University of Alberta. Thanks in particular to Elaine Hull, who not only provided comments on this text but also wrote the study guide to accompany it. A great many colleagues kindly provided me with suggestions, manuscripts, illustration materials, and other help. Among them were Lewis R. Baxter Jr., Bernhardt Bogerts, Bruce Bridgeman, Douglas Chute, Richard Coss, Timothy Crow, Allan Geliebter, Patricia Goldman-Rakic, Laura Grimes, John Haig, Stephen Hobbs, John Hostetler, A. J. Hudspeth, J. G. MacFarlane, T. Nilsson, Sergio Pellis, Howard Poizner, Robert Provine, Joseph Rogers, Paul Sanberg, Evelyn Satinoff, Sue Savage-Rumbaugh, Susan Schiffman, Thomas Stonebraker, Barbara Szekely, Phillip Teitelbaum, Luigi Valzelli, Diana Woodruff-Pak, J. A. Yaryura-Tobias.

Thanks also to the staffs of the libraries at North Carolina State University and at the Marine Biological Laboratory of Woods Hole, Massachusetts, where I spent one summer.

In the production of this text I have had the extraordinary good fortune to work for a second time with Del Mar Associates. Nancy Sjoberg supervised all phases of the production in a manner that was prompt, efficient, and creative. Linda McVay, who rendered the airbrush artwork, converted my crudest sketches into attractive works of art. Jackie Estrada did an excellent and thorough job with the copyediting. Advice from these three led to other drawings that I hadn't even known I wanted until I saw them. Linda Rill selected the color photos. John Odam designed the cover and the color insert sections. I appreciate the good work from all of these people.

Ken King, my editor at Wadsworth, not only continues to be the best editor in the business, but keeps getting better. I thank him for his encouragement, advice, and friendship. I thank my wife, Ann, and my children, David, Sam, and Robin, for their patience, for their support, and for showing interest every time I wanted to talk about the latest bit of esoterica I had read.

I welcome correspondence from both students and faculty using this book. Write to: James W. Kalat, Department of Psychology, Box 7801, North Carolina State University, Raleigh, NC 27695-7801.

Acknowledgments

Figure 1-1: Photo courtesy of the Cincinnati Zoo.

Figure 1-3: Redrawn from "Vom Wirkungsgefüge der Triebe" by E. von Holst and U. von St. Paul, in *Naturwissenschaften*, 1960, 47:409–422. Used by permission of Springer-Verlag.

Figures 1-4 and 1-5: From *Physical control of the mind* by José M. R. Delgado, 1969. Reprinted by permission of José Delgado. Photos provided by José Delgado.

Figures 1-7 and 1-8: Wide World Photos.

Biosketch 2-1: Photo from S. Ramon y Cajal (1960). *Studies on vertebrate neurogenesis*. Courtesy of Charles C Thomas, Publisher, Springfield, Illinois.

Figure 2-5(f): From R. G. Coss, *Brain Research*, 1982. Used by permission of R. G. Coss.

Figure 2-7: From "Spine stems on tectal interneurons in Jewel fish are shortened by social stimulation" by R. G. Coss and A. Globus, in *Science*, 1978, 200:787–790. Copyright 1978 by the American Association for the Advancement of Science. Reprinted by permission of R. G. Coss and AAAS.

Biosketch 3-1: Photo used by permission of Yale University Press.

Figure 3-6: Based on *An approach to neuroanatomical and neurochemical psychophysiology* by L. Valzelli, 1980, Tables 47–50. Used by permission of L. Valzelli.

Figure 3-9: Redrawn from "Autoimmune response to acetylcholine receptors in myasthenia gravis and its animal model" by J. Lindstrom, in H. G. Kunkel and F. J. Dixon (eds.), *Advances in Immunology*, 1979, 27:1–50. Used by permission of J. Lindstrom and Academic Press, Inc.

Biosketch 4-1: Photo and quote used by permission of Paul MacLean.

Figure 4-2: Adapted from H.J. Jerison (1985). Animal intelligence as encephalization. *Phylosophical Transactions of the Royal Society of London*, B, *308*, 21–35. Used by permission of The Royal Society and H.J. Jerison.

Figures 4-5, 4-16, 4-18, 4-20, 12-8, 13-6, 14-1, and 16-1: Photos courtesy of Dr. Dana Copeland.

Figures 4-14 and 6-7: After *Anatomie des Menschen, 3. Band: Periphere Liestungsbahnen II. Centrales Nervensystem, Sinnesorgane, 2. Auflage* by H. Braus, 1960. Used by permission of Springer-Verlag.

Figure 4-21: From *The anatomy of the nervous system* by S. W. Ranson and S. L. Clark, 1959. Reprinted by permission of W. B. Saunders Co.

Figure 4-23: After *The cerebral cortex of man* by W. Penfield and R. Rasmussen, 1950. Used by permission of Macmillan Publishing Co.

Figures 4-25, 4-28, and 6-21: Photos provided by James W. Kalat.

Figure 4-27: From *A stereotaxic atlas of the rat brain* by L. J. Pellegrino and A. J. Cushman, 1967. Reprinted by permission of Plenum Publishing Corp. and Louis Pellegrino.

Figure 4-29: From "Dendritic-tree anatomy codes form vision physiology in tadpole retina" by B. Pomeranz and S. H. Chung, in *Science*, 1970, 170:983–984. Copyright 1970 by the American Association for the Advancement of Science. Reprinted by permission of AAAS and B. Pomeranz. Photos provided courtesy of B. Pomeranz.

Biosketch 5-1: Photo used by permission of Roger Sperry. Sperry quote from a letter by Jerre Levy.

Biosketch 5-2: Photo and quote used by permission of Jerre Levy.

Biosketch 5-3: Photo used by permission of Norman Geschwind. Quote from "Disconnexion syndromes in animals and man" by N. Geschwind, in *Brain*, 1965, 88:237–294, 585–644. Reprinted by permission of Oxford University Press and N. Geschwind.

Figure 5-4: From "Human brain: Left-right asymmetries in temporal speech region" by N. Geschwind and W. Levitsky, in *Science*, 1968, 161:186–187. Copyright 1968 by the American Association for the Advancement of Science. Reprinted by permission of AAAS and N. Geschwind.

Figure 5-5: Redrawn from "Variations in writing posture and cerebral organization" by J. Levy and M. Reid, in *Science*, 1976, 194:337–339. Copyright 1976 by the American Association for the Advancement of Science. Used by permission of J. Levy.

Figure 5-6: Photo courtesy of Ann Premack.

Figure 5-7: Photo courtesy of Sue Savage-Rumbaugh.

Pages 136–138: Quote from tape recording by Nancy Kaplan, provided courtesy of the Duke University Department of Speech Pathology and Audiology.

Biosketch 6-1: Photo and quote used by permission of Susan Schiffman.

Biosketch 6-2: Photo used by permission of Candace Pert.

Figure 6-3(b): Courtesy of Dr. M. Gary Wickham.

Figure 6-9: By permission of A. J. Hudspeth. Photos courtesy of A. J. Hudspeth, R. Jacobs, P. Leake, and M. Miller.

Figure 6-13: After *Human information processing* by P. H. Lindsay and D. A. Norman, 1972. Used by permission of Academic Press and P. H. Lindsay.

Figure 6-18: After "A psychophysical model for gustatory quality" by S. S. Schiffman and R. P. Erickson, in *Physiology and Behavior*, 1971, 7:617–633. Used by permission of Pergamon Press, Inc., and S. S. Schiffman.

Figure 6-19: After "Sensory affect and motivation" by C. Pfaffmann, R. Norgren, and H. Grill, in *Annals of the New York Academy of Sciences*, 1977, 290:18–34. Used by permission of New York Academy of Sciences and Carl Pfaffmann.

Figure 6-20: From "Sensory neural patterns and gustation" by R. P. Erickson, in Y. Zotterman (ed.), *Olfaction and taste*, 1963. Used by permission of Pergamon Press Ltd. and Robert P. Erickson.

Biosketch 7-1: Photos used by permission of Colin Blakemore. Quote used by permission of David Hubel.

Figures 7-3 and 7-7: After "Organization of the primate retina" by J. E. Dowling and B. B. Boycott, in *Proceedings of the Royal Society of London*, B, 1966, 166:80–111. Used by permission of the Royal Society of London and John Dowling.

Figures 7-10 and 7-11: Based on "Receptive fields of single neurons in the cat's striate cortex" by D. H. Hubel and T. N. Wiesel, in *Journal of Physiology*, 1959, 148:574–591. Used by permission of the Journal of Physiology and David Hubel.

Figure 8-4: Reprinted with permission from *Physiology and Behavior, 34*, S. M. Pellis, Y. C. Chen, and P. Teitelbaum, Fractionation of the cataleptic bracing response in rats. Copyright 1985, Pergamon Journals, Ltd. Photo courtesy of P. Teitelbaum.

Figure 8-9: From *A physiological approach to clinical neurology* by J. W. Lance and J. G. McLeod, 1975. Photo courtesy of J. W. Lance.

Biosketch 9-1: Photo used by permission of Michel Jouvet.

Biosketch 9-2: Photo used by permission of William C. Dement.

Figure 9-1: From "Phase control of activity in a rodent" by P. J. DeCoursey, in *Cold Spring Harbor Symposia on Quantitative Biology*, 1960, 25:49–55. Used by permission of Cold Spring Harbor Laboratory and P. J. DeCoursey.

Figure 9-2: From *Sleep and wakefulness* by N. Kleitman, by permission of The University of Chicago Press and N. Kleitman. © 1963 by The University of Chicago. All rights reserved.

Figure 9-3: Photo by Jackie Estrada.

Figure 9-4: From "Deep hypothermia and its effect on the 24-hour clock of rats and hamsters" by C. P. Richter, in *Johns Hopkins Medical Journal*, 1975, 136:1–10. Copyright 1975 by The Johns Hopkins University Press. Used by permission. Photos provided courtesy of C. P. Richter.

Figure 9-7: Records provided by T. E. LeVere.

Figure 9-8: From "Cyclic variations in EEG during sleep and their relation to eye movements, body motility, and dreaming" by W. Dement and N. Kleitman, in *Electroencephalography and Clinical Neuropsychology*, 1957, 9:673–690. Reproduced by permission of Elsevier/North Holland Biomedical Press and W. C. Dement.

Figure 9-9: From "Ontogenesis of the states of sleep in rat, cat, and guinea pig during the first postnatal month" by D. Jouvet-Mounier, L. Astic, and D. Lacote, in *Developmental Psychobiology*, 1969, 2:216–239. Copyright © 1969 by John Wiley & Sons, Inc. Used by permission of John Wiley & Sons.

Biosketch 10-1: Photo from *The way of an investigator* by W. B. Cannon, 1945. Used by permission of Bradford Cannon.

Biosketch 10-2: Photo and quote used by permission of Edward Stricker.

Figure 10-6: From "The role of activation in the regulation of food intake" by D. L. Wolgin, J. Cytawa, and P. Teitelbaum, in D. Novin, W. Wyrwicka, and G. Bray (eds.), *Hunger: Basic mechanisms and clinical implications*, 1976. Copyright 1976 by Raven Press. Reprinted by permission of Raven Press. Photo provided courtesy of P. Teitelbaum.

Figure 10-8: Redrawn from H. Begleiter, Event-related brain potentials in boys at risk for alcoholism, *Science, 225*, September 28, 1984, pp. 1493–1496. Copyright 1984 by AAAS. Used by permission of AAAS and H. Begleiter.

Biosketch 11-1: Photo and quote used by permission of Frank Beach.

Figure 11-6: Redrawn from "Effects of gonadal hormones on urinary behavior in dogs" by F. A. Beach, in *Physiology and Behavior*, 1974, 12:1005–1013. Used by permission of Brain Research Publications, Inc., and F. A. Beach.

Figure 11-7: Redrawn from Figure 12, W. A. Marshall & J. M. Tanner (1986). In F. Falkner & J. M. Tanner (eds.), *Human growth*, 2nd ed., Vol 2, *Postnatal Growth, Neurobiology*, pp. 171–224. New York: Plenum Publishing Corporation. Reprinted by permission of the publisher.

Figure 11-8: From "Rise in female-initiated sexual activity at ovulation and its suppression by oral contraceptives" by D. B. Adams, A. R. Gold, and A. D. Burt, in *New England Journal of Medicine*, 1978, 299:1145–1150. Reprinted by permission, from *The New England Journal of Medicine*.

Figure 11-11: From "Sex-hormone-dependent brain differentiation and sexual functions" by G. Dörner, in G. Dörner (ed.), *Endocrinology of sex*. Copyright 1975 by Johann Ambrosius Barth. Reprinted by permission of Johann Ambrosius Barth.

Biosketch 12-1: Photo from *The Psychobiology of Curt Richter*, Elliott Blass (ed.), 1976. Used by permission of York Press, Inc., and Elliott Blass.

Biosketch 12-2: Photo and quote used by permission of Luigi Valzelli.

Digression 12-1: Photo courtesy of Jules Asher. From G. Kolata, "New Drug Counters Alcohol Intoxication," *Science*, Vol. 234, No. 4781, December 5, 1986, p. 1199. Copyright 1986 by AAAS. Used by permission of AAAS.

Figure 12-1: Courtesy of Raleigh, North Carolina, Police Department.

Figure 12-2: From "Avoidance behavior and the development of gastroduodenal ulcers" by J. V. Brady, R. W. Porter, D. G. Conrad, and J. W. Mason, in *Journal of the Experimental Analysis of Behavior*, 1958, 1:69–72. Copyright 1958 by the Society for the Experimental Analysis of Behavior, Inc. Reprinted by permission of the Society for the Experimental Analysis of Behavior and J. V. Brady.

Figure 12-3: Redrawn from "On the phenomenon of sudden death in animals and man" by C. P. Richter, in *Psychosomatic Medicine*, 1957, 19:191–198. Used by permission of the American Psychosomatic Society.

Figure 12-4: From "Neuronal constellations in aggressive behavior" by José Delgado, in L. Valzelli and L. Morgese (eds.), *Aggression and violence: A psycho/biological and clinical approach*, Edizioni Saint Vincent, 1981. Used by permission of José Delgado.

Figure 12-5: Based on *Brain mechanisms and behaviour* by J. R. Smythies, 1970. Used by permission of Blackwell Scientific Publications Ltd., Oxford, UK.

Figure 12-6: Based on "Psychosomatic disease and the 'visceral brain': Recent developments bearing on the Papez theory of emotion" by P. D. MacLean, in *Psychosomatic Medicine*, 1949, 11:338–353. Used by permission of the American Psychosomatic Society.

Figure 12-7: Redrawn from "Studies on limbic systems ('visceral brain') and their bearing on psychosomatic problems" by P. D. MacLean, in E. D. Wittkower and R. A. Cleghorn (eds.), *Recent developments in psychosomatic medicine*, 1954. Copyright Sir Isaac Pitman & Sons, Ltd. Used by permission of J. B. Lippincott Co. and Sir Isaac Pitman & Sons, Ltd.

Figure 12-9: From "Behavioral changes following rhinencephalic injury in cat" by L. Schreiner and A. Kling, in *Journal of Neurophysiology*, 1953, 16:643–659. Reprinted by permission of the American Physiological Society.

Figure 12-11: Based on Fig. 1, p. 140, of A. Guidotti, P. Ferrero, M. Fujimoto, R. M. Santi, & E. Costa (1986). Studies on endogenous ligands (endacoids) for the benzodiazepine/beta-carboline binding sites. *Advances in Biochemical Psychopharmacology, 41,* 137–148. With permission from Raven Press, New York.

Biosketch 13-1: Photo from *The neuropsychology of Lashley* by F. A. Beach, D. O. Hebb, C. T. Morgan, and H. W. Nissen (eds.), 1960. Reproduced by permission of McGraw-Hill Book Company, Inc.

Biosketch 13-2: Photo used by permission of John Garcia.

Biosketch 13-3: Photo and quote used by permission of Eric R. Kandel.

Digression 13-2: Based on "Learning of leg position by the ventral nerve cord in headless insects" by G. A. Horridge, in *Proceedings of the Royal Society of London*, B, 1962, 157:33–52. Used by permission of the Royal Society of London and G. A. Horridge.

Figure 13-3: Redrawn from "Neuronal mechanisms of habituation and dishabituation of the gill-withdrawal reflex in *Aplysia*" by V. Castellucci, H. Pinsker, I. Kupfermann, and E. R. Kandel, in *Science*, 1970, 167:1745–1748. Copyright 1970 by the American Association for the Advancement of Science. Used by permission of AAAS and V. Castellucci.

Figure 13-5: Adapted from Figure 1(b) in D. Alkon, Calcium-mediated reduction of ionic currents: A biophysical memory trace, *Science, 226,* November 30, 1984, pp. 1037–1045. Copyright 1984 by AAAS. Used by permission of AAAS and D. Alkon.

Figure 13-8: Copyright 1985 by the Society for Neuroscience. Photo courtesy of Dr. Joseph Rogers. Reprinted by permission of Dr. Joseph Rogers.

Biosketch 14-1: Photo courtesy of Patricia S. Goldman-Rakic.

Figure 14-5: Redrawn by permission from *The Annual Review of Neuroscience*, Volume 6, © 1983 by Annual Reviews, Inc..Used by permission of Annual Reviews, Inc. and Jon H. Kaas.

Figure 15-1: Redrawn from E. Janosik and J. Davies, *Psychiatric mental health nursing*, 1986, p. 173. Used by permission of Jones and Bartlett Publishers, Inc.

Figure 15-2: From "Hormones and rhythms in man and animals" by C. P. Richter, in G. Pincus (ed.), *Recent progress in hormone research* (vol. 13), 1957. Used by permission of Academic Press and C. P. Richter.

Figure 15-4: Reprinted by permission of L. R. Baxter Jr. Photo courtesy of L. R. Baxter Jr.

Figure 15-9: From "Differential effects of amphetamines on clinically relevant dog models of hyperkinesis and stereotypy: Relevance to Huntington's chorea" by S. A. Corson, E. O'L. Corson, V. Kirilcuk, J. Kirilcuk, W. Knopp, and L. E. Arnold, in A. Barbeau, T. N. Chase, and G. W. Paulson (eds.), *Advances in neurology, Vol. 1, Huntington's chorea, 1872–1972,* 1973. Copyright 1973 by Raven Press. Reprinted by permission of Raven Press and S. Corson. Photo provided courtesy of S. Corson.

Digression 16-1: Quote from "An interactional description of schizophrenia" by J. Haley, in *Psychiatry*, 1959, 22:321–332. Reprinted by permission of William Alanson White Psychiatric Foundation, Inc.

Figure 16-2: Photos courtesy of B. Bogerts.

Figure 16-3: Photos courtesy of Arnold Scheibel.

Figure 16-4: From "Possible etiology of schizophrenia: Progressive damage to the noradrenergic reward system by 6-hydroxydopamine" by L. Stein and C. D. Wise, in *Science*, 1971, 171:1032–1036. Copyright 1971 by the American Association for the Advancement of Science. Used by permission of AAAS and L. Stein. Photos provided courtesy of L. Stein.

Figure 16-6: From P. Seeman, T. Lee, M. Chau-Wong, and K. Wong, Antipsychotic drug doses and neuroleptic/dopamine receptors," *Nature*, 261, (1976), 717-719. Copyright © 1976 Macmillan Magazines Limited. Reprinted by permission of *Nature* and Philip Seeman.

Color Plates

1, 7, 8, and 9: Dan McCoy/Rainbow

3 and 6: Robert B. Livingston, University of California, San Diego

4: Adapted with the permission of the publisher W. H. Freeman and Company from *Brain, Mind and Behavior* by Floyd E. Bloom et al. Copyright © 1985 Educational Broadcasting Company.

10, 11, and 14: Manfred Kage/Peter Arnold, Inc.

12: D. D. Kunkel, University of Washington/Biological Photo Service

13: Fritz Goro

15: McCoy/Scheibel/Rainbow

16: J. F. McGinty/Peter Arnold, Inc.

17: SIU/Peter Arnold, Inc.

18, 19, and 22: Ed Reschke/Peter Arnold, Inc.

23: Courtesy of L. R. Baxter Jr.

24: Courtesy of Michael E. Phelps and John C. Mazziotta, University of California, Los Angeles, School of Medicine

25: Burt Glinn/Magnum Photos

26: Karen Berman and Daniel Weinberger, National Institute of Mental Health

27: © Tom McHugh/Photo Researchers

28: P. J. Bryant, University of California, Irvine/Biological Photo Service

Contents

Figure 1-1. A biological psychologist tries to explain any behavior, such as the behavior of this mother gorilla toward her baby, not in terms of subjective experiences like "love," or even in terms of past experiences and "reinforcement histories," but in terms of evolution (how did the species develop this behavior?) and physiology (what is going on in the brain and other organs to produce this behavior?). (Photo courtesy of the Cincinnati Zoo.)

The Global Issues of Biological Psychology

CHAPTER

1

MAIN IDEAS

1. Biological psychologists seek to explain behavior in terms of both its physiology and its evolution.

2. Mind and brain are closely related, but we do not know the exact nature of their relationship or what mind really is. Both philosophers and scientists would like to know whether minds could exist independently of brains, whether brains could function equally well if they did not give rise to minds, and what it is about the activity of the brain that is responsible for the mind.

3. Direct electrical stimulation of the brain can induce behavioral changes and subjective experiences. Studies of electrical stimulation of the brain provide strong evidence that the brain is responsible for mental activity.

4. Anything that is characteristic of a species, including a characteristic behavior, is presumed to be an outcome of evolution. In some cases, such as altruistic behavior, it is difficult to imagine how evolution might have favored the behavior.

5. Many experiments in biological psychology use animal subjects. Some of those experiments inflict pain or distress. The ethics of such experiments has become controversial.

It is often said that Man is unique among animals. It is worth looking at this term "unique" before we discuss our subject proper. The word may in this context have two slightly different meanings. It may mean: Man is strikingly different—he is not identical with any animal. This is of course true. It is true also of all other animals: Each species, even each individual is unique in this sense. But the term is also often used in a more absolute sense: Man is so different, so "essentially" different (whatever that means) that the gap between him and animals cannot possibly be bridged—he is something altogether new. Used in this absolute sense the term is scientifically meaningless. Its use also reveals and may reinforce conceit, and it leads to complacency and defeatism because it assumes that it will be futile even to search for animal roots. It is prejudging the issue.

——Niko Tinbergen (1973)

Human beings are part of nature. Although much sets us apart from other animal species, we have much in common with other species, too. To understand who we are, we need to understand our relationship to the rest of the animal kingdom.

To understand the nature of our experiences, our "minds" if you wish, we need to understand the physical structure that is responsible for them. Our experience, our behavior, our sense of personal identity—all are products of the brain. Biological psychology is an attempt to understand how the brain generates those products.

Biological psychology—also known as physiological psychology, behavioral neuroscience, psychobiology, and biopsychology—deals with a number of important practical questions: Can biological measurements determine which people are most likely to develop alcoholism, depression, schizophrenia, or impulsive violent behavior? How may such disorders as insomnia, hyperactivity, and anxiety attacks be prevented? How do tranquilizers, antidepressant drugs, and other medical treatments for psychological disorders work? Is it possible to promote behavioral recovery after brain damage?

In addition to the practical questions, biological psychologists deal with broad philosophical issues: What is the relationship between the mind and the brain? Could a mind exist independently of a brain? If not, then what is it about the physical structure and functioning of the brain that gives rise to the mind?

How does heredity influence behavior? Our capacity for behavior is a product of our evolutionary history. But did that evolutionary history leave us with genes that *force* us to think and act in certain ways? Or did it leave us with genes that merely make it easier for us to develop certain behaviors over others? Or did it leave us with genes that are completely adaptable to the influences of the environment, such that our thinking and behavior are entirely a product of the way we were brought up?

And what about our sense of personal identity? Each of us has a feeling that "I am a single individual." Yet we know that the brain is composed of billions of cells that communicate with one another by paths that are sometimes long and indirect. Under certain circumstances, one part of the brain may fail to communicate with another part of the brain. How, then, does our sense of personal identity arise? And is it an illusion?

Biological psychologists do not have firm answers to any of these questions, but most of them are motivated by curiosity about such questions. Although our scientific investigations may not directly answer the great philosophical questions, they may improve the quality of our speculations.

In this chapter, we shall deal with the global issues of biological psychology. First we shall consider examples of biological explanations of behavior and the philosophical issues related to such explanations. Then we turn to issues concerning evolutionary explanations of behavior. Finally we deal with the ethical issues related to experimentation on animals. In later chapters we shall turn away from these global issues and develop a number of biological explanations in more detail.

BIOLOGICAL EXPLANATIONS OF BEHAVIOR

Throughout this book we shall be trying to explain behavior and experience in biological terms. Biological explanations fall into two major categories: physiological, and genetic-evolutionary. A **physiological explanation** deals with the underlying machinery: What physical processes cause this to happen? A genetic or **evolutionary explanation** deals with the genetic blueprints that led to the physiology: What genes caused the individual to develop this way, and how did that pattern of genes come about? In some cases we deal with only one of those categories of explanation; in other cases we are able to deal with both.

An Example: The Escape Flight of Certain Moths

Let us first consider the example of a moth flying away from a bat. We can ask what machinery causes the moth to do what it does (a physiological question) and why the machinery works the way it does (an evolutionary question). Most of this book will concentrate on vertebrates—humans when possible—but this example of the moth has the advantage that the mechanisms of behavior are understood in considerable detail.

An important problem faced by night-flying moths in many parts of the world is to avoid being eaten by bats. Bats hunt insects at night quite efficiently, sometimes catching ten to twenty per minute (Griffin, Webster, & Michael, 1960). For catching small flying insects at night, the sense of smell is practically useless. Vision would also be useless, even if bats' eyes were much better developed than they actually are. For catching insects, bats have evolved a specialized ability to locate them from echoes, using a well-developed sense of hearing.

A bat produces short bursts of high-pitched sounds, 20,000 to 100,000 Hz (hertz, or cycles per second), and then localizes nearby insects from the echoes. These sounds are mostly above the range of human hearing. Most adults cannot hear pitches as high as 20,000 Hz, although some children can hear pitches as high as 40,000 Hz.

When the bat approaches within 30 to 40 meters of a moth, the moth can hear the bat's sounds. In fact, certain species of moth cannot hear any sound *less than* 20,000 Hz. Those moths fly directly away from every sound they hear, treating it as an indication of a bat. (Some time try jingling some keys around moths. You may be able to generate sounds above 20,000 Hz. If so, depending on the species of moth, you may see some interesting results.)

At the distance of 30 to 40 meters, however, a bat does not hear the echo from the moth. It may by accident continue to approach the moth, but it does not actively home in on the moth until it gets within 3 or 4 meters of it. At that point, the bat gets an echo from the moth and flies toward that echo, with an error of less than two degrees (Masters, Moffat, & Simmons, 1985).

By the time the bat is close enough to locate the moth and to begin chasing it, the bat's sounds become loud enough to the moth's ears that the moth changes its behavior. Instead of flying directly away from the bat, it either dives toward the ground or flies in a random, zigzag manner.

The physiological explanation for the moth's behavior is rather simple in its general principles (Roeder, 1967). The moth has an ear on each side of its body. Unlike human ears, moth ears are simple organs containing only two nerve cells each. These cells are highly sensitive to sounds in the range of 20,000 to 100,000 Hz. If a sound is coming from, say, the left of the moth, the cells in the moth's left ear respond slightly sooner and more frequently than the cells in the right ear. Specialized cells in the moth's nervous system compare the responses of the two ears to determine which ear is responding first and most rapidly; those cells then send messages to the flight muscles that direct the moth's flight away from the more stimulated ear. In this case, the moth turns toward the right and continues turning until the sounds in the two ears are equal.

"Whoops!" you may protest. "If the left ear is responding the same as the right ear, the moth could be flying away from the bat, but it could also be flying directly toward the bat! How does it avoid a suicidal approach?" It so happens that the moth's ears are located just below and behind its wings. If the moth flies toward the bat, the moth hears a flickering of the sound every time it beats its wings. The sound does not flicker when the moth flies away. Presumably the moth uses the flickering as an indication of whether it is flying in the right direction.

As the bat flies closer to the moth, the stimulation of the moth's ears increases and the response of the nerve cells increases. When the bat is within 3 or 4 meters of the moth, the nerve cells in both ears are responding at their maximum level, regardless of the direction of the sound. Because the moth can no longer determine the direction of the bat, it flies in an erratic, unpredictable pattern. The equal, intense stimulation of the two ears may also send a signal that triggers a dive toward the ground. Table 1-1 summarizes the behaviors of the bat and the moth.

Evolutionary explanations of behavior are more speculative than physiological explanations, but in this case it is easy to see why the moth's behavior evolved as it did. First, the moth gains an advantage by having ears

Table 1-1. Bat and Moth Behaviors

Distance from bat to moth	Bat's behavior	Moth's behavior	Moth ear response
More than 40 m	Does not chase	Does not fly away	No response
Between 3 and 40 m	Does not chase	Flies away	Some response; greater in ear closer to bat
Less than 3 m	Chases	Random, evasive flight, or dive to ground	Maximum response in both ears

that can hear *only* ultra-high-pitched sounds, in the range that bats produce. With such ears, the moth can have simple neural connections that cause it to fly away from any sound it hears. The moth does not spend any time determining whether the sound it hears is a bat or something else.

Second, when a bat is distant from the moth, it is to the moth's advantage to fly away from the bat. Not only does the moth's flight increase the distance from the bat, but flying away positions the moth's wings in a way that minimizes the echo they produce. (See Figure 1-2.)

When a bat is within 3 or 4 meters of the moth, it is no longer effective for the moth to fly away, because the bat can already detect the moth's echo. If the bat in fact starts to pursue the moth, the moth is too slow to outfly the bat. Therefore, it would not be advantageous for the moth to have evolved ears that can locate the exact position of a nearby bat. An erratic flight may evade the bat. A dive to the ground may also get the moth out of the reach of the bat.

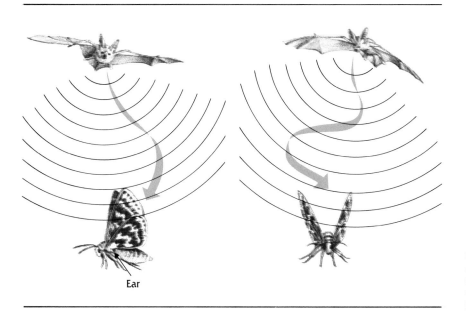

Ear

Figure 1-2. A moth flying away from a bat presents a smaller surface and produces less echo. Note the position of the ear.

Note the relationship of evolution to physiology. Evolution developed the moth's physiology so that the moth hears sounds only in the frequency range of bat calls and so that the moth's ears reach their maximum firing frequency at the point when the bat is close enough to chase the moth.

Note also that we do not have to assume that the moth *knows* why it flies the way it does. Evolution equipped the moth with machinery that automatically produces behaviors that generally prove to be adaptive.

Biological Explanations of Human Behavior

Most of us have no trouble accepting a totally mechanical explanation of the moth's behavior. We may feel differently about a similar explanation of our own behavior, however. Suppose a biological psychologist were to tell you that the anger you experience is merely a reflection of a pattern of activity in one area of your brain, and that the romantic attraction you feel toward someone is the result of activity in another area of the brain. The psychologist goes on to say that you are better at English than at geometry because the left half of your brain is a few millimeters thicker than the right half, and explains each of your other behaviors in terms of other features of your brain. Would you feel any resistance to these explanations?

Such explanations raise difficult philosophical questions, but before we pursue those questions, it is important to make a distinction between two types of biological explanation: biological factors that *force* a behavior to occur and biological factors that *enable* a behavior to occur.

In some cases, the properties of the brain or the rest of the body force a certain behavior to occur. The moth's escape flight is one example. Some human examples: People sweat when they become too hot. The pupil of the eye constricts in the presence of bright light. The leg jerks upward when the knee is tapped in a certain place (the knee-jerk reflex). The flow of saliva increases when we drink unsweetened lemon juice. These behaviors are sure to occur in almost all people except those under the influence of drugs or those with brain damage.

In other cases, a biological influence may make the behavior possible but not absolutely necessary. For example, although a pattern of activity in certain areas of your brain may increase the likelihood of your engaging in aggressive behavior, you may or may not attack someone, depending on what you perceive as the probable consequences of such behavior. An increase in the levels of sex hormones in your blood may increase your sexual motivation, but your actual behavior will depend on your past experiences, the current social setting, and your other, possibly competing, motivations.

The full explanation of your behavior is still biological. Your past experiences exert their effects by means of your brain. Your perception of the current situation is an activity of the brain. So are your competing motivations. The point is that behavior—even moth behavior, but especially human behavior—is the product of many forces. For the sake of simplicity, I shall not always point this out, but you should always bear it in mind when you listen to any biological explanation of behavior.

Table 1-2.   Philosophical Positions on the Mind-Body (or Mind-Brain) Problem

Position	Explanation
Dualism	Holds that mind and brain are fundamentally different and that each can exist independently of the other.
Interactionism	A type of dualism based on the writings of the French philosopher René Descartes. It holds that mind and brain interact with each other and influence each other. (*How* they might do so has always been unclear.)
Parallelism	Another type of dualism, originally proposed by the Dutch philosopher Spinoza. It holds that mind and brain exist separately and do not affect each other. Activities of mind and brain nevertheless agree, much as two accurate clocks may always give the same time, even though neither one influences the other.
Monism	Holds that only one kind of "substance" exists in the universe. Different versions of monism disagree on the nature of that substance.
Mentalism	Version of monism, based on the writings of the Irish philosopher George Berkeley, holding that the physical world exists only in one's mind, or only in the mind of God. Without minds, the physical world could not exist.
Materialism	Version of monism holding that only the material world exists; minds either do not exist at all, or at least do not exist independently.
Epiphenomenalism	A position closely related to materialism. It holds that brain activity produces a mind, but only as an accidental by-product, just as a lawnmower accidentally produces noise. The mind does not influence brain activity or behavior any more than noise influences the functioning of the lawnmower.
Identity position	Version of monism holding that mind and brain are two ways of talking about the same thing. Only one kind of substance exists, but that substance is neither *mind* nor *material* but *mind-material*.
Panprotopsychic identism	A variant form of the identity position, according to which consciousness is present in a primitive, potential form in all matter.
Emergent property position	View that mind is not a property of matter itself, including the matter of the brain, but that it emerges as a new property when the matter is organized in a particular way. For analogy, the properties of water emerge when hydrogen and oxygen are combined, even though neither hydrogen nor oxygen by itself has those properties.

THE MIND-BRAIN RELATIONSHIP

A moment ago I suggested that many of us feel uncomfortable with the idea that our thoughts and actions are the result of physical processes in the brain. Why? Because we believe that our conscious minds control our behavior. For example, it seems to me that I make a conscious decision to do something and then I do it. How can that be, if my action is governed by a series of chemical processes in the brain? Somehow there must be a close relationship between mind and brain, but what is the nature of that relationship? This is the so-called **mind-body problem** or **mind-brain problem**. Some of the most influential philosophical views on the mind-brain problem are summarized in Table 1-2.

The Difficulty of the Problem

One major difficulty in dealing with the mind-brain problem, perhaps the major difficulty, is that many people use the term *mind* in a way that makes it unobservable and unavailable to scientific study. Perhaps it will turn out that "mind" is just another way of saying "brain activities." If, however, the mind is a nonphysical entity separate from the body—as many people assume—then none of us can observe any mind other than our own.

The mind-brain problem has several facets: (1) Can minds have an existence independent of brains? (2) Can brains exist and function without minds? That is, could a nonconscious brain, one that produced no mental experience, function the same way as a conscious brain? Here is another way of asking the same question: "If we built a sufficiently complicated computer, would we accidentally cause it to have a mind? If not—if an extremely complicated computer can get by without a mind—then why do humans have one?" (3) What is it about the structure and organization of the brain that gives rise to mental experience? Does mind depend on a certain, specific set of chemicals or organization of brain cells or pattern of electrical activity, or would any other brain organization be sufficient?

To a large extent, these questions are unanswerable, at least with the kinds of evidence available today. Certain kinds of evidence are relevant, however, including the effects of brain damage. As you will see throughout this book, various kinds of brain damage lead to specific changes in behavior and losses of sensory capacity. Brain damage thus seems largely equivalent to mind damage. A second line of relevant evidence comes from studies of the behavioral effects of electrical stimulation of the brain.

Relevant Data: Control of Behavior by Electrical Stimulation of the Brain

In 1870, Fritsch and Hitzig reported that mild, nondestructive electrical stimulation of portions of the cerebral cortex of a dog could cause muscle movements. At low intensities, the electrical current stimulated discrete, limited movements—always on the side of the body opposite the stimulation. Depending on the exact point stimulated, the dog would move its neck, back, abdomen, tail, leg, or some other part of its body. Repeated stimulation of the same point consistently elicited the same response. Later experiments yielded similar results for many species.

Electrical activity occurs naturally in the brain at all times. Ordinarily, this electrical activity is caused by nerves carrying messages from the sense organs. Their impulses combine with the electrical activity already present in certain areas of the brain to produce activity in other areas, which then activate still other areas. Eventually there is activity in the areas of the brain that control movement. Fritsch and Hitzig had directly stimulated the movement-controlling areas, bypassing all the preliminary stages.

Electrical Stimulation of More Complex Behaviors.   Electrical stimulation of the brain can evoke not only simple muscle movements but also more complex sequences of behavior, particularly if the animal is awake during the stimulation and free to move about. Working with chickens, von

Figure 1-3. Before stimulation (**a**) the rooster ignores the stuffed polecat. With low-level stimulation (**b**) of some point in the brain (not identified), the rooster orients toward the model but does not attack. With stronger stimulation (**c**, **d**), he attacks the model. At the end of the attack, after the stimulation is turned off (**e**), he makes a triumphant call (**f**). (From von Holst & von St. Paul, 1960.)

Holst and von St. Paul (1960) implanted electrodes permanently into lower parts of the brain and cemented the electrodes on the skull to hold them in place. Later they could attach wires to the exposed electrodes and pass a weak electrical current to the brain of an animal while it was awake and moving about. Stimulation of various areas elicited such behaviors as feeding, drinking, cackling, grooming, turning the body to one side, sitting down, sleeping, escape flight, and aggressive attack. (See Figure 1-3.) The behavior elicited depended on the exact location of the electrode and the intensity of the stimulation. (Stronger current could stimulate more distant cells.) The elicited behavior also varied depending on stimuli in the environment. For instance, in later experiments with rats, stimulation at one point caused eating if only food were present and drinking if only water were present (Coons, Levak, & Miller, 1965; Valenstein, Cox, & Kakolewski, 1970). Similarly, Hess (1944) found that electrical stimulation of certain brain areas could induce an animal to fall asleep suddenly.

Stimulation of Still More Complex Behaviors.   José Delgado (1969a) introduced some technological advances that permitted him to investigate the electrical stimulation of a wider variety of behaviors. Inserting permanent electrodes, as in the von Holst and von St. Paul experiments, Delgado then attached the upper tip of each electrode to a miniature electrical stimulator mounted on the skull. Since this stimulator could be activated by remote control with a nearby radio transmitter, an experimenter could stimulate the brain of an animal, usually a monkey, without the limitations that wires would impose on the animal's free movement. (See Figure 1-4.)

Figure 1-4. X-ray of monkey's head showing electrodes implanted into two parts of the brain. (From Delgado, 1969a.)

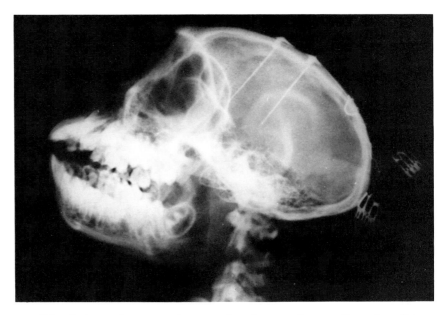

Stimulation of some points produced normal, coordinated walking, walking in circles, or running. Other areas elicited yawning, falling asleep, cessation of spontaneous movement, or loss of appetite. Some areas elicited complicated sequences of movement. In the most spectacular example, a 5-second stimulation of one subcortical area elicited a stereotyped sequence of behavior lasting 10 to 14 seconds: The monkey changed its facial expression, turned its head to the right, stood up on two feet, circled to the right, walked on two feet to a pole in the center of the room, climbed up the pole, and then came down, growled, threatened and sometimes attacked another monkey, and finally approached the group in a friendly manner and resumed its normal behavior. The stimulation was repeated, believe it or not, 20,000 times (until, presumably, the experimenter got bored), and the monkey went through almost exactly the same sequence of behavior every time.

Stimulating certain other areas inhibited aggressive behavior (Delgado, 1963). This was demonstrated with a large, aggressive male named Ali, who shared a large cage with three other monkeys. Ali was friendly toward the larger female, Sarah, indifferent toward the very small male, Lou, and hostile toward the small female, Elsa. An electrode was implanted in a part of Ali's brain called the caudate nucleus, and stimulating it tended to halt his aggressive attacks. The equipment was arranged so that pressing a lever located in the cage would send an impulse to stimulate Ali's caudate nucleus. Eventually, by trial and error, each of the monkeys learned the consequences of pressing the lever, but the only one that pressed it often was, as you might guess, Elsa. Whenever Ali threatened her, Elsa went to the lever. Elsa also discovered that she could make threatening faces at Ali and then stop his attack by pressing the lever. (See Figure 1-5.)

Electrical Stimulation of the Human Brain.   We cannot, of course, experiment on human brains just for research purposes. There are, however,

Figure 1-5. Elsa presses a lever to stimulate a portion of Ali's brain, inhibiting his aggressive attack. (From Delgado, 1969a.)

a variety of medical purposes that allow us to investigate the electrical stimulation of human brains.

Electrical stimulation has most often been used with humans in attempts to treat **epilepsy**, a syndrome caused by abnormal repetitive activity of the nerve cells in the brain. This abnormal activity originates in a damaged or malfunctioning area of the brain called the **focus** of the epilepsy. The focus is located in different places for different individuals. The abnormal repetitive activity spreads outward from the focus until a large portion of the cerebral cortex is involved, possibly causing uncontrollable convulsions. Epilepsy is usually treated with drugs; however, some people have frequent major seizures that do not respond to the usual drug therapies. In such cases, the decision is sometimes made to remove the focus surgically.

The first step is to find the focus. Because the brain has no pain receptors, it can be explored by anesthetizing only the scalp, leaving the brain itself awake and alert during the surgery. The surgeon exposes part of the brain and then applies an electrode to stimulate small areas of the cortex, one after another. Eventually, as the surgeon stimulates some point, the patient says, "That makes me feel the way I feel when I'm about to have one of my seizures." This point can be identified as the focus of the epilepsy and is surgically removed. Ordinarily, the surgery greatly reduces or eliminates the epileptic seizures, and the effects of losing a small piece of brain are usually not serious (Penfield & Roberts, 1959).

Before locating the focus, the surgeon can note the effects of stimulating other parts of the patient's brain. As in nonhuman brains, stimulation of some points produces motor responses. For instance, in one person stimulation caused a series of hand movements; if the man was holding a newspaper at the time, he would fold it and rotate it, or feel around its edge, as long as the simulation continued (Bickford, Dodge, & Uihlein, 1960). The evoked movement was, in general, not subject to voluntary control. In one case stimulation caused a patient to clench his fist. He agreed to try to resist this movement and was warned when the stimulation was about to be applied. Nevertheless, the stimulation caused him to clench his fist, as usual. He remarked, "I guess, Doctor, that your electricity is stronger than my will" (Delgado, 1969a). Stimulation in other locations has elicited hallucinations, arousal, feelings of fear, and many other effects.

Brain stimulation has also been applied for direct therapeutic value, for example in treating **narcolepsy,** a condition in which people fall asleep suddenly during the day. One such patient had an electrode permanently implanted in his skull and attached to a portable device so that when he felt himself starting to fall asleep, he could quickly press a button to stimulate a part of his brain that would arouse him. If he failed to press it in time, one of his friends could go over to press it and turn him back on (Heath, 1963).

Some years ago, a few people were given electrical stimulation of certain parts of the brain, so-called "pleasure areas," in an attempt to provide them with relief from severe pain or depression. Heath (1964) described a patient whose septal area was stimulated (without his knowledge) by remote control during a psychiatric interview. Before the stimulation, he was on the verge of tears as he described his father's illness and his own imagined responsibility for it. After the stimulation, within 15 seconds he suddenly grinned and started discussing a plan to seduce his girlfriend.

Because electrical stimulation of the brain can elicit not only sensations and movements but also emotional changes, it appears that the activity of the brain is responsible for what we call mind. This is, to be sure, not a new conclusion, but the results of brain stimulation provide particularly strong evidence for it.

ISSUES IN THE EVOLUTION OF BEHAVIOR*

Any pattern of genes that is characteristic of most or all members of a species is presumably a product of evolution. We presume that the genes are widespread because the individuals who had them gained some benefit over others who did not have them. Exceptions do occur. For example, a gene that causes one beneficial characteristic may exert other accidental, neutral effects. Thus, we assume that the human liver is brown as an accidental by-product of genes that were selected because of other effects; we do not have to assume that brownness of the liver is particularly advantageous. It is also possible for a gene to be advantageous in the heterozygous condition but harmful in the homozygous condition. For example, people with two genes for sickle-cell anemia (homozygous condition) are likely to die young. However, those with only one sickle-cell gene (heterozygous condition) have greater resistance than others to malaria. Because of that advantage, the sickle-cell gene is fairly widespread in parts of Africa where malaria is common.

Still, as a rule, a widespread, genetically determined characteristic can be presumed to have been advantageous in the history of the species. We can apply this principle to behavior as well as to anatomy. A moth flies away from high-pitched sounds because, in the history of the species, those moths

*Readers who need to freshen their memory on genetics and evolution are referred to the Appendix.

that flew away had a greater chance of passing on their genes than moths that failed to respond.

In many cases, however, it is problematic to discuss the evolution of a particular aspect of behavior. Many people throughout the world are afraid of the dark. Can we draw the conclusion that we have evolved a fear of the dark because such a fear is advantageous? Not necessarily. It is possible that people throughout the world *learn* a fear of the dark and that genetics and evolution have nothing much to do with it. To take a more controversial example, men tend to be more aggressive (at least by certain measures) than women, while women generally spend more time on child care than men do. Can we conclude that evolution has favored these sex differences? Again, we cannot be sure to what extent the behavioral differences are due to genetic differences between the sexes and to what extent they are due to differences in experience. The issue of how heredity and environment (or nature and nurture) interact is a perennial problem in psychology.

Are Humans Still Evolving?

At this point we shall consider just a few of many issues in the evolution of behavior. First, are humans still evolving? You may have heard people say that humans are no longer subject to evolution, or at least that they are much less subject to evolution than in the past, because modern medicine makes it possible for even the "unfit" to survive and because social programs of most civilized countries provide for at least the minimal needs of those who, in an earlier era, might have starved to death or fallen prey to other dangers. (See Figure 1-6.) If everyone survives, not just the fittest, perhaps evolution no longer operates.

What do you think? I hope you will mark your place, set down this book, and just think about this question for a while—perhaps talk it over with a friend—before you read on.

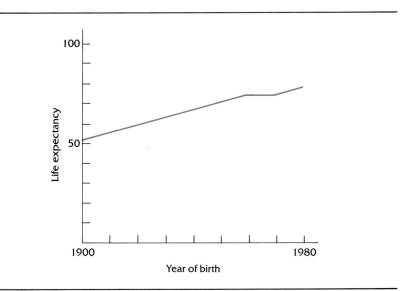

Figure 1-6. Average life expectancies for people born in the United States since 1900. Life expectancies used to be low because so many died in infancy or early childhood. Modern medicine now enables a high percentage of people to reach old age.

The answer to this question is simple: Human evolution has not stopped, and allegations that it has stopped are based on a misunderstanding of evolution. It is wrong to think of evolution as "survival of the fittest." What counts in evolution is reproduction, not just survival. If John survives to the age of 120 but lives his whole life as a hermit, then as far as evolution is concerned, he may as well have died the day he was born. If Joe dies at the age of 19 but has managed to father a dozen healthy children, then he has spread his genes and he is a great success, evolutionarily speaking.

Evolution is merely a cumulative change in the gene pool. If people with one set of genes produce more children, on the average, than people with a different set of genes, then the first set of genes will spread and the species will evolve in the direction of those genes. Of course, it may take many generations for a change to become evident.

If the rate of human evolution has decreased anywhere in the world, it would be in China. The Chinese government, in response to enormous population density, has passed laws that encourage small families and severely penalize families for having more than one or two children. (See Figure 1-7.) If all couples have the same number of children, the prevalence of various genes will not change much from generation to generation, and little evolutionary change will occur. In other countries, where family size varies considerably, evolution continues to take place.

Note that evolution is not synonymous with progress or improvement. The genes that spread may or may not be in the best interest of the species in the long run. For example, among people in the United States in the later part of the twentieth century, highly educated parents are having fewer children than less-educated parents. If we assume (without any good evi-

Figure 1-7. China's one-child family planning policy reduces the chance for changes in the gene pool and thus slows evolution in the Chinese population. In other countries, variations in family size lead to changes in the prevalence of certain genes in the gene pool, thereby producing evolution among these populations. (Wide World Photos.)

dence, I admit) that highly educated people have different genes, on the average, from other people, then evolution at the present time is selecting against those genes.

Could Altruistic Behavior Be a Product of Evolution?

Is it possible for altruistic behavior to evolve, and if so, how? **Altruistic behavior is behavior that benefits an individual other than the one that engages in it.** For example, if you make an anonymous contribution to charity and do not even get a tax break for it, your behavior is altruistic—it does not produce any obvious or direct benefit to you. Similarly, if you see a turtle crossing a highway and you carry it to safety, you are engaging in altruistic behavior. You pick up the turtle in order to help it, not because you expect any benefit to yourself. In fact, you accept a slight risk of being hit by a car.

Altruistic behavior occurs fairly frequently among humans. It also occurs among other species, although it is less common. When a goose sees a hawk overhead, it utters an alarm call that warns other geese, even though it risks attracting the attention of the hawk to itself. When a male wolf wins a fight with another male, it lets the other slink away, even though it could easily kill it and be done with a potential rival forever. Other examples could be given.

It is not clear which, if any, altruistic behaviors in humans or animals have a genetic basis. But never mind that. The fascinating theoretical question is whether evolution could ever favor altruistic behavior. Imagine a gene that somehow increases the probability of an altruistic behavior. An individual who bears that gene incurs some risks and costs while improving the chance that other individuals, who may not bear that gene, will survive and prosper. Evolution should select against that gene, right?

Again, I hope you will stop to think about this question before reading further.

Some people have tried to rescue the possibility of a gene for altruism by supposing that such a gene would enhance the success of the group, even if it did not help the individual (Wilson, 1975). That is, suppose group A includes at least a few individuals with a gene for altruism while group B has no such individuals. Group A may succeed while group B dies out; in this manner the gene may spread.

Except in special cases, such as bees and other social insects, group selection of this type would lead to unstable results. Even if group A displaces group B, a gene for altruism will be selected *against* within group A. In the long run, evolution cannot select for a gene unless, somehow, the individuals with the gene leave behind more offspring than those without the gene.

The most popular resolution to this problem is a theory known as **kin selection** (Trivers, 1972). Suppose a gene causes an individual to behave altruistically toward his or her children and other relatives. That behavior increases the chance that the children and other kin—who may very well have the same gene themselves—will survive and eventually pass on the gene.

Indeed, it may even be evolutionarily advantageous to sacrifice one's own life to save the lives of one's children, and sometimes even one's nephews, nieces, or remoter relatives. Therefore, the theory goes, altruism evolves primarily as a behavior that one shows toward one's immediate family. Once a tendency toward such behavior has evolved, it may occur, more or less accidentally, toward other individuals who are not directly related. Although this theory may not fit all cases of altruistic behavior, it provides a good organizing framework for research.

THE CONTROVERSY OVER THE ETHICS OF ANIMAL RESEARCH

Vincent Dethier once observed that a certain type of little boy likes to tear the wings and legs off insects to see what will happen. Those little boys never come to any good, he said. Some of them become criminals. The others become biologists.

Dethier, himself a biologist, said this in jest. A number of people, however, have seriously equated animal experimentation with cruelty to animals, and heated controversy has arisen about the ethics of using animals in biological and psychological experiments.

Although studies of animals account for only 7 or 8 percent of all published studies in psychology as a whole (Gallup & Suarez, 1980), they account for a much higher percentage of the studies in biological psychology. About 95 percent of the animals used are rats, mice, or birds. The reasons for studying animals are numerous. In some cases investigators prefer to study animals instead of humans because they are interested in the animal species for its own sake or because for some reason it is easier to conduct the study on animals than on humans. For example, if we wanted to study an individual from infancy to old age, or if we wanted to study the effects of genetic changes over several generations, using humans would not be practical because their lifespans are simply too long for convenient investigation.

In other cases, however, animals are preferred because it would be impossible, unethical, or illegal to perform the same experiments on humans. In this book you will read about experiments in which animals were subjected to electrical shocks, brain damage, surgery, stimulation of the brain, injections of drugs or hormones, and other treatments that could not be given to people. If it would be wrong to perform such experiments on humans, many people ask, why is it not also wrong to perform them on animals? (See Figure 1-8.)

It is certainly legitimate to be concerned about this question. Unfortunately, many of those who protest against the use of animals in research have been careless of their facts. It has been charged that laboratory animals are given intense, repeated, inescapable shocks until they can no longer even scream in pain; that they are left to die of hunger and thirst; and that extreme pain and stress are inflicted upon them in attempts to drive them insane. Coile and Miller (1984) examined the psychological studies published over five years and could not find a single example to support any of these charges. No one can say that such experiments have never been conducted in the history of psychology, but they are certainly rare.

Figure 1-8. Animal rights activists maintain that research using animals is inhumane. Because competing values are at stake, no compromise on this issue is fully satisfactory. (Wide World Photos.)

Opponents of animal research have also claimed that such research leads to no useful discoveries. While it is undeniable that much research on animal behavior leads to nothing useful—and the same could be said for research in any other field—animal research has led to the development of antianxiety drugs, new methods of treating pain and depression, an awareness of how certain drugs can impair the development of the fetus, an understanding of the effects of old age on memory, methods to help people overcome neuromuscular disorders, and a number of other valuable advances (N. E. Miller, 1985).

It has further been charged that psychologists have been remiss in failing to consider alternative research methods that do not require animals, such as studying embryos, plants, tissue cultures, and computer simulations. That criticism is simply puzzling (Gallup & Suarez, 1985). Embryos, plants, and tissue cultures do not behave in ways that would make them suitable subjects for psychological experiments. It is impossible to program a computer to simulate a behavior until *after* one understands the behavior. While a computer simulation may be suitable for a classroom demonstration, it is no substitute for using real animals in research.

Although many of the claims made by the opponents of animal research are greatly exaggerated, and a few activists have weakened their credibility (by breaking into animal labs, stealing animals, and vandalizing property, for example), a legitimate moral issue nevertheless remains: Even if animal research sometimes leads to valuable information, and even if severe pain or mistreatment is rare, varying amounts of distress are still being forced upon animals that have no opportunity to refuse to participate. (Of course, the same can be said for animals kept on farms and even many animals kept as pets. But that does not make it right.)

A would-be compromise that sounds good in principle is that investigators should conduct research on animals only if the expected value of the results is greater than the suffering the animals will experience. That principle is not easy to apply, however. It is often difficult to determine the value of the results even after they are obtained, much less before an experiment is conducted. Many important discoveries are made by accident while looking for something else, often something less interesting. Further, we have no agreed-upon measurement of animal suffering. Even if we did, we have no reasonable formula to compare the value of results to the expected suffering. We are not likely to develop a good formula, either. Occasionally, highly important results have emerged from a procedure that was known to produce great pain and that seemed unlikely to produce a valuable outcome (Gallistel, 1981). At other times, what looked like a well-planned experiment turned out to be a waste of time.

Although the judgments are difficult, investigators do try to weigh the expected benefits of proposed research against the costs to the animals. Nearly all investigators do draw a line somewhere and decline to conduct certain kinds of research for ethical reasons, especially when dealing with primates. Moreover, colleges and other research institutions have Laboratory Animal Care Committees that supervise animal research to make sure that the animals are well cared for and that experiments are designed to minimize pain and discomfort. Such committees include veterinarians and community representatives as well as scientists.

Still, many opponents of animal research are not satisfied. Some (the "minimalists") would like to reduce animal research to a minimum, to just those experiments that are clearly worthwhile and that inflict little if any pain. Others (the "abolitionists") wish to prohibit all animal experimentation without exception. Such people generally also advocate vegetarianism and a total ban on the use of animal furs, skins, and other products.

The debate over animal rights is like a number of other moral issues in which legitimate values are in competition—for example, the welfare of a pregnant woman versus the welfare of her fetus that might be aborted, the safety of society versus the rights of people accused of a crime, the desire of society to help a severely psychologically disturbed person versus the right of that person to refuse treatment. When competing values are at stake, agreement is unlikely and no compromise is totally satisfactory.

SUMMARY

1.   Biological explanations of behavior fall into two major categories: physiological explanations (dealing with the internal machinery), and genetic or evolutionary explanations (dealing with the genes that were ultimately responsible for the internal machinery). (p. 3)

2.   Certain moths provide a clear example of both physiological and evolutionary explanations of behavior. A moth's hearing system has evolved to be greatly sensitive to high-pitched sounds (in the range of those emitted by bats) and to be efficient at identifying the direction of the source of those sounds, provided that

it is at least 3 or 4 meters away. This system enables the moth to fly away from bats that are approximately 4 to 40 meters away. (p. 4)

3.   Physiological explanations of human behavior raise the philosophical question known as the mind-body problem. Although a number of answers to this problem have been offered, no solution is widely accepted. (p. 7)

4.   Studies using electrical stimulation of the brain indicate that brain activity controls behavior and that it controls at least certain aspects of emotional and other experience. (p. 8)

5.   The potential to behave in a particular way is the outcome of an evolutionary history; presumably, individuals with that behavior potential had an advantage of some sort over individuals without that potential. (p. 12)

6.   Improvements in health care do not stop human evolution. Evolution is based on differential reproduction, not simply the survival of the fittest. (p. 13)

7.   Some animals behave in what appears to be an altruistic manner, although it is not clear what evolutionary advantage they gain by doing so. The most promising theory is that an altruistic tendency may evolve as an accidental by-product of selection for protecting one's offspring and other close relatives. (p. 15)

8.   Much of our knowledge of biological psychology comes from studies of laboratory animals. The ethics of such research is controversial. (p. 16)

REVIEW QUESTIONS

1.   What are two kinds of biological explanation of behavior? (p. 3)

2.   Physiologically, why is it possible for a moth to determine the direction of a bat that is more than 4 meters away but not a bat that is closer? (p. 5)

3.   Evolutionarily, why is it advantageous for a moth to be able to localize a bat when it is more than 4 meters away but not a bat that is closer? (p. 5)

4.   What are some of the effects of brain stimulation on behavior? (p. 8)

5.   Under what circumstances might someone apply direct electrical stimulation to the human brain? (p. 11)

6.   Why is it misleading to say that human evolution has slowed or stopped because of medical advances that allow almost everyone to survive? (p. 14)

7.   Why is it difficult to imagine how a gene for altruistic behavior could evolve? What is the most satisfactory solution to this problem? (p. 15)

8.   Describe the pros and cons of doing research on animals. (p. 16)

THOUGHT QUESTIONS

1.   Suppose a philosopher asks you what is known about the brain and its control of behavior that philosophers should know about. That is, what scientific information is relevant to the mind-body problem? What would you answer? (Keep this question in mind as you read the rest of the book; see what relevant information you can find.)

2.   Life expectancy appears to be partly under genetic control. People in some families age more slowly than people in other families. Suppose a new gene appears that gives people a relative immunity to the usual diseases and deterioration of old age. People with this gene have a greater than normal chance of living to be 100. Would you expect this gene to be evolutionarily advantageous, disadvantageous, or neutral? In what ways, if at all, can evolution select for genes that do not make their effects felt until old age, after the end of the reproductive period?

TERMS TO REMEMBER

physiological explanation (p. 3)
evolutionary explanation (p. 3)
mind-body (mind-brain) problem (p. 7)
dualism (p. 7)
interactionism (p. 7)
parallelism (p. 7)
monism (p. 7)
mentalism (p. 7)
materialism (p. 7)

epiphenomenalism (p. 7)
identity position (p. 7)
panprotopsychic identism (p. 7)
emergent property position (p. 7)
epilepsy (p. 11)
focus (p. 11)
narcolepsy (p. 12)
altruistic (p. 15)
kin selection (p. 15)

SUGGESTIONS FOR FURTHER READING

Delgado, J. M. R. (1969). *Physical control of the mind*. New York: Harper & Row. Discussion of electrical stimulation of the brain, with optimistic predictions for future benefits to mankind.

Fodor, J. A. (January 1981). The mind-body problem. *Scientific American, 244* (1), 114-123. A brief discussion of major philosophical positions on the mind-body problem.

Rensch, B. (1971). *Biophilosophy*. New York: Columbia. A biologist-turned-psychologist-turned-philosopher attempts to deal with the mind-body problem and other philosophical issues from a scientific standpoint.

Valenstein, E. (1973). *Brain control*. New York: Wiley-Interscience. A treatment of electrical brain stimulation and psychosurgery that comes to much less favorable conclusions than the Delgado book.

Nerve Cells and Nerve Impulses

CHAPTER 2

MAIN IDEAS

1. The cells that compose the nervous system are known as neurons and glia. Only the neurons transmit impulses from one location to another.

2. Many molecules in the bloodstream that are free to enter other body organs are unable to enter the brain.

3. The structure of a neuron is somewhat plastic throughout life. The fibers of a neuron can increase or decrease their branching pattern as a function of experience, age, and chemical influences.

4. The nerve impulse, known as an action potential, is an electrical change across the membrane of a neuron, caused by the sudden flow of sodium ions into the neuron, followed by a flow of potassium ions out of the neuron.

5. Myelin is an insulating sheath that increases the velocity of transmission in certain vertebrate neurons.

6. Many small neurons convey information without action potentials, by means of graded electrical potentials that vary in their intensity.

Until the late 1800s, the best available microscopic views of the nervous system did not reveal much detail about the organization of the brain. Long, thin fibers were observed between one nerve cell and another. Several of the most respected authorities maintained that these fibers actually merged one cell into another; that is, they denied that any gap separated one cell from the next.

In the late 1800s, Santiago Ramón y Cajal (see BioSketch 2-1) found a method of staining a single nerve cell, or **neuron**, without staining its neighbors. For the first time, it became possible to inspect a single neuron in its entirety, and it became clear that cells do not merge into one another. Each cell is distinct; a small gap separates it from each neighboring cell.

Philosophically, we can see some appeal in the old concept that one nerve cell might merge into another. We each experience our conscious awareness as a single thing, not as a combination of many. In a way it seems right that all the cells in the brain should join together physically as a single unit.

Yet we now know that they do not. The adult human brain contains a great many nerve cells—between 30 billion and 100 billion, according to current estimates (Black et al., 1984; Szentágothai, 1983). (Because certain areas of the brain contain a large number of very small cells, it is difficult to get an accurate count.) Those billions of cells all combine to produce both unified experience and coordinated, organized behavior. Before we can begin to contemplate how they act together, we need to know a little about the properties of the individual cell.

In this chapter we shall deal with some detailed information about neuron structure and function, and at times it will not be obvious why a student of psychology needs to know such things. One reason is for building confidence. In order to think about how the brain controls behavior, one needs to know a little about what neurons can and cannot do; moreover, one needs to feel confident that there is not a major gap in one's knowledge. A second reason is that certain interesting points about behavior can be related directly to what we know about the individual neuron. For example, one kind of memory loss (Korsakoff's syndrome; see Chapter 13) is caused by a deficiency in the nutrition of neurons; alcohol exerts certain of its long-term effects by changing the structure of neurons; anesthetic drugs prevent the transmission of information by neurons. To understand these and other examples, one needs a moderate understanding of what neurons are, what they do, and how they do it.

NEURONS AND GLIA

The nervous system consists of two kinds of cells, neurons and glia. Neurons are the cells that convey impulses; they are the cells people usually mean when they refer to "nerve cells." Glia might be thought of as supporting cells; the various types of glia and their functions will be described later.

BIOSKETCH

2-1

Santiago Ramón y Cajal (1852– 1934)

Santiago Ramón y Cajal (kuh-HALL), winner of the 1906 Nobel Prize in Physiology or Medicine, had an inauspicious start in life. At one point he was imprisoned, limited to one meal a day, occasionally kept in solitary confinement, and publicly beaten—at age ten—for the crime of misbehaving in class and not learning his Latin (Ramón y Cajal, 1937). He detested much of his schoolwork, with its strong emphasis on memorization, and spent much of his time observing nature and drawing pictures. His father strongly discouraged his ambition to become an artist and steered him instead toward a career in medicine. Ultimately, Cajal combined these two interests by drawing illustrations of the fine anatomy of the brain and

making great advances in our understanding of the structure of neurons.

After completing his medical education, he began a career of teaching and research, although research was given very little encouragement in Spain in the late nineteenth century. A friend introduced him to a method, discovered by the Italian investigator Camillo Golgi, in which brain tissues were soaked in a combination of bichromate and silver nitrate. This procedure stains a few neurons black over their entire surface while leaving other neurons unaffected. (We still do not know why it stains some neurons and not others.) This staining method reveals the shape of a neuron separate from its background.

Others who had used Golgi's method found it unsatisfactory for tracing the connections of the brain for two reasons: Many axons are too long to see in a single microscopic slide, and the stain does not attach to myelinated axons. Cajal avoided these difficulties by studying immature

brains, at a point when all the axons are short and unmyelinated.

Using this method, Cajal determined that neurons are separate from one another, although the axon of one might come into close contact with another neuron. He also determined, contrary to previous opinions, that dendrites carry impulses toward a cell body and that an axon carries impulses away from it. He provided the first complete descriptions of the shapes of many types of neuron in the brain.

A quote from Cajal (1937):

"How many interesting facts fail to be converted into fertile discoveries because their first observers regard them as natural and ordinary things! . . . It is strange to see how the populace, which nourishes its imagination with tales of witches or saints, mysterious events and extraordinary occurrences, disdains the world around it as commonplace, monotonous and prosaic, without suspecting that at bottom it is all secret, mystery, and marvel."

Neurons resemble other body cells in certain basic properties. We shall therefore begin with some basic information about cells.

The Structures Within an Animal Cell

Figure 2-1 illustrates a generalized animal cell. No actual cell looks quite like this one; it has been stripped of all the specializations that make a blood cell different from a bone cell, a muscle cell different from a liver cell, a neuron different from a skin cell.

Every cell is surrounded by a **membrane,** a structure that limits the flow of materials between the inside of the cell and the outside environment. A few chemicals, such as water, oxygen, and carbon dioxide, flow fairly freely across the membrane, while other chemicals flow poorly or not at all. The fluid inside the cell membrane is known as the **cytoplasm.**

All animal cells (except red blood cells) contain a **nucleus,** a structure that contains the chromosomes. A **mitochondrion** (plural: mitochondria) is

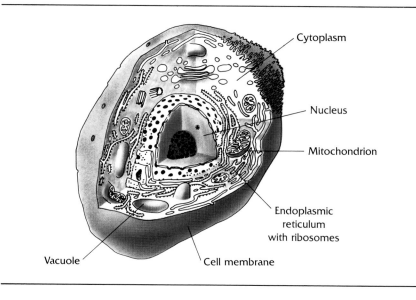

Figure 2-1. Structures inside a representative animal cell.

the site where the cell performs the metabolic activities that provide the energy the cell requires for all its other activities. **Ribosomes** are the sites at which the cell synthesizes new protein molecules. Some ribosomes float freely within the cell; others are attached to the **endoplasmic reticulum**, a network of thin tubes that transport newly synthesized proteins to other locations. **Vacuoles** are fluid-filled bubbles inside the cell. Cells contain a number of other structures that we shall not have occasion to refer to in this text.

The Structure of a Neuron

A neuron contains a nucleus, a membrane, mitochondria, ribosomes, and the other structures typical of all animal cells. The distinctive feature that sets a neuron apart from other cells is its shape (see Color Plate 15). From the central body of the neuron, many small, thin fibers may emanate. Some of those fibers may extend great distances; some may branch widely. The size and shape of neurons vary almost endlessly. The distinctive shape of a given neuron determines its connections with other neurons and thereby determines how it will contribute to the overall functioning of the nervous system.

Figure 2-2 illustrates a **motor neuron,** one that has its cell body in the spinal cord and one fiber extending to a muscle. It would not be fair to call this a "typical" neuron; neurons vary so widely that no one neuron is typical of all others any more than any one vegetable is typical of all others. Nevertheless, the motor neuron is a convenient one to discuss.

The motor neuron, like most neurons, has four major components: the cell body, dendrites, an axon, and presynaptic endings. The **cell body,** or **soma** (Latin for "body"), contains the nucleus, some ribosomes and mitochondria, and other structures found in most cells. Much of the metabolic work of the neuron takes place here. Cell bodies of neurons range in diameter from 0.005 mm to 0.1 mm in mammals and up to a full millimeter in certain invertebrates, such as the squid.

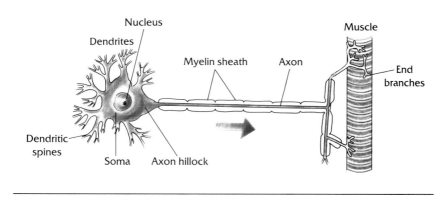

Figure 2-2. A motor neuron.

The **dendrites** are thin, widely branching fibers that get narrower as they get farther from the cell body. (The term *dendrite* comes from a Greek root word meaning "tree"; the shape of a dendrite resembles that of a tree.) The dendrite's surface is lined with specialized junctions at which the dendrite receives information from other neurons. Thus, the greater the surface area of a dendrite, the greater the amount of information it can receive. The surface area of many dendrites is expanded by **dendritic spines**, short outgrowths along the dendrites.

The **axon** is a single fiber that is thicker and longer than the dendrites. (The term *axon* comes from a Greek word meaning "axis"; in some ways it resembles a long axis extending from one pole of the neuron.) Mature neurons have either one axon or none. (In contrast, a neuron may have any number of dendrites.) Certain neurons form more than one axon early in life, although the extra axons are lost as development proceeds (Heathcote & Sargent, 1985).

Many axons begin at a swelling of the cell body known as the **axon hillock**. The axon maintains a constant diameter down its entire length. Generally, an axon carries an impulse from the cell body toward other cells. The axon of a motor neuron conducts impulses from its soma in the spinal cord to muscle or gland cells. In large animals, the length of certain axons may be a meter or more. A neuron without an axon can convey information only to other neurons immediately adjacent to it.

The axon of a motor neuron is covered with an insulating material called a **myelin sheath**. Myelin covers some but not all vertebrate axons. It is not found among invertebrates.

Each branch of an axon swells at its tip, forming a **presynaptic ending**, or *end bulb*. This is the point from which the axon releases chemicals that cross through the *synapse* (the junction between one neuron and the next) and excites the next cell. We shall discuss synapses in detail in Chapter 3.

Table 2-1 lists the anatomical distinctions between dendrites and axons. Occasionally we encounter a structure that strains the definitions. For example, certain neurons, including all the sensory neurons entering the spinal cord, have cell bodies located on a stalk, as shown in Figure 2-5 (**c**), p. 28. One long fiber conveys impulses from the sensory receptor toward the cell body. Because it conveys information toward the cell body, it is acting like a

Table 2-1.   Anatomical Distinctions Between Dendrites and Axon

Dendrites	Axon
A neuron may have many dendrites.	A neuron may have one axon or none. An axon may have many branches.
Usually shorter than the axon. Some neurons have a long "apical" dendrite with branches (see Figure 2-5d).	May be any length, from nonexistent to 1 meter or longer.
Diameter usually tapers toward the periphery of the dendrite.	Diameter usually constant over the length of the axon.
No hillock.	Relatively large axons join the cell body at a distinct swelling called the axon hillock.
Usually branch at acute angles.	Usually branches perpendicular to the main trunk of the axon.
Seldom covered with myelin (an insulating sheath).	Often covered with myelin (vertebrates only).
Usually have ribosomes.	Usually has few ribosomes or none.

dendrite. Yet its structure is clearly that of an axon. In some cases, investigators may disagree on whether to classify something as a dendrite or an axon.

You will note in Table 2-1 the prominent use of the word *usually*. The structure of neurons varies enormously and exceptions can be found to practically any rule about dendrites and axons. Many neurons, especially the smaller ones, violate the rule that dendrites receive information and axons conduct it to other cells. In some cases dendrites and cell bodies transmit information directly to the dendrites and cell bodies of another neuron, without the intervention of an axon.

Variations Among Neurons

For some purposes it is useful to distinguish among three types of neurons: receptor neurons, motor neurons, and interneurons. A **receptor (sensory) neuron** is specialized to be highly sensitive to a specific type of stimulation, such as light, sound waves, touch, or certain chemicals. (See Figure 2-3.) As a rule, each receptor is highly sensitive to one kind of stimulus and relatively insensitive to most others. For example, a few molecules of an airborne chemical can excite the olfactory receptors in the nose but not the receptors in the eye. A single photon of light can affect receptors in the eye but not the olfactory receptors. However, the selectivity is not absolute; all receptors can be stimulated by electricity and other intense stimuli.

A motor neuron receives excitation from other neurons and sends impulses either to muscle cells or to gland cells (see Color Plate 19). **Interneurons** receive information from other neurons (either receptor neurons or interneurons) and send it to either motor neurons or interneurons.

In the simplest possible case (which probably does not exist in reality), a receptor sends impulses to an interneuron, which in turn sends impulses to a motor neuron, as shown in Figure 2-4. Even in the simplest actual cases, however, the interneuron also receives excitation from other interneurons and passes information to still other interneurons in addition to the motor

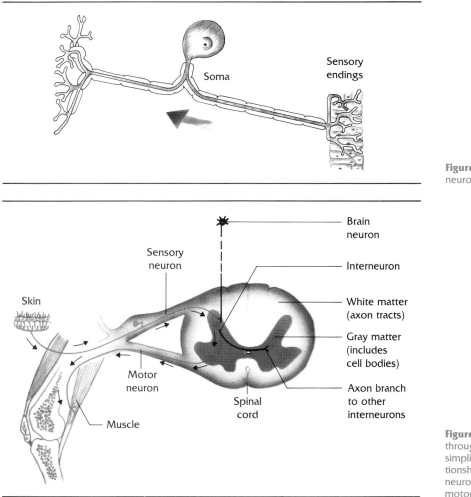

Figure 2-3. A sensory neuron.

Figure 2-4. A reflex arc through the spinal cord, simplified to show the relationship among sensory neuron, interneuron, and motor neuron.

neurons. Many interneurons connect only to other interneurons, not to any receptor or motor neurons. In fact, the human brain (as opposed to the spinal cord) consists almost entirely of interneurons.

Some additional terms you may encounter are *afferent, efferent,* and *intrinsic*. An **afferent neuron** is one that brings information into a structure; an **efferent neuron** is one that carries information away from a structure. A given neuron may be either afferent or efferent, depending on which structure we are talking about. For example, an axon extending from the cerebral cortex to the spinal cord is an *efferent* neuron with respect to the cerebral cortex but an *afferent* neuron with respect to the spinal cord. An **intrinsic neuron** is one whose axons and dendrites are all confined within a given structure. For example, an intrinsic neuron of the cerebral cortex has no dendrites or axons that extend beyond the borders of the cortex.

The shape of neurons varies greatly, as shown in Figure 2-5. The function of a neuron depends on its shape (Palay & Chan-Palay, 1977). Neurons

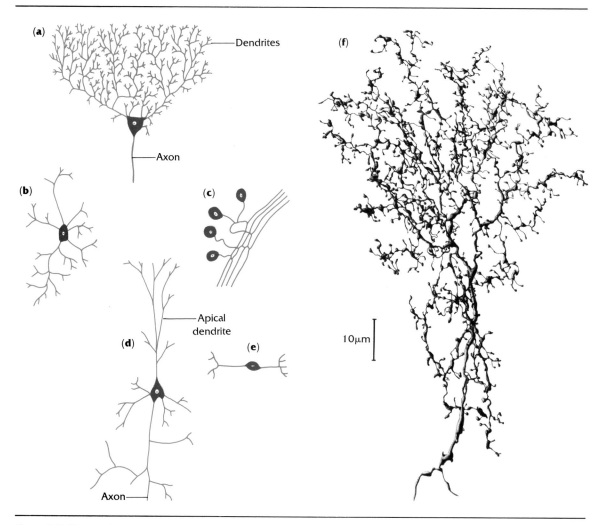

Figure 2-5. Diverse shapes of neurons: (**a**) one of the cell types of the cerebellum, called the Purkinje cell; (**b**) interneuron of spinal cord; (**c**) sensory neurons from skin to spinal cord; (**d**) pyramidal cell of the motor area of the cerebral cortex; (**e**) bipolar cell of retina of the eye; (**f**) Kenyon cell from honeybee. Part (f) courtesy of R. G. Coss.

a, d, and **f** have widely branching dendrites that receive and integrate information from a great many sources. The dendrites of the Purkinje cell of the cerebellum (neuron a) have about 100,000 specialized sites (synapses) for receiving transmissions from other neurons. Neuron b, an interneuron, has an axon and dendrites that branch diffusely within a small radius. It is well suited to exchange information with many other cells and to engage in extensive feedback, influencing some of the same cells that influence it.

The neurons in **c** are the sensory neurons of the spinal cord, already discussed. They receive information from touch receptors at the periphery of the body and convey it over a long axon that does not branch until it reaches the spinal cord. Neuron e, a bipolar cell of the retina in the eye, conveys information about excitation of the visual receptors (see Chapter 7). Note that the bipolar cell's dendrites branch over a limited area and that its axon is short, with only a few branches. If either its dendrites or its axon branched widely, vision would be blurry because information from different parts of the retina would not remain distinct.

The Nourishment of Vertebrate Neurons

Vertebrate neurons depend on **glucose**, a simple sugar, as their main source of nutrition. The same is true of cancer cells and of the testis cells that make sperm. Other cells in the body use a wider variety of fuels.

Why do neurons depend so heavily on glucose? Apparently it is not because neurons are incapable of using anything else. Neurons possess the enzymes necessary to metabolize certain other sugars, plus lactate and two ketone fats, acetoacetate and 3-hydroxybutyrate. The infant brain does, in fact, make use of these alternate fuels. In most parts of the adult vertebrate brain, however, something called the *blood-brain barrier,* to be discussed later, prevents many chemicals from entering the brain. Because of the blood-brain barrier, glucose is the only fuel that enters most neurons in significant quantities (Gjedde, 1984). In certain areas of the brain where the blood-brain barrier is weak, neurons can use ketone fats and other fuels besides glucose (Hawkins & Biebuyck, 1979).

For neurons that depend exlusively on glucose, a shortage of glucose is rarely a problem. The liver can convert many carbohydrates, proteins, and fats into glucose; except in diabetes and other disease states, the glucose level in the blood is always sufficient to meet the brain's needs. An inability to *use* glucose can be a problem, however. In order to use glucose, the body needs vitamin B_1, **thiamine.** If a person's diet is low in thiamine over a period of weeks, the brain's neurons will have increasing difficulty in using glucose. Eventually, neurons may die, giving rise to Korsakoff's syndrome, which we shall discuss in Chapter 13.

Glia

Besides neurons, the other major components of the nervous system are **glia** (or *neuroglia*). (The term *glia* is derived from a Greek word meaning "glue." Glia were once believed to hold neurons together.) On the average, a glial cell is about one-tenth the size of a neuron. Glia are about ten times more numerous than neurons in the human brain, somewhat less in the brains of most other species. Thus, in the human brain, glia occupy about the same total space as the neurons. (See Figure 2-6 and Color Plate 14.)

Glia do not transmit information to other cells. They show electrical activity, but it is a passive activity, driven by the neurons around them. Several anatomical types of glia perform various functions (Varon & Somjen, 1979):

1.   Two kinds of glia build the myelin sheaths that surround and insulate certain vertebrate axons: **oligodendrocytes** (OL-i-go-DEN-dro-sites) in the brain and spinal cord and **Schwann cells** in the periphery of the body. Even the unmyelinated axons of the central nervous system are in contact with oligodendrocytes. For the unmyelinated axons, the function of the oligodendrocytes is mainly to separate one axon from another.

2.   Glia remove waste material, particularly that created when neurons

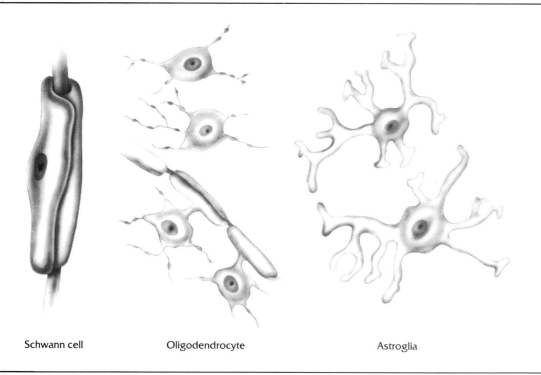

Schwann cell   Oligodendrocyte   Astroglia

Figure 2-6. Shapes of some glial cells.

die. At least two kinds of glia perform this function: the very small **microglia** and the larger, star-shaped **astroglia** (or astrocytes).

3. Where neurons die, glia, especially astroglia, fill up the vacant space and sometimes form scar tissue.

4. **Radial glia**, containing long fibers, guide the migration of neurons and the growth of their axons and dendrites during embryological development. Schwann cells perform a related function after damage to axons in the periphery, guiding a regenerating axon to the appropriate target.

After the brain is mature, it is believed that radial glia transform into astroglia. The astroglia provide structural support to help axons and dendrites hold their shape and position.

Other possible functions of glia are less conclusively demonstrated or less clearly understood. Glia serve as a reservoir of potassium ions and may be a source of proteins and other nutrients needed by neurons. Astroglia may also promote the development of dendrites and axons (Banker, 1980).

The Blood-Brain Barrier

The brain's primary defense against foreign, potentially harmful substances is a set of mechanisms known as the **blood-brain barrier**. Many chemicals, especially proteins and other large molecules, that pass fairly freely into other body cells cannot enter brain cells at all, or do so very slowly. The blood-brain barrier is the main reason why most brain cells depend so heavily on glucose; many other fuels that the cells could use fail to cross the blood-brain barrier.

The strength of the blood-brain barrier varies somewhat from one part of the brain to another. Areas that have a relatively weak barrier can use ketone fats and certain sugars that are unavailable to most of the brain.

One cause of the blood-brain barrier is the arrangement of endothelial cells along the capillaries. In most parts of the body, such cells are separated by gaps large enough to allow the passage of large molecules. In the brain, the endothelial cells are tightly joined to one another. Moreover, the brain's endothelial cells possess active transport mechanisms that pump some molecules in and others out.

Astroglia surround most of these endothelial cells, especially in areas where the blood-brain barrier is strong. Although conclusive evidence is lacking, it is likely that the astroglia strengthen the blood-brain barrier in ways not yet understood (Anders, Dorovini-Zis, & Brightman, 1980; Bradbury, 1979).

The blood-brain barrier is weakened in areas of tumors, infections, and other medical disorders (e.g., Juhler et al., 1984). It is possible to make use of that fact to localize brain damage: An investigator injects a radioactively labeled molecule that is ordinarily unable to cross the blood-brain barrier and then records the radioactivity to determine where it concentrates. The location of the radioactive molecule must be an area with a weakened blood-brain barrier; it is therefore an area of some sort of illness.

Changes in the Structure of Neurons and Glia

In the adult vertebrate brain, most neurons cannot divide to replace neurons that have been lost. In contrast, skin cells and cells in many other parts of the body retain the ability to divide at any time during life.

It was formerly believed that adult vertebrates were incapable of generating any new neurons at all. Gradually, a list of exceptions emerged. The olfactory receptors undergo steady turnover throughout life as old receptors die and new ones take their place (Graziadei & de Han, 1973; Graziadei & Monti Graziadei, 1985). Within the brain itself, additional neurons form throughout life in certain limited areas, at least in the rat brain (Bayer, 1985; Kaplan, 1985). It has not been possible to demonstrate the development of new neurons in the mature primate brain (Rakic, 1985). When new neurons form in the mature rat brain, they are apparently neurons of moderate or small size, rather than those with long axons that link one part of the brain with another. New neurons also form throughout life in certain parts of birds' brains. (See Digression 2-1.)

Although some new neurons do originate in the adult brain, it remains the case that the great majority of mature neurons cannot divide. Cancer is an abnormal proliferation of cells. Because most neurons cannot proliferate, brain cancers are generally—maybe always—limited to glia cells, which can and do divide at any time during life.

Even without the development of new neurons, the structure of the brain can change in two ways: New glia can form, and the dendritic branches of neurons can grow or retract. As a rule, dendrites branch more widely in

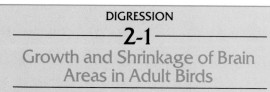

DIGRESSION

2-1

Growth and Shrinkage of Brain Areas in Adult Birds

It was at one time believed that the anatomy of the brain remained basically static once it had reached maturity. We now know that neurons can grow new branches on both their axons and their dendrites and that they can make new connections with other neurons and break old ones. Additional neurons can form in certain areas. One of the best examples of all these changes is the set of changes that take place in the song-producing areas in birds' brains (Nottebohm, 1985).

In canaries and other songbirds, two areas of the brain, identified by the abbreviations HVc and RA, are necessary for the production of song. These areas are larger in the brains of males than those of females, and they are largest in the brains of those males that sing the longest, most varied songs.

The size of the HVc and RA areas also varies over time. They grow large in males in spring, when the males sing frequently, but they shrink in late summer, when song is absent or irregular. Presumably the growth and shrinkage are due to changes in male hormone levels, which are high in early spring and low in late summer. If an experimenter injects male hormones into a female bird, the female's HVc and RA areas increase in size and she begins to sing.

Structurally, what is responsible for the growth and shrinkage? To test the possibility that new neurons form, Nottebohm (1985) injected radioactive thymidine into birds' brains. Because thymidine is a constituent of DNA, it becomes permanently incorporated into any cells that originate shortly after the injection. When Nottebohm later found radioactivity in neurons of the HVc and RA areas, he could infer that new cells had originated there around the time of the injection.

From such studies, Nottebohm found that neurons do indeed form in these areas in adult birds. Moreover, the new neurons make connections with old neurons and contribute to the overall activity of the brain. To his surprise, however, Nottebohm found that such cells formed in both males and females, with or without male hormone injections, regardless of whether the brain areas were expanding at the time or not. Most of these cells were small—apparently local neurons (Paton, O'Loughlin, & Nottebohm, 1985)—and most of them survived less than a year. In other words, there appears to be a constant turnover of small neurons in the song-production areas of the brain, as new neurons replace old ones.

The growth and shrinkage of the HVc and RA areas are not caused by the production and loss of neurons, but by structural changes in permanent neurons. The dendrites lengthen and expand greatly in the male birds in spring, and in females injected with male hormones. The result of such expansion is a greater number of connections with other neurons. In late summer, the dendritic trees contract and the entire brain area becomes smaller.

larger animals than in smaller animals (Purves & Lichtman, 1985); they also branch more widely in certain members of the species than in others. For example, if rats are kept for one month or longer in large cages, in groups of ten to twelve per cage, with a constantly changing variety of objects for them to explore, they develop more glia cells and a wider pattern of dendritic branches than rats kept in individual cages (Uphouse, 1980; Greenough, 1975). The anatomical changes are known to last at least a month, and probably much longer, after the animals have been removed from the enriched environment (Camel, Withers, & Greenough, 1986). Similar results have been reported for Jewel fish (Coss & Globus, 1979) and honeybees (Coss, Brandon, & Globus, 1980). (See Figure 2-7.)

Even in an unchanging environment, dendrites may change their structure. Purves and Hadley (1985) developed a method of injecting a dye into a neuron that enabled them to examine the structure of a living neuron at two times, days to weeks apart. They found that dendritic patterns gradually change. Some branches grow and extend while others retract. Some den-

This insert is divided into two parts (for the second section, see page 224) and includes color illustrations of the nervous system and its functioning. The functioning of the nervous system depends on the fine details of its structure, some of which show up far better in color than in black and white. Certainly, these photos and illustrations portray the details of the brain and nervous system better than they can be described in words. Several also show modern methods used to measure activity in the brain. As these two color sections show, the nervous system is not only a structure of impressive capabilities but also one of great beauty.

Plate 1. The human brain. Note its size relative to that of a hand. Although it weighs only 1,200 to 1,400 grams—about the same as the weight of this book—it contains between 30 billion and 100 billion units called *neurons*, enough to give us a great variety of abilities, including some that go beyond the limits of the largest and most sophisticated computers. (Dan McCoy/Rainbow)

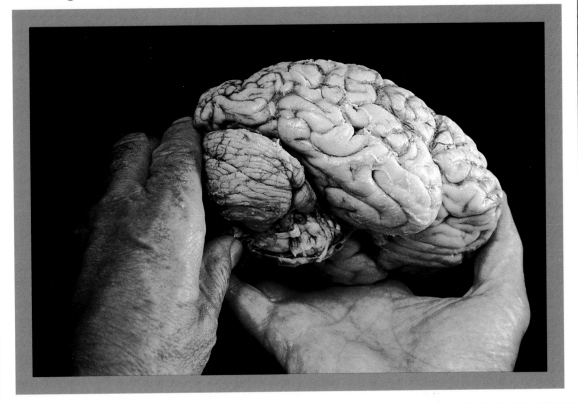

Plate 2. The central nervous system and major branches of the peripheral nervous system. The peripheral nerves carry messages back and forth between the central nervous system (the brain and spinal cord) and the rest of the body.

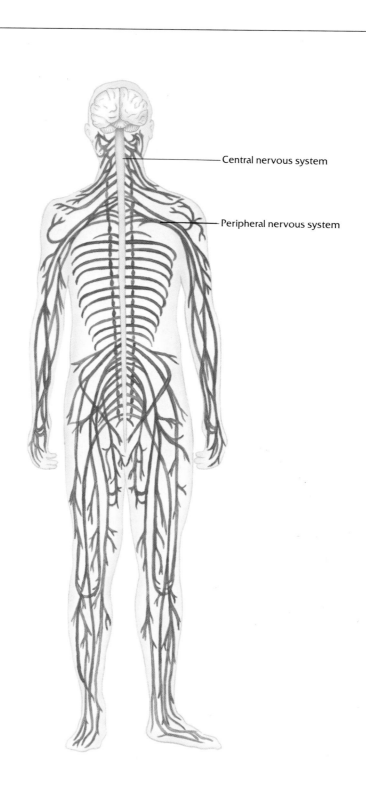

Central nervous system

Peripheral nervous system

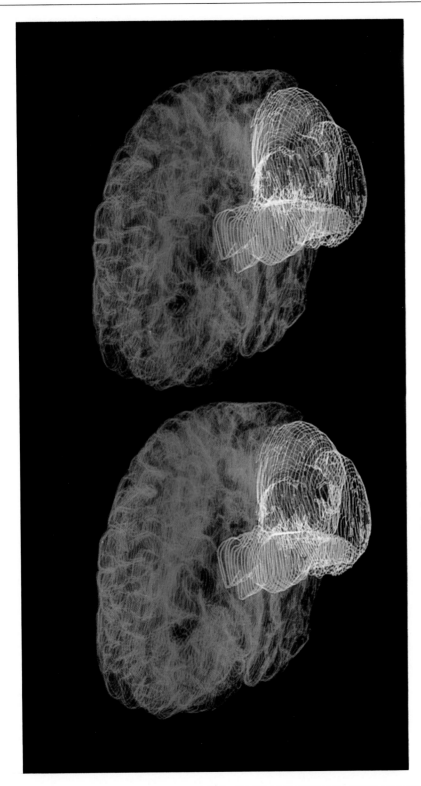

Plate 3. A computer-generated stereoscopic view of the human brain. Insert a card or piece of paper vertically between the two halves of the illustration, separating the view of your left eye from the view of your right eye. Stare at the left half of the illustration with your left eye and the right half with your right eye. Move your head forward or back until you can see a three-dimensional view of the brain. (Robert B. Livingston, University of California, San Diego)

Plate 4. Parts of the human brain, cut and separated. Top two views: The left cerebral cortex, divided to show the outside and inside. Third view: Midline structures (the brainstem), with the eyes and pituitary gland attached. Bottom: A midline view. (Adapted with the permission of the publisher W. H. Freeman and Company from *Brain, Mind and Behavior* by Floyd E. Bloom et al. Copyright © 1985 Educational Broadcasting Company.)

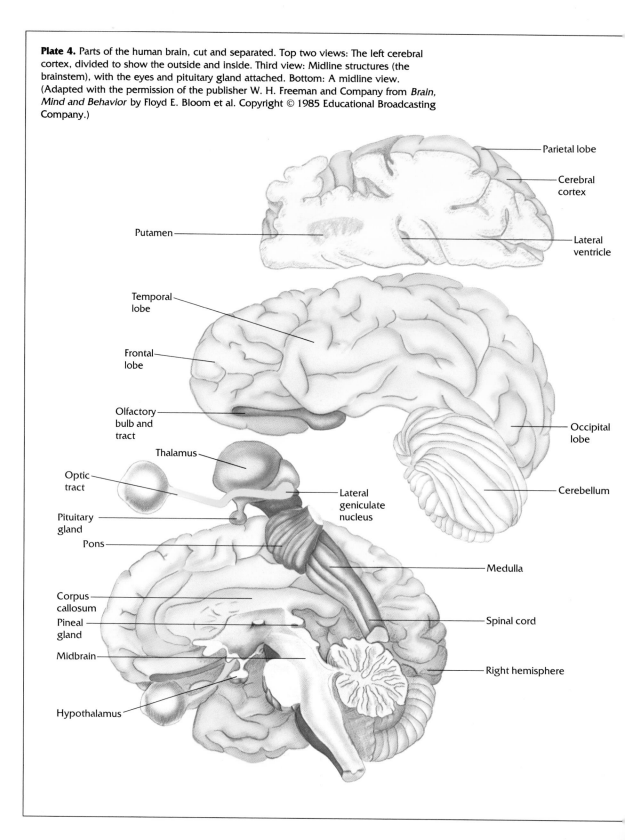

Plate 5. The limbic system, a set of subcortical structures that form a border (or limbus) around the brain stem. These structures, heavily linked with one another, are particularly important for motivated and emotional behaviors, such as eating, drinking, sexual behavior, pleasure, anxiety, and aggressive behavior. The hippocampus and amygdala are also critical for certain aspects of memory.

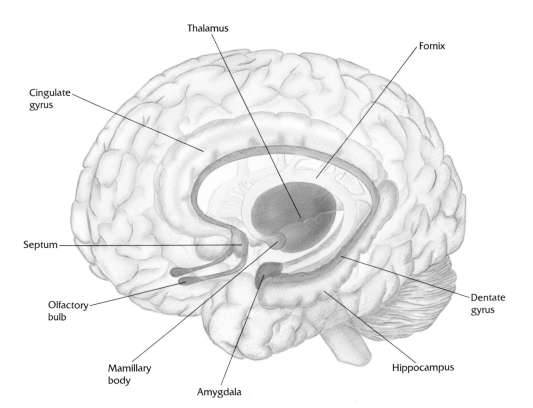

Thalamus

Fornix

Cingulate gyrus

Septum

Olfactory bulb

Mamillary body

Amygdala

Hippocampus

Dentate gyrus

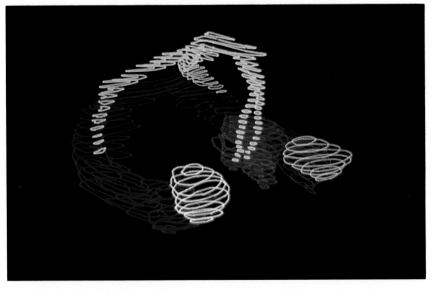

Plate 6. A computer-generated view of the limbic system. (Robert B. Livingston, University of California, San Diego)

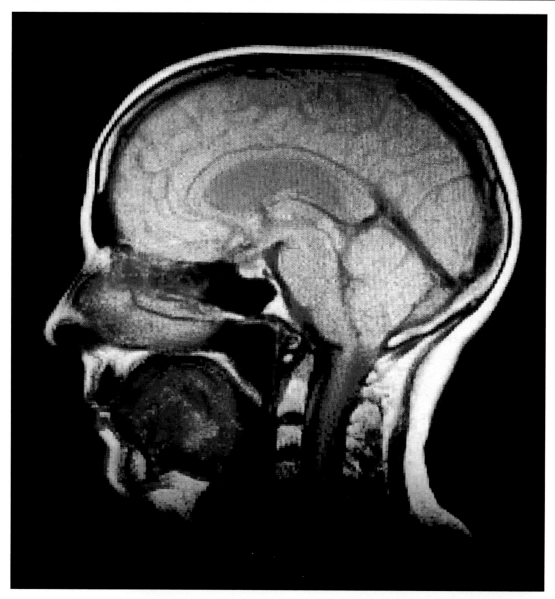

Plate 7. A view of a living brain generated by nuclear magnetic resonance (NMR). Any atom such as hydrogen that has an odd atomic weight has an inherent rotation. An outside magnetic field can align the axes of rotation. A radio frequency field can then make all these atoms move like tiny gyros. When the radio frequency field is turned off, the atomic nuclei release electromagnetic energy as they relax. By measuring that energy, it is possible to form an image of a structure such as the brain without damaging it. (Dan McCoy/Rainbow)

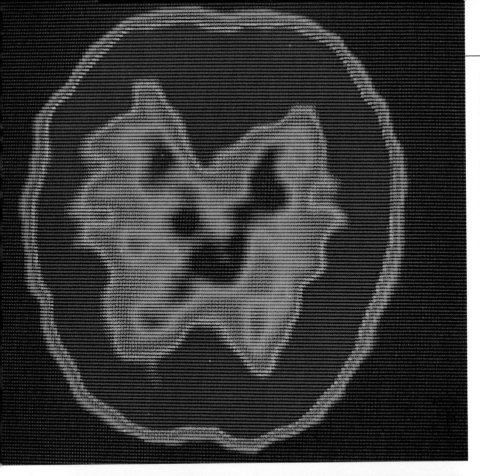

Plate 8. A view of the normal brain generated by positron emission tomography (PET). To generate a PET scan, the person is first injected with a radioactively labeled chemical that will be absorbed by the brain—for example, 2-deoxy-glucose. Because of its similarity to glucose, this chemical is absorbed by brain cells in proportion to the amount of glucose they are metabolizing at a given time. Sensors around the head measure the radioactivity emitted, and a computer generates an image of the brain, indicating the amount of activity in different areas. PET scans are useful for localizing tumors, certain types of epilepsy, and any other disorder that alters the metabolic rate of a given brain area. (Dan McCoy/Rainbow)

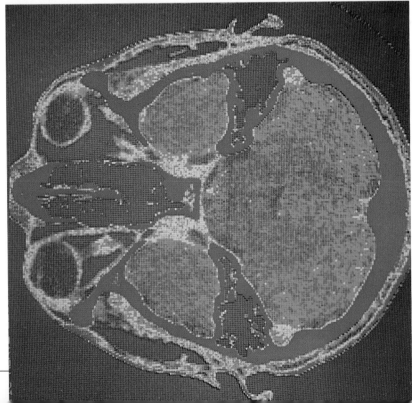

Plate 9. A view of a normal human brain generated by computerized axial tomography (CAT). After a dye is injected into the blood, x-rays are passed through the head in all directions, recorded, and processed by a computer, which can reconstruct a view of the brain at any level. (Dan McCoy/Rainbow)

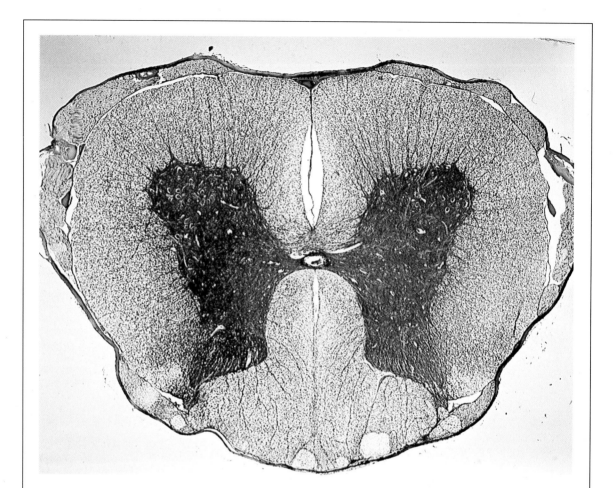

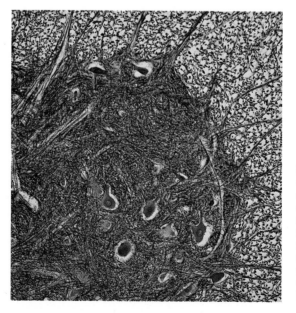

Plate 10. A cross-section through the spinal cord. The H-shaped structure in the center is gray matter, composed largely of cell bodies. The surrounding white matter is composed of axons (extensions of nerve cells). These axons are organized in tracts; some carry information from the brain and higher levels of the spinal cord downward, while others carry information from lower levels upward. These tracts of axons play an essential role in coordinating movements of various parts of the body. (Manfred Kage/ Peter Arnold, Inc.)

Plate 11. At greater magnification, a section of gray matter (lower left) and white matter surrounding it. Note that axons enter the gray matter from the white matter and extend from the gray matter into the white matter. (Manfred Kage/Peter Arnold, Inc.)

drites may grow anew and others may disappear altogether. Evidently, the anatomy of the brain is in constant flux at the microscopic level as neurons change their connections with other neurons.

Alcohol can impair the dendritic branching of neurons. Pregnant rats that are forced to drink large amounts of alcohol give birth to offspring with abnormal patterns of dendritic branching (West, Hodges, & Black, 1981). The dendritic branches of mice retract after the mice are exposed to alcohol, even in adulthood (Riley & Walker, 1978).

Aged humans (those over 70) may have either wider or narrower dendritic branches than middle-aged people. When Buell and Coleman (1981) examined the cortices of people who had died at various ages, they found that normal, alert old people had lost a certain number of neurons. However, the dendrites of their remaining neurons had compensated for the loss by growing longer and branching more widely, thereby increasing their contact with other neurons. Among those older people who had grown senile, the dendrites of the surviving neurons had failed to compensate for the loss of other neurons. In fact, the dendrites were slightly shorter and less branched than the dendrites of middle-aged people.

THE NERVE IMPULSE

A neuron that communicates over long distances must be able to pass impulses along its axon. Axons are specialized to transmit impulses without any loss of strength in the impulse as it travels down the axon.

The Resting Potential of the Neuron

All parts of a neuron are covered by a membrane about 8 nanometers (nm) thick (just less than .00001 mm), composed of two layers of fat molecules with protein molecules embedded in the fats. (See Figure 2-8.) Each of the fat molecules has a water-soluble end and a water-insoluble end. The water-soluble ends point outward (toward the exterior of the cell on one side and

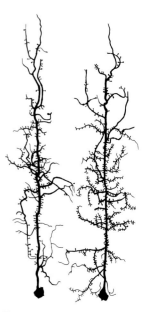

Figure 2-7. Comparison of structures of neurons from the brains of Jewel fish reared in isolation (*left*) and reared with others of their own species (*right*). (Photo courtesy of Richard Coss.)

Figure 2-8. The membrane of a neuron. Embedded in it are channels, composed of protein, that permit certain ions to cross through the membrane.

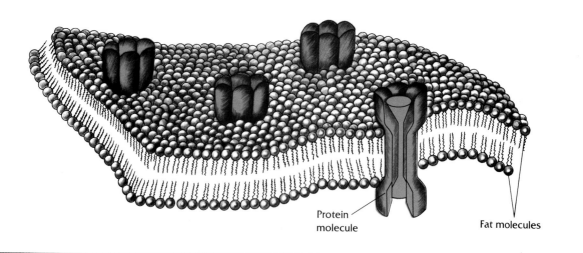

Protein
molecule

Fat molecules

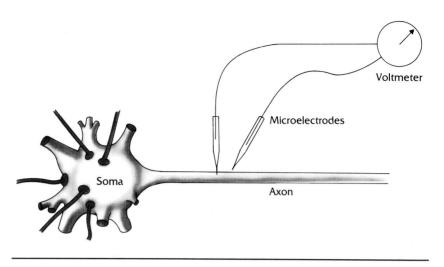

Figure 2-9. Apparatus for measuring the electrical potential across a neuron membrane. The neuron and the voltmeter are *not* drawn to the same scale.

the interior on the other), while the water-insoluble ends point toward one another.

The neuron membrane is **selectively permeable** to the passage of chemicals. That is, it permits some molecules to pass but not others. Water, carbon dioxide, urea, and a few other small molecules cross the membrane fairly freely in either direction at all times. However, most molecules, especially large ones, cannot cross at all. A few important ions, such as potassium, chloride, and sodium, enter at a controlled rate through pores (or gates) in specialized proteins embedded in the membrane. The potassium and chloride pores permit potassium and chloride ions to pass at a moderate rate. When the membrane is at rest, the sodium pores are closed. An occasional sodium ion sneaks through one of the potassium pores, but the total flow of sodium ions is greatly restricted.

In the absence of any outside disturbance, the membrane is electrically **polarized**; that is, the part of the neuron inside the membrane has an electrical potential slightly negative with respect to the outside. We can measure this potential by inserting a very fine electrode into the neuron (see Color Plate 13) and placing a second electrode outside the cell, as illustrated in Figure 2-9. The most common type of electrode for this purpose is a thin glass tube stretched to about 0.5 microns (one micron = .001 mm) in diameter at the tip and filled with a salt solution that can conduct electrical current. Using this apparatus, we find that the inside of the neuron has a potential somewhere in the range of -30 to -90 millivolts (mV) relative to the outside. This is known as the **resting potential** of the neuron.

What causes the resting potential? An important part of the answer is the **sodium-potassium pump**. This pump actively transports sodium ions out of the cell while simultaneously drawing potassium ions into the cell. To be precise, it ejects three sodium ions while bringing in two potassium ions. Since both sodium and potassium ions carry a $+1$ electrical charge, the result of the pump is a net movement of positive ions out of the cell.

Table 2-2.   Average Ion Concentrations Inside and Outside Neurons

Ion	Concentration inside neuron, M*	Concentration outside neuron, M*
Na$^+$ (sodium)	0.010	0.142
K$^+$ (potassium)	0.141	0.005
Cl$^-$ (chloride)	0.004	0.103
HCO$_3^-$ (bicarbonate)	0.010	0.028

*M = molar, a measure of the concentration of a substance in water solution.

The sodium-potassium pump, by itself, would establish only a small difference in charge across the membrane. The selective permeability of the membrane greatly increases the size of the effect. The sodium-potassium pump establishes a **concentration gradient**, with potassium being more highly concentrated inside the neuron and sodium more concentrated outside. Because potassium can cross the membrane at a moderate rate, many of the potassium ions that are pumped into the cell diffuse back out, carrying a positive charge with them. The sodium ions do not balance this flow by entering the cell, because they cross the membrane at a much slower rate. The potassium ions thus are primarily responsible for the resting potential of the membrane.

When the neuron is at its resting potential, sodium, potassium, and other common ions are distributed unequally across the membrane. Typical concentrations for human neurons are given in Table 2-2 (Guyton, 1974).

The concentration of potassium is the result of an equilibrium of competing forces. The sodium-potassium pump actively moves potassium into the neuron. (That is, it does so by expending energy.) The potassium ions then flow passively from their area of greater concentration to the area of lesser concentration. In addition to the sodium-potassium pump and the concentration gradient, a third force is the **electrical gradient**. Because the inside of the cell is negatively charged with respect to the outside, potassium ions are attracted toward the interior of the neuron and thus remain in greater abundance than they would if the concentration barrier were the only factor to contend with.

Similarly, the concentration gradient of sodium ions is the result of the sodium-potassium pump, which actively moves sodium out of the cell, and the very slow passive diffusion of sodium into the cell, driven by both a concentration gradient and an electrical gradient.

Why a Resting Potential?

Presumably, evolution could have equipped us with neurons that were electrically neutral at rest. The sodium-potassium pump does not expend a great deal of energy; still, there must be some advantage to justify even a slight energy expense.

The advantage of the resting potential is that it prepares the neuron to respond rapidly to a stimulus. As we shall see in the next section, an excitation of the neuron opens the sodium gates, enabling sodium to enter the cell explosively. Because the membrane did its work in advance by maintaining the concentration gradient for sodium, the cell is prepared to respond strongly and rapidly to a stimulus.

The resting potential of a neuron can be compared to a poised bow and arrow: If one pulls the bow in advance and then waits, one is ready to fire as soon as the appropriate moment comes. Evolution has applied the same strategy to the neuron.

The Action Potential

The resting potential can remain stable as long as the animal remains healthy and the neuron is not stimulated. In nature, stimulation of the neuron takes place at the synapse. We shall defer consideration of the synapse until Chapter 3; at this point, we shall deal with artificial stimulation of the neuron. (The effects of artificial stimulation are entirely comparable to those of natural stimulation at the synapse.)

Figure 2-10 shows the measured electrical potential inside an axon as a function of time. We can measure the potential with the same apparatus shown in Figure 2-9, with the addition of an extra electrode to stimulate the axon. The extra electrode is placed on the surface of the membrane close to the intracellular electrode.

At time 0, no stimulus is applied to the neuron, and we record its resting potential. At time 1, we stimulate the neuron through the additional electrode, applying a negative charge, which further increases the negative charge inside the neuron. The change is called **hyperpolarization**, meaning increased polarization. As soon as the artificial stimulation ceases, the cell's charge returns to its original resting level (time 2).

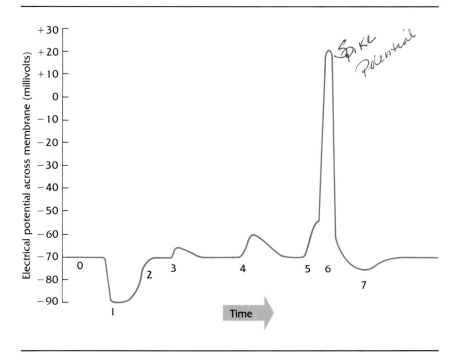

Figure 2-10. Electrical potentials across a neuron membrane during artificial stimulation. Time 1 is a hyperpolarization; 3, 4, and 5 are three degrees of depolarization. See text for a further explanation.

Now, let us apply currents that **depolarize** the neuron—that is, that reduce its polarization toward zero. We apply a small depolarizing current at time 3 and a slightly larger current at time 4. The cell's potential decreases by just a few millivolts and returns to the resting level as soon as the stimulation ceases. However, when we apply just a slightly stronger current (time 5), the cell's potential shoots well beyond the level produced by the current itself (time 6). We say that the cell has reached its **threshold**, a point at which a brief stimulation triggers a rapid, massive electrical change by the membrane. Although it varies from cell to cell, the threshold is generally about 15 mV above the resting potential.

Any subthreshold stimulation produces a small response proportional to the amount of current. Any stimulation beyond the threshold, regardless of *how far* beyond, produces the same response seen at time 6 in Figure 2-10. This response is referred to variously as an **action potential**, an impulse, or a spike. Action potentials occur in axons. As a rule, dendrites produce graded potentials proportional to the magnitude of the stimulation.

Within a given cell, all action potentials are approximately equal in size and shape (amplitude) under normal circumstances. This is known as the **all-or-none law**. To state the all-or-none law more precisely, *the size and shape of the action potential are independent of the intensity of the stimulus that initiated it.*

As a consequence of this law, a neuron's messages are analogous to those of a telegraph. A neuron cannot send larger action potentials any more than a telegraph operator could send louder dots and dashes. In both cases, the message is conveyed by the time sequence of impulses and pauses. For instance, a neuron might signal "dim light" by a low frequency of action potentials and "brighter light" by a higher frequency. It is also possible that impulses in clusters, such as

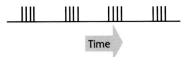

might signal something different from the same number of impulses evenly distributed:

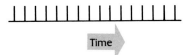

Molecular Basis of the Action Potential

The action potential can be related to the distribution of ions across the membrane. Remember that the sodium-potassium pump keeps the sodium concentration much higher outside the neuron than inside. In addition to this concentration gradient, sodium ions are attracted to the inside of the neuron by an electrical gradient, because of the negative charge inside the neuron. If sodium ions were free to flow across the membrane, they would diffuse into the cell rapidly. Ordinarily, the membrane is almost impermeable to sodium, but at the time of the action potential, the permeability increases sharply.

The membrane proteins that form the sodium gates are **voltage-activated**; that is, their permeability to sodium depends on the voltage difference across the membrane. As the membrane of the neuron becomes even slightly depolarized, the sodium gates begin to open and sodium flows more freely. If the depolarization is slight (less than the threshold), the increased entry of sodium ions is balanced by an increased exit of potassium ions. (Why do potassium ions leave the cell at this time? They do so primarily because the electrical gradient that had held them inside the cell has been weakened. Also, the depolarization of the membrane opens the potassium gates wider as well as the sodium gates.)

When the potential across the membrane reaches threshold, the sodium gates open wide enough that sodium enters the cell faster than potassium can exit. The entering sodium ions depolarize the cell still further, thus opening the sodium gates even wider. Sodium ions rush into the neuron until the electrical potential across the membrane passes beyond zero to a reversed polarity (point 6 on Figure 2-10).

At the peak of the action potential, sodium ions are still more concentrated outside the neuron than inside. An action potential increases the sodium concentration inside a neuron by less than 1 percent in most cases. Because of the persisting concentration gradient, sodium ions should still tend to diffuse into the cell. However, they are no longer attracted to the inside of the cell by an electrical gradient; in fact, the inside of the neuron has become temporarily positive with respect to the outside. This reversed electrical gradient blocks the further entry of sodium.

Moreover, around the time of the peak of the action potential, the sodium gates begin to close, while the potassium gates remain wider open than usual. Sodium ions no longer enter the neuron in significant numbers, but potassium ions rapidly leave because they are much more concentrated inside and because they are no longer attracted by a negative charge. As potassium ions depart, the charge across the membrane returns toward the resting level. In fact, because of the increased permeability to potassium, enough ions may leave to drive the potential beyond the normal resting level to a temporary hyperpolarization (time 7 in Figure 2-10).

Figure 2-11 summarizes the movements of ions during the excitation of a neuron. At the end of this process, the membrane has returned to its resting potential. The inside of the neuron has slightly more sodium ions and slightly fewer potassium ions than before the action potential, but the sodium-potassium pump soon restores the original distribution.

Anything that promotes or interferes with the flow of ions across the membrane can have profound effects on the nervous system. For example, local **anesthetic** drugs such as Novocain and Xylocaine attach to the sodium gates of the membrane, preventing sodium ions from entering (K. W. Miller, 1985). In doing so, such drugs block action potentials in the affected area. If anesthetics are applied to sensory nerves, such as nerves carrying pain messages, they block the messages in those nerves from reaching the brain.

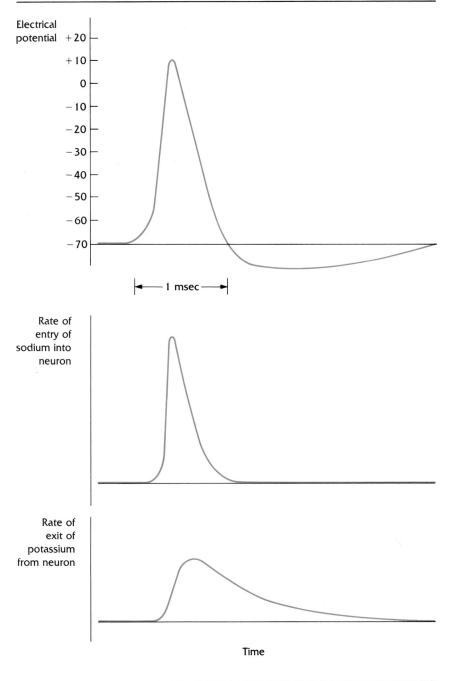

Electrical potential

+ 20
+ 10
0
− 10
− 20
− 30
− 40
− 50
− 60
− 70

|← 1 msec →|

Rate of entry of sodium into neuron

Rate of exit of potassium from neuron

Time

Figure 2-11. The movement of sodium and potassium ions during an action potential.

The Refractory Period

While the electrical potential across the membrane is returning from its peak toward the resting point, it is still above the threshold. Why does the cell not produce another action potential during this period? Evidently, there is a brief period when the cell is resistant to reexcitation. During a period of 1 or more milliseconds after an action potential, the cell is in such a **refractory period**. The first part of this period is called the **absolute refractory period,** during which the membrane cannot produce an action potential in response to stimulation of any intensity. The second part is the **relative refractory period,** during which a stimulus must exceed the usual threshold in order to produce an action potential. During the total refractory period, permeability to sodium ions is low and permeability to potassium ions is higher than normal.

The refractory period sets a maximum on the firing frequency of a neuron. If the absolute refractory period were 1 msec, for example, no stimulus could produce more than 1,000 action potentials per second. Stimuli weaker than the maximum would produce lower frequencies, depending on the relative refractory period.

The refractory period can be used as a tool for studying brain-behavior relationships. To begin, suppose we stimulate some part of the brain and measure the intensity of the evoked behavior, as in Chapter 1, p. 9. Next, we observe that two successive electrical stimulations will evoke the behavior more strongly than a single stimulation. We can represent the sequence as follows, with the horizontal line representing time (in milliseconds) and the vertical lines representing electrical stimuli:

Now we can manipulate the delay between the two electrical pulses in the double stimulation to examine the effect on behavior:

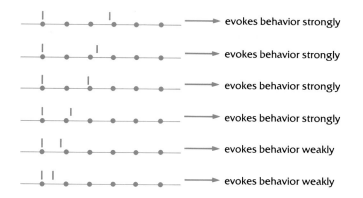

Evidently, two stimuli are better than one *only if* the delay between them is greater than a certain minimum. If the delay is short, the second stimulus reaches the neuron while the membrane is still in its refractory period from the first stimulus. Using this technique, researchers can determine the refractory period of the neurons that govern a particular behavior.

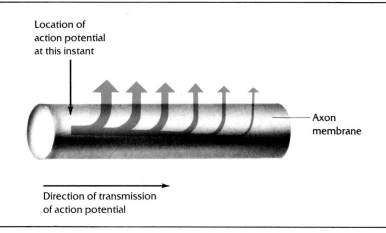

Location of
action potential
at this instant

Axon
membrane

Direction of transmission
of action potential

Figure 2-12. Current that enters an axon at the point of the action potential flows down the axon, thereby depolarizing adjacent areas of the membrane.

Because the refractory period varies from one neuron to another, investigators can use this technique to answer certain questions about how the brain controls behavior. Suppose they find, for example, that the refractory period of the neurons governing one behavior is the same as the refractory period of the neurons governing some other, similar behavior. They would then suspect—though they would not know for certain—that the two behaviors are controlled by the same set of neurons (e.g., Hawkins, Roll, Puerto, & Yeomans, 1983). In another case, investigators may find that the refractory periods for two related behaviors are different. In that case, they may safely conclude that different sets of neurons are responsible for the two behaviors (e.g., Deutsch, 1964).

Propagation of the Action Potential

Up to this point, we have dealt with the action potential as it occurs at one location along the neuron. It is now time to consider how it moves down the axon toward some other cell.

Generally, an action potential begins on the axon hillock. It cannot be conducted any great distance down the axon in the manner that electricity is conducted in a wire, because the axon is a poor conductor of electricity. Rather, each point along the membrane regenerates the action potential in much the same way that it was generated initially.

At the time of the action potential, sodium ions enter one point along the axon, bearing positive charges. That location is temporarily positively charged with respect to neighboring areas along the axon. The positive charge flows both down the axon and across the membrane, as shown in Figure 2-12. If the resistance to electrical flow is great across the membrane and relatively low in the interior of the axon, the charge will flow relatively far along the axon. If, on the other hand, the resistance is slight across the membrane and greater in the interior of the axon—as it is in the thinnest axons—the charge will flow only a short distance along the axon before crossing the membrane.

As the charge passes down the axon, it slightly depolarizes the adjacent areas of the membrane. The areas closest to the action potential are depolar-

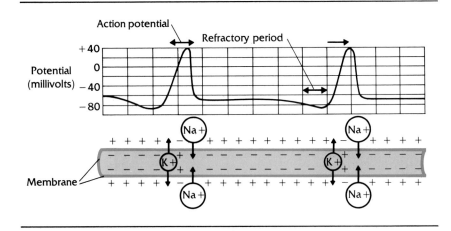

Figure 2-13. Two action potentials as waves traveling along the axon. Note that they are depicted here as a function of location on the axon rather than as a function of time.

ized enough to reach their threshold and to generate an action potential of their own. In this manner the action potential is regenerated. The action potential passes as a wave along the axon. If we could record simultaneously from all points along the axon, the result would resemble Figure 2-13.

The transmission of an action potential down an axon is referred to as the **propagation of the action potential**. The "propagation" of an animal species is the production of babies; in a sense the action potential gives birth to a new action potential at each point along the axon. In this manner, the action potential can be just as strong at the end of the axon as it was at the beginning. The action potential is much slower than electrical conduction, because it requires the diffusion of sodium ions at successive points along the axon. The thinnest axons are the slowest; their action potentials travel at a velocity of less than 1 meter/second. In the thickest unmyelinated axons, action potentials reach a velocity of about 10 meters/second. In axons surrounded by myelin, which we shall discuss in the next section, the velocity may reach or exceed 100 meters/second. In comparison, electricity travels at 300 million meters/second.

Let us reexamine Figure 2-12 for a moment. What is to prevent the electrical charge from flowing in the other direction, opposite the direction that the action potential is traveling? Nothing. In fact, the electrical charge does flow both directions. In that case, what prevents the action potential from traveling both directions? The answer is the refractory period. Normally, an action potential begins at the axon hillock and flows to adjacent areas of the axon. From then on, the action potential can flow in one direction only—away from the axon hillock—because the area behind the action potential is in its refractory period.

The Myelin Sheath and Saltatory Conduction

As noted above, the maximum velocity of action potentials in the unmyelinated axons of vertebrates is about 10 meters/second. At that speed, an impulse from a giraffe's foot would take about a second to reach the brain. Even in smaller animals, a speed of 10 meters/second is too slow for the coordination of certain rapid responses. Myelin sheaths increase speed to make such coordination possible.

Before we discuss how myelin sheaths accelerate action potentials, let us consider the following analogy. Suppose it were my job to carry written messages over a distance of 3 km, without using any mechanical device. One solution would be for me to run with the message over the 3 km distance. That would be analogous to the propagation of the action potential along an unmyelinated axon; it would get the job done, but not very rapidly. An alternative would be for me to tie the message to a baseball and throw it. The problem with that approach is that I cannot throw a ball even close to a distance of 3 km. The ideal compromise would be to station people at moderate distances along the 3 km course and to throw the message-bearing ball from person to person until it reaches its destination.

The principle behind **myelination** of axons is the same. Many vertebrate axons are covered with a myelin sheath, which is a coating made up largely of fats. The myelin sheath is interrupted at intervals of approximately 1 mm by short unmyelinated sections of axon called the **nodes of Ranvier** (RAHN-vee-ay). (See Figure 2-14.)

Suppose an action potential is initiated at the axon hillock. It is propagated along the axon until it reaches the first myelin segment. The action potential then jumps directly over the myelin segment to the first node of Ranvier, and from there to the second node, and so on. The action potential cannot regenerate along the membrane between one node and the next for two reasons: First, the myelin sheath increases the resistance to electrical transmission at every point between the nodes. Second, sodium gates are located in abundance at the nodes but are virtually absent in the myelinated areas between the nodes (Catterall, 1984).

Transmission between one node and the next is by electrotonic conduction. That is the fastest possible method of transmission, although it could not carry a message very far without a great loss of intensity. The electrical charge is still above threshold when it reaches the next node, at which point an action potential of full intensity is regenerated, which can then jump electrically to the following node. This alternation of action potentials at nodes and electrotonic conduction between nodes is referred to as **saltatory conduction**, from the Latin word *saltare* meaning "to jump." Conduction velocity in myelinated axons can be as fast as 120 meters/second.

Some diseases, such as multiple sclerosis, destroy myelin sheaths. The result is at least to slow down action potentials and in many cases to stop them altogether. An axon that has lost its myelin is not the same as one that has never had any myelin; it still lacks sodium gates in the areas previously covered with myelin. Therefore, when the membrane is depolarized in those areas, an action potential cannot arise.

Signaling Without Action Potentials

All that we have just discussed concerning action potentials pertains to certain neurons and not others. Investigators who insert an electrode into a cell body or an axon are likely to find themselves recording from relatively large neurons, simply because it is difficult to insert an electrode into a small cell

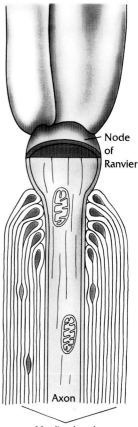

Figure 2-14. An axon surrounded by a myelin sheath and interrupted by nodes of Ranvier. The lower part shows a cross-section through both the axon and the myelin sheath. Magnification × 30,000 (approximately).

without damaging it. A disproportionate amount of our knowledge, therefore, has come from large neurons.

Large neurons with long axons are specialized to transmit messages over long distances, such as from the spinal cord to the muscles, or from one part of the brain to another. A small neuron with a short axon (or no axon at all) communicates over shorter distances, and it differs in several ways from the larger neurons (Bullock, 1979; Pearson, 1979).

A small neuron with no more than a short axon is known as a **local neuron** because it exchanges information only with other neurons in its own vicinity. Local neurons do not produce action potentials. Rather, they produce **graded potentials** (membrane potentials that vary in magnitude). Upon stimulation, a local neuron depolarizes (or in some cases hyperpolarizes) in proportion to the intensity of the stimulus. The change in membrane potential is conducted to adjacent areas of the cell. Unlike action potentials, graded potentials decay in intensity as they pass along the cell.

Actually, all neurons have graded potentials, at least in their dendrites. The distinctive feature of a local neuron is that it has *only* graded potentials; no part of the cell produces action potentials. Those graded potentials are sufficient to convey information to other cells.

In a large neuron with a long axon, the dendrites receive information on one end of the cell and the axon transmits information to its target at the other end. Local neurons do not have such a polarity between one end and the other; they can receive information at various points along their membrane and transmit the information in either direction. A part of a local neuron that receives information may be immediately adjacent to a part that transmits it. In many cases the dendrites of a local neuron may pass information directly to the dendrites of another neuron.

Although our knowledge of local neurons is still fragmentary, it is clear that local neurons are responsible for a great deal of information processing. We shall encounter one of the best-known examples of local-neuron processing when we discuss neural activity in the eye (Chapter 7).

This chapter has concentrated on what happens within a neuron, as if each neuron acted independently. That is a bit like studying the telephone system by examining what happens in a single telephone: Although that is a reasonable place to start, the individual telephone would be of no use unless it were connected to a network of other telephones. Similarly, a neuron contributes to behavior only because of its connections within a vast network. In Chapter 3 we examine what happens at those connections.

--- SUMMARY ---

1.   Santiago Ramón y Cajal used newly discovered staining techniques in the late 1800s to establish that the nervous system is composed of separate cells, now known as neurons. (p. 22)

2.   Neurons receive information from, and transmit information to, other cells. The nervous system also contains cells called *glia* that do not exchange information with other cells. (pp. 22, 29)

3.   Neurons include four major parts: dendrites, a cell body, an axon, and presynaptic endings. Neuron shape varies greatly, depending on the function of the neuron and the connections it makes with other cells. (p. 24)

4.   Because of a set of mechanisms known as the blood-brain barrier, many molecules, especially large molecules, cannot enter the brain. The blood-brain

barrier prevents fuels other than glucose from entering most areas of the brain. For this reason, neurons rely heavily on glucose for their nutrition. (pp. 29, 30)
5.   Certain areas of the brain are capable of generating new neurons even after the brain has reached maturity. (p. 31)
6.   Neurons can alter their shape even after maturity. An enriched environment can lead to longer and more widely branched dendrites. Alcohol can lead to a shrinkage of dendrites. Healthy, alert old people have an increased proliferation of dendritic branches, whereas senile people have slightly shrunken dendrites. (p. 32)
7.   At rest, the inside of a neuron has a negative charge with respect to the outside. Sodium ions are actively pumped out of the neuron, while potassium ions are pumped in. Potassium ions are moderately free to flow across the membrane of the neuron, while the flow of sodium ions is greatly restricted. (p. 34)
8.   When the charge across the membrane is reduced, sodium ions can flow more freely across the membrane. If the change in membrane potential is sufficient to reach the threshold of the neuron, sodium ions enter explosively and the charge across the membrane

is suddenly reduced and reversed. This event is known as the action potential. (p. 36)
9.   The magnitude of the action potential is independent of the size of the stimulus that initiated it. This is known as the all-or-none law. (p. 37)
10.   Immediately after an action potential, the membrane enters a refractory period, a time during which it is resistant to starting another action potential. By measuring the refractory periods of different neurons, it is sometimes possible to determine whether two behaviors depend on the same set of neurons. (p. 39)
11.   The action potential is regenerated at successive points along the axon by a combination of electrical flow through the axon and the diffusion of sodium ions across the membrane. The action potential maintains a constant magnitude as it passes along the axon. (p. 41)
12.   In axons that are covered with myelin, action potentials form only in the nodes that are found between myelinated segments. (p. 43)
13.   Many small local neurons transmit messages over relatively short distances by graded potentials that decay over time and space, instead of by action potentials. (p. 44)

REVIEW QUESTIONS

1.   Identify: nucleus, mitochondrion, ribosomes. (pp. 23–24)
2.   Suppose you were looking at a small fiber in the brain; how could you tell whether it was a dendrite or an axon? (p. 25)
3.   Distinguish among receptor neurons, motor neurons, and interneurons. Distinguish between afferent and efferent. (pp. 26–27)
4.   Describe an example of how the shape of a neuron relates to its function. (p. 28)
5.   What is the primary fuel of neurons in the adult vertebrate brain? Why do most brain neurons use very little of other fuels? (p. 29)
6.   Which vitamin is necessary in order for neurons to use their primary fuel? (p. 29)
7.   What are the functions of glia cells? (pp. 29–30)
8.   What mechanisms cause the blood-brain barrier? Under what circumstances is the barrier weakened? (p. 31)
9.   What is the current belief about whether new neurons can form in an adult vertebrate brain? (p. 31)
10.   What environmental influences can increase or decrease the branching patterns of dendrites? How

does the brain differ between alert and senile old people? (pp. 32–33)
11.   What is the difference between a hyperpolarization and a depolarization? What is an action potential? (pp. 36–37)
12.   State the all-or-none law of the action potential. (p. 37)
13.   Explain the ion movements responsible for the action potential and the return to the resting potential. (p. 38)
14.   Distinguish between the absolute refractory period and the relative refractory period. (p. 40)
15.   Describe how the refractory period can be used in a study to determine whether two types of behavior are controlled by the same neurons or different neurons. (p. 41)
16.   How does an action potential propagate along an axon? (p. 41)
17.   How does myelin increase the velocity of the action potential? (p. 43)
18.   What is a graded potential? How does a local neuron differ from a neuron with a long axon? (p. 44)

THOUGHT QUESTIONS

1.   The fetal alcohol syndrome refers to a condition in which the babies of alcoholic mothers are born with a variety of physical deformities and behavioral ab-

normalities. What abnormalities would you expect to find in the structure of the brains of such children?
2.   Suppose the threshold for some neuron were the

same as that neuron's resting potential. What would happen? At what frequency would the cell produce action potentials?

3.   In the laboratory it is possible to apply an electrical stimulus at any point along the axon and thereby to set up action potentials traveling in both directions from the point of stimulation. An action potential traveling in the usual direction, away from the axon hillock, is said to be traveling in the *orthodromic* di-

rection. An action potential traveling toward the axon hillock is traveling in the *antidromic* direction. If we started an orthodromic action potential at the axon hillock and an antidromic action potential at the opposite end of the axon, what would happen when they met at the center? Why? Can you imagine any research purpose for which one might make use of antidromic impulses?

TERMS TO REMEMBER

neuron (p. 22)
membrane (p. 23)
cytoplasm (p. 23)
nucleus (p. 23)
mitochondrion (p. 23)
ribosomes (p. 24)
endoplasmic reticulum (p. 24)
vacuoles (p. 24)
motor neuron (p. 24)
cell body (soma) (p. 24)
dendrites (p. 25)
dendritic spines (p. 25)
axon (p. 25)
axon hillock (p. 25)
myelin sheath (p. 25)
presynaptic ending (p. 25)
receptor (sensory) neuron (p. 26)
interneurons (p. 26)
afferent neuron (p. 27)
efferent neuron (p. 27)
intrinsic neuron (p. 27)
glucose (p. 29)
thiamine (p. 29)
glia (p. 29)
oligodendrocytes (p. 29)
Schwann cells (p. 29)

microglia (p. 30)
astroglia (p. 30)
radial glia (p. 30)
blood-brain barrier (p. 30)
selectively permeable (p. 34)
polarized (p. 34)
resting potential (p. 34)
sodium-potassium pump (p. 34)
concentration gradient (p. 35)
electrical gradient (p. 35)
hyperpolarization (p. 36)
depolarization (p. 37)
threshold (p. 37)
action potential (p. 37)
all-or-none law (p. 37)
voltage-activated (p. 38)
anesthetic (p. 38)
refractory period (p. 40)
absolute refractory period (p. 40)
relative refractory period (p. 40)
propagation of the action potential (p. 42)
myelination (p. 43)
nodes of Ranvier (p. 43)
saltatory conduction (p. 43)
local neuron (p. 44)
graded potentials (p. 44)

SUGGESTIONS FOR FURTHER READING

Shepherd, G. M. (1983). *Neurobiology.* New York: Oxford University Press. The first seven chapters provide additional details about neurons, the membrane, and the action potential.

Science, September 21, 1984. A special issue devoted to articles about neurons and the nervous system.

Synapses

MAIN IDEAS

1. At a synapse, one neuron releases a chemical known as a synaptic transmitter that excites or inhibits another cell.

2. A single release of transmitter produces only a subthreshold response in the receiving cell. This response summates with other subthreshold responses to determine whether the cell will or will not produce an action potential. The synapses are a major site for the integration of incoming information.

3. Because different transmitters contribute in different ways to the control of behavior, many abnormalities of behavior can be traced to an excess or deficit of transmission at a particular type of synapse.

4. Many of the drugs that affect behavior and experience do so by altering activity at synapses, by any of a number of mechanisms.

Chapter 2 discussed what happens during the excitation or inhibition of a neuron. We did not discuss where this excitation comes from or what happens to it when it reaches the end of an axon. As you might have guessed, the two questions have the same answer: The death of an impulse at the end of one neuron gives rise to the birth of a new response in another neuron, based on activity at specialized junctions called synapses. The synapses are central to all comparison and integration of information in the brain.

CHARLES SHERRINGTON AND THE CONCEPT OF THE SYNAPSE

In the late 1800s, Ramón y Cajal's observations demonstrated that neurons do not physically merge into one another—that a narrow gap separates one neuron from the next. It was not known what takes place at that gap. As far as anyone knew, information might be transmitted across that gap in the same way that it was transmitted along an axon.

Then, in 1906, Charles Scott Sherrington (see BioSketch 3-1) gave that gap a name—**synapse**—and inferred that the synapse must be specialized for the transmission of information. He went on to describe most of the major properties of the synapse. What makes Sherrington's accomplishment particularly impressive is that he based his conclusions almost entirely on behavioral data. Decades later, techniques became available to measure and record the processes that Sherrington had inferred and to demonstrate that most of his conclusions had been correct.

Sherrington conducted most of his experiments on reflexive behavior. In a simple reflex, receptors excite interneurons, which excite effector neurons, which excite muscles, as shown in Figure 2-4, p. 27. Because a reflex depends on communication from one neuron to another at synapses, the properties of a reflex should reflect any special properties of synapses.

In a typical experiment, a dog was strapped into a harness suspended above the ground. Sherrington pinched one of the dog's feet; after a short delay, the dog *flexed* (raised) the pinched leg and *extended* the others. Both the flexion and the extension were reflexive movements; that is, they were produced automatically by the stimulus. Furthermore, Sherrington found the same movements after he made a cut that disconnected the spinal cord from the cerebral cortex; evidently, the flexion and extension were controlled by the spinal cord itself.

Sherrington observed several properties of reflexes that suggested that some special process must occur at the junctions between neurons.

Speed of a Reflex

When Sherrington pinched a dog's foot, the dog flexed that leg after a short delay. During the delay, an impulse had to travel up an axon from a skin receptor to the spinal cord, then another impulse had to travel from the spinal cord back down the leg to a muscle. Sherrington measured the total distance that the impulse traveled from skin receptor to spinal cord to muscle

BIOSKETCH

3-1

Charles Scott Sherrington (1857–1952)

The English physiologist C. S. Sherrington coined the term *synapse* and inferred the synapse's major properties in his 1906 book, *The Integrative Action of the Nervous System*, decades before the technology was available to measure those char-acteristics directly. Sherrington's work, for which he received a Nobel Prize in 1932, inspired the research of many other distin-guished scientists over the next half-century, including Sherring-ton's student John Eccles. It also provided us with the "telephone switchboard" model of the ner-vous system—that is, the idea that we can understand the func-tioning of the nervous system in terms of simple wiring diagrams, the connections between one set of neurons and another. Sherrington himself, however, preferred to apply this model only to the spinal cord, assuming that the brain might follow more complex principles.

Sherrington's interests and ac-complishments ranged far be-yond his work on the synapse. He did medical research on cholera epidemics and wrote a laboratory manual on mammali-an physiology, a book of poetry (*The Assaying of Brabantius and Other Verse*), and a philosophical treatise (*Man on His Nature*). He insisted that his scientific under-standing never caused him to lose his sense of wonder about the universe.

and calculated the speed that the impulse must have traveled to produce a muscle response after the measured delay. He found that the overall speed of conduction through the reflex arc was significantly slower than the known speed of conduction along the axon. Therefore, he deduced, transmission between one neuron and another at the synapse must be slower than trans-mission along an axon.

Synaptic Transmission: Electrical or Chemical?

Although Sherrington had found that transmission was slower at the synapse than along the axon, he still thought it was too fast to be accounted for by any chemical reaction. He suggested that a delay occurred while the synapse was preparing to respond but that the actual synaptic transmission relied on an electrical spark. This is the one major point on which Sherrington turned out to have been wrong.

A young scientist, T. R. Elliott (1905), demonstrated that the hormone *adrenalin* closely mimics the effects of the sympathetic nervous system, a set of nerves that control the internal organs (see Chapter 4). He therefore proposed that those nerves stimulate organs by releasing adrenalin or some-thing similar. He further suggested that synapses in general may operate by releasing chemicals. His evidence was not decisive, however; it might have been the case that adrenalin mimicked certain effects ordinarily produced by electrical stimulation. Sherrington's prestige was so great that most scientists ignored Elliott's results and continued to assume that synapses transmitted information by electrical impulses.

Otto Loewi was one who remained attracted to the idea that synapses operate by releasing chemicals, although he did not see how he could test the idea decisively. In 1920, an idea occurred to him one night; he made a note of the idea, but the next morning he could not understand his note. The following night, the idea returned. Rather than write himself another note, he rushed to the laboratory and performed the experiment at once: He repeatedly stimulated the vagus nerve to a frog's heart, causing the heart rate to decrease. He then collected fluid from that heart, applied it to a second frog's heart, and found that the second heart also decreased its rate of beating. Because the fluid obviously contained chemicals (not electricity!), Loewi concluded that nerves send messages by releasing chemicals.

Curiously, Loewi later remarked (Loewi, 1960) that if he had thought of this idea in the light of day, he probably never would have tried it. Even if synapses did release chemicals, his daytime reasoning went, there was little chance that they would release such an excess of those chemicals that he could easily collect them from the fluid around the heart. Fortunately, by the time he realized the experiment was unlikely to work, it already *had* worked and he was on his way to winning the Nobel Prize.

Although we now know that most synapses operate through the transmission of chemicals, a small number of electrical synapses do exist, particularly in special cases in which it is important for two neurons to synchronize their activities exactly.

Temporal Summation

The reflex arc shows the property of **temporal summation**: the cumulative effects of stimuli appearing at different times. When Sherrington pinched a dog's foot very lightly, the leg did not move. After the same light pinch was repeated several times in rapid succession, however, the leg flexed slightly. The more rapid the series of pinches, the greater the response. Sherrington surmised that a single action potential (resulting from a single light pinch) would cause *some* excitation at the synapse onto the next cell but not enough to produce an action potential in that cell. That is, the excitation would be less than the threshold of the second cell. He suggested that this subthreshold excitation gradually decays during a fraction of a second but is capable of adding with a second small excitation that quickly follows it. A rapid succession of pinches produces a series of action potentials in the receptor neuron, which in turn produces a series of subthreshold excitations of the **postsynaptic cell** (a cell that receives synaptic inputs from **presynaptic cells**). If the excitations occur rapidly enough, they can combine to exceed the threshold and therefore produce an action potential in the postsynaptic neuron.

Decades after Sherrington's work, it became possible to measure some of the single-cell properties that he had inferred. To record the activity evoked in a neuron by synaptic input, researchers can insert a thin **microelectrode** into the cell body. It is necessary that the diameter of the electrode be as small as possible so that it can enter a small cell without damaging it. By far the most popular electrode is a glass tube filled with a concentrated salt solution, such as 2 to 3 molar (M) potassium chloride, and tapering to a tip diameter of 0.0002 mm or less. This electrode, inserted into the neuron, is attached to a wire connected to recording equipment as shown in Figure 3-1. A reference electrode is placed somewhere outside the cell to complete the circuit.

Using these methods, Sir John Eccles was able to demonstrate temporal summation in single cells, displaying the properties that Sherrington had

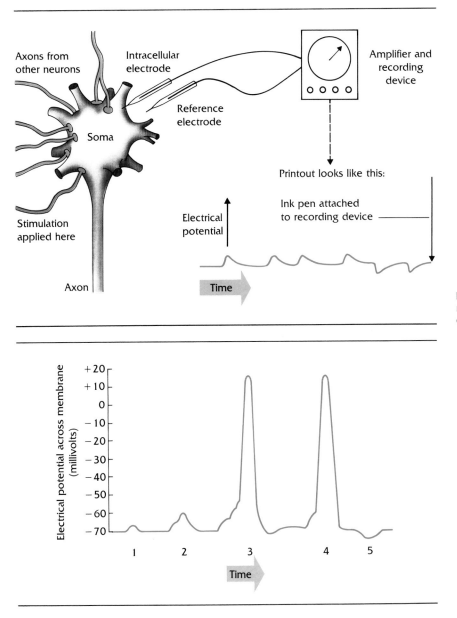

Figure 3-1. Apparatus for recording the response of a cell to synaptic activation.

Figure 3-2. Recordings from a postsynaptic neuron during synaptic activation, showing an EPSP (1), subthreshold temporal summation of EPSPs (2) suprathreshold summation of EPSPs leading to an action potential (3), spatial summation of EPSPs (4), and an IPSP (5).

inferred. Eccles (1964) attached stimulating electrodes to some of the axons that formed synapses onto a neuron. He then recorded from the neuron while stimulating one or more of those axons. After he briefly stimulated one of the axons, he recorded a slight deflection in the electrical potential across the membrane of the postsynaptic cell (point 1 in Figure 3-2). Note that this deflection represents a graded potential of the postsynaptic cell, not an action potential. This temporary, subthreshold excitation is known as an **excitatory postsynaptic potential**, abbreviated **EPSP**. Like an action potential, an EPSP is caused by the entry of sodium ions into the cell (see Chapter 2). However, unlike an action potential, an EPSP is a subthreshold event that decays as a function of time and space. That is, it gradually rises and falls over a period of a few milliseconds, and it decreases in magnitude as it travels along the membrane.

When Eccles stimulated the axon twice in close succession, two consecutive EPSPs were recorded in the postsynaptic cell. If the delay between EPSPs was short enough, temporal summation occurred; that is, the second one added to what was left of the first (point 2 in Figure 3-2). The summation of two EPSPs might or might not be enough to exceed the threshold of the postsynaptic cell, depending on the size of the EPSP, on the time between the two, and on the threshold of the postsynaptic cell. In Figure 3-2, point 3, three consecutive EPSPs combined to exceed the threshold and produce an action potential.

Spatial Summation

The reflex arc also shows the property of **spatial summation**: the cumulative effects of impulses originating in different locations. To study this phenomenon, Sherrington again began with a weak pinch of a dog's foot, too weak to elicit a response. But this time, instead of repeating the pinch, he gave the dog two such pinches simultaneously at different points on the foot. Although either pinch by itself would not elicit a movement, the two together did elicit a response. Sherrington's interpretation was that pinching two points on the foot activated two sensory neurons, each of which sent an axon to the same interneuron. Excitation from either axon alone would excite a synapse on the interneuron, but one excitation would be less than the threshold for an action potential. When both excitations were present at the same time, however, their combined effect exceeded the threshold for producing an action potential (Figure 3-3).

Again, Eccles was able to confirm Sherrington's inference by recording from single cells. He demonstrated the spatial summation of EPSPs: If two axons have excitatory synapses onto a neuron and either one can produce an EPSP, then activation of both simultaneously can produce a larger EPSP. If the combination exceeds the threshold of the cell, an action potential will begin (point 4 in Figure 3-2). Note that temporal summation and spatial summation produce the same result—an action potential is generated in the postsynaptic cell.

Inhibitory Synapses

When Sherrington vigorously pinched a dog's foot, the dog contracted the flexor muscles of that leg and the extensor muscles of the other three legs. At the same time it relaxed the extensor muscles of the stimulated leg and the flexor muscles of the other legs. Sherrington's explanation of this series of coordinated and adaptive movements depended, again, on the synapses and in particular on the wiring diagram of connections among neurons in the spinal cord. When an interneuron (A in Figure 3-4) is stimulated by a receptor neuron, the interneuron sends impulses along branches of its axon to stimulate the motor neurons connected to the flexor muscles on its own side of the cord and the extensor muscles in the other limbs. The result is to raise the stimulated limb while extending the others. The interneuron must also,

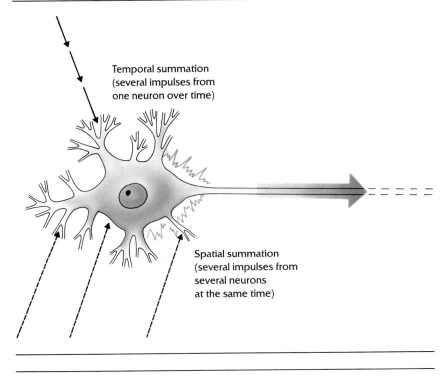

Temporal summation
(several impulses from
one neuron over time)

Spatial summation
(several impulses from
several neurons
at the same time)

Figure 3-3. Temporal and spatial summation.

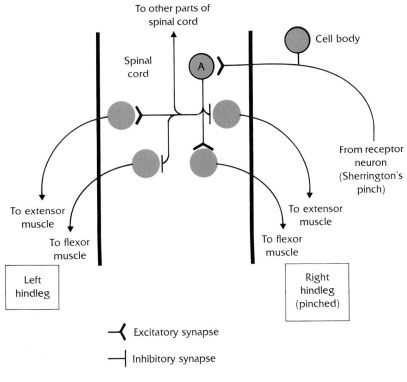

To other parts of
spinal cord

Cell body

Spinal
cord

A

From receptor
neuron
(Sherrington's
pinch)

To extensor
muscle

To flexor
muscle

To extensor
muscle

To flexor
muscle

Left
hindleg

Right
hindleg
(pinched)

Excitatory synapse

Inhibitory synapse

Figure 3-4. System of excitatory and inhibitory synapses in the spinal cord of a dog, as described by Sherrington. Note that excitation in a receptor of one leg leads to flexion of that leg and extension of the other, with inhibition of the antagonistic muscles.

Sherrington inferred, send an inhibitory message to the antagonistic muscles, as shown in Figure 3-4. That is, when it excites a flexor, it inhibits the extensor in the same limb; when it excites an extensor, it inhibits the flexor.

Eccles and other later researchers demonstrated and measured the effects of inhibitory synapses. At these synapses, input from the axon **hyperpolarizes** the postsynaptic cell. That is, instead of decreasing the cell's negative charge, it increases it, thereby decreasing the probability of an action potential by moving the potential further from the threshold (point 5 in Figure 3-2). This temporary hyperpolarization is called an **inhibitory postsynaptic potential, or IPSP**. It resembles an EPSP except that it is a change in the opposite direction. As we shall see later, an IPSP is caused by the exit of potassium ions from the neuron or the entry of chloride ions.

Note that inhibition is more than just the absence of excitation; it is an active "brake" that can suppress irrelevant or competing responses. If the inhibition is strong enough, it can cancel out the simultaneous excitation at other synapses of the same postsynaptic cell.

Relationship Among EPSP, IPSP, and Action Potential

Under normal circumstances, it would be rare for any neuron to be exposed to just one EPSP or IPSP at a time. A neuron may have thousands of synapses along its surface, some excitatory, others inhibitory, and perhaps others silent. Any number and combination of these synapses may be active at any time, giving rise to a continuing combination of temporal and spatial summation. Whether the neuron reaches its threshold and produces an action potential is determined by the momentary balance between EPSPs and IPSPs. The greater the number of EPSPs, the greater the probability of an action potential; the greater the number of IPSPs, the lower the probability of an action potential.

Moreover, the effectiveness of a synapse depends on its location on the postsynaptic cell. An EPSP or IPSP is conducted from its point of origin toward other parts of the neuron by electrotonic conduction, which allows the potentials to decrease over a distance (unlike an action potential). For that reason, a synapse located close to the axon hillock, where action potentials originate, has a greater effect than a synapse located near the far end of a dendrite.

In many neurons, the EPSPs and IPSPs merely modify the frequency of action potentials that the neuron would fire spontaneously. That is, many neurons have a **spontaneous rate** of action potentials, in some cases more than 10 per second, which they produce even during periods of no synaptic input. EPSPs increase the frequency of action potentials in these neurons, while IPSPs decrease it. For example, if the spontaneous rate were 10 per second, a steady stream of EPSPs might increase the rate to 15 or 20 or more, whereas a steady stream of IPSPs might decrease the rate to 5 or fewer action potentials per second.

What All This Means to an Animal

The parts of the neuron that receive synaptic input serve as a focus of convergence and comparison for messages coming from different cells at different times. For instance, a motor neuron projecting to a flexor muscle may respond with EPSPs following a pinch in that leg and with IPSPs following a pinch in another leg. If both legs are pinched simultaneously, the EPSPs compete against IPSPs, and the net result is a complex, not exactly algebraic summation of the two effects. We could regard the summation of EPSPs and IPSPs as a "decision process"; that is, the postsynaptic cell "decides" to fire or not on the basis of the combination of "information" (EPSPs and IPSPs) that it receives.

Although we may think of a neuron as "deciding" whether to fire action potentials, we should not imagine that any neuron decides between eggs and toast for breakfast. A great many neurons are involved in any behavior, and behavior depends on a whole network, not a single neuron. The translation between activity of a neuron and activity of the whole animal is complex. We cannot even assume, for instance, that an inhibitory synapse tends to inhibit behavioral activity. In many cases, one cell has an inhibitory synapse onto a second cell, which in turn inhibits a third cell. The first synapse, by inhibiting an inhibitor, has the net effect of increasing the excitation of the third cell. This principle of double negatives, or inhibition of inhibition, is quite common in the nervous system.

CHEMICAL EVENTS AT THE SYNAPSE

A great many medical conditions and drugs that affect behavior do so by altering the transmission of information at synapses. Consequently, an understanding of the chemical events that take place at a synapse is fundamental to much of current research in biological psychology. The events at a synapse, in summary form, are as follows:

When an action potential reaches the **end bulb** (or tip) of an axon (see Color Plate 16), the end bulb releases a chemical, the **transmitter,** into the **synaptic cleft,** which separates the presynaptic from the postsynaptic cell (which may be either a neuron or a muscle cell). The transmitter diffuses across the cleft and interacts with receptors on the postsynaptic membrane, giving rise to an EPSP or an IPSP. (See Figure 3-5 and Color Plate 12.)

We shall now go through this process in more detail, one step at a time.

Synthesis and Storage of Transmitters

Dozens of chemicals are believed to function as synaptic transmitters in the brain, and research has been gradually adding to the list of known or suspected transmitters (Snyder, 1984). You should become familiar with the following transmitters, as we shall refer to them repeatedly throughout this book:

- **Acetylcholine** (a-SEE-til-KO-leen or ASS-uh-til-KO-leen, abbreviated **ACh**)
- **Dopamine** (DO-puh-meen, abbreviated **DA**)
- **Norepinephrine** (nor-ep-i-NEFF-rin, abbreviated **NE**), also known as **noradrenalin** (nor-a-DREN-a-lin, **NA**)
- **Epinephrine** (ep-i-NEFF-rin), also known as **adrenalin**

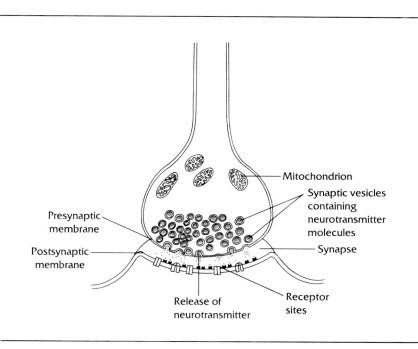

- **Serotonin** (sehr-o-TO-nin, abbreviated **5-HT**, short for 5-hydroxytryptamine)
- Several amino acids, including **glutamate** (GLOO-tuh-mate), **glycine** (GLY-seen), and **aspartate** (ASS-par-tate)
- Several metabolites of amino acids, including **gamma-amino-butyric acid** (abbreviated **GABA** and usually pronounced simply GAH-buh), taurine, and beta-alanine
- **Leu-enkephalin** (loo-en-KEF-uh-lin) and **met-enkephalin**, both of which are opiates (chemicals with effects similar to opium)
- More than 40 **peptides** (chains of a few amino acids), most of which also function as hormones elsewhere in the body

No single neuron releases all these transmitters. In fact, it was long believed that each neuron stores and releases only one transmitter, releasing that same transmitter at all branches of its axon. This generalization was known as **Dale's Law.** We now know that many, perhaps most, neurons release two or more transmitters each, although we still believe that all branches of an axon release the same transmitters. That is, whatever transmitters are released by one branch will also be released by other branches of the same axon (O'Donohue, Millington, Handelmann, Contreras, & Chronwall, 1985).

Dale's law applies to the transmitters that the presynaptic end of a neuron releases, not to the transmitters that the postsynaptic side receives. Although a neuron *releases* only one or two transmitters, it may *receive* a number of different transmitters at various synapses.

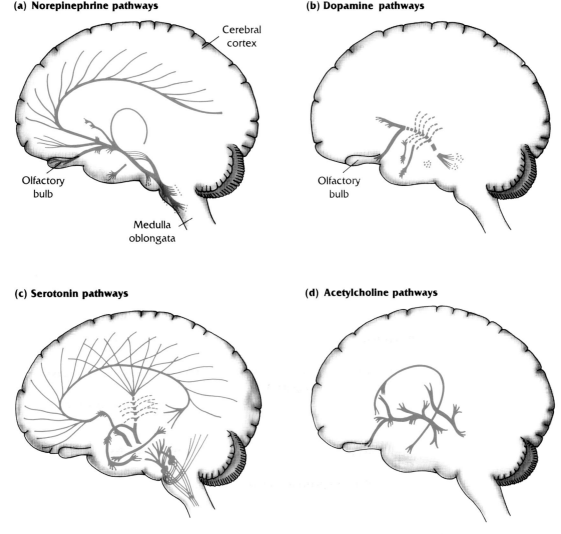

(a) Norepinephrine pathways

Cerebral cortex

Olfactory bulb

Medulla oblongata

(b) Dopamine pathways

Olfactory bulb

(c) Serotonin pathways

(d) Acetylcholine pathways

Figure 3-6. Medial view of the human brain, showing cells and pathways containing high concentrations of (**a**) norepinephrine, (**b**) dopamine, (**c**) serotonin, and (**d**) acetylcholine. (Based on Valzelli, 1980.)

Neurons that release a particular transmitter are clustered together, not scattered randomly throughout the brain. Through a variety of chemical means, it is possible to determine the distribution of certain synaptic transmitters in the brain, as illustrated in Figure 3-6. You need not try to memorize these distributions; just be aware that they differ.

Role of Diet in the Synthesis of Transmitters

Every synaptic transmitter is synthesized in the appropriate neurons from constituents that come from the diet. Under normal circumstances, the brain maintains fairly constant levels of each transmitter even during periods of fasting. Nevertheless, if the diet has a high or low concentration of the

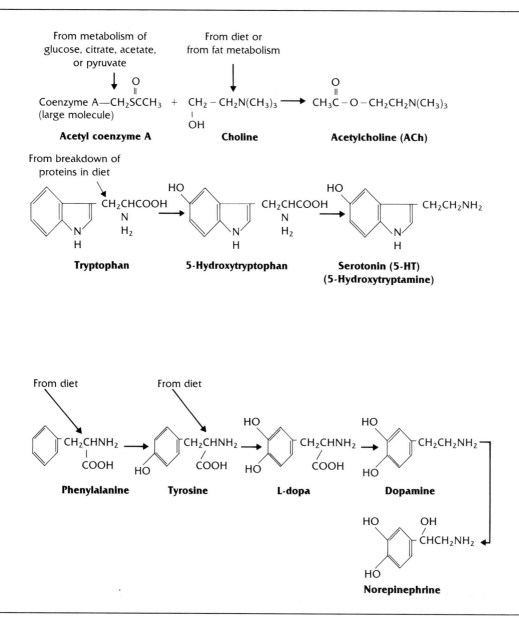

Figure 3-7. Synthesis of four synaptic transmitters. Arrows represent chemical reactions

precursors necessary for making a particular transmitter, the brain may produce a slightly higher or lower than usual amount of that transmitter (R. J. Wurtman, 1982, 1983; Wurtman, Hefti, & Melamed, 1981).

Figure 3-7 illustrates the chemical pathways for the synthesis of acetylcholine, serotonin, dopamine, and norepinephrine. Note that synthesis of both dopamine and norepinephrine follows the same initial pathway, but norepinephrine cells have an additional enzyme not found in dopamine cells that converts dopamine to norepinephrine. Note also that each pathway in Figure 3-7 begins with substances found in the diet. Acetylcholine, for example, is synthesized from choline, which is abundant in cauliflower and milk. Choline can also be made from lecithin, a component of egg yolks, liver, soybeans, butter, peanuts, and several other foods. A meal high in choline or lecithin produces at least a brief increase in the acetylcholine levels of the brain.

It is somewhat more complicated to raise the brain's levels of serotonin. Most proteins contain only small amounts of the amino acid **tryptophan**, the precursor to serotonin. The brain has a special "transport system" that enables tryptophan and a few other amino acids to enter neurons. Tryptophan competes with the other amino acids for access to that transport system, however. After a meal rich in protein, the level of tryptophan reaching the brain may be quite low, because of competition from the other amino acids. One way to increase the entry of tryptophan into the brain is to eat carbohydrates with the protein. Carbohydrates cause an increased release of the hormone **insulin**, which takes a number of competing amino acids out of the bloodstream and into cells throughout the body, thus decreasing the competition against tryptophan for entry into the brain (J. J. Wurtman, 1985).

It is possible to buy tryptophan pills in health food stores. Taking such pills may increase serotonin levels in the brain temporarily. But if one takes frequent, large doses of tryptophan, the liver will build up increased levels of the enzymes that break it down. In the long run, then, one cannot greatly increase brain serotonin levels by taking tryptophan pills.

Release and Diffusion of Transmitters

When an action potential reaches the end of an axon, the depolarization opens calcium pores in the presynaptic membrane. The increased calcium concentration inside the presynaptic cell causes the cell to release a certain amount of its transmitter during the next 1 or 2 milliseconds (msec). The depolarization by itself does not release the transmitter; it promotes the release only indirectly, through its effects on calcium (Zucker & Landò, 1986).

A presynaptic neuron occasionally releases a small amount of synaptic transmitter into the synaptic cleft even when the neuron has not been stimulated. If we record from the postsynaptic cell, we see evidence of this release in the form of periodic EPSPs or IPSPs. Such potentials have a minimum size, known as a **quantum**. The size of the quantum may vary from one synapse to another, but it is constant for a given synapse from one time to another.

If we examine either the spontaneous EPSPs or those evoked by stimulation, we find that the size of the EPSP varies but that all the EPSPs are integral multiples of the quantum. That is, an EPSP may be 30 times the quantum or 31, but never 30.5.

Why is the transmitter always released in quanta? The answer—or at least part of the answer—is that the end bulb of the presynaptic cell contains a large number of **vesicles**, tiny near-spherical packets filled with the transmitter (Figure 3-5). All the vesicles that release a given transmitter from a given neuron are the same size. It would appear therefore that a vesicle is the physical basis for the quantum: The presynaptic cell releases some integral number of vesicles, all the same size, and that is why the stimulation of the postsynaptic cell occurs in units of the quantum.

That may not be the entire story, however. The presynaptic cell also sometimes releases transmitter that was not stored in vesicles (Carroll & Aspry, 1980). Even when this happens, it releases it in quanta—for reasons unknown.

After the presynaptic cell releases the transmitter, the chemical diffuses across the synaptic cleft to the postsynaptic membrane, where it attaches to a receptor. The cleft is only .02 to .05 microns wide, and the transmitter takes no more than 10 microseconds to diffuse across the cleft. The total delay in transmission across the synapse, including the time it takes for the presynaptic cell to release the transmitter, is 0.5 to 2 msec (Martin, 1977; Takeuchi, 1977).

Activation of Receptors of the Postsynaptic Cell

In English, the term *fern* refers to a small plant. In German, *fern* means far away. In French, it means nothing at all. The meaning of any word depends on who hears it or reads it.

The same is true of synaptic transmitters. The meaning of a transmitter depends on the receptor that receives it. At certain synapses, acetylcholine is an excitatory transmitter; it produces an EPSP. At other synapses, acetylcholine is an inhibitory transmitter, because of differences in the receptors. At still other synapses, where the receptors are specialized to receive, say, nor-epinephrine, acetylcholine produces no effect at all.

When transmitters attach to their receptors, some produce **ionic effects** and some produce **metabolic effects**. Let us begin with ionic effects, as illustrated in Figures 3-8 and 3-9. Acetylcholine, glutamate, glycine, and GABA are transmitters with ionic effects. When acetylcholine, for example, attaches to a receptor on the postsynaptic membrane, it opens the gates for a particular ion. At certain sites it opens the gates for sodium ions for about 1–3 msec (Giraudat & Changeux, 1981); they enter the neuron, producing an EPSP (Figure 3-8a). At other synapses, acetylcholine opens the gates for potassium or chloride (Figure 3-8b). Free to flow through the gates in either direction, the ions flow mostly from the area of greater concentration to the area of lesser concentration. For potassium, this means flow from inside the cell to outside; for chloride, it means flow from outside to inside. In both cases, the result is an IPSP, a temporary hyperpolarization of the cell.

Figure 3-9 shows the structure of an acetylcholine receptor. When an acetylcholine molecule attaches to the receptor, it changes the receptor's configuration so as to open the gate to allow a particular ion to pass into or out of the cell (Changeux, Devilers-Thiéry, & Chemouilli, 1984).

Certain other synapses operate by metabolic effects. Many dopamine synapses and most if not all norepinephrine and serotonin synapses fall into this category. The transmitter binds to a membrane receptor, which then stimulates the enzyme adenylate cyclase, which in turn converts ATP to cyclic AMP (adenosine monophosphate) inside the cell (Schramm & Selinger, 1984). Cyclic AMP is referred to as a "second messenger" or "second transmitter" because it then initiates chemical changes in proteins in and

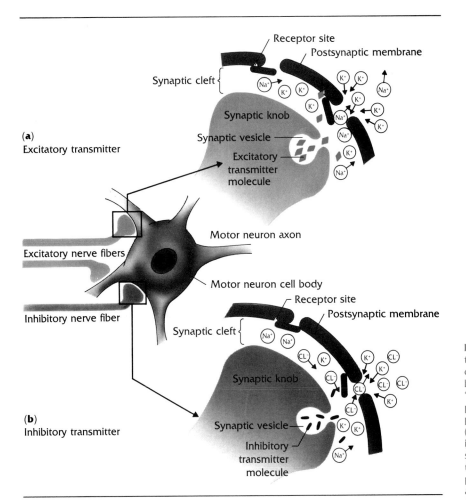

(a)
Excitatory transmitter

(b)
Inhibitory transmitter

Receptor site
Postsynaptic membrane
Synaptic cleft
Synaptic knob
Synaptic vesicle
Excitatory transmitter molecule
Motor neuron axon
Excitatory nerve fibers
Inhibitory nerve fiber
Motor neuron cell body
Receptor site
Postsynaptic membrane
Synaptic cleft
Synaptic knob
Synaptic vesicle
Inhibitory transmitter molecule

Figure 3-8. Some synaptic transmitters, such as acetylcholine, exert ionic effects by selectively opening the "gates" for passage of a particular ion across the postsynaptic membrane. (**a**) Excitatory transmission increases permeability to sodium ions. (**b**) Inhibitory transmission increases permeability to potassium and chloride ions.

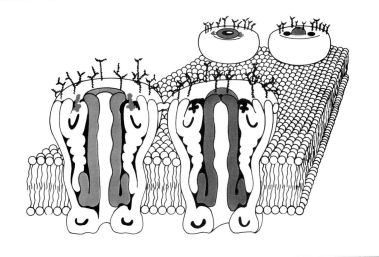

Figure 3-9. Diagram of acetylcholine receptors embedded in a membrane. The receptors on the left have acetylcholine molecules attached to them; consequently, their ion pores are open. (From Lindstrom, 1979.)

near the membrane. Those changes may increase or decrease the permeability of the membrane to one or more ions; they may also alter the sensitivity of the synaptic receptors to later transmitters.

The peptide molecules that serve as transmitters may produce either ionic or metabolic effects (Krieger, 1983; Scheller et al., 1984). In addition, many of them enter the nucleus of the cell, where they initiate changes in the expression of the genes. Compared to other transmitters, peptide transmitters are produced in smaller amounts and are released less frequently. While the ionic effects of a transmitter such as acetylcholine last only milliseconds, the effects of certain peptide transmitters may last minutes or even hours (Shepherd, 1983).

Many authorities distinguish **neuromodulators** from more standard transmitters, but the definition of neuromodulator varies. A common usage is to apply the term to chemicals that increase or decrease the release of transmitters from other neurons, or those that alter the sensitivity of the postsynaptic receptors to other transmitters. Some authorities apply the term *neuromodulator* to chemicals that have widespread effects not limited to a single synapse or even a single neuron.

The study of synaptic mechanisms has been advancing rapidly in recent years. The generalizations given above admittedly overlook a great deal of complexity and variation.

Presynaptic Synapses

Synapses also exist in which the receptor is located on the end bulb at the tip of an axon. Such a receptor is known as a **presynaptic receptor**. At most sites, activation of a presynaptic receptor inhibits the later release of transmitter from the end bulb; sometimes, however, it facilitates release.

In some cases the input to the presynaptic receptor comes from another neuron. For example, a branch of an axon that releases acetylcholine may make an inhibitory contact onto the end bulb of a norepinephrine cell, inhibiting transmitter release (Starke, 1981).

In other cases, the input to the presynaptic receptor comes from the transmitter released by the cell itself (Dubocovich, 1984; Roth, 1984). That is, after the end bulb releases the transmitter, some of the chemical activates a receptive site on the end bulb itself. (See Figure 3-10.) A presynaptic receptor that responds to its own transmitter is known as an **autoreceptor**. Most of the autoreceptors that have been studied so far inhibit the later release of transmitter from that cell. That is, they serve a function of negative feedback; when a cell releases a large amount of the transmitter, the transmitter activates the autoreceptors to inhibit further release.

Disposal of Used Transmitters

A transmitter does not normally linger at the postsynaptic membrane for long. If it did, it might continue exciting or inhibiting the postsynaptic neuron indefinitely. Various types of synaptic transmitters are inactivated in different ways.

After acetylcholine activates a receptor, it is broken down by the enzyme **acetylcholinesterase** (a-SEE-til-kol-lin-ES-ter-aze) into two fragments, ace-

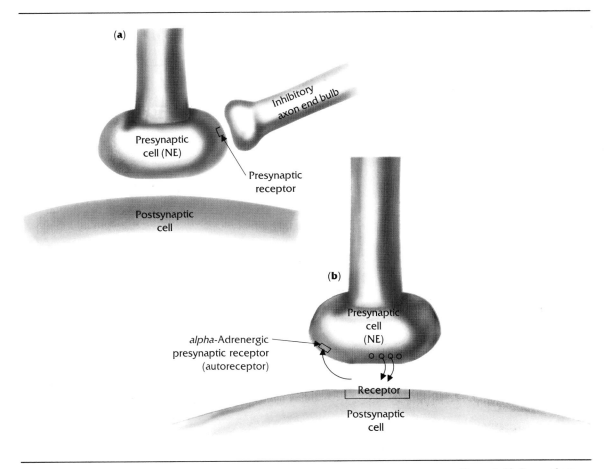

(a)

Inhibitory axon end bulb

Presynaptic cell (NE)

Presynaptic receptor

Postsynaptic cell

(b)

Presynaptic cell (NE)

alpha-Adrenergic presynaptic receptor (autoreceptor)

Receptor

Postsynaptic cell

Figure 3-10. Types of presynaptic receptors. (**a**) A norepinephrine synapse with an inhibitory receptor. (**b**) A norepinephrine synapse with an autoreceptor.

tate and choline. Acetate by itself cannot stimulate the receptor, and choline does so only weakly (Krnjević & Reinhardt, 1979). The acetate and choline diffuse back to the presynaptic neuron, which reabsorbs them and reconnects them to form acetylcholine again. That is, the brain recycles acetylcholine. The process is highly efficient but not perfect; after a rapid series of transmissions at a synapse, the number of quanta released per transmission declines—presumably because the cell has used up its acetylcholine faster than it can reassemble it.

If the enzyme acetylcholinesterase is not present in adequate amounts, acetylcholine may remain at the synapse for an abnormally long time and continue to excite it. This leads to a strategy in some drug therapies: One way to elevate someone's acetylcholine transmission is to give drugs that inhibit acetylcholinesterase.

Serotonin and the **catecholamines** (DA, NE, and epinephrine) are not broken down into inactive fragments at the postsynaptic membrane. They simply detach from the membrane. The presynaptic neuron reabsorbs most of these transmitter molecules intact and then reuses them. A smaller number of the molecules are converted by the enzymes **COMT** (catechol-o-methyltransferase, which affects the catecholamines but not serotonin) and **MAO** (monoamine oxidase, which affects serotonin as well) into inactive chemicals that cannot stimulate the receptor. The inactive chemicals eventually diffuse out of the synaptic cleft and enter the bloodstream. Investigators sometimes measure levels of those chemicals in the blood or urine as an indicator of the amount of transmitter that has been released recently in the brain.

THE ROLES OF DIFFERENT TRANSMITTERS IN BEHAVIOR

Why are synapses so complicated? That is, why do we have dozens of synaptic transmitters, some excitatory, some inhibitory, plus presynaptic receptors and a variety of other complications? Why couldn't nature get along with just one or two transmitters? It is probably for the same reason that the English language could not get along with just one or two letters of the alphabet. The nervous system needs a large number of elements that can be combined in different ways if it is to produce all the complexity of behavior. To be more specific: Different transmitters control different aspects of behavior.

S.P. Grossman (1964a, 1964b) found that an injection of norepinephrine directly into certain areas of a rat's brain would elicit feeding, while an injection of acetylcholine into the same areas would elicit drinking. These results do not mean that norepinephrine and acetylcholine are the only transmitters that control eating and drinking, nor that those are the only behaviors these chemicals contribute to. Nevertheless, Grossman's results have profound implications. If a given transmitter promotes certain kinds of behaviors more than others, then any increase or decrease in the activity of that transmitter should alter behavior. Conversely, for any abnormality of behavior, one possible explanation may be that the brain has had too much or too little transmitter activity at a particular kind of synapse. Finally, the fact that many psychoactive drugs alter synaptic activity may help explain the behavioral effects of these drugs.

Gilles de la Tourette's Syndrome

One behavioral abnormality that is probably related to an abnormality at the synapses is **Gilles de la Tourette's syndrome**. First described by Georges Gilles de la Tourette in 1885, this uncommon condition is characterized by repeated movements such as facial tics, touching others, hitting oneself, squatting, and twirling around while walking. A most striking symptom, which not all people with this syndrome share, is the production of repetitive sounds. The sounds may be obscene words, insults ("you bore . . . you fat bore"), or simply nonsense sounds (Bruun, 1984). The repetitive sounds and movements were once regarded as involuntary, but one lifelong sufferer wrote that he was capable of controlling them (Bliss, 1980). His experience, he said, was of sensations—itches, tickling sensations, and the like—that evoke impulses to make some movement. Just as you might find it possible but difficult to inhibit an impulse to scratch an itchy spot on your skin, he found it possible but difficult to inhibit his repetitive movements.

Gilles de la Tourette's syndrome usually begins in childhood; it is more common in boys than in girls. Once it begins, it is likely to last a lifetime, although the severity will occasionally increase or decrease.

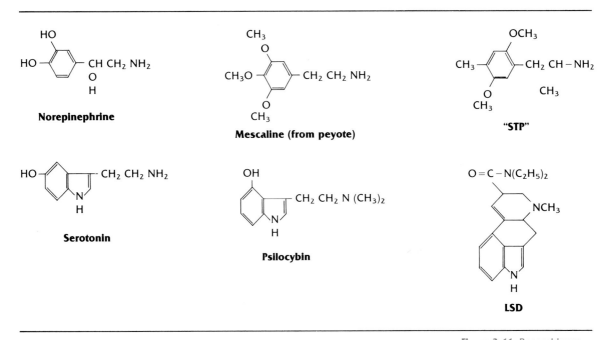

Figure 3-11. Resemblance of four hallucinogenic drugs to two synapatic transmitters.

The cause is not known, but many suspect a genetic basis. About 10 percent of the immediate relatives of someone with Gilles de la Tourette's syndrome have the syndrome themselves, and many others have related disorders such as attention-deficit disorder (see Chapter 15) and multiple tics (Comings & Comings, 1984; Pauls, Kruger, Leckman, Cohen, & Kidd, 1984; Price, Kidd, Cohen, Pauls, & Leckman, 1985).

The symptoms of Gilles de la Tourette's syndrome can be suppressed by **haloperidol**, a drug that blocks dopamine synapses. The treatment is not fully satisfactory because of a variety of side effects from the drug (Bruun, 1984), but the fact that it suppresses the symptoms implies that they are related to some abnormal activity at dopamine synapses. Dopamine is believed, on the basis of other evidence, to be essential for overall body movements such as walking or changing postures. According to one proposal, Gilles de la Tourette's syndrome results when axons in certain areas of the brain release less dopamine than normal; in reaction, the receptors for the dopamine become supersensitive (Devinsky, 1983). Hence, when even small quantities of dopamine reach those receptors, the receptors overrespond and produce impulses to make abnormal movements.

Later in this text we shall encounter explanations of panic disorder, depression, schizophrenia, and other behavioral abnormalities in terms of an excess or deficit of particular transmitters.

Hallucinogenic Drugs

Most of the drugs that produce distortions of sensory experiences resemble certain synaptic transmitters closely enough to attach to their receptors. Figure 3-11 shows the resemblance of norepinephrine and serotonin to four **hallucinogenic drugs**—drugs that can induce hallucinations. The drugs act in various ways: by stimulating the receptors at inappropriate times, by stimulating them for an abnormally prolonged time, or by blocking all stimulation of the receptors (even by the normal transmitters). The mode of action can be fairly complex. For example, LSD apparently blocks serotonin synapses for about 4 hours and also decreases the number of serotonin receptors for a period of days (Jacobs & Trulson, 1979). LSD also acts on other systems, including dopamine synapses.

Hallucinogenic chemicals may have been related to an interesting historical event, the Salem witchcraft trials of 1692. In Salem Village, Massachusetts, a number of people, mostly children and teenagers, reported a set of bizarre symptoms, including convulsions, prickling sensations on the skin, visual hallucinations, pain, nausea, and periods of blindness and deafness. They blamed their symptoms on certain other members of the community, whom they accused of being witches. About twenty people were convicted of witchcraft and hanged.

It has long been assumed that the reported symptoms were hysterical or imaginary, but there is reason to believe they may have been more than that. First, the symptoms showed up in a number of infants and cows, who could hardly be accused of pretending or imagining them or of being victims of a power of suggestion. Second, at least three people reportedly died of the symptoms.

Linnda Caporael (1976) and Mary Matossian (1982) have argued that the symptoms were real and that they were caused by **ergot** poisoning. Ergot is a substance produced by a fungus that sometimes grows on rye. The climate in Massachusetts at the time was probably conducive to the growth of ergot. Ergot poisoning produces convulsions, a sensation in the skin as if ants are crawling inside, pain, nausea, and other symptoms similar to those reported at Salem. Ergot symptoms are generally worse in children than in adults because children eat more in proportion to body weight and therefore consume a larger dose of the harmful chemicals. Ergot is the source from which LSD is made; in nature ergot may spontaneously produce LSD and similar chemicals. Thus, the supposed victims of witchcraft may have actually been suffering from a combination of food poisoning and an LSD experience.

Drugs, Synapses, and Behavior

Not all drugs that affect the brain do so by acting at synapses—alcohol and marijuana do not, for example—but a great many do. An enormous number of drugs that affect synapses are marketed for medical uses, and an ever-changing variety of additional drugs are used for research. (See Digression 3-1.) It would be pointless to try to memorize the names of all the drugs and all their effects. Certain drugs will become more familiar as we discuss their effects in later chapters. Many other drugs are listed in the Glossary, which you can use as a reference source. At this point, let us simply consider a few of the ways in which drugs can affect synapses:

1.   A drug may mimic the effect of a transmitter by directly stimulating the receptor of the postsynaptic cell. For example, nicotine increases heart

DIGRESSION

3-1

Accidental Discoveries of Psychiatric Drugs

We like to think that basic science comes first and that applied science or technology comes afterward, taking the discoveries of basic science and applying them in rational ways to solve practical problems. Yet the history of drug therapies, particularly in psychiatry, includes many examples of the reverse, in which useful drugs were stumbled upon by accident and basic researchers then had to search for an explanation for their success.

Disulfiram, for example, was originally used in the manufacture of rubber. Someone noticed that workers in a certain rubber factory developed a distaste for alcohol (Levitt, 1975). Now better

known by the trade name Antabuse, disulfiram is used to help alcoholics quit drinking alcohol. (See Chapter 10.)

Iproniazid was originally marketed as a rocket fuel. Eventually someone discovered that it was useful therapy for tuberculosis. Later, while experimenting on its effects in treating tuberculosis, someone discovered that it was an effective antidepressant (Klerman, 1975).

The use of bromides to control epilepsy was originally based on a theory, but the theory was all wrong (Friedlander, 1986; Levitt, 1975). In the 1800s it was believed that epilepsy was caused by masturbation. It was also believed that bromides reduced sexual drive. Therefore, the reasoning went, bromides should reduce epilepsy. It turns out that bromides do relieve epilepsy, but they do so for altogether different reasons.

rate, arouses parts of the cerebral cortex, contracts skeletal muscles, and exerts other effects on behavior by directly stimulating certain receptors that normally respond to acetylcholine. Not all acetylcholine receptors respond to nicotine, however. A second type respond to muscarine but not nicotine. The brain also has more than one type of receptor each for norepinephrine, dopamine, and serotonin. Each type of receptor differs from the others in its responses to drugs (Snyder, 1984).

2. A drug can stimulate the release of a transmitter from its storage in presynaptic neurons. A drug with such a mode of action may have a delayed effect that is the opposite of the immediate effect. Amphetamine, for example, increases the release of norepinephrine. Its immediate effect is to increase arousal and produce a generally pleasant feeling, two outcomes dependent on norepinephrine. A few hours after a large dose of amphetamine, however, a person may go into a rebound state of depression, because the brain is unable to resynthesize new norepinephrine fast enough to replace all that was suddenly released.

3. A drug may slow the presynaptic neuron's reuptake of the synaptic transmitters it has released. The consequence is to prolong the effects of the transmitters on the postsynaptic cell. Psychiatric drugs known as **tricyclics** block the reuptake of norepinephrine, dopamine, or serotonin. Cocaine also blocks the reuptake of norepinephrine and dopamine. (Do you see why cocaine produces effects similar to those of amphetamine?)

4. A drug may interfere with an enzyme that inactivates transmitters that have just stimulated postsynaptic receptors. For example, physostigmine blocks the enzyme acetylcholinesterase, which breaks down acetylcholine into acetate and choline. By blocking the breakdown of acetylcholine, physostigmine prolongs the effects at the synapse.

5.   A drug can stimulate or inhibit presynaptic receptors that modify the release of transmitter from an axon.

6.   A drug can inhibit one of the reactions necessary for the production of a particular transmitter. The drug PCPA (para-chloro-phenylalanine) inhibits one of the reactions in the production of serotonin.

7.   A drug can block the receptors for a particular transmitter, preventing the transmitter molecules from activating the receptors. Haloperidol, which is used in the treatment of schizophrenia as well as Gilles de la Tourette's syndrome, blocks dopamine synapses. Accomplishing the same effect in a different way, a drug can directly block the ion pores that a receptor controls (Skok, 1986).

8.   A drug can attach to a receptor that modifies the sensitivity of a neighboring receptor. For example, benzodiazepine tranquilizers (the most common anxiety-reducing drugs) attach to receptors adjacent to GABA receptors, and in the process increase the sensitivity of the GABA receptors. (The full story is a bit more complicated, as we shall see in Chapter 12.)

Bear in mind that just about every drug has multiple effects. When we talk about the effect of amphetamine on norepinephrine, for example, we refer only to amphetamine's most pronounced biochemical effect. It also has less drastic effects on serotonin and acetylcholine synapses, and perhaps on still others. The intensity of such secondary effects may vary from one individual to another, as no two people react to a given drug in quite the same way.

SUMMARY

1.   Charles S. Sherrington first inferred the properties of synapses, based on his observations of reflexes. (p. 48)

2.   A single stimulation at a synapse produces a brief subthreshold excitation or inhibition (EPSP or IPSP) of the postsynaptic cell. Subthreshold effects combine by temporal summation and by spatial summation. (p. 50)

3.   Most synapses operate by the transmission of a chemical, the synaptic transmitter, from the presynaptic cell to the postsynaptic cell. (p. 55)

4.   A large number of chemicals are used as synaptic transmitters. As far as we know, each neuron releases only a single transmitter, or only a single combination of transmitters, from all branches of its axon. (p. 55)

5.   It is possible to increase or decrease the production of a given transmitter, at least briefly, by consuming food with a high or low concentration of the precursors to that transmitter. (pp. 57–58)

6.   At certain synapses, a transmitter exerts its effects by attaching to a receptor that opens the gates to allow a particular ion, such as sodium, to cross the membrane more readily. At other synapses, a transmitter may lead to slower but longer-lasting changes inside the postsynaptic cell. (p. 60)

7.   Presynaptic receptors are receptors on the end bulb of an axon. Activation of such receptors may inhibit or facilitate the release of transmitter from that axon. (p. 62)

8.   After a transmitter has activated its receptor, some of the transmitter molecules are reabsorbed by the presynaptic cell. Other molecules are metabolized into inactive chemicals and eventually excreted. (p. 62)

9.   Different transmitters contribute to behavior in different ways. Certain abnormalities of behavior can be traced to an excess or deficit of chemical activity at particular types of synapses. (p. 64)

10.   Many drugs affect behavior by altering the activity at particular types of synapses. (p. 66)

REVIEW QUESTIONS

1. On the basis of what evidence did Sherrington conclude that transmission at a synapse is different from transmission along an axon? (p. 48)
2. What evidence did later investigators offer to show that transmission at a synapse depends on the release of chemicals? (p. 49)
3. What is the difference between temporal summation and spatial summation? What evidence did Sherrington have for their existence? (p. 50)
4. What evidence did Sherrington have for the existence of inhibitory synapses? What function do they serve? (p. 52)
5. What is meant by the spontaneous rate of a neuron? (p. 54)
6. How can changes in diet modify the levels of certain transmitters in the brain? (p. 57)

7. Distinguish between ionic and metabolic effects at synapses. (p. 60)
8. What ionic movement is responsible for an EPSP? For an IPSP? (p. 60)
9. What is an autoreceptor and how does it contribute to negative feedback? (p. 62)
10. How is acetylcholine inactivated after it is released? How are serotonin and the catecholamines inactivated? (p. 63)
11. What are the symptoms of Gilles de la Tourette's syndrome, and in what way is the syndrome probably related to an abnormality of synaptic transmission? (p. 64)
12. What biological explanation may account for the symptoms attributed to witchcraft in Salem in 1692? (p. 66)

THOUGHT QUESTIONS

1. When Sherrington measured the reaction time of a reflex (that is, the delay between stimulus and response), he found that the response occurred faster after a strong stimulus than after a weak one. How could you explain this finding? Remember that all action potentials—whether produced by strong or weak stimuli—travel at the same speed along a given axon.
2. Suppose axon A enters a ganglion (a cluster of neurons) and axon B leaves on the other side. An experimenter who stimulates A can shortly thereafter record an impulse traveling down B. We would like to know whether B is just an extension of axon A, or whether A formed an excitatory synapse on some neuron in the ganglion, whose axon is axon B. How could an experimenter determine the answer? You should be able to think of more than one good method. Presume that the anatomy within the ganglion is so complex

that you cannot simply trace the course of an axon through it.
3. Neuron X has a synapse onto neuron Y, and Y has a synapse onto Z. Presume for the sake of this question that no other neurons or synapses are present. An experimenter finds that excitation of neuron X causes an action potential in neuron Z with a short delay. However, it is determined that the synapse of X onto Y is inhibitory. Explain, then, how the stimulation of X could possibly produce excitation of Z.
4. Suppose haloperidol, which blocks dopamine synapses, is found to suppress the symptoms of the newly discovered disease X. One possible explanation of its effectiveness is that disease X is caused by supersensitive dopamine receptors. What other explanations are possible?

TERMS TO REMEMBER

synapse (p. 48)
temporal summation (p. 50)
postsynaptic cell (p. 50)
presynaptic cells (p. 50)
microelectrode (p. 50)
excitatory postsynaptic potential (EPSP) (p. 51)
spatial summation (p. 52)
hyperpolarization (p. 54)
inhibitory postsynaptic potential (IPSP) (p. 54)
spontaneous rate (p. 54)
end bulb (p. 55)
transmitter (p. 55)
synaptic cleft (p. 55)
acetylcholine (ACh) (p. 55)

dopamine (DA) (p. 55)
norepinephrine (NE) (p. 55)
noradrenalin (NA) (p. 55)
epinephrine (p. 55)
adrenalin (p. 55)
serotonin (5-HT) (p. 56)
glutamate (p. 56)
glycine (p. 56)
aspartate (p. 56)
gamma-amino-butyric acid (GABA) (p. 56)
leu-enkephalin (p. 56)
met-enkephalin (p. 56)
peptides (p. 56)
Dale's Law (p. 56)

SUGGESTIONS FOR FURTHER READING

Cooper, J. R., Bloom, F. E., & Roth, R. H. (1986). *The biochemical basis of neuropharmacology,* 5th ed. New York: Oxford. Deals primarily with the chemistry of synaptic transmission.

Snyder, S. (Ed.) (1986). *The encyclopedia of psychoactive drugs.* New York: Chelsea House. A collection of volumes on all aspects of drugs. See especially the volume by Sanberg and Krema, *Over-the-counter drugs.*

Anatomy of the Nervous System and Methods of Investigation

CHAPTER

4

MAIN IDEAS

1. Brain size is roughly proportional to body size. Humans have a higher brain to body ratio than most other species.

2. The major divisions of the vertebrate central nervous system are the spinal cord, the hindbrain, the midbrain, and the forebrain.

3. All parts of the cerebral cortex receive fairly direct sensory pathways and send messages that affect movement. Different areas are, however, specialized for different functions.

4. A variety of investigative techniques have been devised to determine the particular behavioral functions served by different areas and systems of the brain.

Trying to learn **neuroanatomy** (the anatomy of the nervous system) from a book is much like trying to learn geography from a book. A book can tell you that Mystic, Georgia is about 40 km north of Enigma, Georgia and that the two cities are connected by a combination of roads, including U.S. Route 129. Similarly, a book can tell you that the habenula is about 4.6 mm away from the interpeduncular nucleus in a rat's brain (slightly farther in a human brain) and that the two structures are connected by a set of axons known as the habenulopeduncular tract, also sometimes known as the fasciculus retroflexus. But these two little gems of information are likely to seem both mysterious and enigmatic unless you have some interest in that area of Georgia or in that area of the brain.

This chapter does not try to provide a detailed road map of the brain. Instead, the chapter is more like a world globe, describing the large, basic structures (analogous to the continents) and a few distinctive features of each. The second half of the chapter describes some representative methods that are used to study the role of various brain structures in the control of behavior. Later chapters fill in some additional detail on specific parts of the brain as they become relevant in the discussion of specific behaviors.

THE EVOLUTION OF THE VERTEBRATE BRAIN

In this book we shall be dealing almost exclusively with vertebrates. **Vertebrates** are animals with a backbone—bony fish, amphibians, reptiles, and mammals. Invertebrates are animals without a backbone—shellfish, worms, insects, crustaceans, and the like. Invertebrates have no spinal cord and usually no single group of neurons numerous enough to call a brain. Invertebrate neurons operate by the same basic principles as vertebrate neurons, and we can learn much from them about nerve conduction, synaptic transmission, and even the possible single-cell mechanisms of learning (Chapter 13). However, their organization into a structural whole is quite different from that of vertebrates.

Evolutionary Differences in Brain Size

Figure 4-1 illustrates the brains of five vertebrate species. In all five we can distinguish three major areas: the *forebrain*, the *midbrain*, and the *hindbrain*. Note that the forebrain forms a larger proportion of the brain of mammals, such as rats and humans, than of fish, amphibians, and reptiles. Early in development, the forebrain begins as a swelling in front, while the midbrain is in the middle and the hindbrain is behind, as the names imply. In mammals, especially humans, however, the forebrain continues to develop and grow until it surrounds the entire midbrain and part of the hindbrain.

Across vertebrates in general, the size of the brain is closely related to the size of the body. As Figure 4-2 illustrates, the logarithm of body weight is an accurate predictor of brain weight. Most mammals and birds form a nearly straight line on this graph, a bit above the line for amphibians, fish, and reptiles (Jerison, 1985). Primates (humans, apes, and monkeys) lie above

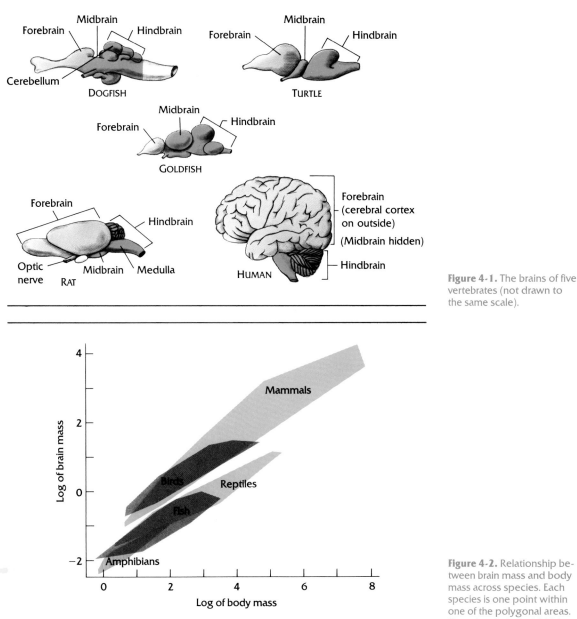

Figure 4-1. The brains of five vertebrates (not drawn to the same scale).

Figure 4-2. Relationship between brain mass and body mass across species. Each species is one point within one of the polygonal areas. (Based on Jerison, 1985.)

the line for other mammals. Dinosaurs, whose brain sizes have been estimated from fossil skulls, had the same brain-to-body ratio as contemporary reptiles.

What causes this relationship between body size and brain size? Certain genes that control the early growth and development of the body influence all parts of the body about equally. Genes that make the limbs, the trunk, and the internal organs grow larger make the brain grow larger as well.

Does it follow from this principle that the largest individuals within a species will have a proportionately larger brain than the smaller individuals? Yes, but only in part. The genes that promote early growth and development affect all parts of the body, but the genes that promote later body growth affect the limbs and other body parts more than the brain. (In humans, the growth spurt of adolescence takes place after the brain is fully developed.) Because the variation in size between one individual and another within a species depends largely on these late-development genes, such body-size variations do not correlate closely with variations in brain size (Riska & Atchley, 1985).

Humans have a higher brain-to-body ratio than most other mammals. Other primates have a high ratio, too, as do dolphins and other species that we regard as relatively intelligent. Reptiles have a lower brain-to-body ratio. Perhaps these ratios help account for the fact that we are more likely to witness a trained dolphin act than a trained alligator act.

You should beware of the idea that brain-to-body ratio is an indicator of intelligence, however. First, it is extremely difficult to measure animal intelligence (Thomas, 1980). Apparent differences in animal intelligence sometimes turn out to be due to sensory differences, motivational differences, or differences in training techniques. The difficulties of comparing intelligence across species are so great that one authority has argued that all nonhuman vertebrates may be equal in intelligence (MacPhail, 1985). While few others agree with MacPhail, it is noteworthy that we cannot refute his position beyond all doubt.

Second, the relative size of the brain in comparison to the body is not the only thing to consider; the absolute size may be important as well. Bernhard Rensch (1964, 1971, 1973) found that within a group of closely related species—various species of rats or chickens, for example—the larger species learned faster and retained what they learned longer than the smaller species, even though all had the same brain-to-body ratio.

Brain size is, of course, not a very informative indicator of what the brain does. Two animal brains of the same overall size may differ greatly in their organization. Species that rely heavily on their sense of smell, such as dogs, rodents, and bears, have large olfactory bulbs. Gorillas and humans, which rely on vision more than smell, have well-developed visual areas in the brain but small olfactory bulbs. Structures essential for localizing sounds are unusually large in dolphins and bats, which find their way about by echolocation (Harrison & Irving, 1966). Raccoons, whose sense of touch is very precise, have an unusually large area of their cerebral cortex devoted to touch (Rensch & Dücker, 1963).

What is the relationship between brain size and intelligence in humans? Very few studies have been conducted on this relationship, and most were done long ago, using crude estimates of brain size and poor measurements of intelligence. What evidence we *do* have suggests a positive but low correlation between brain volume and IQ score, with a correlation coefficient between 0.10 and 0.30 (Van Valen, 1974). The safest statement is that we need better evidence before we can draw a firm conclusion.

BIOSKETCH
4-1

Paul MacLean

Paul MacLean has spent his career contemplating the evolution of the human brain and its implications for the nature of human consciousness. "I can't remember," he says, "a day that I haven't worried about existence, and why we are here, and where we are going."

Born in 1913, MacLean obtained his bachelor's degree at Yale and planned to go to the University of Edinburgh to study philosophy. Before leaving for Edinburgh, however, he became impressed with medicine and somewhat disenchanted with philosophical methods. After completing some premed courses at Edinburgh and medical school at Yale, he served in the U.S. army during World War II. Although his medical training was in internal medicine, he was called upon in the army to spend some time in charge of psychiatric wards. After the war and a year of practice in internal medicine, he decided to pursue his original goal of investigating the brain and its role in psychological functions.

MacLean originated the concept that the brain consists of three major parts: the reptilian, old-mammalian, and new-mammalian brains. He also originated the term *limbic system*, commonly used to refer to a richly interconnected set of subcortical structures of the forebrain.

MacLean's goal has been to understand not just objective behaviors but also conscious experience. In his words, "I am often ashamed of myself because of the name I chose for our laboratory, Laboratory of Brain Evolution and Behavior. I mean, anybody in science talks as though behavior is the only thing that counts, whereas we all know that the only thing that counts is what we are feeling inside ourselves and how we relate to other individuals."

MacLean's Hypothesis

Paul MacLean (see BioSketch 4-1) has likened brain evolution to building a small house, then adding on a new large wing, and then another wing—the overall structure is less unified than if the edifice had been built all at once.

MacLean has hypothesized that the human brain is three brains in one. The "reptilian brain" at the core is composed of structures that are well developed in reptiles (Figure 4-3). The reptilian brain controls breathing, locomotion, fighting, mating, and other fixed, stereotyped behaviors necessary for self-preservation and reproduction. Surrounding the reptilian brain is the "old-mammalian brain," composed of forebrain structures that are better developed in mammals than in reptiles but that are more or less the same in all mammals. The old-mammalian brain, MacLean says, contributes emotional components such as fear, anger, and love. Finally, surrounding the old-mammalian brain is the "new-mammalian brain," which consists of a multilayered cerebral cortex. It is best developed in humans, other primates, dolphins, whales, and a few other mammals. The new-mammalian brain is responsible for the most advanced sensory processing and the most elaborate thought processes. Although the reptilian, old-mammalian, and new-mammalian brains work together, it is possible to imagine conflicts that may arise among them, possibly leading to psychological distress or inefficiency (MacLean, 1970, 1977).

MacLean's hypothesis, like many great generalizations in psychology, is difficult to categorize as simply true or false. If we take the hypothesis

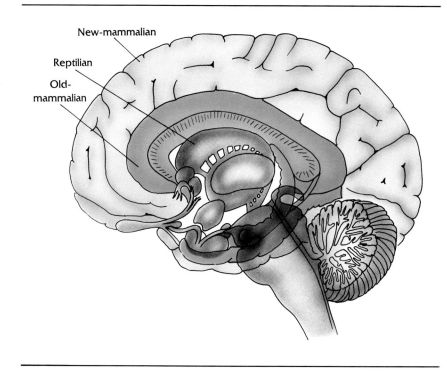

New-mammalian

Reptilian

Old-mammalian

Figure 4-3. The superimposition of new brain structures over older ones, as described by MacLean.

literally, it is easy to find fault with it. Because structures can be lost or modified as well as added (Northcutt, 1985), we have no reason to expect that any part of the human brain would have remained unchanged since the days of our reptilian ancestors. Certainly, no removal of new-mammalian brain can turn a human brain into the equivalent of a rat brain, and no removal of new- and old-mammalian brain can turn a mammalian brain into the equivalent of a reptile brain.

On the other hand, it is clear that the evolution of the human brain has taken place primarily by dramatic elaborations, expansions, and additions in the forebrain, especially the cerebral cortex, while fewer changes have taken place within what MacLean calls the reptilian brain. MacLean's hypothesis may, therefore, be a helpful way of looking at certain trends in brain evolution.

DEVELOPMENTAL CHANGES IN THE VERTEBRATE BRAIN

The central nervous system (brain and spinal cord) begins as a thickening on the surface of the embryo. Long thin lips rise and curl, merging to form a neural tube surrounding a fluid-filled cavity, as shown in Figure 4-4. The tube sinks under the surface of the skin and continues to develop. The forward end enlarges and differentiates into the hindbrain, midbrain, and forebrain. (See Figure 4-5.) The rest becomes the spinal cord. The fluid-filled cavity that the neural tube surrounds becomes the central canal of the spinal cord and the four ventricles of the brain. The fluid inside the canal and **ventricles** is known as the **cerebrospinal fluid (CSF)**.

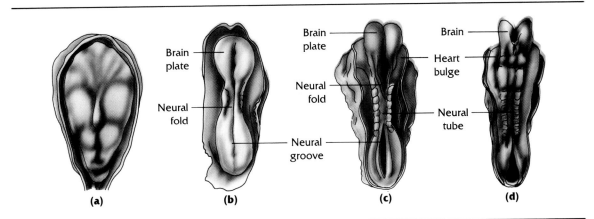

Brain plate

Neural fold

(a)

Brain plate

Neural fold

Neural groove

(b)

Brain plate

Neural fold

(c)

Brain

Heart bulge

Neural tube

(d)

Brain

Heart bulge

Neural tube

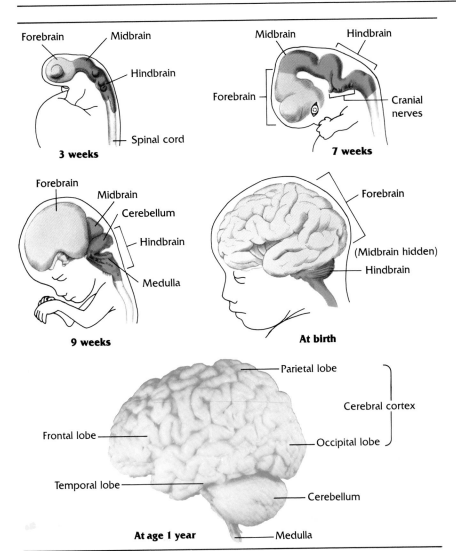

Forebrain   Midbrain

Hindbrain

Spinal cord

3 weeks

Midbrain   Hindbrain

Forebrain

Cranial nerves

7 weeks

Forebrain

Midbrain

Cerebellum

Hindbrain

Medulla

9 weeks

Forebrain

(Midbrain hidden)

Hindbrain

At birth

Parietal lobe

Cerebral cortex

Occipital lobe

Frontal lobe

Temporal lobe

Cerebellum

At age 1 year   Medulla

Figure 4-4. Early development of the central nervous system. The brain and spinal cord begin as folding lips surrounding a fluid-filled canal. Stages shown occur at approximately ages two to three weeks.

Figure 4-5. Human brain at five stages of development. (Photo courtesy of Dr. Dana Copeland.)

At birth, the human brain weighs about 350 g. Certain areas of the forebrain are immature, almost nonfunctional for the first few weeks (Chugani & Phelps, 1986). Development is rapid, however, and areas of the brain that are almost silent at birth approach adult patterns of activity within 7 to 8 months (Chugani & Phelps, 1986). At the end of the first year, the brain weighs 1,000 g, not much less than the adult weight of 1,200 to 1,400 g.

When the cell body of a neuron first develops, the destination of its axon is only partly fixed (Cowan, Fawcett, O'Leary, & Stanfield, 1984). In fact, its axon may never find an appropriate target at all. Initially, a great many neurons form and send out axons toward their targets, which may be other neurons or muscles or gland cells. Those axons that reach the target first form synapses. Those that arrive too late, or that reach the wrong target, die, along with their cell bodies.

Ordinarily, only about half of all newly formed neurons make synapses and survive. If the number of target cells is decreased surgically, fewer of the neurons that would have made synapses with them will survive. If the number of target cells is increased by transplants or other manipulations, more incoming axons than usual survive. Thus, overproduction of neurons followed by cell death is a mechanism for guaranteeing that the number of incoming axons will match the number of available synapses on the target cells.

Not all the synapses that form turn out to be functional. A cell may receive synapses from a variety of sources and later select among them by some unknown means. For example, a cell in the visual system may receive a number of axons relaying information that originated in the left eye and a number relaying information from the right eye. It must then somehow identify some combination of neurons so that it will be looking at the same part of the world in the left eye that it is looking at in the right eye. We shall encounter this specific example of selection among synapses later (Chapter 7), and we shall encounter other examples when we discuss learning (Chapter 13) and recovery from brain damage (Chapter 14).

BASIC SUBDIVISIONS OF THE NERVOUS SYSTEM

The most basic distinction we can draw in the vertebrate nervous system is that between the **central nervous system (CNS)** and the **peripheral nervous system (PNS)**. (See Color Plate 2.) As noted earlier, the CNS consists of the brain (forebrain, midbrain, and hindbrain) and the spinal cord. The PNS encompasses those neurons that connect the CNS to the receptors, muscles, and organs at the periphery of the body.

The Spinal Cord

The **spinal cord** is a segmented structure. Each segment has both a sensory nerve and a motor nerve on its left and right sides, as shown in Figure 4-6. (See also Color Plates 10 and 11.) All the sensory nerves enter the spinal cord on the dorsal (back) side; all the axons of the motor nerves leave on the ventral (stomach) side. (See Table 4-1 and Figure 4-7 for explanations of

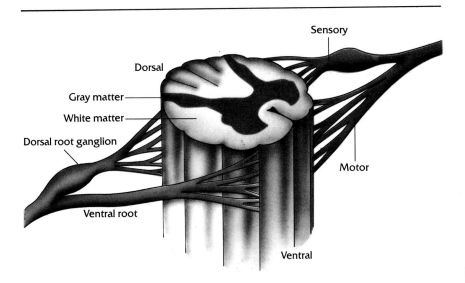

Figure 4-6. A cross-section through the spinal cord.

Table 4-1.   Some Important Anatomical Terms

Term	Definition
Dorsal	Toward the back, away from the ventral (stomach) side. The top of the brain is considered dorsal because that is its position in four-legged animals.
Ventral	Toward the stomach, away from the dorsal (back) side. (*Venter* is the Latin word for "belly." It also shows up in the word *ventriloquist*, literally meaning "stomach-talker.")
Anterior	Toward the front end.
Posterior	Toward the rear end. In humans, the ventral spinal cord is sometimes called *anterior* and the dorsal cord is called *posterior*.
Lateral	Toward the side, away from the midline.
Medial	Toward the midline, away from the side.
Coronal plane	A plane for dividing the brain that shows brain structures as they would be seen from the front.
Sagittal plane	A plane that shows structures as they would be seen from the side.
Horizontal plane	A plane that shows structures as they would be seen from above.
Lamina	A row or layer of cell bodies separated from other cell bodies by a layer of fibers.
Tract	A set of axons within the CNS, also known as a *projection*. If axons extend from cell bodies in structure A to synapses onto B, we say that the fibers "project" from A onto B.
Ipsilateral	On the same side of the body (left or right).
Contralateral	On the opposite side of the body (left or right).
Gyrus	An outswelling on the surface of the brain.
Sulcus	A fold or groove that separates one gyrus from another.

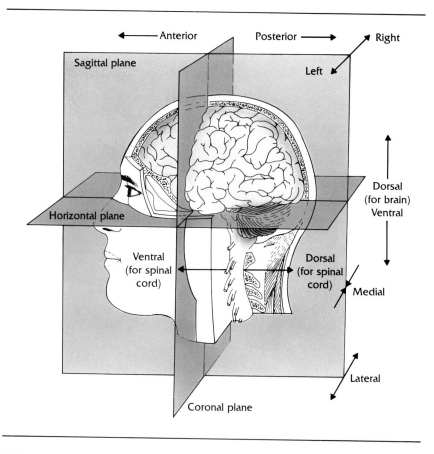

Figure 4-7. Anatomical terms for the human brain. Note that the dorsal-ventral axis for the brain is not parallel to that for the spinal cord; the reason is humans' upright posture. In four-legged animals the cord extends backward instead of downward, and dorsal and ventral mean the same for the cord as for the brain.

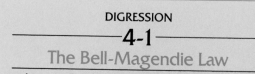

DIGRESSION

4-1

The Bell-Magendie Law

The term *Bell-Magendie Law* refers to one of the first important discoveries about the functioning of the nervous system, the discovery that the dorsal roots of the spinal cord carry sensory information and the ventral roots carry motor information. How it came to be known as the Bell-Magendie Law shows one of the less lovable sides of scientists (Gallistel, 1981).

In 1811, Charles Bell cut the ventral and dorsal roots of experimental animals and drew a vaguely stated, incorrect conclusion that the ventral nerves were responsible for voluntary behavior while the dorsal roots were responsible for involuntary behavior. In 1822, Francois Magendie performed a similar experiment and concluded that the ventral roots were motor and the dorsal roots were sensory.

Bell at that point argued that he should get credit for the discovery because he had said almost the same thing eleven years earlier. He further argued that Magendie never should have performed his experiments at all, first because they were too cruel—all this occurred decades before the use of anesthetics in surgery—and second because he, Bell, had already performed the experiments. He glossed over the fact that his own conclusions had been wrong; he also ignored the contradiction of claiming that Magendie's experiments were cruel but that his own were not.

The result of Bell's arguments was that the scientific world did give him at least shared credit for Magendie's discovery. A further result was that the British government passed laws to prohibit the kinds of experiment that both Bell and Magendie had performed. (The controversy about painful treatment of experimental animals, discussed in Chapter 1, has been going on for a great while.)

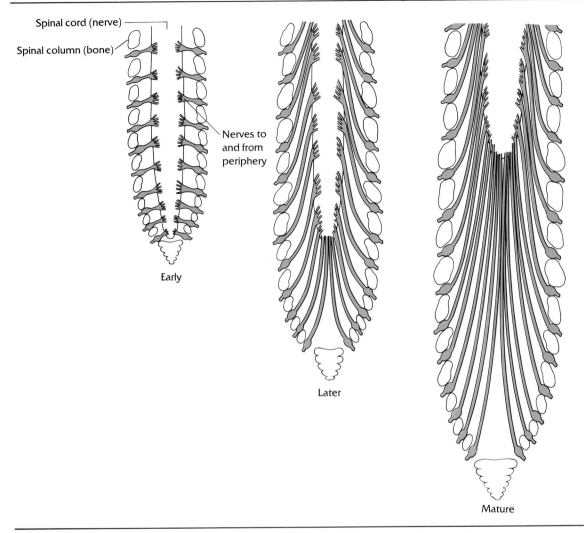

Spinal cord (nerve)

Spinal column (bone)

Nerves to
and from
periphery

Early

Later

Mature

Figure 4-8. Relationship of the spinal cord to the vertebral column, from an early stage of development to maturity.

dorsal, ventral, and other anatomical terms.) The separation of the sensory nerves from the motor nerves on the two sides of the cord is known as the **Bell-Magendie Law**. (See Digression 4-1.) The cell bodies of the sensory nerves are located outside the cord in the **dorsal root ganglion**. Cell bodies of the motor neurons are located within the spinal cord.

Development of the Spinal Cord. Early in embryological development, the bones of the spinal column form around the nerve cord in such a way that the sensory and motor nerves from each segment exit through nearby holes in the spinal column. As prenatal and childhood development proceeds, the bony spinal column continues to grow long after the spinal cord itself has reached its full length. Because the bones continue to stretch while the cord does not, the nerves from the spinal cord must eventually travel some distance down the spinal column before they exit (Figure 4-8).

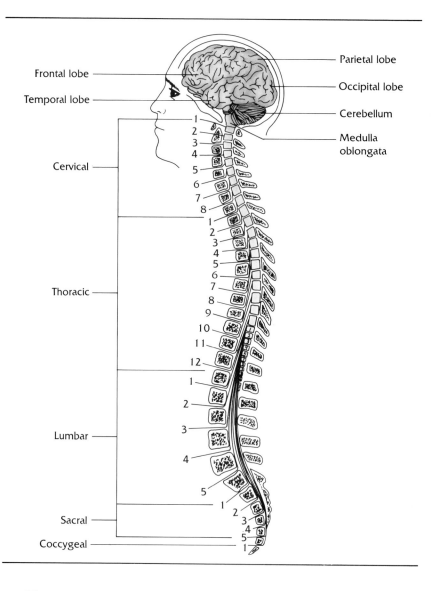

Figure 4-9. The human central nervous system (CNS). Spinal nerves from each segment of the spinal cord exit through the correspondingly numbered opening between vertebrae.

This arrangement applies a small amount of tension on the spinal cord. If the spinal cord is cut, the bottom portion is likely to pull apart from the top portion. That is one of several reasons why humans and other mammals do not recover from a cut through the spinal cord.

Segments of the Spinal Cord.   The spinal cord has thirty-one segments and therefore thirty-one sets of sensory and motor nerves. (See Figure 4-9.) Beginning at the top, we can distinguish eight cervical nerves, twelve thoracic nerves, five lumbar nerves, five sacral nerves, and one coccygeal nerve.

Each spinal nerve innervates a limited area of the body. The skin area innervated by a sensory spinal nerve is called a **dermatome.** Figure 4-10 shows the locations of the dermatomes. For example, the third thoracic nerve

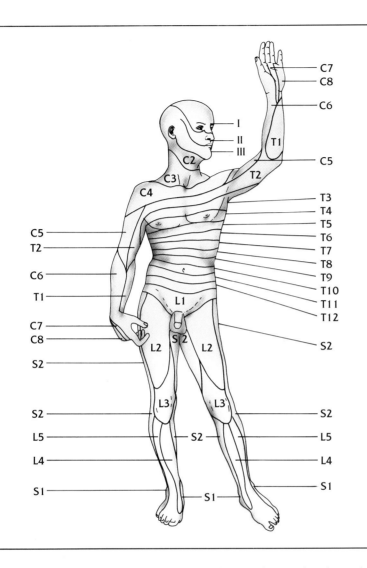

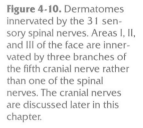

Figure 4-10. Dermatomes innervated by the 31 sensory spinal nerves. Areas I, II, and III of the face are innervated by three branches of the fifth cranial nerve rather than one of the spinal nerves. The cranial nerves are discussed later in this chapter.

(T3) innervates a strip of skin just above the nipples on the chest plus the underarm area. The borders between dermatomes are not so distinct as implied in Figure 4-10, however; there is actually one-third to one-half overlap between adjacent pairs.

The thickness of an area of the spinal cord depends on the density of muscles and receptors in the dermatome attached to it. For example, the cervical area of the spinal cord, which attaches to the forelimbs, is very large in strong-flying birds that have large wings (Sarnat & Netsky, 1981). The thoracic area of the cord is extremely thin in turtles, which have almost no muscles in the corresponding dermatomes.

Spinal Pathways.   The sensory nerves that enter a segment of the spinal cord make synapses with interneurons within the spinal cord. These in turn make synapses with other interneurons and with motor neurons. In the

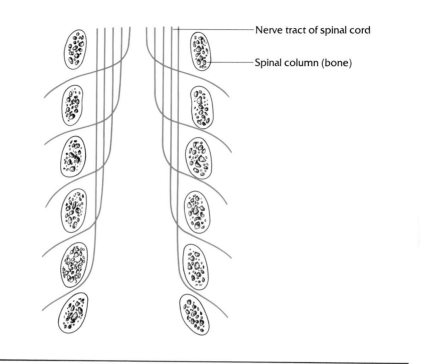

Nerve tract of spinal cord

Spinal column (bone)

Figure 4-11. Lateral displacement of sacral fibers by more anterior fibers in a tract of the spinal cord.

cross-section through the spinal cord shown in Figure 4-6, the H-shaped **gray matter** in the center of the cord is packed with a high density of cell bodies. Many of the interneurons' axons form branches that leave the gray matter and travel toward the brain in the **white matter**. The white matter gets its appearance from the myelinated axons in it. (Myelin is white.) If the spinal cord is cut, the brain loses sensation from and control over all parts of the body served by the spinal cord below the cut.

The white matter contains several separate axon tracts, some carrying impulses from the spinal cord to the brain and others carrying impulses from the brain to the spinal cord. For example, a tract known as the *fasciculus gracilis* conveys sensory information from the lower parts of the body. Within this tract, new fibers that enter the cord at a given segment move to the medial part of the path and displace the fibers that had already entered laterally, as shown in Figure 4-11. Fibers that entered the sacral part of the cord end up in the most lateral positions of this spinal path. As a result, a tumor that forms in the center of the cord may destroy sensations coming from relatively anterior parts of the body while sparing sensations from the lowest segments of the cord (Rowland, 1981).

The Autonomic Nervous System

Associated with the spinal cord, but outside it, lies the **autonomic nervous system**, composed of the **sympathetic** and **parasympathetic nervous systems**. (See Figure 4-12.) The sympathetic nervous system consists of two paired chains of **ganglia** (collections of nerve cells) lying just to the left and right of

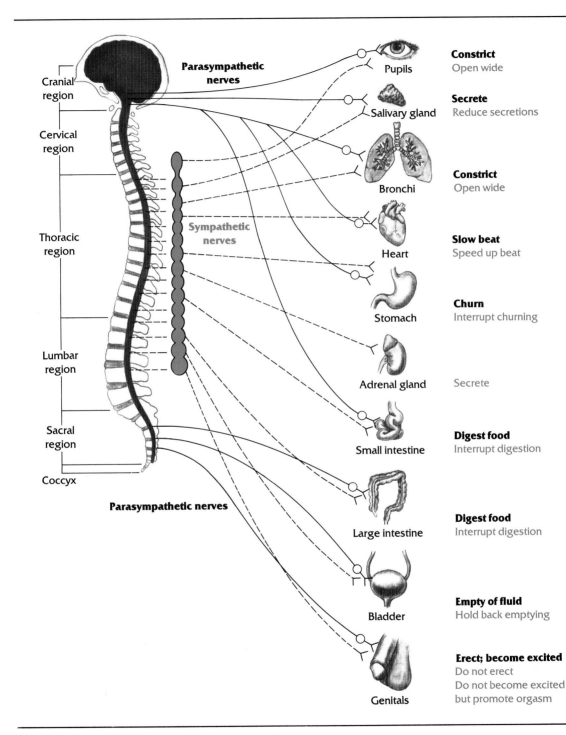

Figure 4-12. The sympathetic and parasympathetic nervous systems.

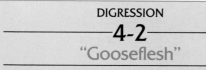

DIGRESSION

4-2

"Gooseflesh"

Erection of the hairs, known as "gooseflesh" or "goosebumps," is controlled by the sympathetic nervous system. What does this response have to do with the "fight or flight" functions that are usually associated with the sympathetic nervous system?

Human body hairs are so short that erecting them accomplishes nothing of importance; the response is an evolutionary relic from ancient ancestors with furrier bodies. Erecting the hairs helps nonhuman mammals to protect their body temperature in a cold environment by increasing their insulation. It also serves several species as a defense against enemies in fight or flight situations. Consider, for example, the Halloween cat, or any other frightened, cornered animal; by erecting its hairs it looks larger and may thereby deter its opponent.

The quills of a porcupine, an effective defense against potential predators, are actually modified body hairs. In a fight or flight situation, sympathetic nervous system activity leads to erection of the quills, just as it leads to erection of the hairs in other mammals (Richter & Langworthy, 1933). The behavior that makes the quills so useful, their erection in response to fear, evidently evolved before the quills themselves did.

the spinal cord in its central regions (the thoracic and lumbar areas) and connected by axons to those spinal cord regions. Axons also extend from the sympathetic ganglia to the internal organs of the body. The sympathetic nervous system prepares the body for "fight or flight" activities: It increases the heart rate and breathing rate and it decreases digestive activity. Because all the sympathetic ganglia are closely linked, they tend to act as a single system. That is, they act "in sympathy" with one another.

The term *para* means "next to"; thus, it is no surprise that the parasympathetic system lies adjacent to the sympathetic system. The parasympathetic nervous system is linked to the cranial nerves of the medulla (which we shall discuss in the next section) and to the sacral nerves in the lower spinal cord. Unlike in the sympathetic system, the parasympathetic ganglia are not arranged in a chain near the spinal cord. Rather, long axons extend from the spinal cord to parasympathetic ganglia close to each internal organ; shorter fibers then extend fom the parasympathetic ganglia into the organs themselves. Because the parasympathetic ganglia are not linked to one another, they sometimes act more independently than the sympathetic ganglia do. Activity of the parasympathetic system decreases heart rate, increases digestive rate, and in general promotes energy-conserving, nonemergency functions.

The sweat glands, the adrenal glands, the muscles that constrict blood vessels, and the muscles that erect the hairs of the skin have sympathetic input only. (See Digression 4-2.) Other organs are controlled by both the sympathetic and parasympathetic systems, but in opposite ways. What the sympathetic system excites, the parasympathetic system inhibits, and vice versa.

The final synapses of the parasympathetic nervous system onto any organ use the transmitter acetylcholine. Most of the final synapses of the sympathetic nervous system use norepinephrine, although a few, such as the ones that control the sweat glands, use acetylcholine. Because the two systems use different synaptic transmitters, certain drugs may excite or inhibit

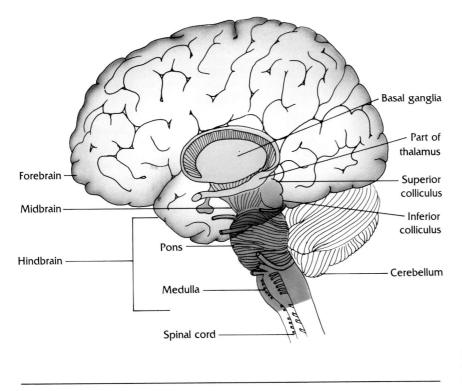

Figure 4-13. Structures of the brainstem (shaded areas).

one system or the other. For example, over-the-counter cold remedies exert their effects largely by blocking parasympathetic activity or by increasing sympathetic activity. This action is useful because the flow of sinus fluids is a parasympathetic response; thus, drugs that block the parasympathetic system inhibit sinus flow. The common side effects of cold remedies also stem from their ability to excite sympathetic responses and block parasympathetic ones: They inhibit salivation, inhibit digestion, and increase heart rate. They also have two effects on sexual responses. Because sexual arousal (erection in the male, vaginal lubrication in the female) depends on the parasympathetic system, cold remedies interfere with such arousal. However, because orgasm depends on the sympathetic system, if one does manage to get aroused, the drugs may speed up orgasm. (Do you now see why nervousness interferes with sexual arousal? And why soft music and other relaxing stimuli promote it?)

The Hindbrain

The **hindbrain** consists of the medulla, the pons, and the cerebellum. As Figure 4-13 shows, the hindbrain plus the midbrain and certain central structures of the forebrain constitute the **brainstem**. (See also Color Plate 4.)

The **medulla**, or medulla oblongata, is located just above the spinal cord; in many ways it might be regarded as an enlarged, elaborated extension

Table 4-2.   The Cranial Nerves

Number and name	Function of sensory component	Function of motor component
1. Olfactory	Smell	(no motor nerve)
2. Optic	Vision	(no motor nerve)
3. Oculomotor	Sensations from eye muscles	Eye movements, pupil constriction
4. Trochlear	Sensations from eye muscles	Eye movements
5. Trigeminal	Sensations from skin of face, nose, and mouth	Chewing, swallowing
6. Abducens	Sensations from eye muscles	Eye movements
7. Facial	Taste from the anterior two-thirds of the tongue, visceral sensations from the head	Facial expressions, crying, salivation, and dilation of blood vessels in the head
8. Statoacoustic	Hearing, equilibrium	(no motor nerve)
9. Glossopharyngeal	Taste and other sensations from throat and posterior third of tongue	Swallowing, salivation, dilation of blood vessels
10. Vagus	Taste and sensations from neck, thorax, and abdomen	Swallowing, control of larynx, parasympathetic nerves to heart and viscera
11. Accessory	(no sensory nerve)	Movements of shoulders and head; parasympathetic to viscera
12. Hypoglossal	Sensation from tongue muscles	Movement of tongue

of the spinal cord, although it is located in the skull rather than in the spine. The medulla controls breathing, heart rate, vomiting, salivation, coughing, sneezing, and other vital reflexes by means of the **cranial nerves.**

Just as the lower parts of the body are connected to the spinal cord via sensory and motor nerves, the skin and muscles of the head and the internal organs are connected to the brain via a set of twelve pairs (one right and one left) of cranial nerves. Most cranial nerves include both sensory and motor components, although some include just one or the other. (See Table 4-2.) Each cranial nerve originates in a nucleus of cells that integrate the sensory information and regulate the motor output. The cranial nerve nuclei for nerves 5 through 12 are located in the medulla and pons of the hindbrain. Those for cranial nerves 1 through 4 are located in the midbrain and forebrain. (See Figure 4-14.)

The **pons** lies anterior to the medulla. The term *pons* is Latin for "bridge"; the name reflects the fact that a great many nerve fibers cross between left and right at the level of the pons. These fibers are principally axons from neurons in the pons, going to the cerebellum. Like the medulla, the pons contains centers for several cranial nerves.

The medulla and pons also contain the **reticular formation** and the **raphe system.** These two systems send axons diffusely throughout the forebrain. They have a great deal to do with arousal and sleep, as we will see in Chapter 9.

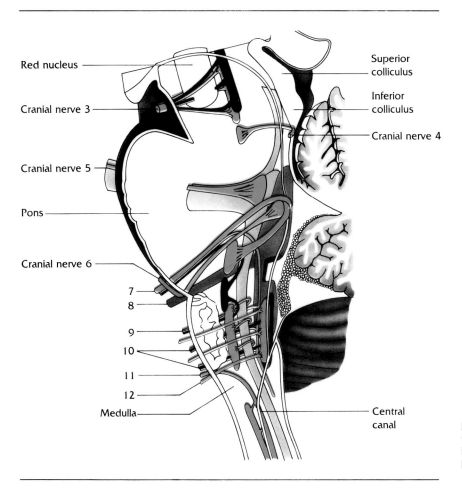

Red nucleus

Superior colliculus

Inferior colliculus

Cranial nerve 3

Cranial nerve 4

Cranial nerve 5

Pons

Cranial nerve 6

7
8

9

10

11

12

Medulla

Central canal

Figure 4-14. Cranial nerves 3 through 12 and their nuclei in the midbrain, medulla, and pons. (Based on Braus, 1960.)

The **cerebellum** is a large structure with a great many deep folds. It is best known for its contributions to the control of movement, which will be discussed in Chapter 8.

The Midbrain

The **midbrain** makes up a smaller proportion of total brain size in humans and most other mammals than it does in birds, reptiles, and amphibians. The roof of the midbrain is called the **tectum**. (*Tectum* is the Latin word for "roof.") The two swellings on each side of the tectum are the **superior colliculus** and the **inferior colliculus** (see Figures 4-13 and 4-14), both of which are part of important routes for sensory information.

Under the tectum is the **tegmentum**. (In Latin, *tegmentum* meant a covering, such as a covering on the floor.) The tegmentum includes the nuclei for the third and fourth cranial nerves, parts of the reticular formation, and extensions of the pathways between the forebrain and the spinal cord or hindbrain. Another structure in the midbrain is the **substantia nigra**, an area that deteriorates in Parkinson's disease (see Chapter 8).

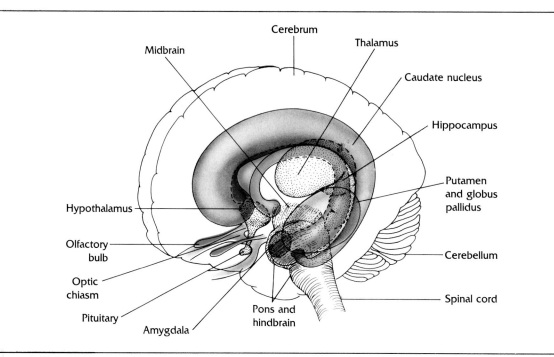

Figure 4-15. Some important subcortical areas of the brain, in perspective.

The Forebrain

The **forebrain** is the largest and most prominent portion of the mammalian brain. The outer portion is the cerebral cortex. (*Cerebrum* means "brain"; *cortex* means "covering.") Under the cerebral cortex lie a number of other forebrain structures, including the thalamus, olfactory bulb, hypothalamus, pituitary gland, basal ganglia, hippocampus, and amygdala. Figure 4-15 shows the positions of these structures in a three-dimensional perspective. Figures 4-16 and 4-17 show coronal and sagittal sections through the human brain. (Review Figure 4-7 for an explanation of coronal and sagittal sections.) Figure 4-16 also includes a view of the ventral surface of the brain.

In describing the forebrain we shall begin with certain subcortical areas and then examine the cerebral cortex in greater detail. We shall return to each of these areas again in later chapters.

Hypothalamus.   The **hypothalamus** is a small area located near the base of the brain (see Figures 4-15 and 4-17.) It has widespread connections with the rest of the forebrain and the midbrain. The hypothalamus contains a number of distinct nuclei (clusters of neurons). Damage to one of the hypothalamic nuclei leads to abnormalities in one or more motivated behaviors, such as feeding, drinking, temperature regulation, sexual behavior, fighting, or activity level.

The hypothalamus also regulates the secretion of hormones through its effects on the pituitary gland. The hypothalamus contains receptors for specific hormones; in response to alterations in the levels of those hormones, the hypothalamus conveys messages to the pituitary gland, partly through

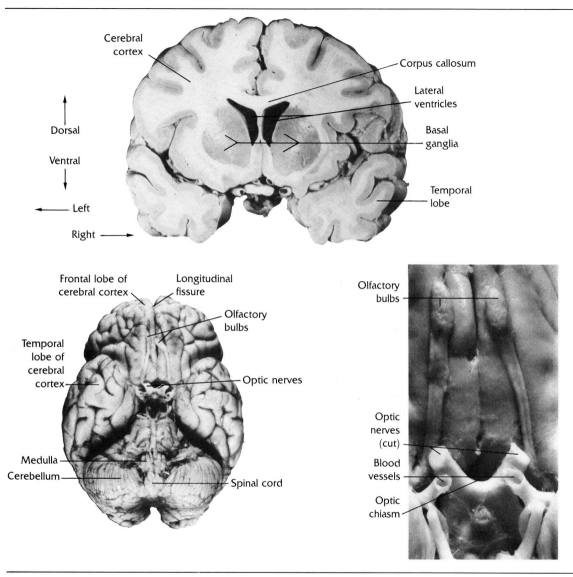

Figure 4-16. Views of the human brain. *Top*: Coronal section. *Bottom*: Ventral surface with close-up of olfactory bulbs and optic chiasm. (Photos courtesy of Dr. Dana Copeland.)

nerves and partly through hypothalamic hormones, to alter the release of hormones by the pituitary.

Pituitary Gland.   The **pituitary gland** is an **endocrine** (hormone-producing) **gland** attached to the base of the hypothalamus by a stalk that contains neurons, blood vessels, and connective tissue. In response to messages from the hypothalamus, the pituitary synthesizes and releases hormones into the bloodstream, which carries them to other organs. The pituitary is sometimes called the "master gland" of the body because its secretions control the timing and amount of hormone secretion by the other endocrine organs, such as the thyroid, the adrenal gland, and the ovaries or

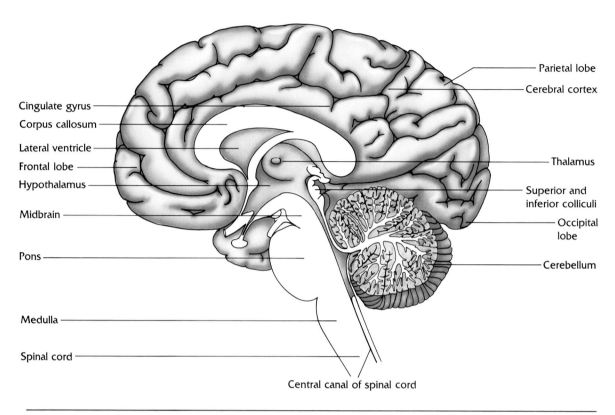

Cingulate gyrus
Corpus callosum
Lateral ventricle
Frontal lobe
Hypothalamus
Midbrain
Pons
Medulla
Spinal cord

Parietal lobe
Cerebral cortex
Thalamus
Superior and inferior colliculi
Occipital lobe
Cerebellum

Central canal of spinal cord

Figure 4-17. A sagittal section through the human brain.

testes. The endocrine organs are subject to long-term regulation by the pituitary gland and short-term regulation by the autonomic nervous system.

Basal Ganglia.   The **basal ganglia** are a group of structures located left and right of the thalamus. The basal ganglia include three major structures: the caudate nucleus, the putamen, and the globus pallidus. Some authorities include several other structures as well.

The basal ganglia are known to be damaged in Parkinson's disease, Huntington's disease, and other conditions that impair the control of movement. The basal ganglia do not control movement directly, however; they send no axons directly to the medulla or spinal cord. Rather, they send messages to the thalamus and the midbrain, which relay information to the cerebral cortex, which in turn sends messages to the medulla or spinal cord. The basal ganglia also contribute to functions other than movement.

Hippocampus.   The **hippocampus** is situated between the thalamus and the cerebral cortex, mostly on the posterior side of the forebrain, as shown in Figure 4-15. Two major axon tracts, the **fornix** and the **fimbria**, link the hippocampus with the hypothalamus and several other structures. We shall discuss the role of the hippocampus in learning and memory when we get to Chapter 13.

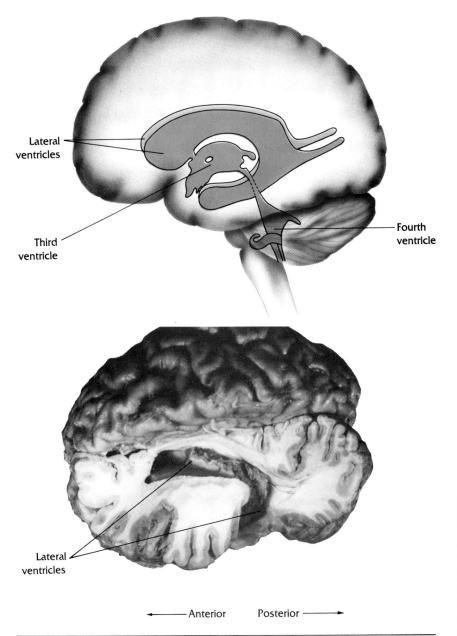

Figure 4-18. *Top:* Diagram showing positions of the four ventricles. *Bottom:* Photo of human brain, viewed from above, with a horizontal cut through one hemisphere to show position of lateral ventricle. (Photo courtesy of Dr. Dana Copeland.) Note that the two parts of this figure are seen from different angles.

Ventricles.   The cerebral ventricles are fluid-filled cavities within the brain. Recall that the nervous system begins its development as a tube surrounding a fluid canal. The canal persists into adulthood as the **central canal** of the spinal cord and, with much expansion, as the ventricles of the brain. Two large lateral ventricles are located in the interior of the two hemispheres of the forebrain. (See Figure 4-18.) Toward the posterior they connect to the third ventricle, which connects to the fourth ventricle in the medulla.

The ventricles and the central canal of the spinal cord contain cerebro-spinal fluid (CSF), a clear fluid similar to blood plasma. CSF is formed by cells that line the four ventricles. It flows from the lateral ventricles to the third and then to the fourth ventricle. From the fourth ventricle, part flows into the central canal of the spinal cord and a larger part goes through an opening to the thin **subarachnoid space** over the brain. It is then gradually reabsorbed into the blood vessels of the brain.

The cerebrospinal fluid cushions the brain against mechanical shock when the head moves. It also provides buoyancy; just as a person weighs less in water than on land, the cerebrospinal fluid helps to support the weight of the brain. The CSF also provides a reservoir of hormones and nutrition for the brain and spinal cord.

Sometimes the flow of CSF is obstructed and it accumulates within the ventricles or in the subarachnoid space, thus increasing the pressure on the brain. When this occurs in infants, the skull bones may spread, causing an overgrown head. This condition is known as **hydrocephalus** (HI-dro-SEFF-ah-luss); it is usually associated with mental retardation.

The Thalamus and Its Relationship to the Cerebral Cortex.   The **thalamus** (from a Greek word meaning "anteroom" or "inner chamber") resembles two footballs joined side by side. Practically all sensory and other information projects first to the thalamus in the center of the forebrain, and then from the thalamus to the cerebral cortex and to a number of subcortical structures. The only exception is olfactory information, which enters the **olfactory bulb** (Figure 4-15) instead of the thalamus. The thalamus is sometimes described as a way station of information on the way to the cerebral cortex or other areas. It is, however, much more than just a passive relay; it processes and integrates information in many ways.

The thalamus consists of a number of separate nuclei, each of which sends its axons to, and receives axons from, a particular part of the cerebral cortex. Figure 4-19 diagrams the routes taken by axons from five of the many parts of the thalamus.

At one time it was believed that the cerebral cortex had three types of areas: sensory areas, motor areas, and association areas. According to this view, sensory nuclei of the thalamus sent input to the sensory areas of the cortex. Several sensory areas then combined to send their input to each association area, which in turn sent input to the motor areas. Finally, the motor areas sent messages that controlled the muscles.

This idea was appealing. The idea of association areas coincided with the idea of a unified consciousness, a single self that is aware of all sensory experiences. Besides, the association areas, which seemed a natural place for learning and memory to occur, formed a larger percentage of the human brain than of the brains of most other species. It seemed that we had a physical explanation for why humans are, at least in our own opinion, so much smarter than other species.

By the 1940s it had become clear that this idea had to be amended at least. The so-called association areas of the cortex receive a great deal of input *directly* from the thalamus. They also receive input from other parts

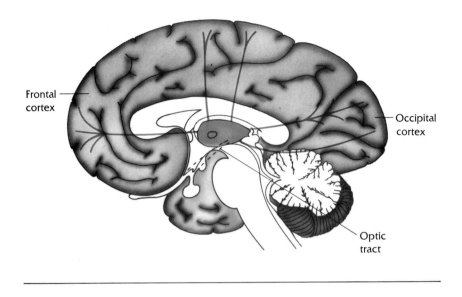

Frontal cortex

Occipital cortex

Optic tract

Figure 4-19. The routes of information from some specific nuclei of the thalamus to limited areas of the cerebral cortex.

of the cortex, but so do the nonassociation areas. Moreover, the association areas form their synapses during the same period of development as the sensory areas (Rakic, Bourgeois, Eckenhoff, Zecevic, & Goldman-Rakic, 1986). If the association areas depended entirely on the other areas for their input, it would seem necessary for them to wait for that input before they began to develop.

Rose and Woolsey (1949) proposed a theory to rescue the concept of association areas. The association areas, they conceded, received input from the thalamus, but that input was from what they called *intrinsic* nuclei of the thalamus—thalamic nuclei that received their own input from other thalamic nuclei, not directly from sensory pathways. In other words, the intrinsic nuclei were association areas of the thalamus, and the cortical areas to which they sent messages were therefore association areas, too.

Later work with more advanced techniques found that the intrinsic nuclei are not associational after all (Diamond, 1979, 1983). They receive much of their input from sensory pathways or from the reticular formation (a diffuse activating system), not just from other thalamic nuclei. It had been easy for an early researcher to overlook certain of these sensory pathways because they consist of small-diameter axons from relatively small neurons (Bishop, 1959).

What once appeared to be an association area next to the visual cortex now appears to be a second visual area, partly independent of the first. The same is true for what used to be regarded as association areas near the auditory cortex and the tactile cortex. Evolution has set down parallel representations of each sensory modality.

Practically all parts of the cerebral cortex receive input from a fairly direct sensory pathway. All areas also receive input from other parts of the cortex, at least from immediately adjacent areas. And all areas send output that controls the muscles, although certain areas definitely send more information than others. In short, according to Diamond (1979), the cortex does not have distinct sensory areas, association areas, and motor areas. Although a given area may have somewhat greater sensory or associational or motor functions than certain other areas, every area of the cortex is at least partly sensory, associational, *and* motor.

THE CEREBRAL CORTEX

The **cerebral cortex** consists of two hemispheres, one on the left side and one on the right, covering all the other forebrain structures. Each hemisphere is organized to receive sensory information mostly from the contralateral (opposite) side of the body and to control muscles mostly on the contralateral side by way of axons to the spinal cord and the cranial nerve nuclei.

The cerebral cortex, the surface of each hemisphere, is gray matter, consisting largely of cell bodies. Large numbers of axons extend inward from the cortex, forming the white matter. (See Figures 4-15 and 4-20.) Neurons in each hemisphere communicate with neurons in the corresponding part of the other hemisphere by two bundles of axons, the **corpus callosum** (Figures 4-15, 4-16, and 4-20) and the smaller **anterior commissure.** (Several other commissures link subcortical structures.)

Portions of the cerebral cortex of humans and most other mammals have six distinct **laminae** (layers), which vary in thickness and prominence from one area of the cortex to another. (See Figure 4-21.) Lamina V, which sends long axons to the spinal cord and other distant areas, is thickest in the motor cortex, the area with the greatest control of the muscles. Lamina IV, which receives axons from the various sensory nuclei of the thalamus, is more prominent in the visual and auditory cortexes than in the motor cortex. Anecdotal reports have found lamina IV to be even thicker than normal in the visual cortex of a person with "photographic memory" and in the auditory cortex of a musician with "perfect pitch" (Scheibel, 1984).

It is possible to distinguish fifty or so areas of the cerebral cortex, based on differences in the thickness of the six laminae and on the appearance of cells and fibers within each lamina. For convenience of discussion, however, we shall group these areas into four *lobes* named for the skull bones that lie over them: occipital, parietal, temporal, and frontal. (See Figure 4-22.)

Occipital Lobe

The **occipital lobe,** located at the posterior (caudal) end of the cortex, is the main target for axons from the thalamic nuclei that receive input from the visual pathways. The very posterior pole of the occipital lobe is known as the *primary visual cortex* or as the *striate cortex* because of its striped appearance in cross-section. Complete destruction of the striate cortex in humans leads to almost complete blindness. Partial destruction of the striate cortex causes loss of vision in part of the visual field.

Vision is not, however, the only function of the occipital lobe. Karl Lashley (1929) found that occipital lobe damage impaired the maze learning of rats that were already blind. Evidently, the occipital cortex contributes something important even in blind rats.

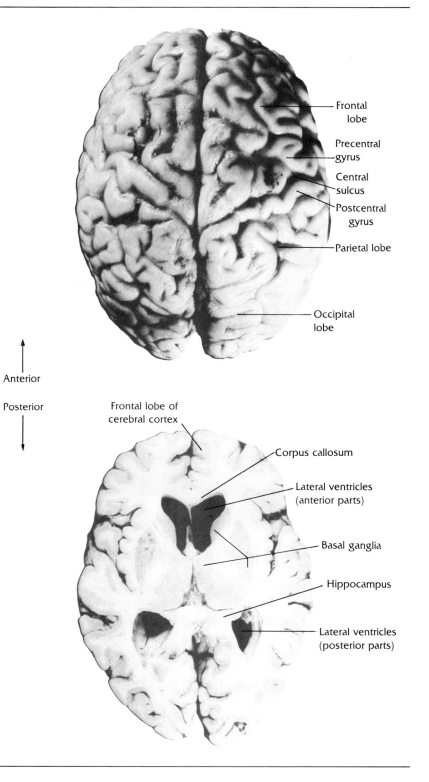

Anterior

Posterior

Figure 4-20. Dorsal view of the surface of the brain and a horizontal section through the brain. (Photos courtesy of Dr. Dana Copeland.)

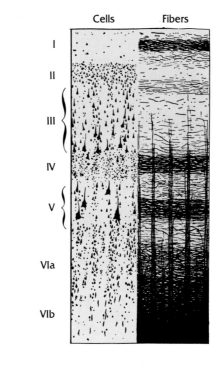

Figure 4-21. The six laminae of the human cerebral cortex: (I) molecular layer (mostly dendrites and long axons, few cells); (II) external granular layer (mostly small pyramidal cells); (III) layer of pyramidal cells; (IV) internal granular layer (small pyramidal and stellate, or star-shaped, cells—the main site for termination of incoming fibers from the thalamus and other structures); (V) inner pyramidal layer (large pyramidal cells); (VI) multiform or spindle-cell layer. (From Ranson & Clark, 1959.)

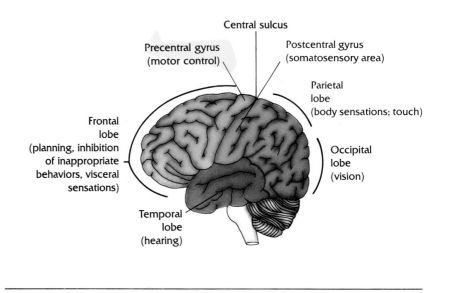

Figure 4-22. Some important subdivisions of the human cerebral cortex, with indications of a few of their primary functions.

Parietal Lobe

The **parietal lobe** lies between the occipital lobe and the **central sulcus**, one of the deepest grooves in the surface of the cortex. The parietal lobe is specialized primarily for dealing with body information, including touch, muscle-stretch receptors, and joint receptors. The area just posterior to the central sulcus is the **postcentral gyrus**, sometimes known as the primary somatosensory area. Direct electrical stimulation of the postcentral gyrus evokes sensations on the opposite side of the body, often described as tingling or not quite natural sensations.

The postcentral gyrus includes four bands of cells running parallel to the central sulcus. Along each band are separate areas that receive information from different parts of the body, as shown in Figure 4-23 (**a**). Two of the bands receive mostly light-touch information, one receives deep pressure information, and one receives a combination of both (Kaas, Nelson, Sur, Lin, & Merzenich, 1979).

The representation of the body in the postcentral gyrus varies from one species to another. The representation of the paws is unusually large in raccoons; the representation of the snout is unusually large in rats. Bats, which use their feet to hang upside down and which use their forelimbs as wings instead of legs, have their body parts represented in a pattern completely different from the one shown in Figure 4-23 (Calford, Graydon, Huerta, Kaas, & Pettigrew, 1985).

Following damage to the parietal lobe, people do not completely lose the sense of touch, nor the muscle and joint senses, at least not permanently. Rather, they suffer a variety of symptoms suggesting difficulty in interpreting such information and in using it to control movement. Some of the common symptoms include (Lynch, 1980):

1. Impairment of ability to identify objects by touch.
2. Clumsiness on the side of the body opposite the damage.
3. Neglect of the opposite side of the body, especially neglect of the left side after right-hemisphere parietal lobe damage (Bisiach & Luzzatti, 1978; Levine, Warach, Benowitz, & Calvanio, 1986). People with such damage may fail to dress the left side of the body and may draw only the right side of an object, read only the right side of a page, and describe by memory only the right side of a familiar scene.
4. Inability to draw maps or to follow maps, to describe how to get somewhere, or to describe what something might look like from a different angle of view.

The parietal cortex is also important for relating visual information to spatial information. Certain parietal cells may be responsible for your knowing that something you have looked at is still the same object after you have tilted your head and looked at it from a different angle (Andersen, Essick, & Siegel, 1985). After parietal lobe damage, a person may find it necessary to focus directly on an object with the center of the retina in order to identify it (Lynch, 1980). To recognize a group of objects, such a person must look at the objects one at a time.

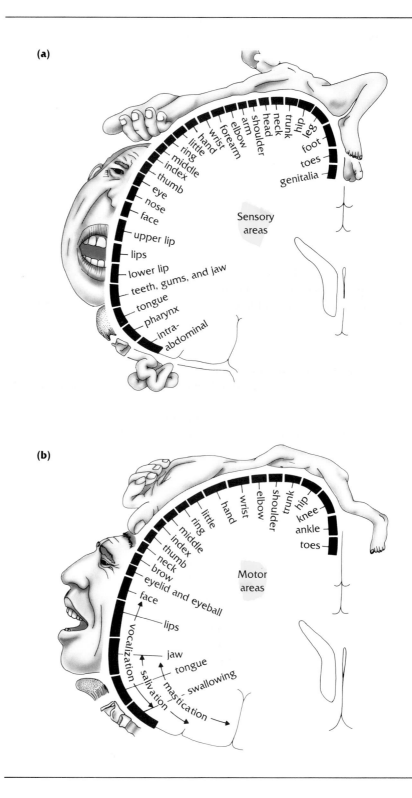

Figure 4-23. Organization of (**a**) sensory areas of the postcentral gyrus and (**b**) motor areas of the precentral gyrus. Each location along either gyrus is primarily involved in sensations or motor control for one area in the opposite half of the body. (After Penfield & Rasmussen, 1950.)

Temporal Lobe

The **temporal lobe** is located laterally in each hemisphere, near the temples. It is the primary cortical target for information originating in the ears and the vestibular organs (which deal with balance and equilibrium). The temporal lobe also contributes to some of the more complex aspects of vision, including perception of complex patterns such as faces. A tumor in the temporal lobe may give rise to elaborate visual hallucinations, whereas a tumor in the occipital lobe ordinarily evokes only the simplest sensations, such as flashes of light. In humans, the left temporal lobe and part of the parietal lobe also contain *Wernicke's area* (see Chapter 5), which is critical for the comprehension of language.

The temporal lobes also play a part in emotional and motivational behaviors. Damage to the temporal lobes can lead to unprovoked laughter, joy, anxiety, or violent behaviors.

Frontal Lobe

The **frontal lobe** extends from the central sulcus to the anterior limit of the brain. The posterior portion of the frontal lobe is the **precentral gyrus**, which is specialized for the control of fine movements, such as moving one finger at a time. It has separate areas responsible for different parts of the body (Figure 4-23b), mostly on the contralateral side of the body but with slight control of the ipsilateral side too. The human left frontal lobe includes *Broca's area*, which is critical for language production (Chapter 5).

The anterior portion of the frontal lobe, known as the **prefrontal cortex,** is a fairly large structure, especially in species with a large brain overall, such as humans. The prefrontal cortex is the only area of cortex known to receive input from all sensory modalities, including olfaction (Stuss & Benson, 1984). We have learned about the functions of this area both from animal studies and from humans with damage in this area. (See Digression 4-3.) Evidently it is critical for memory, emotional expression, and certain personality characteristics such as social inhibitions.

METHODS OF INVESTIGATING HOW THE BRAIN CONTROLS BEHAVIOR

In the nineteenth century, Franz Joseph Gall observed (or so he thought) that people with an excellent verbal memory had bulging, protruding eyes. He drew the inference that verbal memory depended on a part of the brain immediately behind the eyes and that overdevelopment of this part of the brain pushed the eyes forward. If this were so, Gall reasoned, bulges and depressions elsewhere on the skull might also reflect overdevelopment or underdevelopment of underlying brain areas. Thus, by comparing skull features among people and relating them to those people's behavior, it should be possible to identify the activities conducted by each part of the brain. Furthermore, after identifying the functions of all brain areas in this manner, it should be possible to determine the personality of an unknown person by feeling bumps and depressions on his or her head. These were the basic premises of the "science" of **phrenology**. Figure 4-24 shows a typical phrenologist's map of the human skull.

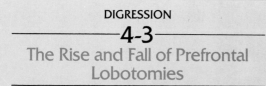

DIGRESSION

4-3

The Rise and Fall of Prefrontal Lobotomies

In the late 1940s and early 1950s, a type of surgery known as **prefrontal lobotomy** was performed on about 40,000 people in the United States (Shutts, 1982). The impetus to performing this operation was a report that damage to the prefrontal cortex of primates in the laboratory had made them tamer without impairing their sensory or motor capacities in any striking way. It was reasoned that the same operation might help people suffering from severe and otherwise untreatable psychiatric disorders.

The largest number of lobotomies in the United States were performed by Walter Freeman, a medical doctor who had never been trained in surgery. His techniques were amazingly crude, even by the standards of his times. After experimenting with several methods, he settled on inserting an ice pick between the eye and the bone case above the eye and then poking the icepick to cut certain parts of the prefrontal areas. Sometimes he used electroconvulsive shock as his only means of anesthetizing the person prior to surgery. Many of the operations were done in Freeman's office or in other sites outside the hospital. (Freeman carried his equipment, such as it was, around with him in his car, which he called his "lobotomobile.")

Freeman and others became increasingly casual about deciding who should get a lobotomy. At first, the technique was used only in cases of severe, untreatable schizophrenia. Lobotomy did manage to calm at least some schizophrenics, although the effects were often disappointing, even

to Freeman and others who performed the operations. (We now know that the frontal lobes of many severe schizophrenics are partly shrunken and less active than normal; lobotomy was therefore damaging a structure that had already been impaired.) As time went on, Freeman tried lobotomy for people with an assortment of other major and minor disorders. Some would, in fact, be considered normal by contemporary standards.

After antischizophrenic and antidepressive drugs became available in the mid-1950s, the use of lobotomy declined sharply. Freeman, who had been praised by some of his colleagues and barely tolerated by others, lost his privilege to practice at most hospitals and faded into the same obscurity as lobotomy itself. Lobotomy has been an exceedingly rare operation since the mid-1950s, although it has not become altogether extinct (Lesse, 1984; Tippin & Henn, 1982).

Because Freeman and others generally conducted only superficial follow-up studies on their lobotomy patients, our understanding of the prefrontal areas remains limited. The common effects of prefrontal damage include apathy, a loss of planning and initiative, memory disorders (Chapter 13), distractibility, generally blunted emotions, and a loss of facial expressions (Stuss & Benson, 1984). People with such damage lose their social inhibitions; they behave in a tactless, callous manner and ignore the rules of polite, civilized conduct. If the damage is extensive, people suffer an inability to suppress one behavior and substitute another (Damasio, 1979). For example, after they have learned to sort a set of cards by color, it is difficult for them to shift to sorting them by the numbers or patterns on the cards.

The phrenologists' conclusions were wrong in all details, and their methods were a classic example of pseudoscience. Identification of many areas on their map of the brain was based on observations of just one or two people. Moreover, they ignored the discrepancies when someone's behavior did not fit the theory.

Nevertheless, certain of the phrenologists' assumptions are similar to the assumptions researchers make today: Different parts of the brain control different aspects of behavior. If brain area A controls behavior X, then individuals with a deficiency of behavior X should have some deficiency in area A. Individuals with a greater than normal amount of behavior X should have an excess of activity in area A; area A may even be larger than normal in such individuals (Scheibel, 1984).

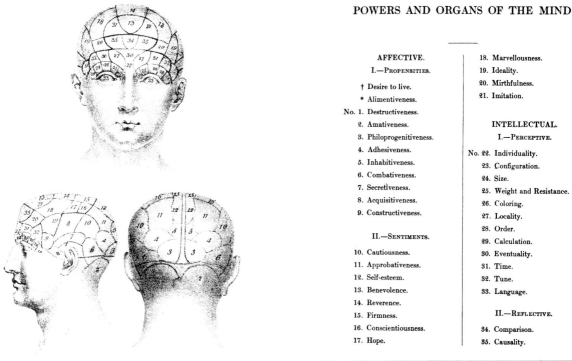

POWERS AND ORGANS OF THE MIND

AFFECTIVE.

I.—PROPENSITIES.

† Desire to live.
* Alimentiveness.
No. 1. Destructiveness.
2. Amativeness.
3. Philoprogenitiveness.
4. Adhesiveness.
5. Inhabitiveness.
6. Combativeness.
7. Secretiveness.
8. Acquisitiveness.
9. Constructiveness.

II.—SENTIMENTS.

10. Cautiousness.
11. Approbativeness.
12. Self-esteem.
13. Benevolence.
14. Reverence.
15. Firmness.
16. Conscientiousness.
17. Hope.

18. Marvellousness.
19. Ideality.
20. Mirthfulness.
21. Imitation.

INTELLECTUAL.

I.—PERCEPTIVE.

No. 22. Individuality.
23. Configuration.
24. Size.
25. Weight and Resistance.
26. Coloring.
27. Locality.
28. Order.
29. Calculation.
30. Eventuality.
31. Time.
32. Tune.
33. Language.

II.—REFLECTIVE.

34. Comparison.
35. Causality.

Figure 4-24. A phrenologist's map of brain areas. (From Spurzheim, 1908.)

Current research differs from phrenology in several major respects, however. The behaviors we try to localize in the brain are such biological functions as vision, control of finger movements, and temperature regulation, rather than such personality traits as self-esteem, reverence, and "marvellousness." We consider not only localized brain areas but also diffuse systems of neurons that may not be confined to one region. And we examine the electrical and chemical activity of brain areas and systems, not just their size. Still, a major goal of current research is to determine what one area of the brain does that differentiates it from other areas. A number of techniques have been developed in pursuit of this goal; a few of the most common are described here.

Lesions and Ablations

A **lesion** is a destruction or functional disruption of the brain. An **ablation** is a removal of part of the brain. Lesions and ablations can be produced intentionally by experimenters with laboratory animals, or they can occur naturally, as when a person has a stroke or a head wound. When a lesion or ablation leads to a deficit in some behavior, it is assumed that the damaged area had an important role in the control of that behavior. The lesion technique has been widely used throughout the history of biological psychology.

The results of lesion experiments can be hard to interpret. As an analogy, suppose no one understood how a television works. To find out, an investigator explodes a small firecracker inside the set, damaging nearby structures, and then examines the effects on the set and tries to characterize any loss to the picture and sound. Later, someone performs an autopsy on the set to determine exactly what physical damage was associated with the impaired functioning.

You can see the problems. With luck, an investigator might find that a firecracker in one area destroys the sound and a firecracker in another area destroys the picture. But that would not tell us *how* either area controlled the picture or sound. Moreover, the loss of sound or picture might not be due to the destruction of a structure in the area but to the interruption of wires that happened to be passing through.

Investigating a brain by making lesions entails similar difficulties, although they are not insuperable. One of the greatest difficulties is to describe the behavioral deficit after a lesion. For example, it would not be satisfactory to say that a lesion interfered with maze learning. We would want to know *how* it interfered. In one study, four monkeys learned a maze that could be solved either by attending to visual cues or by memorizing a pattern of left and right turns (Traverse & Latto, 1986). In fact, different monkeys solved the maze in different ways. When they were then given lesions in the posterior parietal cortex, an area sensitive to body location, the monkeys that had attended to left and right suffered an impairment of their maze performance, while those that had attended to visual cues were unimpaired. An experimenter who had not previously analyzed *how* the monkeys had learned the maze might easily have been confused by the fact that the same lesion impaired performance in some monkeys and not others on the same maze.

After researchers think they know what deficit is associated with a given lesion, a good way to verify their interpretation is to look for a **double dissociation of function**. A double dissociation is a demonstration that lesion 1 impairs behavior A more than behavior B, while lesion 2 impairs behavior B more than behavior A. Such results help researchers ascertain that the behavioral deficits are not simply the product of overall inactivity, blindness, or some other general disorder that should affect both behaviors.

Lesions can be produced in experimental animals in several ways. To remove a large area on the external surface of the brain, an experimenter can cut back a flap of skull and then remove the desired brain tissue with a knife or with vacuum suction. But to damage small structures buried deep in the brain, experimenters need a different method. Most commonly, they use a **stereotaxic instrument**. An animal such as a rat is anesthetized and then placed in position in the stereotaxic instrument, as shown in Figure 4-25. Ear bars and a clamp around the nose and mouth hold the head in place. The position of any part of the brain can be predicted with a fair degree of accuracy from the position of certain landmarks on the head. From the position of the ear bars or from the position of **bregma** (the point of junction of four skull bones, as shown in Figure 4-26), a researcher can calculate the position of any point in the animal's brain.

To calculate the position, the researcher refers to a **stereotaxic atlas** (or map) of the animal's brain. Atlases of this type have been published for the brains of many species. Figure 4-27, from Pellegrino and Cushman's (1967) atlas, illustrates one slice through the brain of an adult rat. The scale at the bottom indicates distances in millimeters left or right from the center of the

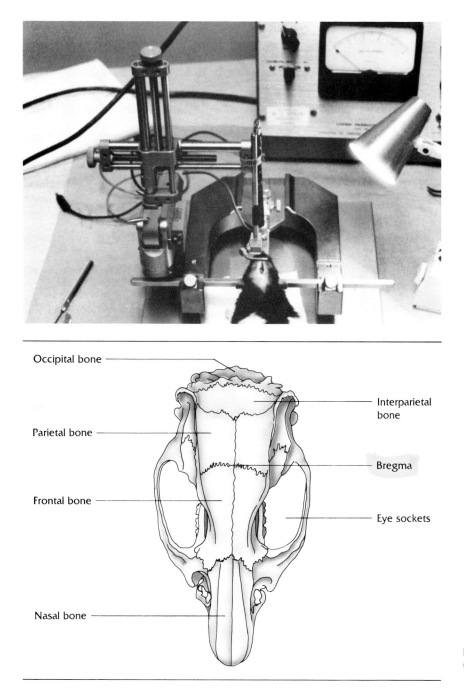

Figure 4-25. A stereotaxic instrument for locating and lesioning brain areas in small animals.

Figure 4-26. Skull bones (rat) and position of bregma.

skull. The scales at the left and right indicate distances dorsal and ventral from the top surface of the brain and from the ear bars, respectively. The notations in the upper corners indicate that this slice is 6.0 mm anterior to the ear bars and 0.2 mm anterior to bregma. Other pages of the atlas present slices at 0.2 mm intervals.

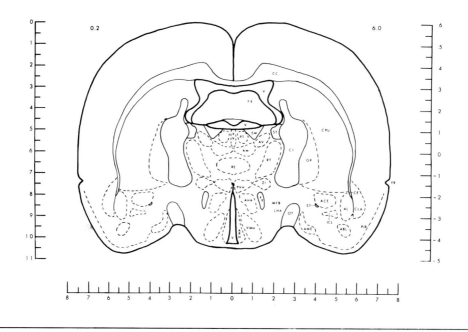

Figure 4-27. A typical page from a stereotaxic atlas of the rat brain showing a coronal section 6.0 mm anterior to the ear bars. The surrounding unlabeled area is the cerebral cortex. Abbreviations refer to various areas of the brain; for example, CC = corpus callosum. (From Pellegrino & Cushman, 1967.)

An experimenter who wants to make a lesion in the ventromedial hypothalamus (VMH in Figure 4-27) places the anesthetized animal in the stereotaxic instrument, cuts back the skin over the skull, dries the skull, and marks points directly above the ventromedial hypothalamus, one on each side of the brain, using measurements from the brain atlas. The experimenter then drills small holes at those points, inserts a thin metal electrode insulated except at the tip, and lowers the electrode to the level of the target. Then the experimenter applies a DC electrical current (typically 0.1 to 0.2 mA for 10 to 20 seconds) or a radio-frequency current to destroy a small amount of brain tissue near the tip of the electrode. Finally, the experimenter removes the electrode and sews up the cut skin over the skull.

The electrode inevitably kills a few cells on the way to and from the target. To find out the effects of such accidental damage and to separate them from the effects of the lesion itself, an experimenter produces a **sham lesion** in a control group. That is, the experimenter goes through all the same procedures but does not apply the electrical current. Any behavioral difference between the lesioned group and the sham-lesion group must be due to the lesion itself and not due to damage caused by passing the electrode up and down through the brain.

Eventually the experimenter must examine the animal's brain to determine whether the lesion was actually located in the intended location or somewhere else. Without some special treatment, a brain looks fairly uniform; it is difficult to identify even the major nuclei and tracts. Therefore, an investigator applies a histological stain to the brain that colors the cell bodies or axons. (Histology is the branch of biology that deals with the structure of

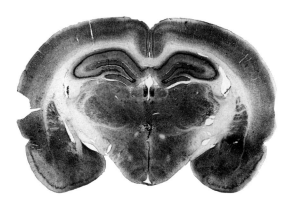

Figure 4-28. A slice of rat forebrain, stained with a Nissl stain, which turn cell bodies blue and leaves axons clear or faintly colored.

tissues.) A photograph of a stained segment of tissue in a rat's brain is shown in Figure 4-28.

Electrical Stimulation of and Recording from the Brain

After an electrode is positioned in the brain, it is possible to use it for purposes other than making a lesion. An experimenter can cement the electrode in place on the skull and then wait for the animal to recover from the surgery, as in Chapter 1. Later, the experimenter can apply brief stimulation through the electrode to excite neurons without damaging them. It is also possible to use the electrode to record the spontaneous activity of the cells it touches.

Researchers always feel more confidence in a conclusion if they can support it through different types of experiments. For example, lesion experiments have shown that damage to the lateral hypothalamus causes an animal to stop eating, while experiments with implanted electrodes have demonstrated that stimulating the same area increases eating. Recording of neurons in this area have revealed that spontaneous activity is high around the time of a meal. All these lines of evidence indicate that the lateral hypothalamus has something to do with eating.

Temporary Lesions

Sometimes it is desirable to examine the effects of inactivating part of the brain without destroying it. One way is to inject a drug such as sodium amytal into either of the two carotid arteries of the head. Because each carotid artery supplies blood to one hemisphere of the brain, the injection inactivates one hemisphere for about 5 to 10 minutes. This technique has occasionally been used with humans to determine which hemisphere controls language for a given individual (Wada & Rasmussen, 1960).

Another method, used only with nonhumans, is to apply a concentrated solution of potassium chloride to the surface of the cerebral cortex. The potassium chloride inactivates the region to which it is applied, and the inactivity spreads to the rest of that hemisphere for about 10 to 20 minutes. This method is called **cortical spreading depression**.

Lesions Induced by Neurotoxins

A **neurotoxin** is a chemical that can produce a selective kind of brain damage that researchers are unable to produce with stereotaxic lesions or with a surgeon's knife. An injection of a large dose of monosodium glutamate (Simson, Gold, Standish, & Pellett, 1977) or kainic acid (Mason & Fibiger, 1979) into some spot in the brain destroys cell bodies in that area but causes little damage to axons passing through. These chemicals can help an investigator separate the contributions of the cells in an area from the contributions of axons from other cells. Kainic acid and similar drugs kill neurons by overstimulating them. They cause such a prolonged depolarization of the cell that sodium ions enter rapidly in massive numbers, in turn attracting chloride ions and water. Ultimately the cell membrane bursts (Rothman, 1985).

The chemical 6-hydroxydopamine selectively destroys synapses that use norepinephrine or dopamine as their synaptic transmitter. The chemical known as AF64A does the same thing for synapses that use acetylcholine (Sandberg, Sanberg, & Coyle, 1984). Such chemicals enable investigators to study the effects of systems that are not restricted to one area of the brain.

Genetic Lesions and Arrested Development

Sometimes an investigator wishes to study the effects of a particular type of cell that is distributed widely and interspersed with other types of cells. To study such effects, a researcher might make use of a genetic mutation. It has been found, for example, that one mutation prevents granule cells from developing in the cerebellum of mice. Such mice have great difficulty maintaining their balance. Their legs tremble constantly, and they can hardly take a step without falling over. Such evidence is at least a start toward understanding the role of the granule cells (Sidman, Green, & Appel, 1965).

Another way to remove a particular type of cell is to interfere with brain maturation at a particular stage. Different cell types mature at different times. If experimenters expose the brain to x-rays or to the neurotoxin MAM (methylazoxymethanol acetate), they can destroy the cells that are dividing and developing at that time, while sparing mature cells (Anderson & Altman, 1972; Sanberg, Pevsner, Autuono, & Coyle, 1985). The researchers can then repeat the experiment at a different age to examine the contributions of a different population of cells.

Correlation of Developing Brain with Developing Behavior

Suppose a certain structure or system in the brain and a certain behavior both reach maturity fairly suddenly at the same time. With caution we can use this as evidence that the structure is responsible for the behavior.

For example, the retina of a frog contains four anatomical types of cells known as constricted tree, E-tree, H-tree, and broad tree, according to their shape. Physiological recordings from cells in the retina reveal that different cells respond best to four different stimuli, edges, convex edges, moving

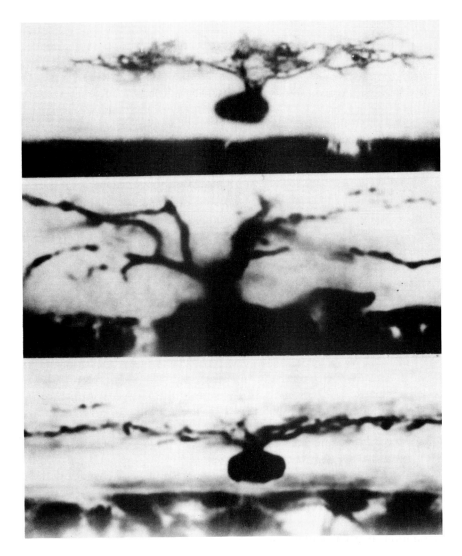

Figure 4-29. Three cell types in the tadpole retina. *From top to bottom*: E-tree, H-tree, and broad tree. (From Pomeranz & Chung, 1970.)

contrast, and dimness. It seems likely that each of the four anatomical types of cells responds best to a different stimulus. But which is which? The question is not easy to answer, because the physiological responses of cells can be recorded only when they are alive and their anatomy can be determined only by staining them after they are dead.

Pomeranz and Chung (1970) were able to relate two of the anatomical types to the types of visual responses by studying the retinas of tadpoles (baby frogs). They noted that tadpoles lack the constricted tree cells and have no cells that respond best to edges. (See Figure 4-29.) They therefore concluded that constricted tree cells respond to edges. Moreover, E-tree cells could be found only in the center of the tadpole's retina, and cells responsive to convex edges could be recorded only in the center of the retina. Thus, E-trees are apparently responsive to convex edges. The researchers were unable to pair up the other two types of cells, however.

The Electroencephalograph

The methods we have discussed so far are difficult to apply to humans. A device called the **electroencephalograph** (**EEG**) enables investigators to make gross determinations of brain activity in humans and other animals without actually cutting into the skull. A few electrodes, generally eight or fewer, are attached with glue or other adhesive to various locations on the surface of the scalp. The output of those electrodes is then amplified and recorded. From an examination of EEG records, an investigator can determine whether the person is asleep, dreaming, awake, or excited. Abnormalities in the EEG record may also suggest the presence of epilepsy, a tumor, or other medical problems located in a brain region under a particular electrode.

With the **evoked potential** method, experimenters use the EEG apparatus to record the brain's activity in response to sensory stimuli. Any sensory stimulus evokes electrical activity with a very short latency (delay) over a limited area of the cerebral cortex. If the individual reacts to the stimulus as meaningful and attention getting, a second electrical response appears with a latency of about 0.3 second.

Labeling Active Brain Areas with Radioactive Chemicals

At any moment, certain areas of the brain are more active than others. For example, the visual cortex becomes more active during visual stimulation and the olfactory bulb becomes more active during olfactory stimulation. When an area of the brain becomes more active, it increases its blood supply, its use of glucose, and its synthesis of proteins. Researchers can capitalize on this fact by administering small amounts of certain radioactive chemicals and then monitoring these chemicals to measure the relative activity of various areas of the brain.

One substance used is radioactive xenon (^{133}Xe). After a person inhales xenon, it dissolves in the blood. Because it does not react chemically with anything in the body, the xenon goes wherever the blood goes. Thus, the radioactivity recorded from a particular part of the brain will be proportional to the amount of blood flow to it. This type of study is referred to as **regional cerebral blood flow**, abbreviated **rCBF**.

The chemical 2-deoxy-D-glucose (abbreviated 2-DG), which is chemically similar to glucose, does not occur naturally in the body, but if it is injected into the bloodstream, it is taken up by neurons when they take up glucose. Because 2-DG is metabolized much more slowly than glucose, it remains in the neuron for hours. An experimenter who injects a radioactive form of 2-DG and measures radioactivity 1 to 4 hours later can find scattered brain areas with large amounts of radioactive 2-DG. Those are the areas that took up large amounts of glucose during the previous several hours, and therefore the areas that were most active during that period. By the same logic, researchers can inject radioactive amino acids and later look for the brain areas that incorporated them into radioactive proteins. Investigators can also inject radioactively labeled drugs to find the receptors to which they attach.

When experiments of this type are conducted on humans, the brain is monitored using a rather large and expensive device known as a **PET** (positron-emission tomography) **scanner**. (See Color Plate 8.) First, radioactively labeled xenon, 2-DG, or whatever is administered to the person. Because the radioactive chemical releases gamma rays, the abundance of gamma rays originating from a given brain area is an indicator of the concentration of that chemical. An array of gamma-ray detectors around the circumference of the head feeds information to a computer that reconstructs the locations from which the gamma rays originated.

PET scans enable researchers to answer some questions that could not previously be addressed with human beings. For example, Chugani and Phelps (1986) performed PET scans on infant brains. They found that the thalamus and brainstem showed fairly high rates of activity by age 5 weeks. Most of the cerebral cortex and the outer part of the cerebellum were immature at 5 weeks but much more advanced by 3 months. The frontal lobes of the cerebral cortex showed little sign of activity until the age of 7½ months.

The brain is a complex structure. You have encountered a great deal of terminology and a good many facts in this chapter. Do not become discouraged if you cannot remember everything. It will help to refer back to this chapter to review the anatomy of certain structures as you encounter their functions again in later chapters. Gradually, the material will become more familiar.

SUMMARY

1. The main divisions of the vertebrate nervous system are the central nervous system and the peripheral nervous system. The central nervous system consists of the spinal cord, the hindbrain, the midbrain, and the forebrain. (p. 72)

2. The size of the vertebrate brain is closely related to body size. Humans and other primates have a higher than usual brain-to-body ratio. The relationship of brain size to intelligence is uncertain. (p. 72)

3. According to Paul MacLean, the vertebrate brain can be conceived of as three parts that evolved at different times to serve different purposes: the reptilian brain, the old-mammalian brain, and the new-mammalian brain. (p. 75)

4. Initially, the brain forms more neurons than will survive to maturity. The ones that fail to make synapses onto the proper target cells die. (p. 78)

5. Each segment of the spinal cord has a sensory nerve on each side and a motor nerve on each side. Several spinal pathways convey information to the brain (p. 78)

6. The sympathetic nervous system (one of the two divisions of the autonomic nervous system) activates the body's internal organs for vigorous activities. The parasympathetic system promotes digestion and other nonemergency processes. (p. 84)

7. The hindbrain consists of the medulla, pons, and cerebellum. The medulla and pons control breathing, heart rate, and other vital functions through the cranial nerves. The cerebellum contributes to movement. (p. 87)

8. The subcortical areas of the forebrain include the hypothalamus, pituitary gland, basal ganglia, hippocampus, and thalamus. (p. 90)

9. Each area of the cerebral cortex receives input from a nucleus of the thalamus or from the olfactory bulb. Each cortical area has sensory, associational, and motor functions, although the degree of each varies. (p. 94)

10. The occipital lobe of the cortex is primarily responsible for vision. The parietal lobe deals with touch information and contains the postcentral gyrus. The temporal lobe is responsible for hearing, among other functions. The frontal lobe includes the precentral gyrus, which controls fine movements. Damage to the prefrontal area of the frontal lobe leads to a loss of

planning, a loss of facial expression, and difficulty in suppressing inappropriate behavior. (pp. 96–101)

11.   One of the most common methods of studying the functioning of the brain is by examining the effects of lesions (brain damage). A stereotaxic device can enable an investigator to implant electrodes deep in the brain to make lesions or to stimulate neurons or record from them. (p. 103)

12.   Several chemicals can be used to produce temporary or permanent impairment of part of the brain; certain chemicals have selective effects on cell bodies or on a particular kind of synapse. (p. 107)

13.   The electroencephalograph and the PET scan are methods of studying the brain without damaging it. (p. 110)

REVIEW QUESTIONS

1.   What accounts for the tendency of brain size to be roughly proportional to body size across a large number of species? (p. 73)

2.   What is MacLean's hypothesis concerning the evolution of the brain? (p. 75)

3.   How do the ventricles and the central canal of the spinal cord originate? (p. 76)

4.   What mechanism in development assures that the number of axons innervating a structure will match the number of synaptic sites available? (p. 78)

5.   What is the Bell-Magendie Law? (p. 81)

6.   Why do nerves from the adult spinal cord travel down within the bones of the spinal column before they exit to the periphery? (p. 81)

7.   What are the functions of the sympathetic and parasympathetic nervous systems? Where are their ganglia located? (pp. 84–86)

8.   Why do certain drugs excite either the sympathetic or the parasympathetic nervous system but not the other? (p. 87)

9.   Name the principal structures of the hindbrain and the midbrain. (pp. 87–90)

10.   What do the cranial nerves do? (p. 88)

11.   Cover the labels in Figures 4-16 through 4-19 and identify the structures shown. (pp. 91–95)

12.   What do the ventricles contain? (p. 94)

13.   In what way is the olfactory bulb similar to a nucleus of the thalamus? (p. 94)

14.   Why have investigators rejected the view of separate sensory, association, and motor areas of the cortex? What view has taken its place? (p. 94)

15.   List the four lobes of the cerebral cortex and describe the major function of each. (pp. 96–101)

16.   What are some of the difficulties in interpreting the results of a lesion experiment? (p. 103)

17.   Describe the method for inserting an electrode into an area of an animal's brain that cannot be seen from the surface. (p. 104)

18.   Describe methods that can be used to study the functioning of the intact human brain. (pp. 107–111)

THOUGHT QUESTIONS

1.   Suppose a surgeon wanted to relieve someone's severe and otherwise untreatable pain by cutting through the spinal tract that conveys pain. He or she would, of course, cut from the outside inward and would try to cut only the part that is carrying unbearable pain sensations. Is it possible to relieve pain from the upper body while sparing pain from the lower body, or vice versa, or neither or both? Why?

2.   One of the many kinds of cells to be found in the cerebral cortex is the stellate cell, which is an unusually small neuron. Stellate cells are more numerous in

adults than in children and more numerous in humans than in other species. How might one determine what special role, if any, stellate cells have in the control of behavior? Describe at least three possibilities. (For one attempt to answer this question, see Scheibel & Scheibel, 1963).

3.   Multiple sclerosis is a disease that destroys the myelin sheaths of axons. Why should we expect that evoked potentials would have longer than normal latencies in people with multiple sclerosis?

TERMS TO REMEMBER

neuroanatomy (p. 72)
vertebrates (p. 72)
central nervous system (CNS) (p. 76)
ventricles (p. 76)
cerebrospinal fluid (CSF) (p. 76)
peripheral nervous system (PNS) (p. 78)
spinal cord (p. 78)

Bell-Magendie Law (p. 81)
dorsal root ganglion (p. 81)
dermatome (p. 82)
gray matter (p. 84)
white matter (p. 84)
autonomic nervous system (p. 84)
sympathetic nervous system (p. 84)

parasympathetic nervous system (p. 84)
ganglia (p. 84)
hindbrain (p. 87)
brainstem (p. 87)
medulla (p. 87)
cranial nerves (p. 88)
pons (p. 88)
reticular formation (p. 88)
raphe system (p. 88)
cerebellum (p. 88)
midbrain (p. 89)
tectum (p. 89)
superior colliculus (p. 89)
inferior colliculus (p. 89)
tegmentum (p. 89)
substantia nigra (p. 90)
forebrain (p. 90)
hypothalamus (p. 90)
pituitary gland (p. 91)
endocrine gland (p. 91)
basal ganglia (p. 92)
hippocampus (p. 92)
fornix (p. 92)
fimbria (p. 92)
central canal (p. 93)
subarachnoid space (p. 94)
hydrocephalus (p. 94)
thalamus (p. 94)

olfactory bulb (p. 94)
cerebral cortex (p. 96)
corpus callosum (p. 96)
anterior commissure (p. 96)
laminae (p. 96)
occipital lobe (p. 96)
parietal lobe (p. 99)
central sulcus (p. 99)
postcentral gyrus (p. 99)
temporal lobe (p. 101)
frontal lobe (p. 101)
precentral gyrus (p. 101)
prefrontal cortex (p. 101)
phrenology (p. 101)
prefrontal lobotomy (p. 102)
lesion (p. 103)
ablation (p. 103)
double dissociation of function (p. 104)
stereotaxic instrument (p. 104)
bregma (p. 104)
stereotaxic atlas (p. 104)
sham lesion (p. 106)
cortical spreading depression (p. 108)
neurotoxin (p. 108)
electroencephalograph (EEG) (p. 110)
evoked potential (p. 110)
regional cerebral blood flow (rCBF) (p. 110)
PET scanner (p. 111)

SUGGESTIONS FOR FURTHER READING

Blakemore, C. (1977). *Mechanics of the mind.* New York: Cambridge. An interesting, highly readable introduction to brain functioning.

Goldberg, S. (1979). *Clinical neuroanatomy made ridiculously simple.* Miami, FL: Medmaster. A short paperback that reviews those features of the human CNS that are most frequently important in medicine.

Morihisa, J. M. (1984). *Brain imaging in psychiatry.* Washington, D.C.: American Psychiatric Press. Provides information on PET scans and similar methods.

Any college library will include textbooks devoted to the anatomy of the brain. Check the subject catalog under *neuroanatomy, nervous system,* and *brain.*

CHAPTER 5

Lateralization, Language, and Brain Disconnection Syndromes

MAIN IDEAS

1. The left and right hemispheres communicate by means of the corpus callosum. After damage to the corpus callosum, each hemisphere has access to information only from the opposite half of the body and the opposite visual field.

2. The left hemisphere is specialized for language in most people. The right hemisphere is specialized for certain complex visual-spatial tasks.

3. Handedness is only partly determined by the genes. It is apparently influenced by hormones and other factors that control the development of other parts of the body as well.

4. Two areas in the left hemisphere are important for language. After damage to Broca's area, a person has difficulty speaking and has trouble either using or understanding prepositions and other grammatical connectives. After damage to Wernicke's area, a person has trouble understanding language and recalling the names of objects, although he or she can still pronounce words fluently and string them together grammatically.

The human brain consists of neurons numbering in at least the tens of billions. Those neurons are assembled in discrete brain areas, each of which has its own specialized function. Yet each of us has an experience of unity. Although your brain parts are many, your consciousness is one.

That unity of consciousness comes about through the connections between various brain parts. What would happen if certain connections were broken? In that case, although different parts of the brain would continue to carry on their activities, they would be unable to communicate with one another. One part of the brain would not know what another part of the brain was doing.

Such disconnections do occur in humans. Before we can discuss them, however, we must consider some background material concerning the differences between the two hemispheres of the brain and the connections of the eyes to the brain.

THE LEFT AND RIGHT HEMISPHERES OF THE BRAIN

The left hemisphere of the cerebral cortex is connected to sensory receptors mainly in the right half of the body, and it has the main control of muscles on the right side of the body. The right hemisphere is connected to sensory receptors mainly on the left half of the body and controls muscles on the left side. (Why we evolved this way, no one knows.) Each hemisphere has only limited sensory input and motor control on its own side of the body. The degree of ipsilateral control (control of the same side of the body) varies from one individual to another.

Each hemisphere is also connected to the eyes in such a way that it gets input from the opposite half of the visual world—that is, in such a way that the left hemisphere sees the right side of the world and the right hemisphere sees the left side of the world. For rabbits and other species that have the left eye facing to the left side of the world and the right eye facing the right side of the world, the connections from eye to brain are easy to describe: The left eye connects to the right hemisphere and the right eye connects to the left hemisphere. In humans, however, both eyes face forward. You can see the left side of the world almost as well with your right eye as with your left eye. Therefore, in order for the right hemisphere to see the left side of the world, it has to be connected to parts of both eyes, not simply to the left eye.

Figure 5-1 illustrates the connections from the eyes to the human brain. Vision starts with stimulation of the receptors that line the **retina** on the back of each eye. Light from the right half of the world (the right **visual field**) shines onto the left half of the retinas of both eyes, while light from the left visual field shines onto the right half of both retinas. The left half of each retina connects to the left hemisphere; thus, the left hemsphere sees the right visual field. Similarly, the right half of each retina connects to the right hemisphere, which sees the left visual field. A small vertical strip down the center of each retina, covering about 5 degrees of visual arc, connects to both hemispheres (Innocenti, 1980).

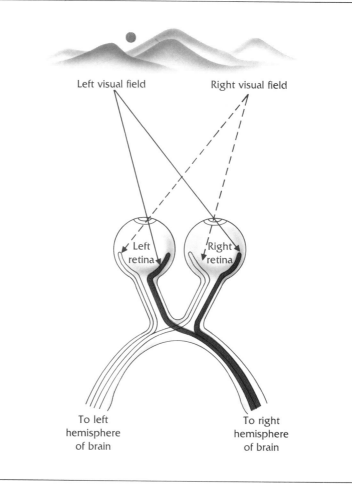

Figure 5-1. Route of visual input to the two hemispheres of the brain. Note that the left hemisphere is connected to the left half of each retina and thus gets visual input from the right half of the world, while the opposite occurs with the right hemisphere.

Information about each visual field projects to just one side of the cerebral cortex. The auditory system handles information differently. Although each ear receives sound waves from just one side of the head, it sends input to both sides of the brain, though somewhat more strongly to the opposite side. (The reason for this is that people localize sounds in space by comparing the input from the two ears. Any part of the brain that contributes to localizing sounds must receive input from both ears.)

Effects of Cutting the Corpus Callosum

Ordinarily, the left and right hemispheres exchange information through the **corpus callosum** (refer back to Figures 4-17 and 4-18) and several smaller bundles of fibers. Each hemisphere has access to the information that passed initially to the opposite hemisphere.

That exchange of information is blocked if the corpus callosum is damaged. A small number of people have had their corpus callosum cut as a therapy for severe epilepsy. Epilepsy is usually treated with drugs. Some rare

BIOSKETCH
5-1

Roger W. Sperry

In 1981 Roger W. Sperry, a pioneer in the study of the split-brain phenomenon, shared the Nobel Prize for physiology and medicine with David Hubel and Torsten Wiesel, whose work is discussed in Chapter 7. Sperry received a bachelor's degree in humanities and a master's degree in psychology from Oberlin College and a Ph.D. in zoology from the University of Chicago. Since 1954 he has been a professor of psychobiology at the California Institute of Technology.

Sperry gained wide acclaim for two separate lines of research. In his early research on the growth and repair of nerve circuits, he found that nerves from the sense organs attach in a very precise way to the brain. If he cut the sensory nerves from the skin or from the eye, each fiber grew back to the same brain area as before, even if the skin or eye had been flipped upside down in the meantime (Attardi & Sperry, 1963; Sperry, 1952, 1959). This contradicted the earlier belief that nerve connections to the brain were mostly haphazard, with the brain eventually learning to organize all the nerves.

Later Sperry and his students pioneered the study of the split-brain phenomenon, first for 10 years in cats and monkeys, and then in humans.

Science is not just a matter of finding the right answers; it also requires asking the right questions. One of Sperry's former students, Jerre Levy (see Bio-Sketch 5-2), recalls that Sperry constantly goaded his students with such challenging questions as "What is it that the right hemisphere actually does best?" and "Why do you suppose people have asymmetric brains?" His central question for his students was always "What are you trying to discover and why and what difference will it make?"

Sperry has tried to channel his own research within the broader context of the mind-brain relationship. Rejecting the view that science and ethics are totally separate realms, Sperry (1975) has noted: "When subjective values have objective consequences . . . they become part of the content of science. . . . Science would become the final determinant of what is right and true, the best source and authority available to the human brain for finding ultimate axioms and guideline beliefs to live by, and for reaching an intimate understanding and rapport with the forces that control the universe and created man."

individuals, however, fail to respond to any of the antiepileptic drugs. If their seizures are sufficiently severe and frequent to be incapacitating, they and their attending physicians may be willing to try almost anything to relieve the epilepsy. In certain cases, surgeons have cut the corpus callosum. The idea is to prevent epileptic seizures from crossing from one hemisphere to the other, so that when epileptic seizures do occur, they should be less severe because they will affect only half the body.

In cases where this operation has been performed, it has relieved the epilepsy better than expected. Not only are the epileptic seizures limited to one side of the body, but they also occur less often than before the operation. Moreover, the people suffer little or no impairment of overall intellectual performance, motivation, emotion, or language. They can walk, swim, and carry on other motor activities that make use of both sides of the body.

When this so-called "split-brain surgery" was first performed, the behavioral effects were so subtle that it took sophisticated experimental designs by Roger Sperry (BioSketch 5-1) and his students (Nebes, 1974) to reveal them. In one typical experiment, a split-brain patient stared straight ahead as pictures were flashed on the left side of a screen. (See Figure 5-2.) When the corpus callosum is destroyed, any information that enters one hemi-

Figure 5-2. A split-brain patient stares at a central point as a display is flashed briefly on one side or the other. Thus, input is restricted to one cerebral hemisphere at a time.

sphere cannot pass to the other. Thus, the information went only to the right hemisphere. The picture stayed on the screen long enough for the person to see it clearly in the left visual field but not long enough for the person to move his or her eyes in order to bring the picture into the other visual field. The experimenter then told the person (both hemispheres could hear the instructions) to put one hand behind a cloth curtain, to feel the ten or more objects behind the curtain, and to hold up the object that had just been shown on the screen. Split-brain patients consistently performed correctly if permitted to use their left hand (controlled by the right hemisphere, which saw the display on the screen). But if they were told to use their right hand, accuracy fell to the chance level. If the experimenter flashed the display on the right side of the screen, however, the right hand performed correctly and the left hand failed.

For most people, the ability to speak depends on the left hemisphere of the cerebral cortex. In split-brain people, when a display was flashed in the right visual field, thus going to the left hemisphere, the person could name the object easily. But when it was flashed in the left visual field, thus going to the right hemisphere, the person could not name it or describe it, although he or she was quite capable of pointing to it with the left hand. It was even possible for the person to say, "I don't know what it is," while simultaneously pointing to the correct choice with the left hand. (Of course, a split-brain person who *watched* the left hand pick up an object in the center or right visual field could then name the object.)

Functions of the Right Hemisphere of the Cerebral Cortex

When it was discovered that the left hemisphere controls speech, most observers thought of the right hemisphere as something like a vice-president.

That is, it supported the "major" hemisphere in various ways but was definitely subordinate to it. Later studies, including some with split-brain patients, indicated that the right hemisphere is capable of more than researchers had assumed.

First, although it usually cannot control speech (or writing), the right hemisphere does understand simple speech. A split-brain person who hears a verbal description of an object can feel some objects with the left hand (right hemisphere) and pick up the described object. Such a person can do the same after seeing the name of the object in only the left visual field. In a few split-brain patients, the left hand can write or can arrange letter blocks to describe information known only by the right hemisphere (Gazzaniga, LeDoux, & Wilson, 1977; Levy, Nebes, & Sperry, 1971). They can do so even though their left hemisphere is in complete control of spoken language.

Furthermore, the right hemisphere can perform certain functions better than the left hemisphere. One such function is the control of emotional expressions. After damage to the right hemisphere, people have trouble both in producing facial expressions of emotion and in understanding other people's facial expressions (Borod, Koff, Perlman-Lorch, & Nicholas, 1986; Kolb & Taylor, 1981; Rinn, 1984). Even in normal people, the left side of the face (controlled by the right hemisphere) generally smiles more broadly and in other ways expresses more emotion than the right side of the face (Sackeim, Gur, & Saucy, 1978).

The right hemisphere apparently contributes to emotional content even in speech. People who have suffered damage to the right hemisphere speak with less than the normal amount of inflection and expression (Shapiro & Danly, 1985). They also have trouble interpreting the emotions that other people express through their tone of voice (Tucker, 1981).

Another function the right hemisphere performs better than the left is complex visual recognition. It has been known for some time that many people who suffer damage to the right hemisphere have difficulty finding their way between one place and another and have trouble recognizing faces. Split-brain patients have given us additional information about these specialized functions of the right hemisphere.

For example, a split-brain person can work puzzles better with the left hand than with the right. Although the right hand can write words much better than the left, the left hand does better at drawing a box, a bicycle, and similar objects. (Bear in mind, this applies to split-brain people, not to normals.)

In one experiment, split-brain subjects were asked to feel a three-dimensional object without looking at it (Levy-Agresti & Sperry, 1968). Then they were shown two-dimensional representations of objects and were told to point to the two-dimensional pattern corresponding to the felt object. The subjects were much more accurate when using the left hand for this task than when using the right. Thus, the right hemisphere appears to be specialized for complex visual and spatial tasks.

The right hemisphere is not necessary for *all* visual and spatial tasks, however. In one study, stroke patients who had suffered damage to the right hemisphere performed about as well as normals at estimating the positions of nine major cities on an outline map of the United States. They were also as good as normals at estimating the distances between points on a sheet of paper. They were greatly impaired, however, when they had to combine both of these tasks in their head, by imagining the positions of those same nine cities and estimating the distances between them (Morrow, Ratcliff, & Johnston, 1986). Evidently, the right hemisphere is more essential for those tasks that require internal representations of visual and spatial information—imagination, we might say.

Do Split-Brain People Have Two Minds or One?

The two hemispheres of a split-brain person can process information and answer questions independently of each other. In fact, they seem at times to act as if they are separate people sharing one body. One person sometimes found himself buttoning his shirt with one hand while unbuttoning it with the other hand. Another person would pick up a newspaper with the right hand, only to have the left hand (controlled by the less verbal hemisphere) put it down. Repeatedly the right hand picked it up; an equal number of times the left hand put it down, until finally the left hand threw it to the floor (Preilowski, 1975).

One split-brain person described his experience—or, rather, his left hemisphere described his experience—as follows (Dimond, 1979): "If I'm reading I can hold the book in my right hand, it's a lot easier to sit on my left hand, than to hold it with both hands. . . . You tell your hand—I'm going to turn so many pages in a book—turn three pages—then somehow the left hand will pick up two pages and you're at page 5, or whatever. It's better to let it go, pick it up with the right hand, and then turn to the right page. With your right hand you correct what the left has done."

Such conflicts are reported to be more common in the first months after the surgery than later on. Gradually the hemispheres find ways to cooperate with each other, sometimes in surprising ways. One person who was being tested with the standard apparatus shown in Figure 5-2 suddenly seemed able to name what he saw in either visual field. However, the right hemisphere could answer correctly only when the answers were restricted to two possibilities (such as yes/no or true/false) and only when the subject was allowed to correct himself immediately after making a guess. Suppose something was flashed in the left visual field. The experimenter might ask, "Was it a letter of the alphabet?" The left (speaking) hemisphere would take a guess: "Yes." If that was correct, the person would get credit for a correct answer. But if the left hemisphere guessed incorrectly, the right hemisphere, which saw the display on the screen and heard the left hemisphere's guess, knew the guess was wrong. The right hemisphere would then make the face frown. (Both hemispheres can control facial muscles on both sides of the face.) The left hemisphere, feeling the frown, would say, "Oh, I'm sorry, I meant no." If such corrections are permitted, split-brain patients are able to guess the correct answers consistently.

In certain cases the two hemispheres have been able to exchange information so quickly that it has been suggested that they may be passing information through subcortical structures of the brain that were not divided

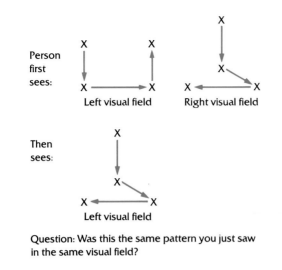

Person first sees:

Left visual field   Right visual field

Then sees:

Left visual field

Question: Was this the same pattern you just saw in the same visual field?

Figure 5-3. Task on which split-brain people perform better than normals.

when the corpus callosum was cut. For example, when subjects focus on a dot on a screen while a red or a green patch is flashed on each side of the screen, they cannot say whether the patches on the two sides of the screen were the same color. They can, however, press a button to indicate that at least one patch was green and a different button to indicate that neither patch was green (Sergent, 1986).

As a rule, having a split brain confers a disadvantage on a person's behavior, when it has any effect at all. Under unusual conditions, however, it yields an advantage by enabling the two halves of the brain to pay attention to different things at the same time. In one experiment, subjects are asked to watch a screen while a dot flashes about among four points in the left visual field and another dot simultaneously flashes about among four different points in the right visual field, as shown in Figure 5-3. Then another dot is flashed about among four points in one visual field or the other and the subjects must determine whether it has traced the same pattern as the dot previously seen in the same visual field. For a normal person, this is a nearly impossible task, as the unified brain becomes confused between what has been presented in the two visual fields. Split-brain subjects get the correct answer about 75 percent of the time, however (Holtzman & Gazzaniga, 1985), since each hemisphere sees only one visual field and suffers no interference or confusion.

Does the split-brain person have one mind or two? Investigators are not in complete agreement, and the question is complicated by our inability to say exactly what we mean by *mind*. Still, it appears that each hemisphere can answer certain questions on its own and that the two hemispheres sometimes exchange information by facial signals or other means that two separate people might use for communication. Thus, the two hemispheres of a split-brain person seem to be at least partly independent.

Evidence for Hemispheric Specializations in Intact People

Although the differences between the two hemispheres are more apparent after damage to the corpus callosum, certain differences can be demonstrated even in an intact person. The differences seen in intact people are, however, generally so small and inconsistent that they emerge only as statistical trends over a large number of people.

For example, a large group of right-handed college students were given a sound (such as "een") and were shown a large array of words, arranged randomly and some of them written on an angle. The students' task was to find up to eight words that rhymed with the sound. Half were told to scan the page left to right, while the other half were told to scan right to left; apparently all of them followed the instruction. Although the same number of rhyming words were available on both the left and right sides, the students found a mean of 43 percent of the words on the right side and 38 percent on the left (Levy & Kueck, 1986). This difference, statistically significant but not enormous, is typical of results in this field. It indicates that reading, presumably controlled by the left hemisphere, is slightly more effective when a person is gazing to the right, which is the field of vision of the left hemisphere.

A related example: When one hemisphere becomes more active, the eyes tend to turn toward the visual field of that hemisphere. Thus, when people are trying to solve a verbal problem, such as "What does this proverb mean?"—a left-hemisphere task—they gaze to the right more often than they gaze to the left. When trying to answer spatial questions, such as "Imagine your home and try to count the number of windows," they are more likely to turn their eyes to the left (Kinsbourne, 1972). These results apply only to right-handers; left-handers give inconsistent results. Even in right-handers the effect is not dependable, however. People are more likely to gaze in the predicted direction if the experimenter stands behind them instead of in front of them (Ehrlichmann & Weinberger, 1978). When standing in front, the experimenter may distract people or inhibit their natural behaviors.

Another example is that speaking triggers activity in the hand controlled by the hemisphere that controls speech. Most people engage in a great many hand gestures while they are speaking, often without being aware that they are doing so. Most right-handers move their right hand more actively while they speak; left-handers vary in which hand they move more actively (Kimura, 1973a, 1973b).

Here is a demonstration you can try yourself: Count how many times a child can tap one finger within 1 minute. Collect the same data for the index finger of each hand. Now take the measurements again while the child taps the finger and talks at the same time. For most right-handers, talking decreases the tapping rate with the right hand more than it does with the left hand (Kinsbourne & McMurray, 1975). Evidently, it is more difficult to do two things at once if both activities depend on the same hemisphere. (Adults may tap too fast for you to count the taps accurately. Have the person tap with a pencil on a piece of paper; later you can count the markings.)

Another demonstration: Find a stick that you can balance on one hand, but only with difficulty. See how long you can balance it with each hand while talking and compare it to the times without talking. Most right-handers find that talking interferes with their performance with the right hand but not with the left (Hicks, 1975). Again, left-handers are more variable.

Why Lateralization?

Why do we have a division of labor between the hemispheres? Whatever the reason, it is not altogether specific to humans, and it may be related to vocal communication. The Japanese macaque, a species of monkey, makes several kinds of vocalizations. Its ability to discriminate among the different vocalizations depends mostly on the left hemisphere of the brain (Heffner & Heffner, 1984). We do not know whether its production of vocalizations also depends on the left hemisphere. The ability of certain songbirds to sing does depend mostly on the left hemisphere; left-hemisphere damage prevents song and right-hemisphere damage does not (Nottebohm, 1970).

We can infer something about the advantages of lateralization by examining those uncommon people whose speech is controlled by both hemispheres of the brain. R. K. Jones (1966) performed surgery on four adult patients who had tumors or blood clots near the left-hemisphere speech center. Ordinarily a surgeon would hesitate to remove a tumor near the speech center for fear of damaging speech, but these four patients happened to have speech centers in both hemispheres. (This was determined by anesthetizing one hemisphere at a time with sodium amytal. Because anesthesia to either hemisphere produced the same effects on speech, it was inferred that both hemispheres controlled speech equally.)

The result was that, after surgical damage to the left speech center, each patient soon began to speak again, presumably by using the intact speech center in the right hemisphere. Furthermore, before the operation all four patients stuttered; afterward they all stopped stuttering!

The apparent implication is that the presence of two speech centers causes stuttering, perhaps because competing impulses from the two centers arrive at the speech muscles slightly out of synchrony. This suggestion makes sense of another interesting fact about stuttering: Stutterers usually do not stutter when singing or when speaking rhythmically. Many stutterers find that if they tap a foot in a regular rhythm and speak one word per tap, the stutter disappears. Either singing or rhythmic speaking could provide a basis for timing and synchronizing the impulses from the two hemispheres and thereby avoid conflict between impulses from the two hemispheres.

Jones's report on these surgical cases inspired further research on whether stutterers indeed have bilateral control of speech. Many studies have compared healthy stutterers (without epilepsy or other brain abnormalities) to nonstuttering control subjects on a variety of measures of hemispheric dominance for speech. One measure is the dichotic listening task, which tests whether the person reponds more readily to words heard in the left or right ear. In general, such studies have found that the difference between stutterers and nonstutterers, as groups, is not large; however, a greater percentage of stutterers than nonstutterers have right-hemisphere dominance for speech, or mixed dominance, or dominance that changes from one testing period to the next (Quinn, 1972; Pinsky & McAdam, 1980; Rosenfield & Goodglass, 1980; Sussman & MacNeilage, 1975). The apparent fluctuation of dominance is interesting, since most stutterers do not stutter equally at all times. Overall, it is likely that mixed dominance for speech is a contributing factor for some stutterers but not for others. As with many other behaviors, different people may do the same thing for different reasons.

DEVELOPMENT OF LATERALIZATION AND ITS RELATIONSHIP TO HANDEDNESS

Because in most people language depends primarily on the left hemisphere, it is natural to ask whether the left hemisphere is anatomically different from the right. If so, is this difference present before speech develops, or is it a result of speech, and what is the relationship between handedness and hemispheric dominance for speech?

Anatomical Differences Between the Hemispheres

For many years it was widely believed that the left and right hemispheres were anatomically the same, in spite of their differences in action. Then Geschwind and Levitsky (1968) reported that one section of the temporal cortex, called the planum temporale (PLAY-num tem-poh-RAL-ee), is larger in the left than in the right hemisphere for 65 percent of people (Figure 5-4). The size is about equal for 24 percent and larger in the right hemisphere for

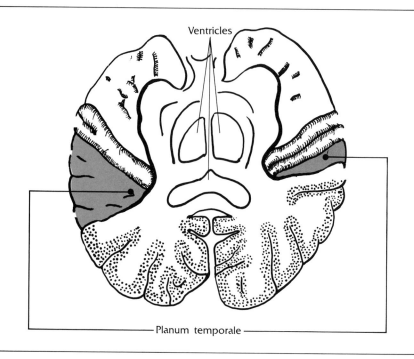

Ventricles

Planum temporale

Figure 5-4. Horizontal section through a human brain just above the surface of the temporal lobe. Note that the planum temporale, an area critical for speech comprehension, is substantially larger in the left hemisphere than in the right hemisphere. (From Geschwind & Levitsky, 1968.)

11 percent. The size differences for this area are reasonably large; in fact, they are visible to the naked eye if one knows where to look. The planum temporale includes areas known to be important for language.

The planum temporale is evidently larger in the left than in the right hemisphere even before language develops. Witelson and Pallie (1973) examined the brains of fourteen infants who had died before the age of 3 months. In twelve of the fourteen, the planum temporale was larger in the left than in the right hemisphere—on the average, about twice as large. Children who suffer brain damage in the first 4 years of life show more language impairment after left-hemisphere damage than after right-hemisphere damage (Aram & Ekelman, 1986).

Indeed, hand preference, which is related to speech lateralization, begins to emerge at an earlier age than one might suppose. Infants younger than 3 months old hold a rattle longer in their right hand than in their left hand before dropping it (Caplan & Kinsbourne, 1976).

One convenient indicator of the size of the planum temporale is the length of the Sylvian, or lateral, fissure (one of the major fissures, or folds, on the side of the cortex). In humans, the Sylvian fissure is 14 percent larger on the left side than on the right, on the average. In chimpanzees, it is only 5 percent larger; in monkeys, the two sides are practically equal (Yeni-Komshian & Benson, 1976). We do not know why even this slight difference is found between the hemispheres in chimpanzees, but whatever the reason, it seems that the human specializations for language were elaborations of tendencies already present in our remote primate ancestors.

Maturation of the Corpus Callosum

The corpus callosum completes its maturation gradually over the first 5 to 10 years of human life, making it one of the last structures of the brain to reach full maturity (Trevarthen, 1974). The developmental process is not so much a matter of growing new axons, however, as it is of selecting certain axons and discarding others.

At an early stage of development, the brain generates far more axons in the corpus callosum than it will have at maturity (Ivy & Killackey, 1981; Killackey & Chalupa, 1986). The reason for this is that any two neurons that are connected via the corpus callosum need to have corresponding functions. For example, suppose a given neuron in the occipital cortex of the left hemisphere responds to light in the very center of the retina. It should be connected to a right-hemisphere neuron that responds to light in that same location. During early embryological development, the genes cannot specify exactly where those two neurons will be. Therefore, a great many connections are made across the corpus callosum, but only those axons that happen to connect very similar cells survive (Innocenti & Caminiti, 1980).

But how does a neuron "know" whether or not it is connected to another neuron with properties similar to its own? Apparently, a neuron recognizes whether the input from the other neuron is synchronized with its own activity. Cats ordinarily have a certain number of connections across the corpus callosum to link the visual areas of the brain. If either or both of their eyelids are sewn shut for the first 3 months of life, they develop fewer than the normal number of axons across the corpus callosum. The same result occurs if their eye muscles are damaged early in life so they cannot focus both eyes in the same direction at the same time (Innocenti, Frost, & Illes, 1985). In other words, experience sharpens the selection of axons across the corpus callosum, enabling the right axons to survive. Abnormal experiences lead to a reduction in the number of axons, and to other abnormalities.

Because the connections across the human corpus callosum take years to develop their mature adult pattern, the behavior of young children resembles that of split-brain adults in some situations. A 9-week-old infant who has one arm restrained will never reach across the midline of the body to pick up a toy on the other side (Provine & Westerman, 1979). Apparently each hemisphere at that age has little access to the sensory information or motor control of the opposite hemisphere. By age 17 weeks, however, infants will reach across the midline to pick up a toy more often than not.

In one study, 3- and 5-year-old children were asked to feel two fabrics, either with the same hand or with the opposite hands, and say whether they were the same or different kinds of material. The 5-year-olds did equally well with one hand or with two. The 3-year-olds made 90 percent more errors with different hands than with the same hand (Galin, Johnstone, Nakell, and Herron, 1979). The likely interpretation is that the corpus callosum matures sufficiently between ages 3 and 5 to make the comparison of stimuli across the two hands much easier by age 5.

Development Without a Corpus Callosum

Rarely, the corpus callosum fails to form, for genetic or other poorly understood reasons. People who never had a corpus callosum differ from those who have undergone split-brain surgery (Jeeves, 1984). They can read words that they see in either visual field and name objects that they touch with either hand. Like split-brain patients, however, they are slow on tasks that require them to coordinate both hands, such as threading beads. And they show one peculiarity not typical of split-brain patients: Whenever they move the fingers of one hand, they involuntarily move the fingers of the other hand, too. Apparently, if the corpus callosum fails to develop normally, the two hemispheres develop abnormally as well. It is likely that each hemisphere gains a significant amount of control of the sensory and motor pathways on both sides of the body.

Handedness and Its Relationship to Language Dominance

About 10 percent of all people are left-handed or ambidextrous. (For purposes of this discussion we shall consider ambidextrous people to be left-handed. Indeed, most left-handers are partly ambidextrous.) Because artworks drawn or carved with the right hand differ from those drawn with the left hand, an examination of paintings and artifacts leads to the conclusion that about 90 percent of people have been right-handed in all parts of the world since prehistoric times (Coren & Porac, 1977).

The brain of a left-handed person is different from that of a right-handed person, but it is not simply a mirror image. For about 99 percent of right-handed people, the left hemisphere is strongly dominant for speech. The planum temporale and certain other areas are decidedly larger in the left hemisphere than in the right, and left-hemisphere damage greatly impairs language while right-hemisphere damage barely affects it. It is only in a rare left-hander that the right hemisphere has the same degree of dominance as the left hemisphere does for right-handers. A common estimate is that the left hemisphere is dominant for speech in 60 to 70 percent of left-handers, while the right hemisphere is dominant in the others (Levy, 1982). These figures may be misleading, however. Most left-handers, both those with left dominance and those with right dominance, have at least partly bilateral representation of language (Satz, 1979). Damage to either hemisphere impairs language. The corpus callosum is about 11 percent thicker in left-handers than in right-handers, presumably facilitating cross-hemisphere communication and bilateral representation of functions (Witelson, 1985).

Why are certain people left-handed and others right-handed? Although genetics has something to do with it, it is not the only determinant. The chance of having a left-handed child is higher if both parents are left-handed, but the family data on handedness do not suggest any simple Mendelian effects.

Geschwind and Galaburda (1985) proposed that handedness is largely under the control of hormones and other factors that modify the development of other parts of the body as well as the brain. All of the following are positively correlated with one another: left-handedness; being male; neuronal abnormalities in the left hemisphere; probability of dyslexia (see Digression 5-1); stuttering; probability of excellence at mathematics, architecture, and other right-hemisphere talents; childhood allergies; migraine headaches in adulthood; and disorders of the immune system. That is not to say that if you are left-handed you will develop all the other attributes on this list. The point is that anyone who has any one of the characteristics on the list has an increased chance of showing any of the others. The factors that lead to each of them must overlap the causes of the others.

One of those factors, according to Geschwind and Galaburda, may be the male hormone **testosterone**. Testosterone or related hormones may delay the maturation of the left hemisphere. Ordinarily, that is not a problem. Males, who are subject to greater influences of testosterone than females, are likely to develop a somewhat larger right hemisphere and smaller left hemisphere than females, although both hemispheres function quite adequately in most individuals of either sex. But now suppose that the influence of testosterone were exaggerated in a given individual—not necessarily because the testosterone levels themselves were unusually high, but because of increased sensitivity to testosterone or because of other unidentified influences. The result could be impairment of left-hemisphere functions, better-than-average development of right-hemisphere functions, and greater-than-average survival of corpus callosum axons that are ordinarily lost in early development.

What does this have to do with the immune disorders and other medical problems linked with left-handedness and the rest? Testosterone is known to retard the growth of the thymus gland and other structures of the immune

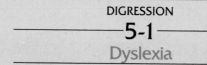

DIGRESSION

5-1

Dyslexia

Dyslexia means an inability to read. Like the terms *backache* and *headache*, it refers to symptoms, not causes. Different people may suffer from backache or headache for a variety of unrelated reasons. The same is true of dyslexia. It is likely that many people suffering from dyslexia have abnormalities in the brain, perhaps a failure of parts of the brain to mature. When we say this, however, it should be understood that we are talking about just one of the possible reasons for reading failure, ranging from poor eyesight to poor instruction.

It is possible to distinguish three major types of dyslexia in people whose nonreading academic skills are normal or above normal (Boder, 1973; Pirozzolo, 1979):

People with *auditory dyslexia* have trouble sounding out words. Although they know the sounds of the letters C, A, and T, they cannot sound out the word CAT. They may read more successfully by memorizing each word as a whole, just as Chinese readers learn the meaning of each symbol (Rozin, Poritsky, & Sotsky, 1971). This is the most common type of dyslexia.

People with *visual dyslexia* have trouble recognizing words as a whole and can read them *only*

by sounding them out. They have all the predictable difficulties with words that are spelled irregularly, such as *knife, phlegm,* and *business.* Even with the simplest text they read slowly. Visual dyslexics are much worse than other readers at identifying words outside the *fovea,* the very center of the visual field (Pirozzolo, 1979). Whereas a normal reader can read a group of words at a glance, the visual dyslexic person must look at words one at a time. Visual dyslexics are also prone to making errors on the return-sweep eye movements at the end of a line. Instead of bringing their eyes to the next line, they may undershoot or overshoot.

The third group cannot recognize words as a whole, nor can they sound them out. This more severe type of dyslexia is, fortunately, rare.

Only on occasion is it possible to determine what, if anything, may be wrong in the brains of dyslexic people. Kemper (1984) reported autopsies on the brains of three dyslexic boys, ages 14 to 20, who died in accidents. He found thinner than normal cerebral cortex, especially around Wernicke's area, and other minor abnormalities in the appearance and location of neurons. Witelson (1977) has inferred from behavioral studies that dyslexic people have both hemispheres specialized for visual-spatial processing; in effect, they have two right hemispheres.

system, as well as the left hemisphere. The result is greater vulnerability to a variety of disorders.

Geschwind and Galaburda's hypothesis is a most provocative one that has inspired new research on handedness and its correlates. For example, left-handers are more responsive than right-handers, on the average, to a variety of drugs, including aspirin, tranquilizers, and antidepressives (Irwin, 1985).

The role of testosterone in all this is not certain; as we shall see in Chapter 11, the female hormone estradiol has more easily demonstrable effects on the development of the cerebral cortex than testosterone does. No doubt we shall continue to see new research that will expand and modify our current understanding of handedness, and of the role of hormones in brain development.

Hemispheric Dominance and Handwriting Posture

Jerre Levy (see BioSketch 5-2) demonstrated that the position in which one holds one's hand for writing is related to the way language is organized in the brain (Levy & Reid, 1976, 1978). More than half of all left-handers hold a pen in a hooked or inverted manner to write. (See Figure 5-5.) They can

BIOSKETCH
5-2

Jerre Levy

Jerre Levy, a native of Demopolis, Alabama, did her undergraduate studies at Tulane University and the University of Miami. After receiving a Ph.D. from the California Institute of Technology in 1970, she served on the psychology faculty at the University of Pennsylvania and later at the University of Chicago.

As a graduate student she worked with Roger Sperry (see BioSketch 5-1), dealing with humans who had undergone the split-brain operation. Her investi-gations concentrated particularly on the functions of the right hemisphere of the cerebral cor-tex. Split-brain patients are very scarce, however, and after leav-ing Cal Tech, Levy turned her at-tention to the related topic of handedness. Among her contri-butions have been: (1) a theoret-ical model regarding the genetic basis of handedness (Levy & Nagylaki, 1972); (2) a demon-stration that right-handers con-sistently prefer pictures with the "more important" content on the right side of the picture (as one views it), while about half of left-handers have the opposite preference (Levy, 1976); and (3) the discovery that the hand posture used in writing depends on which hemisphere is domi-nant for reading.

Levy states: "I was one of those children who drive their parents to distraction with per-sistent 'whys' in response to every answer received. I have changed little since childhood, the major difference being that I now drive myself to distraction with my questions. . . . I believe that real meaning and satisfac-tion from living must come from a conscious attempt to continue in our individual lives the evolu-tion that made us human. I chose the field that I did not only be-cause of curiosity regarding man's origins, but also because of concern for his destiny, and though I am not so arrogant as to believe that what I do can make any real difference, my val-ues compel me, nevertheless, to make the attempt."

give good reasons for this posture: It enables them to see what they have written more clearly, and it prevents smearing of the ink. If that were the whole story, however, we should expect all left-handers to hold their pens that way. In fact, nearly half of left-handers hold their pen in the noninverted manner. Moreover, a few rare right-handers write in an inverted position, even though they do not gain the benefits the left-handers claim. Why do some invert the pen while others do not?

Levy and Reid (1976, 1978) initially proposed that left-handers who write in the inverted posture have their language areas located in the left hemisphere, whereas those who write in the noninverted posture have their language areas located in the right hemisphere. The rare right-handed people who invert the pen, according to Levy and Reid's observations, are those who have right-hemisphere dominance for language. Perhaps, Levy and Reid reasoned, people who write in the inverted manner do so because they are somehow using the left hemisphere to control writing with the left hand or are using the right hemisphere to control writing with the right hand.

Later investigations have failed to confirm this hypothesis in its original form. First, available evidence suggests that only the right hemisphere can control handwriting with the left hand (Gur, Gur, Sussman, O'Connor, & Vey, 1984; Levy & Wagner, 1984). Second, remember that most left-handers have largely bilateral control of language; it turns out that in ad-dition a person may have certain aspects of language localized mainly in one hemisphere while other aspects depend on the opposite hemisphere. For

| Sinistral noninverted writer | Sinistral inverted writer | Dextral inverted writer | Dextral noninverted writer |

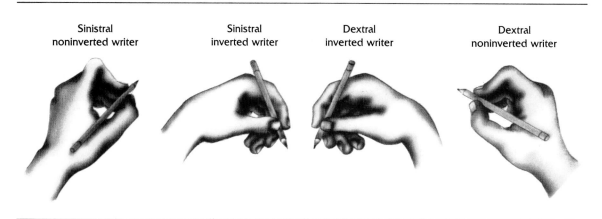

Figure 5-5. Typical inverted and noninverted handwriting positions. (From Levy & Reid, 1976.)

that reason, the apparent relationship between inverted writing posture and hemispheric control of language varies from one study to another, depending on the methods used to determine which hemisphere controls language (Levy, 1984). Up to this point, the studies have not led to a simple conclusion.

It remains the case, nevertheless, that inverted writers differ from noninverted writers in their responses to a variety of neurological tests, especially when tested with visual stimuli in the left and right visual fields (e.g., Levy & Wagner, 1984). Exactly how the brain differs between inverted and noninverted writers is not yet clear, but differences of some sort apparently do exist.

THE EVOLUTIONARY BASIS OF LANGUAGE

How did human language evolve? We should expect to find some precursors to human language in monkeys and apes, if only because evolution usually modifies existing systems rather than adding anything totally new. That is, the ancient ancestors we share in common with other primates must have had some abilities that could be modified into human language, and theoretically those precursors should still be evident in such contemporary primates as chimpanzees.

Many early attempts to teach chimpanzees to talk and to understand speech ended in failure (Premack, 1976). Differences between the chimpanzee and human vocal apparatus account for the chimps' failure to learn to speak (Bryan, 1963), although they do not explain the chimps' failure to understand speech.

The first success in teaching chimpanzees an approximation to human language was reported by Gardner and Gardner (1975), who trained a chimp named Washoe to use American Sign Language (ASL), the language of the American deaf. Washoe's trainers used a combination of imitation, reward, and occasionally putting Washoe's hands into the appropriate positions. By the end of 51 months of training, her vocabulary had reached 132 words.

Figure 5-6. One of the Premacks' chimps, Elizabeth, reacts to colored plastic chips that read "Not Elizabeth banana insert—Elizabeth apple wash." (Photo courtesy of Ann Premack.)

At about the same time as the Gardners' experiment, David and Ann Premack (1970, 1972) began training a chimp named Sarah to communicate using plastic chips. The Premacks taught Sarah (and later other chimpanzees) to interpret commands given by a column of chips and to use the chips to construct her own sentences. (See Figure 5-6.) Each chip represented a word or concept, as in Chinese. The Premacks' method allowed Sarah less spontaneity and creativity than Washoe had with sign language; however, it enabled Sarah to achieve more complicated linguistic structures. Sarah eventually used correct word order, negatives, questions, the symbols for *same* and *different*, plurals, the expression *is the name of*, compound sentences, and *if-then* constructions.

In a still more elaborate project on chimpanzee language, chimps have been trained to punch buttons bearing symbols to type out messages on a computer (Savage-Rumbaugh, Rumbaugh, & Boysen, 1978). The computer creates a visual display of the typed message; it also responds appropriately to all meaningful requests. These chimps have learned to make requests of the computer (e.g., "Please machine give me apple" or "Please machine turn on movie"). They also have learned to type messages to communicate with other chimps (e.g., "Please share your chocolate with me").

Have such chimpanzees really learned a little human language, or have they just learned a complicated set of tricks to get rewards? That is, we humans may interpret a set of symbols as "Elizabeth apple wash," but do the symbols really mean the same thing to the chimpanzee? Although chimpanzees learn to use symbols, they do not learn them the way children do. They need special training sessions in which they are reinforced for using the

Figure 5-7. A pygmy chimpanzee communicates by pressing a symbol that represents a concept. (Photo courtesy of Sue Savage-Rumbaugh.)

correct symbols. They do not learn simply by imitation, they seldom string symbols together to make original sentences, and they use their symbols almost exclusively to request, not to describe. For these reasons, a number of observers have expressed skepticism about whether the chimpanzees are learning anything that approximates human language (Terrace, Pettito, Sanders, & Bever, 1979).

More recently, studies of the rare pygmy chimpanzee have achieved results that may reduce the skepticism (Savage-Rumbaugh, McDonald, Sevcik, Hopkins, & Rubert, 1986). Pygmy chimpanzees have a social order that resembles that of humans in several regards. They have close male-female bonds, the males contribute much to infant care, adults share food with one another frequently, and they make elaborate vocalizations. In captivity, a few of them have learned to press symbols that light up when touched; each symbol represents a word. (See Figure 5-7.) Unlike common chimpanzees, pygmy chimpanzees sometimes learn the meaning of a symbol just by watching another chimp use it, and they use the symbols to name objects even when they are not requesting them. One pygmy chimp named Kanzi, having learned to use symbols to ask people to chase him around the room, spontaneously put together a set of symbols to ask one person to chase another person. After some experience with the symbols, two of the young pygmy chimps began to show a surprising degree of understanding of spoken English. (Although people had been speaking English naturally around the chimps, they had made no effort to train the chimps to understand it.)

Overall, two points are clear: (1) Our primate relatives—especially pygmy chimpanzees, it seems—have at least certain primitive abilities to use arbitrary symbols for communication. Human language presumably evolved from that base. (2) Humans learn and use language better than other animals. Therefore, it makes sense to look for specializations of the human brain that enable it to use language effectively.

EFFECTS OF BRAIN DAMAGE ON HUMAN LANGUAGE

Investigations of how the brain controls language are necessarily limited to humans. Most of our knowledge—until recently, almost all of our knowledge—has come from studies of brain-damaged people. Consequently, we can describe the brain mechanisms of language only at a fairly gross level, lacking the detail that can come from studies of single cells.

Broca's Area

Occasionally a person suddenly loses all ability to speak. In 1861, one patient who had been mute for 21 years was taken to the French surgeon Paul Broca because of gangrene. Broca was impressed that the man seemed psychiatrically and neurologically normal except for his inability to speak. When the patient happened to die shortly thereafter, Broca did an autopsy on the man's brain and found a lesion restricted to a small part of the frontal lobe of the left cerebral cortex (Schiller, 1979). In later years Broca examined the brains of other patients whose only problem had been a language impairment of sudden origin; in more than 95 percent of cases he found damage in that same small area, which is now known as **Broca's area**. The usual cause of the damage was a stroke (an interruption of blood flow to part of the brain). Figure 5-8 shows the location of Broca's area.

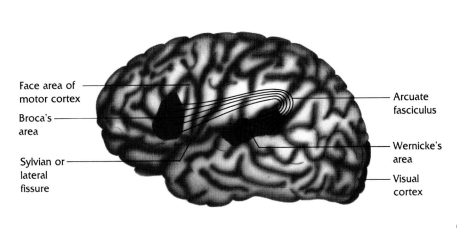

Figure 5-8. Location of the major language areas of the human cerebral cortex.

Later studies confirmed that Broca's area is damaged in most patients who suffer an inability to speak. The term **aphasia** refers to a loss of language due to brain damage. The kind of aphasia produced by damage to Broca's area is sometimes known as *Broca's aphasia*.

It has subsequently been found that damage limited just to Broca's area produces only a mild, temporary speech impairment. A long-lasting and severe loss of speech is more often associated with extensive damage that includes Broca's area, part of the left motor cortex, some areas farther posterior in the left cortex, and sometimes parts of the thalamus or basal ganglia (Damasio & Geschwind, 1984; Ludlow et al., 1986). Furthermore, when normal people speak, they have increased cerebral blood flow in Broca's area, the motor cortex and surrounding areas, the left thalamus, and the basal ganglia (Wallesch, Henriksen, Kornhuber, & Paulson, 1985). Apparently speech depends on a fairly large circuit that includes these other areas as well as Broca's area.

The effects of damage in Broca's area vary in degree, depending on the size and exact location of the damage. The effects in general include (Geschwind, 1970, 1972):

1. *Difficulty in language production.* Some people with Broca's aphasia cannot speak at all, although they may be able to make a variety of sounds and sometimes even hum or sing. Those with less extensive damage can speak, but with difficulty; words are spoken slowly and articulated poorly. The problem is not simply a lack of control of the throat; such people have trouble writing as well. In addition, deaf people with damage in and around Broca's area find it difficult to produce sign language (Bellugi, Poizner, & Klima, 1983). They can make only a few brief signs, even though their ability to use their hands in other ways may be unimpaired.

2. *Telegraphic speech.* When someone with Broca's aphasia speaks at all, the speech is meaningful but it omits prepositions, conjunctions, helper verbs, quantifiers, and tense and number endings. These omitted words and endings are sometimes known as the *closed* class of grammatical forms in the sense that it is almost impossible to add new prepositions, conjunctions, and the like to our language. In contrast, we readily add new nouns and verbs. Someone with Broca's aphasia can speak nouns and verbs more easily than other words.

The problem is not simply that Broca's aphasics want to minimize the labor of pronouncing a great many words. Such people find it difficult to repeat a phrase using many prepositions and conjunctions, such as "No ifs, ands, or buts," although they can successfully repeat "The general commands the army." Furthermore, patients who cannot read aloud "To be or not to be" can read "Two bee oar knot two bee" (Gardner & Zurif, 1975). Clearly, the trouble depends on the meanings of words, not just their pronunciation.

3. *More adequate language comprehension.* People with Broca's aphasia understand both spoken and written language better than they can produce it. They have occasional trouble hearing the articles (*a*, *an*, and *the*) in a stream of speech, although they can understand them if they hear them

(M. Grossman, Carey, Zurif, & Diller, 1986). A more serious impairment is that they have trouble understanding the same word categories that they cannot say. That difficulty is not always obvious in normal conversation. (You might try scratching out all the prepositions, conjunctions, and so forth from a few paragraphs of your choosing. Can you make sense of what's left?)

In the process of guessing the meaning, Broca's aphasics sometimes change the meaning, especially if the sentence is strange or irregular. For example, when they are asked to repeat an implausible sentence, they do not repeat it verbatim but instead change it to something more plausible. A Broca's aphasic may change "The bicycle is riding the boy" to "The bicycle is riding by the boy" (Ostrin & Schwartz, 1986).

People with Broca's aphasia have their greatest trouble understanding a sentence whose meaning depends on word order or other grammatical devices. For example, they have difficulty understanding the sentence, "The girl that the boy is chasing is tall" (Zurif, 1980). They are not sure who is chasing whom and which one is tall.

In certain respects, children 2 to 3 years old resemble Broca's aphasics: Both have poor articulation, both understand speech better than they produce it, and both use mostly concrete nouns with few prepositions, conjunctions, and the like. Although it is tempting to suppose that the maturation of language has something to do with maturational changes in Broca's area, we have no firm evidence of any anatomical change in Broca's area during the period of speech acquisition (Milner, 1976).

Wernicke's Area

In 1874 Carl Wernicke (pronounced WER-nih-kee in the United States although the German pronunciation is VER-nih-keh), a 26-year-old junior assistant in a German hospital, discovered that damage in another area of the brain produced a very different kind of language impairment. Patients could produce language, but they had trouble comprehending the verbal and written communications of others. This brain area, now known as **Wernicke's area** (Figure 5-8), is located in the left temporal lobe not far from the auditory part of the cerebral cortex. Damage to Wernicke's area produces *Wernicke's aphasia*, which has the following symptoms:

1. *No difficulty with articulation.* In contrast to Broca's aphasics, Wernicke's aphasics speak rapidly, articulately, and fluently, except when they pause to try to think of the name of something.

2. *Poor language comprehension.* Wernicke's aphasics have great trouble understanding both spoken and written speech. Many people, when they are speaking to someone suffering from this condition, try to help the person by simply speaking very slowly, mostly by drawing out the vowels. That strategy turns out not to help at all. It does help, however, to pause extra-long at the boundaries between phrases; for example: "The truck (pause) chased the car (pause) that hit the bus" (Blumstein, Katz, Goodglass, Shrier, & Dworetsky, 1985).

3. *Difficulty finding the right word.* People suffering from Wernicke's aphasia have **anomia** (ay-NOME-ee-uh), a difficulty in recalling the names

of objects and in constructing relative clauses. A typical result is as follows: "Yes, all the little, little pe-, ah, puh, ah, places the, the ah, big big of-fi-ces then have undergone this here ah, the, ah, the, ah, there and they're there, but they can't hear, hi, hi, can't see them because it's s-so-so big, other big buildings are there" (Martin & Blossom-Stach, 1986).

Although people with Wernicke's aphasia speak grammatically, what they say makes little sense. Even when they do manage to find some of the right words, they fail to arrange the words properly, saying, for example, "The Astros listened to the radio tonight" (instead of "I listened to the Astros on the radio tonight") or "The car was towntown for a photograph, to a friend on a bookstore, and a restaurant" (Martin & Blossom-Stach, 1986).

The following is a conversation between a woman with Wernicke's aphasia and a speech therapist who is trying to teach her the names of some objects. Although her speech comprehension is better than that of many Wernicke's aphasics, she has a severe difficulty with naming. (This dialogue was provided by the Duke University Department of Speech Pathology and Audiology.)

Therapist: *(Holding picture of an apron) Can you name that one?*

Woman: *Um . . . you see I can't, I can I can barely do; he would give me sort of umm . . .*

T: *A clue?*

W: *That's right . . . just a like, just a . . .*

T: *You mean, like, "You wear that when you wash dishes or when you cook a meal . . ."?*

W: *Yeah, something like that.*

T: *Okay, and what is it? You wear it around your waist, and you cook . . .*

W: *Cook. Umm, umm, see I can't remember.*

T: *It's an apron.*

W: *Apron, apron, that's it, apron.*

T: *(Holding another picture) That you wear when you're getting ready for bed after a shower.*

W: *Oh, I think that he put under different, something different. We had something, you know, umm, you know.*

T: *A different way of doing it?*

W: *No, umm . . . umm . . . (Pause)*

T: *It's actually a bathrobe.*

W: *Bathrobe. Uh, we didn't call it that, we called it something else.*

T: *Smoking jacket?*

W: *No, I think we called it, uh . . .*

T: *Lounging . . .?*

W: *No, no, something, in fact we called it just . . . (Pause)*

T: *Robe?*

W: *Robe. Or something like that.*

The conversation proceeded similarly through pictures of a bird, a thermos, a bride, an airplane, and an arm; the woman could not name any of them, although she seemed to recognize the names when she heard them. The therapist then began to review:

T: *(Apron picture) The thing you wear when you're cooking.*

W: *(Silence)*

T: *Apron.*

W: *Apron.*

T: *(Robe picture) What's this?*

W: *Apron, umm, umm . . .*

T: *Robe.*

W: *Robe.*

T: *(Apron picture) What's this?*

W: *(Silence)*

T: *That's the apron again.*

W: *Apron, apron, apron.*

T: *(Robe picture) And this?*

W: *Apron.*

T: *That's the robe.*

W: *Robe. Robe, robe. Apron, robe, apron, robe.*

T: *(Apron picture) Now this one again.*

W: *Apron.*

T: *(Robe picture) Uh-huh.*

W: *Robe.*

T: *(Bird picture) Okay. Now this is . . .*

W: *Apron, robe . . .*

T: *Bird.*

W: *Bird. Bird.*

T: *(Apron picture) What's this first one again?*

W: *(Sigh)*

T: *That's the apron.*

W: *Apron, apron, apron, apron.*

T: *(Bird picture) And that's the . . .*

W: *(Silence.)*

Unlike hearing people, deaf people who suffer damage to Wernicke's area do not lose their ability to understand sign language. Rather, they lose that ability after damage in the parietal lobe, the area responsible for the sense of touch (Bellugi, Poizner, & Klima, 1983).

Disconnections of Broca's Area and Wernicke's Area from Each Other and from Other Areas

Carl Wernicke suggested that Wernicke's area, located near the auditory cortex in the temporal lobe, was involved in transferring sounds into language comprehension, and that Broca's area, located near the motor cortex in the frontal lobe, was involved in converting language representations into the muscle movements necessary for speech. Wernicke further argued that Wernicke's area must be connected to Broca's area and that at least one of the two areas must be connected to the visual and auditory areas of the cortex. If so, he reasoned, specific behavior deficits should result from any damage to one of those connections. This theory, expanded and repopularized by Norman Geschwind (BioSketch 5-3) a century later (Geschwind, 1970, 1972), offers explanations for many specific impairments related to language.

A set of fibers called the **arcuate fasciculus** (AR-kyoo-ate fuh-SIK-yoo-lus) (see Figure 5-8) connects Wernicke's area to Broca's area. Damage to the arcuate fasciculus gives rise to a condition known as **conduction aphasia** (Damasio & Damasio, 1980). Pronunciation remains normal, because Broca's area is intact. Language comprehension is nearly normal, because Wernicke's area is intact. However, the person has difficulty repeating what others say and carrying on a continuous conversation. What the person hears and understands (by means of Wernicke's area) cannot get to Broca's area to influence speech.

When people with conduction aphasia speak, they may have trouble finding words, especially the names of objects. That is, they resemble Wernicke's aphasics, even though Wernicke's area is intact. The reason is simply that the intact Wernicke's area cannot convey the names of objects to Broca's area. Table 5-1 contrasts Broca's aphasia, Wernicke's aphasia, and conduction aphasia.

The presentations of the next three clinical syndromes begin with a behavioral description. After reading the first paragraph of each, try to guess

Norman Geschwind (1926–1984)

One of the perennial debates in biological psychology is: To what extent does a behavior depend on specific locales in the brain, and to what extent does it depend on the brain as a whole? Norman Geschwind (GESH-wind) was taught, like other students in the 1940s and 1950s, that the brain works as a whole and that earlier writings emphasizing localization were simply mistaken. When he read the old German and French neurological works for himself, however, he was impressed with their evidence for specific localization

of speech and other functions (Galaburda, 1985). Beginning in the 1960s Geschwind led a revival of interest in localizations of function in the human brain and in the effects of disconnecting one area from another.

Geschwind received his A.B. and M.D. degrees from Harvard University. He worked at Harvard Medical School, MIT, and the Beth Israel Hospital in Boston. He dealt mostly with patients who had localized brain damage and showed such disturbances as aphasia (language loss) and apraxia (disorder of voluntary movement). He also investigated the anatomical asymmetries of the brain underlying cerebral dominance. His interpretations emphasized damage that disconnects one part of the brain from another.

For many years both psychologists and medical doctors have

been exhorted to "think of the patient as a whole" and not as an assemblage of parts. Geschwind (1965), however, remarked that this principle leads to much confusion when dealing with brain-damaged people: "We were constantly dealing with questions such as 'If he can speak normally and he knows what he's holding in his left hand, why can't he tell you?' We had to point out that . . . that part of the patient which could speak normally was not the same part of the patient which 'knew' (nonverbally) what was in the left hand. . . . I am not advancing 'the atomistic approach' as a basic philosophical postulate to replace 'the holistic approach,' but am rather suggesting that failure to consider the applicability of either type of analysis will in one situation or another lead to errors."

Table 5-1. Three Types of Aphasia

Area damaged	Pronunciation	Content of speech	Comprehension
Broca's area (Broca's aphasia)	Very poor	Speaks mostly nouns and verbs; omits prepositions and other grammatical connectives	Has trouble only if understanding depends on prepositions, sentence grammar, or word order
Wernicke's area (Wernicke's aphasia)	Unimpaired	Speech is grammatical but sometimes nonsensical; has trouble finding the right word, especially names of objects	Seriously impaired
Arcuate fasciculus (conduction aphasia)	Unimpaired	Can't repeat what others say; has trouble with names of objects	Slightly impaired in some cases

where the brain damage might be before you read the neurological explanation of each clinical syndrome.

Word Blindness Without Inability to Write.   The person has suddenly lost the ability to read. Language is normal in all other ways; even writing is spared, although the person cannot read what he or she has just written.

This condition is known as **word-blindness**, or **alexia**. Vision is intact in the left visual field but is lost in the right visual field.

The cause? The left visual cortex has been destroyed (by stroke, perhaps), as has the posterior part of the corpus callosum, known as the *splenium*, which contains the fibers from the visual areas of the cortex. The person can see only with the right visual cortex (left visual field), and information in the right visual cortex cannot get to the language areas in the left hemisphere (Greenblatt, 1973; Hécaen & Kremin, 1976; Staller, Buchanan, Singer, Lappin, & Webb, 1978). Spontaneous writing is normal because vision is not necessary for writing; a normal person can, after all, write with his or her eyes closed. Reading is impaired, however, because it requires transfer of information from vision to the language areas of the brain.

Most people suffering from word blindness can name the objects they see in the left visual field. This may seem surprising, since the fibers that transmit visual information across the corpus callosum have been damaged. Geschwind (1970, 1972) has suggested that the right hemisphere may in some manner convert the visual identification of an object into touch or other kinds of sensory representations that can be sent across the intact anterior corpus callosum. Because the right hemisphere cannot convert written words or letters into any nonvisual code, the left hemisphere has no access to them. For the same reason, most people with word blindness cannot name the colors they see.

Certain people have had their posterior corpus callosum cut, for the same medical reasons as the total split-brain patients discussed earlier. When they see something in the left visual field (right hemisphere), they can sometimes transfer enough information across the anterior corpus callosum for the left hemisphere to describe the object partially, but not necessarily to name it (Sidtis, Volpe, Holtzman, Wilson, & Gazzaniga, 1981). They often describe it as a "tip of the tongue" experience; a patient might say, "I saw an article of clothing . . . it's worn by men, mostly in fall . . . Oh, it's a hunter's cap." It is as if the information is flowing piecemeal across the corpus callosum and the left hemisphere must infer what the object is.

Tape-Recorder Speech.   Certain people with a rare pattern of extensive brain damage have no spontaneous speech at all and no evidence of language comprehension (Geschwind, Quadfasel, & Segarra, 1968; Ross, 1980; Whitaker, 1976). Such people do not follow verbal instructions or engage in conversation. However, they do repeat much of what others say and may even complete familiar quotes that someone else starts. If someone else says, "Roses are red . . .," the person repeats this and then completes the poem. In short, the person's only use of speech is to repeat it, like a parrot or a tape recorder.

What is the neurological basis of this disorder? The entire language circuit of such people, from auditory cortex through Wernicke's and Broca's areas to the motor cortex, is intact. However, much of the rest of the cerebral cortex has been destroyed, including all the areas that surround the language circuit. Because the language areas are disconnected from all the motor control areas, other than those that control the speech muscles, the person cannot respond to any instructions. Because the motivations originating elsewhere in the brain have no access to the language circuit, the person has no spontaneous speech.

Ability to Follow Instructions with the Right Hand but Not the Left. Following a particular kind of brain damage, a person can follow someone's verbal instructions, such as "Comb your hair," or "Wave good-bye," with the right side of the body but not the left. The left hand is capable of the movements, however. Such a person may make those movements spontaneously with the left hand. He or she can also use the left hand to imitate those movements when someone else makes them.

The problem here is simply damage to the corpus callosum (Geschwind, 1975). Verbal messages can get from the language areas in the left hemisphere to the motor cortex in the left hemisphere, which controls the right half of the body. The right motor cortex, controlling the left half of the body, is intact and can generate the movements either spontaneously or by imitation. Verbal information from the left hemisphere cannot reach the left side of the body, however.

A person with damage to the corpus callosum can nevertheless follow verbal instructions that require using muscles on both sides of the face, such as "Smile," or "Raise your eyebrows." The reason is that each hemisphere has a fair degree of control of the facial muscles on both sides of the face, especially the upper face, and in fact many of the muscles near the midline of the body (Rinn, 1984).

Therapy and Recovery from Aphasia

Aphasia that results from brain damage may or may not be permanent. After either a stroke or a wound to the head, the resulting aphasia gradually decreases in many cases and disappears altogether in some (Mohr et al., 1980). Recovery is better after subcortical lesions that cause aphasia than after lesions of the cerebral cortex (Olsen, Bruhn, & Öberg, 1986). If the left hemisphere is damaged in early childhood, the right hemisphere assumes a certain amount of the left hemisphere's normal functions, at the expense of its own. After left-hemisphere damage, a child recovers language better than an adult would, but his or her visual-spatial abilities fail to develop as well as normal (Lansdell, 1969).

Speech therapists work with aphasic patients to get them to practice and improve whatever language skills they retain. Although it is generally agreed that patients improve more if they get therapy promptly, speech therapy is helpful even for patients who do not receive it until years after their stroke or injury (Helm-Estabrooks & Ramsberger, 1986). If the person regains no use of spoken language after severe brain damage, it is sometimes possible to teach him or her to use cut-out colored paper symbols as words, in a manner similar to that used by the Premacks with chimpanzees. Patients who cannot speak or understand speech can learn to arrange simple sentences, such as "Andrea give John water," and to use paper symbols for more complex concepts as well (Gardner, Zurif, Berry, & Baker, 1976; Glass, Gazzaniga, & Premack, 1973)

SUMMARY

1.   Visual information from each visual field crosses through the pupils and lenses of the eyes to reach the opposite side of the retina. In humans, stimulation of the left half of each retina (from the right visual field) sends impulses to the left hemisphere of the brain. Stimulation of the right half of each retina (from the left visual field) sends impulses to the right half of the brain. (p. 115)

2.   The corpus callosum, a set of axons connecting the two hemispheres, has been surgically cut in a small number of people to relieve severe, otherwise untreatable epilepsy. (p. 116)

3.   After the corpus callosum is cut, the left hemisphere can answer questions verbally and can control the right hand. The right hemisphere can control the left hand. Each hemisphere sees the opposite side of the world and feels the opposite side of the body. Neither hemisphere has direct access to the knowledge of the other. (p. 118)

4.   The left hemisphere of most people is specialized for language. The right hemisphere is specialized for control of complex visual-spatial functions, especially those that require internal representations of visual and spatial information. (p. 119)

5.   Although the two hemispheres of a split-brain person are sometimes in conflict, they find many ways to cooperate and to cue each other. (p. 120)

6.   The brain of a left-handed person is not simply the mirror image of the brain of a right-handed person. Left-handers tend to have more nearly bilateral control of speech and other functions. They are more likely to stutter, and to have a variety of other medical and psychological anomalies, some of them advantages and others disadvantages. According to one hypothesis, all these effects may be exaggerations of the normal effects of testosterone on development. (pp. 126–127)

7.   Chimpanzees can learn to communicate by sign language or by other nonvocal means. Although their productions are often impressive, they are less likely to make original sentences than children with similar vocabularies. (p. 131)

8.   After damage to Broca's area, people find it difficult to speak or write. They find it especially difficult to use prepositions, conjunctions, and other grammatical connectives. They also fail to understand speech when its meaning depends on grammatical connectives, sentence structure, or word order. (p. 134)

9.   After damage to Wernicke's area, people have trouble understanding speech and find it difficult to recall the names of objects. (p. 135)

10.   Other specialized problems, such as word blindness, arise if Wernicke's area and Broca's area are disconnected from other parts of the cerebral cortex, such as the visual area, the auditory area, or the motor-control area. (p. 138)

REVIEW QUESTIONS

1.   Why is the left hemisphere of the brain simply connected to the right eye in rabbits, but not in humans? (p. 115)

2.   In the human eye, what part of each retina connects to the left hemisphere? to the right hemisphere? What part of the visual field does the left hemisphere see? What part does the right hemisphere see? (p. 115)

3.   Can a split-brain person name something after feeling it with the left hand? with the right hand? Why? (p. 118)

4.   What kinds of tasks can the right hemisphere perform better than the left hemisphere? (p. 119)

5.   Describe one way in which the two hemispheres of a split-brain person cooperate. (p. 120)

6.   Describe one task that apparently demonstrates differences between the left hemisphere and the right hemisphere in intact people. (p. 122)

7.   What is a possible biological factor predisposing a person to stutter? (p. 123)

8.   What evidence do we have that the left hemisphere differs from the right hemisphere even before a child develops language? (p. 125)

9.   How does experience affect the development of the corpus callosum? (p. 125)

10.   In what way is the behavior of a young child similar to that of a split-brain person? (p. 126)

11.   List some of the biological characteristics that are more prevalent among left-handers than among right-handers. According to Geschwind and Galburda, what may account for these increased prevalences? (p. 127)

12.   Why are the results so variable in studies that attempt to link handwriting posture to hemispheric dominance for language? (p. 129)

13.   What is one reason why chimpanzees learn sign language better than spoken language? (p. 130)

14.   What do young children often do in their speech that chimpanzees seldom do? (p. 132)

15.   Where are Broca's area and Wernicke's area? (p. 133)

16.   In what ways is language impaired after damage to Broca's area and neighboring areas? In what ways is it impaired after damage to Wernicke's area? (pp. 134, 135)

17. Describe the effects of disconnecting Wernicke's area from Broca's area. (p. 138)

18. What brain damage accounts for word blindness? (p. 140)

19. If an aphasic patient fails to recover speech, what method can help the patient communicate? (p. 141)

THOUGHT QUESTIONS

1. As discussed on p. 121, certain split-brain patients can press a button with the right hand to answer a question about information presented to the left visual field. How does the left hemisphere (which controls the right hand) know what was in the left visual field? Sergent (1986) suggests that the information passes from the right hemisphere to the left hemisphere via subcortical connections in the brain. Can you imagine any other possible explanation? If so, can you imagine a way to test whether your hypothesis is plausible?

2. Most people with Broca's aphasia suffer from partial paralysis on the right side of the body. Most people with Wernicke's aphasia do not. Why?

3. In a syndrome called *word deafness*, a person cannot understand spoken language, although both language and hearing are normal in other respects. What would be a possible neurological explanation?

TERMS TO REMEMBER

retina (p. 115)
visual field (p. 115)
corpus callosum (p. 116)
testosterone (p. 127)
dyslexia (p. 128)
Broca's area (p. 133)

aphasia (p. 134)
Wernicke's area (p. 135)
anomia (p. 135)
arcuate fasciculus (p. 138)
conduction aphasia (p. 138)
word-blindness (alexia) (p. 140)

SUGGESTIONS FOR FURTHER READING

Aitchison, J. (1983). *The articulate mammal: An introduction to psycholinguistics* (2nd ed). New York: Universe Books. Discusses language and the biological specializations that make language possible.

Geschwind, N. (1979). Specializations of the human brain. *Scientific American, 241* (3), 180–199. Discusses the effects of brain damage on language.

Springer, S. P., & Deutsch, G. (1981). *Left brain, right brain.* San Francisco: W. H. Freeman. Discusses the split-brain phenomenon and the specializations of the two hemispheres evident in normal people.

CHAPTER 6

Sensory Systems

MAIN IDEAS

1. Our senses have not evolved to give us complete information about all the stimuli in the world, but to give us the information most useful to us.

2. Each sensory nerve carries information about one type of sensation. Whenever a given nerve is excited, even if it is artificially excited by electricity, the brain's interpretation of its message is the same.

3. Each sensory system has receptors that are highly sensitive to a given type of energy. The receptors transduce that energy into action potentials, which code the information in a manner that the brain can process.

A ccording to an American Indian saying, "A pine needle fell. The eagle saw it. The deer heard it. The bear smelled it" (Herrero, 1985). Different species are sensitive to different information. Bees and many other insects can see short-wavelength (ultraviolet) light that is invisible to humans; conversely, humans see long-wavelength (red) light that these insects cannot see. Bats produce sonar waves at 20,000 to 100,000 Hz and localize insect prey by listening to the echos. Most adult humans cannot hear any sounds in that range, although children may hear the lower part of that range (Griffin, Webster, & Michael, 1960).

Many animal species are sensitive to only a small range of stimuli, the stimuli that are most useful to their way of life. For example, a frog's eyes include cells that respond selectively to small, dark moving objects—such as insects (Lettvin, Maturana, McCulloch, & Pitts, 1959). The ears of the cricket frog, *Acris crepitans*, are highly sensitive to sounds around the frequencies 550 and 3550 Hz—the frequencies found in the adult male's croak. The frog's ear is poorly sensitive to other sounds. In frog species in which the male produces other sounds, the ears are "tuned" to respond to the particular sounds those males make (Capranica & Frishkopf, 1966; Capranica, Frishkopf, & Nevo, 1973). Similarly, 17-year locusts are highly sensitive to the songs produced by their own species and are virtually deaf to other sounds (Simmons, Wever, & Pylka, 1971).

We generally assume that human sensory systems simply reflect the physical world. Granted, human visual and auditory abilities are broader and less specialized than those of frogs and locusts, perhaps because a wider range of stimuli are biologically relevant to us than to them. However, even humans have some important sensory specializations. For example, we can detect the sweet taste of certain nutritious substances and the bitter taste of poisons at low concentrations (Richter, 1950; Schiffman & Erickson, 1971). Conversely, we fail to taste many substances that are neither helpful nor harmful (for instance, sand and cellulose). Our olfactory systems are sensitive to a wide variety of gases but completely insensitive to others, including some that it would be useless for us to detect (nitrogen, for example). Thus, this chapter is not about how our sensory systems enable us to perceive Reality with a capital R, but how they enable us to get information that is biologically useful.

RECEPTION, TRANSDUCTION, AND CODING

When physical energy such as light or sound reaches the sense organs, it must be converted to a form that can be processed in the brain. That conversion has three steps: **Reception** is simply the absorption of physical energy. **Transduction** is the conversion of that physical energy to an electrochemical pattern in the neurons. **Coding** is the one-to-one correspondence between some aspect of the physical stimulus and some aspect of the nervous system's activity. For example, light rays strike retinal receptors (reception); the light energy is converted to a change in the receptors' membrane polarization

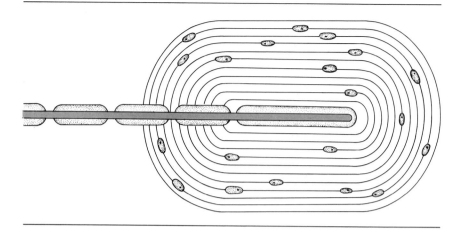

Figure 6-1. A Pacinian corpuscle. Pressure on the
corpuscle causes a depolarization in the axon.

(transduction); and the resulting train of impulses in the optic nerve has a
frequency that increases as the intensity of the light increases (coding).

Reception and Transduction

Reception, in the simple sense of absorbing energy, is a rapid process. Each
type of receptor is adapted to receive a particular form of energy. Visual
receptors can absorb and respond to as little as a single photon of light,
although they are relatively insensitive to air vibrations, chemicals, and other
stimuli that excite other receptors. Auditory receptors can detect air vibrations only slightly more intense than the vibrations produced by blood traveling through the vessels of the ear. Other receptors are uniquely sensitive to
chemical stimuli and touch stimuli.

Transduction is the process of converting received energy into nerve
activity. The stimulation of a receptor produces a **generator potential**, a local
current similar to an EPSP (see Chapter 3). If the generator potential is
intense enough, it may trigger an action potential.

As an example of transduction, consider the Pacinian corpuscle (Figure
6-1 and Color Plate 18), a receptor that detects pressure on the skin. Inside
the onionlike surround is a neuron membrane that conducts no current when
at rest. When mechanical pressure bends the membrane, its resistance to
sodium flow decreases, and sodium ions enter, depolarizing the membrane.
That depolarization is the generator potential (Loewenstein, 1960).

Coding

At one time people believed that the brain's representation of a physical
stimulus would have to resemble the stimulus itself. That is, to see a table
you would need a pattern of activity in a set of neurons that were arranged
in the shape of a table. That view has long been discarded. The word *table*
does not look like a table or sound like a table. A computer stores a record
of the word *table* by means of a series of electromagnetic pulses that physically resemble neither tables nor the spoken or written word for tables.
Similarly, the brain can store its representation for *table* in any code, pro-

vided only that a one-to-one relationship exist between the stimulus itself and the brain's code for it.

One important aspect of all sensory coding is *which* neurons are active. A given frequency of impulses may mean one thing when it occurs in one neuron and something quite different when it occurs in another. This basic insight was described by Johannes Müller in 1838 as the **law of specific nerve energies**: *Each sensory nerve is ordinarily excited by only one kind of energy (light or air vibrations, for example), and the brain interprets any stimulation of that nerve as being that kind of energy.*

That is, the action potentials of the auditory nerve are physically the same as those of the optic nerve. The brain experiences them differently only because it somehow knows which one is the auditory nerve and which one is the optic nerve. If you poke your eye or rub it hard, you may see spots or flashes of light even if the room is totally dark. The reason is that the mechanical pressure excites some receptors in the retina of the eye; anything that excites those receptors is perceived as light. (If you wish to try this experiment, be sure to press gently on your eyeball with your eye shut and without contact lenses on the eye.)

Furthermore, if it were possible to take the nerves from your eyes and ears and cross-transplant them so that the visual receptors were connected to the auditory nerve and vice versa, you would literally "see" sounds and "hear" lights. The implication of all this is that perceptions depend on which neurons are active and how active each one is at a given time.

Although the law of specific nerve energies is still considered fundamentally correct a century and a half after it was first stated, we must add some important qualifications. First, certain cells with a spontaneous rate of firing may signal one kind of stimulus by an increase in firing and a different kind by a decrease in firing. For instance, certain cells in the visual system increase their firing rate in response to red light and decrease below the spontaneous rate in response to green light. The same cell, therefore, may contribute to the perception of both red and green.

Second, it is possible that the "rhythm" of impulses may code certain kinds of information. For example, the following three records of impulses over time may convey different information, even though they represent the same mean frequency in the same cell:

Third, although the law of specific nerve energies applies to the nerve as a whole, it may not apply equally well to individual axons within the nerve. That is, the brain knows, for example, that activity in any of the taste nerves

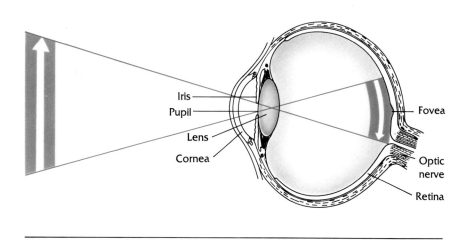

Figure 6-2. Diagrammatic cross-section of the vertebrate eye, showing the projection of an image onto the retina.

means taste, not light or sound. But does it also know that activity in one axon means salty taste, while activity in another axon means sweet taste? Or do all the axons contribute to all the tastes? That issue remains an unresolved controversy, especially for the senses of taste and smell.

VISUAL CODING AND THE RETINAL RECEPTORS

Figure 6-2 illustrates the basic structures of the eye. Light enters through the **pupil** and is focused by the cornea and lens onto the receptors in the **retina**. As in a camera, the light rays are focused so that the image is reversed. Light from the left side of the world strikes the right half of the retina, and vice versa. Light from above strikes the bottom half of the retina; light from below strikes the top half of the retina.

In the past, both scientists and philosophers used to worry about how the brain turns the image right side up again. The answer in its simplest terms is that the image does not need to be right side up. The bottom part of the retina does not "know" that it is on the bottom. The same is true of the brain. If a surgeon could somehow twist your entire brain 180 degrees, while leaving intact all the nerve connections between the brain and the sense organs, the world would not suddenly look upside down to you. In fact, it would not look different at all. Again consider the computer analogy: When a computer stores instructions for what to write on the top and bottom of the page, the instructions for the top of the page do not need to be located physically above those for the bottom of the page.

An area called the **fovea** (meaning *pit*) in the center of the retina is specialized for acute, detailed vision. Because blood vessels and ganglion cell axons are almost absent near the fovea, the fovea has the most unimpeded vision available in the eye. The tight packing of receptors further aids perception of detail. You have heard the expression "eyes like a hawk." One way in which hawks, eagles, and other birds of prey have superior vision is that they have two foveas per eye. Each of their eyes has one fovea pointing ahead

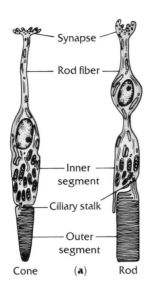

Synapse

Rod fiber

Inner segment

Ciliary stalk

Outer segment

Cone (a) Rod

(b)

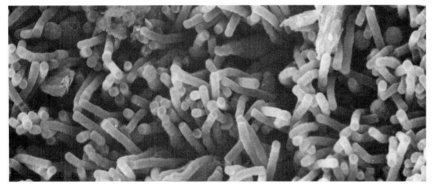

Figure 6-3. (a) Diagram of a cone and a rod. (b) Electron micrograph of human retina. (Courtesy of Dr. M. Gary Wickham.)

and one pointing to the side (Wallman & Pettigrew, 1985). The two foveas enable such birds to perceive detail in their peripheral vision.

Receptor Types in the Retina

The retina contains two types of receptors: **rods** and **cones**. (See Figure 6-3.) Table 6-1 presents the functional distinctions between the two. Note that the cones, which are specialized for color vision, are more sensitive to detail and are located near the center of the retina, whereas the rods are more sensitive to dim light and are found toward the periphery of the retina. These differences are reflected in several aspects of our experience. For detailed vision we try to focus an object on the fovea, where cones are concentrated and acuity is the greatest. To perceive the dimmest lights, such as faint stars in the night sky, we often find it better to look slightly to the side so that the light rays from the target fall outside the fovea.

Table 6-1.   Functional Distinctions Between Rods and Cones

Characteristic	Rods	Cones
Location	*LIGHT* Absent from fovea; increasingly common toward periphery	*DETAIL* More common toward center of the retina
Sensitivity to detail (acuity)	Low because many rods funnel onto a single postsynaptic neuron	Greater because fewer cones funnel onto a single postsynaptic neuron
Sensitivity to dim light	Greater	Lesser
Contribute to color vision?	No	Yes
Species more abundant in	Rodents, other nocturnal animals	Birds, primates

We can see dim lights better in the periphery of the retina for two reasons. One is simply that rods are more sensitive to light than cones are. The second is that near the fovea only a small number of receptors convey input to a given postsynaptic cell, but in the periphery great numbers of rods funnel their input into each postsynaptic cell. That is, in the periphery, the summation of many inputs increases detection of dim light, at the expense of perceiving details.

Because the number of cones decreases toward the periphery of the retina, we are color-blind in the extreme periphery. You can demonstrate this for yourself as follows: Mix several colored pencils behind your back and pick one at random. Hold it behind your head and move it very slowly into your field of vision. If you have normal peripheral vision, you will be just able to detect the presence of the pencil and its brightness at a point where you cannot yet perceive its color.

Chemical Basis for Receptor Excitation

Both rods and cones contain photopigments (chemicals sensitive to light), which consist of the chemical 11-*cis*-retinal (a derivative of vitamin A) bound to proteins called *opsins*. The 11-*cis*-retinal is stable in the dark, but the addition of even a single photon of light is sufficient to convert it to another form, all-*trans*-retinal (Wald, 1968). (The light is absorbed in this process; it does not continue to bounce around in the eye.) Although 11-*cis*-retinal is so sensitive that a single photon is sufficient to activate it, it seldom discharges a false alarm in the absence of light. The average molecule of this chemical has about a 50 percent chance of a spontaneous activation within a thousand years. Because each rod has an estimated 200 billion of these molecules, however, the average rod cell has about one spontaneously active molecule per minute (Yau, Matthews, & Baylor, 1979).

The conversion of 11-*cis*-retinal to all-*trans*-retinal releases energy that decreases the permeability of the receptor's membrane to sodium. (This is the *transduction* process.) The result is a graded hyperpolarization of the receptor—not a depolarization. The greater the light, the greater the hyperpolarization. Ordinarily, even in the dark, the receptor is in a steady state of partial depolarization and is constantly sending inhibitory synaptic transmission to the *bipolar cells*, which are the next cells in the pathway of the visual system. When light hyperpolarizes the receptor, it slows the rate of inhibitory transmission to the bipolars and thereby leads to a net excitation of the bipolars.

COLOR VISION

Color vision may have evolved independently more than once. Insects can distinguish among different wavelengths of light, although their distinctions differ from ours. Fish, too, evolved color vision, perhaps because their survival requires them to perceive contrast in a range of environments. In bluish waters, blue-sensitive cones can detect dark but not light objects. In greenish waters, green-sensitive cones can detect light but not dark objects. A combination of blue- and green-sensitive cones enables fish to perceive patterns under more varied conditions than they could with either type of cone alone (Levine & MacNichol, 1982).

Although the extent of color vision varies widely among vertebrates, at least rudimentary color vision is widespread. Species active during the day, including monkeys and most birds, have many cones and well-developed color vision. Cows, contrary to a somewhat popular opinion, also have good color vision (Dabrowska, Harmata, Lenkiewicz, Schiffer, & Wojtusiak, 1981).

Color vision is based on differential responses of various receptors to light of different wavelengths. The shortest visible wavelengths, about 400 nm (1 nm = 10^{-9} m), are perceived as violet; progressively longer wavelengths are perceived as blue, green, yellow, orange, and red (near 700 nm). (See Color Plate 20.) Discrimination among colors poses some special coding problems for the nervous system. A cell in the visual system, like any other neuron, can vary only its frequency of action potentials or, in a cell that has graded potentials, its membrane polarization. If the cell's response indicates the brightness of the light, then it cannot simultaneously be a code for color. Conversely, if each response indicates a different color, the cell can have no way to signal brightness. The inevitable conclusion is that no one neuron can simultaneously indicate brightness and color; our perceptions must depend on patterns of responses by a number of neurons.

The Young-Helmholtz (Trichromatic) Theory

The **Young-Helmholtz theory** of color vision, also known as the **trichromatic theory**, was first proposed by Thomas Young and later modified by Hermann von Helmholtz, both in the nineteenth century. According to this theory, we perceive color by means of three kinds of cones, with each kind maximally sensitive to a different set of wavelengths. (*Trichromatic* means three colors.) Figure 6-4 shows wavelength-sensitivity functions for three cone types. We can call them the *short-wavelength*, the *medium-wavelength*, and the *long-wavelength* cones. Note that each cone is sensitive to a broad range of wavelengths, not just to a narrow band.

According to the Young-Helmholtz theory, we discriminate among wavelengths by means of the ratio of activity across the three types of cones. That is, light at 500 nm excites the medium-wavelength cone to about 65 percent of its maximum, the long-wavelength receptor to 40 percent of its

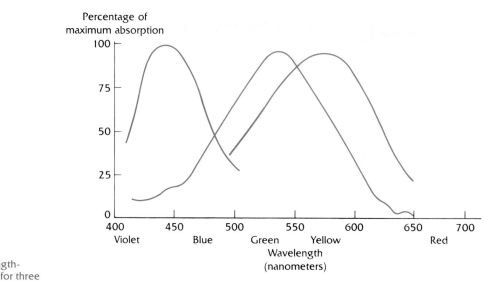

Percentage of
maximum absorption

Figure 6-4. Wavelength-
sensitivity functions for three
cone types.

maximum, and the short-wavelength receptor to 30 percent of its maximum. This ratio of responses among the three cones defines the color perception. Increased intensity of light would increase the activity of all three but would not greatly alter the ratio.

Note that the response of any one neuron is ambiguous. A given response by the middle-wavelength cone might indicate low-intensity 540 nm light, or brighter 500 nm light, or still brighter 460 nm light. The nervous system can determine the color and brightness of the light only by comparing the responses of the three types of cones. A certain degree of color vision would be possible with just two types of cones, but not with just one. Rats, in fact, have just one kind of cone (Neitz & Jacobs, 1986). Although their cones probably enable rats to see better during the day than they would if they had only rods, rats are unable to discriminate between one color and another.

Originally, the Young-Helmholtz theory was based strictly on psychophysical observations, such as the demonstration that all colors can be produced by mixing appropriate amounts of just three wavelengths. Modern methods have clearly established physical differences among three kinds of cones. Although all cones contain the 11-*cis*-retinal, the opsins bound to it are different in the three kinds of cones. The opsins modify the sensitivity of the photopigment to light to produce the three different peaks of wavelength absorption (Wald, 1968).

The Opponent-Process Theory

After the information leaves the cones, it is coded in a manner more consistent with the **opponent-process theory** of Ewald Hering, a nineteenth-century rival of Helmholtz. According to the opponent-process theory, we perceive

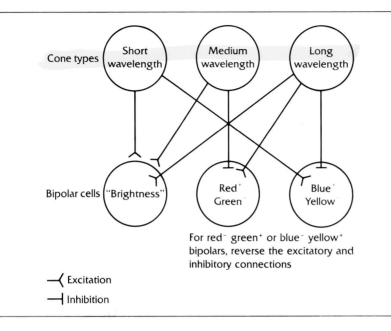

Cone types

For red⁻ green⁺ or blue⁻ yellow⁺ bipolars, reverse the excitatory and inhibitory connections

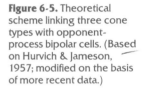

color in terms of three dimensions, white versus black, red versus green, and blue versus yellow; that is, any visual perception could be represented as a point on each of those three dimensions. Hering supported his view with psychophysical observations, such as the phenomenon of color afterimages: If you stare at something yellow for about a minute and then look at a white background, you see blue. Similarly, if you stare at blue, red, or green, you see a yellow, green, or red afterimage, respectively. (See Color Plate 21.) According to Hering, these afterimages represent rebounds away from the fatigued process and toward its opposite (Hurvich & Jameson, 1957).

Beyond the level of the cones, color coding in many neurons in the visual system resembles Hering's opponent processes (DeValois & Jacobs, 1968). Many bipolar cells are excited by green light on the retina and inhibited by red light, or are excited by red light and inhibited by green. Other bipolars are excited by yellow or blue and inhibited by the other.

Although it is not known exactly how the three kinds of cone connect to the bipolar cells, Figure 6-5 illustrates one possibility. Note that the activity of the "red⁺ green⁻" cell depends on the ratio of activity between the medium-wavelength and long-wavelength cones. The long-wavelength cone that excites it is actually more sensitive to yellow light than to red. Yellow light is not the maximum stimulus for the "red⁺ green⁻" cell, however, because yellow light stimulates the medium-wavelength cone as well. Red light produces a greater ratio of response by the long-wavelength cone in comparison to the medium-wavelength cone.

The Retinex Theory

If a room is illuminated with bright red lights, or if you wear red-tinted glasses, your retina will receive mostly red light from all objects in the room.

According to either the Young-Helmholtz theory or the opponent-process theory, you should perceive everything as various shades of red. In fact, however, you continue to perceive greens, yellows, blues—the entire range of colors. You have **color constancy**—the ability to perceive an object as the same color under different lights.

If you then focus on one of those green, yellow, or blue objects in isolation, shutting off all light from surrounding objects, something strange happens: It suddenly looks red! Evidently, color constancy depends on simultaneous contrast between an object and objects of other colors.

To account for this observation, Edwin Land, inventor of the Polaroid Land camera, proposed the **retinex theory**. According to the retinex theory, we perceive color through the combined activities of the retina and the cortex. The cerebral cortex compares the wavelengths of light coming from different parts of the retina at a given time and from that comparison determines a perception of color for each object (Land, Hubel, Livingstone, Perry, & Burns, 1983; Land & McCann, 1971).

Certain areas of the cerebral cortex follow the retinex theory, while others do not. The occipital lobe of the cerebral cortex contains at least four visual areas, known as V1 through V4. Color-sensitive neurons in area V1, located at the extreme occipital pole, change their response depending on the wavelength of light falling on certain parts of the retina. Those cells follow the opponent-process theory. On the other hand, neurons in area V4, located three strips anterior in the occipital cortex, follow the retinex theory. Certain cells there respond to the presence of green objects, others to yellow objects, and so forth. Such cells continue to respond to those objects even if the light falling on the objects is, say, mostly red. The cells' activity depends on the contrast between one area of the retina and another, not just on the wavelengths coming from a given spot on the retina (Zeki, 1980, 1983).

Because of the differences between areas V1 and V4, damage to the two areas can produce different impairments of color vision. After damage to area V1, monkeys have trouble distinguishing one color from another under any circumstances. After damage to area V4, they can learn to distinguish between, say, green and orange patches under normal white light. Having done so, however, the monkeys become confused if the overhead white light is changed to green or red (Wild, Butler, Carden, & Kulikowski, 1985). They have lost their color constancy.

SOMATOSENSATION

The **somatosensory system,** the sensation of the body and its movements, is not one sense but many. We can distinguish discriminative touch (by which we can identify the shape of an object), deep pressure, the sense of position and movement of joints, cold, warmth, pain, and tickling.

The skin is packed with a variety of touch receptors. Figure 6-6 shows some of the major receptor types found in the skin of mammals, and Table 6-2 lists some of their probable functions (Iggo & Andres, 1982). Other receptors, not included on the list, respond to deep stimulation, movement of joints, and movement of muscles.

A touch receptor may consist of a simple bare ending, an elaborated

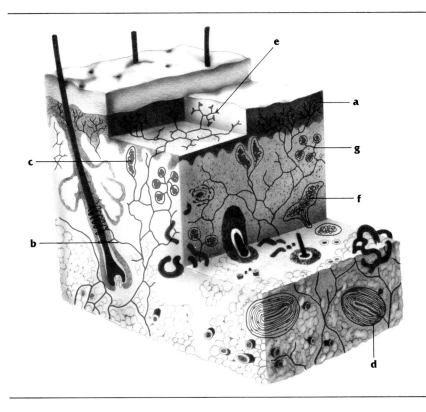

Figure 6-6. Sensory receptors in mammalian skin. (**a**) Free nerve endings; (**b**) hair-follicle receptors; (**c**) Meissner's corpuscles; (**d**) Pacinian corpuscles; (**e**) Merkel's disks; (**f**) Ruffini endings; (**g**) Krause end bulbs. The functions of these receptors are listed in Table 6-2.

Table 6-2.   Touch Receptors and Their Probable Functions

Receptor	Location	Responds to	Rate of adaptation to a prolonged stimulus
Free nerve ending (unmyelinated or thinly myelinated fibers)	?	Pain, warmth, cold (?)	?
Hair-follicle receptors	Hair-covered skin	Movement of hairs	Rapid
Meissner's corpuscles	Hairless areas	Sudden displacement of skin; low-frequency vibration (flutter)	Rapid (?)
Pacinian corpuscles	Both hairy and hairless skin	Sudden displacement of skin; high frequency vibration	Very rapid
Merkel's disks	Both hairy and hairless skin	Indentation of skin	Slow
Ruffini endings	Both hairy and hairless skin	Stretch of skin *Temp.*	Slow
Krause end bulbs	Hairless areas, perhaps including genitals; maybe some hairy areas	? *Temp.*	?

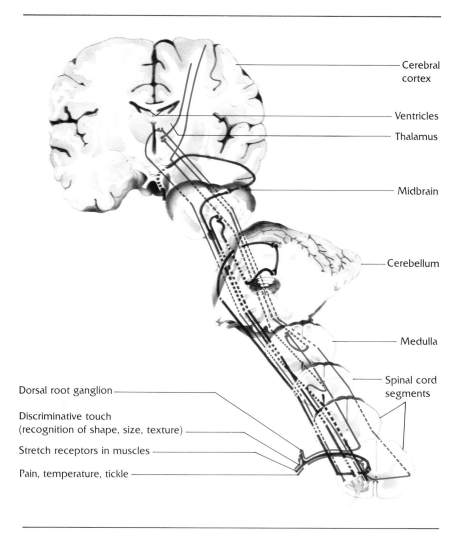

Cerebral cortex

Ventricles

Thalamus

Midbrain

Cerebellum

Medulla

Spinal cord segments

Dorsal root ganglion

Discriminative touch (recognition of shape, size, texture)

Stretch receptors in muscles

Pain, temperature, tickle

Figure 6-7. Some major pathways ascending the spinal cord. Note that all sensory input enters by way of the dorsal roots of the spinal cord and that different kinds of sensory information travel through different pathways. (Based on Braus, 1960.)

neuron ending, or a bare ending surrounded by nonneural cells that modify its function. Some of the more sensitive areas of skin, such as the fingertips, have as many as 700 touch cells in 2 square millimeters of surface. Although different receptor types are believed to be associated with different types of sensation, certain of the receptors are not yet well understood.

Information from the various touch receptors enters the spinal cord and passes toward the brain. Figure 6-7 depicts a few of the major sensory paths. The point of this figure is certainly not for you to try to memorize these paths but merely to demonstrate that different types of sensory information have different routes to the brain. Because of this separation, it is possible for localized damage to disrupt, say, the fine sense of touch without interfering with the sensation of temperature, or vice versa. On the other hand, because pain and temperature are carried in the same path, any injury that impairs one will also impair the other.

Information that travels up different routes in the spinal cord also reaches different parts of the thalamus and cerebral cortex. For example, one area of the thalamus responds to activity of the Pacinian corpuscles. Within that area, different parts respond to different parts of the body. At least three other nearby areas of the thalamus respond to different receptors or combinations of receptors (Dykes, Sur, Merzenich, Kaas, & Nelson, 1981).

The various areas of somatosensory thalamus send their impulses to different areas of the somatosensory cortex, located in the parietal lobe. The somatosensory cortex includes four parallel strips, each of which has its own representation of the entire body (see Chapter 4). Two of the strips respond mostly to touch on the skin; the other two respond mostly to deep pressure and movement of the joints and muscles (Kaas, 1983).

In short, various aspects of somatosensation remain at least partly separate from one another at all levels, from the receptors to the somatosensory area of the cerebral cortex.

HEARING

Hearing can be regarded as a modified touch sensation. The receptors in the ear detect vibration and mechanical distortion, much the way that receptors on the skin do. In fact, many investigators believe that the mammalian ear evolved from the *lateral line system* of fish, a long row of touch receptors on each side of the body.

The human auditory system is sensitive to air vibrations ranging from about 15 to 20 Hz to somewhat less than 20,000 Hz in an average adult. Perception of high pitch decreases with age—preschool children are better than adults at hearing pitches of 20,000 Hz and above (B. A. Schneider, Trehub, Morrongiello, & Thorpe, 1986). For middle-aged adults, the upper limit for hearing decreases by about 80 Hz every six months (von Békésy, 1957). The upper limit drops even faster for those exposed to loud noises.

You may have heard of something called a "Rube Goldberg" device. Rube Goldberg was a cartoonist (1883–1970) who drew enormously complicated inventions to perform simple tasks. For example, a person's tread on the front doorstep would pull a string that raised a cat's tail, awakening the cat, which would then chase a bird that had been resting on a balance, which would swing up to strike a doorbell. The functioning of the ear may remind you a little of a Rube Goldberg device, since sound waves are transduced into action potentials through a many-step, roundabout process. Unlike Rube Goldberg's inventions, however, the ear actually works.

The first step in hearing is the entry of air vibrations into the auditory canal, as shown in Figure 6-8. At the end of the auditory canal, vibrations strike the **tympanic membrane**, or eardrum, which vibrates at the same frequency as the sound waves that strike it. The tympanic membrane is attached to three bones in the middle ear that transmit the vibrations to the *oval window* of the inner ear. These bones are sometimes known by their English names—hammer, anvil, and stirrup—and sometimes by their Latin names—malleus, incus, and stapes. The tympanic membrane has an area about twenty times larger than the footplate of the stirrup. As in a hydraulic

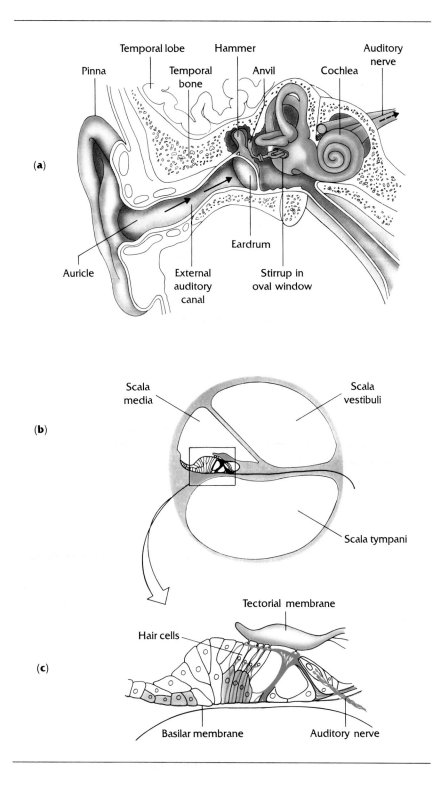

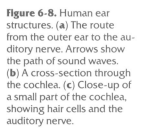

Figure 6-8. Human ear structures. (**a**) The route from the outer ear to the auditory nerve. Arrows show the path of sound waves. (**b**) A cross-section through the cochlea. (**c**) Close-up of a small part of the cochlea, showing hair cells and the auditory nerve.

pump, the vibrations of the tympanic membrane are transformed into more forceful vibrations when they reach the smaller stirrup. The net effect of the system is to convert the air waves into waves of greater pressure on the small oval window. This is important because more force is required to move the viscous fluid inside the oval window than to move the eardrum, which has air on both sides of it.

The sensory receptors for hearing are located in the inner ear in a snail-shaped structure called the **cochlea** (KOCK-lee-uh, Latin for "snail"). A cross-section through the cochlea, as in Figure 6-8 (**b**), shows that it contains three long fluid-filled tunnels, the scala vestibuli, scala media, and scala tympani. The stirrup contacts the oval window at the entrance to the scala vestibuli, from where vibrations are transmitted to the rest of the cochlea. When the vibrations reach the **basilar membrane**, which forms the floor of the scala media, they displace the **hair cells** that lie along the basilar membrane (Figure 6-8c). As the scala media is pushed up and down by the pressure waves, the hair cells are bent between the tectorial and basilar membranes. The hair cells respond within microseconds to a displacement as small as the diameter of one atom, thereby stimulating action potentials in the auditory nerve, the eighth cranial nerve (Hudspeth, 1985). Figure 6-9 shows electron micrographs of the hair cells of three species.

Pitch Perception

Our ability to understand speech or to enjoy music depends on our ability to differentiate among sounds of different pitches, even when the sounds are presented for brief periods in rapid succession. How do we do so?

According to one early theory, the **frequency theory**, the basilar membrane vibrates in synchrony with a sound and causes hair cells to produce action potentials at the same frequency. For example, a sound at 500 Hz would cause 500 action potentials per second in the auditory nerve. The downfall of this theory in its simplest form is that humans can distinguish pitches up to 20,000 Hz, and the refractory period of neurons would prevent any cell from approaching that rate of firing. In fact, few neurons can sustain a firing rate of more than 200 to 300 action potentials per second.

According to the **place theory**, an alternative proposed by Hermann von Helmholtz, the basilar membrane is like the strings of a piano: Each portion along the membrane is tuned to a specific pitch and vibrates whenever that pitch is present. Thus, according to this theory, a sound at any pitch activates the hair cells at only one place along the basilar membrane. The nervous system distinguishes among pitches on the basis of which neurons are activated. The downfall of this theory in its original form is that no portion of the basilar membrane has physical properties like those that cause a piano string to resonate to a tone. Moreover, the various parts of the basilar membrane are bound together, so no one part could resonate without carrying neighboring parts with it.

According to the currently prevalent theory (Corso, 1973; Gulick, 1971), the mechanism for discriminating pitch is different for low pitches than for high pitches. For low-pitched sounds (up to about 100 Hz), the

Figure 6-9. Hair cells from a frog sacculus (**a, b**), an organ that detects ground-borne vibrations; the cochlea of a cat (**c**); and the cochlea of a fence lizard (**d**). Kc = kinocilium, one of the components of a hair bundle. (From Hudspeth, 1985.)

frequency theory seems to apply. The basilar membrane vibrates in synchrony with the sound waves, and hair cells generate one action potential per wave. Weak sounds activate only a small number of hair cells, while stronger sounds activate greater numbers. Thus, at low pitches the frequency of impulses identifies the pitch and the number of cells firing identifies the loudness.

For pitches near 100 Hz or higher, a given neuron cannot fire at the same rate as the frequency of the sound waves. A neuron may nevertheless produce action potentials phase-locked to the peaks of the sound waves (that is, always occurring at the same phase in the sound wave), as illustrated here:

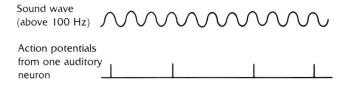

Additional auditory neurons also produce action potentials phase-locked with peaks of the sound wave but not necessarily in phase with the action potentials of the first neuron:

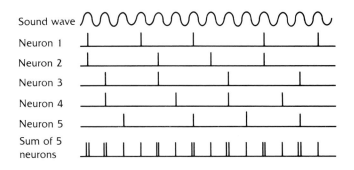

If we consider the auditory nerve as a whole, including a large number of individual fibers, we find that each wave of sound produces a *volley* of impulses by various fibers; that is, at least a few neurons fire synchronously with each wave in, say, a 600 Hz tone. Although no individual fiber can produce impulses at a rate of 600 per second, the auditory nerve as a whole can have volleys of impulses at 600 per second. This is referred to as the **volley principle** of pitch discrimination (Rose, Brugge, Anderson, & Hind, 1967).

(Do such volleys really contribute to pitch perception? Investigators can indeed demonstrate volleys of impulses, and they generally assume that any information produced by neurons, the brain can use. In this case, however, we must admit that we do not know how the brain uses the volleys, if it does. How does a structure somewhere in the brain "read" the impulses across many neurons to detect a volley?)

At some tone near 5,000 Hz even the volley principle becomes inadequate, as even staggered volleys of impulses cannot keep pace with the sound waves. Before this point is reached, however, another mechanism comes into play, similar to the mechanism postulated by the place theory.

The basilar membrane is thin (about 0.15 mm) and stiff at one end of the cochlea, the **base**, where the stirrup meets the cochlea. It is wider (0.5 mm) and only one-hundredth as stiff at the other end of the cochlea, the **apex** (von Békésy, 1956; Yost & Nielsen, 1977). (See Figure 6-10.) It may seem surprising that the basilar membrane is thinnest at the base, where the cochlea itself is widest. The difference is made up of a bony shelf that attaches to the basilar membrane. When a vibration strikes the basilar membrane, it

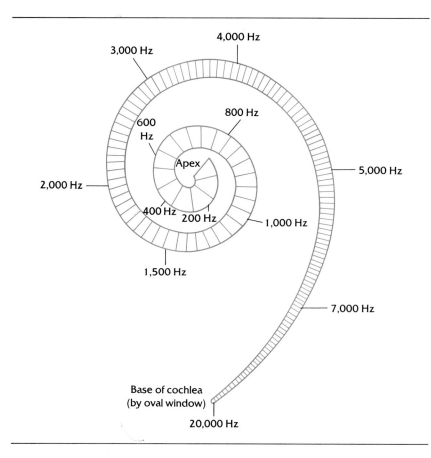

Figure 6-10. The basilar membrane of the human cochlea. High-pitched sounds produce their maximum displacement near the base. Low-pitched sounds produce their maximum displacement near the apex.

sets up a *traveling wave*. As the wave travels along the membrane, it produces some displacement at all points, but the amount of displacement varies because of variations in the thickness and stiffness of the membrane.

Vibrations at different frequencies set up traveling waves that peak at different points along the basilar membrane, as shown in Figures 6-10 and 6-11. The traveling wave for a low-frequency vibration peaks at or near the apex, where the membrane is large and floppy. For progressively higher frequencies, the point of maximum displacement gets closer to the base. In fact, the highest frequencies produce practically no displacment of the membrane near the apex. The waveforms in Figure 6-11 are drawn fairly broadly, in order to be easily visible. In healthy tissues, however, the waves are sharply defined, falling rapidly on both sides of the maximum displacement (Zwislocki, 1981).

To summarize, we identify the lowest pitches by means of the frequency of impulses. We discriminate among high pitches in terms of the place along the basilar membrane at which the receptors show their greatest activity; the higher the pitch, the closer the maximum displacement to the base of the cochlea. We discriminate intermediate pitches (about 60 to 5,000 Hz) through a combination of frequency (perhaps aided by the volley principle) and place.

Varieties of Deafness

Complete deafness is rare. About 99 percent of deaf people can hear at least certain pitches if they are loud enough. We distinguish two categories of hearing impairment, nerve deafness and conductive deafness.

Nerve Deafness. **Nerve deafness,** or **inner-ear deafness,** results from damage to the cochlea, the hair cells, or the auditory nerve. The damage can occur in any degree. It is possible for the damage to be confined to one part of the cochlea or to neurons in one part of the cochlea. The result is an impairment in hearing pitches in one range of frequencies—most often the high frequencies. Although nerve deafness is permanent, hearing aids can compensate for the loss.

Some degree of nerve deafness is common in old age (Corso, 1985). Nerve deafness can come about in young people as a result of heredity, exposure of one's mother to rubella (German measles) during pregnancy, certain diseases including multiple sclerosis, and prolonged exposure to loud noises.

Conductive Deafness. **Conductive deafness,** or **middle-ear deafness,** occurs if the bones of the middle ear do not transmit sound waves properly to the cochlea. Such deafness can be caused by certain diseases and infections or by a tumorous growth of bones in and around the middle ear. Conductive deafness is sometimes temporary. If it persists, it can sometimes be corrected by surgery.

Because people with conductive deafness have a normal cochlea and auditory nerve, they can hear sounds that bypass the middle ear. For example, they can hear their own voices, which can be conducted through the bones of the skull directly to the cochlea.

Localization of Sounds

Determining the direction and distance of a sound is not a simple process. Unlike touch, for which receptors are spread over the whole body, or even vision, in which each eye has receptors focused on separate points in space, audition requires a comparison between the two ears—which are in effect just two points in space—to locate the sources of stimuli. And yet this system can be made accurate enough for owls to hunt mice on dark nights, solely by their sounds, identifying not only the left-right direction of a sound source but its elevation as well (Knudsen & Konishi, 1978).

Information from the two ears progresses through several stages on the way to the brain, as illustrated in Figure 6-12. Virtually all aspects of the auditory system, from the external ear to the auditory cortex, show adaptations that facilitate the localization of sounds.

Two methods are used for sound localization (Yost & Nielsen, 1977). The first is the difference in loudness between the two ears. The head impedes the passage of sound waves, especially if the wavelength is shorter than the width of the head; that is, for short-wavelength (high-frequency) sounds, the head creates a *sound shadow* (Figure 6-13). Consequently, the sound is

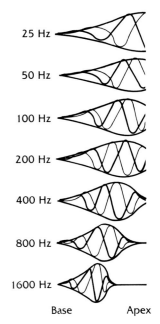

25 Hz

50 Hz

100 Hz

200 Hz

400 Hz

800 Hz

1600 Hz

Base   Apex

Figure 6-11. Traveling waves in the basilar membrane set up by different frequencies of sound. Note that the peak displacement is closer to the base of the cochlea for high pitches and is toward the apex for lower pitches.

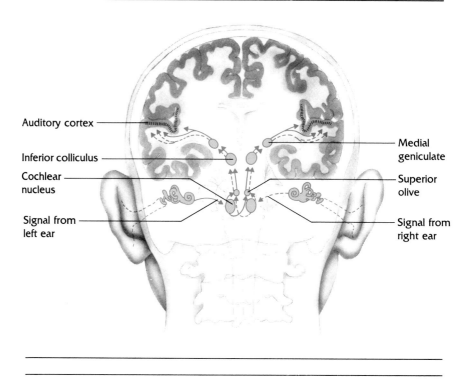

Auditory cortex

Inferior colliculus

Cochlear
nucleus

Signal from
left ear

Medial
geniculate

Superior
olive

Signal from
right ear

Figure 6-12. Route of auditory impulses from the receptors in the ear to the auditory cortex. The cochlear nucleus receives input from only the ipsilateral ear. All later stages have input originating from both ears.

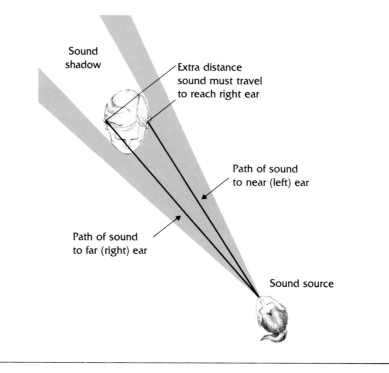

Sound
shadow

Extra distance
sound must travel
to reach right ear

Path of sound
to near (left) ear

Path of sound
to far (right) ear

Sound source

Figure 6-13. Differential loudness as a cue for sound localization. The sound shadow shown does not include the effects of diffraction or "bending" of sound waves around the head. (After Lindsay & Norman, 1972.)

Recordings over time for:

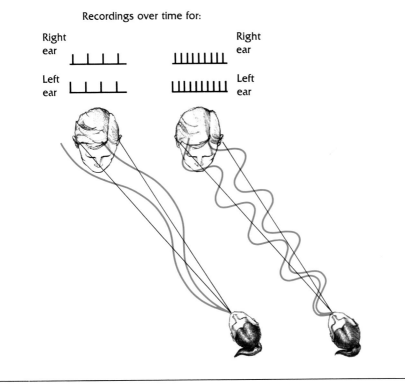

Right
ear

Left
ear

Right
ear

Left
ear

Figure 6-14. Phase differences between the ears as a cue for sound localization. Note that low pitches arrive at the ears only slightly out of phase. The ear for which the receptors fire first (here, the left one) is interpreted as being closer to the sound. The greater the difference between the ears, the farther the sound must be to the side. However, with higher-pitched sounds, as in the right part of the figure, the phase differences become too large to be useful, as it is ambiguous whether the sound wave in one ear is half a cycle ahead of the other ear or half a cycle behind.

louder for the closer ear. In adults, this mechanism produces accurate sound localization for pitches above 3,000 Hz and progressively less accurate localization for lower pitches.

The second method of localization is the *phase difference* for sound waves arriving at the two ears. Figure 6-14 shows that when sound waves travel farther to reach one ear than the other, they reach the two ears at slightly different times and thus are slightly out of phase. For low-frequency sounds (Figure 6-14, *left*) the phase differences are detectable and unambiguous; receptors in the ear closer to the sound source fire slightly ahead of those in the farther ear, for each sound wave. At higher frequencies (Figure 6-14, *right*) the waves may be out of phase by half a cycle or more by the time they reach the ears. It is then ambiguous whether receptors in the left ear are firing before or after those in the right. Phase differences provide accurate localization for sounds less than about 1,500 Hz but not for higher pitches.

In short, humans localize low pitches (up to 1,500 Hz) by phase differences between the ears and high pitches (above 3,000 Hz) by intensity differences. Humans have trouble localizing intermediate pitches accurately.

The usefulness of both methods of localization depends on the size of the head. For a small species such as the mouse, the ears are so close together that the animal cannot detect phase differences between sounds even at low pitches. Small animals therefore have trouble localizing low-pitched tones; large animals are more successful.

For higher-pitched tones, the head produces a strong sound shadow for sounds with wavelengths less than the width of the head. The smaller the head, the shorter the wavelength has to be for the animal to localize it by a difference in loudness. In other words, the smaller the animal, the higher the frequency has to be for loudness to be a cue to direction. Thus, small-headed species such as mice cannot use phase differences for localization at all and can use loudness differences only for higher pitches than humans can.

During the course of evolution, each species seems to have evolved a sensitivity to those pitches that it can easily localize. Rodents and other small animals are less sensitive to low-pitched sounds than humans are, but they are more sensitive to higher pitches, up to 40,000, 60,000, or even 100,000 Hz. The hearing range of larger mammals is shifted toward lower pitches. The upper limit for elephants is just 10,000 Hz (Heffner & Heffner, 1982). These findings underscore the point made at the beginning of this chapter: Each species is most sensitive to the information that is most useful to it.

The two methods of sound localization depend on different brain structures. Localization based on loudness depends on the lateral part of the superior olive (in the medulla); localization based on phase differences depends on the medial part. Small-headed species, such as the mouse, which cannot use phase differences to localize sound, have no medial superior olive at all; they have just the lateral superior olive (Masterton, 1974).

VESTIBULAR SENSATION

The sense of balance is controlled in part by **vestibular sensation.** (Vision and touch also contribute.) Vestibular sensation arises from a set of structures in the inner ear immediately adjacent to the cochlea. (See Figure 6-15.) The vestibular system consists of two **otolith** organs and three **semicircular canals** (Parker, 1980). Although we seldom pay much attention to vestibular sensation, it plays an important role in balance and coordination of movement.

Like the hearing receptors, the vestibular receptors are touch receptors modified to detect a specialized stimulus. One of the otoliths has a horizontal patch of hairs; the other has a vertical patch. Calcium particles lie next to the hair cells of the otoliths. When the head tilts in different directions, the calcium particles push against different sets of hair cells and excite them.

The three semicircular canals are oriented in three different planes. These canals also contain hair cells. A movement of the head in any possible direction excites a different population of hair cells in the canals. Action potentials initiated by cells of the vestibular system travel via part of the eighth cranial nerve to the brainstem and cerebellum.

OLFACTION

Vision depends on four distinguishable types of receptors—rods and three kinds of cones. Touch also depends on distinct receptor types. Hearing does not. All the hair cells along the basilar membrane are physically the same as

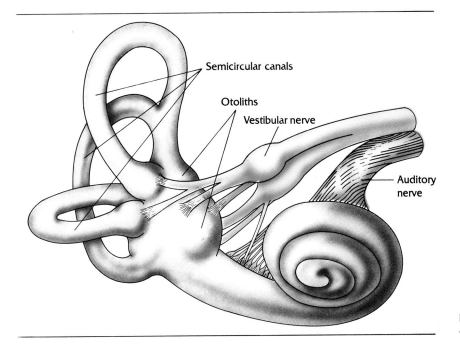

Semicircular canals

Otoliths

Vestibular nerve

Auditory nerve

Figure 6-15. The vestibular apparatus.

one another; they vary in their responses only because the membrane attached to them varies in its stiffness. Moreover, the hair cells do not fall into any discrete categories based on their responses. Rather, they form a continuum from those responsive to the lowest pitches to those responsive to the highest pitches.

What about olfaction and taste? Do our chemical receptors fall into a few distinct categories, like those of vision and touch? Or do they form a continuum of properties, like the receptors for hearing? To this point, the answers to those questions remain controversial.

The receptors for smell are the **olfactory cells** that line the olfactory epithelium in the rear of the nasal air passages. (See Figure 6-16). The olfactory receptors are regarded as relatively primitive neurons. They maintain some of the primitive properties of the "all-purpose chemical receptors" that cover the entire skin surface of sea anemones (Parker, 1922).

In mammals, each olfactory cell has cilia (threadlike structures) that extend from the cell body into the moist surface of the nasal passage (Getchell, Margolis, & Getchell, 1985). An axon stretches from the other end of the cell body to the olfactory bulb, from which connections extend to the cerebral cortex, hippocampus, amygdala, and hypothalamus (Scalia & Winans, 1976). In most mammalian species, olfaction is critical for sexual arousal, which is partly under the control of the hypothalamus (see Digression 6-1).

The Labeled-Line Theory of Olfaction
According to one theory of olfaction, the **labeled-line theory of olfaction,** olfactory receptors fall into a few distinct types. According to this theory,

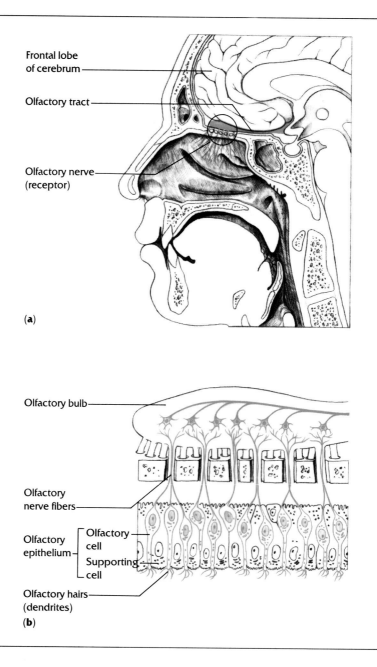

Frontal lobe
of cerebrum

Olfactory tract

Olfactory nerve
(receptor)

(a)

Olfactory bulb

Olfactory
nerve fibers

Olfactory
epithelium — Olfactory
cell
Supporting
cell

Olfactory hairs
(dendrites)

(b)

Figure 6-16. Olfactory receptors. (**a**) Location of receptors in nasal cavity. (**b**) Closeup of olfactory cells.

each odorous chemical fits into one and probably only one receptor site, in a lock-and-key fashion (Amoore, 1963). Once a receptor is excited, it sends a message that represents a specific odor. In other words, olfaction is a response to a few primary odors. All other, nonprimary odors are simply combinations of primary odors.

If so, how many primary odors are there, and how can we identify them? One way would be to demonstrate that all human olfactory experiences can

6-1
Pheromones

A **pheromone** is an odorous chemical released by one animal that induces a change in the behavior of another animal. Most mammalian species use pheromones in sexual attraction; they can determine from another animal's smell whether it is a male, a female in estrus, or a female not in estrus. Pheromones can also produce longer-lasting effects (Bronson, 1974): The odor of a group of female mice can stop another female mouse's estrous cycles, and the odor of a male can restore the estrous cycle. However, just after the female becomes pregnant, the odor of an unfamiliar male can cause her to abort.

Do humans secrete and respond to pheromones? Many women produce vaginal secretions containing fatty acids similar to the sex pheromones of monkeys. They release the fatty acids in the greatest quantity at about the middle of the menstrual cycle, when estrogen levels are highest and the probability of becoming pregnant is highest.

The fact that women produce such chemicals does not necessarily indicate that either men or women respond to them, however. No evidence to this point has shown any significant response by men. A possible effect on other women relates to the timing of menstrual cycles. Many of the women who live together in a college dormitory gradually synchronize their menstrual cycles, unless they are taking birth control pills. (Why this happens, no one knows. Females of other species do not typically synchronize their cycles.) To test whether pheromones are responsible for the synchronization, Russell, Switz, & Thompson (1980) exposed volunteer women to the underarm odor of a donor woman who was selected because she had regular 28-day cycles and did not shave her underarms or use deodorants. A swab of her underarm secretions was applied to the upper lip of each recipient woman three times a week. Recipients were instructed not to wipe it off for at least 3 hours. As you might expect, this experiment had a high drop out rate; six of the eleven volunteers quit the study. Of the five who completed it, four became synchronized to the donor woman's menstrual cycles.

be matched by mixtures of a few odorous chemicals. Those chemicals would then be good candidates as the primary odors. No one has accomplished this feat, however. Another approach has been to study specific anosmias. **Anosmia** is a loss of olfaction; a **specific anosmia** is a loss of the ability to smell a specific chemical. For example, Amoore (1967) demonstrated that about 2 to 3 percent of all people are insensitive to the smell of isobutyric acid, the smelly component of sweat. Because it is possible to lose the ability to smell just this one chemical, there must be a receptor specific to isobutryric acid. Amoore (1977) has also found specific anosmias for five other odors, which he has labeled musky, fishy, urinous, spermous, and malty. Although evidence is less firm, twenty-six other odors have emerged as possible specific anosmias. If this approach is valid, the number of primary odors must be fairly large.

The Across-Fiber Pattern Theory of Olfaction

The alternative to the labeled-line theory is the **across-fiber pattern theory of olfaction**. According to this theory, olfactory receptors need not fall into any limited number of categories and no odor is more primary than any other. Rather, all receptors contribute to the identification of all odors. Each odor gives rise to a unique pattern of activity across all the fibers and is recognized by that pattern.

Recordings from olfactory receptors have indicated that each receptor does respond to a great many chemicals, that most odorous chemicals excite large populations of olfactory receptors, and that the pattern across cells is different for each odor (Moulton, 1976; Tanabe, Iino, & Takagi, 1975). On the other hand, it would be going too far to say that all receptors contribute equally to the identification of all odors. Most odorous chemicals give rise to a greater level of activity by receptors in one area of the nasal passages than in others. Furthermore, chemicals that smell similar to each other produce their greatest excitation in overlapping areas (Laing, 1984).

Variations in Olfactory Sensitivity

People who have an impairment of the sense of smell are less noticeable than those who have impairments of vision or hearing. This impairment can cause a loss of pleasure, however, particularly in the enjoyment of eating. Although humans rely on olfaction less than most other mammals, the sense of smell is more important to us than we sometimes realize.

Olfaction can be impaired at least briefly by a number of medical conditions, including vitamin B_{12} deficiency. A loss of olfaction is a common, if often unreported, side effect of many drugs used in medicine (Schiffman, 1983). Olfactory sensitivity also declines in old age. The minimum concentration of an odorant that older people (in their 80s) can detect is about four times as high as the minimum that college students can detect (Schiffman, Moss, & Erickson, 1976). Older people also have more trouble discriminating one odor from another (Schiffman & Pasternak, 1979).

TASTE

Taste is commonly believed, on the basis of little evidence, to be a relatively simple sense, producing only four experiences: sweet, sour, salty, and bitter. If so, we might expect taste to be well understood by now, especially since the taste receptors are much more accessible to investigation than the receptors for vision and hearing. But in fact, many of the most basic questions about taste remain unanswered.

The receptors for taste are not true neurons but modified skin cells. The relationship of taste receptors to skin cells is particularly evident in fish, which have taste receptors scattered over their entire body surface, from nose to tail (Bardach & Villars, 1974). Mammalian taste receptors are located in **taste buds**, located in **papillae**, or folds on the surface of the tongue (see Figure 6-17 and Color Plate 17). A given papilla may contain any number of taste buds from none to ten or more (Arvidson & Friberg, 1980), and each taste bud contains about fifty receptor cells. Each of the neurons carrying impulses from the taste bud receives synaptic contacts from a number of receptors (Altner, 1978).

Taste Receptors

It is not known exactly how many types of taste receptors exist on the tongue. We do know a certain amount about a receptor for salty tastes, and we have reason to believe at least two kinds of sweetness receptors exist. Additional receptors must exist as well, although we do not know how many.

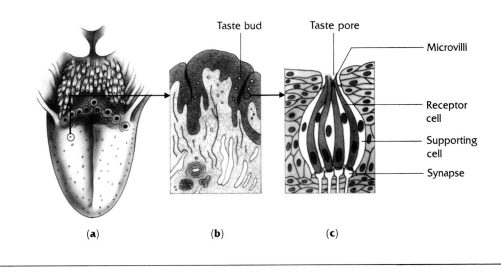

(a)   (b)   (c)

Taste bud   Taste pore

— Microvilli

— Receptor cell

— Supporting cell

— Synapse

Figure 6-17. (a) Upper surface of the tongue. (b) Enlargement showing taste buds on a papilla. (c) Enlarged section through a taste bud.

The receptors for salty tastes operate on a simple principle. Recall that a neuron produces an action potential when sodium ions cross its membrane. A saltiness receptor cell, which detects the presence of sodium, does not need a specialized membrane site sensitive to sodium. It simply permits sodium ions on the tongue to cross its membrane. The higher the concentration of sodium on the tongue, the greater the response of this receptor. Chemicals such as amiloride, which prevents sodium from crossing the membrane, reduce the intensity of salty tastes (Desimone, Heck, Mierson, & Desimone, 1984; Schiffman, Lockhead, & Maes, 1983). The chemical bretylium tosylate, which facilitates the passage of sodium across the membrane, intensifies salty tastes (Schiffman, Simon, Gill, & Beeker, 1986).

We know that sweetness receptors are distinct from other receptors, because certain chemicals can alter the response of sweetness receptors without affecting other taste receptors (see Digression 6-2). Humans evidently have at least two types of sweetness receptors—one for such substances as sucrose that have only a sweet taste, and one for such substances as saccharin that have both a sweet and a bitter taste. Preexposure to caffeine enhances both the sweetness and the bitterness of saccharin without affecting the purely sweet taste of sucrose or the purely bitter taste of quinine. Preexposure to adenosine decreases both components of the saccharin taste, again without affecting either sucrose or quinine (Schiffman, Diaz, & Beeker, 1986). Moreover, preexposure of the tongue to sucrose decreases its later response to other sweet tastes, and preexposure to quinine decreases its response to other bitter tastes, but neither one decreases the response to combined sweet-bitter substances (Birch & Mylvaganam, 1976). Evidently saccharin and similar chemicals excite a special sweet-bitter receptor that is different from the receptors that sucrose and quinine excite. Additional sweetness receptors may exist as well (Schiffman, Reilly, & Clark, 1979).

DIGRESSION

6-2

Miracle Berries and the Modification of Taste Receptors

Although the **miracle berry**, a plant native to West Africa, is practically tasteless, it temporarily changes the taste of other substances. Miracle berries contain a protein, **miraculin**, that modifies sweet receptors in such a way that they can be stimulated by acids (Bartoshuk, Gentile, Moskowitz, & Meiselman, 1974). For about half an hour after exposing one's tongue to miracle berries, all acids (which are normally sour) taste sweet. They continue to taste sour as well.

Miraculin was, for a time, commercially available in the United States as a diet aid. The idea was that dieters could coat their tongue with a miraculin pill and then eat and drink unsweetened, slightly acidic substances. Such substances would taste sweet without providing many calories.

A colleague and I once spent an evening ex-

perimenting with miracle berries. We drank straight lemon juice, sauerkraut juice, even vinegar. All tasted extremely sweet. Somehow we forgot how acidic these substances still were. We awoke the next day to find our mouths full of ulcers.

Other taste-modifying substances include an extract from the plant *Gymnema sylvestre* that makes people temporarily insensitive to both sweet and bitter tastes (Bartoshuk et al., 1974), and the chemical theophylline, which reduces sensitivity to certain bitter tastes, or at least decreases rejection of them (Kodama, Fukushima, & Sakata). After eating artichokes, some people report a sweet taste from water (Bartoshuk, Lee, & Scarpellino, 1972). Sodium lauryl sulfate, a constituent of toothpaste, intensifies sour and bitter tastes while weakening sweet tastes (Schiffman, 1983). For that reason, orange juice and similar juices taste unpleasant shortly after one uses toothpaste.

BIOSKETCH

6-1

Susan S. Schiffman

Taste and olfaction are areas of knowledge in which some long-accepted views have been called into question. Susan Schiffman has been one of the contributors to the intellectual ferment in this area.

Born in Chicago, Susan Stolte Schiffman received a B.S. degree from Syracuse University and a Ph.D. in psychology from Duke University in 1970. After two years of postdoctoral study at the Center for the Study of Aging in the Duke Medical Center, she joined the Duke Psychiatry Department.

For many years, theorists had held that the sense of taste was based on four primaries (sweet, sour, salty, and bitter) and that smell was based on perhaps seven primary odors. Schiffman began to analyze these senses in a different way, looking for continuous dimensions underlying taste and smell rather than primaries. "The chemical senses are a good research topic," she has said, "because they offer an opportunity to bring together knowledge from many disciplines—chemistry, physics, biology, mathematics, and psychology."

Schiffman has combined her basic science research with an interest in practical applications. Her research has branched out to include taste and smell abnormalities in old age and in obesity,

methods for combating obesity, a search for new nonfattening sweeteners, and the properties of the receptors for sweet and salty tastes. Much of her research has been conducted in cooperation with cereal and perfume manufacturers and other industries. "I have learned as much from outside academia as from within," she says. "Many industrial firms have great research equipment and the money to apply to a problem. For instance, for some of my odor studies I needed extremely pure, highly expensive chemicals. The cost would be prohibitive in a university laboratory, even with a large research grant. But industrial firms are willing to support the research if the information might help develop products that they can market."

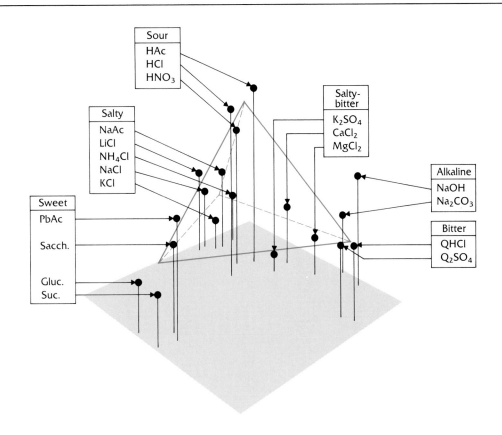

Figure 6-18. Representation of taste stimuli based on judgments of similarity among tastes. The greater the distance between points, the greater is the difference in taste. (From Schiffman & Erickson, 1971.)

How many other types of taste receptors are there? One way to find out how many types to look for is to learn more about how people categorize taste experiences. If, for example, they describe all tastes as mixtures of four basic tastes, then four types of taste receptors should be sufficient.

Susan Schiffman (see BioSketch 6-1) asked people to taste a large number of compounds and to describe the similarity between each pair, using a rating scale. From the similarity ratings, a computer was used to plot out a spatial representation of all the stimuli, such that the more similar the tastes of two stimuli, the closer they were to each other on the plot. Beginning mostly with stimuli described as sweet, sour, salty, or bitter, Schiffman found the distribution shown in Figure 6-18. Note that sweet, sour, salty, and bitter substances fell at the four points of a tetrahedron. Two alkaline substances fell outside the tetrahedron, however. In later research, Schiffman found other substances that fell well outside the tetrahedron, including monosodium glutamate, sodium succinate, and certain amino acids and dipeptides (Schiffman & Erickson, 1980; Schiffman, McElroy, & Erickson, 1980). Many people reported difficulty finding words to describe those tastes. In short, four receptors may not be enough to account for all taste experiences.

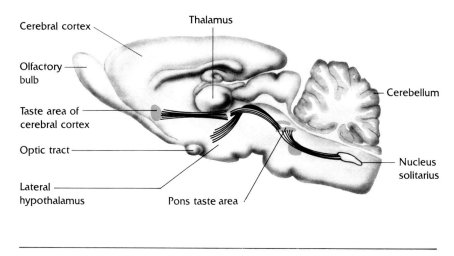

Figure 6-19. Major routes of impulses related to the sense of taste in the rat brain, beginning in the tract from the nucleus solitarius. The thalamus and cerebral cortex receive impulses from both left and right sides of the tongue. This figure represents a unilateral schema of a bilateral system. (After Pfaffmann, Norgren, & Grill, 1977.)

The Route of Taste Information from the Tongue to the Cortex

Information from the receptors in the anterior two-thirds of the tongue is carried to the brain along the chorda tympani, a branch of the seventh cranial nerve (the facial nerve). Taste information from the posterior tongue and the throat is carried along branches of the ninth and tenth cranial nerves. Those three nerves project to different parts of the **nucleus solitarius** in the medulla (Travers, Pfaffmann, & Norgren, 1986). From the nucleus solitarius, information branches out, reaching (among other areas) the pons, the lateral hypothalamus, the amygdala, part of the thalamus, and two areas of the cerebral cortex, one of which is responsible for taste and one of which is responsible for the sense of touch on the tongue (Pritchard, Hamilton, Morse, & Norgren, 1986; Yamamoto, 1984). Figure 6-19 diagrams a few of these major connections for the rat brain.

The various taste areas of the brain contribute to behavior in different ways. The hypothalamus apparently relates taste to hunger and satiety. Hypothalamic cells respond more vigorously to a taste when the animal is hungry. Their response to the taste of a particular food declines especially after the animal has just eaten a fair amount of that food (Rolls, Murzi, Yaxley, Thorpe, & Simpson, 1986). The decline may be responsible for *sensory specific satiety*—the tendency to get satiated on a food one has just eaten and to prefer to switch to something else.

After damage to the taste areas of the thalamus or the cerebral cortex, animals maintain their normal taste preferences but they forget aversions they have learned because of previous pairings of tastes with illness (Kiefer, Leach, & Braun, 1984; Lasiter, Deems, & Glanzman, 1985). Evidently, the thalamus and cerebral cortex contribute to learning about tastes.

In contrast, the nucleus solitarius apparently participates directly in only the identification of tastes. Its responses do not vary depending on hunger or previous learning (Yaxley, Rolls, Sienkiewicz, & Scott, 1985).

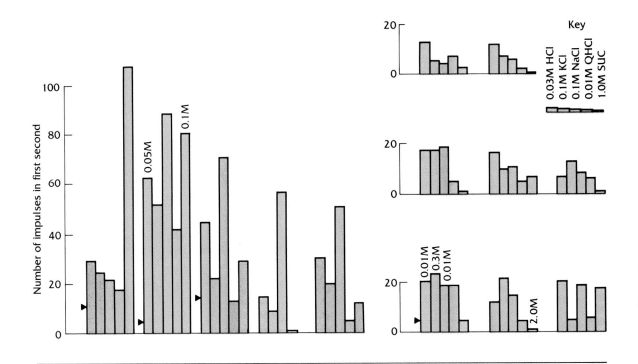

Figure 6-20. The response of single neurons in rats' nucleus solitarius (in impulses per second) during the first second after stimuli were applied to the tongue. Small triangles indicate spontaneous activity. (From Erickson, 1963.)

The Coding of Taste Information

Different receptors are specialized to respond to salty, sweet, sweet-bitter, bitter, sour, and possibly other substances. According to the **labeled-line theory of taste**, each type of receptor has its own route to the brain. That is, each axon carries information about just one of the primary tastes, and each neuron anywhere in the brain's taste system is also coded to respond to just one of the primary tastes. Support for this theory comes from demonstrations that most taste-sensitive neurons respond better to one taste than to others (Pfaffmann, Frank, & Norgren, 1979; Smith, Van Buskirk, Travers, & Bieber, 1983a). It is possible to identify neurons as salty-best, sweet-best, and so forth.

Although each neuron responds best to one taste, most taste neurons respond *somewhat* to all tastes, including salty, sweet, sour, and bitter (Scott & Perrotto, 1980; Yamamoto, Yuyama, Kato, & Kawamura, 1985). Furthermore, the taste neurons do not seem to fall into any small number of types. Figure 6-20 shows the response of thirteen taste neurons to five stimuli on the tongue: hydrochloric acid (HCl), potassium chloride (KCl), sodium chloride (NaCl), quinine hydrochloride (QHCl), and sucrose (SUC). Note that neurons with the same preferred stimulus differ from one another in how they respond to the other four stimuli. If we categorize these cells simply as "salty-best," "sweet-best," and so forth, we overlook some major differences among the cells within each group (Erickson, 1963; Scott, Yaxley, Sienkiewicz, & Rolls, 1986; Woolston & Erickson, 1979).

As in the case of olfaction, there is an **across-fiber pattern theory of taste** that contrasts with the labeled-line theory. According to the across-fiber pattern theory, each taste evokes a unique pattern of responses across all the neurons in any given taste-sensitive part of the brain. In other words, a given level of response by a given cell means nothing except in the context of what other cells are doing, just as the meaning of the letter *h* depends on its context.

The difference between the labeled-line theory and the across-fiber pattern theory is subtle. Both theories agree, for example, that the cells that respond best to NaCl respond somewhat to sucrose also. The issue is whether their response to sucrose contributes in any way to the sweet taste of sucrose. The labeled-line theory says no: Sweetness depend only on the response of sweet-best cells. The across-fiber pattern theory says yes: All cells contribute to all tastes.

A middle position may be possible. Scott and Chang (1984) have suggested that the sweet-best cells contribute to all taste sensations but that they contribute to sweet tastes more than to others. That is, if we could somehow eliminate all the sweet-best cells, we would impair sweet tastes more than other tastes (Smith, VanBuskirk, Travers, & Bieber, 1983b).

PAIN

Pain is a sensation with strong motivational properties. Actually, we should distinguish several kinds of pain, including mechanically induced pain, chemically induced pain, intense heat, and intense cold (LaMotte & Collins, 1982). The perceived intensity of pain varies from person to person and from time to time, even if the actual intensity of the stimulus is the same (Liebeskind & Paul, 1977). For example, some soldiers and athletes report little pain from serious injuries; occasionally they do not even notice an injury until the action is over. Other people report far more severe pain than their injuries seem to justify.

Unmyelinated axons and some thinly myelinated axons carry pain information to the spinal cord, releasing a synaptic transmitter known as **substance P** to the neurons they contact in the spinal cord. The spinal cord neurons in turn send their information up two spinal pathways to the ventrobasal nucleus of the thalamus (Tasker, 1976), which in turn sends information to the somatosensory cortex. Substance P is the probable synaptic transmitter for these synapses in the brain, too.

Relieving Pain by Depleting Its Synaptic Transmitter

Pain serves an important function in alerting us to an injury. Rare individuals who are born with a defective sense of pain run the risk of injury from cuts and burns because they do not immediately pull away from stimuli that cause pain in others. Prolonged and severe pain, on the other hand, ceases to be informative and merely interferes with ongoing behavior. People have long been interested in ways of relieving pain. Anesthesia is a valuable method during surgery, although it is of little use for long-term control of pain. In severe cases, surgeons have sometimes cut the spinal pathways that conduct pain to the brain. Such a drastic method certainly has limitations and draw-backs, however.

One approach to pain relief, currently of theoretical rather than practical interest, is to deplete substance P from pain-transmitting neurons. **Capsaicin**, the constituent that gives jalapeño peppers their hot taste, causes the sudden release of substance P from storage in the vesicles. After an injection of capsaicin, animals show a reaction of pain and irritation for about 5 to 10 minutes, corresponding to the period of release of substance P. Afterward, they become relatively insensitive to pain for a long time, sometimes months, because the nerves have little substance P left to release (Gamse, Leeman, Holzer, & Lembeck, 1981; Jancsó, Kiraly, & Jancsó-Gábor, 1977; Yarsh, Farb, Leeman, & Jessell, 1979). You should not try to use jalapeño peppers as a home remedy for pain, however. If the dose of capsaicin necessary to produce this effect in humans is similar to the 50 mg/kg used with rats, a person would have to sit down to a meal of about a pound and a half of jalapeños to deplete stores of substance P. Also, that dose of capsaicin is believed to be capable of damaging myelin sheaths.

Relieving Pain by Stimulating Neural Systems That Inhibit It

Melzack and Wall (1965) proposed a highly influential theory of pain known as the **gate theory**. According to this theory, axons from nonpain receptors and certain axons descending from the brain can excite a set of neurons that inhibit transmission from the pain axons in the spinal cord. That is, other kinds of sensation can close certain gates to prevent pain information from reaching the brain. In its original form, the theory specified a number of other details that later research did not support. Still, the theory inspired a great deal of research.

It is now clear that other kinds of brain activity can indeed inhibit pain perception, although they do not necessarily have their effects in the spinal cord. It has been known for centuries that opiate drugs, including morphine, can relieve pain. In the 1970s, researchers found that the brain releases its own opiatelike substances, which attach to the same receptor sites in the brain that morphine affects (See BioSketch 6-2). The brain's opiates are known as **endorphins**, a contraction of *endogenous morphines*. Several types of endorphins are known, including the hormones *beta-endorphin* and *dynorphin* and two peptides that are presumed to act as synaptic transmitters: **met-enkephalin** and **leu-enkephalin**.

Enkephalin-containing neurons are concentrated in the same areas of the brain as substance P (McLean, Skirboll, & Pert, 1985). Evidently enkephalin inhibits the firing of pain-conducting cells containing substance P. In addition, activity of enkephalin cells on their own contributes to reward. This effect can be contrasted to the effects of morphine, which besides producing pleasant effects by mimicking enkephalin in the brain also produces unpleasant effects on the digestive system (Bechara & van der Kooy, 1985). Enkephalin produces only the pleasant effects, not the unpleasant ones.

A number of sensory stimuli can cause the release of enkephalin and thereby decrease response to painful stimuli. For example, stimulation of

Candace
Pert

"People are too easily influenced by negative data," says Candace Pert. "It is often hard to make thing work right. If you can never prove your idea, maybe the idea was wrong, but maybe you never did the experiment right."

Practicing what she preaches, she spent six months in the laboratory as a graduate student getting completely negative results, until she finally found a way to demonstrate what she knew must be there—identifiable opiate receptors in the brain. Why was she so sure that such recep-

tors must exist? She dates her confidence to an experience she had just after graduating from Bryn Mawr College in 1970 and before entering the Ph.D. program in pharmacology at Johns Hopkins Medical School. While in a hospital, receiving frequent morphine injections for pain caused by a horseback-riding accident, she read Goldstein's *Principles of Drug Action*, which argued that there must be opiate receptors in the brain. The experience inspired her with a confidence about finding opiate receptors, which kept her going through all the discouraging early results. Within a short time, she was widely recognized as one of the top pioneers in this field of research.

Pert regards synaptic receptors as the interface between

biochemistry and behavior. Although her methods are primarily biochemical, her interests are largely psychological, dating back to the psychology seminars she took as an undergraduate, and to the experience of watching the human brain mature in the developing behavior of her children. She believes that studies of synaptic receptors and changes in their conformation may make major contributions to our understanding of learning and mental illness. They can also make contributions in more surprising areas: Some of her studies on brain receptors identified a peptide that apparently blocks the AIDS virus from entering cells (Kolata, 1987). That peptide has been given preliminary trials with AIDS patients.

the vagina decreases pain in both women and female nonhuman animals (Komisaruk & Wallman, 1977; Komisaruk & Whipple, 1986). Listening to "thrilling" music—the kind that sends a tingling sensation down your back or all over your body—also decreases pain (Goldstein, 1980). The drug **naloxone**, which blocks enkephalin synapses, blocks both the tingling sensation and the pain-killing effect of music.

Certain kinds of skin stimulation can also block pain (Watkins & Mayer, 1982). Two examples are acupuncture, an ancient Chinese technique of gently twisting thin needles placed in the skin, and **transcutaneous electrical nerve stimulation**, the application of prolonged, weak electrical shock to the arms, legs, or back. (See Figure 6-21.)

Footshock or other painful stimuli can under certain circumstances decrease the painfulness of future stimuli. The effects depend, however, on the circumstances. For example, exposure to intermittent or low-intensity continuous shock decreases rats' sensitivity to pain, through the release of enkephalin or related substances. Exposure to continuous, high-intensity shock also decreases pain sensitivity, but it does so through a different, unidentified route that does not require any endorphin (Terman & Liebeskind, 1986). That is, the pain-numbing effect of the high-intensity shock is not altered by the anti-opiate drug naloxone. Evidently both an opiate-dependent and a nonopiate mechanism can decrease pain.

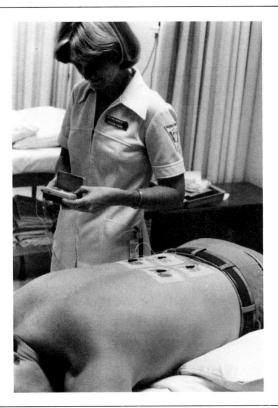

Figure 6-21. A physical therapist administering transcutaneous electrical nerve stimulation for relief of back pain.

Furthermore, the opiate-dependent mechanism for decreasing pain is affected by factors other than the stimuli on the skin. The mere presence of a cat causes the release of endorphins by rats, and thereby decreases their response to pain (Lester & Fanselow, 1985). A mouse defeated in a battle with another mouse adopts a characteristic submissive posture: It sits upright with limp forepaws, tilts its head to an angle, and retracts its ears. It turns away from its opponent and squeals when approached, even before it is bitten. Moreover, it shows a decreased response to pain. Both the submissive posture and the decreased response to pain depend on the release of endorphins (Miczek, Thompson, & Shuster, 1986). The endorphin release, in turn, depends not on the pain or damage the mouse receives in battle but on the fact that the mouse has "lost." A victorious mouse that has suffered equal injuries shows none of these effects.

Why do endorphin systems exist? That is, why did vertebrates evolve mechanisms that inhibit pain during and following such stimuli as footshock or defeat in battle? One possibility is that it may be useful to relieve the pain after it has alerted the individual to danger.

It is unsafe to assume that the endorphin systems are altogether helpful, however. After exposure to inescapable shock or defeat in battle, when animals experience an opiate-dependent analgesia, they also "give up." Not only does the animal fail to fight back against renewed attacks by the victorious opponent, but it also fails to take simple steps to escape and avoid shock (Maier, Sherman, Lewis, Terman, & Liebeskind, 1983). Such animals also have a decreased immune response and decreased resistance to the growth of tumors (Shavit, et al., 1985). In short, although mild activation of the endorphin systems appears to be beneficial, vigorous activation may actually impair an animal's efforts at survival.

SUMMARY

1. Each type of receptor transduces a particular kind of energy into a generator potential. (p. 146)
2. Sensory information is coded so that the brain can process it. The coded information bears no physical similarity to the stimuli being coded. (p. 146)
3. According to the law of specific nerve energies, the brain interprets any activity of a given sensory neuron as representing the kind of sensory information that neuron is tuned to. (p. 147)
4. The fovea is the part of the retina where receptors can detect the greatest detail. (p. 148)
5. The retina has two kinds of receptors, rods and cones, which differ in their acuity, their ability to detect dim light, and their responses to color. (p. 149)
6. The retina has three kinds of cones, as predicted by the Young-Helmholtz theory. Beyond the level of the retina, color is coded by opponent processes. Certain areas of the cerebral cortex responsible for color constancy have properties consistent with the retinex theory. (p. 151)
7. Touch depends on several types of receptors. Various types of touch information are kept distinct by each level of the nervous system, including the cerebral cortex. (p. 154)
8. Hearing and vestibular sensation may be regarded as modified touch sensations. (pp. 157, 166)
9. We detect the pitch of low-frequency sounds by

the frequency of action potentials in the auditory system. We detect the pitch of high-frequency sounds by the area of greatest response along the basilar membrane. (p. 159)
10. Deafness can be caused by damage to the nerve cells or by damage to the bones that conduct sounds to the nerve cells. (p. 163)
11. We localize high-frequency sounds on the basis of differences in loudness between the ears. We localize low-frequency sounds on the basis of differences in phase. (p. 163)
12. Controversy continues as to whether olfaction and taste are coded by labeled lines or by patterns across the entire population of fibers. (pp. 167–169, 175)
13. The intensity of pain varies from person to person and from time to time, even when the physical stimulus is the same. (p. 176)
14. Pain can be relieved by depleting the supplies of substance P, the synaptic transmitter of pain, or by increasing the activity of endorphins, chemicals that inhibit the activity of pain-detecting neurons. (p. 177)
15. The release of endorphins can be increased by various sensory stimuli and experiences. Intense, inescapable shock or defeat in a fight may evoke the release of enough endorphin to impair productive activity. (pp. 178–179)

REVIEW QUESTIONS

1. What is the difference between transduction and coding? (p. 145)
2. What is the law of specific nerve energies, and how must it be modified in light of modern knowledge of the nervous system? (p. 147)
3. What are the differences between rods and cones? (p. 149)
4. Why is perception of dim light better toward the periphery of the retina than in the fovea? (p. 150)
5. How does 11-cis-retinal contribute to the detection of light? (p. 150)
6. Describe the Young-Helmholtz theory, the opponent-process theory, and the retinex theory. (p. 151)
7. In what way is the sense of touch several senses instead of just one? (p. 154)
8. Differentiate among the frequency theory, the volley principle, and the place theory of pitch perception. (pp. 159–161)

9. How do our mechanisms of pitch perception vary among low, medium, and high-pitched tones? (p. 159)
10. What are the two major categories of deafness, and what causes each? (p. 163)
11. What mechanisms enable an animal to localize sounds? How does the effectiveness of each method depend on the size of the animal's head? (p. 163)
12. What does the vestibular system detect? (p. 166)
13. Distinguish between the labeled-line theory and the across-fiber pattern theory as they apply to both olfaction and taste. (pp. 167, 175)
14. What is the main idea of the gate theory of pain? (p. 177)
15. How can an investigator use naloxone to determine whether a given effect depends on endorphins? (p. 178)
16. What harm can result from a great release of endorphins? (p. 180)

THOUGHT QUESTIONS

1. How could you test for the presence of color vision in a bee? Examining the retina will not help; invertebrate receptors resemble neither rods nor cones. It is possible to train bees to approach one visual stimulus and not another. The difficulty is that if you trained some bees to approach, say, a yellow card and not a green card, you would not know whether they solved the problem by color or by brightness. Because brightness is different from physical intensity, you cannot equalize brightness by any physical measurement, nor can you assume that two colors that are equally bright to humans are also equally bright to bees. How might you get around the problem of brightness to study the possibility of color vision in bees?

2. Why do you suppose the human auditory system evolved sensitivity to sounds in the range of 20 to 20,000 Hz instead of some other range of frequencies?

3. The text explains how we might distinguish loudness for low-pitched sounds on the basis of the frequency theory. How might we distinguish loudness for high-pitched sounds?

TERMS TO REMEMBER

reception (p. 145)
transduction (p. 145)
coding (p. 145)
generator potential (p. 146)
law of specific nerve energies (p. 147)
pupil (p. 148)
retina (p. 148)
fovea (p. 148)
rods (p. 149)
cones (p. 149)
Young-Helmholtz (trichromatic) theory (p. 151)
opponent-process theory (p. 152)
color constancy (p. 154)
retinex theory (p. 154)
somatosensory system (p. 154)
tympanic membrane (p. 157)
cochlea (p. 159)
basilar membrane (p. 159)
hair cells (p. 159)
frequency theory (p. 159)
place theory (p. 159)
volley principle (p. 161)
base (p. 161)
apex (p. 161)
nerve (inner-ear) deafness (p. 163)

conductive (middle-ear) deafness (p. 163)
vestibular sensation (p. 166)
otolith (p. 166)
semicircular canals (p. 166)
olfactory cells (p. 167)
labeled-line theory of olfaction (p. 167)
pheromone (p. 169)
anosmia (p. 169)
specific anosmia (p. 169)
across-fiber pattern theory of olfaction (p. 169)
taste buds (p. 170)
papillae (p. 170)
miracle berry (p. 172)
miraculin (p. 172)
nucleus solitarius (p. 174)
labeled-line theory of taste (p. 175)
across-fiber pattern theory of taste (p. 176)
substance P (p. 176)
capsaicin (p. 177)
gate theory (p. 177)
endorphins (p. 177)
met-enkephalin (p. 177)
leu-enkephalin (p. 177)
naloxone (p. 178)
transcutaneous electrical nerve stimulation (p. 178)

SUGGESTIONS FOR FURTHER READING

Goldstein, E. B. (1984). *Sensation and perception* (2nd ed.) Belmont, CA: Wadsworth. A general textbook on the sensory systems, emphasizing vision and hearing.

Zwislocki, J. J. (1981). Sound analysis in the ear: A history of discoveries. *American Scientist, 69,* 184–192. An excellent review of transduction and coding of auditory information.

Higher Processing of Visual Information

MAIN IDEAS

1. Within the retina, a process called lateral inhibition acts to enhance the contrast between a brightly lit area and a neighboring dimmer area.

2. Information from the retina is transmitted to a number of areas of the brain that process the information in different ways.

3. Certain cells in the visual cortex respond specifically to light patterns in a particular shape, such as bars and edges.

4. The properties of cells in the visual system can be altered by specific experiences or deprivations of experience early in life.

By looking at Figure 7-1 you can experience some optical illusions. They are called optical illusions because most people perceive something different from what is actually there. The various theories about these optical illusions, despite their disagreements, all agree that the causes are within the brain, not within the eyeballs. (If you look at one line of the Müller-Lyer illusion with one eye and the other line with the other eye, you will still see the illusion.)

A different kind of optical illusion does depend on processes within the eyeball, however. In Figure 7-2, you may see dark diamonds at the crossroads among the black squares. Cells within each eye are responsible for those perceptions.

The point of all this is simply that our perceptions are not the same thing as the stimuli that strike our receptors. After the transduction and coding of sensory information discussed in Chapter 6, sensory information reaches the brain, where higher and more complex processing takes place. Although such processing occurs in all sensory modalities, we shall illustrate with just one example, vision.

LEVELS OF PROCESSING IN THE VISUAL SYSTEM
The human retina contains roughly 120 million rods and 6 million cones. If we were aware of the activity in every receptor, we would be flooded with information. We do not need or want information about 126 million points of light. We merely need to know what objects are out there and where they

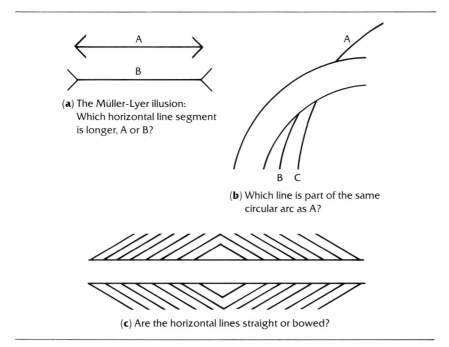

(**a**) The Müller-Lyer illusion: Which horizontal line segment is longer, A or B?

(**b**) Which line is part of the same circular arc as A?

(**c**) Are the horizontal lines straight or bowed?

Figure 7-1. Three optical illusions. (**a**) Lines A and B are the same length. (**b**) B is the extension of A. (**c**) The lines are straight.

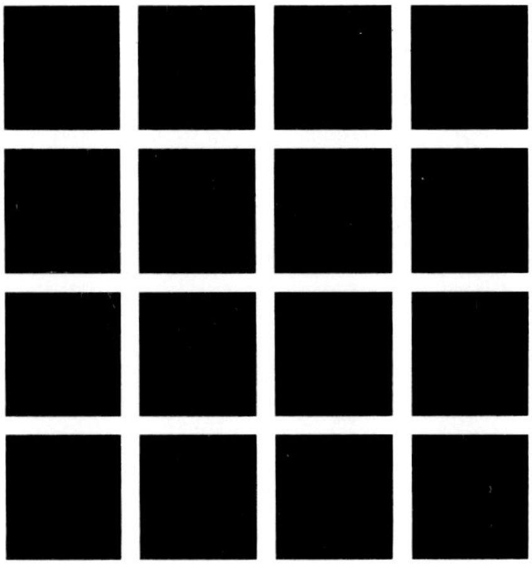

Figure 7-2. Another kind of optical illusion. Do you see dark diamonds at the "crossroads"?

are. Imagine, as an analogy, that Senator Philip Buster receives thousands of letters from constituents on some issue. The senator directs staff members to summarize the information; for example, "55 percent of the letters were in favor of legalizing miracle berries for the following reasons . . ., and 45 percent were opposed for the following reasons . . ." The summary digests a tall stack of mail into a single page. Although a great deal of detailed information has been lost, the important patterns have been emphasized.

The information provided by our visual receptors is analogous to the stack of letters; much of it is repetitive. The brain needs to summarize the information—to highlight the important patterns, such as the borders between objects.

Visual information goes through several layers of processing. The rods and cones in the retina send information to other neurons toward the center of the eyeball itself, rather than directly back to the brain, as one might suppose. The receptors make synaptic contact with **horizontal cells** and **bipolar cells.** (See Figure 7-3 and Color Plate 22.) The bipolars make synapses onto **amacrine cells** and **ganglion cells,** also located in the eyeball. The ganglion cell axons group together to form the **optic nerve,** which turns around to exit through the back of the eye. The point at which it leaves is called the **blind spot** of the eye because it has no receptors. Blood vessels also enter the eye through the blind spot. Curiously, people are never spontaneously aware of having a blind spot. In fact, even people with very large blind spots, caused by glaucoma or other eye diseases, are seldom aware of them.

In Figure 7-3, note that light passes through several layers of cells before it reaches the receptors. Those cells are, however, sufficiently transparent that they distort vision only to a minimal extent.

After the optic nerve leaves the retina, it travels back on the lower surface of the brain (refer back to Figure 4-16). Most of the axons go to the lateral geniculate nucleus of the thalamus, some fibers go to the superior colliculus, and a smaller number go to several other areas. The occipital lobe of the cerebral cortex receives input from the lateral geniculate. Parts of

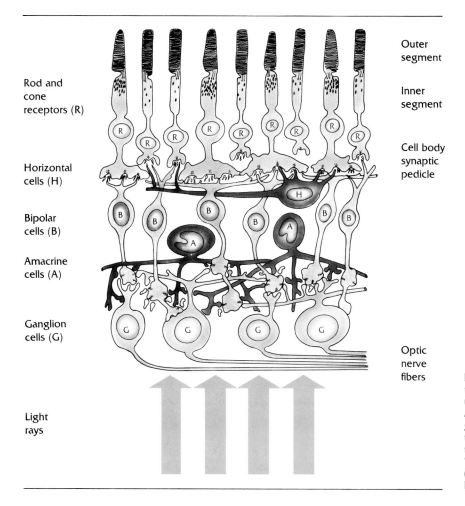

Rod and cone receptors (R)

Outer segment

Inner segment

Horizontal cells (H)

Cell body synaptic pedicle

Bipolar cells (B)

Amacrine cells (A)

Ganglion cells (G)

Optic nerve fibers

Light rays

Figure 7-3. Nerve cells of the retina. The top of the figure is the back of the retina. All the optic nerve fibers group together and then turn around to exit through the back of the retina, in the "blind spot" of the eye. (Adapted from Dowling and Boycott, 1966.)

the temporal lobe and parietal lobe receive input from the occipital lobe and from areas of the thalamus other than the lateral geniculate. Figure 7-4 outlines a few of the major connections. Each area processes visual information in different ways. We shall begin with the retina and proceed through all the other areas in order.

LATERAL INHIBITION

Lateral inhibition—inhibition of cells to the side—is a method of sharpening the contrast at borders and of enhancing the response of the nervous system to changes. It was first discovered in studies of *Limulus*, the horseshoe crab (Hartline, 1949). When light shines on a visual receptor, activity in that receptor increases. If light is added onto neighboring receptors, activity in those receptors increases but activity in the first receptor decreases (Figure 7-5). That is, activity in any receptor decreases the activity of other receptors to the side. That decrease is the effect of lateral inhibition.

The basic results for the vertebrate eye resemble those for *Limulus*, although the anatomy is quite different. To understand the principle, let us

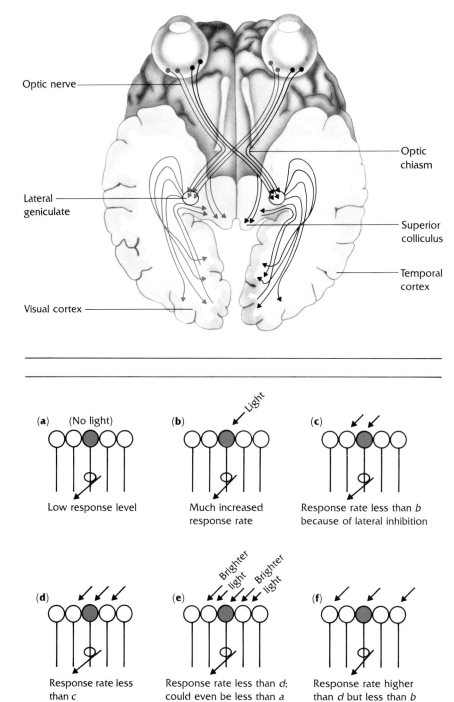

Figure 7-4. Major connections in the visual system of the brain.

Figure 7-5. Six representations of a patch of receptors from the *Limulus* retina. Light shines on the receptors as shown by the arrows; activity is recorded from the receptor in the center.

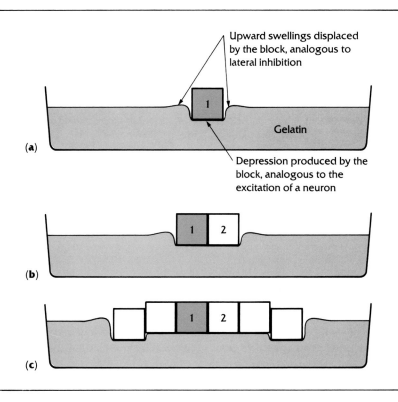

Upward swellings displaced by the block, analogous to lateral inhibition

Gelatin

(a)

Depression produced by the block, analogous to the excitation of a neuron

(b)

(c)

Figure 7-6. Blocks on a surface of gelatin. An analogy to lateral inhibition.

consider an analogy: If I place a wooden block on a surface of gelatin, the block depresses the gelatin beneath it while raising the surrounding surface (Figure 7-6a). The depression is analogous to the excitation of a neuron; the rise in the surrounding gelatin is analogous to lateral inhibition of surrounding neurons. Next I place a second block next to the first. As the second block sinks into the gelatin, it raises the first (Figure 7-6b). Finally, I try placing a row of blocks on the gelatin. The blocks at the beginning and end of the row sink deeper than the others (Figure 7-6c). Why? Because each block in the interior of the row is subject to an upward pressure from both sides, while the blocks at the beginning and end of the row are subject to that pressure from one side only.

In the vertebrate retina, lateral inhibition is accomplished by the horizontal cells. Each receptor cell (such as R11 in Figure 7-7) transmits excitation to one or more bipolar cells (B8, in this case). It also excites a large, blob-shaped horizontal cell (H), which *inhibits* a large number of bipolar cells. The horizontal cell is a *local circuit* cell (see p. 44); instead of using action potentials, it transmits a graded potential that decays over distance. When stimulated by a receptor, the horizontal cell inhibits nearby bipolar cells strongly, while its inhibition of more distant bipolars is weaker, because of the decay.

In short, stimulation of a receptor produces net excitation of one or more bipolar cells and inhibition of their neighbors, by means of the horizontal cells.

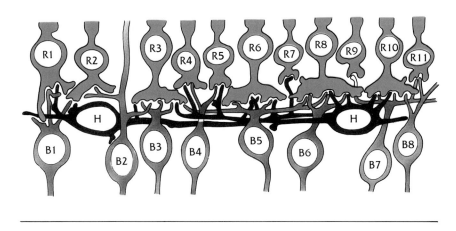

Figure 7-7. Diagram of connections in the vertebrate retina. Receptors excite horizontal and bipolar cells; horizontal cells inhibit bipolars. (Based on Dowling & Boycott, 1966.)

The function of lateral inhibition is to sharpen borders. In Figure 7-7, suppose a border between dark and light falls between receptors R2 and R3. Cell R2 and those to the left of it are in the dark; all cells from R3 to the right are in the light. Bipolar cells B2 and B3 will respond more vigorously than the bipolars farther to the right. Why? Because they receive lateral inhibition only from one side (the right), while bipolars B4 and onward receive lateral inhibiton from receptors on both sides.

Similarly, bipolar B1 will be *less* active than other bipolars to the left of it (not shown in the figure), and will be less active than if light were falling nowhere on the retina. The reason is that B1 is receiving lateral inhibition through the horizontal cell without receiving excitation from any receptor.

Lateral inhibition is an important first step in the organism's summarizing of visual information and extracting meaning from it. Lateral inhibition emphasizes the borders between light and dark, which are normally the edges of an object.

THE CONCEPT OF A RECEPTIVE FIELD

In tracing what happens to visual information as it passes from the retina to various points in the brain, we must make extensive use of a concept known as the **receptive field**. The receptive field of a neuron is an area of the body in which stimulation of some kind excites or inhibits the cell, directly or indirectly. For a neuron in the visual system, the receptive field is an area of the retina. In other systems of the brain, a neuron's receptive field may be part of the basilar membrane, part of the skin, or part of any other receptive structure.

Examine cell B3 in Figure 7-7. Cell B3 can be excited when light strikes receptor R3. It is inhibited when light strikes any of the receptors R1–R8. We say that receptors R1 through R8 constitute the receptive field of cell B3. That is, stimulation anywhere in that area affects the cell by either exciting or inhibiting it. Figure 7-7 shows cells along only one dimension. If we present the entire retina in two dimensions, the receptive field of a cell such as B3 looks like the drawing in Figure 7-8.

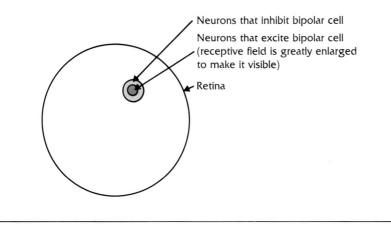

Neurons that inhibit bipolar cell

Neurons that excite bipolar cell
(receptive field is greatly enlarged
to make it visible)

Retina

Figure 7-8. Diagram of the retina, showing a typical receptive field of a bipolar cell (greatly magnified).

We can describe the receptive field of a visual cell in two ways. The first is to describe it as an area of the retina, as in Figure 7-8. The second is to describe it as an area of the visual field. Since every spot on the retina receives its input from one point in the visual field, the two ways are equivalent.

To determine the receptive fields of neurons in the visual system, an investigator can shine light on specific receptors in the retina while recording from a cell in the brain. If the light on a receptor either increases or decreases the firing rate of a brain cell, then that receptor is part of the cell's receptive field. If the light has no effect, the receptor is outside the receptive field.

Receptive Fields Beyond the Bipolar Cells

A group of bipolar cells send their output to ganglion cells; in turn, a group of ganglion cells send their output to later cells, and so on. The neurons at each level have receptive fields made up by combining the receptive fields of all incoming fibers.

For analogy, consider the ZIP codes of U.S. mail. The code 94002 includes one small city, Belmont, California. The code 940.. includes a number of small cities just south of San Francisco. The code 94... includes San Francisco, Oakland, and a number of cities on all sides of them. The code 9.... includes the entire states of California, Oregon, Washington, Alaska, and Hawaii. Just as each higher level of the ZIP code includes all the lower levels, and therefore covers a larger area, each higher neuron in the visual system gets its input from the neurons at the previous level and therefore has a larger receptive field than any of the previous neurons. The analogy breaks down in one regard, however: ZIP codes simply add together, whereas an area that is part of the excitatory receptive field of a lower-level neuron might be in the inhibitory field of a higher-level neuron.

Ganglion Cells

In cats, monkeys, and many other mammals, the receptive field of a ganglion cell is similar to that of a bipolar cell. The center of the receptive field is either excitatory or inhibitory, and a surrounding region is the opposite

Table 7-1.   Three Types of Ganglion Cells

Characteristics	W cells	X cells	Y cells
Percent of total ganglion cells	40%	55%	5%
Typical cell body size	Small <25 microns	Medium 25 microns	Large 35 microns
Typical receptive field (spread of dendrites)	Very large >500 microns	Small 65 microns	Large 500 microns
Axon diameter	Small	Medium	Large 4–6 microns
Conduction speed	Slowest	Medium	Fastest
Response to stationary stimulus	Sluggish	Sustained	Brief
Location in retina	Fairly evenly distributed	Mostly in or near fovea	Fairly evenly distributed
Destination of axons	Lateral geniculate, superior colliculus, and elsewhere	Lateral geniculate	Lateral geniculate, superior colliculus

(Kuffler, 1953). The major difference is that the ganglion cell's receptive field is larger, since it is formed from the receptive fields of all the bipolar cells that feed into it.

At least three kinds of ganglion cells can be distinguished, known as W, X, and Y cells. Table 7-1 lists the distinctions among them (based on Sherman & Spear, 1982; Fukuda, Hsiao, & Watanabe, 1985). The three types are largely independent of one another; few neurons anywhere in the visual system get input from more than one of the three types. We presume that the three types have different functions in behavior. According to one theory, Y cells are responsible for basic form recognition and X cells control perception of fine detail. Another view is that X cells analyze spatial patterns and Y cells analyze temporal patterns. The role of W cells is uncertain.

Cerebral Cortex

Axons from the ganglion cells form the optic nerve, which exits from the eye. Branches of the optic nerve extend to the lateral geniculate nucleus of the thalamus and to the superior colliculus. A smaller number extend to the pulvinar nucleus of the thalamus and to the midbrain. Receptive fields of neurons in the lateral geniculate are similar to those of the ganglion cells but are slightly larger (Hubel & Wiesel, 1961). We shall return to the superior colliculus later.

Axons from the lateral geniculate extend to the **visual cortex** in the occipital lobe (refer to Figure 7-4). Actually, the cortex has at least six visual areas (van Essen, Newsome, & Bixby, 1982). The lateral geniculate axons extend to two of them, the **striate cortex** and the **parastriate cortex** (Figure 7-9). The striate cortex gets its name from its large fourth layer of incoming axons that give it a striped appearance. All the axons are arranged in a geometrical order such that neighboring areas of the cortex receive their input from neighboring areas of the retina.

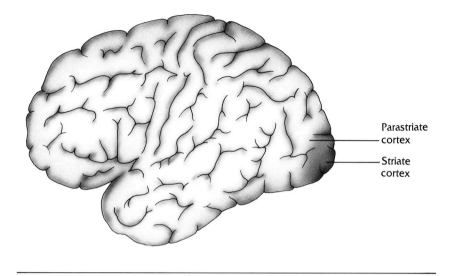

Parastriate
cortex

Striate
cortex

Figure 7-9. Location of striate and parastriate cortex in the occipital lobe of the brain.

Receptive fields of cells in the visual cortex are larger than those of the cells at lower levels. They also differ in two other regards. First, every cell in the lateral geniculate and lower levels is **monocular**—that is, it responds to one eye only. The same is true of visual cortex cells of such species as rabbits that have their eyes on the sides of their head. In cats and primates, however, which have both eyes facing the same direction, most visual cortex cells have **binocular** receptive fields. That is, they respond to portions of both eyes. Second, visual cortex cells have receptive fields shaped like a bar or an edge, unlike the circular receptive fields of the lateral geniculate and retinal cells (Hubel & Wiesel, 1959).

David Hubel and Torsten Wiesel, pioneers in this area of research (see BioSketch 7-1) have distinguished three categories of visual cortex cells: simple, complex, and hypercomplex.

Simple Cells. The receptive fields shown in Figure 7-10 are typical of **simple cells**, found exclusively in the striate cortex. Each simple cell can be excited by a point of light anywhere in the excitatory part of its receptive field (pluses) and inhibited by light anywhere in the inhibitory part (minuses). Light covering the entire excitatory area produces more excitation than just a single point of light does. For example, a cell with a receptive field like that depicted in Figure 7-10 (c) is maximally responsive to a vertical bar of light in a specific location on the retina. The response of the cell decreases sharply if the bar of light is moved slightly to the left or to the right or if it is tilted even a few degrees away from the vertical (because light then strikes the inhibitory regions as well). Different cortical cells have different preferred orientations for bars of light, including vertical, horizontal, and intermediate angles. Most cells near the fovea prefer vertical and horizontal lines; the periphery includes more cells that prefer other angles (Schall, Vitek, & Leventhal, 1986).

David Hubel

Since the late 1950s, David Hubel and Torsten Wiesel have pioneered a method of studying the physiology of vision by inserting an electrode near or into a neuron of the visual system and recording the response of that neuron to light patterns on the retina.

In one of their earliest studies, Hubel and Wiesel were measuring the responses of cortical cells in a cat's brain when they exposed the retina to slides of small black dots. A crack in one of their slides stimulated a greater response than any of the dots. Partly on the basis of this lucky accident, they began examining the response of the cells to more complex stimuli.

Among their discoveries were the following: Cells in the visual cortex respond to light shining in particular patterns, especially lines and edges, on the retina. Most of those cells respond to light in both eyes. Cells responsive to a bar of light in a particular orientation are clustered together in columns in the visual cortex. Abnormal early experience can change some of the properties of visual cortex cells. For such discoveries, Hubel and

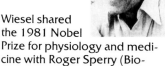

Torsten Wiesel

Wiesel shared the 1981 Nobel Prize for physiology and medicine with Roger Sperry (Bio-Sketch 5-1).

Hubel's advice for aspiring young investigators: "Brain science is difficult and tricky, for some reason; consequently one should not believe a result (one's own or anyone else's) until it is proven backwards and forwards or fits into a framework so highly evolved and systematic that it couldn't be wrong."

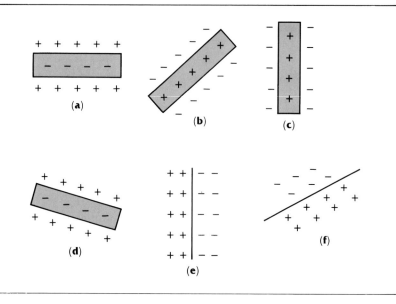

Figure 7-10. Typical receptive fields for simple visual cortex cells of cats and monkeys. (Based on Hubel & Wiesel, 1959.)

Figure 7-11 illustrates how the orientation of a stimulus affects the response of a simple cell. The illustrated cell detects vertical lines in its receptive field. Lines at other orientations are less effective. Diffuse light covering both the excitatory and the inhibitory fields yields little or no net excitation.

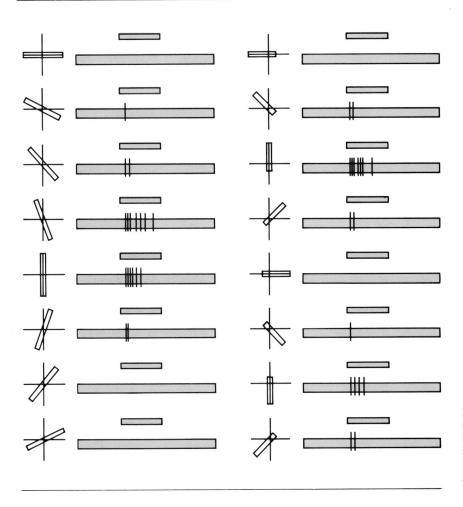

Figure 7-11. Responses of a cat's cortical cell to a bar of light presented at varying angles. The short horizontal lines indicate the time when light is on. (From Hubel & Wiesel, 1959.)

The receptive fields of the simple cells are presumably formed by combining the receptive fields of cells in the lateral geniculate. For example, suppose four cells in the lateral geniculate—A, B, C, and D—have receptive fields located on the retina as shown in Figure 7-12. If those four cells send their axons to one simple cell in the cortex, the receptive field of that cell will be the sum of those of the lateral geniculate cells. That is, it will have a bar-shaped excitatory field and a surrounding inhibitory field.

Complex cells.   **Complex cells,** which can be found in either the striate or parastriate cortex, have a larger receptive field than simple cells. Unlike the receptive fields we have encountered up to this point, the receptive fields of complex cells cannot be mapped into fixed excitatory and inhibitory zones. A complex cell is practically unaffected by any small point of light anywhere in the retina. It does, however, respond to a pattern of light in a preferred orientation (for instance, a vertical bar) and with a preferred direction of movement. Any stimulus with the right orientation and movement

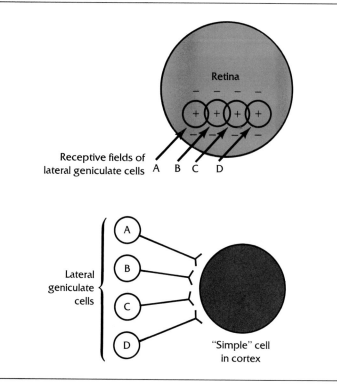

Receptive fields of
lateral geniculate cells A   B C   D

Lateral
geniculate
cells

A
B
C
D

"Simple" cell
in cortex

Figure 7-12. The receptive fields of a simple cell is the sum of the receptive fields of the lateral geniculate cells that innervate.

within the large receptive field excites the cell, regardless of the exact location of the stimulus within that receptive field. (See Figure 7-13.)

We have two ways of determining whether a given cell in the visual cortex is a simple cell or a complex cell: (1) Find a bar of light to which the cell vigorously responds. Move the light slightly to one side or the other. If the cell responds only to light in one location, it is a simple cell. (2) Shine small spots of light instead of a bar. If any spot produces significant excitation or inhibition, the cell is a simple cell.

Hypercomplex cells. **Hypercomplex cells** resemble complex cells except for one additional feature: A hypercomplex cell has a strong inhibitory field at one end of its bar-shaped receptive field. The cell responds to a bar-shaped pattern of light anywhere in its broad receptive field, provided that the bar does not extend beyond a certain point. Table 7-2 summarizes the properties of simple, complex, and hypercomplex cells.

Another Interpretation: Spatial Frequency Detectors

Each cell in the visual cortex responds vigorously to a bar of light with a particular location, orientation, and other properties. Does this mean that perceiving a certain bar-shaped pattern of light is the *same thing as* activity of a certain cell somewhere in the brain? If so, are there other cells, at increasingly more complex levels, responsible for such specific perceptions

Table 7-2.   Summary of Cells in the Primary Visual Cortex

Characteristic	Simple cells	Complex cells	Hypercomplex cells
Location	Striate cortex	Striate and parastriate cortex	Striate and parastriate cortex
Binocular input?	Yes	Yes	Yes
Size of receptive field	Smallest	Medium	Largest
Response to single point of light	Excited or inhibited, depending on location	No response	No response
Best stimulus	Bar of light in particular location	Bar of light anywhere in receptive field	Same as complex cell but with strong inhibitory field at one end
Sensitive to orientation of stimulus?	Yes	Yes	Yes

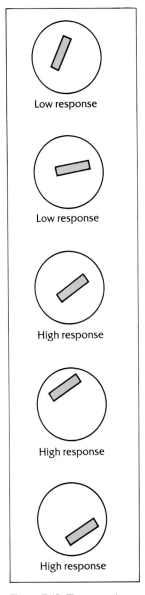

Figure 7-13. The receptive field of a complex cell in the visual cortex. It is like a simple cell in that its response is greatly affected by the angle of orientation of a bar of light. It is unlike a simple cell in that the complex cell's response is unaffected by the position of the bar within the receptive field.

as recognizing your grandmother, identifying your psychology professor, and so on? Such specialization is unlikely, for several reasons. A principal reason is that no kind of brain damage prevents you from recognizing, say, your grandmother without also disrupting other visual perceptions.

Somehow the responses of a whole population of neurons must be collectively responsible for visual perceptions. Although it is possible to break down any visual scene into a large number of component lines and bars, other kinds of analyses are easier. One branch of mathematics, Fourier analysis, has shown that it is possible to take any graphical function, no matter how complicated, and break it down into the sum of sine waves. Figure 7-14 shows an example of a **sine-wave grating**. Note that the brightness alternately increases and decreases like a sine wave. Now examine Figure 7-15. The graph at the top can be analyzed into the five sine waves beneath it.

Suppose that each neuron in the visual cortex responds to a different sine-wave grating—that is, a grating with a specific spatial frequency. In that case, the response of the total ensemble can reconstruct the original stimulus. If we further assume that some neurons are tuned to a specific horizontal sine-wave grating and that others are tuned to a vertical grating, then the population as a whole can encode a full two-dimensional scene. And the combination of two eyes allows three-dimensional perception.

Do the cells in the visual cortex in fact have these properties? Investigators who have shined sine-wave gratings on the retina have found that each neuron in the visual cortex responds best to sine waves with a particular period and that different cells vary in their preferred sine-wave periods (DeValois, Albrecht, & Thorell, 1982; Maffei & Fiorentini, 1973). At this point, we are not sure whether it is best to describe cells in the visual cortex as bar detectors, as sine-wave detectors, or as detectors of some other aspect of the stimulus.

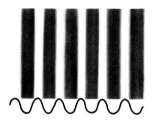

Figure 7-14. A sine-wave grating of light and darkness.

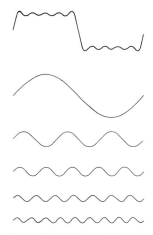

Figure 7-15. Through Fourier analysis, the graph at the top can be demonstrated to be composed of the five sine waves below it.

Columnar Organization of the Visual Cortex

Cells with various properties are not distributed at random throughout the visual cortex. When researchers insert an electrode perpendicular to the surface of the cortex and penetrate the cortex, they encounter a column of neurons, all of which have certain properties in common. Depending on which stimulus attribute is being studied, the researchers may find that the cells respond best to bars with the same angle of orientation (Hubel & Wiesel, 1977) or to sine-wave gratings of the same period (Tootell, Silverman, & DeValois, 1981). The cells in a column also share the same degree of binocularity—that is, whether they are equally responsive to both eyes or more responsive to one eye than to the other.

If the experimenters then penetrate the cortex at a nearby point, they will find another column of cells, again sharing the same properties with one another but different from the cells of the first column. For example, if the first column responded best to horizontal lines, the adjacent column might respond best to lines tilted a few degrees away from horizontal.

VISUAL PROCESSING BEYOND THE OCCIPITAL CORTEX

Information from the striate and parastriate cortex goes to several areas in the temporal and parietal cortex, as illustrated in Figure 7-16 (based on Desimone, Schein, Moran, & Ungerleider, 1985; and Woolsey, 1981). It would be pointless to try to memorize Figure 7-16. The point of the figure is simply that several areas beyond the occipital cortex process visual information. Each of these areas processes the information in a different way, for different functions.

The **inferior temporal cortex** is specialized for advanced analysis of visual patterns. Cells in this area have large receptive fields, having a median width of 26 degrees of the visual field, always including the fovea (Desimone & Gross, 1979). Although most of these cells respond at least moderately well to a wide variety of stimuli, a small number respond preferentially to certain highly complex patterns. One study found two cells in macaque monkeys that respond more vigorously to the sight of a hand than to any other stimulus, and twenty cells that respond most vigorously to a face (Desimone, Albright, Gross, & Bruce, 1984).

The response of a cell in the inferior temporal cortex depends on the shape of the object in its visual field but is not much affected by changes in the object's size or location. Thus, in macaques face-sensitive cells respond both to profiles facing left and profiles facing right. This area of the brain may be essential for the visual *constancies*—that is, our ability to recognize an object as the same even as it moves closer or farther or as it rotates. As might be expected, damage in this area impairs the ability to recognize objects but does not cause blindness at any point in the visual field (Ungerleider & Pribram, 1977).

Cells in the **middle temporal cortex** and **superior temporal cortex** are mostly insensitive to the size, shape, color, or brightness of an object and respond equally over enormous receptive fields (Bruce, Desimone, & Gross, 1981; Gross, Bruce, Desimone, Fleming, & Gattass, 1981; Saito et al., 1986). Their response depends primarily on the speed and direction of an

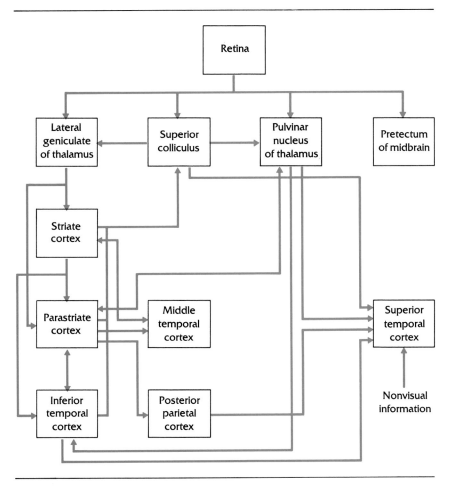

Figure 7-16. Some of the visual areas of the primate brain.

object. They may be responsible not only for our perception of whether an object is moving left or right but also for our perception of whether the object is moving toward us or away.

The **posterior parietal cortex** apparently has much to do with attention to visual objects, especially attention in preparation for a movement. Cells in this area are particularly active when an animal is staring at an object or moving its eyes or paws toward an object (Mountcastle, Lynch, Georgopoulos, Sakata, & Acuna, 1975). Certain cells in this area suppress their activity during eye movements. In that manner, they may be able to distinguish whether an object is really moving or whether it just appears to be moving because of eye movements (Sakata, Shibutani, Kawano, & Harrington, 1985). People who have suffered damage to the posterior parietal cortex on one side of the brain often fail to pay attention to the opposite visual field, even though they are capable of seeing it (Pierrot-Deseilligny, Gray, & Brunet, 1986).

In short, the visual areas of the temporal and parietal cortex are not necessary for seeing, in the most limited sense, but they *are* necessary for recognizing complex objects, determining their movement, and directing attention toward them.

ROLE OF THE SUPERIOR COLLICULUS

The optic nerve branches after entering the brain, with some branches going to the lateral geniculate and others to the superior colliculus (refer to Figure 7-4). To some extent, the superior colliculus duplicates the function of the lateral geniculate, contributing to pattern perception (Casagrande et al., 1972). It is also in a position, however, to take the same information that goes to the lateral geniculate (and eventually the visual cortex), and process it in a different way. Unlike the lateral geniculate, the superior colliculus is not purely a visual structure; especially in its deeper layers, it contains cells that respond to visual, auditory, and touch stimuli (Wurtz & Albano, 1980). For example, a given cell might respond to a visual stimulus 30 degrees to the right of the animal's center, to an auditory stimulus from the same direction, and to a whisker touch from the same direction (Drager & Hubel, 1975). The superior colliculus contributes to eye and head movements in response to each of those stimuli. After the superior colliculus is anesthetized, eye movements become shorter and slower than normal (Hikosaka & Wurtz, 1986).

Why does the brain need two (or more) systems to process visual information in parallel? The complex and hypercomplex cells are well adapted to detect certain patterns in their large receptive fields; the visually responsive cells in the temporal cortex and parietal cortex have even larger receptive fields. Because their receptive fields are so large, such cells are ill suited to perceive the exact location of an object. The superior colliculus specializes in determining location.

Schneider (1969) demonstrated that lesions of the superior colliculus produce effects very different from lesions of the visual cortex. After damage to the visual cortex, hamsters failed to learn to discriminate between a speckled pattern and diagonal stripes (to approach one and not the other for reward). (See Figure 7-17.) Hamsters with damage to the superior colliculus eventually succeeded in this task. They often walked almost to the wrong stimulus before turning around and wandering back to the right one—that is, they had difficulty orienting to the correct stimulus from a distance—but they did master the discrimination of pushing only the door with the correct stimulus on it. On the other hand, hamsters with damage to the superior colliculus seemed totally blind in the presence of a visible sunflower seed, failing to orient toward it and approach it directly. Although hamsters with visual cortex lesions had trouble with complicated visual discriminations, they had no trouble turning toward a seed and finding it.

To summarize: If a task requires an animal to determine *what* pattern it sees (for example, stripes versus dots), visual cortex lesions cause greater impairment than superior colliculus lesions. If the task requires the animal to determine *where* the pattern is, then superior colliculus lesions cause greater impairment.

Humans who have suffered damage to part of the visual cortex seem completely blind—and describe themselves as completely blind—in the af-

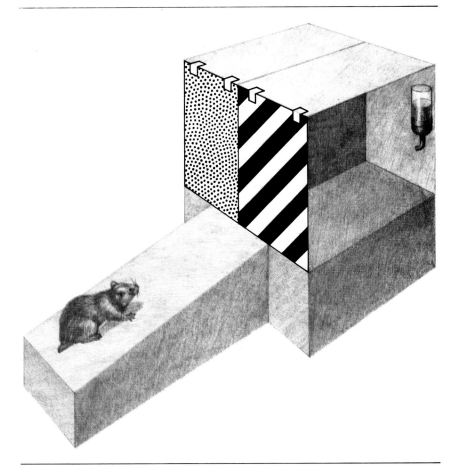

Figure 7-17. Apparatus used to test the effects of lesions on the ability of hamsters to make visual discriminations.

fected area of the visual field. Is their blindness in fact complete, or could the superior colliculus (or other subcortical visual areas) provide certain aspects of vision?

After damage to the right visual cortex, a person cannot identify an object in the left visual field in any way. However, such a person who is told to guess *where* the object is can point toward it with surprising accuracy—surprising even to himself or herself (Perenin & Jeannerod, 1978; Weiskrantz, Warrington, Sanders, & Marshall, 1974). One person was able to point at targets in his blind area even though his unimpaired vision was limited to 9 degrees of the visual field (Bridgeman & Staggs, 1982). With training, such people can improve their accuracy in moving their eyes toward visual stimuli that they still claim not to see (Zihl, 1980).

The ability to point toward objects in a damaged visual field has been known as **blindsight**. Most investigators have assumed that it depends on the superior colliculus, although no one has offered any direct evidence of superior colliculus participation. Not everyone concedes this point, however. Campion, Latto, & Smith (1983) suggested that apparent blindsight could be due to a small number of spared cells in the otherwise damaged visual cortex, or to scattering of light into the unimpaired area of the visual field. To show that the *scattering* hypothesis is plausible, they covered up the right visual field of some normal volunteers (by cards that covered half of each eye) and then flashed a point of light in that field. These people were able to point toward the light with reasonable accuracy. Evidently enough light scattered into the left visual field for them to guess the direction of origin of the light.

EFFECTS OF EXPERIENCE ON THE DEVELOPMENT OF THE VISUAL SYSTEM

How does a cell in the cortex develop its property of responding only to, say, a vertical line 5 degrees above the fovea? How do other cells develop their even more complex properties of responding to a hand or a face, or an object moving toward the eyes? Similar questions could be asked about the cortical cells that respond to auditory and touch stimuli. Are all the properties of each cell built in at birth, or do they develop as a result of the individual's experiences? The apparent answer is that certain properties are partially present at birth or shortly later but that experience sharpens and modifies those properties within limits.

Kittens normally open their eyes for the first time at age 9 days. Hubel and Wiesel (1963) opened the eyes of an 8-day-old kitten and recorded the response of cortical cells to light stimulation of the retina. They found simple and complex cells with receptive fields similar to those of a normal adult cat. However, many of the kitten's cells responded sluggishly or lacked the clearly defined bar-shaped receptive fields found in the simple and complex cells of adults. If a kitten is reared in a normal environment, one-fourth of the total cells are mature at age 2 weeks and three-fourths at age 5 weeks. If a kitten is reared in the dark, however, only 2 percent of the total cells are mature at age 5 weeks (Buisseret & Imbert, 1976). Evidently, visual experience is necessary not only to promote development but also to prevent deterioration to a point beneath where the infant began.

A young animal that is exposed to abnormal visual experiences develops visual cortex cells with abnormal properties. For example, if a kitten is reared in an environment with only horizontal lines, nearly all its simple and complex cortical cells will develop a preferential sensitivity to horizontal lines (Blakemore, 1974; Stryker, Sherk, Leventhal, & Hirsch, 1978). When the cat is later exposed to vertical lines and objects, it virtually ignores them, even after years of living in a normal environment (Mitchell, 1980). Evidently, the abnormal visual experience early in life alters the properties of cells in the visual cortex in such a way that they become most sensitive to the kinds of visual patterns present in the kitten's environment.

The development of the visual cortex apparently depends in part on a competition among incoming axons. For example, if a kitten or infant monkey is reared with both eyes sutured shut, its cortical cells develop abnormal properties but they remain somewhat sensitive to light in either eye. Yet if one eye is open while the other eye is closed for the first few months, most cells in the visual cortex become totally unresponsive to the closed eye

(Wiesel, 1982). That is, input from the active eye competitively displaces input from the inactive eye. Cells that receive their direct input from the closed eye become responsive mostly to corpus callosum axons carrying information from the open eye (Cynader, Leporé, & Guillemot, 1981).

To further explore the role of competition, Guillery (1972) sutured one of a kitten's eyes shut and then surgically damaged a small spot on the retina in the active eye (Figure 7-18). Nearly all the visual cortex cells became unresponsive to the closed eye. However, those cells that were connected to the damaged area of the open eye remained responsive to the closed eye. That is, cells lost responsiveness to the sutured, inactive eye only if they got input from a healthy part of the active eye.

Another kind of competition takes place in the posterior parietal cortex. Cells in that area, you will recall, are active when an individual attends to a visual object. These cells ordinarily respond to somatic (touch) information as well. If monkeys are reared with their eyes closed for the first 7 to 11 months, many cells in the posterior parietal cortex become responsive only to somatic information (Hyvärinen, Hyvärinen, & Linnankoski, 1981). After the monkeys' eyes are opened, even though the cells in the visual cortex respond to light the monkeys fail to attend to what they see. Even after months of opportunity for vision, they have to feel their way around and they frequently bump into objects or fall off tables.

Similar Processes in Humans

Nature sometimes performs experiments on humans that no investigator could perform on purpose. For example, occasionally infants have suffered a loss of vision that could be surgically corrected early in life. Although such children can see after the operation, they find it difficult to determine what they are seeing. Like the monkeys reared without vision, they have trouble using vision to find their way around (Valvo, 1971). In some cases they may even choose to close their eyes and revert to the use of touch and sound cues to maneuver through a hallway or down the stairs.

Certain children are born cross-eyed or wall-eyed; that is, their eyes never look in the same direction at the same time. This condition is known as **strabismus**. When kittens are made strabismic by cutting certain eye muscles early in life, each of their cortical cells develops sensitivity to one eye or the other; almost none remain responsive to both eyes. The same seems to be true in humans. Although children with strabismus continue to see with each eye, they cannot develop binocular depth perception or any other binocular interaction, even after a surgical operation in adulthood to reposition the eyes in their normal locations (Banks, Aslin, & Letson, 1975; Mitchell, 1980). Presumably they could have developed binocular vision if the operation had been performed early enough in life.

Finally, uncorrected astigmatism early in life can permanently distort vision. **Astigmatism** is a blurring of vision for either horizontal or vertical lines, but not the other, caused by an asymmetric curvature of the eyes. If the blurring is not corrected by eyeglasses by age 5 to 7, the person remains permanently less sensitive to the lines that were blurry early in life (Mitchell,

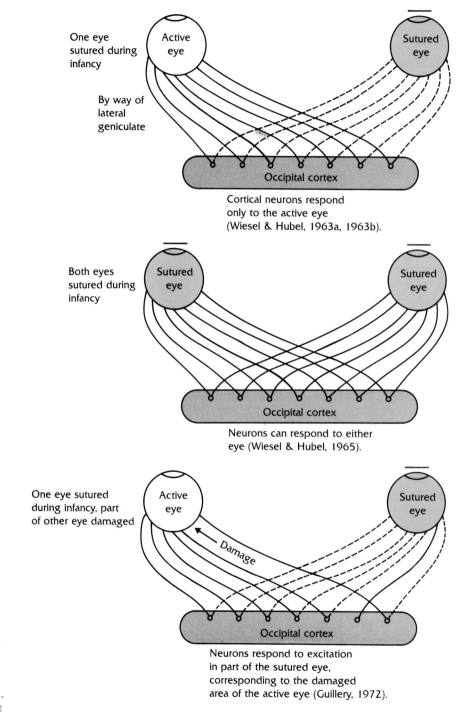

Figure 7-18. The effects of reduced activity in either or both eyes on the responsiveness of neurons in the occipital cortex. Occipital cortex neurons lose responsiveness to an inactive input only if there is competition from a more active input.

1980). The probable explanation is that in humans, as in cats and monkeys, visual cortical neurons become more responsive to the stimuli that have been most prominent in early development.

Why Did We Evolve Modifiability of the Visual Cortex?

In certain species, such as rabbits, the properties of cells in the visual cortex are apparently fixed at birth and are not greatly affected by the kinds of experiences that change the cells of cats and primates. Why have certain species evolved cortical cells that are fixed at birth while others have evolved cortical cells that are modifiable?

Modifiability probably relates in part to the development of binocular depth perception. Unlike the eyes of rabbits, those of cats, monkeys, and humans both face the same direction; most of the cells in the visual cortex get some input from both eyes. For the input to produce depth perception, a cortical cell must get its input from *corresponding areas* of the two eyes— that is, from areas that both focus on the same point in the visual field. How can the nervous system pick out which point on one retina corresponds to a given point on the other retina? Although it is possible to get the correspondence approximately right at the time of birth, it is not possible to get it exactly right, because the distance between the two eyes varies from one person to another. Thus, nature's solution has been to let early experience fine-tune the properties of the cortical cells.

SUMMARY

1. Information travels from the visual receptors to the bipolar cells and from them to the ganglion cells, whose axons exit the eye as the optic nerve. (p. 184)

2. Each receptor excites one or more bipolar cells plus a large horizontal cell that inhibits many bipolar cells. The result is lateral inhibition—excitation of a receptor produces net excitation of the closest bipolar cells and inhibition of neighboring bipolars. (p. 184)

3. Lateral inhibition functions to enhance the contrast at borders between light and dark. (p. 185)

4. Each cell of the visual system has a receptive field—an area of the retina that excites or inhibits its activity. (p. 188)

5. Cells at higher levels of the visual system have larger receptive fields than cells at lower levels. (p. 189)

6. Bipolar cells, ganglion cells, and lateral geniculate cells have circular receptive fields in which the center is excitatory and the surround inhibitory, or vice versa. There are three kinds of ganglion cells, designated as W, X, and Y. (p. 190)

7. Most cells in the visual cortex have binocular receptive fields. (p. 191)

8. In the striate cortex and parastriate cortex, most cells have a receptive field shaped like a bar or an edge. (p. 191)

9. A simple cell has a fixed excitatory area and a fixed inhibitory area; a complex cell responds equally to a given pattern in any location within its receptive field. (pp. 191–193)

10. It is possible to characterize visual cortical cells in terms of their responses to sine-wave gratings instead of their responses to bars and edges. (p. 195)

11. The striate and parastriate cortex contain columns of cells that share certain properties with one another. (p. 196)

12. The inferior temporal cortex is important for recognizing complex visual patterns. It may be essential for recognizing an object after changes in its location or orientation. (p. 196)

13. The middle and superior temporal cortex are particularly sensitive to the direction that a visual object moves. (p. 196)

14. The posterior parietal cortex contains cells that are responsive mostly when an individual is attending to a visual object in preparation for a movement toward it. (p. 197)

15. The superior colliculus contributes to the perception of the location of an object. It also participates in eye movements and other movements directed toward a target in visual space. (p. 198)

16. Cells in the visual cortex have partially mature properties even before the start of visual experience. In cats and primates, experience is necessary to maintain and sharpen the sensitivities of those cells. (p. 200)

17. If one eye is active early in life and the other is

not, axons from the active eye increase their influence on the visual cortex, at the expense of the axons from the inactive eye. (p. 201)

18.   Visual deprivation or other abnormal visual experiences early in life can permanently alter the development of the visual cortex of humans as well as laboratory animals. (p. 201)

REVIEW QUESTIONS

1.   What is lateral inhibition and what does it contribute to perception? (p. 185)
2.   How does a horizontal cell produce lateral inhibition in the vertebrate eye? (p. 187)
3.   Describe the connections from the receptors to the various structures of the visual system of the brain. (pp. 184, 185)
4.   How can one find the receptive field of a cell in the visual system? (p. 188)
5.   What are the differences among a simple cell, a complex cell, and a hypercomplex cell? (pp. 191–194)
6.   What is the appeal in describing cells of the visual cortex as detectors of sine-wave gratings? (p. 195)
7.   In what way do cells in a column of the visual cortex resemble one another? (p. 196)
8.   What additional visual processing takes place in the inferior temporal cortex, the middle and superior temporal cortex, and the posterior parietal cortex? (p. 196)
9.   What is the function of the superior colliculus? (p. 198)
10.   Describe the controversy over the basis for blindsight. (p. 199)
11.   What changes occur in the visual cortex cells of kittens and monkeys early in life if they are reared in a normal environment? What changes occur if the animals' eyes are kept closed? (p. 200)
12.   Describe evidence that input from one eye competes against input from the other eye for influence on cells in the visual cortex. (p. 201)
13.   Give an example of the permanent influence of early visual experience on the development of vision in children. (p. 201)

THOUGHT QUESTIONS

1.   Can you explain the dark diamonds you see in Figure 7-2 in terms of lateral inhibition?
2.   In Figure 7-7, suppose cells B1 and B2 have the same spontaneous rate of firing. Cell R3 excites B2 but not B1; through the horizontal cell it inhibits both of them. When light shines on R3, what will happen to the firing rate in B1? In B2? Will the immediate effects differ from those a few milliseconds later? (Remember that R3 excites B2 through a direct synapse. The inhibitory process requires two synapses, the one from R3 to the horizontal cell and the one from the horizontal cell to the bipolars.)
3.   After a receptor cell is stimulated, the bipolar cell receiving input from it shows an immediate burst of response. A fraction of a second later, the bipolar's response rate decreases, even though the stimulation from the receptor cell remains constant. How can you account for that decrease? Hint: What does the horizontal cell do?
4.   Cortical cells have receptive fields with preferred orientations of horizontal, vertical, and intermediate angles. Why would it be unsatisfactory for an animal to have only two kinds of cells, horizontal and vertical, without the intermediates? Note: Such an animal would not necessarily be blind to intermediate angles. Even a 45-degree line could give rise to a slight response by both cells. (Hint: How could the animal tell the difference between a line at a 5-degree angle and one at a 10-degree angle? between a 45-degree angle and a 135-degree angle?)

TERMS TO REMEMBER

horizontal cells (p. 184)
bipolar cells (p. 184)
amacrine cells (p. 184)
ganglion cells (p. 184)
optic nerve (p. 184)
blind spot (p. 184)
lateral inhibition (p. 185)
receptive field (p. 188)
visual cortex (p. 190)
striate cortex (p. 190)
parastriate cortex (p. 190)
monocular (p. 191)

binocular (p. 191)
simple cells (p. 191)
complex cells (p. 193)
hypercomplex cells (p. 194)
sine-wave grating (p. 195)
inferior temporal cortex (p. 196)
middle temporal cortex (p. 196)
superior temporal cortex (p. 196)
posterior parietal cortex (p. 197)
blindsight (p. 199)
strabismus (p. 201)
astigmatism (p. 201)

SUGGESTIONS FOR FURTHER READING

Ali, M. A., & Klyne, M. A. (1985). *Vision in vertebrates*. New York: Plenum.

Harris, C. S. (Ed.). (1980). *Visual coding and adaptability*. Hillsdale, NJ: Erlbaum. Includes reviews of some active topics of recent research.

Hubel, D. H., & Wiesel, T. N. (1979). Brain mechanisms of vision. *Scientific American, 241* (3), 150–162. Highly recommended.

CHAPTER 8

The Control of Movement

MAIN IDEAS

1. It is possible to analyze a sequence of movements into its component elements. Depending on one's purposes and methods of study, one can analyze a sequence into muscle movements, into somewhat larger units (reflexes, oscillators, and servomechanisms), or into purposive actions.

2. All the motor neurons that send messages to the muscles have their cell bodies in the spinal cord or the medulla.

3. The cerebellum and the basal ganglia contribute to the control of movement in several

ways, including control of the direction, intensity, and duration of movements. They help to combine individual movements into coordinated wholes.

4. Disorders of the basal ganglia, including Parkinson's disease and Huntington's disease, impair both movement and cognitive patterns.

5. Two systems originating in the cerebral cortex, the pyramidal system and the extrapyramidal system, contribute to the control of different types of movement.

W hy is it that all animals, except one-celled animals and probably sponges, have a nervous system, while plants do not? It is because animals move and because they need to coordinate each movement with other movements and with sensory stimuli. Plants do not move; a tree that had brilliant thoughts could do nothing about them.

Like most generalizations, this one has exceptions: One is the sensitive plant *Mimosa*, which curls its leaves in response to touch or vibration and sometimes changes its responses in ways that resemble learning (Sanberg, 1976). Although the mechanisms are not well understood, we may assume that the plant has a system that functions similarly to nerves.

Although the ultimate function of nerves is to control movement, most psychologists pay little attention to movement. Compared to the study of visual perception, or learning, or social interactions, or motivation and emotion, the study of muscle contractions seems somehow less impressive, less glamorous, less "psychological."

And yet, consider: Although it takes a typist at least one-fourth of a second to type a single letter in response to a stimulus, many skilled typists type an average of eight or more characters per second (Salthouse, 1984). (Evidently they start each character well before finishing the previous character.) A professional baseball player will at least sometimes hit a ball thrown at 90 miles per hour, even though his eyes cannot move fast enough to maintain focus on the ball for the last 5 or 6 feet of its travel (Bahill & LaRitz, 1984). Highly skilled movements have to be planned ahead and executed as a coordinated unit, sometimes with almost no margin for error. To understand how they occur is a significant challenge for psychology as well as biology.

MUSCLES AND THEIR MOVEMENTS

All animal movement depends on the contraction of muscles. Vertebrate muscles fall into three categories (see Figure 8-1): **smooth muscles**, which control movements of internal organs; **skeletal**, or **striated**, **muscles**, which control movement of the body with respect to the environment; and **cardiac muscles** (the muscles of the heart), which have properties intermediate between those of smooth and skeletal muscles.

In contrast to a neuron, which can respond to a synaptic transmitter with either depolarization or hyperpolarization, a muscle has only one response: depolarization. Because a muscle has only one direction of movement, contraction, a single muscle cannot mediate alternating or opposing movements. Opposing movements depend on **antagonistic muscles**. A leg, for example, has a **flexor** muscle that raises it and an **extensor** muscle that lowers it. Walking, or any other coordinated sequence of movements, requires a regular alternation between contraction of one set of muscles and contraction of another.

Skeletal muscles are of three types (Hennig & Lømo, 1985). One type makes only slow movements, but does not fatigue. That type is responsible

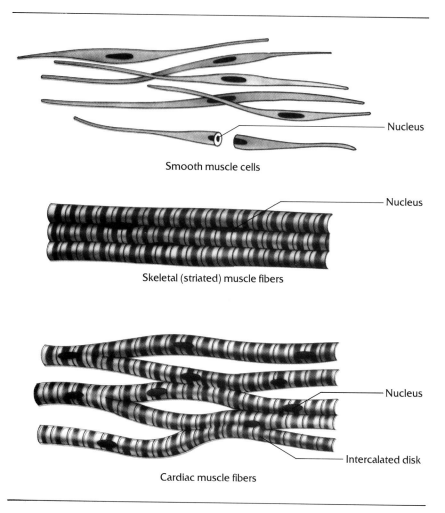

Smooth muscle cells

Nucleus

Nucleus

Skeletal (striated) muscle fibers

Nucleus

Intercalated disk

Cardiac muscle fibers

Figure 8-1. The three main types of vertebrate muscles.

mostly for postural adjustments and the like. A second type can make fast movements; it too is resistant to fatigue. It is responsible for most everyday movements. The third type makes forceful, rapid movements but fatigues quickly. In mammals, all three types are intermingled; in fish, they are separated and easy to distinguish visually: The slow muscles are red, the faster but still fatigue-resistant muscles are pink, and the fastest but rapidly fatiguing muscles are white.

Any muscle fiber contracts more vigorously at high temperatures than at low temperatures. Nevertheless, a fish, whose body temperature follows that of its surroundings, can swim just as fast at 10°C. as at 20°C. It does so by recruiting different muscles (Rome, Loughna, & Goldspink, 1984). At any temperature, a fish uses its red muscles for slow movements, red and pink for faster movements, and all three types—red, pink, and white—for its fastest bursts of activity. At high temperatures, the fish needs only red muscle activity and some pink muscle activity until its swimming speed becomes quite rapid. At lower temperatures, it begins to recruit the pink and white muscles sooner, relying on them even at moderate speeds. By recruiting the right combination of muscle types, the fish can keep its activity well coordinated and vigorous at any temperature. Fish fatigue faster at the lower temperatures, however, because of their increased dependence on white muscle fibers.

MOTOR PROGRAMS AND THEIR COMPONENTS

Movement is organized in terms of hierarchies called motor programs. A **motor program**, also known as a *fixed action pattern*, is a sequence of movements composed of many units, occurring either sequentially or simultaneously. Each unit is composed of many muscle movements. Gallistel (1980) has argued that the units of movement fall into at least three categories: reflexes, oscillators, and servomechanisms.

Reflexes

A **reflex** is a simple, automatic response to a stimulus, such as the knee-jerk reflex or the contraction of the pupils in response to light. Simple reflexes have historically served an important role in the theories of Descartes, Sechenov, Pavlov, Skinner, and others who have argued that behavior is governed by mechanical causes.

Certain reflexes are present in infants but not in older children or adults. For example, if an object is placed firmly in an infant's hand, the infant will reflexively grasp it tightly. If someone touches the cheek of an awake infant, the head will turn toward the stimulated cheek and the infant will begin to suck. If the sole of the foot is stroked, the infant will extend the big toe and fan the others (the **Babinski reflex**). Although such reflexes fade away as the infant grows older, the reflexive connections behind them remain intact. They are not lost but rather suppressed by axons from the maturing brain. If the cerebral cortex is damaged, the infant reflexes return. In fact, neurologists generally test for infant reflexes to find out whether the cerebral cortex has been damaged. The infant reflexes sometimes also return temporarily if the cerebral cortex is inactivated by alcohol, carbon dioxide, or other chemicals. (You might try testing for infant reflexes in a friend who has consumed too much alcohol.)

The stretch reflex illustrates the role of certain receptors in and near the muscle. (See Figure 8-2.) Any sudden slight stretch of the extensor muscle excites the **muscle spindle**, a stretch receptor parallel to the muscle (Merton, 1972; Miles & Evarts, 1979). Impulses from the muscle spindle ascend the sensory axon to the spinal cord, where they excite the motor neurons. The motor neurons in turn send impulses to contract the extensor muscle, thereby opposing the original stretch.

The same mechanism is responsible for the familiar knee-jerk reflex. This reflex contributes to walking: When a leg is lifted, the stretching of the spindle elicits the extensor reflex, which puts the foot and lower leg in position to bear weight.

Another receptor, the **Golgi tendon organ**, located at both ends of a muscle, controls the strength of contraction of the muscle, during both reflexive and voluntary movement. The more vigorously the muscle contracts,

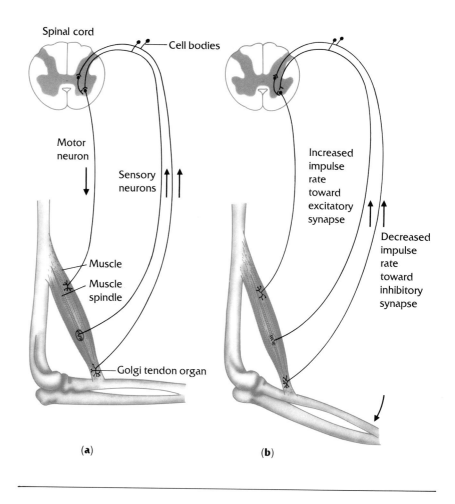

Figure 8-2. Contraction of a flexor muscle in the arm is regulated by two types of receptors. At rest (**a**) there is some activity in both the spindle and the Golgi tendon organ. A slight stretch of a muscle (**b**) due to a spontaneous fluctuation in the transmission reaching it leads to increased activity of the muscle spindles (stretch receptors) and decreased activity of the Golgi tendon organs (tension receptors).

the greater the response of the Golgi tendon organs. Their impulses travel to the spinal cord, where they inhibit the motor neurons, thus leading to a decrease in the contraction of the muscle. That is, the Golgi tendon organs act as a brake against an excessively vigorous contraction.

Oscillators

Oscillators are repetitive sequences of movements, including alternations between two movements. An oscillator, like a reflex, occurs with little variation from one occurrence to another. Examples include wing-flapping in birds and insects, fin movements in fish, and the repetitive shaking movements that a wet animal makes to dry itself off. Oscillators may be triggered by an external stimulus or may begin without obvious provocation. The main distinction from a reflex is that an oscillator is a rhythmic repetition of movements that is generated internally, not triggered by a rhythmic stimulus in the environment.

One example of an oscillator is the **scratch reflex**. C. S. Sherrington found that when he lightly irritated a dog's skin, the dog would raise a limb and scratch the irritated area. The scratching movement, with its well-timed alternation of extensor and flexor muscles, occurred at a constant rate of four to five scratches per second. As the degree of irritation increased, the length and strength of each scratching movement increased, but the rhythm stayed the same. The nerve impulses in the sensory nerves did not follow the rhythm of four to five per second. Therefore, Sherrington reasoned, the scratching rhythm was generated by some set of cells in the spinal cord, not by the sensory input. He postulated that a "motor program" in the spinal cord cells produced the rhythmic scratching movements. The role of the sensory stimuli is to trigger the motor program, not to guide the movements.

Servomechanisms

Both reflexes and oscillators produce ballistic movements. A **ballistic movement** is one that, once triggered, proceeds automatically, like a thrown ball. A ballistic missile, for example, is simply aimed and launched; once it is on its way, the people who launched it cannot alter its aim or velocity. A *guided* missile, on the other hand, can receive radio signals to correct its trajectory while it is on the way to the target.

A **servomechanism** is somewhat like a guided missile; it is a mechanism that can redirect movements on the basis of feedback from previous behaviors. For example, when a soprano holds a single note for a prolonged time, the pitch of her voice will inevitably waver slightly from the intended note. When she hears a slight change of pitch, she compensates and quickly brings her voice back to the original note. The importance of the feedback becomes apparent if we distort it. If a device records the soprano's singing and plays it back to her through earphones after a delay of a few seconds, her voice may drift off the intended note for several seconds before she hears her error. She then begins to correct her error, but by the time she hears her correction, several seconds later, she has already overcorrected. Her voice swings back and forth widely around the intended note. This procedure, called *delayed auditory feedback*, disturbs anyone's speech patterns, although one can learn to minimize the effect.

Even when behavior is guided by sensory feedback, however, it may not require feedback on a moment-by-moment basis. In order for people to type, play musical instruments, or engage in coordinated athletic activities, they have to organize a sequence of movements as an integrated whole. A skilled typist types a word or even a phrase at a time, not one letter at a time. An expert gymnast plans a complex series of movements as a unit and performs them as a unit.

Perhaps the best evidence that we plan a sequence of movements as a unit comes from an examination of the errors people make. The fact that someone who intended to say "our dear old queen" has actually uttered "our queer old dean" indicates that the phrase was spoken as a whole, not as one word or one sound at a time (Lashley, 1951).

Furthermore, certain sequences of coordinated behavior can proceed remarkably well even after sensory feedback has been greatly reduced. For

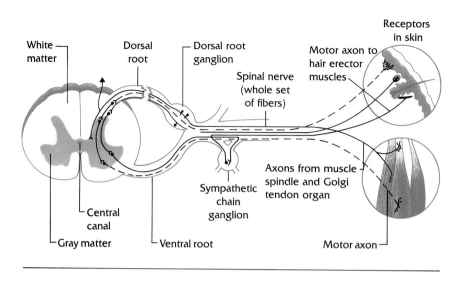

Figure 8-3. A cross-section through the spinal cord. All sensory nerves enter the spinal cord through the dorsal root. Thus, a cut through the dorsal root (as shown) permanently deprives the animal of touch sensations from part of the body, while the motor nerves remain intact.

example, it is possible to eliminate most of the normal touch feedback from arm and leg movements by surgery. Recall that all the sensory nerves entering the spinal cord enter in the dorsal root, while all the motor nerves from the spinal cord leave through the ventral root. Because of this anatomical segregation, it is possible to cut all the sensory nerves for a part of the body without harming the motor nerves. (See Figure 8-3.) Although the animal loses all sensation in the affected part of the body, it suffers no paralysis.

Taub and Berman (1968) cut all the afferent nerves from one arm of a monkey. (Such a limb is referred to as **deafferented**.) After the operation, the monkey did not spontaneously use the limb for walking, for picking up objects, or for any other voluntary behaviors. The investigators initially assumed that the monkey could not use the limb because of the lack of sensory feedback. In a later experiment, however, they cut the afferent nerves of both forelimbs; a monkey with this more extensive damage recovered use of both deafferented limbs. Coordination of the limbs recovered gradually over 2 to 6 months, not completely to normal but to a fair approximation: The monkey could walk moderately fast, it could climb upward or sideways on the walls of metal cages, and it could even pick up a raisin between its thumb and forefinger.

Apparently, a monkey with one deafferented forelimb fails to use it not because it cannot use it but merely because it finds it easier to rely on the normal limb. When both limbs are deafferented, the monkey is forced to use both. Evidently, walking is possible without touch feedback from the limbs.

We should not conclude, however, that sensory feedback is unimportant for walking or similar behaviors. Deafferented monkeys are certainly slower and less precise in their movements than normal monkeys. Also, such monkeys have at least indirect feedback, because they can feel their body move forward after certain movements and feel it fall after others.

Putting the Units Together

A behavioral sequence may include a combination of elements. For example, when a person walks, the flexion and extension of each leg alternate in an oscillating manner, while the intensity of each leg movement is modified by reflexes each time the leg hits the ground. For a locust in flight, the movement of the wings is controlled by an oscillator; superimposed on these movements are reflexive adjustments for any displacement by the wind (Gallistel, 1980).

Certain sequences of behavior are governed by a motor program, which may include any combination of reflexes, oscillators, and servomechanisms in an integrated whole. A motor program can be either learned or built into the nervous system, but once it is established it may be fairly inflexible.

One example of a motor program is amphibian locomotion (Weiss, 1941). A salamander moves its four legs in a fixed order. Weiss cut off the two forelimbs and grafted them on again, facing backward. The nerves that had been cut during this procedure eventually grew back and reestablished connections to the muscles. From that time on, for the rest of the salamander's life, its locomotion was maladaptive. Each muscle moved at the time when it would normally have moved if it had been in its normal position. In the reversed position, however, the forelimbs moved one way while the hindlimbs moved the other way, and the salamander as a whole hardly moved at all. Evidently, a motor program sent a pattern of impulses to the legs that could not be modified.

Another example of a motor program is the grooming behavior of mice (Fentress, 1973). Periodically during the day, a mouse sits up, licks its paws, wipes its paws over its face, closes its eyes as the paws pass over them, licks the paws again, and so forth. The mouse begins with a series of rapid rubs on the nose and then follows with longer, slower strokes. Even mice that lack forelimbs assume the typical posture for grooming and then wiggle their stumps back and forth. Periodically they extend their tongues and close their eyes in synchrony with the movements of the limb stumps, just as if intact paws were passing back and forth over the face. Moreover, they begin with rapid stump movements and then shift to slower movements, like normal mice. In short, mice seem to have a motor program for this complex sequence of movements; once triggered, it runs to completion even if the sensory feedback is abnormal.

In humans, yawning may qualify as a motor program (Provine, 1986). A yawn is composed of the opening of the mouth, a prolonged inhalation, often accompanied by stretching, and a shorter exhalation. Yawns are very consistent in duration, with a mean of just less than 6 seconds.

By comparing species, we can gain some insight into how a motor program can be gained or lost through evolution. For example, if you hold almost any bird several feet above the ground and then drop it, the bird will stretch out its wings and flap them. Provine (1979, 1981) found the same movements in chickens with featherless wings or amputated wings, even though the wing movements failed to break their fall. On the other hand, penguins, emus, and rheas, which have not used their wings for flight in countless generations, do not extend or flap their wings when they are dropped (Provine, 1984). Although their ancient ancestors presumably had this motor program, it has been lost over the course of evolution.

What Are the Units of Movement?

Although Gallistel's analysis of movement in terms of reflexes, oscillators, and servomechanisms is useful, it is not the only way to analyze movement. For example, we could describe the behavior of a cat that stalks and captures a mouse in at least two ways: First, we could describe it as a series of meaningful acts—for example, the cat follows the scent of the mouse until it sees or hears the mouse, then runs toward the mouse, dodging obstacles, until the mouse is close, and then springs onto the mouse and captures it with claws or teeth. Second, we could describe the behavior as a sequence of simple units—an oscillator that alternates contraction and flexion of each limb, reflexive adjustments to correct the strength of each muscle contraction, and so forth. In a sense, both of those descriptions are equivalent. But which way does the nervous system organize behavior—by purposeful units, by muscle contractions, or by some other means?

Apparently, different parts of the nervous system organize behavior in different ways; some operate in terms of large purposeful combinations, some in terms of individual movements, and probably some in terms of intermediate levels as well. Consider an example that illustrates organization by purposes: If brain damage prevents a particular pattern of muscle contractions, an animal will substitute a different pattern that achieves the same end. Thus, if a rat learns to run through a maze and then damage to the cerebellum prevents it from running, it will walk, hobble, stagger, or if need be roll through the maze to reach the goal box (Lashley & McCarthy, 1926).

On the other hand, certain drugs and certain kinds of brain damage produce movement patterns that are more easily analyzed in terms of movements than of purposes. After an injection of the drug haloperidol, rats show an abnormally strong resistance to being pushed along a horizontal surface. They grip with their toes, extend their legs, stiffen their body, and arch their spinal column. Although this appears to be a single, coordinated, purposeful act, it is composed of two independent movements (Pellis, Chen, & Teitelbaum, 1985). A tight abdominal bandage that minimizes touch stimulation of the hindquarters abolishes all resisting movements with the rear half of the body but does not affect use of the front half. (See Figure 8-4.) A tight bandage around the head coupled with damage to the vestibular system abolishes all resisting movements by the front half, without affecting use of the rear half. It makes more sense to describe the rat's behavior as the summation of two reflexive responses than as a single purposive whole.

After an injection of apomorphine (a drug that stimulates dopamine synapses), or during a stage of recovery after damage to the lateral hypothalamus, rats engage in a variety of stereotyped behaviors, including walking forward, circling, pivoting tightly, moving their forequarters from side to side, and other behaviors. If they walk into a corner or to the end of a tube, they may get trapped there, unable to turn around or back up. All those stereotyped behaviors can be shown to be combinations of just three elements: maintaining contact between the snout and any firm surface, walking

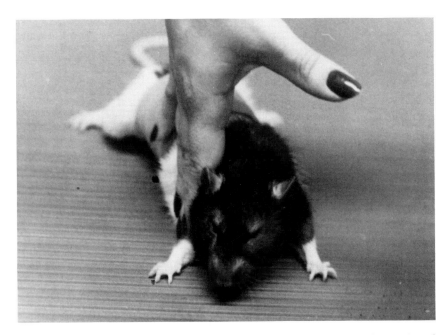

Figure 8-4. A rat that has been given haloperidol moves little on its own, but vigorously resists being pushed to the side. After its abdomen has been tightly bandaged, however, it resists only with its forelimbs. (From Pellis, Chen, & Teitelbaum, 1985.)

forward, and turning. That is, apparently complex actions can be analyzed as three simple movements, combined in varying strengths (Szechtman, Ornstein, Teitelbaum, & Golani, 1985).

The same principles apply to humans. Patients suffering from Parkinson's disease (discussed later in this chapter) often respond to their medications with stereotyped behaviors that resemble the stereotyped behaviors of drugged rats (Schallert, DeRyck, & Teitelbaum, 1980).

THE ROLE OF THE SPINAL CORD AND THE MOTOR NERVES IN MOVEMENT

As we have seen, all sensory neurons enter the dorsal side of the spinal cord, and all motor neurons leave through the ventral side. Each motor neuron has its cell body within the spinal cord, while its axon extends all the way to the muscle it innervates. Various diseases of the spinal cord can thus impair the control of movement. (See Table 8-1.)

Each muscle is composed of many individual muscle fibers innervated by **motor neurons**, as illustrated in Figure 8-5 and Color Plate 19. In the skeletal muscles of mammals and birds, a given axon may innervate more than one muscle fiber, although no muscle fiber can receive input from more than one axon. The eye muscles have a ratio of about one axon per three muscle fibers; the biceps muscles of the arm have a ratio of one axon for more than a hundred fibers (Evarts, 1979). Generally, when each axon innervates relatively few muscle fibers, as in the eye muscles, movements can be made with greater precision than when a single axon innervates a great many fibers.

The **nerve-muscle junction**, the point where an axon meets a muscle fiber, is merely a special kind of synapse. In skeletal muscles, every axon releases acetylcholine at the nerve-muscle junction, and the acetylcholine

Table 8-1.   Some Disorders of the Spinal Cord

Paralysis	Total lack of movement in one part of the body. Paralysis follows damage to the motor neurons in the spinal cord or to their axons in the periphery.
Spastic paralysis	Inability to move one part of the body voluntarily, although reflexive movements and tremors remain. The cause is damage to axons extending from the brain to the spinal cord, with the motor neurons themselves remaining intact.
Paraplegia	Loss of sensation and voluntary muscle control in both legs. The cause is a cut through the spinal cord above the segments attached to the legs. Reflexes remain in the legs. Although no messages can pass between the brain and the legs, the genitals still respond reflexively to touch. Paraplegics can function sexually and can satisfy their partners even though they feel nothing themselves. They sometimes experience orgasm during dreams, independent of genital arousal (Money, 1967).
Quadriplegia	Loss of sensation and muscle control in all four extremities, due to a cut through the spinal cord above the level controlling the arms.
Hemiplegia	Loss of sensation and muscle control in the arm and leg on one side, due to a cut halfway through the spinal cord or (more commonly) to damage to one of the hemispheres of the cerebral cortex.
Tabes dorsalis	A late stage of syphilis. The dorsal roots of the spinal cord deteriorate gradually, impairing sensation in the legs and pelvic region, reflexes in the leg, walking, and bladder and bowel control.
Poliomyelitis	Paralysis caused by a virus that damages cell bodies of motor neurons.
Amyotrophic lateral sclerosis (Lou Gehrig's disease)	Gradual weakness and paralysis, starting with the arms and later spreading to the legs. Both motor neurons and axons from the brain to the motor neurons are destroyed. The cause is unknown.

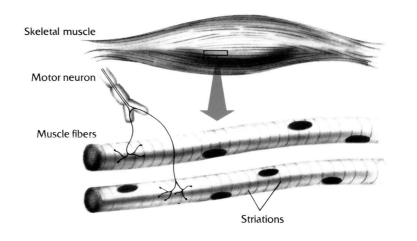

Figure 8-5. Structure of a skeletal muscle. A motor neuron can innervate more than one muscle fiber, but there is only one axon innervating a skeletal muscle fiber at one time in mammals or birds.

always has an excitatory effect; that is, the transmitter always causes the muscle to contract. Muscle relaxation occurs passively by the cessation of transmission; the nerve sends no special message to induce relaxation.

Myasthenia gravis (MY-us-THEE-nee-uh GRAH-viss) is an autoimmune disease in which the body forms antibodies against the acetylcholine receptors at nerve-muscle junctions (Lindstrom, 1979). Most patients have measurable blood levels of antibodies that will destroy those receptors (Drachman, Adams, & Josifer, 1982). Myasthenia gravis is a rare condition, responsible each year for the deaths of about two or three people per 100,000 over the age of 75, and an occasional younger person (Chandra, Bharucha, & Schoenberg, 1984).

The symptoms of myasthenia gravis are weakness and rapid fatigue of all movements. Any repeated movement gets weaker rapidly unless the person pauses to rest. Because the muscles have fewer than the normal number of acetylcholine receptors, the receptors that remain can move the muscle normally only if they receive the maximum amount of transmitter. After the motor neuron has fired a few times in quick succession, later action potentials release fewer quanta of acetylcholine. The same is true for healthy people, but they notice no change in their movement because they have an abundance of acetylcholine receptors. In people with myasthenia gravis, transmission at the nerve-muscle junction is precarious at best, and even a slight decline in acetylcholine availability has powerful effects (Drachman, 1978).

Myasthenia gravis can be treated with drugs that suppress the immune system (Niakan, Harati, & Rolak, 1986). That approach has its limitations, of course, because suppression of the immune system leaves the patient vulnerable to other illnesses. Many patients are also given drugs that inhibit the enzyme acetylcholinesterase, which breaks down the transmitter acetylcholine. The result is to prolong the action of acetylcholine at the nerve-muscle junction. It is necessary to monitor the dose carefully, however, as an excess can impair use of the muscles just as badly as myasthenia gravis itself.

THE ROLE OF THE CEREBELLUM IN MOVEMENT

The cerebellum, as we noted in Chapter 4, is important for motor control, and possibly for certain cognitive functions as well (Leiner, Leiner, & Dow, 1986). The term *cerebellum* is Latin for "little brain." Although it is smaller than the rest of the brain, it contains so many neurons and so many connections that its potential for information processing is comparable to that of the cerebral cortex.

The cerebellum receives input from the spinal cord, from each of the sensory systems by way of the cranial nerve nuclei, and from the cerebral cortex. Thus, it is well suited to relate movement to sensory information. The output fibers from the cerebellum project mostly to the thalamus and the *red nucleus*, a structure in the midbrain. From the thalamus, information from the cerebellum is conveyed to the cerebral cortex. Several other paths extend from the cerebellum, including one that extends directly to the nucleus of the third cranial nerve, which controls eye movements.

For a long time it was believed that the role of the cerebellum was merely to improve the coordination of muscles and to maintain equilibrium. The cerebellum does make those contributions, but it has other functions as well. In particular, it is now known that cerebellar neurons are active prior to movements, not just during and after them. Thus, the cerebellum seems to generate and plan movements as well as coordinate them.

Hans Kornhuber (1971, 1974) proposed that the cerebellum plays a key role in all voluntary ballistic movements—that is, those not dependent on moment-by-moment sensory feedback. This role includes the development of learned motor programs that turn slow, deliberate movements into rapid, well-practiced habits. Evidence for this role has come from individuals who have experienced damage to the cerebellum; such people must carefully plan each movement, even those that used to come automatically.

Variations in the cerebellum across animal species also support Kornhuber's viewpoint. The cerebellum is proportionately larger in birds than in most mammals; birds certainly make a great many rapid, ballistic movements in flight and when landing on perches. The sloth, on the other extreme, is a mammal proverbial for its slowness. When Murphy and O'Leary (1973) made cerebellar lesions in sloths, they found no observable change in the animals' movement patterns.

In humans, damage to the cerebellum causes difficulty with a variety of rapid movements, including speaking, writing, typing, playing a musical instrument, and athletic skills. Affected people make errors in the direction, intensity, velocity, and timing of movements. Although they can still perform the necessary movements individually, they cannot link them together smoothly (Brooks, 1984; Dichgans, 1984). Ordinarily, certain movements accompany one another. For example, when pulling the right arm back in preparing to throw a ball, a normal person will put more weight on the right leg, raise the left leg and the left arm, and shift the pelvis and the neck. After cerebellar damage, a person may throw with the right arm without making the appropriate movements with the rest of the body.

A consistent deficit after cerebellar damage is **dysdiadochokinesia** (dis-die-ah-doe-koh-kih-NEE-zee-uh), an inability to perform rapid alternating movements, such as clapping hands. (You might want to learn this term, if only to impress your friends. The next time some basketball player has trouble dribbling a ball, you can smugly announce that the problem is dysdiadochokinesia.)

The cerebellum is particularly important for the control of **saccades** (sa-KADS or sa-KAHDS), rapid eye movements from one fixation point to another. Saccadic eye movements depend on impulses from the cerebellum and the frontal cortex to the cranial nerves. All saccades are rapid and ballistic. Only one speed is available for moving the eyes from one fixation point to another. The distance determines the speed. If you attempt to move your eyes slowly from one point to another, your eye muscles divide the total movement into a large number of short movements with pauses between them. Each of the short movements, however, is rapid and ballistic.

A normal, healthy person moves his or her eyes from one fixation point to another by a single movement or by one large movement plus a small

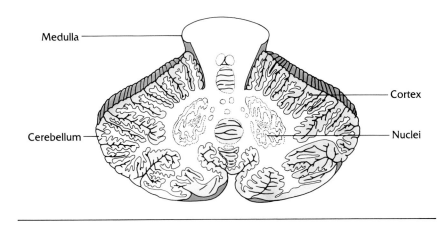

Medulla

Cortex

Cerebellum

Nuclei

Figure 8-6. Cross-section through the cerebellum and medulla, showing the location of the cerebellar nuclei relative to the cerebellar cortex.

correction at the end. Someone with mild cerebellar damage, however, has difficulty programming the angle and distance of eye movements (Dichgans, 1984). The eyes make many short movements until by trial and error they eventually focus on the intended spot. Someone with more extensive damage to the cerebellum may have no voluntary eye movements at all.

Another test of cerebellar damage is the *finger-to-nose test*. The person is instructed to hold one arm straight out and then, at command, to touch his or her nose as quickly as possible. A normal person does so in three steps: First, the finger moves ballistically to a point just in front of the nose. This *move* function depends on the *cortex* (outer covering) of the cerebellum, which has cells that send messages to the *nuclei* in the interior of the cerebellum. (See Figure 8-6.) Second, the finger remains steady at that spot for a fraction of a second. This *hold* function depends on just the nuclei themselves (Kornhuber, 1974). Finally, the finger is slowly moved to the nose by a slower movement that does not depend on the cerebellum.

After damage to the cortex of the cerebellum, a person has trouble with the initial, rapid movement. Either the finger does not go far enough or it goes too far, striking the person in the face. After damage to certain nuclei of the cerebellum, the person may have difficulty with the hold segment—after the finger reaches a point just in front of the nose, it wavers wildly.

The symptoms of cerebellar damage markedly resemble those of alcohol intoxication. Drunken individuals as a rule are clumsy, their speech is slurred, and their eye movements are inaccurate. A police officer testing someone for possible drunkenness may use the finger-to-nose test or other tests that are also used for diagnosing damage to the cerebellum. The reason for the resemblance is that the cerebellum is one of the first areas of the brain to show the effects of moderate degrees of alcohol intoxication.

THE ROLE OF THE BASAL GANGLIA IN MOVEMENT

The term **basal ganglia** applies collectively to a group of large subcortical structures in the forebrain (see Figure 8-7): the caudate nucleus, the putamen, the globus pallidus, the substantia nigra, and the subthalamic nucleus

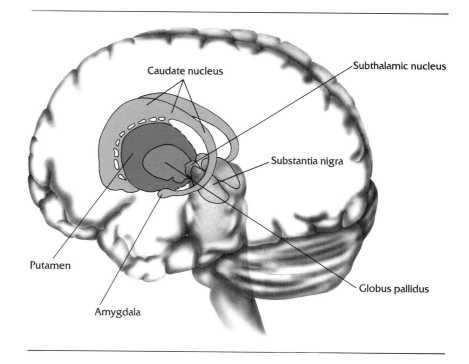

Figure 8-7. Location of the basal ganglia.

(DeLong et al., 1984). These structures receive their input from parts of the thalamus and from all parts of the cerebral cortex.

The basal ganglia contribute to both movement and cognitive functions. In the control of movement, they are apparently not responsible for selecting which muscles will be active at a given time. Rather, they control the direction and amplitude of movements—especially postural movements, more than finger or hand movements. After damage to the basal ganglia, people can still make all the movements they could have made before the damage, but the movements are weak, slow, and poorly coordinated (DeLong et al., 1984; Marsden, 1984).

Two medical disorders associated with damage to the basal ganglia are Parkinson's disease and Huntington's disease.

Parkinson's Disease

Parkinson's disease is an affliction that occurs mostly in the elderly. Among people over age 75, it is responsible for the death of about one person per thousand, with a higher rate among whites than blacks in the United States (Chandra, Bharucha, & Schoenberg, 1984). The main symptoms are slow movements, difficulty initiating movements, rigidity, and tremors. Many people with Parkinson's disease become severely depressed. At this point it is not known to what extent the depression is an understandable reaction to a serious illness and to what extent it is a symptom of the illness itself (Dakof & Mendelsohn, 1986).

The immediate cause of Parkinson's disease is the degeneration of a path of dopamine-containing axons from the **substantia nigra** to the caudate

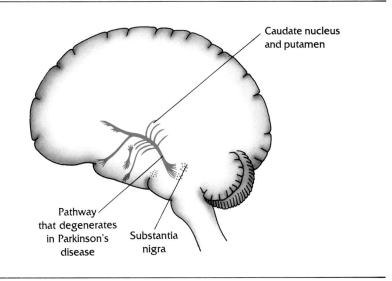

Caudate nucleus
and putamen

Pathway
that degenerates
in Parkinson's
disease

Substantia
nigra

Figure 8-8. Brain pathways involved in Parkinson's disease.

nucleus and putamen. (See Figure 8-8.) (What causes this path to degenerate is another story, to be discussed shortly.) In the absence of treatment, these axons continue to degenerate, the condition worsens, and ultimately the person dies.

Treatment for Parkinson's Disease. Because we do not know how to stop the axons from degenerating, the goal of therapy has been to replace the missing dopamine. A patient cannot, however, simply take dopamine pills or injections, because dopamine does not cross the blood-brain barrier. L-DOPA, a precursor to dopamine (refer back to Figure 3-6), does, however, cross the barrier. Most people with Parkinson's disease take L-DOPA pills daily, often in conjunction with other drugs. (See Figure 8-9.) The L-DOPA, after reaching the brain, is converted into dopamine. It relieves the symptoms of Parkinson's disease and may return the person to years of active life. It does not cure the problem, however, and the gradual destruction of the dopamine-containing axons continues.

Moreover, L-DOPA produces harmful side effects, including nausea, restlessness, low blood pressure, and occasionally hallucinations and delusions. The side effects can be relieved somewhat by additional drugs that prevent L-DOPA from being converted to dopamine before it enters the brain (Dakof & Mendelsohn, 1986).

The side effects of L-DOPA generally grow worse after someone has taken the medication for a long time. However, it is difficult to be sure whether the side effects worsen *because* the person has taken the L-DOPA for so long or simply because the underlying disease has grown worse in the meantime. Because of this uncertainty, it remains controversial whether physicians should prescribe L-DOPA at once for Parkinson's patients or whether they should delay giving the medication and interrupt it for "drug holidays," in hopes of minimizing the side effects.

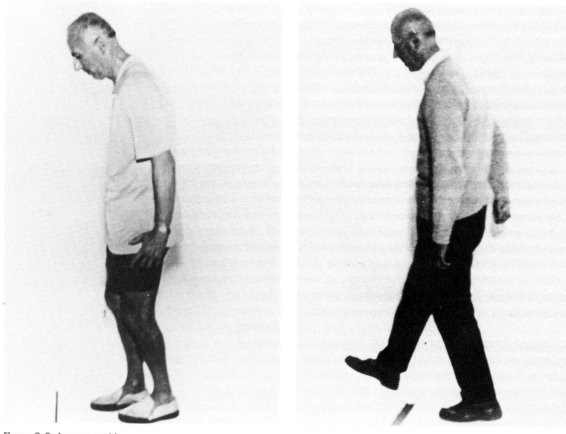

Figure 8-9. A person with Parkinson's disease before (*left*) and after (*right*) treatment with L-DOPA. (From Lance & McLeod, 1975.)

Possible Causes of Parkinson's Disease.   Parkinson's disease is one of the few neurological or psychological disorders that do not run in families. Even having an identical twin with Parkinson's disease does not increase one's risk of getting it oneself (Duvoisin, Eldridge, Williams, Nutt, & Calne, 1981). It would seem, then, that it is caused by something in one's environment.

A potentially important clue to the origin of Parkinson's disease was discovered by accident (Ballard, Tetrud, & Langston, 1985). In 1982, several young adults (ages 22 to 42) in northern California developed symptoms of Parkinson's disease after using a heroin substitute, which all of them had bought from the same dealer. (See Digression 8-1.) At first, their physicians resisted considering their condition to be Parkinson's disease, because that disorder usually develops slowly in old age, while these patients had developed it rapidly at a young age. Eventually, however, it became clear that the symptoms matched Parkinson's disease exactly. Before the investigators had a chance to alert the community to the danger of the heroin substitute, a number of other people had used it. Some of them developed severe, eventually fatal Parkinson's disease. Others developed milder symptoms. Still others have developed no symptoms so far, although their substantia nigra has suffered damage that puts them intermediate between normal and Par-

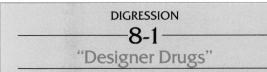

DIGRESSION
8-1
"Designer Drugs"

The United States enforces laws against the manufacture, sale, or use of a great many drugs believed to be harmful. Heroin is one such drug. One way to evade the law is to sell a drug that produces similar effects but that is chemically different, even if the difference is as minor as, say, substituting a methyl group for a single hydrogen ion. The laws apply to heroin and other drugs that have been chemically identified and listed by the federal government. They do not apply to new drugs that have never been sold before, that the government may not even have heard of.

Because of this enormous loophole in the legal system, certain drug dealers manufacture "designer drugs"—drugs that may produce effects similar to heroin (or whatever) and that remain technically legal until the government obtains enough of it to determine what it is and pass a law against it. Although the risk to the drug dealer is low, the risk to the user is unknown and may in certain cases be quite severe.

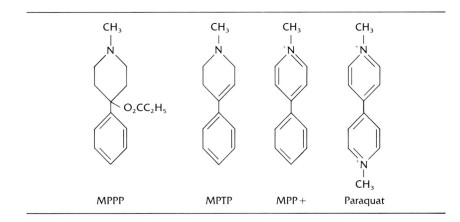

MPPP   MPTP   MPP+   Paraquat

Figure 8-10. The chemical structures of MPPP, MPTP, MPP+, and paraquat, a common pesticide.

kinson's disease (Calne et al., 1985). These patients are considered to be at serious risk for developing Parkinson's disease later in life.

Apparently, the drug dealer had attempted to make a drug known as MPPP but had in fact made a mixture of MPPP and MPTP. MPTP is converted by the body to MPP+, which is selectively toxic to the substantia nigra. A number of studies have now confirmed that injections of MPTP can produce symptoms of Parkinson's disease in monkeys and other animals (Snyder & D'Amato, 1986).

No one supposes that illegal drug use is responsible for most cases of Parkinson's disease. A more likely hypothesis is that MPTP or similar chemicals may be present in the environment as pollutants of the air or water. Perhaps certain people accumulate enough of such chemicals to inflict partial damage on their substantia nigra. When they grow old, that early damage combines with the natural loss of cells that occurs in old age to produce the symptoms of Parkinson's disease.

What might be the source of MPTP in the environment? A number of herbicides and pesticides, including *paraquat*, have a chemical structure similar to that of MPTP and MPP+. (See Figure 8-10.) Barbeau (as described by Snyder & D'Amato, 1986) found that among geographical regions near Montreal, Quebec, the areas that used paraquat most frequently had rates of Parkinson's disease seven times higher than the areas that used it least. If future research confirms a relationship between Parkinson's disease and toxic chemicals, society may be able to take steps to reduce the future prevalence of Parkinson's disease.

One special reason to be concerned about paraquat is that in 1978, the United States government financed a program of spraying Mexican marijuana fields with paraquat in an effort to eradicate the plant. Many of the marijuana leaves were sold in spite of the contamination, however, and were presumably smoked. An estimated 9,000 people in the United States may have been exposed to at least 100 μg of paraquat through the marijuana (Landrigan, Powell, James, & Taylor, 1983).

Huntington's Disease

Huntington's disease, also known as *Huntington's chorea*, is a severe neurological disorder related to damage in the caudate nucleus and putamen. The motor symptoms usually begin with a facial twitch; later, tremors spread to other parts of the body. Eventually, walking, speech, and other voluntary movements become impossible.

In addition, people with Huntington's disease suffer psychological disorders, which may be noticed before the motor symptoms. Among the psychological symptoms are impaired memory and judgment, delusions, emotional outbursts, socially inappropriate behaviors, and a lack of self-grooming (Sanberg & Coyle, 1984).

The most common age of onset is 30 to 50, although cases are known with onset in childhood or in old age. Once the symptoms emerge, both the psychological and the motor symptoms grow progressively worse over a period of about 15 years, culminating in death (Chase, Wexler, & Barbeau, 1979). About 50 people per million in the United States eventually develop Huntington's disease.

Nature of the Brain Damage in Huntington's Disease. Huntington's disease is characterized by a progressive loss of neurons especially in the caudate nucleus, putamen, and globus pallidus, with some loss in the cerebral cortex. The overall brain weight may decline by 15 to 20 percent before death (Sanberg & Coyle, 1984). Unlike with Parkinson's disease, in which only dopamine fibers degenerate, the damage in Huntington's disease is to many types of neurons. Because so many cell types are lost, no drug therapy is remarkably effective.

An injection of **kainic acid** into the caudate nucleus and putamen of rats produces both a pattern of behavior and a pattern of brain damage that mimic Huntington's disease (Sanberg & Johnston, 1981). The same occurs after injections of **quinolinic acid** (Beal et al., 1986). Both kainic acid and quinolinic acid resemble the synaptic transmitter *glutamate;* they damage neurons by overstimulating them. The body itself normally produces small amounts of quinolinic acid. It is therefore possible that the brain damage of Huntington's disease is caused by overstimulation or oversensitivity to this or similar chemicals.

Plate 12. A synapse, magnified thousands of times by an electron microscope. The synapse is the point at which one neuron communicates with another by releasing a chemical that has been stored in vesicles. The vesicles are seen here as the many round structures in the middle cell. The dark junction at the bottom of that cell is a synapse, where the vesicles are releasing their contents to the next cell. (The color has been added; electronmicrographs are ordinarily colorless.) (D. D. Kunkel, University of Washington/Biological Photo Service)

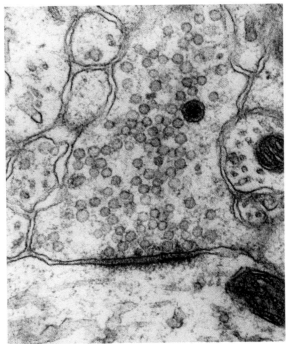

Plate 13. A microelectrode and neurons, magnified hundreds of times by a light microscope. Brain tissue has been sliced and stained to make the neurons easy to see. In the living organism, microelectrodes like this one can be used to record the electrical activity of a neuron. Such studies are responsible for much of our knowledge of how neurons work and what information they receive and send. (Fritz Goro)

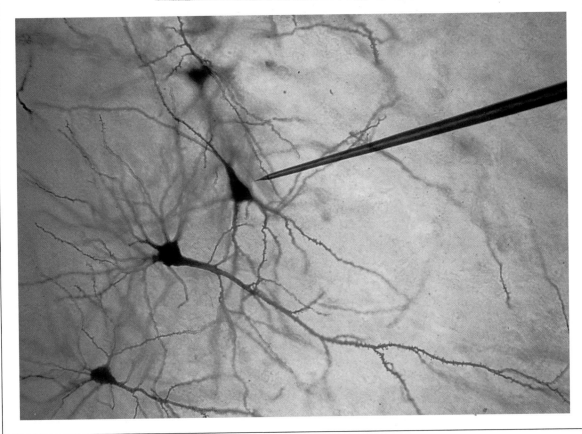

Plate 14. Glia cells (below). Glia, also known as neuroglia, perform a number of important roles in the nervous system even though they do not communicate information on their own. Among other functions, they guide the growth and migration of neurons, produce the myelin sheaths that insulate certain vertebrate axons, and remove waste products from the brain. (Manfred Kage/ Peter Arnold, Inc.)

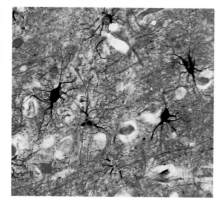

Plate 15. Neurons (right), the cells that compose the nervous system. The distinctive characteristic of each neuron is its shape, which determines the cells from which it can receive information and the cells to which it can send information. Because neurons differ greatly in their branching patterns, some pool information from a great many sources and send their output over distances of a meter or more. Others have a much more restricted input and output, limited only to immediately adjacent cells. (McCoy/Scheilbel/Rainbow)

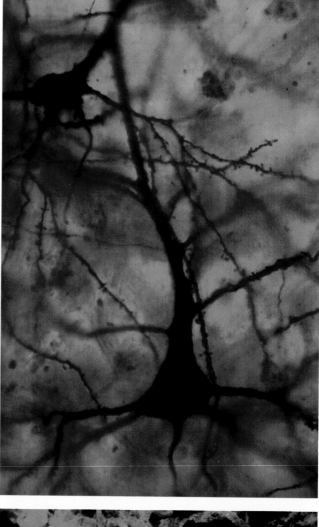

Plate 16. Axon end bulbs (upper left of photo). An axon is a single, long, thin extension of the neuron that carries information toward other cells. At the tip of each of its branches, it swells to form an end bulb, the point from which it releases chemical transmitters into synapses. (J. F. McGinty/Peter Arnold, Inc.)

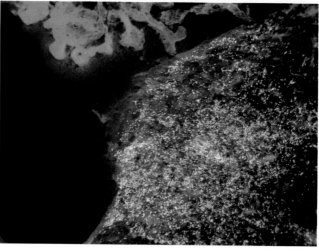

Plate 17. A taste bud (below). A taste bud contains about 50 receptor cells, each of which responds to various chemicals, sending messages that the brain ultimately interprets as a taste experience. (SIU/Peter Arnold, Inc.)

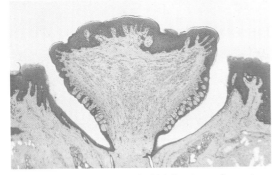

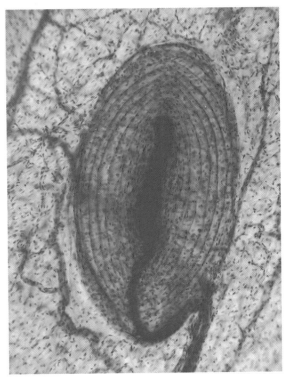

Plate 18. A Pacinian corpuscle (right), a type of receptor that responds best to any sudden displacement of the skin or to high-frequency vibrations. If constant pressure is applied to the skin, the Pacinian corpuscles quickly stop responding. Other receptors in the skin have different patterns of reponse to various kinds of touch. The onionlike outer structure of the Pacinian corpuscle provides a mechanical support to the neuron inside it, so that the neuron will be bent by a sudden stimulus but not a sustained one. (Ed Reschke/Peter Arnold, Inc.)

Plate 19. An axon innervating skeletal muscle fibers. A single axon may innervate a number of muscle fibers, but each fiber receives its input from only one axon. Movements can be much more precise where each axon innervates only a few fibers, as is the case with the eye muscle, than where it innervates many fibers, as is the case with the biceps muscle. (Ed Reschke/Peter Arnold, Inc.)

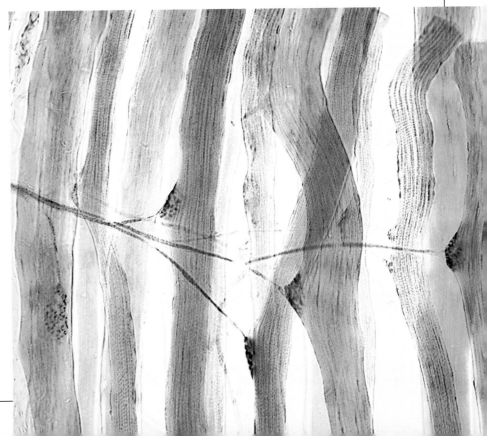

Plate 20. A beam of light separated into its wavelengths, revealing the spectrum of colors.

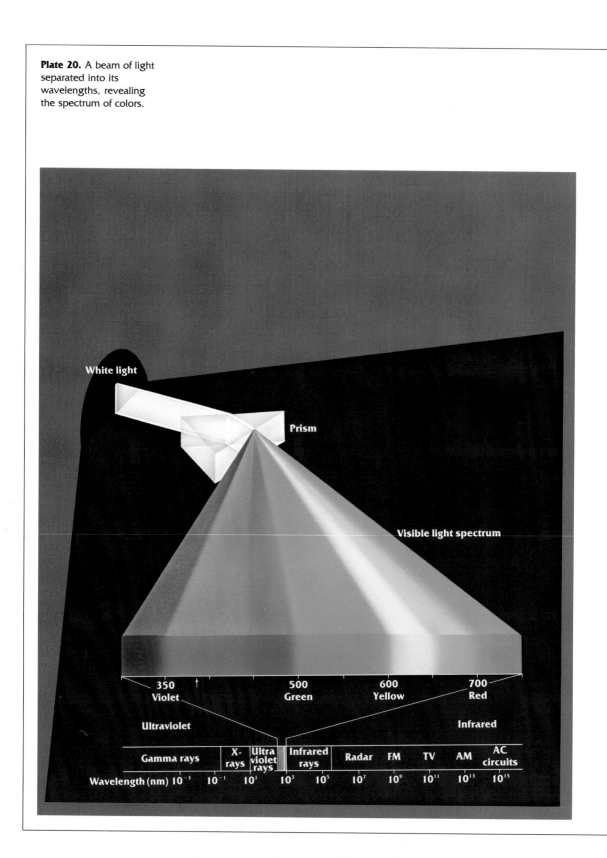

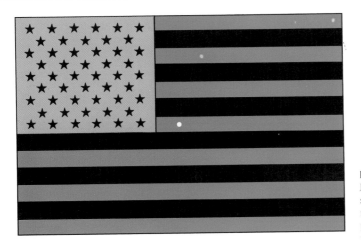

Plate 21. Stimulus for demonstrating negative color afterimages. Stare at one point of the flag under bright light for about a minute and then look at a white field. You should see a red, white, and blue flag.

Plate 22. A cross-section through the retina. Light enters from the top and passes through several layers of cells and axons before it reaches the rods and cones, the tightly packed receptors at the back of the retina. The receptors are seen here as nearly vertical lines on the lower half of the photo. Above the receptors is a layer composed largely of bipolar cells; above that is a thinner layer of ganglion cells. Axons from the ganglion cells group together to form a long length-wise band near the top of the photo. That band courses to the blind spot of the retina, where the axons from all the ganglion cells leave the retina and extend toward the brain via the optic nerve. (Ed Reschke/Peter Arnold, Inc.)

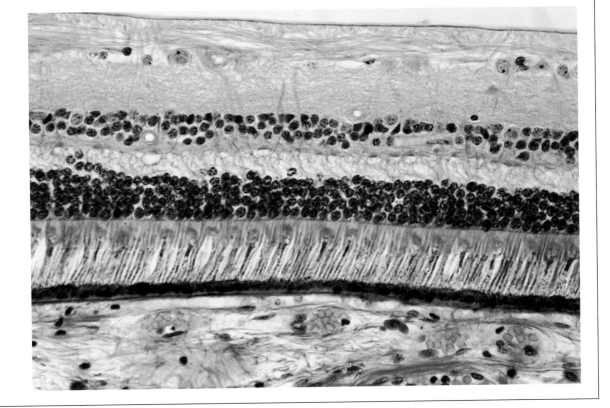

Plate 23. (A color version of 15-4.) Three PET scans per day (showing three horizontal planes) for a patient who went through rapid and enormous changes in mood. The patient was depressed on May 17 and May 27; brain metabolic rates were low on those two days. On May 18 the patient was in a cheerful, active, hypomanic mood, and the brain metabolic rate was high. (Courtesy of L. R. Baxter Jr.)

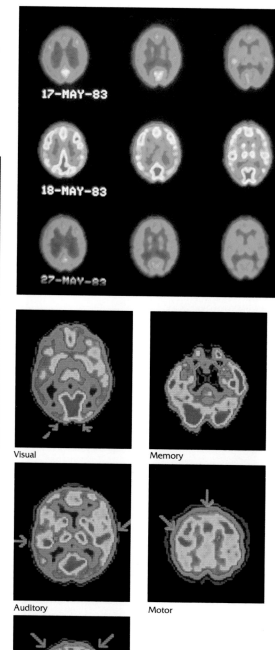

17-MAY-83

18-MAY-83

27-MAY-83

Plate 24. PET scans of normal people, showing differences during various tasks. Red indicates the greatest level of brain activity; blue indicates the least. *Left column:* Brain activity during passive exposure to a visual task and an auditory task and during performance of a cognitive task, an auditory memory task, and a task of moving fingers of the right hand in a fixed sequence. *Center and right columns:* Brain activity without auditory input, while listening to language, to music, or to both. Arrows indicate regions of greatest activation. Note that different areas of the brain are activated by different tasks. (Courtesy of Michael E. Phelps and John C. Mazziotta, University of California, Los Angeles, School of Medicine)

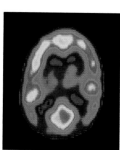

Resting state

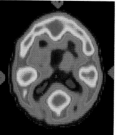

Language and music

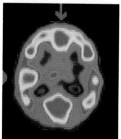

Language

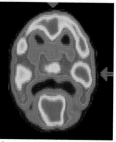

Music

Visual

Memory

Auditory

Motor

Cognitive

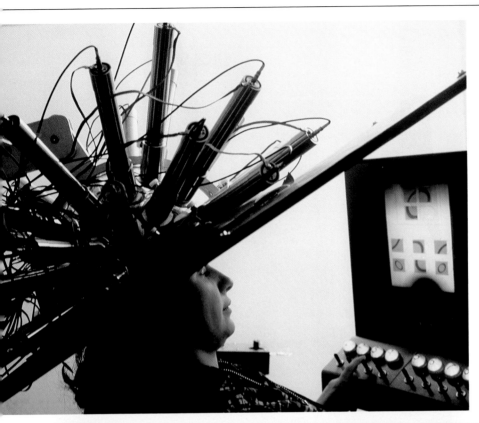

Plate 25. Person engaged in a cognitive task while attached to an apparatus that records regional cerebral blood flow (rCBF) in the brain. (Burt Glinn/Magnum Photos)

Plate 26. Regional cerebral blood flow in normal people (top) and in patients with schizophrenia (bottom). The two views on the left show activity during a simple numbers matching task. The two views on the right show activity during performance of a test that activates the prefrontal cortex of normal subjects. Note that it fails to enhance activity in the schizophrenic subjects. (Karen Berman and Daniel Weinberger, National Institute of Mental Health)

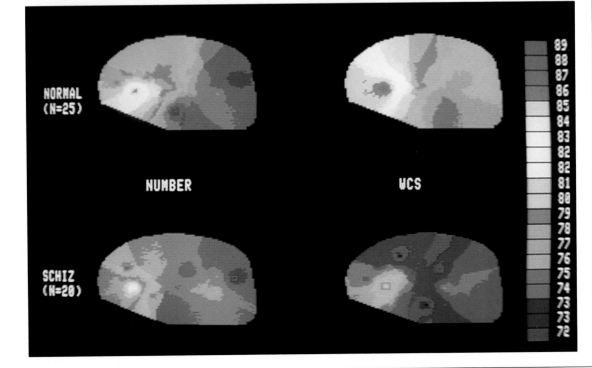

NORMAL (N=25)

SCHIZ (N=20)

NUMBER

WCS

89
88
87
86
85
84
83
82
82
81
80
79
78
77
76
75
74
73
73
72

Plate 27. Ventral view of *Aplysia*, a mollusc used in many studies of the physiology of learning. Unlike the vertebrate nervous system, the nervous system of *Aplysia* is the same from one individual to another. Furthermore, because many cells are easily recognizable, it is possible for investigators to determine the properties of a given cell in a given animal and then to find that same cell in a different animal. Such studies have led to a detailed understanding of how a cell changes its properties during learning. (© Tom McHugh/Photo Researchers)

Plate 28. *Hermissenda*, a mollusc used in many studies of the physiology of learning. *Hermissenda* has the same advantages as *Aplysia* for studies of single cells. Experimenters working with *Hermissenda* have studied different types of learning from those studied in *Aplysia* and have uncovered different single-cell changes in learning. Evidently learning relies on different mechanisms in different situations. (P. J. Bryant, University of California, Irvine/ Biological Photo Service)

Heredity and Presymptomatic Testing for Huntington's Disease.
Huntington's disease is controlled by an autosomal dominant gene. That is, a person who has the gene will eventually develop the disease and will transmit the gene to about half of his or her children, on the average.

Imagine that you are 20 years old and that you have just learned that one of your parents has Huntington's disease. You now know that you have a 50 percent chance of developing it yourself, probably about 20 years in the future. In addition to your grief about your parent's agony, your life will change in two ways. First, you will constantly worry about your own health. Whenever you do something clumsy or you experience a slight tremor anywhere in your body, you will not be able to ignore it the way anyone else would; you will fear that it is the start of Huntington's disease. Second, you may have trouble deciding whether to have children. You may decide that you would not want to have children if you have the gene for Huntington's disease. But you do not know whether you have the gene, and you may not find out until you are 40 or older. In fact, because the disease sometimes begins in old age, you may never be confident that you are safe.

For these reasons it would be desirable to conduct a **presymptomatic test**—a test of whether you are likely to develop the disease, conducted before any symptoms are present. One presymptomatic test is to administer small doses of L-DOPA. This drug, while relieving the symptoms of Parkinson's disease, aggravates the symptoms of Huntington's disease. The idea behind this test is to give a dose so small that it would have no effect on a normal person. Such a dose may induce temporary symptoms of Huntington's disease if it is given to someone who has a gene for the disease. When given to certain young adults whose parents have Huntington's disease, this test has shown some success in identifying which of them will eventually develop the disease themselves (Klawans, Goetz, Paulson, & Barbeau, 1980). One major drawback to the test is the worry that injections of L-DOPA may accelerate the onset of the disease.

A different kind of presymptomatic test, still in the experimental stages, examines the genes directly. The gene for Huntington's disease is located on human chromosome number 4. At this time, scientists cannot pinpoint exactly where the gene is on that chromosome or what the gene looks like. They do know, however, that it is close to the G8 marker on chromosome 4 (Folstein et al., 1985; Gusella, Wexler et al., 1983). G8 is a gene that comes in four forms—called *A*, *B*, *C*, and *D*—that can be distinguished under a microscope. Although the G8 gene itself has nothing to do with Huntington's disease, it is inherited along with any Huntington's disease gene that is near it.

The logic of the test is as follows: Suppose a few close relatives who developed Huntington's disease all have, say, at least one copy of the *C* form of the G8 gene. (Because everyone has two copies of chromosome 4 per cell, each of those people will have a second form of G8 as well, which may or may not be a *C*.) We can presume that the gene for Huntington's disease is on the same chromosome with the *C* form in this family. Now suppose that one of these people, who has a *C* and a *D* form, has children with someone

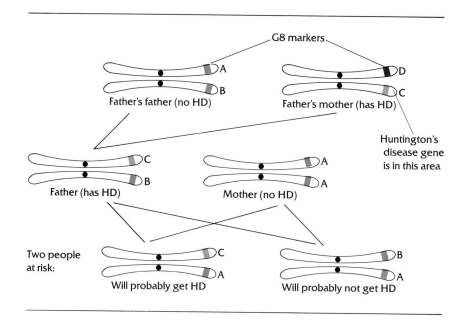

Figure 8-11. Example of use of the G8 chromosome marker for presymptomatic detection of Huntington's disease. In this family, the Huntington's disease gene is linked to marker C.

else who has two *B* forms. We can now examine their children's chromosomes. Those who have a *B* and a *C* probably have the gene for Huntington's disease. Those who have a *B* and a *D* should be safe. Figure 8-11 illustrates the strategy of the test.

This test can be used only if investigators can examine the chromosomes of a number of related people with Huntington's disease. Even under the best circumstances it cannot be 100 percent accurate, because of the possibility of *crossing over* of the genes (see Appendix). That is, the two number 4 chromosomes may exchange pieces. Researchers hope to be able to improve the test and eventually to locate the gene for Huntington's disease itself.

If an accurate presymptomatic test becomes available, ethical issues will arise in its use. If you knew one of your parents had Huntington's disease, would you want to find out for sure whether you will get it, too? Most people believe they would want to know, but it may be different when they actually find themselves in that situation. If people are given the test, they may need counseling to help them deal with the results.

THE ROLE OF THE CEREBRAL CORTEX IN MOVEMENT

Since the pioneering work of Fritsch and Hitzig (1870), it has been known that direct electrical stimulation of the motor cortex can elicit movements. Electrical stimulation generally leads to a coordinated movement that includes at least a few muscles. It is difficult, in fact, to induce an isolated movement of a single muscle (Asanuma, 1981).

The cerebral cortex does not contain any of the motor programs for movement. The spinal cord and medulla contain the programs that actually pattern the muscle movements. The cerebral cortex merely selects which programs will be active at any given moment. The cerebral cortex is particularly important for the control of complex and varied actions. It contributes little to the control of coughing, sneezing, swallowing, gagging, laughing, or crying (Rinn, 1984). (Perhaps this lack of control by the cerebral cortex has something to do with why it is so hard to perform those actions voluntarily.)

The Pyramidal System

We distinguish two major systems in the mammalian cerebral cortex that control the motor neurons of the spinal cord and the medulla: the pyramidal system and the extrapyramidal system. The **pyramidal system** consists of a set of cells whose axons cross between the left and right sides of the nervous system in distinctive swellings called **pyramids** in the medulla, as shown in Figure 8-12 (**a**). About 50–60 percent of those axons originate in the precentral gyrus of the frontal lobe (see Chapter 4), which is also known as the **primary motor cortex**. Most of the rest of the pyramidal axons originate either in the postcentral gyrus (the primary somatosensory cortex) or in parts of the frontal cortex anterior to the primary motor cortex (Wiesendanger, 1984).

The axons of the pyramidal system extend directly, without synaptic interruption, from the cerebral cortex to interneurons in the medulla and spinal cord. Those interneurons in turn control the motor neurons that send the final messages to the muscles.

Different points of origin of the pyramidal system control different aspects of movement. The primary motor cortex is responsible for fine control of movement, such as movements of individual fingers or other precision movements. The primary motor cortex on each side of the brain controls movements almost exclusively on the opposite side of the body. A notable exception is that the primary motor cortex on each side has control of certain bilateral facial movements, including eyelid and eyebrow movements (Rinn, 1984; Roland, 1984).

During a simple, repetitive movement, only cells in the primary motor cortex are active. If the movement has to be planned or integrated with sensory information, cells become active in two anterior areas—the **premotor cortex** and the **supplementary motor cortex** (Roland, 1984). These areas become active, for example, if someone has to move a finger around in a maze in response to someone else's directions. They show specific patterns of activity depending on whether the movement is guided by visual, auditory, or tactile stimuli (Kurata & Tanji, 1986). They are active during the planning of a movement, even if the movement itself is never carried out.

After damage to the pyramidal system, a person suffers a complete but temporary paralysis. Over the following weeks, reflexes return, followed by voluntary movements. Although the control of fine movements may never recover completely, it sometimes returns to a surprising degree (Wiesendanger, 1984). The recovered movements may depend on undamaged portions of the pyramidal system or on the other major motor system of the cortex, the extrapyramidal system.

The Extrapyramidal System

The **extrapyramidal system** is defined simply as those cortical areas other than the pyramidal system that also control movement. As illustrated in

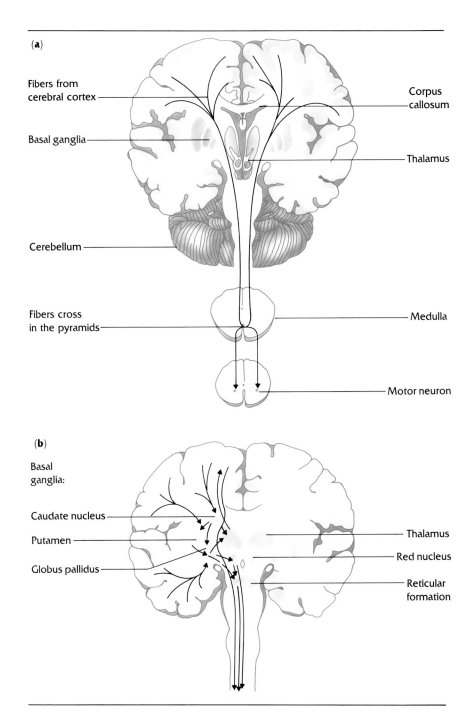

(a)

Fibers from cerebral cortex

Basal ganglia

Cerebellum

Fibers cross in the pyramids

Corpus callosum

Thalamus

Medulla

Motor neuron

(b)

Basal ganglia:

Caudate nucleus

Putamen

Globus pallidus

Thalamus

Red nucleus

Reticular formation

Figure 8-12. (**a**) The pyramidal system. (**b**) The extrapyramidal system.

Figure 8-12 (**b**), the fibers of the extrapyramidal system take a less direct route to the spinal cord than those of the pyramidal system. All parts of the cerebral cortex send information to, and receive information from, the basal ganglia (Selemon & Goldman-Rakic, 1985). Fibers from the basal ganglia, the cerebellum, and diffuse areas of the cerebral cortex extend to the red nucleus and the reticular formation. Fibers from the red nucleus and the reticular formation, as well as from the vestibular nucleus (not shown in Figure 8-12), send impulses to the spinal cord and the medulla.

The extrapyramidal system differs from the pyramidal system in a number of ways. One is that the extrapyramidal axons originate from sources controlled by all of the cerebral cortex plus the basal ganglia, instead of just limited parts of the cerebral cortex. Another difference is that the extrapyramidal paths go through a chain of several neurons, while the pyramidal axons extend all the way from the cerebral cortex to the spinal cord. A third is that whereas the pyramidal system controls fine, discrete movements of individual body parts, the extrapyramidal system controls postures, general body movements, and movements of muscles closer to the center of the body. For example, damage to the pyramidal system impairs finger movements more than walking; damage to the extrapyramidal system impair walking, turning, and standing up more than it affects finger movements.

These differences are not absolute; damage to either system can impair any movement; the differences between the two systems are a matter of degree. Moreover, the two systems are closely connected to each other. Most movements in healthy individuals reflect a combination of pyramidal and extrapyramidal influences.

Apraxia

In certain cases, damage in the cerebral cortex can lead to complex deficits known as **apraxia**, a difficulty in organizing movements purposively. A person with apraxia may, for example, perform some action spontaneously and then prove unable to do the same thing in response to someone's verbal instructions. Certain patients say they know what to do but cannot organize the movements to do it (Faglioni & Basso, 1985). For example, one patient described by Brown (1972) was told to put a letter into an envelope. He spent a long time trying many unusual ways of folding the letter and never did get it into the envelope. Then he was told to dial the operator on the telephone. He picked up the receiver and rotated it in his hand, apparently uncertain about which end should go to his ear. Later he was told to light a cigarette. He went through the motions slowly and eventually attempted to light the wrong end of the cigarette, using the wrong end of the match.

In general, apraxic movements are slow, hesitant, poorly planned, and abnormally repetitive. Frequently they stop in the middle of a sequence. Also, apraxic movements are often improperly organized with regard to spatial relationships. For example, when attempting to copy a drawing, an apraxic person may start too close to one side of the paper and thus be unable to fit the picture on the page.

Different instances of apraxia may be associated with a great many types of brain damage, and in many cases no one knows exactly where the damage is located or how such damage led to the behavioral troubles. In some cases, however, the damage is surprisingly simple. Here is an example of apraxia that can be explained in terms of known damage to a part of the brain (Geschwind, 1975):

Following brain damage, a man could not follow verbal instructions to use either arm or either leg in isolation, nor any other single set of muscles by itself, although he could make all the same movements spontaneously. He did, however, follow instructions to stand, walk, bow, kneel, or to make other postural movements of the whole body. He could follow instructions to take a boxer's position, but not to punch with one hand.

His brain damage was simple: The language areas in his left cerebral cortex were disconnected from his pyramidal system but not from his extra-pyramidal system. That is, the damage interrupted fibers from the language areas to the primary motor cortex. Because the primary motor cortex itself and the entire pyramidal system were intact, his spontaneous movements were normal. Although the language areas could not send messages to the pyramidal system, they could communicate with the extrapyramidal system. In response to verbal instructions, the extrapyramidal system could initiate gross movements and postures, but not the movements of an individual limb.

Let us return for just a moment to the point raised in the introduction to this chapter: the fact that the control of movement is an important topic for psychology as well as for biology. The differences between the pyramidal and extrapyramidal systems and between the cerebellum and the basal ganglia relate directly to the ways in which behavior is organized. In discussing movement, we have to consider such topics as the distinction between voluntary and involuntary, the development of behavior, the effects of practice on motor skills, and the relationship between language and action. In short, the control of movement is an integral topic not only of biological psychology but of psychology in general.

SUMMARY

1.   Vertebrates have skeletal, cardiac, and smooth muscles. Skeletal muscles are of three types: slow and nonfatiguing, faster and nonfatiguing, and fastest but rapidly fatiguing. It is possible to recruit different combinations of muscles in order to maintain consistent movement under varying conditions. (p. 207)

2.   Movements can be analyzed into three types of unit—reflexes, oscillators, and servomechanisms. (p. 209)

3.   Although most movements depend on sensory feedback, animals can learn to make nearly normal movements after a great restriction of sensory feedback. (p. 211)

4.   Motor programs, which may include combinations of reflexes, oscillators, and servomechanisms, are organized sequences of movements that are produced in a consistent, fairly inflexible manner. (p. 213)

5.   Experiments on the effects of haloperidol and apomorphine reveal that certain apparently purposive movements are composed of separate elements that may be facilitated or interfered with separately from one another. (p. 214)

6.   All motor neurons exit the medulla or the ventral roots of the spinal cord. (p. 215)

7.   Myasthenia gravis is a disease in which the body's immune system attacks the nerve-muscle junctions. The disease is treated by suppressing the immune system and by prolonging the actions of acetylcholine at the nerve-muscle junction. (p. 217)

8.   The cerebellum helps to generate ballistic movements and helps to link individual movements into rapid, coordinated sequences. (p. 218)

9.   The basal ganglia are a group of large subcortical structures that control the direction and amplitude of movements, especially postural movements. (p. 219)

10.   Parkinson's disease is associated with degeneration of dopamine-containing axons from the substantia nigra to the caudate nucleus and putamen. It is generally treated with L-DOPA, which the brain can convert into dopamine. (p. 220)

11.   Parkinson's disease is not hereditary. It may be caused by exposure to certain chemicals including MPTP and related compounds. (p. 222)

12.   In Huntington's disease, numerous brain cells,

especially in the basal ganglia, die. It is possible to mimic the disease in animals by injections of kainic acid or quinolinic acid. (p. 224)

13. Much research attention has been given to attempts to develop a presymptomatic test for Huntington's disease. (p. 225)

14. The pyramidal system is a set of neurons, located mostly in the primary motor cortex and adjacent areas, whose axons extend directly to interneurons in the medulla and spinal cord. The pyramidal system controls fine movements, especially of the extremities. (p. 227)

15. The extrapyramidal system is an interconnected set of neurons, originating from all parts of the cerebral cortex and the basal ganglia, that send messages through several synapses to the medulla and spinal cord. The extrapyramidal system controls postural movements and trunk movements more than finger or hand movements. (p. 228)

16. Apraxia is an inability to organize certain movements purposively or to make them in response to instructions. (p. 229)

REVIEW QUESTIONS

1. How does a fish manage to swim at the same speed at different temperatures, even though the temperature affects the vigor of contraction of each muscle? (p. 208)
2. What is the difference between reflexes, oscillators, and servomechanisms? (pp. 209–211)
3. How do muscle spindles and Golgi tendon organs contribute to the control of muscle contractions? (p. 213)
4. What is a motor program? Give an example. (p. 209)
5. Give an example of a behavior that is suitable to analyze in terms of purposes, and a behavior that is more suitable to analyze in terms of movements. (p. 214)
6. Why can the eye muscles be moved with greater precision than the biceps muscles? (p. 215)
7. What transmitter is released at the nerve-muscle junction of skeletal muscles? (p. 215)

8. What causes myasthenia gravis? How can the condition be treated? (p. 217)
9. What are the behavioral effects of damage to the cerebellum? (p. 218)
10. What aspect of movement is controlled by the basal ganglia? (p. 219)
11. What are the symptoms of Parkinson's disease? What treatment is commonly used? What is a possible environmental cause? (p. 220)
12. What are the symptoms of Huntington's disease? What treatment can induce a similar state in laboratory animals? What methods may make it possible to identify which people will get the disease, before the symptoms become apparent? (p. 224)
13. What are the differences between the pyramidal system and the extrapyramidal system? (p. 227)
14. What is meant by the term *apraxia*? Describe an example. (p. 229)

THOUGHT QUESTIONS

1. A person with damage to the afferent nerves from one arm does not use that arm. The physician's advice is to tie the other arm behind the person's back. Why?
2. The presymptomatic test for Huntington's disease that uses the G8 marker is useless if the parent with Huntington's disease has two G8 markers that are alike—for example, two *D*'s. Why is that? Can you

imagine other circumstances in which the test would be useless?
3. Human infants are at first limited to gross movements of the trunk, arms, and legs. The ability to move one finger at a time matures gradually over more than the first year. What hypothesis would you suggest about which brain areas controlling movement mature early and which ones mature later?

TERMS TO REMEMBER

smooth muscles (p. 207)
skeletal (striated) muscles (p. 207)
cardiac muscles (p. 207)
antagonistic muscles (p. 207)
flexor (p. 207)
extensor (p. 207)
motor program (p. 209)
reflex (p. 209)
Babinski reflex (p. 209)

muscle spindle (p. 209)
Golgi tendon organ (p. 209)
oscillators (p. 210)
scratch reflex (p. 211)
ballistic movement (p. 211)
servomechanism (p. 211)
deafferented limb (p. 212)
motor neurons (p. 215)
nerve-muscle junction (p. 215)

myasthenia gravis (p. 217)
dysdiadochokinesia (p. 218)
saccades (p. 218)
basal ganglia (p. 219)
Parkinson's disease (p. 220)
substantia nigra (p. 220)
Huntington's disease (p. 224)
kainic acid (p. 224)
quinolinic acid (p. 224)

presymptomatic test (p. 225)
pyramidal system (p. 227)
pyramids (p. 227)
primary motor cortex (p. 227)
premotor cortex (p. 227)
supplementary motor cortex (p. 227)
extrapyramidal system (p. 227)
apraxia (p. 229)

SUGGESTIONS FOR FURTHER READING

Evarts, E. V. (1979). Brain mechanisms of movement. *Scientific American, 241* (3), 164–179. A good overview of brain mechanisms, written for a general audience.

Gallistel, C. R. (1980). *The organization of action: A new synthesis.* Hillsdale, NJ: Erlbaum. Provocative analysis of movement in terms of reflexes, oscillators, and servomechanisms; includes reprints of some classic articles.

Geschwind, N. (1975). The apraxias. *American Scientist, 63,* 188–195. Discusses movement disorders in relationship to localized human brain damage.

Daily Rhythms of Activity and Sleep

CHAPTER 9

MAIN IDEAS

1. Wakefulness and sleep, as well as temperature and other body activities, vary on a cycle of approximately 24 hours. This cycle is generated by the body itself.

2. People can suffer insomnia if their biological rhythm is out of phase with the prescribed time for sleeping.

3. Sleep progresses through four stages, which differ in brain activity, heart rate, and other signs of arousal.

4. A special type of stage 1 sleep, known as paradoxical sleep or REM sleep, is light sleep in some ways and deep sleep in others. It is associated with dreaming, especially with vivid dreaming.

5. The reticular formation is important for arousal of the brain. Certain areas of the brain are believed to be important for the control of sleep, although the exact nature of their contribution is not yet clear.

Suppose you have just made a journey as an astronaut to the planet Daynite in another solar system. Daynite rotates on its axis only once a year; that is, it always keeps the same side facing its sun, and no part of the planet alternates between day and night. Nearly all the animal and plant life lives in a "twilight zone" around the border between light and dark. The animals, having had a very different evolutionary history than any species on earth, exhibit numerous peculiarities. One is that none of them ever sleep.

Although you may be surprised to find animals that never sleep, your reaction hardly compares to the reaction of the Daynitian astronauts who simultaneously make their first visit to Earth. They marvel that about once every 365th of a year each animal lies down and stops moving. After these strange Earthlings appear to have been dead for a few hours, they spontaneously come back to life again! The Daynitians wonder, "What on Earth is going on?"

For the purposes of this chapter, let us adopt the perspective of the Daynitians. Let us ask why animals as active as we are spend one-third of our lives doing so little.

ENDOGENOUS CIRCADIAN AND CIRCANNUAL RHYTHMS

Because the light and temperature at any point on the Earth vary from day to night and from one season to another, the activity of any animal sensitive to light and temperature will rise and fall on a regular basis. Animals do more than just respond to changes in their environment, however; they anticipate the changes. Migratory birds start flying south in the fall even if the weather has remained unseasonably warm in their northern home. Squirrels begin storing nuts and putting on extra layers of fat in preparation for winter, long before food becomes scarce. Animals that mate during only one season of the year go through extensive changes in both their anatomy and their behavior as the reproductive season approaches. Humans who keep regular sleep and waking habits begin to arouse from a night's sleep before the alarm sounds and before the room becomes light.

How do animals, including humans, know what time of day or what time of year it is? In the pioneering work on this topic, Curt Richter (1922) found that rats increase their activity once every 2 to 4 hours, coincident with an increase in stomach contractions, even in an unchanging environment. He later found that female rats greatly increase their activity every fourth or fifth day, at the fertile period of their estrous cycle. These were the first demonstrations that the body could generate long rhythms independent of rhythmic sensory input.

Even the year-long rhythms underlying migration, hibernation, and the like are governed partly by mechanisms within the animal. A migratory bird prepares to fly south when the period of light each day declines to a certain level. (Temperature has nothing to do with the timing of migration, as indeed it should not. A sudden cold spell in July or a warm spell in September is a poor predictor of the weather to come.) But although the duration of light is

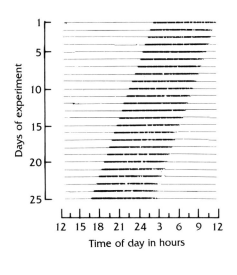

Figure 9-1. Activity record of a flying squirrel kept in constant darkness. The darkened bars indicate periods of activity as measured by a running wheel. Note that the free-running rhythm of activity and rest in this animal under conditions of constant darkness has a period of slightly less than 24 hours in duration. (From DeCoursey, 1960.)

a powerful factor in the timing of migration, it is not the only one. After a bird migrates to the tropics, how does it know when to return to the north? In the tropics, the daily duration of daylight varies only slightly from one time of year to another. Many birds have an internal timing mechanism that can ready them for the approximate time of migration. In one experiment, willow warblers (a European species) were captured from the wild and kept in cages with 12 hours of light alternating with 12 hours of darkness each day (Gwinner, 1986). For the next three years, the birds showed a characteristic *migratory restlessness* every fall and every spring, although their self-generated "years" ran faster than the true calendar. The birds gradually drifted out of phase with the time in the real world.

Evidently, a mechanism somewhere in the bird's body generates a rhythm that prepares the bird for the changes in the seasons. We refer to that rhythm as an **endogenous circannual rhythm**. (*Endogenous* means "generated from within." *Circannual* comes from the Latin words *circum*, for "about," and *annum*, for "year." An endogenous circannual rhythm is thus a self-generated rhythm that lasts about a year.) Similar mechanisms underlie a mammal's seasonal changes in reproduction, body fat, and hibernation. In nature, the daily onset of light and darkness fine-tunes such mechanisms to prevent them from running too fast or too slow.

Similarly, animals produce **endogenous circadian rhythms**—rhythms that last about a day. (*Circadian* comes from *circum*, for "about," and *dies*, for "day.") Figure 9-1 represents the activity of an animal kept in total darkness for 25 days. Each horizontal line represents one 24-hour day. A thickening in the line represents a period of activity by the animal. Even in this unchanging environment, the animal generates a regular rhythm of activity and sleep. The self-generated cycle may be slightly shorter than a true 24 hours, as in Figure 9-1, or slightly longer, depending on whether the

environment is constantly light or constantly dark, and on whether the species is normally active in the light or in the dark (Carpenter & Grossberg,
1984). The cycle may also vary from one individual to another, even in the
same environment. Nevertheless, the rhythm is highly consistent for a given
individual in a given environment.

Although the circadian rhythm can persist in the absence of light, light
is critical for periodically resetting the **biological clock** that underlies the
rhythm. As an analogy, consider a wristwatch. I used to have a wind-up
wristwatch that lost about 2 minutes per day. If I continued to wind the
watch but never reset it, it would be an hour slow after one month. We could
say that it had a **free-running rhythm** of 24 hours 2 minutes. The biological
clock is similar to the wristwatch. Because its free-running rhythm is not
exactly 24 hours, it has to be reset daily. The mechanism that resets it is often
referred to by the German term **Zeitgeber** (TSITE-gay-ber), meaning "time-
giver." Light is the dominant Zeitgeber for land animals (Rusak & Zucker,
1979); although temperature, social stimuli, and other events may help to
reset the clock, the influence of light generally overrules all else. (The tides
are a more important Zeitgeber for certain aquatic animals.)

Humans, too, can generate circadian activity rhythms different from 24
hours, if they stay in caves or other artificial environments that isolate them
from sunlight and other cues to time. In fact, even if other time cues are
present, the absence of light may free the endogenous rhythms to drift out of
phase with real time. One blind person reported that he could sometimes
sleep and wake normally but at other times felt sleepy all day and wakeful
all night. Investigators found that he had a free-running rhythm of 24.9
hours for body temperature, alertness, and other functions (Miles, Raynal,
& Wilson, 1977). Although he could wake and sleep on schedule whenever
his endogenous rhythm was in phase with the outside world, he experienced
severe troubles when it was out of phase.

Attempts to Train the Biological
Clock to Produce a Different Period

Is it possible to change a person's biological clock so that it will produce
a different endogenous rhythm? If humans moved to a planet with, say,
20-hour days or 30-hour days, would they adjust easily or would they have
to undergo countless generations of evolutionary change before they felt
really at home? In an effort to answer such questions, two volunteers spent
a month deep in an isolated part of Mammoth Cave in Kentucky (Kleitman,
1963). The temperature (12°C) and relative humidity (100 percent) were
constant at all times and the only light they saw was the artificial light
controlled by a fixed schedule.

Throughout the month in the cave, the agreed-upon schedule was a
28-hour day, with 19 hours of activity alternating with 9 hours of sleep. One
subject (R in Figure 9-2) adjusted reasonably well to the new schedule; his
temperature cycles matched his activity cycles. However, he was always
sleepy well before the scheduled bedtime and he had trouble awakening at
the scheduled times. The other subject (K in Figure 9-2) was much less

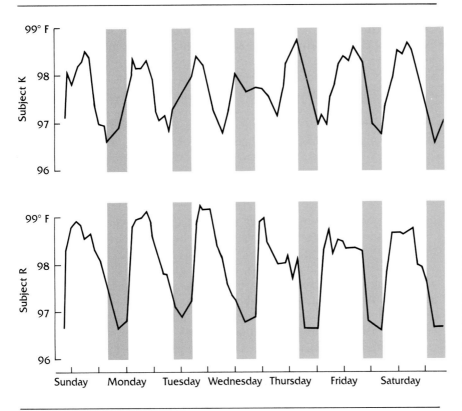

Figure 9-2. Curves of weekly body temperature of two men under an artificial routine of 19 hours of wakefulness and 9 hours of sleep. Shaded areas represent time in bed. K's weekly record has seven 24-hour curves, but R adapted fairly well to the 28-hour schedule; his temperature minima are in the shaded areas. (From Kleitman, 1963.)

successful. He continued to feel sleepy only at his usual bedtime, once every 24 hours; he had great trouble getting to sleep when the artificial cycle was out of phase with his original cycle. Even by the end of the month, he showed no sign of adjusting to the 28-hour schedule.

Other experimenters have also attempted to train people or laboratory animals to follow a cycle other than 24 hours. As a rule, the adjustment is more successful if the imposed cycle is close to 24 hours. In one experiment, a group of twelve young people lived in a cavelike environment, isolated from natural light and other time cues, for 3 weeks. They agreed to go to bed when the clock said 11:45 P.M. and to awake when it said 7:45 A.M. Although they did not know it, the clock started as a normal clock and then gradually ran faster, until it was completing a day in only 22 normal-sized hours. When the clock was completing a day in 23 hours, the people were alert during their wakeful periods and reported no trouble awakening on schedule or falling asleep on schedule. On a 22-hour schedule, however, only one subject kept pace with the clock. For the others, alertness rose and fell on a free-running 24-hour cycle that quickly drifted out of phase with the waking-sleeping schedule (Folkard, Hume, Minors, Waterhouse, & Watson, 1985). Evidently, humans find it difficult to adjust to a waking-sleeping cycle much different from 24 hours per day.

One Biological Clock or More?

Suppose visitors from outer space were to examine an office building for evidence of circadian rhythms. They would find that the amount of noise is higher between 8 A.M. and 5 P.M. than during the rest of the day. During those hours they would also note an increased use of electricity and running water, an increased level of illumination, and increased use of the telephones. The heating system is less active, however, than it is at night. Now, our visitors want to know, does the building have just a single mechanism, a clock perhaps, that turns on the lights, the noise-maker, the electricity-user, and so forth, from 8 to 5, and then turns on the heater at night? Or does the building have a number of separate mechanisms? In short, the fact that our body's various daily rhythms are more or less synchronized with one another does not tell us whether they are controlled by the same underlying mechanism. To find out, an investigator would need to ask whether the various rhythms can ever get out of synchrony and whether any factor can alter one rhythm without altering the others.

Mammals, including humans, have circadian rhythms in their waking and sleeping, frequency of eating and drinking, body temperature, secretion of certain hormones, volume of urination, sensitivity to certain drugs (Moore-Ede, Czeisler, & Richardson, 1983b), frequency of yawning (Anías, Holmgren, Urbá Holmgren, & Eguíbar, 1984), and multiple other variables Does a single clock underlie all the separate rhythms? Or does the body have more?

Humans appear to have at least two clocks. In several experiments, people have been cut off from sunlight and other contact with the outside world and have been allowed to sleep and awaken at whatever time they choose, neither knowing nor caring what time it is in the outside world. Although most people under such circumstances maintain a consistent 24- to 25-hour cycle, an occasional individual starts living on a peculiar cycle, such as 29 hours of wakefulness alternating with 21 hours of sleep. Their cycles of eating, drinking, urination, and hormone secretions stay in phase with their cycles of waking and sleeping. Their body temperature does not, however. Ordinarily, the temperature in the interior of the body (not the skin) rises during the middle of the day to just over 37°C and falls at night to just over 36°C. Body temperature continues to follow a 24- to 25-hour cycle even when the person is following an idiosyncratic cycle for waking and sleeping (Aschoff, Gerecke, & Wever, 1967; Aschoff & Wever, 1976; Czeisler, Weitzman, Moore-Ede, Zimmerman, & Knauer, 1980). Evidently, humans have at least two mechanisms underlying circadian rhythms, one that controls activity levels and one that controls body temperature. This conclusion is indirectly supported by the finding that certain kinds of brain damage can disrupt the circadian rhythm of drinking in monkeys without disrupting their circadian rhythm of temperature (Fuller et al., 1981).

Resetting the Biological Clock: Jet Lag and Related Phenomena

When evolution built in humans' biological clock, it missed. Instead of giving us a 24-hour clock, it gave us about a 24½- or 24¾-hour clock. We have to readjust our internal workings every day to stay in phase with the outside

Figure 9-3. Long-distance travelers are troubled by jet lag because crossing time zones disrupts their biological clock. (Photo by Jackie Estrada.)

world. On weekends, when most of us are freer to follow the dictates of our nature, we tend to stay awake later than usual and awaken later than usual. By Monday morning, when the electric clock says the time is 7 A.M., the biological clock says it is about 5 A.M. (Moore-Ede, Czeisler, & Richardson, 1983a).

Jet Lag.   Because the human biological clock tends to run slower than 24 hours, most of us find it easier to adjust to crossing time zones going west than going east. Going west, we stay awake later at night and awaken later in the morning than we would have at home. Going east, we go to sleep earlier and awaken earlier. In one study, a group of healthy young men reported psychological discomfort and unsatisfactory sleep after crossing seven times zones going east; they took 11 days to return to normal. Such discomfort is known as **jet lag** (Figure 9-3). A trip west over seven time zones produced no serious complaints (Désir et al., 1981).

Shift Work.   People who have to sleep irregularly—such as train and truck drivers, medical interns, and shift workers in certain factories—find that their duration of sleep depends on their time of going to sleep. When they go to sleep in the morning or early afternoon, after working all night, they sleep only briefly (Frese & Harwich, 1984). They sleep the longest when they go to sleep in the early or middle part of the night, while their body temperature is still gradually decreasing. Body temperature reaches its minimum in the early morning hours. If they do not get to sleep until after their temperature has begun to rise, they sleep a much shorter time (Winfree, 1983).

One Type of Insomnia.   Certain people can reset their biological clocks to adjust to new time zones or other demands more easily than other people can. Rare individuals seem virtually unable to adjust to an eastward shift in time zones. If forced to move east, they develop a long-lasting insomnia. They may also develop insomnia by staying up late a few nights in a row and thereby unintentionally resetting their biological clocks.

People suffering insomnia for this reason may not even realize how it came about. They know that they cannot get to sleep until late at night and that they cannot awaken until late in the morning. The condition may persist for years. Sleeping pills offer only temporary relief. The solution is to take off some time from work and to make a point of going to sleep each night 2 or 3 hours *later* than the night before, until eventually they get their sleep time back to where they want it to be (Weitzman et al., 1981). In effect, they go seven-eighths of the way around the world west in order to get one-eighth of the way east. (Naturally, such a person should be advised to keep very regular sleep habits from then on.)

The Search for the Biological Clock

The biological clock might depend on any number of possible mechanisms. We might imagine a device that counts heartbeats or breaths, for example, as an indication of the passage of time. Such a mechanism would be inaccurate, however; its speed would depend on the activity of the individual.

Richter found that the biological clock is insensitive to most forms of interference. An animal's circadian rhythm of activity and sleep remains intact after blinding or deafening, although it may drift out of phase with the real world because of the loss of Zeitgebers. The circadian rhythm is hardly disturbed at all by procedures that greatly modify the total level of activity, including food or water deprivation, x-rays, tranquilizers, LSD, alcohol, anesthesia, lack of oxygen, long periods of forced activity, long periods of forced inactivity, most kinds of brain damage, or the removal of any of the hormonal organs (Richter, 1967). Although electroconvulsive shock inactivates an animal for about a week, when the animal does become active again, its activity returns at the normal time of day, just as if the previous week had been a normal one. Certain drugs, including caffeine, other stimulants, and barbiturates, can act as Zeitgebers to reset the clock (Ehret, Potter, & Dobra, 1975; Mayer & Scherer, 1975). Still, the biological clock is remarkably immune to interference.

The only interventions Richter (1965, 1970) found that disturbed the biological clock significantly were substitution of heavy water (D_2O) for normal water in the diet and damage to the hypothalamus. Exposure to heavy water can impair the ability of the biological clock to generate 24-hour rhythms; the basis for this effect is not well understood. Later researchers determined more precisely the area of the hypothalamus where damage disrupts the biological clock: It is a small area called the **suprachiasmatic** (soo-pruh-kie-as-MAT-ik) **nucleus**, abbreviated **SCN**. The SCN receives part of its input directly from branches of axons from the retina. If the connections from those axons to the SCN are damaged, light can no longer reset the biological clock, even though the individual can still see.

The SCN generates rhythms itself. If neurons of the SCN are removed from an animal's brain, or if they are left in place but are disconnected by cuts from the rest of the brain, the SCN neurons nevertheless produce a pattern of impulses that follows a circadian rhythm (Green & Gillette, 1982; Inouye & Kawamura, 1979). After damage to the SCN, animals lose their circadian rhythms of activity but not necessarily their rhythms of body temperature (Turek, 1985). In certain cases, damage to the SCN leads to a temporary loss of the temperature cycle, or to a weakening of it, or to a change in its speed (Prosser, Kittrell, & Satinoff, 1984). Evidently, the SCN contains the biological clock for activity, while a second biological clock, responsible for temperature variations, lies partly outside the SCN but is heavily influenced by a healthy SCN.

Knowing that the suprachiasmatic nucleus generates a circadian rhythm does not tell us *how* it does so, however. Richter (1975) tested the effects of greatly reduced body temperature on the biological clock. All chemical reactions and most of the body's activities proceed more rapidly at higher temperatures. One would expect, therefore, that if the biological clock operates by monitoring the rate of a chemical reaction or any other repetitive process, a decrease in body temperature should slow down the clock. On the other hand, from the standpoint of understanding the animal's adaptation to its environment, we might predict that temperature should have little effect on the clock: If a cold-blooded animal such as a fish is to keep track of time at all, it should do so in a way that will not be confused by changes in the temperature of the environment (Rozin, 1965, 1968).

To test the effect of temperature, Richter put some rats and hamsters in a refrigerated jar for several hours, lowering their body temperatures to just above freezing. Because hamsters normally hibernate during the winter, it is not unusual for them to drop to a low body temperature and later recover. Rats, which do not hibernate, are more difficult to revive after a period of refrigeration, but it is sometimes possible.

While the animals were maintained at near-freezing, their breathing ceased altogether, electrical activity in the brain ceased altogether, and metabolic rate (the rate of utilization of energy) dropped to practically zero. Heart rate decreased to zero in the hamsters and to zero or almost zero in the rats. The animals were in suspended animation, almost as if they were dead. After 1 to 4 hours in this state, the animals were removed from refrigeration and gently warmed and artificially respirated. Although not all recovered, many did.

The question then was: At what time would the animals awaken the following day? Because all had been blinded weeks before, their activity followed self-generated cycles close to 24 hours in duration. Each animal's cycle was consistent enough that the time when activity would begin on each day could be accurately predicted. Since each animal had been completely inactivated for 1 to 4 hours, Richter expected that the next day's activity period would start 1 to 4 hours later than it would have otherwise. That is exactly what happened for six of the rats and thirteen of the hamsters. The results for one of these hamsters are shown in Figure 9-4 (a).

However, an additional eight rats and fourteen hamsters awakened *at the normal time* the following day! Figure 9-4 (b) shows the results for a hamster whose heart had been stopped for just over 4 hours. Although it

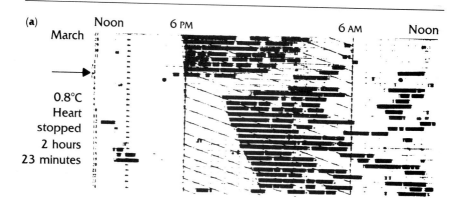

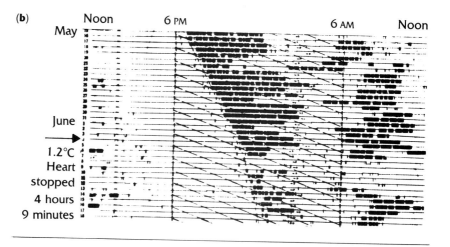

Figure 9-4. Activity records for two hamsters whose body temperatures were reduced to about 1°C for 2 to 4 hours on one day. Each line represents a day. For the hamster in (**a**) the onset of the next activity period was delayed by about the same duration as the period of refrigeration. The hamster of (**b**), however, had its onset of activity at the usual time the following day. (From Richter, 1975.)

was less active than usual on the next several days, its activity began at the same time as usual. Complete or near-complete cessation of heart rate, breathing, and brain activity had failed to reset the clock. To say it in a flashier way, while this animal was for all practical purposes dead, it continued to keep track of what time it was!

Richter's results suggest that the workings of the biological clock are largely independent of temperature. The results of other experiments have indicated that while this is largely true, it is not entirely true. Gibbs (1983) lowered the body temperature of a number of hamsters to temperatures ranging from 10°C to 20°C for times ranging from 3 hours to 24 hours. He found that the decrease in body temperature did slow the hamsters' biological clocks at least slightly and that the clocks seemed to get slower and slower as the duration of cold was increased. That is, 12 hours of cold produced more than four times the effect of 3 hours of cold. It is as if the biological clock could coast on its inertia for a couple of hours but then began to slow down if it was kept cold for a still longer period.

THE FUNCTIONS OF SLEEP

The suprachiasmatic nucleus and other mechanisms of the biological clock control the timing of sleep, but they are not responsible for sleep itself, any more than they are responsible for eating, drinking, urinating, or any other activity that follows a circadian rhythm.

Presumably, animals would not have evolved mechanisms that provide alternating periods of activity and sleep unless sleep serves some important function. Although we know that we need sleep, we do not fully understand why we need to sleep. Certain peculiarities about the need for sleep set it apart from such needs as hunger and thirst. For example, people who go without sleep all night report that as morning arrives, they actually begin to feel less sleepy. Apparently, the need to sleep is tied to the biological clock: The need to sleep is greatest at certain times of day.

The Repair and Restoration Theory of Sleep

According to the **repair and restoration theory of sleep,** the function of sleep is to enable the body to make repairs after the exertions of the day. Many restorative processes occur during sleep, such as digestion, removal of waste products, replenishment of the supply of synaptic transmitters (Hartmann, 1973; Stern & Morgane, 1974), and protein synthesis (Adam, 1980). Such restorative functions occur during the wakeful state as well, however. The fact that restorative functions occur during sleep does not necessarily mean that sleep exists primarily to facilitate those functions.

One way to evaluate the importance of the restorative functions is to observe the effects of sleep deprivation. People who have gone without sleep for a week or more, either as an experiment or as a publicity stunt, report dizziness, impaired concentration, irritability, hand tremors, and hallucinations (Dement, 1972; Johnson, 1969). In one experiment rats were deprived of sleep by a platform that rotated to force them to walk whenever they started to sleep. The rats gradually became weakened, with skin damage, swollen paws, and decreased brain activity. Within 5 to 33 days, all the rats died or reached the verge of death (Rechtschaffen, Gilliland, Bergmann, & Winter, 1983).

Such results confirm that sleep does serve restorative functions. Still, it does not follow logically that sleep is analogous to stopping to catch one's breath after, say, running a race. If sleep is restorative in that simple sense, we should expect that people would sleep significantly more after a day of great physical or mental exertion than after an uneventful day. What effect does exertion have on sleep?

The answer is that it has a little effect, but not a great deal. After a day of running a 92 km marathon, people sleep poorly the first night because of

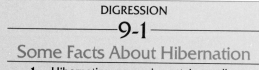

DIGRESSION

9-1

Some Facts About Hibernation

1. Hibernation occurs in certain small mammals such as ground-squirrels and bats. It is a matter of definition whether we can say that bears hibernate. Bears sleep most of the winter, but they do not lower their body temperatures the way smaller animals do.

2. Hamsters sometimes hibernate. If you keep your pet hamster in a cold, poorly lit place during the winter, and it appears to die, make sure it is not just hibernating before you bury it!

3. Hibernation retards the aging process.

Hamsters that spend longer times hibernating have proportionately longer life expectancies than other hamsters (Lyman, O'Brien, Greene, & Papafrangos, 1981).

4. Hibernating animals produce a chemical that suppresses metabolism and temperature regulation. Swan and Schätte (1977) injected extracts from the brains of hibernating ground-squirrels into the brains of rats, a nonhibernating species. The rats decreased their metabolism and body temperature. Similar brain extracts from nonhibernating ground-squirrels had no similar effect on the rats.

---

multiple aches and pains, and then sleep longer than usual the next three nights (Shapiro, Bortz, Mitchell, Bartel, & Jooste, 1981). People in one experiment spent a day visiting an exhibition, a shopping center, a museum, an amusement park, a zoo, and a movie and taking several scenic drives. After this most active and stimulating day, they fell asleep faster than usual but slept only the same duration as usual (Horne & Minard, 1985). Apparently, how much sleep we need does not depend strongly on how active we are during the day.

Moreover, a few people manage to satisfy their restorative needs in far less than the customary 7 to 8 hours. Two men have been reported to average only 3 hours of sleep per night and to awaken feeling refreshed (Jones & Oswald, 1968). A 70-year-old woman was reported to average only 1 hour of sleep per night; many nights she felt no need to sleep at all (Meddis, Pearson, & Langford, 1973). If it is possible to satisfy the restorative functions associated with sleep in such a short time, then perhaps sleep is maintained by additional factors besides the need for recuperation.

The Evolutionary Theory of the Need for Sleep

Given that the duration of sleep bears little relationship to the activity of the previous day, several theorists have offered an alternative explanation of why we sleep. According to the **evolutionary theory of sleep** (Kleitman, 1963; Webb, 1974), the function of sleep is similar to that of hibernation. Hibernation is a special adaptation of certain mammalian species to a season when food is scarce (see Digression 9-1). Their heart rate, breathing, brain activity, and metabolism decrease greatly; they generate only enough body heat to prevent themselves from freezing.

Hibernation is a true need; a ground-squirrel that is prevented from hibernating can get as disturbed as a person who is prevented from sleeping. However, the function of hibernation is not to recover from the exhaustion of the summer; it is simply to conserve energy during a time when the environment is hostile. Similarly, according to the evolutionary theory, the primary function of sleep is to force us to conserve energy at times when we

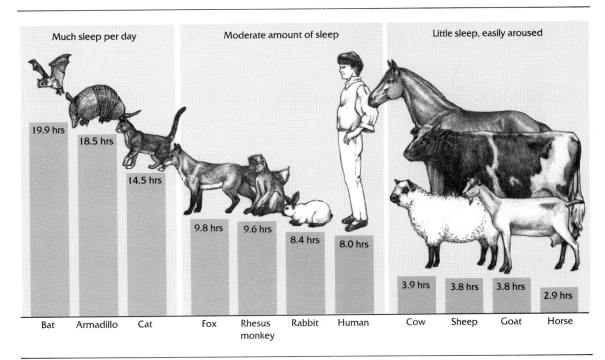

19.9 hrs
18.5 hrs
14.5 hrs
9.8 hrs
9.6 hrs
8.4 hrs
8.0 hrs
3.9 hrs
3.8 hrs
3.8 hrs
2.9 hrs

Bat | Armadillo | Cat | Fox | Rhesus monkey | Rabbit | Human | Cow | Sheep | Goat | Horse

Figure 9-5. Hours of sleep per day for varying animal species. Animals that are seldom attacked sleep a great deal; animals in danger of being attacked sleep very little.

would be relatively inefficient. The evolutionary theory does not deny that we need to sleep; it merely asserts that evolution built that need into us for a special reason.

The evolutionary theory predicts that animal species should vary in how much sleep they need depending on how much time they need to spend searching for food each day, how safe they are from predators when they sleep, and other aspects of their way of life. In general, the data support these predictions (Allison & Cicchetti, 1976; Campbell & Tobler, 1984).

Horses, cows, and other animals that graze most of the day sleep relatively few hours. Cats and other predators that usually eat just one short, nutrition-packed meal per day sleep much longer. Species that are frequently attacked by predators and whose only defense is their ability to run away (e.g., rabbits, sheep, and goats) sleep relatively few hours per night and awaken at slight noises. Cats, dogs, and other species that are seldom attacked spend more hours sleeping and are not awakened easily by stray sounds. Bats, which live in caves that offer excellent protection against predators, are also heavy sleepers. (See Figure 9-5.)

Although the evolutionary theory of sleep has considerable appeal, it, too, has its critics (e.g., Hauri, 1979). In particular, they argue, the theory seems to predict that sheep, goats, and similar species should not sleep at all, since they are vulnerable to attack when they sleep. The fact that they do sleep suggests that sleep has additional functions besides conservation of energy.

The evolutionary theory makes one prediction that has not been tested: A species that has spent much of its evolutionary history in an environment

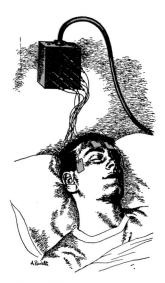

Figure 9-6. Apparatus for EEG (electroencephalo-graph) recording from a person's scalp.

that does not change during the day might not sleep at all, or at least should not sleep with any regularity. For example, deep-sea fish and cave-dwelling fish live in an environment with no light and almost no changes in temperature. Little is known about the sleep habits of such species. In fact, little is known about the sleep of fish in general (Campbell & Tobler, 1984).

THE STAGES OF SLEEP

Advances in scientific research are usually the result of improvements in our ability to measure something. Sleep research is no exception. The **electroencephalograph (EEG)**, mentioned in Chapter 4, records a gross average of the electrical potentials of the cells and fibers in a particular part of the brain by means of an electrode attached to the scalp. (See Figure 9-6.) It displays a net average of all the neurons' potentials. That is, if half the cells increase their electrical potentials while the other half decrease, the EEG recording is a flat line. The EEG record rises or falls only when a number of cells are **synchronized**, or doing the same thing at the same time. You might compare it to a record of the noise in a crowded football stadium: It shows only slight fluctuations from time to time until some event gets everyone yelling at once.

Figure 9-7 (**a**) shows an EEG record and a record of eye movements from a male college student during a period of relaxed wakefulness. Note the steady series of waves at a frequency of about ten per second, known as **alpha waves**. Alpha waves are characteristic of the relaxed state, not of all wakefulness.

Figure 9-7 (**b**) is from the same young man just after he had fallen asleep. This period of sleep is called stage 1 sleep. The waves are irregular with low amplitude. The brain activity is said to be **desynchronized**; the neurons are not all doing the same thing at the same time. The EEG in stage 1 resembles that of a person who is awake and alert.

Figures 9-7 (**c**), (**d**), and (**e**) present the records for stages 2, 3, and 4, respectively. In each succeeding stage, heart rate, breathing rate, and brain activity are slower than in the previous stage. Stages 2 to 4 are known collectively as **slow-wave sleep (SWS)**. Each succeeding stage has an increasing percentage of slow, large-amplitude waves. By stage 4, more than half the record includes large waves of at least a half-second duration. Such slow waves indicate that neuronal activity is highly synchronized. In stage 1 or in alert wakefulness, because the cortex receives much input, various cells are rapidly excited and inhibited out of phase with one another. By stage 4, sensory input to the cerebral cortex has been greatly reduced, and the few remaining sources of input can synchronize a large number of cells. As an analogy, imagine the barrage of stimuli arriving at the brain of an alert person as being like dropping hundreds of rocks into a pond over the course of a minute; the resulting waves will largely cancel one another out. Although the surface of the pond will be choppy, it will have few large waves. Contrast that to the effect of dropping just one rock: The surface will have smoother, more regular waves, like those seen in stage 4 sleep.

On going to sleep, a person begins in stage 1 and slowly progresses through stages 2, 3, and 4 in order. External stimuli can halt this progression,

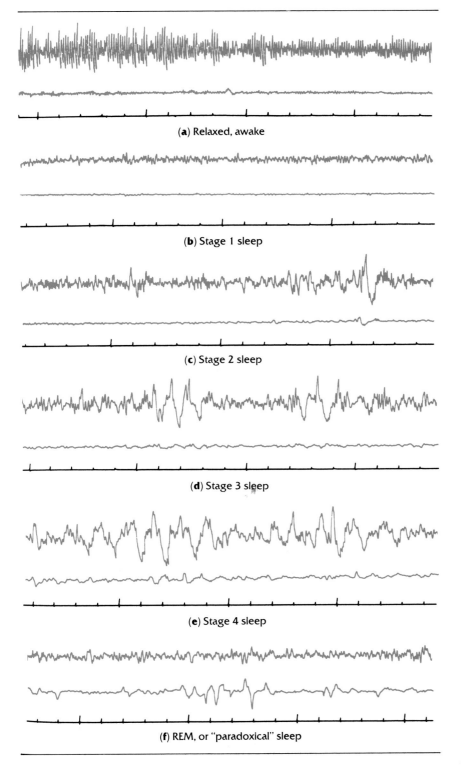

(a) Relaxed, awake

(b) Stage 1 sleep

(c) Stage 2 sleep

(d) Stage 3 sleep

(e) Stage 4 sleep

(f) REM, or "paradoxical" sleep

Figure 9-7. EEG records from a male college student. For each part of the record, the top line is the EEG from one electrode on the scalp; the middle line is a record of eye movements; the bottom line is a time marker, indicating one-second units. Note the presence of slow waves in stages 2, 3, and 4. (Records provided by T. E. LeVere.)

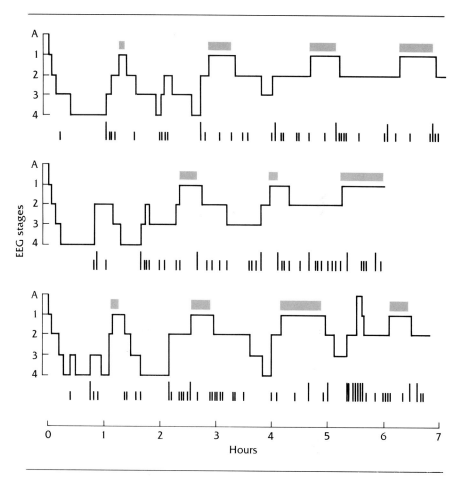

Figure 9-8. Sequence of sleep stages on three representative nights. A = awake; 1, 2, 3, 4 = the four stages of sleep. The horizontal color bars indicate periods of rapid eye movements. The vertical lines indicate body movements; the short lines are minor movements and the long lines are changes in body position. (From Dement & Kleitman, 1957a.)

however. For example, noises during stage 3 can prolong this stage or cause a reversion to stage 2, stage 1, or even wakefulness.

About 60 to 90 minutes after going to sleep, a person begins gradually to progress from stage 4 back through stages 3, 2, and 1. Figure 9-8 shows typical sequences. After returning to stage 1, the person then progresses back to stage 4, then back to stage 1 again, and so on. The whole sequence repeats throughout the night, with each cycle lasting about 90 to 100 minutes. Early in the night, stages 3 and 4 predominate. Later in the night, the duration of stage 4 grows shorter and the duration of stage 1 grows longer.

Paradoxical, or REM, Sleep

The first episode of stage 1 sleep during the night differs in important ways from most of the later episodes. The later periods of stage 1 sleep have been called **paradoxical sleep** by Michel Jouvet (BioSketch 9-1) because they are in some ways the deepest sleep and in other ways the lightest. (The term *paradoxical* means "apparently self-contradictory.") During paradoxical sleep, the EEG shows a desynchronized pattern resembling wakefulness. Heart rate and breathing rate are higher and more variable than in stages 2

BIOSKETCH
9-1

Michel Jouvet

Michel Jouvet, born in 1925, was active in the French Resistance during World War II. After the war he entered the University of Lyons, where he received an M.D. in 1956.

Jouvet's entry into sleep research was partly accidental. After spending a year working with H. W. Magoun at UCLA,

Jouvet returned to France planning to test the learning abilities of cats after removal of the cerebral cortex. That question proved to be difficult to investigate, since the decorticate cats were inactive and unresponsive to stimulation.

As often happens in the midst of an "unsuccessful" experiment, Jouvet stumbled on some interesting, unexpected results. In trying to measure activity changes in an inactive animal, Jouvet had used electrical recording to measure slight movements of the cat's muscles while simultaneously recording EEG

from the hindbrain. He found that during certain periods of apparent sleep, the cat had extreme relaxation of the neck muscles and high brain activity, similar to wakefulness. Jouvet named this condition "paradoxical sleep" and began to study its properties.

Since 1968, Jouvet has been the chief of the department of experimental medicine at Claude-Bernard University in France. In addition to his sleep research, Jouvet was the first investigator to establish (in 1959) criteria for "cerebral death" in humans.

through 4. In those regards paradoxical sleep is light. However, a person in this stage is more difficult to awaken than in any other stage. Furthermore, the postural muscles of the body, such as those that support the head, are more relaxed than in any other stage. In these regards paradoxical sleep is deep. This stage of sleep is also associated with erections in males and vaginal moistening in females. It is not obvious whether we should consider erections and vaginal secretions as indications of deep or light sleep. In short, paradoxical sleep is, as the name implies, a combination of deep sleep, light sleep, and ambiguous features. Consequently, most investigators now avoid using the terms *deep* and *light* sleep.

In addition to these steady characteristics, paradoxical sleep has certain intermittent characteristics, including facial twitches, finger twitches, and rapid eye movements. Because the eyes move back and forth, this stage has become widely known as **rapid eye movement (REM) sleep** (Aserinsky & Kleitman, 1955; Dement & Kleitman, 1957a). The term *REM sleep* is more commonly used than the term *paradoxical sleep* when referring to humans. The term *paradoxical sleep* is preferred when dealing with certain animals, especially those animals that have no eye movements. This stage is also sometimes known as *desynchronized sleep, D sleep,* or *active sleep.*

Figure 9-7 (f) provides an EEG record for a period of REM sleep. The EEG looks about the same as in the first stage 1 period; the difference is in the eye movement record below it. Eye movements are common during REM sleep; they seldom occur during the other stages of sleep, which are sometimes known as **non-REM sleep.**

REM sleep is associated with dreaming, although the relationship is not perfect. Researchers can determine the sleep stage of a person by monitoring EEG records and eye movements. William Dement (see BioSketch 9-2) and Nathaniel Kleitman (1957b) awakened adult volunteers during various

BIOSKETCH

9-2

William C. Dement

As a medical student at the University of Chicago, William Dement became active in Nathaniel Kleitman's sleep laboratory. He observed sleepers' periods of rapid eye movements and demonstrated that they usually occurred while a person was dreaming. It was soon apparent that REM sleep, as described by Dement in humans, was the same as paradoxical sleep, which Michel Jouvet had described in cats.

Dement became the founder and director of the Sleep Disorders Clinic at Stanford University, where he has conducted basic research on sleep and has worked with people suffering from a variety of sleep disorders including insomnia, apnea (inability to breathe while sleeping), and narcolepsy (sudden attacks of sleep during the day). He is the author of more than 200 articles and a popular book, *Some Must Watch While Some Must Sleep* (1972). In that book he remarks, "Although [sleep] illnesses have always plagued mankind, they have remained until now cloaked in ignorance. There is no medical tradition for dealing with them, nor is there even a reasonably accurate folklore.... At this very moment, clinical sleep researchers are feverishly discovering and defining new illnesses of sleep and clarifying the old illnesses, while most physicians in the 'real world' are still prescribing barbiturates and amphetamines for nearly everything. We have much work yet to do in both research and education. To paraphrase Robert Frost, we have miles to go before we sleep."

stages of sleep. They found that people awakened during REM sleep reported dreams about 80 to 90 percent of the time. Those dreams often included elaborate visual imagery and complicated plots. People awakened during slow-wave sleep reported dreams less frequently. The percentage of dream recall in non-REM sleep varies from one investigation to another, from less than 10 percent to more than 70 percent. Much of this discrepancy depends on whether investigators include vague, thoughtlike experiences as dreams or whether they limit dreams to complex experiences with well-defined visual imagery (Foulkes, 1967).

By awakening people during REM sleep, investigators have been able to answer questions that were previously a matter for speculation. For example, as far as we can determine, all normal humans dream. Everyone studied in the laboratory has had periods of REM sleep. When people who claim they never dream are awakened during an REM period, they generally report dreams. Most of their dreams are less vivid than those of other people, however. Apparently, they believe they do not dream only because their dreams are not very memorable.

Furthermore, it can be shown that dreams last about as long as they seem to last—contrary to a once-popular belief that a dream lasts only a second or two. Dement and Wolpert (1958) awakened people after they had been in REM sleep for varying periods of time. The length of the dreams they reported corresponded closely to the length of the REM period prior to awakening, up to a limit of about 15 mintutes. Beyond 15 minutes the volunteers did not report still longer dreams, perhaps because they had already forgotten the beginning of the dream by the time they got to the end of it.

The Effects of REM Sleep Deprivation

Why do we dream? To study dreaming, researchers have had to substitute the more answerable, though still difficult, question, what function does REM sleep serve? Dement (1960) observed the behavior of eight men who agreed to be deprived of REM sleep for 4 to 7 consecutive days. During that period they slept only in a laboratory. Whenever the EEG and eye movements indicated that a given subject was entering REM sleep, an experimenter promptly awakened him and kept him awake for several minutes. The subject was then permitted to go back to sleep until he started REM sleep again.

Over the course of the 4 to 7 nights, the experimenters found that they had to awaken the subjects more and more frequently. On the first night, an average subject had to be awakened twelve times. By the final night, this figure had increased to twenty-six. That is, the subjects had increased their "attempts" at REM sleep.

During the deprivation period, the subjects reported mild, temporary personality changes. Most reported increased anxiety, irritability, and impaired concentration. Five of the eight experienced increased appetite and weight gain. Control studies found that a similar number of awakenings not linked to REM sleep did not produce similar effects. The disturbances were therefore due to REM deprivation, not just the total number of awakenings.

After the deprivation period, seven subjects continued to sleep in the laboratory. During the first uninterrupted night, five of the seven spent more time than usual in REM sleep—29 percent of the night was devoted to REM sleep, as compared with 19 percent before the deprivation. One of the seven showed no increase. (The seventh subject came to the laboratory that night so drunk that his results were considered unreliable.)

Similar experiments have been done with laboratory animals, for which it is possible to impose much longer periods of REM deprivation. Cats have been deprived of REM sleep for up to 70 consecutive days (see Dement, Ferguson, Cohen, & Barchas, 1969). Do not imagine shifts of experimenters monitoring a cat 24 hours a day and prodding it whenever it enters REM sleep. Rather, they use a rather diabolical scheme in which the cat stays on a tiny island surrounded by water. Although the cat can maintain its balance when it is awake or in non-REM sleep, as soon as it enters REM sleep its postural muscles relax, and it loses its balance and falls into the water. It can have no more than a couple of seconds of REM sleep at a time before awakening. Over the course of days, cats placed in this situation make progressively more attempts to enter REM sleep. At the end of the deprivation period, the cats show a rebound increase in the time spent in REM sleep. The greater the deprivation, up to about 25 to 30 days, the greater the rebound. Deprivation beyond 30 days does not increase the rebound further, possibly because at that point the cat is making so many attempts at REM sleep that it is getting in a great many very short REM periods prior to all the interruptions. During the REM deprivation, a cat's behavior is abnormal in several regards. For example, many male cats will sexually mount almost anything that moves.

These and similar studies indicate a specific need for REM sleep in addition to the need for sleep in general. Exactly why animals need REM sleep is unclear, however. Before we speculate on that point, let us consider how individuals and species differ in the time they devote to REM sleep.

Individual and Species Differences in REM Sleep

One way to shed light on the function of REM sleep is to see whether there are any consistent differences between those that get a great deal of REM sleep and those that get little.

If we compare species, the only pattern that stands out is that the percentage of REM sleep is greatest in those species that have the greatest total amount of sleep. Cats, which spend up to 16 hours a day sleeping, have a great deal of REM sleep. Rabbits, guinea pigs, and sheep, which sleep much less, have very little REM sleep.

Fish and reptiles sleep, but they do not have separate REM and non-REM states. Is the one sleep state they do have REM or non-REM? It is not easy to decide (Meddis, 1979). We cannot use EEG criteria because these animals lack a well-developed cerebral cortex and they do not produce EEG waves comparable to those of mammals. We cannot use eye movements as a criterion because even when fish and reptiles are awake they have few eye movements. And we can hardly waken a fish to ask it about its dreams. Although the question seems most difficult, it is not just a matter of idle curiosity. If we knew which sleep state fish and reptiles have, we would know whether to try to explain the evolution and function of REM sleep in mammals, or the evolution and function of non-REM sleep.

Within a species, infants have a greater percentage of REM sleep than adults. Figure 9-9 demonstrates this relationship for cats. The same is true for humans and most other mammalian species. REM sleep occupies an even greater percentage of total sleep time in premature infants (Astic, Sastre, & Brandon, 1973; Dreyfus-Brisac, 1970). We must admit some difficulty distinguishing between an infant in REM sleep and an infant who is awake but has his or her eyes closed (Lynch & Aserinsky, 1986). For that reason, the data on infants may not be entirely accurate.

Among adult humans, those who get the greatest amount of sleep per night (9 or more hours) have the highest percentage of REM sleep. Those who get the least total sleep (5 hours or less) spend the lowest percentage of their sleep on REM. From all these data, a pattern seems to emerge: Across species, across ages, and across individuals, the greater the total amount of sleep, the greater the percentage of REM sleep.

In other words, the amount of REM sleep varies more than the amount of non-REM sleep, from one individual to another and from one time to another. Perhaps the need for non-REM sleep is greater than the need for REM sleep. After people or other species have been deprived of sleep for a day or more, their sleep on the first uninterrupted night has an increased duration of non-REM sleep. REM sleep does not show such a large immediate rebound effect (Borbély, 1982).

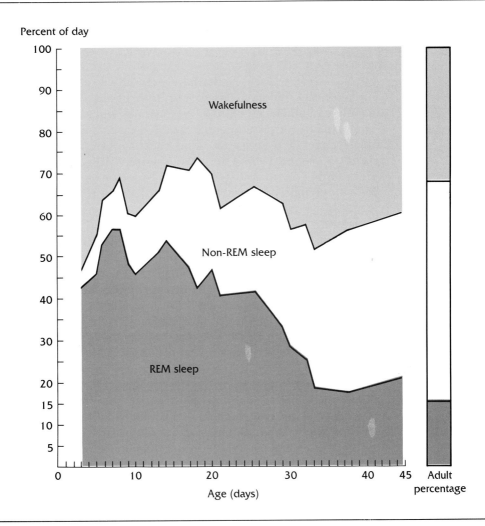

Percent of day

Figure 9-9. Percentage of time spent in wakefulness, non-REM, and REM sleep as a function of age in cats. (From Jouvet-Mounier, Astic, and Lacote, 1969.)

What Is the Function of REM Sleep?

REM sleep, or paradoxical sleep, appears to be paradoxical in yet another sense: Although deprivation studies indicate a need for REM sleep, the body apparently adds extra REM sleep time only after it has first satisfied its need for non-REM sleep.

Speculations on why we need REM sleep have been numerous. It has been linked to the consolidation of memory, brain growth, the need for periodic arousal of the brain during the night, suppression of inappropriate associations in the brain, and the dampening of excessively strong motivations. At this point, we have no solid evidence for any of these interpretations. The function of REM sleep remains uncertain, and a subject for continuing research.

A BIOLOGICAL PERSPECTIVE ON DREAMING

"Dreams are real while they last. Can we say more of life?"

—Havelock Ellis

For many years psychologists have been heavily influenced by Sigmund Freud's theory of dreams, which was based on the assumption that dreams are caused by hidden and often unconscious wishes. Although Freud was certainly correct in asserting that dreams depend on the dreamer's personality and recent experiences, his theory of the mechanism of dreams was based on a now-obsolete view of the nervous system (McCarley & Hobson, 1977). He believed, for example, that brain cells were inactive except when nerves from the periphery brought them energy. Freud was also hampered by relying on dream reports that his patients gave him hours or days after the dream occurred.

Given a more modern understanding of the brain and the capacity to awaken someone during REM sleep and get an almost immediate dream report, contemporary investigators can offer new interpretations of dream phenomena. According to the **activation-synthesis hypothesis,** various parts of the brain are activated during REM sleep, and the brain synthesizes some sort of story to make sense of all the activity (Hobson & McCarley, 1977; McCarley & Hoffman, 1981). From this hypothesis we can expect to find a correspondence between brain activity during REM sleep and the content of dreams.

For example, almost any external stimulus that occurs during REM sleep is incorporated into a dream. If water is dripping on your foot, you may dream about swimming or about walking in the rain. Even in the absence of external stimuli, bursts of activity occur spontaneously in certain parts of the cerebral cortex. The most common sites of activity are the visual, auditory, and motor cortexes; not surprisingly, almost all dreams include visual imagery and more than half include hearing or movement. Occasional bursts of vestibular sensation are also common during REM sleep; they may be responsible for the common dreams of falling, flying, or spinning.

Many people dream that they are trying to move but cannot. It is tempting to relate this dream to the fact that the major postural muscles are virtually paralyzed during REM sleep. On the other hand, people do sometimes dream they are moving, in spite of the actual paralysis.

The eye movements during REM sleep also relate to the content of the dream (Roffwarg, Dement, Muzio, & Fisher, 1962). For example, one person awakened after a period of vertical eye movements reported a dream of walking up stairs. Another person awakened after a period of rapid left and right movements reported dreaming about watching a train speed by. Another person awakened after periods of very slow eye movements alternating with rapid jerks of the eyes to the left reported dreaming about reading poetry.

In short, during REM sleep the brain receives occasional external stimuli and is subject to spontaneous activation of various cortical areas. A dream may be the brain's attempt to make sense of that shifting array of stimuli.

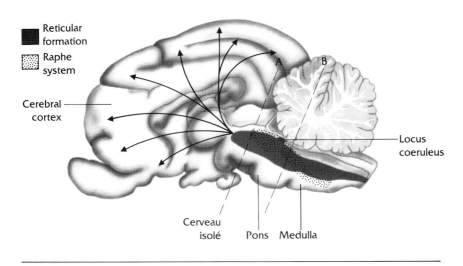

Reticular
formation

Raphe
system

Cerebral
cortex

Locus
coeruleus

Cerveau
isolé   Pons   Medulla

Figure 9-10. Location of systems in cat brain that play critical parts in wakefulness and sleep. A cut at line A leads to prolonged sleep; a cut at line B leads to prolonged wakefulness.

BRAIN MECHANISMS IN SLEEP

Suppose I buy a new radio. After I play it for 4 hours, it suddenly stops. In trying to explain why it stopped, I would try to discover whether its batteries were dead or whether it needed repair. Suppose I discover that the radio will operate again a few hours later even without repairs or a battery change. I also discover that the radio always stops whenever I play it for 4 hours. I begin to suspect that the manufacturer designed it this way on purpose, perhaps to prevent me from wearing it out too fast or to prevent me from listening to the radio all day. I might then try to find the device in the radio that turns it off whenever I play it for 4 hours. Notice that I am asking a new question. When I thought that the radio stopped because it needed repairs or new batteries, I would not have thought to ask which device turned the radio off. I ask that question only when I think of the stoppage as something other than an accidental, passive process.

The same is true for sleep. If we think of sleep only as a passive cessation of activity, similar to catching one's breath after running a race, we do not ask which part of the brain is responsible for sleep. But if we think of sleep as a specialized state evolved to serve particular functions, we may look for the devices that control it.

Wakefulness and the Reticular Activating System

Making a cut through the midbrain, separating the forebrain and part of the midbrain from the rest of the midbrain, pons, medulla, and spinal cord (line A in Figure 9-10), produces the **cerveau isolé** preparation (French for "isolated forebrain"). The cerveau isolé animal goes into a prolonged state of sleep. The brain shows no signs of wakefulness in the EEG for the next week or so, and only brief periods of wakefulness later.

All sensory stimuli other than vision and smell enter the nervous system at levels below the cut; thus, the cut isolates the brain from most sources of sensory stimulation. It may seem obvious, therefore, that the cut produces prolonged sleep by isolating the brain from the sensory stimuli that normally activate it. However, the effect of this cut is very different from the effect of cutting off all the individual sensory sources. Because each sensory tract enters the brain through a well-defined path, it is possible to cut each individual sensory tract while sparing the rest of the spinal cord and brain stem. After this series of lesions, the animal becomes unresponsive to sensory stimulation other than vision and smell but continues to have normal periods of sleep and wakefulness. Apparently the cerveau isolé cut decreases wakefulness by some means other than just reducing sensory input.

In 1949 Moruzzi and Magoun found that wakefulness depends not on the various sensory tracts themselves but on a system called the **ascending reticular activating system (ARAS)**, often known simply as the **reticular formation**. Although the reticular formation is largely dependent on the sensory tracts for its input, it is also capable of generating activity on its own. High-frequency stimulation of the reticular formation awakens a sleeping individual or increases alertness in one already awake. It also desynchronizes the EEG. Damage to the reticular formation or a cut that separates it from the anterior parts of the brain leads to prolonged sleep or inactivity. Clearly it is critical for wakefulness and alertness.

Figure 9-10 shows the position of the reticular formation within the pons in a cat brain. The borders as shown are only approximate. The term *reticular* is based on the Latin word *rete*, meaning "net." As the name implies, the reticular formation is diffuse, lacking sharp boundaries. It extends forward at least into parts of the thalamus and hypothalamus; some authorities maintain that it extends all the way into the cerebral cortex. (For more information, see Morgane and Stern, 1974.)

As the term *reticular* also implies, the individual neurons are heavily interconnected, as in parts of a net. The reticular formation is characterized by neurons with long dendrites that branch diffusely. The connections among neurons do not form straight chains but include multisynaptic paths and looping axon branches. The reticular formation on close inspection gives an appearance that is more irregular and disorderly than most of the rest of the brain.

The input and output of the reticular formation are diffuse also. The cranial nerves send input to the ascending reticular formation in addition to their primary targets. Thus, the ARAS can be activated by practically any stimulus. The ARAS also generates spontaneous activity of its own. Cells in the ARAS, in turn, send impulses diffusely throughout the cerebral cortex.

(The reticular formation has descending paths as well. These paths receive input mostly from extrapyramidal sources, as described in Chapter 8, and project to cells in the medulla and spinal cord.)

The ARAS differs in an important way from the sensory systems. The lateral geniculate nucleus of the thalamus, for example, receives input mostly from the retina and sends its output mostly to the occipital cortex. Similarly, structures in other sensory systems receive limited kinds of input and project their axons to limited targets. The input to the ARAS, in contrast, is so mixed and its output so scattered that the system would be useless for conveying any precise information. The ARAS is poorly designed for conveying specific information but well designed for controlling arousal and wakefulness. Any strong stimulation—sound, touch, pain, whatever—activates the ARAS, thereby diffusely activating the entire cerebral cortex.

Sleep-Inducing Areas in or Near the Pons

We discussed the effects of a cut through the midbrain of a cat at line A in Figure 9-10. If, instead, we make the cut at line B, we still isolate the brain from most sensory input, but the effect of this cut, instead of increasing sleep, is to increase wakefulness! A cat with such a cut stays awake 70 to 90 percent of the time, which is about twice as long as a normal cat (Batini, Magni, Palestini, Rossi, & Zanchetti, 1959; Batini, Moruzzi, Palestini, Rossi, & Zanchetti, 1958, 1959; Batini, Palestini, Rossi, & Zanchetti, 1959). Evidently the cut at B has spared enough of the ARAS to permit wakefulness but has damaged a system that promotes sleep; that is, a sleep-promoting area must exist mostly below the cut.

The sleep-promoting area is probably the **raphe system** (see Figure 9-10). *Raphe* is a Greek word meaning "seam" or "stitching." (You may hear *raphe* pronounced many ways, including RAY-fee, RAH-fay, and ruh-FAY.) The seam referred to here is the line joining the halves of the hindbrain. The raphe system, located medially in the hindbrain, includes several distinct nuclei ranging from the posterior medulla to the anterior midbrain. The raphe nuclei are close to the ARAS.

After damage to the raphe system, a cat or rat remains awake for a day or more (Jouvet & Renault, 1966; Żernicki, Gandolfo, Glin, & Gottesmann, 1984). Sleep gradually returns, although the animal may never again sleep as much as it used to.

If the raphe system is responsible for sleep, we should expect stimulating it to put an animal to sleep. Although such stimulation can induce sleep, it does so only under a narrow range of conditions, such as stimulation of a particular area at a frequency of 1 to 3 Hz (Kostowski, Giacalone, Garattini, & Valzelli, 1969).

Brain Areas That May Trigger REM Sleep

Jouvet (1960) was the first to suggest that a particular area of the brain, probably in the hindbrain, might trigger a series of events that produce REM sleep. REM sleep begins with a distinctive pattern of high-amplitude electrical potentials that can be detected first in the reticular formation of the pons, then in the lateral geniculate of the thalamus, and finally in the occipital cortex (Brooks & Bizzi, 1963; Laurent, Cespuglio, & Jouvet, 1974). Those potentials are known as **PGO waves**—for pons-geniculate-occipital. The PGO waves begin at or just before the start of REM sleep; they continue during REM sleep. Each PGO wave is synchronized with an eye movement (Cespuglio, Laurent, & Jouvet, 1975).

When an animal compensates for a loss of REM sleep, it compensates for the lost PGO waves more precisely than it compensates for the lost REM time (Dement, Ferguson, Cohen, & Barchas, 1969). During a prolonged period of REM deprivation, PGO waves begin to emerge during stages 2 to 4 sleep—a time when they do not normally occur—and even during wakefulness, often in association with strange behaviors, as if the animal were having a hallucination. At the end of the deprivation period, when the animal is permitted to sleep without interruption, the REM periods have an unusually high density of PGO waves.

Where in the hindbrain are the cells that trigger the PGO waves, and with them REM sleep? The search for those cells has proved elusive so far. Jouvet (1960) originally pointed to the **locus coeruleus** (see Figure 9-10). (Locus coeruleus is Latin for "blue place"; the locus coeruleus looks blue in fresh brain tissue.) Jouvet suggested that one part of the locus coeruleus generated impulses to the cortex that produced REM sleep, while another part sent impulses to the spinal cord to inhibit the motor neurons. For example, cats that had received damage to the caudal portion of the locus coeruleus still had periods of REM sleep, but their muscles did not relax. In their sleep they would walk, chase, attack, and perform other actions as if they were acting out dreams (Jouvet & Delorme, 1965).

Later studies confirmed that the motor neurons of the spinal cord receive a steady stream of inhibitory impulses during REM sleep; however, these impulses do not appear to be coming from the locus coeruleus (Glenn & Dement, 1985; Henley & Morrison, 1974). Similarly, although the PGO waves originate somewhere in the pons, they apparently do not originate in the locus coeruleus.

A later hypothesis focused attention on the **FTG neurons** of the pons—cells of the *gigantocellular tegmental field*. It was suggested that the FTG cells become active only during REM sleep, when their widely, diffusely branching axons might control activity throughout the cortex (Hobson, 1977; Hobson, McCarley, & Wyzinski, 1975). One possibility was that a feedback relationship between the locus coeruleus and the FTG cells might generate cycles of REM sleep alternating with non-REM sleep (McCarley & Hobson, 1975).

That hypothesis, too, seems inadequate. The FTG neurons that are active during REM sleep are just as active or more active during wakeful movements (Siegel, McGinty, & Breedlove, 1977; Siegel, Wheeler, & McGinty, 1979). None of them seems specific to REM sleep. Moreover, damage to the FTG neurons does not interfere with REM sleep (Sastre, Sakai, & Jouvet, 1979). Apparently those cells have something to do with movement, or perhaps the inhibition of movement, rather than with REM sleep (Chase, 1983).

In short, the cells that trigger REM sleep have not yet been found. Either researchers have been looking in the wrong place, or the cells are small and hard to identify, or REM sleep depends on a wide population of cells, not a small set of triggering cells.

The Biochemistry of Sleep

The cells of the raphe system use serotonin as their predominant transmitter. The locus coeruleus uses norepinephrine almost exclusively. Because of these specificities, many investigators have looked for effects of those transmitters on sleep.

The results have been discouragingly inconsistent. After damage to cells of the raphe system, or after chemical depletion of the transmitter serotonin, a number of investigators have reported decreases in the duration of sleep (Laguzzi & Adrien, 1980; Pujol, Buguet, Froment, Jones, & Jouvet, 1971). On the other hand, other investigators have reported that a permanent depletion of serotonin had no effect, or only a temporary effect, on sleep (Morgane, 1981). It is not clear which differences in procedures are responsible for the discrepancies in results.

The possible relationship of serotonin to sleep has prompted some investigators to try precursors to serotonin as possible sleeping pills. The amino acid L-**tryptophan**, after entering the brain, is converted to serotonin. In doses of 1–15 g, taken just before bedtime, tryptophan helps some people get to sleep, particularly young people who are otherwise healthy. (These doses contrast to the 0.5 to 2 g per day present in the average human diet.) For those with long-lasting or relatively severe insomnia, tryptophan may be helpful after prolonged use, particularly after alternating periods of use with periods of nonuse (Schneider-Helmert & Spinweber, 1986). The benefit of tryptophan is that, as a natural product and a normal part of the diet, it produces no apparent side effects. Nor does the body develop as much tolerance to its effects as it does to the effects of most other sleeping pills. Tryptophan is not beneficial for everyone, however. Before trying tryptophan or any other sleeping pill, a person should explore the reasons behind his or her sleeping difficulties.

The possible role of norepinephrine in sleep, particularly in the onset of REM sleep, is even more difficult to determine with confidence. Damage to the locus coeruleus or depletion of its transmitter norepinephrine sometimes leads to an increase in REM sleep, suggesting that norepinephrine inhibits REM sleep (Hartmann, Chung, Draskoczy, & Schildkraut, 1971). However, other studies have reported no effect, brief effects, or effects in the opposite direction (Jones, Harper, & Halaris, 1977). One attempt to integrate all the data is a suggestion that neither norepinephrine nor serotonin directly triggers sleep or any stage of sleep (Koella, 1984); rather, it may be that they modulate vigilance levels during both wakefulness and sleep.

Acetylcholine may be a better candidate for the trigger of REM sleep. Drugs that stimulate acetylcholine synapses lead to an immediate onset of REM sleep (Shiromani, Siegel, Tomaszewski, & McGinty, 1986). A small glycopeptide, designated **Factor** S, which can be isolated from the nervous system or bloodstream of sleeping animals, can induce sleep, mostly slow-wave sleep, when it is injected into other animals (Inoué, Uchizono, & Nagasaki, 1982; Krueger, Pappenheimer, & Karnovsky, 1982). It may be that several synaptic transmitters or hormones contribute to the regulation of sleep.

ABNORMALITIES OF SLEEP

Sleep abnormalities are associated with a wide variety of psychological and neurological disorders. In one study of 100 patients suffering from chronic insomnia, 95 were found to be suffering from one or more psychiatric dis-

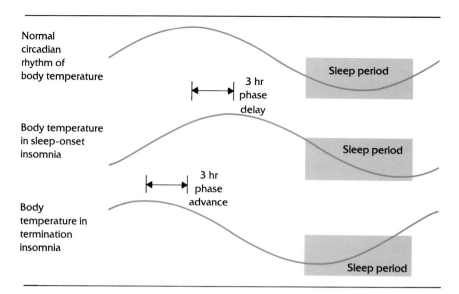

Normal circadian rhythm of body temperature

Sleep period

3 hr phase delay

Body temperature in sleep-onset insomnia

Sleep period

3 hr phase advance

Body temperature in termination insomnia

Sleep period

Figure 9-11. How a delay of advance in the circadian rhythm of body temperature can relate to insomnia.

orders (Tan, Kales, Kales, Soldatos, & Bixler, 1984). The most common were depression and substance abuse.

In addition to sleep abnormalities associated with more severe disorders, sleep disorders may occur as someone's primary complaint. It is estimated that 8 to 15 percent of adults in the United States have chronic sleep complaints (Weitzman, 1981).

Insomnia

Insomnia (sleeplessness) has many causes. It can result from excessive noise, worries and stress, drugs and medications, uncomfortable temperatures, sleeping in an unfamiliar place, or trying to go to sleep at the wrong time in one's circadian rhythm (Kales & Kales, 1984). A friend of mine suffered insomnia for months until he realized that he dreaded going to sleep at night because he dreaded waking up in the morning and doing his daily jogging. After he switched his jogging time to late afternoon, he no longer had any trouble sleeping. Before trying sleeping pills or any other method of combating insomnia, a person should carefully identify the reasons for his or her sleep troubles.

It is convenient to distinguish three categories of insomnia: onset insomnia, maintenance insomnia, and termination insomnia. People with **onset insomnia** have trouble falling asleep. Those with **maintenance insomnia** awaken frequently during the night. And those with **termination insomnia** wake up too early and cannot get back to sleep. It is possible to have more than one of the three types of insomnia.

Certain cases of insomnia are related to abnormalities of biological rhythms (MacFarlane, Cleghorn, & Brown, 1985a, 1985b). As mentioned earlier in this chapter, it is possible for the circadian rhythm of temperature to get out of phase with the circadian rhythm of waking and sleeping. Ordinarily, people fall asleep while their temperature is declining and awaken while it is rising, as in Figure 9-11 (**a**). Some people's body temperature rhythm is *phase-delayed*, as in Figure 9-11 (b). If they try to go to sleep at the normal time of day, their body temperature is higher than normal for going to sleep. Such people are likely to experience onset insomnia. Other people's body temperature rhythm is *phase-advanced*, as in Figure 9-11 (c). They are likely to suffer termination insomnia. Those who suffer from sleep-maintenance insomnia may have extensive irregularities of their circadian rhythms.

REM sleep occurs mostly during the rising phase of the temperature cycle. For most people, this is the second half of the night's sleep, as shown in Figure 9-11 (a). For people with termination insomnia, or anyone else who falls asleep after the temperature cycle has already hit its bottom, REM sleep may start shortly after the person falls asleep (Czeisler, Weitzman, Moore-Ede, Zimmerman, & Knauer, 1980). Because depression is often associated with sleep-termination insomnia, many depressed people enter REM sleep earlier in the night than nondepressed people do.

One special cause of insomnia is **sleep apnea,** which is an inability to breathe while sleeping (Weitzman, 1981). Many people breathe irregularly during REM sleep, and about 10 to 15 percent of all adults have occasional periods of at least 10 seconds without breathing. Sleep apnea to that degree is considered normal and has no relationship to insomnia (Kales & Kales, 1984). A few people, however, have such periods more frequently or for longer times, sometimes a minute or more before they awaken, gasping for breath (Weitzman, 1981). Such people may stay in bed more than 8 hours per night but sleep only about half that time.

Obesity is one of several possible causes of sleep apnea. Some obese people, especially men, have trouble finding a sleeping position that enables them to breathe easily.

Another factor occasionally linked to insomnia is **nocturnal myoclonus,** a periodic involuntary movement of the legs and sometimes arms (Weitzman, 1981). The legs may kick once every 20 to 30 seconds for a period of minutes or even hours, mostly during non-REM sleep. Nocturnal myoclonus is more common in older people than in younger people and is particularly rare before age 30. A mild to moderate degree of nocturnal myoclonus, like sleep apnea, occurs in about as many normal people as in insomniacs (Kales & Kales, 1984). Although severe nocturnal myoclonus may be related to insomnia, we do not know whether it is a cause of poor sleep or a result of it.

Still another cause of insomnia is, paradoxically, sleeping pills. Although barbiturates and tranquilizers may help a person get to sleep, someone who has taken such drugs a few times may develop a dependence on them for getting to sleep. Such a person who tries going to sleep without the drug may go into a withdrawal state that prevents sleep (Kales, Scharf, & Kales, 1978). He or she may react to the sleeplessness by taking the sleeping pills again, setting up a cycle from which it is difficult to escape.

Certain short-acting tranquilizers, such as midazolam and triazolam, have become popular because their effects wear off before the next morning. Unlike certain other drugs, they do not leave the person sleepy the next day. On the other hand, because their effects wear off so quickly, they may produce withdrawal effects during the night. As a result, someone who takes such drugs may awaken very early as a side effect of the drug and find it impossible to get back to sleep (Kales, Soldatos, Bixler, & Kales, 1983).

A final point regarding tranquilizers as sleeping pills: Certain tranquilizers may either phase-advance the biological clock or phase-delay it, depending on the time of day when a person takes them (Turek & Losee-Olson, 1986). Especially if such pills are taken to combat the sleep disorders of jet lag, it is possible for them to aggravate the problem instead of relieving it, depending on when the person takes the pills and which direction the person has flown.

Narcolepsy

Narcolepsy is a condition characterized by unexpected periods of sleep in the middle of the day (Dement, 1972; Kellerman, 1981; Weitzman, 1981). Four symptoms are generally associated with narcolepsy:

1.   Gradual or sudden attacks of sleepiness.
2.   Occasional **cataplexy**—an attack of muscle weakness while the person remains awake. Cataplexy is generally triggered by strong emotions such as anger or great excitement.
3.   Sleep paralysis, a complete inability to move just as the person is falling asleep or waking up.
4.   *Hypnagogic hallucinations*, which are dreamlike experiences that the person has trouble distinguishing from reality.

All these symptoms have been interpreted as an intrusion of REM sleep into the wakeful state.

Narcolepsy has a hereditary basis. It is usually treated with stimulant or antidepressant drugs, although the drugs are only moderately successful.

Night Terrors, Sleep Talking, and Sleepwalking

Night terrors are experiences of intense anxiety from which a person generally awakens screaming in terror. A night terror should be distinguished from a *nightmare*, which is simply an unpleasant dream; it occurs during REM sleep in people of any age. A night terror occurs during non-REM sleep and is far more common in children than in adults.

Many people talk in their sleep occasionally, including many who never know it. *Sleep talking* has about the same chance of occurring during either REM sleep or non-REM sleep (Arkin, Toth, Baker, & Hastey, 1970).

Sleepwalking occurs mostly in children, especially ages 2 to 5, and is most common early in the night, during stage 3 or stage 4 sleep. Its causes are not known, other than the fact that it runs in families.

Although sleepwalking is generally harmless, both to the sleepwalker and to others, a few individuals experience a dangerous combination of night terrors and sleepwalking at the same time. One adult man was reported to walk in his sleep several times a week, thrashing violently with his arms. Another stopped his car one night, fell asleep, and then started driving in his sleep, eventually causing an accident that killed three people (Hartmann, 1983).

SUMMARY

1. Animals, including humans, have internally generated rhythms of activity and other functions, approximating both a 24-hour cycle and a one-year cycle. (p. 234)

2. Although the biological clock can continue to operate in constant light or constant darkness, the onset of light at a particular time can reset the clock. (p. 236)

3. The biological clock can keep pace with an external rhythm of light and darkness slightly different from 24 hours, but it ignores the external rhythm if the discrepancy is more than 1 or 2 hours. (p. 237)

4. Under certain circumstances, the circadian rhythm of temperature may get out of phase with the activity-sleep rhythm; the two rhythms may even follow different periods. (p. 238)

5. It is easier for people to phase-delay their clock (to follow a cycle longer than 24 hours) than to phase-advance the clock (to follow a cycle shorter than 24 hours). (p. 239)

6. The biological clock is apparently a property of the suprachiasmatic nucleus, a part of the hypothalamus. (p. 240)

7. The biological clock is not greatly affected by large changes in body temperature, at least for 1 to 4 hours. (p. 241)

8. Sleep probably serves at least two functions: repair and restoration, and conservation of energy during a period of relative inefficiency. (p. 243)

9. During a 90- to 100-minute period, human sleep progresses through stages 1 through 4 and then back to 1. Stage 4 has the least brain activity and the lowest heart rate. (p. 246)

10. A special type of stage 1 sleep is REM sleep (or paradoxical sleep), characterized by a high level of brain activity, often vivid dreams, muscle relaxation, and resistance to being awakened. (p. 248)

11. Although people and animals show signs of needing REM sleep, investigators are still unsure what function it serves in the body. (p. 251)

12. Dreams can be regarded as the brain's response to sensory stimulation and spontaneous neural activity during sleep. (p. 254)

13. Wakefulness and arousal are largely the products of the reticular activating system, which receives information from all sensory systems and sends information diffusely throughout the forebrain. (p. 256)

14. The raphe system is believed to be important for generating sleep, although its exact role in sleep remains controversial. (p. 257)

15. Although REM sleep is believed to begin with waves of activity in the pons, no population of cells in the pons has been conclusively identified as the triggering mechanism of REM sleep. (p. 257)

16. Research has variously linked sleep—and REM sleep in particular—to serotonin, norephinephrine, acetylcholine, and Factor S. The amino acid L-tryptophan, a precursor to serotonin, has been reported to help certain people to get to sleep (p. 259)

17. Insomnia can have several causes. In certain cases it results from a shift in phase of the circadian rhythm of temperature relative to the circadian rhythm of sleep and wakefulness. (p. 260)

18. Tranquilizers entail certain risks when they are used as sleeping pills, including the risk of withdrawal symptoms when the person stops using them. (pp. 261–262)

REVIEW QUESTIONS

1. Why is it advantageous for a migratory bird to have an internal mechanism that predicts the changing seasons, instead of relying entirely on changes in the light/dark patterns in the environment? (p. 235)

2. What evidence indicates that the body has an internal biological clock, instead of timing its activities entirely on the basis of light and other external cues? (p. 235)

3. What stimulus is the most effective Zeitgeber for resetting the biological clock? (p. 236)

4. Which direction of travel is most likely to produce jet lag? (p. 239)

5. If someone reports persistent trouble getting to sleep on time and waking up on time, and this person is known to suffer severe jet lag when traveling east, what advice would you give? (p. 240)

6. What is the evidence that the suprachiasmatic nucleus generates circadian rhythms of activity? (p. 240)

7. Why would we expect the biological clock to be sensitive to temperature, and what is the evidence that it is not? (p. 241)

8. State the strengths and weaknesses of the repair and restoration theory and the evolutionary theory of the need for sleep. (p. 243)

9. Why are the waves on an EEG larger in amplitude when brain activity decreases? (p. 246)

10. What are the differences among sleep stages 1, 2, 3, and 4? (p. 246)

11. Which sleep stages are most common early in the night? Which ones predominate later in the night? (p. 248)

12. What are the characteristics of REM sleep? (p. 249)

13. What are the effects of REM sleep deprivation? (p. 251)

14. What seems to determine which individuals and species will get the greatest percentage of REM sleep? (p. 252)

15. According to the activation-synthesis theory of dreams, what determines the content of a dream? (p. 254)
16. How is the structure of the reticular formation adapted to its function of overall arousal of the brain? (p. 256)
17. What is the evidence that a part of the brain, probably the raphe system, promotes the onset of sleep? (p. 257)
18. Why do some people use L-tryptophan as a sleeping pill? (p. 259)

19. Describe some of the possible causes of insomnia. (p. 260)
20. What are the disadvantages of using sleeping pills to combat insomnia? (p. 261)
21. Describe the characteristics of narcolepsy. (p. 262)
22. Are night terrors more common in REM sleep or non-REM sleep? What about sleep talking? sleepwalking? (p. 262)

THOUGHT QUESTIONS

1. What evolutionary advantage might there be in the fact that sheep, guinea pigs, and rabbits have very little REM sleep? (Hint: In which stage of sleep is it hardest to waken an individual?)
2. When cats are deprived of REM sleep for various periods, the amount of rebound increases for the first 25 to 30 days but does not increase further with a longer deprivation. What prevents the need from ac-

cumulating beyond that point? Make use of PGO waves in your answer.
3. The content of dreams is related to the direction and speed of eye movements. How could you design an experiment to test whether the dream content controls the eye movements or whether the eye movements control the dream content?

TERMS TO REMEMBER

endogenous circannual rhythm (p. 235)
endogenous circadian rhythm (p. 235)
biological clock (p. 236)
free-running rhythm (p. 236)
Zeitgeber (p. 236)
jet lag (p. 239)
suprachiasmatic nucleus (SCN) (p. 240)
repair and restoration theory of sleep (p. 243)
evolutionary theory of sleep (p. 244)
electroencephalograph (EEG) (p. 246)
synchronized (p. 246)
alpha waves (p. 246)
desynchronized (p. 246)
slow-wave sleep (SWS) (p. 246)
paradoxical sleep (p. 248)
rapid eye movement (REM) sleep (p. 249)
non-REM sleep (p. 249)
activation-synthesis hypothesis (p. 254)

cerveau isolé (p. 255)
ascending reticular activating system (ARAS) (p. 256)
reticular formation (p. 256)
raphe system (p. 257)
PGO waves (p. 257)
locus coeruleus (p. 258)
FTG neurons (p. 258)
L-tryptophan (p. 259)
Factor S (p. 259)
insomnia (p. 260)
onset insomnia (p. 260)
maintenance insomnia (p. 260)
termination insomnia (p. 260)
sleep apnea (p. 261)
nocturnal myoclonus (p. 261)
narcolepsy (p. 262)
cataplexy (p. 252)
night terrors (p. 262)

SUGGESTIONS FOR FURTHER READING

Dement, W. C. (1972). *Some must watch while some must sleep.* San Francisco: Freeman. Readable review of pioneering work on sleep and sleep stages.

Kales, A., & Kales, J. D. (1984). *Evaluation and treatment of insomnia.* New York: Oxford. Review of research on the causes and treatment of insomnia.

Motivation and the Regulation of Internal Body States

CHAPTER

10

MAIN IDEAS

1. Many physiological and behavioral processes act to maintain a nearly homeostatic condition, that is, near-constancy of certain body variables.

2. Mammals regulate body temperature by such physiological processes as shivering and by such behavioral processes as selecting an appropriate environment. Brain areas that control body temperature respond both to their own temperature and to the temperature of the skin and spinal cord.

3. Thirst responds to at least two variables: the osmotic pressure of the blood, which may withdraw water from the cells, and the total volume of blood. Thirst may also act to anticipate and prevent water need as well as react to such a need.

4. Hunger and satiety are regulated by a number of factors, including taste, stomach distention, and glucose availability to the cells.

5. Because certain people may be biologically predisposed toward alcoholism, it may become possible to identify those who are most at risk before they have begun to abuse alcohol.

Whrat is life? Life is many things and can be defined in different ways depending on whether our interest is medical, legal, philosophical, or poetic.

At the most basic biological level we can say that *life is a coordinated set of chemical reactions*. Not every coordinated set of chemical reactions is alive, but life cannot exist without a coordinated set of chemical reactions.

Every chemical reaction in the body takes place in a water medium at a rate that depends on the concentration of molecules in the water, the identity of those molecules, the temperature of the solution, and the presence of any contaminants. In order to continue the chemical reactions we call "life," we need to prepare the ingredients according to a most precise recipe. A great deal of our motivated behavior is organized to keep those ingredients present in the right proportions and at the right temperature.

HOMEOSTASIS

Walter B. Cannon (1929; see BioSketch 10-1) introduced the term **homeostasis** (HOM-ee-oh-STAY-sis) to refer to a group of biological processes that tend to keep certain body variables near a "set" level. To understand how a homeostatic process works, we can use the analogy of the thermostat in a house. Someone fixes a set range of temperatures on the thermostat. When the temperature in the house drops below that range, the thermostat triggers the furnace to provide heat until the house temperature returns to the set range. If the house also has an air-conditioning system, the set range for temperature has a maximum as well as a minimum. When the temperature rises above the maximum, the thermostat triggers the air conditioner to cool the house until the temperature returns to the set range.

Similarly, animals have homeostatic processes that trigger certain activities when some variable passes beyond the limits of its set range. In many cases the range is so narrow that we refer to it as a **set point**. For example, if calcium is deficient in the diet and its concentration in the blood begins to fall below its set point of 0.16 g/l, additional calcium is released into the blood from storage deposits in the bones. If the calcium level in the blood rises above 0.16 g/l, part of the excess is stored in the bones and part is excreted in the urine and feces. Analogous mechanisms maintain constant blood levels of water, oxygen, glucose, sodium chloride, protein, fat, and acidity (Cannon, 1929).

Certain motivations, including temperature regulation, hunger, and thirst, can be regarded as homeostatic processes, although they do not operate like the thermostat that controls the temperature of a house (Hogan, 1980; Satinoff, 1983). A thermostat compares the temperature at a single point in the house to the set range; if it finds a discrepancy, it turns on the heating system or the cooling system. Biological motivations are more complex. The body monitors its need for heat, cold, food, or water by monitoring a number of different variables in different parts of the body and by trigger-

BIOSKETCH
10-1

Walter B. Cannon (1871– 1945)

Walter B. Cannon was one of the pioneers who organized the field of biological psychology and structured the issues that have occupied other twentieth-century investigators in this field. Although Cannon received an M.D. from Harvard in 1900, he never actually practiced medicine. He was professor of physiology at Harvard from 1900 until his retirement.

Cannon was the first to characterize the sympathetic nervous system as being responsible for fight-or-flight activities. His research ranged over such topics as digestion, hunger, thirst, the effects of emotional excitement on the body, the nature of shock from war injuries, and the chemical basis of nerve impulses. He was responsible for the concept of *homeostasis*. His explanations of behavior focused mainly on structures outside the brain. For example, he explained hunger in terms of stomach contractions and thirst in terms of dryness of the mouth.

Cannon was an explorer in all senses of the word. He and his wife were the first humans to climb a mountain in Montana that is now known as Mt. Cannon.

In his autobiography, Cannon (1945) described the role of hunches and sudden inspiration in his scientific research: "As a matter of routine I have long trusted unconscious processes to serve me.... [One] example I may cite was the interpretation of the significance of bodily changes which occur in great emotional excitement, such as fear and rage. These changes— the more rapid pulse, the deeper breathing, the increase of sugar in the blood, the secretion from the adrenal glands—were very diverse and seemed unrelated. Then, one wakeful night, after a considerable collection of these changes had been disclosed, the idea flashed through my mind that they could be nicely integrated if conceived as bodily preparations for supreme effort in flight or in fighting."

ing a number of responses, each partly independent of the others. The set point for temperature varies from one time of day to another. The set point for body weight may vary from one time of year to another, at least in certain animal species. Most species, humans included, eat more and gain more weight when they can find tasty food than when they can find only bland food. Although the body maintains fairly steady levels of temperature, body water, weight, and so forth, the regulation is flexible.

TEMPERATURE REGULATION

Fish, amphibians, and reptiles are **poikilothermic**; their body temperature is the same as that of their environment. Mammals and birds are **homeothermic**; they maintain the same body temperature despite large variations in the temperature of the environment. Every mammal and bird keeps its body temperature quite close to the set point under normal circumstances. As we discussed in Chapter 9, that set point depends on the time of day. In humans, it varies from a little over 37°C in the middle of the afternoon to just over 36°C in the middle of the night.

Why have we evolved mechanisms to control body temperature? What difference would it make if body temperature fluctuated over a range of 20 degrees or more each day?

Part of the answer has to do with the effect of temperature on chemical reactions. Although the rates of all chemical reactions increase when the temperature rises, the rates of different reactions do not increase equally. For instance, imagine a sequence of chemical reactions of this form:

$$A \xrightarrow{1} B \xrightarrow{2} C$$

The letters stand for chemicals and the numbers stand for reactions. Suppose that a 10-degree increase in temperature triples the rate of reaction 1 but only doubles the rate of reaction 2. As a result, chemical B may be generated faster than it can be converted to chemical C. The resulting accumulation of B might be harmful. In short, a constant body temperature makes it possible to evolve precise coordinations among the various reactions in the body.

A constant body temperature also makes it easier for the animal to stay active when the environment turns cold. Recall from Chapter 8 that for fish and reptiles to be active at low temperatures, they have to recruit muscle fibers that fatigue rapidly. By maintaining a constant internal temperature, birds and mammals can be equally active and equally resistant to fatigue at all environmental temperatures.

Brain Mechanisms of Temperature Regulation

The body defends the temperature at its core—including the brain and the other internal organs—more carefully than it defends the temperature of the skin. When the body cools below the set point, the blood vessels to the skin constrict, preventing the blood from being cooled by the cold air around the skin. Although the skin may grow very cold, the brain, heart, and other internal organs remain warm. To generate more heat, the muscles contract rhythmically (shivering), or the animal as a whole may run about. The fur of a mammal becomes erect, increasing insulation from the cold environment.

If the body begins to overheat, more blood than usual flows to the skin, where it can be cooled by contact with the air (which is almost always cooler than the body). An animal may decrease its production of heat by decreasing body activity. An animal may sweat, pant heavily, or lick its body; evaporation of the saliva cools the body.

All these physiological changes depend predominantly on certain areas within the **hypothalamus**, a small structure at the base of the brain. (See Figure 10-1.) The hypothalamus contains a number of nuclei (clusters of neuron cell bodies), each of which apparently serves a different function. The most critical area for temperature control is the **preoptic area**, adjacent to the anterior hypothalamus. (It is called *preoptic* because it is located next to the optic chiasm, where the optic nerves cross.) After damage to the preoptic area, a mammal is impaired in its temperature regulation. Its body temperature fluctuates over a range of 10 degrees or more, even in an unchanging environment (Satinoff, Liran, & Clapman, 1982). Because it does not shiver, its body temperature plummets in a cold environment (Satinoff, Valentino, & Teitelbaum, 1976).

The preoptic area monitors body temperature partly by monitoring its own temperature (Nelson & Prosser, 1981). Heat that an experimenter applies directly to the preoptic area causes an animal to pant or sweat, even in a cool environment. If the same area is cooled, the animal shivers, even in a

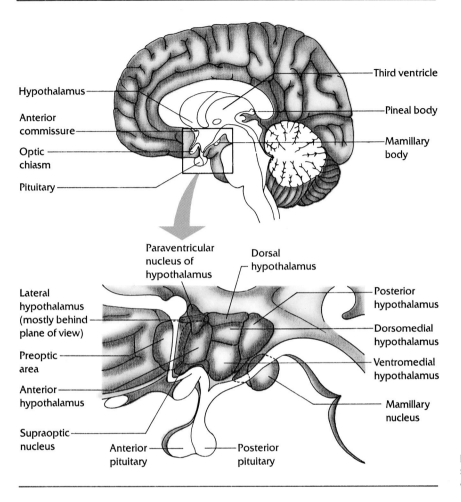

Lateral hypothalamus (mostly behind plane of view)

Preoptic area

Anterior hypothalamus

Supraoptic nucleus

Paraventricular nucleus of hypothalamus

Dorsal hypothalamus

Posterior hypothalamus

Dorsomedial hypothalamus

Ventromedial hypothalamus

Mamillary nucleus

Anterior pituitary

Posterior pituitary

Hypothalamus

Anterior commissure

Optic chiasm

Pituitary

Third ventricle

Pineal body

Mamillary body

Figure 10-1. Major subdivisions of the hypothalamus and pituitary.

warm room. The cells of the preoptic area also receive input from temperature-sensitive receptors in the skin and spinal cord. The animal shivers most vigorously when both the preoptic area and the other receptors are cold; it sweats or pants most vigorously when both are hot.

Although the preoptic area is the dominant area of the brain for temperature control, it is not the only area. Temperature-sensitive cells exist in other parts of the hypothalamus, elsewhere in the brain, and even in the spinal cord. At least fragmentary shivering, sweating, and so forth can occur after preoptic area damage.

Behavioral Mechanisms of Temperature Regulation

Although the body temperature of fish, amphibians, and reptiles matches that of their environment, their temperature seldom fluctuates wildly. They regulate their temperature by choosing their environment (Crawshaw, Moffitt, Lemons, & Downey, 1981). A desert lizard burrows into the ground in the middle of the day, when the surface is too hot, and again in the middle of the night, when the surface is too cold. While on the surface, it will choose a spot in the sun or in the shade in order to keep its body temperature fairly constant.

Mammals, too, use behavioral means to regulate their body temperature. They do not sit on an icy surface shivering when they can build a nest, nor do they sweat and pant in the sun when they can find a shady spot. The more they can regulate their temperature behaviorally, the less they need to rely on physiological changes (Refinetti & Carlisle, 1986a).

During infancy, behavioral mechanisms compensate for inadequate physiological mechanisms. For example, infant rats have no fur for insulation. An infant rat isolated in a cold room cannot generate heat nearly as fast as it loses it. A litter of ten to twelve infant rats, however, can huddle together and collectively maintain a normal body temperature. As the ones on top cool off, they burrow into the center of the mass, while the warm ones near the center passively float to the top (Alberts, 1978).

Adult mammals, after damage to the preoptic area, can also regulate their temperature by behavioral means. In a cold environment, they will press a lever to keep a heat lamp on long enough to keep their body temperature near normal (Satinoff & Rutstein, 1970; Van Zoeren & Stricker, 1977). Their temperature regulation is not as good as normal, however; the variation between day and night is exaggerated, for example (Szymusiak, DeMory, Kittrell, & Satinoff, 1985). Behavioral regulation of temperature is partly under the control of the preoptic area, partly under the control of the posterior hypothalamus (Refinetti & Carlisle, 1986b), and partly under the control of other parts of the brain.

Fever

People with bacterial and viral infections generally have a fever—an increase in body temperature. As a rule, the fever is not part of the illness; it is part of the body's defense against the illness.

When the body is invaded by bacteria, viruses, fungi, or other foreign bodies, it mobilizes, among other things, its *leukocytes* (white blood cells) to attack them. The leukocytes release a protein, known as *endogenous pyrogen* or *leukocytic pyrogen*, which in turn causes the production of **prostaglandin E**. The prostaglandin E then acts on cells in the preoptic area (by means unknown) to cause them to raise body temperature (Dascombe, 1986; Dinarello & Wolff, 1982). Although it is still possible for fever to occur after damage to the preoptic area, such a fever is weaker than usual.

Newborn rabbits, whose hypothalamus is immature, do not get fevers in response to infections. If they are given a choice of environments, however, they will select an unusually warm environment and thereby raise their body temperature (Satinoff, McEwen, & Williams, 1976). That is, they will develop a fever by behavioral rather than physiological means. Fish and reptiles do the same, if they can find a warm enough environment (Kluger, 1978).

Does a fever do the animal any good? Certain types of bacteria grow less vigorously at high temperatures than at normal mammalian body temperatures (Kluger & Rothenburg, 1979). Animals that develop moderate fevers, up to about 2.25 degrees above normal temperature, have a better chance of surviving a bacterial infection than animals that fail to develop a fever (Kluger & Vaughn, 1978). If the fever goes higher than that, the animal's probability of survival declines.

THIRST

Water constitutes an estimated 70 percent of the human body. Because the rate of all chemical reactions in the body depends on the concentration of the chemicals in water, the body's water must be regulated within narrow limits.

Scientific interest in the biological basis of thirst began in the eighteenth century (Fitzsimons, 1973). All early theories implicitly acknowledged that thirst depended on brain activity, although the theories differed on which stimulus was critical to the brain. According to one set of theories, the critical variable was the total amount of water in the blood and other tissues. According to the other set, the critical variable was whether the throat was moist or dry. Both theories remained reasonably prominent until 1919, when Walter B. Cannon argued forcefully for the dry-throat theory. Cannon pointed out that thirst usually occurs at a time when salivation is at a minimum and that anesthesia of the throat blocks thirst.

Today, we regard dryness of the throat as only a minor contributor to thirst. Although an individual with inactive salivary glands does drink more than usual during a meal just to wash down its food, such an individual drinks only a normal amount over the course of a day. If an animal's esophagus is cut and connected to a tube that empties outside the body, the water that moistens its throat fails to replenish body water supplies, and the animal drinks vastly more than a normal animal (Blass & Hall, 1976).

We must, however, clarify what we mean by "the amount of water in the body." There are actually two components to body water: the concentration of water in the body's cells and the total volume of fluid in the blood.

Osmotic Thirst

The body gains water through drinking and eating. It loses water through breathing, urination, defecation, sweating, and evaporation through the mouth. Because the gains and losses ordinarily balance each other out, the concentration of all solutes combined in the body fluids remains at a nearly constant level, about 0.15 M (molar) in mammals. (A concentration of 1.0 M has a number of grams of solute equal to the molecular weight of that solute, dissolved in 1 liter of solution.) This fixed concentration of solutes can be regarded as a set point, similar to the set point for temperature. Any deviation from the set point activates mechanisms that act to restore the concentration of solutes to the set point.

The solutes produce an **osmotic pressure**. Osmotic pressure is, loosely speaking, the force with which a solution holds its water and attracts water from an adjacent solution. The osmotic pressure of a solution is proportional to the total number of molecules in the solution per unit volume. To illustrate: Suppose a solution that is highly concentrated and therefore has a high osmotic pressure is adjacent to a solution that has a lower concentration and osmotic pressure. If a membrane between the two solutions allows only

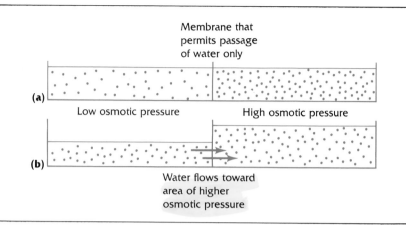

Membrane that
permits passage
of water only

(a)

Low osmotic pressure   High osmotic pressure

(b)

Water flows toward
area of higher
osmotic pressure

Figure 10-2. Two dishes of solution separated by a semipermeable membrane. (a) Two solutions of unequal osmotic pressure are introduced. (b) Water flows toward the area of higher osmotic pressure.

water to cross it, there will be a net flow of water from the solution with low osmotic pressure into the solution with higher osmotic pressure. (See Figure 10-2.) Note that because of the way *osmotic pressure* is defined, water flows toward the area of higher osmotic pressure, not away from it as you might initially imagine.

If the concentration of solutes increases in the body, the osmotic pressure of its fluids increases. This can occur either because the body lost water or because it gained solutes. Generally, the body compensates by excreting a concentrated urine, to rid the body of excess solutes, and by drinking, to increase water. The thirst that results in this manner is known as **osmotic thirst.**

Osmotic thirst occurs when osmotic pressure outside the cells causes water to flow out of the cells. For example, if concentrated sodium chloride is injected into the blood, the sodium does not readily cross the membranes of cells. Because the osmotic pressure is higher outside the cells than inside, water flows out of the cells, shrinking the volume of the cells. The result is increased thirst (Fitzsimons, 1961). An injection of concentrated glucose does not have the same effect because the glucose readily crosses the membrane. Therefore, no gradient of osmotic pressure withdraws water from the cell.

Osmotic thirst depends largely on the **lateral preoptic area** of the hypothalamus (Blass & Epstein, 1971; Peck & Novin, 1971), which overlaps the brain area responsible for temperature regulation. If an investigator applies a drop of concentrated salt solution directly to the lateral preoptic area, the animal soon begins to drink. An application of distilled water to the same area causes the animal to stop drinking. Evidently, cells in the lateral preoptic area sense their own state of hydration and osmotic pressure—just as the cells that control temperature monitor their own temperature.

A lesion in the lateral preoptic area decreases an animal's drinking response to an injection of sodium chloride into the blood (Blass & Epstein, 1971; Peck & Novin, 1971). We cannot say that the animal fails to respond to the sodium chloride, however; it merely responds in a different way from normal animals. After a normal animal has been injected with concentrated sodium chloride, it first drinks copious quantities of water. Minutes or even hours later, it excretes great quantities of fairly dilute urine, relieving itself of both the sodium chloride and the excess water. After an animal with lateral preoptic area damage receives a similar injection of sodium chloride, it becomes inactive. It excretes small quantities of highly concentrated urine, removing much of the sodium chloride and only a little body water. Hours later, it drinks a modest amount of water, restoring the normal balance (Stricker, 1976; Stricker & Coburn, 1978). It has achieved the same result as a normal animal by using a different strategy.

A normal, healthy animal resorts to the same strategy as that of the lesioned rat if its water tastes bad. A rat that is offered only a quinine solution reacts to an injection of sodium chloride by excreting a highly concentrated urine and then, hours later, drinking a little of the quinine solution (Rowland & Flamm, 1977).

In short, an animal with damage to its lateral preoptic area is not incapable of drinking. It reacts in a way similar to normal rats whose water tastes bad.

Hypovolemic Thirst

The other type of thirst, besides osmotic, is **hypovolemic** (HI-po-vo-LEE-mik), which means "based on low volume." The body needs to maintain an adequate blood pressure. If blood volume, and therefore pressure, is too low, the blood cannot carry enough water and nutrients to the cells. Blood volume may drop sharply after a deep cut, after internal hemorrhaging, or after heavy menstrual flow in certain women. The body then needs to replenish not only its water but also the salts and other solutes that have been lost. The result is hypovolemic thirst.

It is unsatisfactory to study hypovolemic thirst simply by withdrawing blood from an animal. An animal that rapidly loses a large amount of blood may go into a state of shock. Two ways to withdraw blood gradually are injections of polyethylene glycol or dilute formaldehyde just under the skin (Stricker & Macarthur, 1974). Either solution stays where it is injected for hours and causes fluid from the blood to accumulate in that area.

After a reduction of blood volume, an animal increases its drinking. It will drink only a little pure water, however, because a large amount of water would dilute its body fluids. Instead, it will drink large amounts of a salt water solution at a concentration similar to that of its blood (Stricker, 1969). If it is offered one tube containing pure water and another containing highly concentrated salt water, it will alternate between the two to produce a mixture that matches the content of its blood.

Hypovolemic thirst differs from osmotic thirst in several ways. (See Table 10-1.) Besides the fact that it is caused by a loss of blood volume instead of a change in osmotic pressure, and that it can be satisfied better by salt water than by pure water, it apparently depends on cells in several areas surrounding the third ventricle of the brain, rather than the lateral preoptic area. Because those areas lie outside the usual blood-brain barrier, they are

Table 10-1.   Comparison of Osmotic and Hypovolemic Thirst

Type of thirst	Stimulus	Best relieved by drinking	Brain areas implicated
Osmotic	High concentration of solutes in cells; loss of water from cells	Water	Lateral preoptic area of the hypothalamus
Hypovolemic	Low blood volume	Water with salt or other solutes	Areas surrounding third ventricle

in a good position to monitor all the contents of the blood (Buggy, Fisher, Hoffman, Johnson, & Phillips, 1975; Mangiapane, Thrasher, Keil, Simpson, & Ganong, 1983; Miselis, Shapiro, & Hand, 1979).

Possible Hormonal Triggers of Hypovolemic Thirst

Hypovolemic thirst depends on at least one, probably two, stimuli. One stimulus is signals from the **baroreceptors**—receptors on the largest blood vessels that detect their blood pressure. When these receptors report a decrease in blood pressure, thirst increases (Rettig, Ganten, & Johnson, 1981; Zimmerman, Blaine, & Stricker, 1981).

The other possible mechanism is hormones released by the kidneys. When blood volume drops, the kidneys detect the change and respond by releasing a hormone, renin. Renin cleaves a portion off angiotensinogen, a large protein that circulates in the blood, to form angiotensin I, which is quickly converted to angiotensin II. The hormone angiotensin II then causes a constriction of blood vessels, compensating for the drop in blood pressure. (See Figure 10-3.)

When angiotensin reaches the brain, it may directly excite the cells in areas around the third ventricle—the areas known to be critical for hypovolemic thirst (Fitzsimons, 1971). Injections of angiotensin to those areas can prompt drinking, while injections to other areas have no effect on drinking (Mangiapane & Simpson, 1980).

The controversy concerning this research has been whether a drop in blood volume ever elicits enough angiotensin to produce a significant increase in drinking. It is agreed that hypovolemia produces angiotensin, but it is not clear whether it produces as much angiotensin as the amount investigators have used to inject into the brain to produce thirst. Several studies have reported that the blood levels are never high enough to stimulate thirst (Abraham, Baker, Blaine, Denton, & McKinley, 1975; Stricker, 1977; Stricker, Bradshaw, & McDonald, 1976). Other studies, however, have reported that the blood angiotensin does reach high enough levels (Johnson, Mann, Rascher, Johnson, & Ganten, 1981).

A possible resolution to this controversy is that the effects of angiotensin may be **synergistic** with the effects of the baroreceptors (Epstein, 1983; Rowland, 1980). If two effects are synergistic, they produce together more than twice the effect of either one acting by itself. That is, it may take less angiotensin to stimulate thirst if the baroreceptors are also indicating low blood pressure than if they are indicating normal blood pressure.

Sodium-Specific Cravings

A healthy body has ample means of protecting its sodium. When sodium intake is low, the adrenal glands produce the hormone **aldosterone**, which causes the kidneys to conserve sodium when excreting urine. But suppose an individual loses sodium by bleeding, sweating, or other means and then drinks water, replacing the fluid volume but not the sodium. Under those circumstances of increased need for sodium, the individual experiences an increased preference for salty foods. That increased preference develops automatically, apparently without any trial-and-error learning (Richter, 1936). In fact, sodium-deficient animals have an increased preference for all salty-tasting substances, including lithium salts, which are poisonous (Nachman, 1962). Sodium-specific cravings differ from specific hungers for other vitamins and minerals, which animals have to learn by trial and error (Rozin & Kalat, 1971).

The aldosterone evoked by the sodium deficiency is largely responsible for the salt craving (Stricker, 1983). Angiotensin II also contributes to the preference for salty tastes. By itself, it can produce a moderate increase in such preference (Dalhouse, Langford, Walsh, & Barnes, 1986). The effects of aldosterone and angiotensin are strongly synergistic; together, they produce a greater effect than either one can alone (Fluharty & Epstein, 1983; Stricker, 1983).

Drinking Associated with Eating

Most research on drinking has focused on drinking as a homeostatic process, as a means of compensating for a deficit. In a natural setting, however, a great deal of drinking is not homeostatic. It does not just react to deficits; it anticipates and prevents them.

A normal rat, given unlimited access to both food and water, does most of its drinking just before and after its meals. That is adaptive, since the meal will increase the concentration of solutes in the body. But the rat does not wait until those solutes enter the cells; it drinks long before the food is digested. (The same is, of course, true of humans.) Although the exact mechanisms are not well understood, it appears that when food enters the stomach, it stimulates the vagus nerve and causes the release of histamine. Both the vagus stimulation and the histamine lead to an increase in drinking (Kraly, 1984).

HUNGER

Imagine that your automobile needed a balanced diet, including varying proportions of twenty or more different kinds of fuel, and that the particular balance it needed varied from time to time. Imagine further that you never knew exactly what you were getting at any fuel station. Sometimes the pumps might contain gasoline, sometimes kerosene, sometimes alcohol, and sometimes old brown sludge. To say the least, you would have trouble judging how much fuel to add at any time.

The problem of regulating human food intake is even more complicated. In addition to needing a balanced diet and never knowing exactly what is in

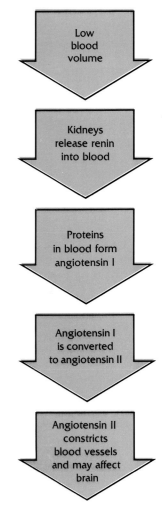

Figure 10-3. Hormonal response to hypovolemia.

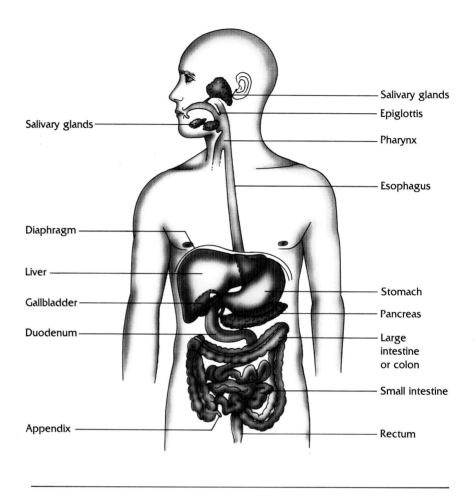

Salivary glands

Salivary glands

Epiglottis

Pharynx

Esophagus

Diaphragm

Liver

Gallbladder

Duodenum

Appendix

Stomach

Pancreas

Large intestine or colon

Small intestine

Rectum

Figure 10-4. The human digestive system.

the food, we need different amounts of any one nutrient depending on what other nutrients we are getting. For example, the more carbohydrates we eat, the more thiamine (vitamin B_1) we need. Perhaps the amazing fact about feeding is not that many people eat poor diets but that anyone ever gets the right amount and balance of foods.

The Digestive System

Before discussing hunger, let us quickly review the digestive system. (See Figure 10-4.) Most foods consist of large molecules that cannot be used directly by the cells. The function of the digestive system is to break down the food into smaller, more easily used molecules.

Digestion begins in the mouth, where food is mixed with saliva, which contains enzymes that help break down carbohydrates. When swallowed, the food travels down the esophagus to the stomach, where it is mixed with hydrochloric acid and several enzymes, which are mostly effective for the digestion of proteins. Between the stomach and the intestines is a round sphincter muscle that closes off the entrance to the intestines. This muscle periodically opens to allow food to enter the intestines, a bit at a time. Thus, the stomach serves as a storage place for food as well as a digestive organ.

Food then passes to the small intestine. The small intestine contains a large number of enzymes that help to digest proteins, fats, and carbohydrates. It is also the main site for the absorption of digested foodstuffs; little is absorbed through the walls of the esophagus or stomach. The large intestine absorbs water and minerals and lubricates the remaining materials to pass them as feces.

Digested materials absorbed through the small intestine are carried by the blood for use throughout the body. If more carbohydrates, proteins, and fats are absorbed than the body can use at one time, the excess is stored as fat. Later, when the body needs additional nutrients, fat reserves are converted into glucose, the body's primary fuel, which is mobilized into the bloodstream.

Physiological Mechanisms of Hunger and Satiety

Newborn rats, which grow at a most rapid rate, follow a simple rule on the consumption of mother's milk: They nurse whenever it is available, as long as it is available, and as much as is available (Blass & Teicher, 1980). They stop nursing only if the milk backs up from their stomach into the esophagus so that they cannot breathe!

Bears, even as adults, are not much different from newborn rats (Herrero, 1985). Bears survive mostly on nuts and berries, which are in season for only a few days or weeks at a time. When the nuts and berries are available, bears stuff them down nonstop all day long, gaining enough weight to hold them through weeks or months of little food.

Humans, however, as well as adult rats and most other mammals, eat discrete meals. Even people who are free to eat as much as they want, whenever they want, eat two to four meals a day, instead of grazing gradually, like horses, or eating until the food backs up into the esophagus, like infant rats. Something within us tells us when to start eating and when to stop. In fact, it is likely that we have several such mechanisms.

Oral Factors.   People eat partly for the sake of taste. In one experiment, college students consumed lunch five days a week without tasting it. Each swallowed one end of a rubber tube and then pushed a button to pump a liquid diet into his or her stomach (Jordan, 1969; Spiegel, 1973). After a few days of practice, each subject established a consistent pattern, pumping in a constant volume of the diet each day and maintaining a constant body weight. Most subjects found the untasted meals unsatisfying, however. Many reported a desire to taste or chew something. Moreover, when they were allowed to drink the liquid diet in the normal manner while also receiving it through the stomach tube, they drank almost as much as if they were receiving nothing through the tube (Jordan, 1969).

Eating is sustained not only by taste but by other facial sensations as well. A rat explores a potential food with its mouth and whiskers before it starts to eat. The tactile sensations are conveyed to the brain via the fifth cranial nerve (the trigeminal nerve). After that nerve is cut, a rat decreases its exploration of foods and its biting of them. It can still eat moist, soft foods, using its jaw as a scoop, but it loses weight. It not only fails to eat properly, but it will not press a bar as much as normal for food reinforcement. Evidently, a loss of sensation from the mouth leads to a decrease in food-related motivation (Zeigler, Jacquin, & Miller, 1985).

Although taste and other mouth sensations contribute to the regulation of eating, they are not sufficient by themselves to end a meal. In **sham-feeding** experiments, everything an animal swallows leaks out a tube connected to the esophagus or stomach. Under such conditions, animals swallow several times as much as normal during each meal (Antin, Gibbs, Holt, Young, & Smith, 1975).

Calibration for Calories.   The fundamental purpose of eating is to maintain a constant level of nutrition in the cells. But different meals differ in their concentration of nutrients. Theoretically, we should stop eating an energy-rich lasagna meal sooner than we stop a meal of, say, celery and cucumbers. Do we? Do humans and other animals learn to calibrate how many calories are in each bite, and then adjust the size of each meal accordingly?

They cannot do so at once. In one experiment, adult humans consumed a liquid meal once a day for two to three weeks (Wooley, Wooley, & Dunham, 1972). Although the taste was about the same every time, half the meals were high in calories and half were low. After each meal, subjects were asked to guess whether they had just eaten a high-calorie meal or a low-calorie meal. Their guesses were correct less than 60 percent of the time.

Similarly, when laboratory animals are given a new diet that is richer or less rich in calories than their previous diet, they take several days to compensate by increasing or decreasing their intake (LeMagnen, 1967). Apparently, they cannot tell how rich the food is in calories just by tasting it. However, over the course of a few days they gradually learn to calibrate how many calories are present in a given quantity of food and to adjust their intake (Deutsch, 1983).

Stomach Distention.   At the time a meal ends, little of its nutrition has entered the blood or the cells. Most of the food is still in the stomach, although some may have entered the small intestine. Accumulating evidence points to **distention** (filling up) of the stomach as the primary mechanism determining the size of a meal under normal conditions.

In one experiment, Deutsch, Young, and Kalogeris (1978) attached an inflatable cuff at the connection between the stomach and the small intestine. When they inflated the cuff, it closed off the passage of food from the stomach to the duodenum. They carefully demonstrated that the cuff was not traumatic to the animal and did not interfere with feeding, even when inflated. Then they demonstrated that with the cuff inflated, a animal would eat a normal-size meal and then stop; that is, it could get satisfied even though the food could not go beyond the stomach. Those results imply that satiety signals can arise from the stomach, perhaps in conjunction with the mouth and esophagus. They also imply that stimulation of later parts of the digestive system is not necessary for satiety.

If the experimenters withdrew 10 ml of food from the stomach, the animal ate an extra 8 ml in compensation (Deutsch et al., 1978). Apparently, an animal eats until its stomach is full, and it can eat again to return the stomach to full. The term *full*, however, does not refer simply to bulk. A rat will eat a larger quantity of low-calorie food than of high-calorie food, partly because high-energy foods of any kind—carbohydrate, protein, or fat— delay the emptying of the stomach (McHugh & Moran, 1985).

The stomach conveys satiety messages to the brain via two nerves, the vagus nerve and the splanchnic nerve. The **vagus nerve** (cranial nerve number 10) conveys information about the stretching of the walls of the stomach. Animals with a damaged vagus nerve eat until they overfill the stomach (Gonzalez & Deutsch, 1981). The **splanchnic** (SPLANK-nik) **nerves** (from parts of the thoracic and lumbar spinal cord) may convey information about the nutrient contents of the stomach (Deutsch & Ahn, 1986).

Might it be possible to increase satiety by artificially distending the stomach? In one study, rats were offered a high-fat diet, on which they gained weight. Then the experimenters implanted water-filled balloons to occupy about one-third of each rat's stomach. The rats ate smaller meals than before and lost weight over a period of weeks (Geliebter, Westreich, Hashim, & Gage, 1987). It is not clear whether such a procedure would be safe or effective with obese humans, however. (One reason for caution is that the rats' stomachs grew as a result of the balloon implants.)

The Duodenum and the Hormone CCK.   The **duodenum** (doo-uh-DEE-num) is the first part of the small intestine; it is the first structure of the digestive system that absorbs a significant amount of nutrients. When a bulk substance (nutrient or nonnutrient) enters the duodenum, the animal decreases or stops its eating (Ehman, Albert, & Jamieson, 1971; Vanderweele, Novin, Rezek, & Sanderson, 1974).

Gibbs, Young, and Smith (1973) suggested that **CCK** (cholecystokinin), which is released as a hormone by the duodenum and also used as a synaptic transmitter in the brain, may play an important role in satiety. They noted, for example, that the introduction of food into the duodenum causes the duodenum to release CCK. When CCK is injected into a rat prior to a meal, the rat will eat less than normal. The greater the volume of the injection, the smaller the meal (Antin, Gibbs, & Smith, 1978). After a large enough dose of CCK, a rat that has not fed will go through a sequence of grooming itself and then resting or sleeping, just as it would after a normal meal (Antin, Gibbs, Holt, Young, & Smith, 1975).

Later research has confirmed an important contribution of CCK to satiety. For example, obese mice have been found to be deficient in CCK (Straus & Yalow, 1978).

Nevertheless, the route by which CCK contributes to satiety is not certain. We need not immediately assume that CCK travels directly to receptors in the brain to trigger satiety. One possibility is that CCK has little to do with satiety under most normal circumstances. By this interpretation, injections of CCK decrease meal size only by making an animal nauseous. Studies have disagreed as to whether CCK induces nausea—specifically, whether rats learn an aversion to tastes that are followed by an injection of CCK (Holt, Antin, Gibbs, Young, & Smith, 1974; Moore & Deutsch, 1985; Verbalis, McCann, McHale, & Stricker, 1986).

Another possibility is that CCK does contribute to satiety under normal conditions but does so indirectly, by influencing the stomach rather than the brain. The effects of CCK on meal size are reduced or abolished by cutting the vagus nerve to the stomach (Hommer, Palkovits, Crawley, Paul, & Skirboll, 1985; Smith, Jerome, Cushin, Eterno, & Simansky, 1981). It may be that CCK acts primarily as a short-term signal from the duodenum to the stomach to inhibit the muscles that open the passage from the stomach to the duodenum. That is, food that enters the duodenum triggers the release of CCK, which delays further emptying of the stomach (McHugh & Moran, 1985). Thus, CCK increases satiety by prolonging stomach distention.

In support of that interpretation, one study found that an injection of CCK had no effect on human appetite at the start of a meal. It did, however, shorten the meal (Pi-Sunyer, Kissileff, Thornton, & Smith, 1982). In other words, CCK has little satiety effect by itself; it magnifies the satiety-producing effect of food in the stomach.

Blood Glucose.   Digested food enters the bloodstream, much of it in the form of glucose. Glucose is an important source of energy for all parts of the body and by far the most important fuel of the brain. Jean Mayer (1953) proposed that the supply of glucose to the cells is the primary basis for hunger and satiety. When the cells have too little glucose, the individual gets hungry. When they have enough, the individual becomes satiated.

It has indeed been found that an artificially produced increase in blood glucose decreases feeding (Davis, Wirtshafter, Asin, & Brief, 1981; Tordoff, Novin, & Russek, 1982), whereas a drug that prevents glucose from entering the cells leads to increased feeding (Thompson & Campbell, 1977). These results support the theory that eating is controlled partly by the availability of glucose to the cells. On the other hand, glucose is certainly not the only factor. Even fructose, a sugar that does not cross the blood-brain barrier, and which cannot be converted to glucose, can suppress hunger (Stricker, Rowland, Saller, & Friedman, 1977). So can a variety of other nutrients. Thus, hunger and satiety must not be based on glucose exclusively, but on the availability of all types of nutrients combined (Friedman & Stricker, 1976).

Moreover, the level of glucose in the blood varies little under normal conditions (LeMagnen, 1981). Even during a period of prolonged fasting, the liver can convert stored glycogen, fats, and proteins into glucose to maintain blood glucose levels.

Still, the availability of glucose to the cells can vary significantly as a function of changes in blood levels of insulin. The hormone **insulin** increases the entry of glucose into the cells, the conversion of glucose to fats, and the storage of fats. When insulin levels are high, a larger than normal percentage

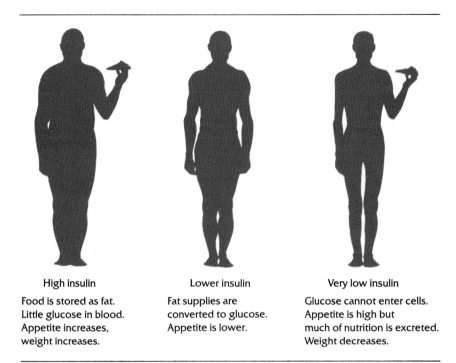

High insulin	Lower insulin	Very low insulin
Food is stored as fat. Little glucose in blood. Appetite increases, weight increases.	Fat supplies are converted to glucose. Appetite is lower.	Glucose cannot enter cells. Appetite is high but much of nutrition is excreted. Weight decreases.

Figure 10-5. Effects of insulin on glucose, appetite, and weight.

of any meal is stored as fat, and the individual is ill equipped to make use of its fat stores for fuel (Figure 10-5). As a result, a low amount of glucose circulates in the blood and little of it reaches the cells. Appetite increases. For example, insulin levels are higher for humans during daytime than at night, so a larger percentage of what we eat during the day is stored as fat. As a result, appetite returns within several hours after a meal (LeMagnen, 1981). When insulin levels are low, such as for humans at night, the glucose in the blood is not converted to fat to be stored; on the contrary, fat supplies are converted to glucose. For that reason, we can go through the night without eating, without feeling hungry.

When insulin levels are extremely low, as in cases of diabetes, glucose levels in the blood are high but the glucose cannot enter the cells. People and animals suffering from diabetes eat larger than normal amounts because their cells are starving (Lindberg, Coburn, & Stricker, 1984). Nevertheless, they lose weight; a great deal of the nutrition they consume is excreted, unused. (Note the paradox that both high levels of insulin and very low levels can lead to increased eating, although they do so for different reasons. To maintain a normal body weight, it is best to have steady, intermediate levels of insulin.)

People produce increased levels of insulin when they eat, and even when they are getting ready to eat. Up to a point, that is useful, since it prepares the body to let more glucose enter the cells and to store the excess part of the meal as fats. Obese people, however, overrespond, producing greater amounts of insulin than people of normal weight (Johnson & Wildman, 1983). It may be that their high levels of insulin cause large amounts of food to be stored as fat, and therefore cause their appetite to return sooner than normal after a meal.

Metabolic Rate.   Weight is the outcome of both the amount of food consumed and the amount of energy used. It is possible for obese people to lose weight by following habits of regular exercise to burn off more calories (Thompson, Jarvie, Lahey, & Cureton, 1982); unfortunately, most people with serious weight problems find it difficult to stick to an exercise program for long.

Most of the calories consumed by people are used not for exercise but for **basal metabolism,** the constant processes that generate heat in the body. People differ significantly in their basal metabolism. People with higher metabolic rates do not maintain a higher body temperature; they produce more heat than others but radiate it to their environment. People with lower metabolic rates generate less heat but conserve it better.

Because of such differences in metabolic rates, it is possible for one person to gain weight while eating only a moderate amount, and for another person to remain thin while eating much more. Metabolic rates vary depending on many factors, probably including genetics (Bogardus et al., 1986). Similarly, genetic differences strongly influence body weight. According to one study of 540 adopted children in Denmark who had reached adulthood, their weight correlated strongly with that of their biological relatives, not with that of their adoptive relatives (Stunkard et al., 1986). The implication is that genetic differences in metabolic rate lead to differences in adult body weight. We cannot draw that conclusion with confidence until someone conducts a longitudinal study, linking early-onset differences in metabolic rate with later-developing differences in body weight. Still, a relationship between the two seems likely.

Unfortunately for those interested in losing weight, a decrease in food intake leads to a compensatory decrease in metabolic rate (McMinn, 1984). That is, if you adhere to a low-calorie diet, your metabolic rate will decrease and you will burn fewer calories. This is not to say that people cannot lose weight, but just that it becomes more difficult after the first few pounds.

Brain Mechanisms in Hunger and Satiety

The brain must respond to messages concerning the availability of glucose and other nutrients, the distention of the stomach, and other signals, by sending impulses that control eating behavior. Although many brain areas contribute, most of the research has focused on the hypothalamus.

The Lateral Hypothalamus.   After damage to the **lateral hypothalamus,** an animal refuses food and water and starves to death unless it is force-fed, in which case it gradually recovers, as discussed in Chapter 14. Electrical stimulation of the lateral hypothalamus, on the other hand, causes an animal to eat (Brügger, 1943). For these reasons, this area was for many years thought of as the hunger center of the brain.

Damage to the lateral hypothalamus interferes with more than just feeding, however. Animals with lesions are underaroused (Figure 10-6), un-

Figure 10-6. A cat with a lesion in the lateral hypothalamus grasps and picks up a mouse that was placed against its snout; then the cat falls asleep. (From Wolgin, Cytawa, & Teitelbaum, 1976.)

derresponsive to sensory stimuli (Marshall & Teitelbaum, 1974), and inactive. Such animals, ordinarily unresponsive to food as well as other stimuli, increase their eating in response to a mild tail-pinch (O'Brien, Chesire, & Teitelbaum, 1985). Evidently the lack of arousal is part of the feeding problem.

It is not the whole problem, however, and the mechanisms of arousal are partly separable from the mechanisms of feeding. The loss of arousal and responsiveness is due mostly to destruction of axons passing through the lateral hypothalamus, rather than to the loss of cells there. It is possible to destroy cells without harming the passing fibers. Experimenters can inject kainic acid, which destroys cell bodies but not axons (Grossman, Dacey, Halaris, Collier, & Routtenberg, 1978; Stricker, Swerdloff & Zigmond, 1978), or they can make lesions in the lateral hypothalamus of 10-day-old rats, before the fibers have grown into the area (Almli, Fisher, & Hill, 1979). The result of either method is impaired eating without a significant loss of arousal or responsiveness to stimuli. Evidently the cell bodies of the lateral hypothalamus contribute to feeding, while the passing fibers contribute to overall arousal (including the arousal necessary for feeding).

The question remains, *how* does the lateral hypothalamus contribute to feeding? Part of the answer is that the lateral hypothalamus controls certain internal secretions. Activity of the lateral hypothalamus increases the release of insulin and digestive juices in the stomach (Morley, Bartness, Gosell, & Levine, 1985). That is, after damage to this brain area, an animal has low levels of insulin and digestive juices. It has difficulty digesting its foods and little motivation to do so, since its fat reserves are being converted into blood glucose, in response to the drop in insulin levels. The animal has fairly high levels of blood sugar even without eating.

DIGRESSION

10-1

Anorexia Nervosa

Anorexia nervosa is a condition characterized by avoidance of eating and loss of weight, sometimes to the point of risking death. It is found in about half of 1 percent of girls in their late teens (Crisp, Palmer, & Kalucy, 1976). It is never known to occur before puberty and seldom begins later than the early 20s, although it may continue for many years after starting at a young age. Anorexia nervosa is rare among men; it is also far less common among black women than among white women, for reasons unknown (Pumariega, Edwards, & Michell, 1984).

Those afflicted with anorexia nervosa do not suffer from a lack of hunger or a lack of interest in food. Rather, they have a pathological desire to be extremely thin. Anorexia nervosa is closely related to **bulimia**, a condition characterized by alternation between brief binges of excessive eating and periods of near-starvation, sometimes with forced vomiting. Many women with anorexia have bouts of bulimia as well. It may be that anorexia and bulimia are just alternative expressions of the same underlying disorder.

Anorexia is caused in part by certain family dynamics, including pressure to be thin and a pressure to be perfect. Many women with anorexia report a resistance to becoming an adult woman, with the possibilities of sexual intercourse and pregnancy (Rowland, 1970).

In addition to the strong psychological and sociological determinants, a biological predisposition may be present as well. Women with anorexia nervosa have low levels of reproductive hormones, resembling the patterns found in girls before puberty (Brauman & Gregoire, 1979). Although the hormonal abnormalities are partly a result of the loss of weight, they may also reflect an underlying disorder that preceded the weight loss. A majority of women with anorexia stop menstruating before or at the same time that they start losing weight (Eisenberg, 1981; Schwabe, 1981), and their reproductive hormones reach levels lower than those found in women who lose the same amount of weight because of illness. Furthermore, after women with anorexia recover their normal weight, they often fail to recover hormonally. Even if their hormones approximate normal levels, they may continue to react abnormally to hormone injections (Gold et al., 1986).

Many drugs and hormonal treatments have been tried as therapies for anorexia nervosa, although none so far have shown large, consistent benefits (Johnson, Stuckey, & Mitchell, 1983). The most common treatment is behavior modification, combined with individual and family counseling (Hsu, 1986). Under any treatment, a full return to normalcy is rare in less than 4 or 5 years (Crisp, Hsu, Harding, & Hartshorn, 1980; Schwartz & Thompson, 1981).

In certain respects the opposite of anorexia nervosa is the rare, little-known **Kleine-Levin syndrome**, which occurs mostly in young men. Its symptoms include excessive eating, weight gain, lack of energy, and excessive time in bed, with low sleep efficiency (Orlosky, 1982; Reynolds, Black, Coble, Holzer, & Kupfer, 1980). Although it has been speculatively linked to abnormalities of the hormone testosterone, little is known about its causes.

Lateral hypothalamic damage has seldom been reported in humans. Anorexia nervosa, a condition in which people stop eating and lose weight, has only superficial similarities to the effects of lateral hypothalamic damage; the causes for the loss of eating are quite different (Stricker & Andersen, 1980). (See Digression 10-1.)

The Ventromedial Hypothalamus. Adjacent to the lateral hypothalamus is the **ventromedial hypothalamus** (refer to Figure 10-1). Damage in that area, including axons passing through and around it, produces effects that are nearly the opposite of those produced by damage to the lateral hypothalamus. The animal eats and drinks excessive amounts and gains weight, sometimes a great deal of weight. (See Figure 10-7.) An adult female rat may double or triple her weight after the lesion. Certain humans with damage in

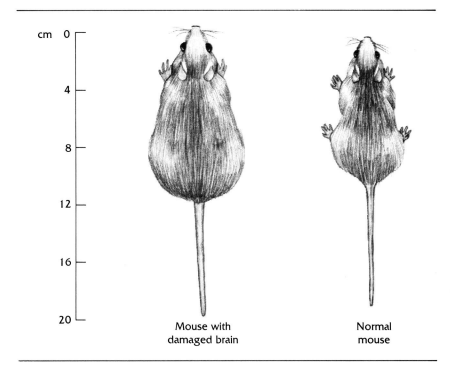

Figure 10-7. Obesity in a mouse caused by a lesion of the ventromedial hypothalamus.

Mouse with
damaged brain

Normal
mouse

Table 10-2.   Effects of Lesions in Certain Areas of the Hypothalamus

Hypothalamic area	Effect of lesion
Preoptic area	Deficit in physiological mechanisms of temperature regulation
Lateral preoptic area	Deficit in osmotic thirst
Areas surrounding third ventricle	Deficit in hypovolemic thirst
Lateral hypothalamus	Undereating, weight loss, low levels of insulin (because of damage to cell bodies) Underarousal, underresponsiveness (because of damage to passing axons)
Ventromedial hypothalamus	Overeating, weight gain, high levels of insulin

the ventromedial hypothalamus have been known to gain more than 10 kg per month (Al-Rashid, 1971; Killeffer & Stern, 1970; Reeves & Plum, 1969). Table 10-2 summarizes the effects of lesions in several areas of the hypothalamus.

In addition to eating excessively and gaining weight, rats with ventromedial hypothalamic damage show several other changes in behavior:

1. They drink excessive amounts of water (Wishart & Walls, 1975).
2. They are less responsive than normal rats to the satiating effects of glucose. The introduction of large amounts of glucose into their diges-

tive system decreases their food intake less than it does with normal rats (Panksepp, 1973).

3. They are finicky eaters. Although they overeat on a normal diet, they overeat even more on a particularly tasty diet (Ferguson & Keesey, 1975; Teitelbaum, 1955). Some dispute exists about whether they are more likely than normal rats to reject a slightly bitter diet (Weingarten, Chang, & Jarvie, 1983).

4. Although they overeat when food is readily available, they work less hard than normal rats to get food (Miller, Bailey, & Stevenson, 1950; Teitelbaum, 1957).

Exactly why do animals with damage to the ventromedial hypothalamus overeat? Apparently it is not, as was once thought, that such animals are deficient in satiety. If they were unresponsive to the satiating effects of a meal, each meal should be larger than normal. In fact, however, each meal is of normal size. The animals overeat because they eat *more frequent* meals than normal, especially during the daylight hours, when rats are ordinarily inactive (Duggan & Booth, 1986).

They eat more frequently for two reasons. The first is that their stomachs empty faster than those of other rats, especially during the daylight hours (Duggan & Booth, 1986). The faster the stomach empties, the sooner an animal is ready for its next meal. The second reason is that damage to the ventromedial hypothalamus leads to a lasting increase in the production of insulin. (This is the opposite of the effect of damage to the lateral hypothalamus.) Rats with such damage have higher than normal insulin levels at all times and respond to meals with even larger insulin increases (King, Smith, & Frohman, 1984). Because of the increased insulin, a larger than normal percentage of each meal is stored as fat. If animals with this kind of damage are kept on a strict diet and are prevented from eating more than they had prior to the lesion, they gain weight anyway! Friedman and Stricker (1976; see BioSketch 10-2) have therefore proposed that the animal does not gain weight because it overeats; rather, it has to overeat because it is storing excessive fat even without overeating. It has no more usable fuel in its bloodstream than a starving animal. What it eats is largely converted to fat; to have enough fuel for its current use, it must continue to eat.

ALCOHOL ABUSE

Not all motivations are homeostatic. We have dealt so far with the consumption of water, sodium, and food. Each of these is regulated by homeostatic or near-homeostatic processes. For contrast, we turn to alcohol consumption, an apparently nonhomeostatic behavior that can take precedence over many biological needs.

Alcohol abuse is a peculiarly human phenomenon. Although it is possible to get rats and other species to drink alcohol under certain circumstances, sometimes even in large quantities, only humans spontaneously develop an alcohol habit that grossly interferes with normal living. Even among humans, only a minority of drinkers develop a serious problem. Why do certain people become alcoholics, while others continue to drink in moderation?

BIOSKETCH 10-2

Edward Stricker

Edward Stricker received a B.S. degree in chemistry from the University of Chicago at the age of 19 and a Ph.D. in psychology from Yale. After doing postdoctoral research at the University of Colorado and the University of Pennsylvania and serving four years on the faculty at McMaster University, he went to the University of Pittsburgh, where he is now professor of psychology, biology, and psychiatry.

Stricker has been a prominent researcher on temperature regulation, hypovolemic thirst and sodium-specific hunger, the effects of damage to the ventromedial hypothalamus, and recovery from brain damage (Chapter 14). Although this may seem a diverse list, Stricker insists that, "In fact, I have only studied one problem, homeostasis, and have focused on the general principles and similarities that cut across levels and systems."

Although much of Stricker's research might be considered physiology more than psychology in the usual sense, his long-range interests include a strong emphasis on human behavior. He says, "I believe that by studying the biochemistry of the catecholaminergic neurons that are so importantly involved in motivation, we are essentially studying the biochemistry of motivation, including human behavior. I foresee a time when we will be discussing motivation in terms of the underlying biochemistry just as we now can discuss movement of a limb in terms of its underlying anatomy."

The Effects of Alcohol on the Body and on Behavior

Most drugs that affect behavior—for example, opiates, cocaine, LSD, amphetamine—alter the activity at a particular type of synapse. In contrast, ethyl alcohol (the kind that people drink) does not attach to any receptor. It inhibits the flow of sodium across the membrane, expands the surface of all membranes, and generally interferes with nervous system activity.

Alcohol by itself does not make people feel happy. Rather, it increases people's susceptibility to social influences. That is, although you are unlikely to elevate your mood much by drinking alone, drinking at a party may reduce your inhibitions and help you enjoy the party more. Alcohol also helps people to forget their tension, anxiety, and other problems (Cowan, 1983).

Chronic problem drinkers have bouts of drinking that go far beyond social facilitation. Many, especially the older ones, suffer a variety of cognitive deficits, including reasoning impairments and *perseveration* (a tendency to repeat a given response even when it is inappropriate). Problem drinkers who abstain from alcohol will gradually improve in performance of cognitive tasks, especially if they quit drinking before age 40 (Goldman, 1983). Prolonged, severe alcohol abuse may lead to vitamin B_1 deficiency, which in turn leads to *Korsakoff's syndrome*, characterized by a permanent memory impairment (see Chapter 13).

Most severe alcoholics suffer from other psychological disorders as well. According to one study of people hospitalized for alcoholism, more than three-fourths also had depression, phobias, anxiety problems, antisocial personality, and other disorders (Hesselbrock, Meyer, & Keener, 1985).

Antabuse, a Drug Treatment for Alcohol Abuse

After a person drinks ethyl alcohol, enzymes in the liver and elsewhere metabolize it to **acetaldehyde**, a poisonous substance. The enzyme **acetaldehyde dehydrogenase** then converts acetaldehyde to **acetic acid**, which the body can use as a source of energy:

$$\text{Ethyl alcohol} \longrightarrow \text{Acetaldehyde} \xrightarrow{\text{Acetaldehyde dehydrogenase}} \text{Acetic acid}$$

Over a long period of time, acetaldehyde can cause cirrhosis of the liver and damage to other organs. Even in the short term, it can cause illness if its concentration in an organ is high enough.

Most people have sufficient levels of acetaldehyde dehydrogenase to prevent acetaldehyde from accumulating to toxic levels. The levels of this enzyme do vary, however. Most mice, as well as members of most other nonhuman species, have relatively low levels. Consequently, when they drink alcohol, they build up high levels of acetaldehyde, grow ill, and learn to avoid drinking alcohol. One genetic strain, however, the C57 strain, has high levels of acetaldehyde dehydrogenase (Horowitz & Whitney, 1975). These mice quickly convert acetaldehyde to harmless acetic acid. Unlike other mice, they will drink large quantities of alcohol.

It is possible to decrease a person's levels of acetaldehyde dehydrogenase by means of the drug *disulfiram*, which goes by the trade name **Antabuse**. Antabuse inactivates all copper-containing enzymes, including acetaldehyde dehydrogenase. For about 24 hours after taking an Antabuse pill, people must avoid all contact with alcohol, at the risk of grave illness. They must even avoid shampoos that contain alcohol, as alcohol that is absorbed through the scalp can be dangerous, too.

Antabuse is sometimes used to help people stop abusing alcohol (Peachey & Naranjo, 1983). The idea is that such a person will learn an aversion to the taste of alcohol because of the illness that follows. In fact, however, the drug may be effective mostly because of its threat value. Many of the people who take Antabuse abstain from drinking completely and therefore never experience the illness that alcohol would cause them (Fuller & Roth, 1979). Those who do drink in spite of taking the pill do get ill, but they are as likely to stop taking the pill as to stop drinking alcohol. Evidently, Antabuse functions mostly as a way for an alcoholic to make a daily reaffirmation of a decision to abstain from alcohol.

Possible Biological Predispositions to Alcohol Abuse

At this point, no one can predict with much accuracy who will become a severe alcohol abuser and who will not. We can identify certain risk factors, however. First, the risk of alcoholism is greater for those who grow up in a culture or subculture that tolerates public drunkenness and for individuals who are victims of child abuse or witnesses to hostility between their parents. Environmental influences of this type are certainly important. Our interest in this book, however, is to identify possible biological influences.

A predisposition toward alcoholism can, it appears, be inherited. According to one long-term study of adopted boys in Boston, boys who were close biological relatives of alcoholics had an increased probability of eventually becoming alcoholics themselves, even if they were adopted by nonalcoholics (Vaillant & Milofsky, 1982).

Still, not all children of alcoholics become alcoholics, and it is not obvious how the genes predisposing to alcohol abuse might exert their effects. Research has been conducted, therefore, on the children of alcoholics.

The design of several studies has been to compare young adults who have an alcoholic father with young adults who are not closely related to any alcoholic. (Children of alcoholic mothers are excluded to avoid the potential effects of alcohol during pregnancy.) The assumption behind such studies is that a fair number of the sons of alcoholics are at risk of becoming alcoholics themselves; they might be considered *prealcoholics*. Fewer of the sons of nonalcoholics will go on to become alcoholics themselves. Therefore, any observable differences between the sons of alcoholics and the sons of nonalcoholics are probably also differences between prealcoholics and nonprealcoholics.

In two similar studies (O'Malley & Maisto, 1985; Schuckit, 1984), sons of alcoholics and sons of nonalcoholics drank high or low amounts of alcohol, without knowing what amount they had drunk. Then they were asked to estimate how intoxicated they were. In both studies, the sons of alcoholics rated themselves as *less* intoxicated and *less* impaired. Nevertheless, in their actual performance on a timed motor task—inserting pegs into matching holes on a pegboard—they were *more* impaired than the sons of nonalcoholics (O'Malley & Maisto, 1985). Here is a possible interpretation: Those who are not at risk for alcoholism drink a moderate amount and begin to feel tipsy. They decide they have had enough and stop at that point. Those who are at greater risk for alcoholism drink the same amount and feel little effect. They continue drinking until they begin to feel the effects, by which point they may have already impaired both their coordination and their judgment. Perhaps it is easy for such people to develop a habit of drinking excessively.

Sons of alcoholics differ from sons of nonalcoholics in another way that is more difficult to interpret. Using an electroencephalograph, it is possible to record **evoked potentials** from the brain in response to sensory stimuli. One component of an evoked potential, known as the **P300 wave**, is a positive wave occurring about 300 msec after a meaningful stimulus. The amplitude of the P300 wave is greatest when people have some reason to pay attention to a stimulus; it is least for a repeated stimulus that signals nothing. The P300 wave is weaker in alcoholic men than in nonalcoholic men; furthermore, it is weaker in the 7- to 13-year-old sons of alcoholic men than in the sons of nonalcoholics (Begleiter, Porjesz, Bihari, & Kissin, 1984). (See Figure 10-8.) How a weak P300 wave may predispose someone to alcoholism is hardly obvious, but it may indicate a biological difference that emerges early in life.

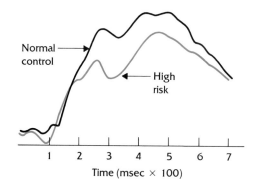

Figure 10-8. Evoked responses from two groups of young men in response to a visual stimulus. (Based on Begleiter et al., 1984.)

By attending to evoked potentials and to measurements of how young people react to alcohol and perhaps other stimuli, future research may be able to identify people at risk for alcoholism at an early age. These methods will have to be refined, however, to make their predictions more accurate.

SUMMARY

1. Homeostasis is a tendency to maintain a body variable near a set point. Temperature, hunger, and thirst are not exactly homeostatic, because the set point varies from time to time. (p. 266)
2. A constant body temperature enables an animal to evolve chemical reactions that are precisely coordinated. It also enables the animal to be equally active and equally resistant to fatigue at all environmental temperatures. (p. 267)
3. The preoptic area of the hypothalamus is critical for temperature control. It monitors both its own temperature and that of the skin and spinal cord. (p. 268)
4. Even homeothermic animals rely partly on behavioral mechanisms for temperature regulation, especially in infancy and after damage to the preoptic area. (pp. 269–270)
5. Fever is caused by the release of prostaglandin E, which stimulates cells in the preoptic area. A moderate fever may help an animal combat an infection. (p. 270)
6. Osmotic thirst is thirst caused by an increase in the osmotic pressure of the blood, which draws water out of the cells. After damage to the lateral preoptic area of the hypothalamus, an animal drinks less in response to osmotic thirst, although it still maintains a normal osmotic pressure. (p. 271)
7. Hypovolemic thirst is thirst caused by a loss of blood volume. Animals with hypovolemic thirst drink

more water containing solutes than pure water. Hypovolemic thirst depends on brain areas surrounding the third ventricle. (p. 273)
8. Two stimuli have been identified for hypovolemic thirst—signals from the baroreceptors, and the hormone angiotensin II, which increases when blood pressure falls. The two stimuli may act synergistically. (p. 274)
9. A loss of sodium salts from the body gives rise to sodium-specific cravings. The hormones aldosterone and angiotensin II act synergistically to stimulate such cravings. (p. 275)
10. Most drinking takes place around the time of a meal, stimulated by food in the stomach. (p. 275)
11. People and animals eat partly for the sake of taste. With much practice, they may learn to calibrate the density of calories in different foods, so that they may eat different amounts of different diets. (p. 277)
12. The primary factor that limits the size of a meal is distention of the stomach. Nerves from the stomach report information concerning both mechanical distention and nutrient content. (p. 278)
13. When food reaches the duodenum, it stimulates the release of CCK, which decreases food intake by inhibiting the further release of food from the stomach, and possibly by other means. (p. 279)
14. Hunger increases when little glucose and other fuels reach the cells; it decreases when much glucose is

available to the cells. Such fluctuations ordinarily depend on the hormone insulin, which promotes the storage of food supplies as fat. (p. 280)

15. People differ in their metabolic rates, partly for genetic reasons. It is likely that a low metabolic rate leads to weight gain. (p. 282)

16. Damage to cells in the lateral hypothalamus leads to decreased eating and loss of weight, partly because of decreased digestive juices and partly because of a drop in insulin levels. (pp. 282–283)

17. Damage to the ventromedial hypothalamus leads to more frequent meals and weight gain, partly because of more rapid stomach emptying and partly because of an increase in insulin levels. (p. 284)

18. Antabuse blocks one step in the breakdown of alcohol and thereby leads to a build-up of toxic acetaldehyde. It is sometimes used to help people break an alcohol habit. (p. 288)

19. A hereditary tendency exists for alcohol abuse. One way in which that tendency is manifested is apparently that people at risk for alcoholism feel less intoxication than normal when drinking moderate amounts of alcohol. (p. 289)

REVIEW QUESTIONS

1. In what ways are certain motivations homeostatic, and in what ways are they unlike the thermostat that controls temperature in a house? (p. 266)

2. What evidence do we have that the preoptic area controls body temperature? (p. 268)

3. In what way can an animal continue to regulate body temperature after damage to the preoptic area? (p. 269)

4. What processes in the brain are responsible for fevers? (p. 270)

5. What is the difference between osmotic and hypovolemic thirst? (pp. 271–273)

6. Why does an injection of sodium chloride produce thirst, while an injection of an equal amount of glucose does not? (p. 272)

7. In what way does an animal with damage to the preoptic area of the hypothalamus resemble an animal that has access only to bad-tasting water? (p. 273)

8. Which hormones synergistically promote a craving for salty tastes? (p. 275)

9. By what mechanisms may eating lead to drinking, even before any osmotic changes have occurred in the cells? (p. 275)

10. What evidence points to distention of the stomach as a major contributor to satiety? (p. 278)

11. What causes the release of the hormone CCK? By what mechanism does CCK probably act in limiting meal size? (p. 279)

12. Why is it that high levels of insulin and very low levels of insulin *both* lead to an increase in eating? (p. 281)

13. Describe several biological reasons why certain people may become overweight. (Make reference to stomach emptying speed, CCK, insulin levels, and genetic differences in metabolic rate.) (pp. 278–282)

14. What are the effects of damage to the lateral hypothalamus on eating? (p. 282)

15. Through what two mechanisms does damage to the ventromedial hypothalamus lead to weight gain? (p. 286)

16. What are the steps in metabolic breakdown of ethyl alcohol by the liver? (p. 288)

17. How does Antabuse help people break a habit of alcohol abuse? (p. 288)

18. What methods can be used to try to identify people at greater than average risk of alcoholism? (p. 289)

THOUGHT QUESTIONS

1. Speculate on why human body temperature is 37°C. Is that figure just an accident? Would it have been just as easy to evolve temperature regulation around a body temperature of 21°C or 47°C? Why, would you suppose, do birds have higher body temperatures than mammals? If you were asked to predict the body temperature of beings on some other planet, what would you want to know about conditions on that planet before making your prediction?

2. Certain women during menstruation or pregnancy crave salt. Why?

3. In late autumn, migratory and hibernating species deposit extra fat. Would you expect their insulin levels to be high or low at this time? What levels would you predict after migration or hibernation has actually begun?

TERMS TO REMEMBER

homeostasis (p. 266)
set point (p. 266)
poikilothermic (p. 267)
homeothermic (p. 267)

hypothalamus (p. 268)
preoptic area (p. 268)
prostaglandin E (p. 270)
osmotic pressure (p. 271)

SUGGESTIONS FOR FURTHER READING

Logue, A. W. (1986). *The psychology of eating and drinking.* New York: Freeman. Discussion includes anorexia nervosa, bulimia, and alcohol abuse.

Stellar, J. R., & Stellar, E. (1985). *The neurobiology of motivation and reward.* New York: Springer-Verlag. A general treatment emphasizing hunger and thirst.

Vaillant, G. E. (1983). *The natural history of alcoholism.* Cambridge, MA: Harvard. Report of a long-term study of alcoholic men.

CHAPTER 11

Sexual Behavior

MAIN IDEAS

1. Hormones alter the readiness for a type of behavior, such as sexual behavior, on a relatively long-term basis.

2. Sex hormones have organizing and activating effects. Organizing effects are permanent effects on anatomy and the brain, exerted during a critical period of early development. Activating effects are transient effects exerted at any later time.

3. In mammals, the presence or absence of testosterone determines whether the gonads and hypothalamus will develop in the male or the female manner, although for certain effects testosterone must first be converted to estradiol within the cell.

4. In mammals, the presence or absence of estradiol determines sex differences in the cerebral cortex.

At the start of the last chapter, life was defined as a coordinated set of chemical reactions. That bare minimum definition omits a critical element: reproduction. Standard biological definitions of life stipulate that a system can be considered alive only if it has the potential to metabolize energy and to reproduce.

We allow for certain exceptions to this definition. Although mules are infertile, no one doubts that they are alive. The same is true for worker bees, the very young and the very old of all species, and various other individuals. Still, in order for a species to survive, at least certain members of the species must reproduce often enough to replace all the individuals that die.

For humans, nearly all other vertebrates, and a large proportion of invertebrates, reproduction occurs sexually. A sperm from the male and an ovum from the female combine to produce a new individual not quite the same as either parent. The constant reshuffling of genes enables the species to adapt evolutionarily to a changing environment. It also provides enough variability among individuals to make it difficult for any one strain of virus or bacterium to wipe out the entire population.

Reproduction is not always easy, however. To reproduce, an individual must find a healthy, sexually mature member of the opposite sex of its own species. It must persuade that partner to accept it as a mate, and then synchronize its behavior with that of its partner so that both are ready to engage in the sex act at the same time. Finally, once the young have made their appearance, in most species one or both of the partners must provide care for the young until they are ready to care for themselves.

HORMONES

Hormones are important in the control of many behaviors; several hormones were discussed in Chapter 10. Hormones are so important to sexual behavior, however, that this is the best context for discussing hormones in general. A **hormone** is a chemical that is released by one organ and conveyed by the blood or lymphatic system to other organs, whose activity it influences. Figure 11-1 presents the major **endocrine** (hormone-producing) **glands**. Table 11-1 lists some important hormones and their principal effects.

Mechanisms of Hormone Actions

The effects of hormones on behavior overlap greatly with the effects of synaptic transmitters. A number of chemicals, including epinephrine, norepinephrine, angiotensin, and CCK, are believed to function both as synaptic transmitters and as hormones. The difference between a synaptic transmitter and a hormone is that a synaptic transmitter is released in small amounts directly adjacent to the target cell, while a hormone is released in larger amounts to be carried by the blood to targets throughout the body. Consequently, hormones promote a long-term readiness to respond, rather than a brief response to a single stimulus. For example, hormones increase the readiness to respond sexually but do not determine the choice of one sex

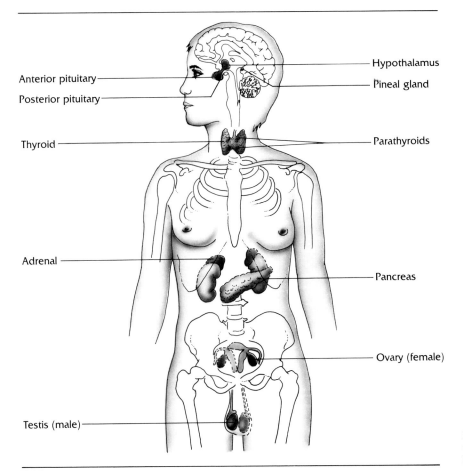

Anterior pituitary

Posterior pituitary

Thyroid

Adrenal

Testis (male)

Hypothalamus

Pineal gland

Parathyroids

Pancreas

Ovary (female)

Figure 11-1. Some important endocrine glands of humans.

partner over another. Hormones prepare birds to migrate but do not help them maneuver their flight around an obstacle.

Hormones affect the nervous system via at least two mechanisms (Plapinger & McEwen, 1978). First, **peptide hormones** and hormones derived from amino acids attach to receptors on the cell membrane, where they induce a series of chemical reactions that alter the cell's permeability to ions for a period of minutes to hours. Epinephrine (also known as adrenalin) is one example. Epinephrine and similar chemicals exert their effects in the same way when they act as synaptic transmitters.

Second, **steroid hormones**, which can alter transmission across the membrane like the other hormones (Nabekura, Oomura, Minami, Mizuno, & Fukuda, 1986), also enter the cell and attach to the chromosomes, altering the expression of the genes. Two classes of steroid hormones, the **estrogens** (more abundant in females) and the **androgens** (more abundant in males), turn on the genes that control certain sexual characteristics, such as breast development or growth of facial hair. The genes that those hormones activate are called **sex-limited genes**. Although they are present in both sexes, the steroid hormones limit their effects to one sex or the other.

Table 11-1.   Partial List of Hormone-Releasing Glands

Organ	Hormones	Hormone functions
Hypothalamus	Various releasing hormones	Promote or inhibit release of various hormones by pituitary
Anterior pituitary	TSH (thyroid-stimulating hormone)	Stimulates thyroid gland
	LH (luteinizing hormone)	Increases production of progesterone (female), testosterone (male)
	FSH (follicle-stimulating hormone)	Increases production of estrogen and maturation of ovum (female) and production of sperm (male)
	ACTH	Increases secretion of steroid hormones by adrenal gland
	Prolactin	Increases milk production
Posterior pituitary	Oxytocin	Controls uterine contractions and milk production
	Vasopressin	Constricts blood vessels, raises blood pressure
Pineal gland	Melatonin	Contributes to regulation of sleep-activity cycles
Thyroid	Thyroxine Triiodothyronine	Increase metabolic rate, growth, and maturation
Parathyroid	Parathyroid hormone	Increases blood calcium, decreases potassium
Adrenal cortex	Aldosterone	Reduces excretion of salts by kidney
	Cortisol	Stimulates liver to elevate blood sugar; increases metabolism of proteins and fats
Adrenal medulla	Epinephrine Norepinephrine	Similar to effects of sympathetic nervous system
Pancreas	Insulin	Increases entry of glucose to cells, increases storage as fats
	Glucagon	Increases conversion of stored fats to blood glucose
Ovary	Estrogens	Promotes ovulation and female sexual characteristics
	Progesterone	Maintain pregnancy
Testis	Androgens	Promote sperm production, growth of pubic hair, male sexual characteristics

Control of Hormone Release

The release of certain hormones varies from time to time, under the control of the hypothalamus, which acts by way of the **pituitary gland**. The pituitary consists of two distinct glands, the **anterior** and the **posterior pituitary**, which release different sets of hormones (Table 11-1). The hypothalamus communicates with the anterior pituitary by secreting special hormones, called **releasing hormones**, into the blood supply to the anterior pituitary. Axons from certain parts of the hypothalamus release *oxytocin* and *vasopressin* into the posterior pituitary, which in turn stores them and eventually releases them.

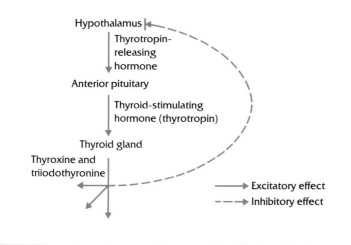

Hypothalamus

Thyrotropin-
releasing
hormone

Anterior pituitary

Thyroid-stimulating
hormone (thyrotropin)

Thyroid gland

Thyroxine and
triiodothyronine

→ Excitatory effect
- - → Inhibitory effect

Figure 11-2. The regulation of thyroid hormones.

The hypothalamus acts to maintain fairly constant circulating levels of certain hormones. For example, when the level of thyroid hormone is low, the hypothalamus releases one of its hormones, known as *thyrotropin-releasing hormone*, which stimulates the anterior pituitary to release *thyroid-stimulating hormone* (also known as *thyrotropin*), which in turn causes the thyroid gland to secrete more thyroid hormones. After the level of thyroid hormones has risen, the hypothalamus decreases its release of thyrotropin-releasing hormone. (See Figure 11-2.)

Sex hormones rise and fall during the menstrual cycle of women and other female primates. (See Figure 11-3.) After the end of a menstrual period, *follicle-stimulating hormone* (FSH) promotes the growth of follicles in the ovary. Toward the middle of the menstrual cycle, the follicles produce increasing amounts of one type of estrogen, **estradiol**. Ordinarily, estradiol inhibits the release of *luteinizing hormone* (LH) from the pituitary. Near the middle of the menstrual cycle, however, for reasons not well understood, the increase in estrogen levels causes a sudden surge of LH release as well as an increase of FSH (top graph in Figure 11-2). These hormones cause one of the follicles in the ovary to release an **ovum** (egg). They also cause the remnant of the follicle (now called the *corpus luteum*) to release the hormone **progesterone**, which prepares the uterus for the implantation of a fertilized ovum. Progesterone also inhibits the further release of LH. By the end of the menstrual cycle, the levels of LH, FSH, estradiol, and progesterone have all declined (Feder, 1981). If the ovum is fertilized, the levels of estradiol and progesterone increase gradually thoughout pregnancy. If the ovum is not fertilized, the lining of the uterus is cast off (menstruation), and the cycle is ready to begin again.

In real life, the cycle is a little less predictable than all this may sound. Bright light can speed up the cycle, darkness can retard it, and various kinds of stress can alter it in many ways. In other mammalian species, reproductive hormones are governed by social stimuli. Female rabbits, for example, ovulate only when a male is present.

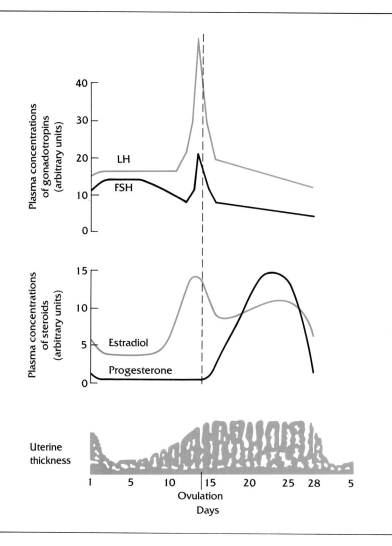

Figure 11-3. Blood levels of certain hormones over the menstrual cycle.

ORGANIZING EFFECT OF SEX HORMONES

We generally refer to the androgens, a group of hormones including testosterone and several others, as "male hormones," and to the estrogens, a group of hormones including estradiol and others, as "female hormones." Those designations are only partly correct. Both males and females produce both types of hormones, although males produce more androgens than estrogens and females produce more estrogens than androgens.

We distinguish two effects of sex hormones: organizing and activating. At an early stage of development, sex hormones produce **organizing effects**, determining whether the body will develop as a male or as a female. The organizing effects change the individual's anatomy, more or less permanently. Later in life, hormones may temporarily *activate* a particular behavior, but the effects last only a little longer than the hormones themselves. (We shall have more to say about activating effects a little later.)

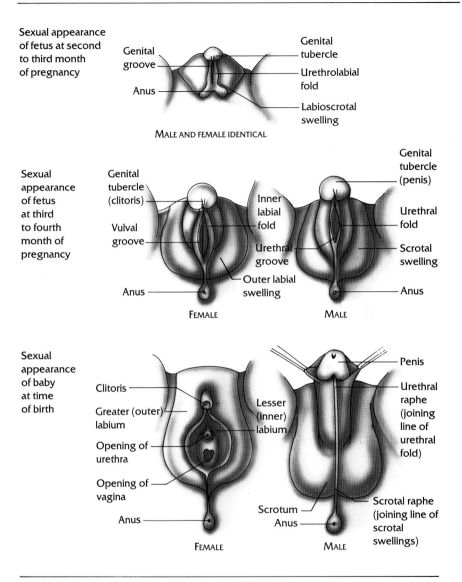

Sexual appearance of fetus at second to third month of pregnancy

Genital groove
Anus
Genital tubercle
Urethrolabial fold
Labioscrotal swelling

MALE AND FEMALE IDENTICAL

Sexual appearance of fetus at third to fourth month of pregnancy

Genital tubercle (clitoris)
Vulval groove
Anus
Inner labial fold
Urethral groove
Outer labial swelling

FEMALE

Genital tubercle (penis)
Urethral fold
Scrotal swelling
Anus

MALE

Sexual appearance of baby at time of birth

Clitoris
Greater (outer) labium
Opening of urethra
Opening of vagina
Anus

Lesser (inner) labium

FEMALE

Penis
Urethral raphe (joining line of urethral fold)
Scrotal raphe (joining line of scrotal swellings)
Scrotum
Anus

MALE

Figure 11-4. Differentiation of human genitals from a single set of precursors. (Based on Netter, 1965.)

During an early stage of prenatal development, every mammalian fetus has the precursors to both the Müllerian ducts (found in mature females) and the Wolffian ducts (found in mature males). It also has a set of external structures that could differentiate into either female genitals or male genitals. (See Figure 11-4.) From this initial unisex appearance, the fetus develops in either the female or the male direction, depending on the influence of hormones.

Sex Differences in the Gonads and Hypothalamus

In addition to the obvious differences in the gonads, the sexes differ in the anatomy of the hypothalamus. One portion of the medial preoptic area of the hypothalamus is dependably larger in males than in females—two to three times larger in humans, and even larger in certain other species (Hines, Davis, Coquelin, Goy, & Gorski, 1985; Swaab & Fliers, 1985). Other parts of the hypothalamus show smaller differences. Furthermore, the female hypothalamus sends a pattern of neural and hormonal activity that enables the pituitary to release hormones in a cyclic pattern; the male hypothalamus cannot do so. These differences between the sexes emerge at an early age, presumably organized by early hormones.

The presence or absence of **testosterone** is apparently decisive in determining the development of both the genitals and the hypothalamus. A female rat that is injected with testosterone during the first 10 days after its birth is partly masculinized, even though she is given no additional hormones after that. Her clitoris grows larger than normal; her other reproductive structures look intermediate between female and male. At maturity, her pituitary and ovaries produce steady levels of hormones instead of the cycles that are characteristic of females. Anatomically, certain parts of her hypothalamus resemble those of a male more than those of a female. Her behavior is also masculinized: She mounts other females and makes copulatory thrusting movements, rather than arching her back and allowing males to mount her. In short, the early testosterone promotes the male pattern and inhibits the female pattern (Gorski, 1985; Wilson, George, & Griffin, 1981).

Early treatment with estradiol or other estrogens does not have the reverse effect. A male that is injected with small amounts of estrogens still develops as a male, although large quantities can demasculinize him (Diamond, Llacuna, & Wong, 1973). Furthermore, if the gonads are removed from either a male or a female rat just after birth, depriving the animal of its own hormones, the young rat develops looking and behaving like a female. (It may need at least a small amount of estrogen to develop a fully normal female pattern, however.)

In short, in the presence of little or no sex hormones, a mammal develops the female pattern of external genitals and hypothalamus. Add estrogens, within normal limits, and the result is still female. Add testosterone and the result is male. Testosterone exerts long-lasting effects only if it is present during an early *critical period*—age 0 to 10 days for a rat, about the third and fourth months of pregnancy for a human (Money & Ehrhardt, 1972).

According to studies carried out on rodents, testosterone exerts part of its effect on the hypothalamus through a surprising route: After it enters a neuron, it is converted to estradiol! Testosterone and estradiol are chemically very similar, as you can see in Figure 11-5. Other types of androgens that cannot be converted into estrogens are less effective in masculinizing the hypothalamus. Moreover, drugs that prevent testosterone from being converted to estradiol block the organizing effects of testosterone on sexual development.

Why, then, is the female not masculinized by her own estradiol? During the early critical period, immature mammals of most species have in their bloodstream a protein called **alpha-fetoprotein**, which is not present in adults (Gorski, 1980; MacLusky & Naftolin, 1981). Alpha-fetoprotein

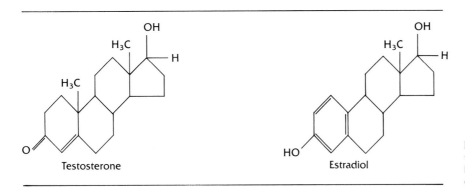

binds with estrogen, impeding it from leaving the bloodstream and entering the cells that are developing in this early period. Nonrodents have additional mechanisms for inactivating estrogen; for example, it is likely that infant primates break down estrogens into inactive substances. In any event, testosterone is neither bound to alpha-fetoprotein nor metabolized; it is free to enter the cells, where enzymes convert it into estradiol. That is, testosterone is a way of getting estradiol into the cells at a time when estradiol itself cannot leave the blood.

This explanation of testosterone's effects enables us to make sense of an otherwise puzzling fact: Although normal amounts of estradiol have little effect on early development, an injection of a large amount actually masculinizes development. The reason is that normal amounts are bound to alpha-fetoprotein or metabolized, whereas large amounts may exceed the body's capacity for inactivation; the excess is thus able to enter the cells and masculinize them.

Once testosterone or estradiol gets into a cell, we know relatively little about how it changes the cell's properties. It does appear that testosterone exerts at least part of its effects on neurons that use dopamine as their synaptic transmitter. During the early critical period for sexual differentiation of the brain, drugs that disrupt activity at dopamine synapses lead to a permanent decrease in male sexual ability (Hull, Nishita, Bitran, & Dalterio, 1984). Evidently, the drugs bypass testosterone and act directly on the cells that testosterone affects.

Sex Differences in the Cerebral Cortex

On the average, the cerebral cortex is thicker on the right side for males and thicker on the left side for females. Although this sex difference in the cortex is not large, and not altogether consistent from one individual to another, it is found in rats as well as humans.

Early sex hormones influence the cortex and the hypothalamus in different ways. While testosterone determines the developmental pattern of the hypothalamus by conversion to estradiol, circulating levels of estradiol are more decisive for the development of the cortex. Compared to the hypothalamus, the cerebral cortex has lower levels of the enzyme *aromatase*, which converts testosterone to estradiol (MacLusky, Naftolin, & Goldman-Rakic, 1986). Therefore, more of the testosterone entering the cells of the cortex

Table 11-2.   Organizing Effects of Sex Hormones on Early Mammalian Development

	Time of maturation	Role of estradiol	Role of testosterone
Hypothalamus	Earlier	Would masculinize if it could enter neurons, but in normal amounts it cannot	Enters cells, where aromatase converts it to estradiol, which masculinizes development
Cerebral cortex	Later	Enters cells freely, inhibits development, increases cell loss in certain areas; may facilitate myelination	Less is converted to estradiol; effects are uncertain

remains testosterone. Furthermore, by the time the cortex is developing, estrogens are freer to enter the cells than they were when the hypothalamus was developing. Levels of alpha-fetoprotein have declined in rats; metabolic breakdown of estrogen has declined in primates.

More neurons form in early development than will survive to maturity, in the cortex as well as other areas. Estradiol increases the rate of loss of neurons. Because females have more estradiol receptors in the right hemisphere and males have more in the left, infant females lose more neurons in the right hemisphere and infant males lose more neurons in the left hemisphere (Sandhu, Cook, & Diamond, 1986). If the ovaries are removed from a female rat just after birth, her cerebral cortex grows thicker than normal (Pappas, Diamond, & Johnson, 1979). On the other hand, although estrogen inhibits the survival of neurons, it accelerates the growth and myelination of axons in certain parts of the brain (Curry & Heim, 1966; Toran-Allerand, 1976).

The role of testosterone is less certain. It is known to decrease the loss of neurons in the spinal cords of infant rats (Nordeen, Nordeen, Sengelaub, & Arnold, 1985) and in parts of the brains of birds (Konishi & Akutagawa, 1985). It may not have such effects on the mammalian cerebral cortex, however. Early **castration** (removal of the testes) of a male has no clear effect on development of the cortex (Diamond, Johnson, & Ehlert, 1979). Table 11-2 summarizes the organizing effects of sex hormones on early mammalian development.

Organizing Effects of Hormones on Nonreproductive Characteristics

Hormones given during the critical period may also have an organizing effect on nonreproductive characteristics that differ between the sexes, including size, strength, vulnerability to certain diseases, and response to drugs (Bardin & Catterall, 1981). For example, female dogs exposed to androgens during the critical period assume the male position for urination (Beach, 1974a). (See Figure 11-6.)

Female monkeys exposed to testosterone during their critical period are masculinized in several ways. They attempt to copulate with other females and not with males. They engage in more rough-and-tumble play than other females during youth, are more aggressive, and make more threatening facial gestures (Quadagno, Briscoe, & Quadagno, 1977; Young, Goy, & Phoenix,

Adult female
Full squat

Adult female
Squat lift

Adult male
Full elevation

Adult male
Partial elevation

Figure 11-6. Urination postures of dogs. Adult female dogs that had been exposed to androgens shortly before and after birth urinated in the adult male position on 62 percent of occasions. (From Beach, 1974a.)

1964). Similar effects on play and aggressive behavior have been noted in dogs (Beach, Buehler, & Dunbar, 1982; Reinisch, 1981) and ferrets (Stockman, Callaghan, Gallagher, & Baum, 1986). In humans, too, males and females differ in their play patterns and aggressive behavior, even at an early age. It would be consistent with the data on other species to suppose that prenatal hormones predispose humans toward these differences. Directly relevant data are sparse and hard to interpret, however (Hines, 1982). In humans it is difficult to separate the roles of early upbringing from those of hormones or other biological determinants.

The hormones present during the critical period may also be important determinants of life expectancy. It is well known that women live longer than men, on the average. It has been suggested that men die earlier because they work harder or worry more. However, females outlive males in most

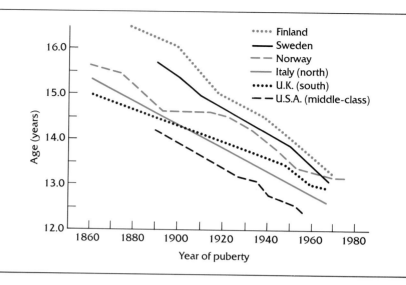

mammalian species, and it is difficult to believe that male bears work harder than females, or that male porcupines worry more than females. When Dörner and Hinz (1975) measured the effects of early sex hormones on lifespan in rats, they found that females injected with testosterone in the early critical period had lifespans similar to those of males, while males castrated early lived longer than normal males and (in this study) even longer than females. Similarly, castrated male cats live longer than intact ones (Hamilton, Hamilton, & Mestler, 1969). In humans, mentally retarded men who have been castrated survive longer than similar men who have not been castrated; removal of the ovaries does not affect survival of women (Hamilton & Mestler, 1969).

PUBERTY

Puberty is the onset of sexual maturity. On the average, puberty begins at about age 12 to 13 for girls and a year later for boys. Over the last century, the age of puberty has gradually decreased in the United States and Western Europe (Marshall & Tanner, 1986). (See Figure 11-7.) Why it has been decreasing, we do not know, although we can speculate on the effects of improved diet and increasing exposure to artificial lighting. Exposure to bright or prolonged lighting is known to advance the onset of puberty in several species (Steger, 1976).

Puberty begins when the hypothalamus begins to release bursts of one of its releasing hormones, *luteinizing hormone releasing hormone*, at a rate of about one burst per hour. It is not known what stimulates the hypothalamus to do so, but once it begins, it continues throughout the fertile period. This hormone stimulates the pituitary to secrete LH and FSH, which in turn stimulate the gonads to release estradiol or testosterone (Goldman, 1981). Estradiol causes breast development and broadening of the hips. Testosterone causes lowering of the voice, beard growth, broadening of the shoulders, and growth of hair on the chest, in the underarms, and in the pubic area.

Both boys and girls undergo a growth spurt in response to the increase in hormones.

Although a certain amount of variation is normal in the age of puberty, puberty is considered *precocious* if it begins before age 8 in girls, 9 in boys. Although children who begin puberty that early show an immediate growth spurt, their growth stops early and they are generally short as adults. A 6- or 7-year-old child in puberty develops acne and secondary sexual characteristics that often provoke teasing from other children and lead to social awkwardness. If precocious puberty is recognized quickly, the child can be given drugs that inhibit the release of LH and FSH, thus postponing puberty until a more appropriate age (Pescovitz, Cutler, & Loriaux, 1985).

ACTIVATING EFFECTS OF HORMONES

Long after the early hormones have determined the structure of the gonads and the nervous system, current levels of testosterone or estradiol exert **activating effects** on sexual behaviors. Activating effects temporarily modify sexual or other activities; they do not permanently alter anatomy, as organizing effects do.

Activating Effects on Sexual Behavior

After removal of the testes from a male rat or the ovaries from a female rat, sexual behavior declines as the sex hormone levels in the blood decline. It may not disappear altogether, partly because the adrenal glands also produce some testosterone and estradiol. Not only can hormones influence behavior; behavior and sensory stimuli can alter the production of hormones, too. (See Digression 11-1.)

Dogs and cats are less dependent on current levels of sex hormones than rodents are (Beach, 1967, 1970). (See BioSketch 11-1.) Male dogs maintain sexual behavior at a somewhat decreased level for several years after castration. Male cats maintain a certain amount of sexual activity if they have had sexual experience prior to the castration. Female dogs and cats engage in no sexual activity after removal of their ovaries, however. And even with their ovaries intact, they engage in sexual activity only during **estrus** ("heat"), the time when they are fertile and when their estrogen levels are highest.

Primates (monkeys, apes, and humans) are still less dependent on current levels of sex hormones than dogs and cats. Male monkeys maintain moderate levels of sexual activity after castration (Phoenix, Slob, & Goy, 1973), and some female monkeys show limited sexual behavior after removal of the ovaries. Furthermore, intact females of certain monkey species engage in a fair amount of sexual activity outside their fertile periods (Czaja & Bielert, 1975; Eaton & Resko, 1974).

The dependence of sexual activity on current hormone levels is least in humans, although an influence is certainly demonstrable. Among males, sexual interest and the potential for sexual activity are highest at the age when testosterone levels are highest (about ages 15 to 25). Men with low testosterone levels generally have lower than average frequencies of erection and sexual activity, although both frequencies increase after the men receive testosterone injections (Davidson, Camargo, & Smith, 1979).

DIGRESSION
11-1

Behavior Can Influence Hormones, Just as Hormones Can Influence Behavior

The mating behavior of the ring-necked dove offers a striking example of how hormones and behavior interact with each other. A newly mated pair of doves goes through a well-synchronized series of behaviors, as outlined in the following table:

	Male	Female
Day 1	Aggressive behavior	Nonaggressive
Days 2–6	Courtship (nest coos) Copulation Nest building (brings twigs)	Courtship (nest coos) Copulation Nest building (arranges twigs)
Day 7		Lays two eggs
Next 2 weeks	Sits on eggs during middle of the day	Sits on eggs from late afternoon to next morning
Next 3 weeks	Tends and feeds chicks	Tends and feeds chicks

The behaviors of the male and female are tightly synchronized. If the female assumes the receptive posture for copulation too early, the male may copulate but then quickly deserts her (Erickson & Zenone, 1976). But properly timed copulation establishes a "pair bond" that keeps the couple together through the mating season and sometimes even into later years.

Both birds normally ignore nesting materials on day 1, begin to build a nest on day 2 or 3, and, if a nest is not completed by day 6 or 7, work frantically on nest building at that time. Neither pays much attention to a nest with eggs before day 7, but both take turns sitting on eggs after that time. Both produce a "crop milk" that they feed chicks that hatch 14 days after the eggs are laid, but they do not provide milk if chicks hatch much earlier.

Although it is possible to give hormone injections that induce any of the observed behaviors, it is also the case that each change in the birds' behavior induces a change in their hormone secretions. The sequence of behaviors depends on a system in which each behavior causes the production of hormones that prepare a bird for the next stage of behavior. On day 1, the male struts around and makes a cooing display. The male behavior seems to excite the female; her ovaries increase production of estrogen (Erickson & Lehrman, 1964). By day 2 she is ready for courtship and soon after that for copulation. If a researcher simply injects an isolated female wih estrogen, she is ready for courtship and copulation almost as soon as a male appears. Thus, the function of the male's behavior on the first day is to stimulate the female's hormonal secretions.

Meanwhile, the male seems to be excited by observing the female on day 1; he has an increased production of androgens. By day 2 he is ready for nest building. Based on studies in other bird species (Adkins & Pniewski, 1978), it is likely that different aspects of the male's courtship and nesting behaviors depend on different forms of androgen.

A week of courtship and nest building causes the female to produce first estrogen and then a combination of estrogen and progesterone. If we give estrogen injections to an isolated female for a week, with additional progesterone on the last two days, she becomes ready to incubate eggs even if she has neither seen nor heard a male. Evidently, the courting and nesting experiences produce hormonal changes that make her ready for the next behavioral stage.

Similarly, 14 days of sitting on eggs (or of watching another bird sit on eggs through a piece of glass) causes either the male or the female to produce the hormone prolactin, which stimulates the production of crop milk and disposes the bird to take care of baby doves. If a dove is isolated from other birds and from nests and eggs, a researcher can still get it to take care of baby doves by injecting it repeatedly with prolactin.

In short, one behavior causes a hormonal change, which disposes the bird toward a second behavior, which causes a further hormonal change, and so on to the end of the sequence (Lehrman, 1964; Martinez-Vargas & Erickson, 1973).

BIOSKETCH
11-1

Frank A. Beach

Frank A. Beach founded the study of the effects of hormones on behavior. Born in 1911, Beach studied to be an English teacher and received his B.S. degree from Kansas State Teachers College in Emporia, Kansas. Unable to find a permanent high school teaching job during the Depression, he went to graduate school in psychology at the University of Chicago, where he received his Ph.D. in 1940. He later held positions at the American Museum of Natural History, Yale University, and the University of California at Berkeley.

Beach was a very independent student (Beach, 1974b). While an undergraduate, he did experiments on shock-avoidance learning in rats, although no one on the faculty had ever done a rat experiment. Having had little guidance on shock levels or other procedures, he set the shock level as high as possible, and then—to be sure the rat could not miss the shock—he flooded the maze floor with water. When the rat got the shock, it flew into the air and let out a shriek probably heard throughout Kansas. Beach never found out what the rat had learned, but Beach learned to avoid shock experiments.

Later, at the University of Chicago, he educated himself on procedures for brain surgery with rats. More successful this time, he did his Ph.D. dissertation on the effects of brain lesions on maternal behavior in rats. His experiences as a student gave him the courage to continue trying the new. Eventually, when he heard a lecturer say that no one knew anything about the effects of hormones on behavior, he set out to investigate that frontier. His first book, *Hormones and Behavior* (1948) summarized all that was known in that field at the time and organized the field for all future investigators.

Anyone who devotes his or her life to basic research faces a moral decision. In Beach's words, "To what degree should my choice of research work be governed by human needs, by social imperatives, and how am I going to justify spending all of my energies on any research that does not bear directly on pressing human problems . . .? The solution, or rationalization, that I have finally come up with is that it is a perfectly worthwhile way of spending one's life to do your level best to increase human knowledge, and it is not necessary nor is it always even desirable to be constrained by possible applicability of what you find to immediate problems. This may sound very peculiar to some young people, but it is a value judgment which I myself have made and which I can live with."

Decreases in testosterone levels decrease sexual activity. After castration, for example, most men report a decrease in their sexual interest and activity. Occasional attempts have been made to reduce androgen levels by means of drugs in order to suppress sexual behavior by men with a history of sexual offenses, such as exhibitionism and child molesting (Berlin & Meinecke, 1981; Money, Wiedeking, Walker, & Gain, 1976). A majority of the treated men cease their offensive behaviors as long as they continue taking the drugs.

After **hysterectomy** (removal of the uterus and ovaries), about one-third of women report a decreased sexual response (Zussman, Zussman, Sunley, & Bjornson, 1981), partly because their decreased hormone levels make intercourse unpleasant, and sometimes even painful. Natural fluctuations in women's hormone levels have a weak relationship to women's sexual arousal. According to two studies, women not taking birth control pills initiate more sexual activity (either with a partner or by masturbation) about midway between menstrual periods than at other times during the month (Udry & Morris, 1968; Adams, Gold, & Burt, 1978). (See Figure 11-8.) The

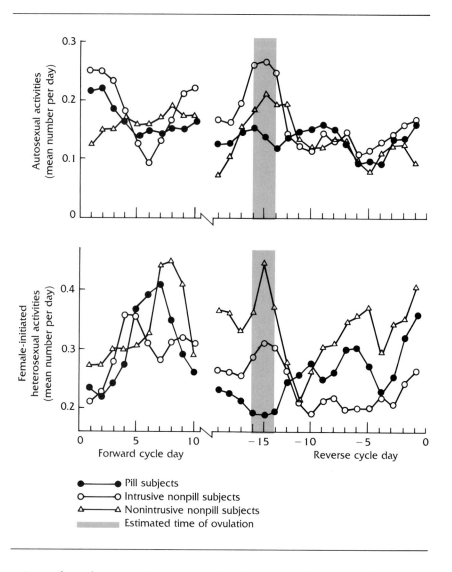

Figure 11-8. Fluctuation of autosexual activities (masturbation and sexual fantasies) and female-initiated heterosexual activities during the monthly cycle. Results are plotted separately for women taking birth control pills, women using "intrusive" birth control methods (diaphragm, foam, or condom), and women using "nonintrusive" methods (IUD or vasectomy). (From Adams, Gold, & Burt, 1978.)

point midway between the menstrual periods is the time of ovulation and generally the time of the highest estrogen levels.

By what mechanism do sex hormones alter behavior? They do so partly by changing sensations. The *pudendal nerve* transmits tactile stimulation from the pubic area to the brain. Estrogens increase the area of skin that excites the pudendal nerve (Komisaruk, Adler, & Hutchison, 1972). Among humans, women's sensitivity to visual, auditory, and olfactory stimuli is heightened at the time of ovulation, presumably because of the increased levels of estrogens (Parlee, 1983).

Activating Effects on Aggressive Behavior

Most of the fighting that takes place within most animal species is activated by sex hormones. In many species, reproductively mature males fight one another vigorously during the mating season, to protect their territories and their mates. Fighting is rare among females, prepubertal males, and males outside the reproductive season (Goldstein, 1974; Moyer, 1974). A castrated male fights little; testosterone injections restore aggressive behavior (Brain, 1979).

Testosterone probably enhances the probability of human violent behavior also, although the evidence is not overwhelming. Throughout the world, males engage in more violent behavior than females (Maccoby & Jacklin, 1974; Moyer, 1974). Moreover, the highest incidence of violence, as measured by crime statistics, is in men 15 to 25 years old, who also have the highest levels of testosterone in the blood.

In one study, the testosterone levels in the blood of young men correlated $+.66$ with their replies on a hostility questionnaire, which included such items as "Whoever insults me or my family is asking for a fight," and "Sometimes people bother me just by being around" (Persky, Smith, & Basu, 1971). Another study found a significant correlation between the testosterone levels of male prisoners and those men's histories of violence prior to imprisonment (Kreuz & Rose, 1972). The five men with the highest testosterone levels had committed a total of two murders, one attempted murder, one assault, and four armed robberies. The five men with the lowest levels of testosterone had committed larceny or burglary but no murders, assaults, or armed robberies.

DETERMINANTS OF GENDER IDENTITY

Gender identity—the sex with which one identifies and the sex that one calls oneself—is a uniquely human characteristic. Gender identity is closely related to, but not identical with, the concept of **sex role**, the set of activities and dispositions presumed to be common for one sex or the other in a particular society. While someone who adopts the female gender identity is likely to accept the female sex role, for example, it is also possible to reject all or part of that sex role. Someone may say, "Yes, I am a woman, but I like sports and mathematics and I refuse to do housework."

Sex roles are determined to a large extent by one's culture and upbringing. For example, cooking is regarded as women's work by certain societies and as men's work by others. Even within our own society, what we regard as normal behavior for a man or a woman may change sharply from one generation to the next.

Gender identity is undoubtedly also governed heavily by one's upbringing. From an early age, a girl is told, "You are a girl, and later if you decide to marry, you will marry a boy." She is dressed in girl's clothing and placed mostly in the company of other girls. Boys are given the reverse treatment. And yet, a few people are clearly dissatisfied with their assigned sex, a small number of them (transsexuals) to such an extreme degree that they insist on a sex change. Others (homosexuals) have no desire to become a member of the opposite sex, but they direct their sexual interests toward members of their own sex. Might some biological factor, such as prenatal hormones, influence gender identity, or homosexual versus heterosexual orientation?

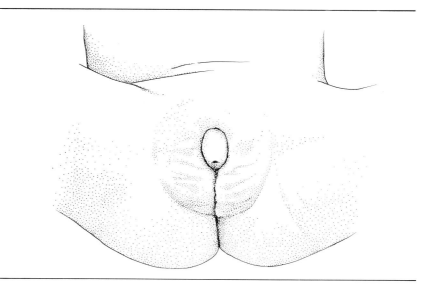

Figure 11-9. External genitals of a genetic female, age 3 months, masculinized by excess androgens from the adrenal gland before birth (the adrenogenital syndrome).

Intersexes or Pseudohermaphrodites

Recall that testosterone masculinizes the development of the gonads and the hypothalamus during a critical period in early development. If a genetic female is exposed to more testosterone than the average female but less than the average male, she may develop an appearance intermediate between male and female. The same is true of a genetic male who is deprived of some, but not all, of his own testosterone.

One way that this occurs to a small extent in rats is that a fetus may be exposed to a small proportion of the hormones of the fetuses next to it in the uterus. A female rat fetus that develops between two males has her external genitals slightly masculinized (Clemens, Gladue, & Coniglio, 1978). As an adult, she makes sexual approaches toward other females somewhat more often than a normal female rat does (Meisel & Ward, 1981). A male rat fetus that develops between two females grows up to be less aggressive than other males, although this effect may have more to do with increased estradiol levels than decreased testosterone (Vom Saal, Grant, McMullen, & Laves, 1983).

Rarely, human fetuses are exposed to an abnormal hormonal environment prior to birth. For example, a female fetus or her mother may have an adrenal gland that produces an excess of testosterone and other androgens. Also, certain drugs given to prevent miscarriage contain chemicals that may masculinize the development of a few female fetuses. If, for any reason, a female fetus is exposed to elevated androgen levels, the results is partial masculinization of her external anatomy, as illustrated in Figure 11-9. Note in the figure that the genitals show a structure intermediate between a clitoris and a penis and swellings intermediate between normal labia and a normal scrotum.

Individuals whose genitals do not match the normal development for their genetic sex are referred to as **hermaphrodites** (from Hermaphroditus, son of Hermes and Aphrodite, in Greek mythology). It is possible to distinguish several types of hermaphrodites. The so-called true hermaphrodite, a rarity, has some normal testicular tissue and some normal ovarian tissue— for example, a testis on one side of the body and an ovary on the other (Simpson, 1976). Individuals whose development is intermediate between male and female, like the one in Figure 11-9, are variously called **intersexes, pseudohermaphrodites,** or simply hermaphrodites.

When a baby is born with a pseudohermaphroditic appearance, a decision must be made: Shall we call it a boy or a girl? Human societies do not recognize *neuter* as an option, and experience has shown that it is harmful to a child's mental health to raise it indecisively, leaving it in doubt as to which sex it is.

Sex Assignment of Human Pseudohermaphrodites.   One way to resolve the question might be to do a chromosome test and determine whether the baby is genetically male or female. Most authorities reject that approach. Given that nearly all pseudohermaphrodites are infertile, the important thing is not whether the sex one calls oneself matches one's chromosomes but whether it matches one's external appearance and one's behavior.

Another approach is to apply some testosterone directly to the genital region to produce a temporary puberty. The result can give some hint of what will happen later during natural puberty. If the clitoris/penis shows a great deal of growth, the baby can be called a male; otherwise, assuming growth will not occur during natural puberty either, it can be considered a female.

Most authorities now favor a much simpler decision rule: When in doubt, call the child a female. Corrective surgery can reduce the genital growth to clitoral size; a vagina can be either lengthened or constructed artificially; and at puberty, estrogen injections can be given if necessary to stimulate breast growth. Any beard or chest hair that starts to grow can be removed. On the other hand, it is very difficult to surgically alter a hermaphrodite to look like a boy. No one has yet found a satisfactory way to lengthen a penis or to create a new one through surgery.

However, to raise all pseudohermaphrodites as females assumes that gender identity depends entirely on how a child is reared—that is, that the child will accept whichever sex is assigned. Is that true?

Gender Identity of Human Pseudohermaphrodites.   Although most pseudohermaphrodites are reared as females, a number have also been reared as males. Researchers have therefore been able to examine how well various children who started life about the same in appearance adapted to the assignment of male or female. Unfortunately, none of the findings have been scientifically conclusive. Let us examine the existing evidence and some of the difficulties in interpreting it:

1.   Many of the pseudohermaphrodites reared as females are tomboyish (Ehrhardt & Money, 1967; Money & Ehrhardt, 1968). During childhood and early adolescence, they show less interest in dolls and more interest in vigorous sports than most other girls. This tendency parallels the finding that female monkeys exposed to testosterone during the critical period also

engage in much aggressive play. We cannot conclude, however, that tomboy-ishness reflects a direct effect of testosterone on the brain—either in monkeys or in humans. As a result of the early effects of testosterone on the body, pseudohermaphrodites grow taller and more muscular than most females. Thus, they may develop a strong interest in vigorous sports simply because they are bigger and stronger than most other girls.

2.   Intersexes reared as females tend, from an early age, to fantasize more often about a career and less often about marriage and family than most other girls (Ehrhardt & Money, 1967; Matheis & Förster, 1980; Money & Ehrhardt, 1968). They are also more likely, as adults, to develop a homosexual or bisexual orientation (Money, Schwartz, & Lewis, 1984). Again, it is tempting to suggest an explanation in terms of prenatal hor-mones, but we cannot be sure. Were the girls aware they were unlikely to have children? Such knowledge could minimize their motherhood fantasies. Did the girls' large, relatively muscular, somewhat masculine appearance influence the way they were treated by boys and by other girls? If so, might that treatment have led to a homosexual or bisexual orientation?

3.   About 90 to 95 percent of all adult pseudohermaphrodites are sat-isfied with the sex to which they were assigned at birth; the other 5 to 10 percent express serious dissatisfaction with their assigned sex and may even request a sex reassignment (Money, 1970). Neither the 90 to 95 percent figure nor the 5 to 10 percent figure leads to any unambiguous conclusion. Unless we assume that pseudohermaphroditic babies are assigned a sex at random, it is likely that most of them were assigned the sex that most nearly matched their appearance at birth, which in turn matched their prenatal hormone pattern. Those who eventually reject their assigned sex could be either cases in which the doctor guessed wrong or cases in which the parents reared the child in an inconsistent or unsatisfactory way. If the pseudoher-maphrodite eventually accepts the assigned sex, we can explain the agree-ment either in terms of rearing or in terms of prenatal hormones, as outlined in Figure 11-10.

Discrepancies of Sexual Appearance by Genetic or Other Accidents

Most of the evidence from pseudohermaphrodites does not tell us anything indisputable about the roles of rearing and hormones in determining gender identity. From a scientific viewpoint, the only decisive way to settle the issue would be to take a completely normal male baby and raise him as a female, or to raise a normal female baby as a male. If the process succeeded, we would know that upbringing determines gender identity and that hormones do not. Although no one could perform such an experiment intentionally, it is possible to take advantage of experiments that have occurred by accident in nature. Here, we shall consider three examples in which children were (presumably) exposed to the hormonal pattern of one sex and then reared (unambiguously, as far as we know) as the opposite sex.

Penis Development Delayed Until Puberty.   Certain genetic males in the Dominican Republic were born with a gene that prevented penis growth

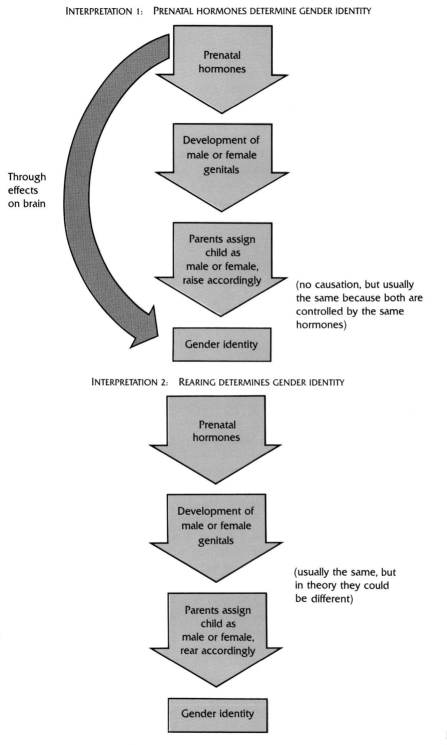

Figure 11-10. What controls gender identity?

early in life, although their testosterone levels may have been normal. As infants, they were regarded as girls with slightly swollen clitorises and were reared as females. At puberty, their penises suddenly grew, and each was reassigned as a male. Most of them developed clear male gender identities and directed their sexual interest toward females (Imperato-McGinley, Guerrero, Gautier, & Peterson, 1974). One interpretation of these results is that the prenatal hormones favored a male gender identity, despite the children's being reared as females. Another possibility is that gender identity is established by social influences around the time of puberty. In either case, the results make it difficult to argue that early rearing experiences are the sole determinant of gender identity, unless we assume that these children were actually recognized as different from the start and were reared in an abnormal way. (We can only speculate as to whether it would be equally easy for someone reared as a male to switch to a female identity.)

Boys with Much Breast Development at Puberty.   Although it is common for teenage boys to add some fat in the breasts and to experience some breast tenderness, in rare cases a boy has as much breast development as a girl. In one study of ten such boys, three had a history of dressing like girls, acting effeminate, and showing a homosexual or bisexual preference *before* the start of breast development (Money & Lewis, 1982). Although it is always dangerous to draw conclusions from a small number of individuals, these results suggest that some unrecognized hormonal abnormality predisposed the boys to a largely feminine gender identity and to later breast development.

Accidental Removal of the Penis.   Potentially the most decisive case of all is an ongoing one involving a genetic boy who is being reared as a girl. It all began when a physician, while trying to circumcise the baby boy using an electrical procedure, accidentally used too high a current and burned off the entire penis. The parents elected to rear the child as a female, with the appropriate corrective surgery. What makes this a particularly decisive case is that the child has a twin brother (whom the parents did not let the physician try to circumcise). If both twins develop satisfactory gender identities, one as a girl and the other as a boy, it will appear that rearing has been decisive and that prenatal hormones have not. To whatever extent the twin reared as a girl may prove dissatisfied with her assigned sex, we would probably assume that prenatal hormones have played a role. As a prepubertal child, she seemed to have a normal female gender identity, though with strong tomboyish tendencies (Money & Schwartz, 1978). A long-term follow-up should prove most interesting.

Possible Biological Bases of Homosexuality in Humans

Why is it that whereas most people seek sex partners of the opposite sex, a few prefer partners of their own sex? No doubt many factors are at play, and different factors are active in different people. Although the emphasis here is on the search for possible biological factors, experiential factors are certainly important as well.

Male Homosexuality.   At one time, psychiatrists and clinical psychologists considered all male homosexuals to be neurotic and attributed their sexual development to a domineering, close-binding mother and a detached, rejecting father (Van den Aardweg, 1984). Eventually, psychotherapists realized that they were overlooking a large population of nonneurotic homosexuals. Simply put, neurotic homosexuals consult psychiatrists and clinical psychologists; well-adjusted homosexuals do not. Further, a domineering mother and a rejecting father are common only in the families of neurotic homosexuals. Well-adjusted homosexual men generally have normal relationships with quite normal parents (Siegelman, 1974).

Might biological factors predispose certain men toward homosexuality? A genetic predisposition may exist, although the evidence is not solid. About 20 percent of the brothers of homosexual men are themselves homosexual, in comparison to about 4 percent of the total male population (Pillard & Weinrich, 1986). Of course, this evidence does not distinguish between the contributions of genetics and of a shared environment. If any genes do promote homosexuality, it is not clear why evolutionary pressures would not select strongly against a gene that decreases the probability of reproduction.

A stronger candidate as a possible biological factor in homosexuality is the pattern of hormones during early development. Although adult male homosexuals have, on the average, slightly lower testosterone levels than heterosexuals (Starká, Sipová, & Hynie, 1975), the differences are too small and too inconsistent to account for differences in behavior. Prenatal hormones are, however, a different story. It is possible to imagine that low levels of testosterone, or low sensitivity to testosterone, may feminize certain aspects of brain maturation in a genetic male, possibly leading to a homosexual preference later in life. Although no available evidence supports this hypothesis directly, several lines of research indicate that it is plausible and worthy of further investigation.

In one set of studies, male rats castrated on the day of birth and injected with testosterone at maturity responded sexually to male partners and not to females (Dörner, 1967, 1974). That is, the pattern of sexual behavior of these genetic males was determined by their *perinatal hormones* (hormones present around the time of birth), not by their adult hormones. Testosterone in adulthood increased sexual arousal but did not determine which type of sexual behavior would occur.

In another line of research, Ward (1972, 1977) exposed pregnant rats to a "stressful" experience during the final week of pregnancy by confining them in tight Plexiglas tubes for 135 minutes daily under bright lights. Such stress decreases brain levels of aromatase, the enzyme that converts testosterone into estradiol, which is necessary for masculinization of the hypothalamus (Weisz, Brown, & Ward, 1982). The stress caused the mothers to produce large amounts of adrenal hormones, which crossed into the fetuses' bloodstreams and may have competitively inhibited the actions of testosterone. The stress also caused the male fetuses to produce their peak testosterone levels a day or two earlier than usual, before the critical period for brain differentiation (Ward & Weisz, 1980).

Because the stress took place before birth and rats' genitals differentiate after birth, each male developed a penis and testes of nearly normal size. Behavior was modified, however, presumably because of early effects on the hypothalamus. As adults, the prenatally stressed males responded to injections of either testosterone or estrogen with an increase in female sexual behavior, arching their backs to receive a male partner. Few attempted to copulate with female partners. Although the prenatally stressed males were altered in their sexual behaviors, their behavior was typically male in certain other regards, such as level of activity in an open field (Meisel, Dohanich, & Ward, 1979). Evidently, different aspects of sex-differentiated behavior are organized at different times in development, or are perhaps sensitive to different types of androgens.

Even for sexual behavior, the effects of the prenatal stress varied, depending on social experiences after birth. Prenatally stressed males reared in isolation or with other prenatally stressed males became deficient in male sexual behavior. Those reared with normal males and females approached normal sexual responsiveness to females, even though they also responded sexually to other males (Dunlap, Zadina, & Gougis, 1978; Ward & Reed, 1985).

It is difficult to know how relevant these rat data are to humans. Relevant human data are difficult to obtain, not only for ethical reasons but also because it is difficult to reconstruct for any homosexual (or heterosexual) adult the hormonal environment that may have been present during a critical stage of prenatal development. The only feasible approach is indirect: Researchers can test whether a homosexual man's hypothalamus responds to certain hormones in a manner more characteristic of females than of males. One difference between the female and male hypothalamus is that an injection of estrogen causes an increased release of luteinizing hormone (LH) in the female but a decreased release in the male. Two studies have found an intermediate response by exclusively homosexual males: Estrogen causes an increase in LH, but less of an increase than females show (Dörner, Rohde, & Krell, 1972; Gladue, Green, & Hellman, 1984). Although these results are suggestive, they leave many questions unanswered. For example, we do not know which came first, the homosexual behavior or the responsiveness to estrogen.

Female Homosexuality.   Biological psychologists have devoted more research to male homosexuality than to female homosexuality. In animals, testosterone during the early critical period can masculinize the sexual behavior of a genetic female as well as her anatomy. Dörner once injected an infant female rat with testosterone and deprived an infant male of his own testosterone by castration. When the rats reached maturity, Dörner (1974) placed them together and got the result shown in Figure 11-11. The female mounted the male and the pair went through an inverted sequence of sexual behavior.

In humans, too, early exposure to androgens can partially masculinize a girl's anatomy and increase the probability of eventual homosexual or bisexual behavior. However, as noted earlier, it is hard to know whether to attribute such behavior to direct effects on the brain or to the fact that other

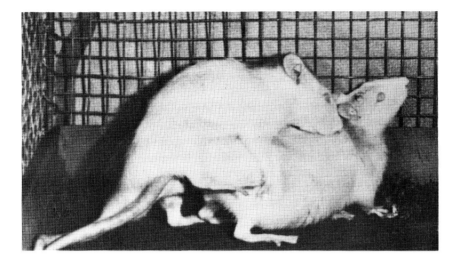

Figure 11-11. A female rat mounting a male. The female was injected with androgens during an early critical period; the male was castrated at birth and injected with androgens at adulthood. (From Dörner, 1974.)

people react differently to a relatively large, muscular woman than to other women. Furthermore, even if the effect does depend on the brain, we cannot conclude much about homosexual women in general. Prenatal exposure to androgens is so rare that it is not likely to account for many cases of female homosexuality.

OTHER ABNORMALITIES OF SEXUAL DEVELOPMENT

Certain individuals with a normal male XY chromosome pattern have the genital appearance of a female. This problem is known as **androgen insensitivity** or **testicular feminization**. Although such individuals produce normal amounts of androgens, their body lacks the mechanism that enables androgens to bind to genes in a cell's nucleus. Consequently, the androgens are without effect and the external genitals develop almost like those of a normal female. Two abnormalities appear at puberty: First, in spite of breast development and broadening of the hips, menstruation does not begin, because the body has two internal testes instead of ovaries and a uterus. (The vagina is short and leads to nothing.) Second, pubic hair does not develop, because pubic hair depends on androgens in females as well as males.

A woman with androgen insensitivity develops with a fully normal female gender identity. If her condition is medically identified, she is typically given surgery to lengthen the very short vagina and to remove the internal testes, because internal testes are likely to develop tumors and other health problems.

Abnormal sexual development can also result from abnormalities of the sex chromosomes. Normally, a female has two X chromosomes (XX pattern), while a male has an X and a Y (XY pattern). Occasionally, however, the chromosomes separate improperly during reproduction and a child is born with an abnormal chromosome pattern, such as XO, XXY, or XYY.

A female with **Turner's syndrome** has an XO chromosome pattern— one X chromosome and no other sex chromosome. Such females are sterile, short, and immature in appearance. Sometimes, but not always, they have webbed necks and receding chins. Although they do not undergo puberty spontaneously, they do respond to estrogen pills with breast development and other female secondary sexual characteristics. Their overall intelligence is normal, but they are apt to have specific disabilities with map reading and similar spatial orientation tasks (Alexander, Ehrhardt, & Money, 1966; Alexander, Walker, & Money, 1964; Steffen, Heinrich, & Kratzer, 1978). Their dreams are so deficient in visual imagery that they resemble those of blind people (Kerr, Foulkes, & Jurkovic, 1978).

A male with **Klinefelter's syndrome** has an XXY chromosome pattern (Nielsen, 1969). Most often, such a man has a small penis and testes, breast development during puberty, a high-pitched voice, obesity, and little beard growth. He is sterile and is likely to have little sex drive.

An XYY male is taller than average. Because several reports found more XYY males in prisons than in the rest of the population, it was speculated that the extra Y chromosome had made those men into "super-males"— extra-tall and extra-aggressive. Careful studies of XYY prisoners have revealed, however, that most had been convicted of nonviolent crimes, such as car theft, larceny, embezzlement, and reporting false alarms to the police; few had committed any violent crimes (Owen, 1972; Witkin et al., 1976). It is possible that the XYY male has an increased probability of imprisonment not because of high aggressiveness but because of low intelligence (Witkin et al., 1976). Low intelligence may predispose individuals to crime because of social factors, such as decreased employment opportunities. It may also increase the probability that someone who commits a crime gets caught.

PARENTAL BEHAVIOR

Sexual behavior has a way of leading to babies. Among mammals, a mother that has just given birth is subject to massive hormonal changes, and it is natural to expect that those hormonal changes may predispose her to maternal behavior.

This hypothesis is largely correct; hormones greatly facilitate at least the early stages of maternal behavior. During late pregnancy and just after giving birth, a mother has high levels of estrogen, progesterone, oxytocin, and prolactin. An injection of these hormones can induce maternal behavior even in a virgin female rat, although the behavior generally does not appear until a day or two after the injection (Bridges, DiBiase, Loundes, & Doherty, 1985; Lamb, 1975; Moltz, Lubin, Leon, & Numan, 1970; Pedersen, Ascher, Monroe, & Prange, 1982). Each hormone controls somewhat different aspects of the maternal behavior. For example, progesterone is important for nestbuilding in mice, while prolactin is important for retrieval of young (Zarrow, Gandelman, & Denenberg, 1971).

The hormones prepare a mother to respond to babies; once she has done so, she may be permanently changed. A female rat that has had even one and a half hours of experience of mothering her young responds in a maternal manner to other young even after a 25-day delay, which stops her from producing milk and returns her hormones to their normal state (Bridges, 1975).

Although hormones facilitate maternal behavior, they are not indispensable for it. If a female rat that has never been pregnant is left with some 5- to

10-day-old babies, her interest in them increases over several days. (Because the babies cannot survive without parental care and food, an experimenter must periodically replace them with new, healthy babies.) After about six days, the adoptive mother builds a nest, assembles the babies in the nest, licks them, and does everything else that a normal mother would, except nurse them. Ovarian hormones aid in this process, but they are not necessary. For example, female rats with or without intact ovaries respond maternally, although those with intact ovaries show more complete parental behavior (Mayer & Rosenblatt, 1979).

Even male rodents can be induced to parental behavior, although they never produce hormonal patterns resembling those of a new mother. Ordinarily, a male mouse kills babies. If he copulates with a female and stays with her during pregnancy, however, he accepts the young and helps to take care of them (Elwood, 1985). A male rat that is caged with infants by himself (with no adult female) gradually comes to show parental behavior toward the infants (Brown, 1986; Rosenblatt, 1967). In this regard his behavior is like that of a previously inexperienced female, except that the female shows a greater total amount of parental care.

In short, 5 to 10 days of exposure to infants can substitute for the hormonal changes that accompany pregnancy and delivery. Would this effect of exposure ever influence behavior in nature? After all, a baby that needed six days to induce an adult to take care of it would die before the adult got mobilized. Rosenblatt's (1970) answer is that maternal behavior goes through two stages. During the first few days after giving birth, hormones facilitate maternal behavior. After those first few days, the mother's familiarity with the young becomes a sufficient basis to maintain maternal care, with or without hormones. The advantage of this system is that maternal care lasts longer than the hormonal changes that accompany giving birth.

SUMMARY

1. Hormones can affect the activity of a neuron either by altering membrane receptors or by altering the expression of genes. (p. 295)

2. The hypothalamus controls activity of the pituitary gland by means of nerve impulses and releasing-hormones. The pituitary in turn disperses hormones that alter the activity of other hormone-producing glands. (p. 296)

3. The organizing effects of a hormone are effects exerted during an early critical period that bring about relatively permanent alterations in anatomy or in the potential for function. (p. 298)

4. In the absence of sex hormones, or with the addition of small amounts of estrogens, the gonads and hypothalamus of an infant mammal will differentiate like those of a female. In the presence of certain amounts of testosterone, the infant will develop as a male. (p. 300)

5. At least in rodents, and probably in primates also, testosterone is converted to estradiol within the cells, and it is estradiol that actually masculinizes the development of the hypothalamus. Estradiol in the blood does not masculinize development, either because it is bound to proteins in the blood or because it is metabolized. (p. 300)

6. Certain differences exist in the cerebral cortexes of males and females. These differences are due to the actions of estradiol, which inhibits the survival of the neurons it binds to, mostly in the right hemisphere. (p. 301)

7. Sex hormones have organizing effects on nonreproductive behaviors also, including play and aggressiveness. (p. 302)

8. Puberty begins when the hypothalamus begins to release bursts of luteinizing hormone releasing hormone. Factors that control the timing of that release are not yet understood. (p. 304)

9. In adulthood, current levels of sex hormones control the activation of sex behavior. Primates, especially humans, are less tightly controlled by their current hormone levels than most other mammalian species. (p. 305)

10. It is difficult to determine the role, if any, of prenatal hormones in the development of gender identity. (p. 309)

11. Pseudohermaphrodites are people who were subject to a hormonal pattern intermediate between male and female during their prenatal critical period for sexual development. (p. 310)

12. Although most pseudohermaphrodites accept their assigned sex, many are somewhat or greatly dissatisfied. (p. 312)

13. Certain adolescents develop a sexual appearance that does not match their sex of rearing. Observations of such individuals suggest that their sexual orientation may have been influenced, directly or indirectly, by prenatal hormones. (p. 314)

14. In male rats, procedures that prevent testosterone from masculinizing the brain during a prenatal period lead to an adult pattern of sexual responsiveness toward other male rats. The relationship of this finding to human homosexuality is still speculative. (p. 315)

15. Abnormal chromosome patterns, such as XO and XXY, lead to sterility and sometimes behavioral abnormalities. (p. 317)

16. Hormones released around the time of giving birth facilitate maternal behavior in female mammals. Nevertheless, mere prolonged exposure to young is also sufficient to induce parental behavior, even in males of certain species. (p. 318)

REVIEW QUESTIONS

1. What are the similarities and differences between hormones and synaptic transmitters? (p. 294)

2. What is the difference between the organizing and activating effects of a hormone? (p. 298)

3. What are the effects of testosterone in the early critical period on the development of the gonads and the hypothalamus? What are the effects of estradiol? (p. 300)

4. What are the effects of testosterone and estradiol on the early development of the cerebral cortex? Why is it possible for circulating estradiol to have greater effects on the cortex than on the hypothalamus? (p. 301)

5. Name some nonreproductive characteristics that are subject to long-term influences of prenatal sex hormones. (p. 302)

6. What hormonal change is associated with the onset of puberty? (p. 304)

7. What can be done for a child with precocious puberty? (p. 305)

8. What differences exist among mammalian species in their dependence on current hormone levels for sexual behavior? (p. 305)

9. What may cause a fetus to develop as a pseudohermaphrodite, or intersex? (p. 310)

10. Why are each of the observations on gender identity in pseudohermaphrodites scientifically inconclusive? (pp. 311–312)

11. What kind of evidence may be more decisive than observations of pseudohermaphrodites in evaluating the possible contribution of prenatal hormones to gender identity? (p. 312)

12. What event in early development can cause a male rat to develop sexual responsiveness to other males and not to females? Through what hormonal mechanism does this event probably work? (p. 315)

13. What is responsible for maternal behavior in the first few days after giving birth? What is responsible for parental behavior later? (p. 318)

THOUGHT QUESTIONS

1. What would happen to the release of thyroid-stimulating hormone from the pituitary after damage to the thyroid gland? What would happen to pituitary hormones after damage to the ovaries?

2. Occasionally a woman takes birth control pills (high in estrogen) after unknowingly becoming pregnant. Would the estrogen pose any threat to the normal sexual development of a male fetus? a female fetus? Explain.

3. The presence or absence of testosterone determines whether a mammal will differentiate as a male or a female; estrogens have no effect. In birds, the story is the opposite: The presence or absence of estrogen is critical (Adkins & Adler, 1972). What problems would determination by estrogen create if that were the mechanism for mammals? Why do those problems not arise in birds? (Hint: Think about the difference between live birth and hatching from an egg.)

4. On the average, pseudohermaphrodites have IQ scores in the 110–125 range, well above the mean for the population (Dalton, 1968; Ehrhardt & Money, 1967; Lewis, Money, & Epstein, 1968). One possible interpretation is that a hormonal pattern intermediate between male and female promotes great intellectual development. Another possibility is that pseudohermaphroditism may be more common in intelligent families than in less intelligent ones, or that the more intelligent families are more likely to bring their pseudohermaphroditic children to an investigator's attention. What kind of study would be best for deciding between these hypotheses? (For one answer, see Money & Lewis, 1966.)

TERMS TO REMEMBER

hormone (p. 294)
endocrine glands (p. 294)
peptide hormones (p. 295)
steroid hormones (p. 295)
estrogens (p. 295)
androgens (p. 295)
sex-limited genes (p. 295)
pituitary gland (p. 296)
anterior pituitary (p. 296)
posterior pituitary (p. 296)
releasing hormones (p. 296)
estradiol (p. 297)
ovum (p. 297)
progesterone (p. 297)
organizing effects (p. 298)
testosterone (p. 300)

alpha-fetoprotein (p. 300)
castration (p. 302)
puberty (p. 304)
activating effects (p. 305)
estrus (p. 305)
hysterectomy (p. 307)
gender identity (p. 309)
sex role (p. 309)
hermaphrodite (p. 310)
intersex (p. 311)
pseudohermaphrodite (p. 311)
androgen insensitivity (p. 317)
testicular feminization (p. 317)
Turner's syndrome (p. 317)
Klinefelter's syndrome (p. 318)

SUGGESTIONS FOR FURTHER READING

Adler, N. T. (Ed.) (1981). *Neuroendocrinology of reproduction*. New York: Plenum. Collection of review articles on many aspects of hormones and sexual behavior.

Money, J., & Ehrhardt, A. A. (1972). *Man & woman, boy & girl*. Baltimore: Johns Hopkins. Discusses roles of hormones and social environment in the development of human sexual behavior.

CHAPTER 12

Emotional Behavior

MAIN IDEAS

1. Emotional states are associated with activation of the autonomic nervous system.

2. Several psychosomatic illnesses can be traced to autonomic nervous system activity.

3. A set of forebrain structures known as the limbic system is important in emotional behaviors.

4. Aggressive behavior is associated with activity of the amygdala and with decreased turnover of serotonin.

5. Anxiety is associated with high levels of sympathetic nervous system arousal and high levels of norepinephrine activity; it can be inhibited by GABA synapses.

6. Pleasure is associated with activity of certain brain pathways in areas that are rich in catecholamines and with activity of endorphin synapses.

Y ou have just landed on the planet Zypton, which is inhabited by silicon-based animals that have very different body functions from Earth animals. Your task, as the only psychologist-astronaut on the mission, is to determine whether these animals have emotions. They have no recognizable facial expressions. In fact, they don't have faces. They also don't have hearts . . . or hormones. They do have behavior, however. What behavior would qualify as emotional?

The question is not whether the animals have experiences similar to how humans feel when they are sad, angry, and so on. You cannot know what it feels like to be one of those animals, if indeed they have any conscious experience at all. You are looking for behaviors that have certain features that can be designated as emotional. What are those features?

You are entitled to speculate on this question; psychologists have no widespread agreement on what they mean by *emotion*. Let me offer one possibility, however: Part of what we mean by emotion is *a temporary change in the intensity of behavior*, generally an increased intensity (Tomkins, 1980). A fearful individual moves away from the feared object with great intensity; an angry individual moves to attack something or someone with great intensity. Intensification may not be the whole story—for example, it is possible to feel happy or sad without doing anything at all—but at least it is a part of the story that is easy to deal with biologically.

EMOTION AND AUTONOMIC NERVOUS SYSTEM AROUSAL

The intensity of behavior is largely governed by the autonomic nervous system. The sympathetic nervous system prepares the body for intense, vigorous activity. The parasympathetic nervous system increases digestion and other processes associated with relaxation. Perhaps the strongest impetus for parasympathetic activity is removal of a stimulus that excited sympathetic activity. That is, when a stimulus for sympathetic activity is suddenly removed, a rebound overactivity of the parasympathetic system follows. Consequently, people sometimes faint just after escaping from something frightening. (At this point, you might wish to review the structure and function of the sympathetic and parasympathetic nervous systems, p. 84).

The *polygraph* test—the so-called "lie detector test"—is really a test of sympathetic nervous system arousal (see Figure 12-1): It measures heart rate, breathing rate, and electrical conduction of the skin (which is a measure of the slight sweating caused by sympathetic nerves to the skin). The theory behind the polygraph test is that people become nervous when they lie and that their nervousness is revealed in the response of their sympathetic nervous system.

Because lying is only loosely related to nervousness, the polygraph is not a highly reliable indicator of truthfulness. The polygraph is nevertheless an excellent indicator of nervousness, which is closely related to arousal of the sympathetic nervous system. Activity of the sympathetic nervous system

Figure 12-1. The polygraph test. (Courtesy of Raleigh, North Carolina, Police Department.)

leads to increased heart rate, sweating, adrenal secretions, and other preparations for vigorous activity.

Activity of the sympathetic nervous system is evoked not simply by a set of stimuli but by the individual's interpretation of those stimuli or reaction to them. (That is one reason why it is difficult to estimate someone's stress level just by counting stressful events.) In one study, a group of boys who were given a task and told it was a test reacted with increased heart rates. A second group given the same task but told it was a game reacted with decreased heart rates (Darley & Katz, 1973).

In another study, a group of people who received inescapable shocks, and who knew the shocks were inescapable, had decreased heart rates—a typical parasympathetic response to uncontrollable distress. (We might regard this as a different kind of "nervousness.") Another group, who were misled into believing that they might find some way to avoid the shocks, had faster heart rates (Malcuit, 1973). In other words, a given task or a given set of shocks could either increase or decrease sympathetic arousal, depending on what response people thought the situation called for.

The Role of the Autonomic Nervous System in Ulcers

Ulcers form when excess digestive secretions (a parasympathetic response) eat away at the lining of the stomach or duodenum. A connection between ulcers and strong emotions, such as those created by job stress, has long been noted. Because of the difficulties in studying ulcer formation in humans, experiments have been conducted on animals.

In a pioneering experiment, monkeys were exposed to work-related stress (Brady, Porter, Conrad, & Mason, 1958). Pairs of monkeys were confined to chairs, as shown in Figure 12-2. One foot of each monkey was attached to an electrode that delivered a shock every 20 seconds unless one of the monkeys, dubbed the *executive monkey* of the pair, pressed the lever in front of it. If the executive pressed the lever at least once every 20 seconds,

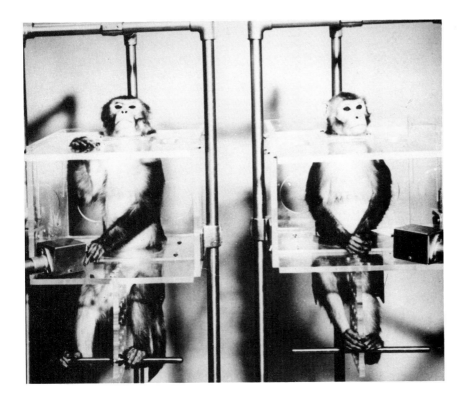

Figure 12-2. An "executive" monkey (left) and a "passive" monkey (right). When the executive presses the lever, it temporarily prevents electric shocks for both monkeys. Note the more relaxed bearing of the passive monkey. (From Brady et al., 1958.)

neither monkey received any shocks. But if it waited any longer, both monkeys would receive a shock and would continue receiving a shock every 20 seconds until the executive pressed the lever again. The second monkey, whom we shall call the *passive* monkey, had no control over the shocks. The procedure lasted 6 hours at a time, twice a day, seven days a week. Within an hour or two of the first session, each executive monkey had learned the response well and prevented the shocks almost completely from then on.

The result, as expected, was that the executive monkeys got ulcers and the passive monkeys did not. Why? Actually, because the experimental design was imperfect, the results are not easy to interpret. The monkeys were not randomly assigned to the executive and passive roles but rather were assigned on the basis of how well they learned the avoidance response. It may be the case that the animals that learn to respond rapidly are also the ones most likely to develop ulcers. Regardless of how seriously we take that flaw, the experiment does not fully explain why the executives got ulcers and the passives did not. The key factor might be the emotional strain, but it might just as easily be physical exertion. A second experiment sheds important light on the results of the first.

Foltz and Millett (1964) repeated the executive monkey experiment except that they used the same passive monkey with three different executives. After one executive had served for a few weeks, it was replaced by a second executive, which, being inexperienced in the apparatus, took a couple of hours to learn what to do. The passive monkey gyrated vigorously in its chair, screaming and gesturing wildly toward the new executive, until it started preventing the shocks consistently. Later, when a third (untrained) executive replaced the second one, the passive monkey went through the same routine, and soon developed a severe case of ulcers.

Evidently, the ulcers did not come from "being in charge" but from a state of high arousal, whatever its cause. An executive monkey gets ulcers because it has to work nonstop for 6 hours at a time; a passive monkey may get ulcers if it receives a number of uncontrollable shocks.

Similar experiments have been conducted on rats. Unlike the monkeys, the executive rats did not avoid the shocks consistently. The passive rats developed more ulcers than the executives, presumably because they could neither control the shocks nor predict their onset (Weiss, 1968, 1971a, 1971b). Note that the ulcers do not result from the shocks themselves but from the passive rats' lack of an adequate coping response.

Ulcers do not form during the stress periods themselves, while the animals are receiving shocks or pressing levers to avoid them, but during the rest periods afterward (Desiderato, MacKinnon, & Hissom, 1974). The shock period greatly activates the sympathetic nervous system; during the rest period, the parasympathetic system rebounds to a period of overactivity. Because of the overactive parasympathetic system, digestive juices are released in such excess that they damage the insides of the stomach and intestines, causing ulcers.

Given this explanation of ulcers, how could a person at high risk for developing ulcers, unable to prevent a stressful experience, avoid developing ulcers? One method would be to taper off gradually after a stressful experience, instead of slipping directly from high arousal into rest. Some light exercise might be helpful, for example. A second method would be to eat something to help absorb the excess digestive secretions.

Voodoo Death and Related Phenomena

Almost everyone knows of someone with a strong will to live who survived well beyond others' expectations or of someone who gave up and died of relatively minor ailments. The extreme case of the latter is *voodoo death*, in which a healthy person dies apparently just because he or she believes that some curse has destined death.

Such phenomena were generally ignored by scientists until Walter Cannon (1942) published a collection of reasonably well-documented reports of voodoo death. A typical example was a woman who ate a fruit and then was told that it had come from a taboo place. Within hours she was dead. The common pattern in such cases was that the intended victim knew about the magic spells and believed in them. In each case the hexed victim believed that he or she was sure to die soon. The friends and relatives believed the same thing and began to treat the victim as a dying person. The victim was overwhelmed with a feeling of hopelessness, refused food and water, and died usually within 24 to 48 hours. In some manner the terror and feeling of hopelessness led to death. (For more examples, see Cannon, 1942; Cappannari, Rau, Abram, & Buchanan, 1975; Wintrob, 1973.) Similar exam-

Curt P. Richter

Born in 1894, Curt Richter studied engineering in Germany, then returned to the United States to receive a bachelor's degree from Harvard and a Ph.D. in psychology from Johns Hopkins University under the supervision of John B. Watson. He remained at Johns Hopkins for his entire academic career. He published his first scientific article in 1919; he continued publishing well into the 1980s, writing over 300 articles on a wide variety of topics.

Richter directed his research toward discovering new phenomena rather than testing theories about well-known phenomena. In most of his studies he observed the spontaneous behavior of rats and other animals under relatively unconstrained conditions. Many times he was able to identify effects that neither he nor anyone else would have expected before the experiment began.

Richter pioneered the scientific study of spontaneous activity, biological rhythms, and food selection in animals. He made major contributions to the study of brain damage, endocrine disorders, rat extermination, skin resistance to electrical current in

humans, and the effects of domestication on animals. He made suggestions regarding biological predispositions to alcoholism and manic-depressive psychosis. His discovery of sudden death in rats is described in this chapter.

What would motivate someone to continue laboratory research, mostly by himself, well into his 80s? In Richter's case it is simply the joy of discovery. "I enjoy research more than eating," he once said.

A selection of Richter's articles is available in the collection *The Psychobiology of Curt Richter*, edited by E. M. Blass (1976).

---

ples occur in our own society—not that people die because they believe they are hexed, but people sometimes die quickly because they expect to.

What is the cause of death in such cases? Curt Richter (see BioSketch 12-1) accidentally stumbled on a possible answer while studying the swimming abilities of rats. Ordinarily, rats can swim in turbulent warm water nonstop for 48 hours or more. (See Figure 12-3.) However, Richter (1957a) found that a rat would die quickly if he cut off its whiskers just before throwing it into the tank. (A rat's whiskers are critical to its ability to find its way around.) The rat would swim frantically for a minute or so and then suddenly sink to the bottom, dead. Richter found that many, but not all, laboratory rats died quickly under these conditions. Wild rats, which are known to be more nervous and emotional than domesticated laboratory rats, *all* died quickly under the same conditions. According to the results of autopsies, the rats had not drowned; their hearts had simply stopped beating.

A rat is capable of swimming without its whiskers. If its whiskers are trimmed hours or days in advance, a rat can swim for hours. Evidently, the sudden death resulted from combining the dewhiskering operation with immersion into the water. That combination greatly stimulated the rat's sympathetic nervous system and greatly elevated its heart rate. After the rat swam frantically for a minute or so and found no escape, its parasympathetic system became highly activated, both as a rebound from the stong sympathetic activation and as the natural response to a terrifying, apparently inescapable situation. The parasympathetic response was so great that it stopped the rat's heart altogether.

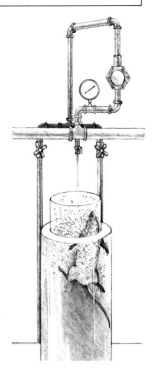

Figure 12-3. Rat swimming in turbulent-water tank. (From Richter, 1957a.)

To confirm the role of apparent escapability or inescapability, Richter performed an additional experiment. As before, he cut a rat's whiskers before putting it into the water. Before the rat sank, however, he rescued it and allowed it to revive on a safe, dry platform. Later, when he put it back into the water, it swam successfully for many hours. The rescue had apparently immunized the rat against extreme terror in this situation and therefore also immunized it against an extreme parasympathetic rebound. Richter's results suggest that voodoo death and perhaps many other cases of sudden death in a frightening situation may be due to excessive activity by the parasympathetic nervous system, either as a rebound effect or as a response to a frightening, hopeless situation.

The Autonomic Nervous System and Other Psychosomatic Illnesses

Most peoples' autonomic responsiveness is highly consistent over time. Those with a relatively high degree of sympathetic responsivity respond more rapidly to stimuli than most other people, though sometimes less accurately. They tend to show more emotional expression and more overall activity. They are more gregarious, more distractible, and less patient (Shields, 1983). In other words, reactivity of the sympathetic nervous system is related to much of what we call *personality*.

It is also related to vulnerability to other diseases besides ulcers. People with a high sympathetic response to stressors may be more vulnerable than others to heart disease (Krantz & Manuck, 1984). Stress, particularly uncontrollable stress, increases the growth of tumors in laboratory animals (Sklar & Anisman, 1981), and probably in humans as well. Although the route by which stress affects tumor growth is not certain, it probably does so by releasing high amounts of adrenal hormones (Axelrod & Reisine, 1984), which in turn weaken the response of the immune system. For example, during exam periods, medical students have a decrease in their blood levels of both interferons and natural killer cells, two active agents of the immune system (Glaser, Rice, Speicher, Stout, & Kiecolt-Glaser, 1986). The sympathetic nervous system can also affect the immune system directly by its innervation of the thymus gland, spleen, and lymph nodes.

Biofeedback: An Attempt to Control the Autonomic Nervous System

For a long time, psychologists assumed that it was impossible to exert direct, voluntary control over heart rate, intestinal contractions, and other processes controlled by the autonomic nervous system. People can, of course, control such processes indirectly—by exercising to increase heart rate, for example—but it remained doubtful that a person could control these processes while the skeletal muscles remain at rest.

In the early 1960s, Neal Miller, Leo DiCara, and others gave rewards to laboratory rats and rabbits for certain responses that are ordinarily considered involuntary. In a typical experiment, a device was implanted to measure and record the contractions of a rat's intestines. The experimenters then began rewarding certain rats for increases in intestinal contractions, others for decreases. Over the course of an hour or so, the rats gradually shifted their degree of intestinal contractions in the rewarded direction. Note that the reward served not only as a reinforcement but also as a kind of sensory feedback: The presence or absence of reward can indicate to an animal whether or not it has made the desired response. Miller (1969) and others reported that they had successfully trained animals in this manner to increase or decrease heart rate, intestinal contractions, production of urine by the kidneys, and so forth.

Later studies on animals failed to replicate the original results. In experiments on more than 2,500 rats, with varying procedures, rewards proved ineffective at altering autonomic responses (Dworkin & Miller, 1986). Perhaps the original results were in error; perhaps such findings occur only under limited circumstances. In either event, they are far from reliable.

In the meantime, however, before it became clear that the animal results were unreplicable, the original studies had inspired applications to humans. In a procedure known as **biofeedback**, people are given continuous information about an internal process that they are trying to control. For example, a person with high blood pressure sees a bright light or some other signal whenever blood pressure drops below some target level. The person attempts to keep the light on, by whatever means, for as long as possible. Biofeedback has certainly proved itself useful for a few applications, including retraining muscle use after a stroke. In the control of heart rate and blood pressure, however, the effects turn out to be too small and too temporary to be of any significant medical value (Blanchard & Young, 1973, 1974).

When people alter their heart rate and other responses during biofeedback, they do so in large part by changing the tension in their skeletal muscles. People can learn to control their responses to stress by progressively relaxing their skeletal muscles (McGuigan, 1984). As their muscles relax, their emotions become calmer, too.

GENERAL THEORIES OF EMOTION

Although we can agree that emotion is closely related to autonomic arousal, the nature of that relationship needs to be explored. Does an emotional experience cause autonomic arousal, or does the autonomic arousal cause an emotional experience? Or are emotion and autonomic arousal the same thing? Or might it be the case that they occur independently, even though they ordinarily occur at the same time?

The primary difficulty in addressing such questions is that emotional *experience* is an internal process observable only by the person who has it. In other words, the relationship between emotions and autonomic arousal is part of the overall mind-brain problem that we addressed back in Chapter 1. Any theories we suggest are necessarily hard to test.

The James-Lange Theory

The fact that theories are hard to test has not stopped psychologists from proposing them. The earliest theory of emotion was the **James-Lange theory**, proposed by William James and C. G. Lange independently in 1884. The James-Lange theory reverses the commonsense notion that emotions cause arousal and action. According to the James-Lange theory, arousal and action lead to emotion. Perhaps a better way of saying it is that emotion is a label we give to certain kinds of arousal and action. When I notice that I am running away, I decide that I must be afraid. When I notice that I am attacking, I conclude that I must be angry.

Although it is difficult to test the James-Lange directly, the theory does lead to at least two testable predictions: (1) The more intense one's arousal, the greater one's emotion. (2) If one can discern a difference between emotions, the emotions must be associated with different types of physiological arousal or overt action.

The first of these predictions is partly, but only partly, correct. Drugs and other treatments that enhance autonomic arousal also augment emotional behaviors and people's ratings of the intensity of their emotions. Spinal cord damage, which reduces people's perception of their autonomic arousal, also weakens emotions in many cases (Reisenzein, 1983). On the other hand, it is significant that emotions persist at all after spinal cord damage, and in many cases people claim that their emotions are still as strong as ever (Lowe & Carroll, 1985).

The second prediction is also only partly correct. Different emotions are associated with different physiological changes, but the differences are not large (Ekman, Levenson, & Friesen, 1983). For example, the electrical resistance of the skin declines more during sadness than during other emotions. Hand temperature increases more during anger than during other emotions. Heart rate increases more with fear and anger than with happiness. Although these differences are statistically reliable, they are neither large nor consistent or easy to perceive in oneself. It is doubtful that people determine whether they are happy, sad, or angry by observing their skin temperature, heart rate, or electrical resistance.

Schachter and Singer (1962) offered a theory similar to the James-Lange theory. According to their modification, people (and perhaps other animals, too) seek to understand the source of their autonomic arousal. Different people may experience a given state of arousal as fear, anger, or happiness depending on what they think caused the arousal. If they attribute the arousal to a pill they took, they may not experience the arousal as emotion at all. In other words, the autonomic arousal may largely determine the degree of emotion, but cognitive factors determine *which* emotion a person will feel.

[margin note: Cognitive arousal theory]

The Cannon-Bard Theory

Not all agree that autonomic arousal is indispensable to emotion. According to the **Cannon-Bard theory**, as proposed by Walter Cannon (1927) and modified by Philip Bard (1934), emotions and autonomic changes occur simultaneously but independently. That is, a pattern of sensory information may excite activity in both the autonomic nervous system and the cerebral cortex, so that a person could experience an emotion even if he or she received no sensations from the autonomic nervous system.

Which theory is correct, the James-Lange theory, a modification of it, the Cannon-Bard theory, or some other? This question is not a popular topic of current research. It is easier to deal with the biological factors that increase or decrease a given emotion—anxiety, for example—than to determine what anxiety itself really is. The general theories of emotion are nevertheless part of psychology's heritage, and some of the work researchers do on specific emotions may ultimately shed some light on the more general issues.

THE LIMBIC SYSTEM AND EMOTIONS

Emotional behavior depends largely on an area of the brain that we have come to know as the **limbic system,** composed of the hypothalamus, the amygdala, and several other cortical and subcortical structures (see Color Plates 5 and 6). In pioneering studies, Bard (1929, 1934) found that when he removed the entire cerebral cortex of cats, they displayed exaggerated aggressive behaviors and postures in response to a variety of stimuli. After a touch, a sharp air puff, or any other unpleasant stimulus, a cat would arch its back, erect its hair, growl, claw, and bite. The attacks were not well directed toward any target, however.

Bard referred to the attacks as **sham rage.** Sham rage can be elicited easily after damage to the entire cerebral cortex, most of the thalamus, and in fact all of the brain anterior to the hypothalamus. If the damage extends to the hypothalamus, however, no stimulus can evoke a full-blown attack. Bard concluded that the hypothalamus and other nearby structures are necessary for the expression of rage and that the cerebral cortex ordinarily serves the function of inhibiting, directing, and organizing the attacks.

Later, Delgado (1969a, 1969b) stimulated certain spots in the anterior and medial hypothalamus of cats. The cats hissed and growled, arched their backs, and bared their teeth, although, like Bard's cats, they did not direct their expression at any target. (See Figure 12-4.)

Later studies found that electrical stimulation in parts of a cat's hypothalamus or amygdala could elicit elements of attack. If the cortex and thalamus had been removed, the result was sham rage. If the entire brain was intact, however, the cat directed its attack toward a nearby rat or mouse. A blindfolded cat did not attack, however (Flynn, 1973; Flynn, Edwards, & Bandler, 1971). Apparently the thalamus and cortex integrate the emotional patterns of the hypothalamus with sensory information to produce emotional behavior.

In 1937, J. W. Papez (PAIPS) proposed that the hypothalamus and several other subcortical structures (see Figures 12-5 and 12-6) compose a circuit responsible for emotions. Papez based his theory partly on the fact that cells in much of the limbic system respond to taste, smell, and pain stimuli, all of which evoke strong emotional reactions. These three sensory modalities also have the properties of slow onset, slow offset, and vagueness about location—properties that characterize emotions as well.

Paul MacLean (1949, 1958, 1970) revived and revised Papez's theory on the basis of later evidence. MacLean gave Papez's circuit the name *limbic system.* (The term *limbic* comes from the Latin word *limbus,* meaning "border." The structures of the limbic system form a border around certain midline structures.) The limbic system has been fairly consistent throughout mammalian evolution. While great differences were emerging among species

Figure 12-4. Sham rage in a cat (not directed toward any object) evoked by radio stimulation of the medial hypothalamus. (From Delgado, 1981.)

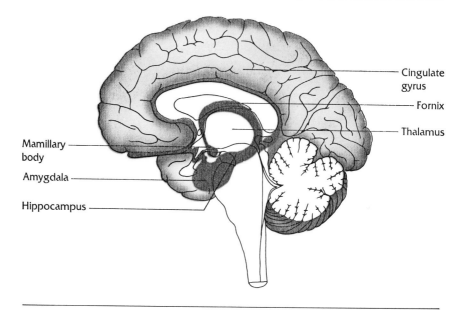

Figure 12-5. Sagittal section close to the midline of the human brain, showing some structures of the limbic system. Only a small part of the hippocampus is visible at the midline; most of it is located in the interior of each hemisphere. (Based on Smythies, 1970.)

Cingulate gyrus

Fornix

Thalamus

Mamillary body

Amygdala

Hippocampus

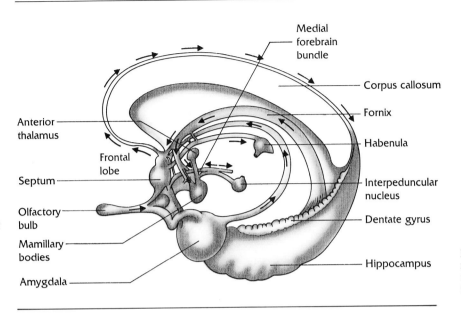

Figure 12-6. Some of the major pathways and connections of the limbic system. (Based on MacLean, 1949.)

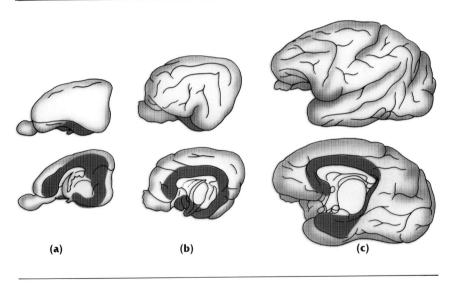

Figure 12-7. Brains of (**a**) a rabbit, (**b**) a cat, and (**c**) a monkey, showing both the lateral surface (top) and the medial surface (bottom). The limbic system (dark areas) shows less variation across mammalian species than does the cerebral cortex. (From MacLean, 1954.)

in the size of their cerebral cortex, the size of the limbic system stayed more nearly constant. (See Figure 12-7.)

According to MacLean, the strongest evidence for the role of the limbic system in emotion comes from observations of people with an epileptic focus or other abnormality in the temporal lobe or elsewhere in the limbic system. Although most people with temporal lobe epilepsy have no emotional experiences associated with their epileptic seizures, a substantial minority experience aggressive impulses, fear, a dissociation of experience similar to multiple personality (Schenk & Bear, 1981), uncontrollable laughter (Swash, 1972), sexual arousal (Rémillard et al., 1983), or a feeling of extreme blissful happiness including a sense of oneness with the universe and the Creator (Cirignotta, Todesco, & Lugaresi, 1980). The latter experience is named *Dostoyevskian epilepsy* after the Russian novelist who had this type of epilepsy.

Within the limbic system MacLean (1970) distinguished three circuits. One circuit, including the **amygdala** and the hippocampus, affects behaviors related to self-preservation. (*Amygdala* is the Latin word for "almond"; it got its name because it reminded some neuroanatomist of the shape of an almond.) Damage to various parts of the amygdala can make an animal excessively tame, unaggressive, and emotionally unresponsive (Zagrodzka & Fonberg, 1979; Aggleton & Passingham, 1981). Monkeys and cats with amygdala damage sometimes attempt to eat feces, burning matches, and other objects that they would ordinarily reject. High levels of activity in the amygdala or hippocampus are often associated with fear, even with panic.

A second circuit in the limbic system includes the cingulate gyrus of the cerebral cortex, the septum, and several other structures. (The septum is a fairly large structure in the rat brain but a much less imposing structure in humans.) This circuit seems to relate to pleasure, especially sexual enjoyment. Electrical or chemical stimulation in this region in rats often causes penile erection, self-grooming, and related behaviors.

A third system, according to MacLean, includes parts of the hypothalamus and anterior thalamus. Believed to be important for cooperative social behavior and certain aspects of sexuality, it is larger in primates than in most other mammalian species.

ANGER AND AGGRESSIVE BEHAVIOR

During World War II, almost every major nation was at war. In Germany, the Nazis under Hitler were exterminating the Jews. The United States was preparing a nuclear bomb, which it later dropped on two cities in Japan. In the midst of all this violence, Mohandas K. Gandhi, the world's foremost advocate of nonviolence, was in jail in a remote village in India for leading a protest march against British rule in that country. Gandhi was charged with "disturbing the peace." The irony of the situation was not lost on Gandhi. When asked what he thought of Western civilization, he replied, "It might be a good idea."

Although a certain level of aggressive behavior is normal and even helpful, human aggressive behavior often goes beyond that level. Every year, criminals, terrorists, and national armies kill untold numbers of people; an all-out nuclear war could end human civilization (if, unlike Gandhi, we are willing to consider ourselves civilized). Clearly, the investigation of aggressive behavior is of practical as well as theoretical importance.

The Function of Aggressive Behavior

Fighting among animals within a species is not a purposeless behavior and is not necessarily disadvantageous to the species as a whole. The usual basis for animal fighting is defense of territory or defense of one's young. For

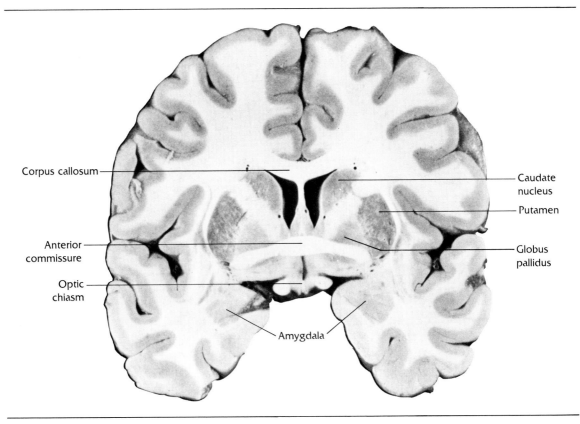

Corpus callosum

Caudate nucleus

Putamen

Anterior commissure

Globus pallidus

Optic chiasm

Amygdala

Figure 12-8. Coronal section through the human brain, showing the location of the amygdala. (Photo courtesy of Dr. Dana Copeland, Wake County Medical Center.)

example, early in the reproductive season pairs of birds stake out a territory in which they gather food and rear their young. The male will attack any other male of its own species that enters the territory, and it will attack especially vigorously if the intruder comes near the nest. Depending on the species, the female may or may not attack intruders. As with human sports, the home team usually wins. The winner drives the loser out of the territory, generally without inflicting much injury. The winner thereby gains complete control over the food supply in its area, removes potential competition for its mate, and avoids a high population density that might attract predators.

Attack can also be provoked, in humans as well as other species, by painful or otherwise unpleasant stimuli, including heat or foul odors (Berkowitz, 1983). Presumably, attack provoked by pain is similar to fighting in self-defense.

The Amygdala and Aggressive Behavior
The amygdala (Figure 12-8) is important for feeding, drinking, sexual behavior, and other behaviors. Here we focus on its role in aggressive behavior.

Nonhuman animals. Electrical stimulation of the amygdala can lead to vigorous attacks on other individuals or (less often) to an inhibition of attack. Damage to the amygdala usually leads to tameness and placidity,

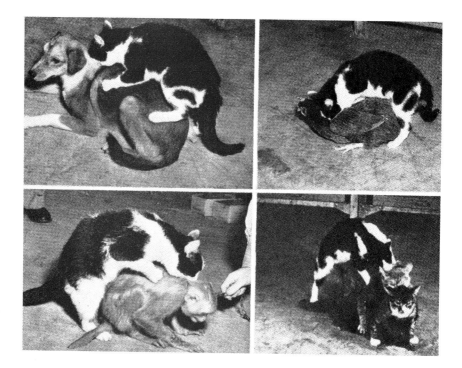

Figure 12-9. Male cats with lesions of the amygdala and surrounding areas sexually mounting a dog (upper left), a hen (upper right), and a monkey (lower left). In the lower right, four male cats with amygdala lesions are simultaneously mounting each other. (From Schreiner & Kling, 1953.)

although damage in certain nuclei of the amygdala can enhance aggression. Animals with an epileptic focus in the amygdala generally have an increase in aggressive behavior (Pinel, Treit, & Rovner, 1977). **Rabies**, a disease caused by a virus that attacks much of the brain but especially the temporal lobe (including the amygdala), leads to furious, violent behavior (Lentz, Burrage, Smith, Crick, & Tigor, 1981). (*Rabies* is the Latin term for "rage.")

The effect of damage to the amygdala is not, however, simply a matter of constantly causing or preventing a certain emotion. It is more a matter of changing how animals interpret information. For example, male cats with amygdala lesions may sexually mount other males, members of other species, or even inanimate objects (Schreiner & Kling, 1953). (See Figure 12-9.) They are not hypersexual in the sense of having an increase in total sexual activity; they merely become indiscriminate in their selection of partners (Aronson & Cooper, 1979). Similarly, certain monkeys with amygdala lesions have trouble interpreting social stimuli from other monkeys; because of their misinterpretations, they may attack inappropriately or fail to defend themselves when attacked.

Rosvold, Mirsky, and Pribram (1954) made an amygdala lesion in the most dominant and aggressive monkey of a group of eight. After the lesion, it quickly sank to the lowest status in the dominance hierarchy. Then they made a lesion in the amygdala of the most dominant remaining monkey, who quickly fell to seventh place. When they then made a lesion in the third monkey, however, it did not drop significantly in status or in aggressive behavior. One possible explanation was that the lesions had invaded slightly different parts of the brain in the three monkeys. Another possibility was that the effect of the lesions was modified by the social environment. The first two monkeys returned to an environment with aggressive competitors, the third, to one without aggressive competitors. It may have been harder for the first two monkeys to maintain aggressive behavior, in the face of clear competitors, than for the third. Figure 12-10 shows the monkeys' dominance hierarchies before and after the three lesions.

Humans.   Irritation of the temporal lobe can provoke violent behavior in humans as well as other species. About 10 percent of people with temporal lobe epilepsy have occasional outbursts of unprovoked violent behavior (Bear & Fedio, 1977; Goldstein, 1974; Pincus, 1980). (An epileptic attack occurs when a large group of neurons suddenly produce synchronous action potentials. Depending on the location of the epileptic focus—the place where the attack originates—the symptoms can range from uncontrollable flailing of the arms and legs to merely a brief loss of consciousness. When the focus is in the temporal lobe, the result is hallucinations, lip smacking or other repetitive acts, and in certain cases emotional behaviors.)

Here is an example of a patient with temporal lobe epilepsy that led to sudden outbursts of unprovoked violent behavior (Mark & Ervin, 1970):

> Thomas was a 34-year-old engineer, who, at the age of 20, had suffered a ruptured peptic ulcer. He was in a coma for 3 days, which caused some brain damage. Although his intelligence and creativity were unimpaired, there were some serious changes in his behavior, including outbursts of violent rage, sometimes against strangers and sometimes against people he knew. Sometimes his episodes began when he was talking to his wife. He would then interpret something she said as an insult, throw her against the wall and attack her brutally for 5 to 6 minutes. After one of these attacks he would go to sleep for a half hour and wake up feeling refreshed.
>
> Eventually he was taken to a hospital, where epileptic activity was found in the temporal lobes of his cerebral cortex. For the next seven months, he was given a combination of tranquilizers, antiepileptic drugs, and other medications. None of these treatments reduced his violent behavior. He had previously been treated by psychiatrists for 7 years without apparent effect. Eventually he agreed to a surgical operation to destroy a small part of the amygdala on both sides of the brain. Afterwards he had no more episodes of rage.

Excessive violent behavior is not, of course, necessarily associated with brain abnormalities. Because it is *sometimes* associated with brain abnormalities, however, certain medical therapies have been introduced on an experimental basis. Maletzky (1973) studied twenty-two men with a history of three or four unprovoked violent attacks per month. (Five had committed murder.) All had been treated with psychotherapy and tranquilizers for years, without benefit. (In fact, the tranquilizers had increased the violent behavior of several.) Maletzky gave each of them daily doses of Dilantin, a common antiepileptic drug. Although only fourteen of the twenty-two showed EEG abnormalities suggesting epilepsy, nineteen showed a clear decrease in violent behavior while taking Dilantin. Other investigators have

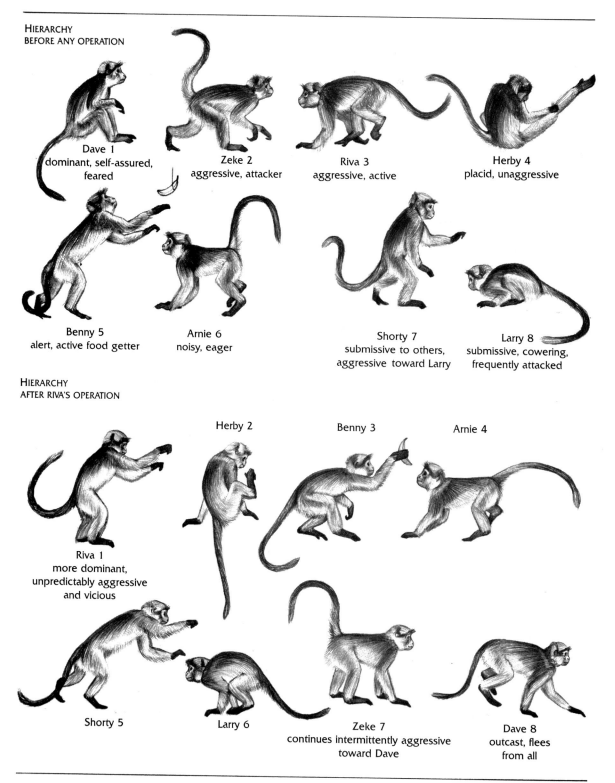

HIERARCHY
BEFORE ANY OPERATION

Dave 1
dominant, self-assured,
feared

Zeke 2
aggressive, attacker

Riva 3
aggressive, active

Herby 4
placid, unaggressive

Benny 5
alert, active food getter

Arnie 6
noisy, eager

Shorty 7
submissive to others,
aggressive toward Larry

Larry 8
submissive, cowering,
frequently attacked

HIERARCHY
AFTER RIVA'S OPERATION

Herby 2

Benny 3

Arnie 4

Riva 1
more dominant,
unpredictably aggressive
and vicious

Shorty 5

Larry 6

Zeke 7
continues intermittently aggressive
toward Dave

Dave 8
outcast, flees
from all

also reported that antiepileptic drugs decrease violent behavior in certain people (Stephens & Shaffer, 1973; Tunks & Dermer, 1977; Neziroglu, 1979).

In cases in which people with a history of unprovoked violence have failed to respond to antiepileptic drugs, a few surgeons have resorted to surgical destruction of parts of the amygdala or other brain areas (Balasubramaniam & Kanaka, 1976; Mark & Ervin, 1970; Narabayashi, 1972). They have reported success in reducing or eliminating the violent outbursts, with only occasional unwelcome side effects, including overeating or diabetes. It is not clear, however, that such patients have been tested very carefully for possible side effects.

Is brain surgery justifiable when the goal is only to change behavior? Such surgery, known as **psychosurgery**, has a history dating back to lobotomies that hardly inspires confidence. Opponents of psychosurgery charge that because it is conducted to protect society, not to help the patient, it could easily be abused. Defenders of psychosurgery reply that when that person is a danger to others, the only decision is whether the freedom is to be limited by the medical profession or the legal profession. At present, all forms of psychosurgery, including amygdala surgery for violent behavior, are performed only rarely. The controversy is likely to be with us for some time, however.

Serotonin Synapses and Aggressive Behavior

Although it is unlikely that aggressive behavior, or any other behavior, is controlled by just one synaptic transmitter system, several lines of evidence point to serotonin as a transmitter of particular importance in aggressive behavior. The main conclusion is that decreased release of serotonin is associated with an increase in aggressive behavior.

Nonhuman Animals. One part of the evidence for this conclusion comes from the work of Luigi Valzelli. (See BioSketch 12-2.) Valzelli found that four weeks of social isolation induces male mice of certain genetic strains, but not others, to attack other male mice (Valzelli, 1973). If the isolation induces aggressive behavior in a strain, it also induces a decrease in serotonin turnover in the brain. That is, although the brain may have a normal amount of serotonin, it fails to release it and synthesize new serotonin to take its place. Turnover can be inferred from the concentration of **5-HIAA**, a serotonin metabolite, in the blood or urine. Across strains of mice, the greater the decrease in serotonin turnover, the greater the increase in aggression by the male mice (Valzelli & Bernasconi, 1979). Female mice do not become aggressive in any genetic strain, nor do they show a decrease in serotonin turnover.

Similar results occur in rats. After male rats are socially isolated and then put with mice, rats that show a decrease in serotonin turnover attack and kill the mice. Certain other rats show an increase in serotonin turnover; they become friendly and almost motherly toward the mice (Valzelli & Garattini, 1972).

Consistent with these results, drugs that inhibit the release of serotonin increase aggressive behavior in animals. The drug **PCPA** (para-chloro-phe-

Figure 12-10. (opposite page) The dominance hierarchy for eight male monkeys before brain operations (top) and after amygdala lesions were made first in Dave, second in Zeke, and third in Riva (bottom). (From Rosvold, Mirsky, & Pribram, 1954.)

Luigi Valzelli

During the 1950s and 1960s, when scientific research careers were extremely rare in Italy, and when drug research throughout the world dealt mostly with biochemistry and medical uses, Luigi Valzelli became an Italian scientist specializing in the effects of drugs on behavior. Having received an M.D. degree from the University of Milan, he helped to establish a private research institute, where he has conducted a long series of careful experiments. He is the author of hundreds of scientific publications in four languages.

Although his publications deal with many topics, one theme stands out: The effects of a drug vary from individual to individual in predictable ways. For example, certain male mice become very aggressive after a month of social isolation, while other mice do not. The aggressive mice react differently from the others to amphetamine, caffeine, antidepressants, and other drugs. Similarly in humans, he suggests, it is likely that the effects of a drug depend on people's behavior and personality in regular and predictable ways.

Valzelli's motivations for research range from the greater understanding of brain chemistry to the control of human violent behavior to more philosophical goals. He describes one of his main motivations as "the exploration of the borders between the self and the body and the hope to understand even a little bit of such a mysterious boundary." He goes on to say, "I am also convinced that psychology and psychiatry may both be assumed at the key of understanding history, philosophy, and the evolution of man . . . perhaps the 'essence' of man."

nylalanine) blocks the synthesis of serotonin. After receiving an injection of PCPA that cuts their serotonin production in half, male and sometimes even female rats will attack and kill mice (Valzelli, Bernasconi, & Garattini, 1981). Once the aggressive behavior begins, it may continue even after the serotonin levels return to normal (Valzelli, Bernasconi, & Dalessandro, 1983).

Testosterone, amphetamine, benzodiazepines, and cannabinols (the active agents in marijuana) all increase the probability of violent behavior in animals. Although they work through partly different routes, these drugs have one point in common (Essman & Essman, 1986): All four decrease the turnover of serotonin in the brain. Further, their effects are magnified by phenylalanine, which also decreases the production of serotonin.

Finally, diets low in tryptophan, a precursor to serotonin, increase aggressive behavior in animals. Administration of tryptophan or closely related chemicals decreases aggression (Broderick & Bridger, 1984).

Humans.   In humans as in rats, amphetamine lowers serotonin turnover and increases violent behavior. Several medical conditions, including Gilles de la Tourette's syndrome, are associated with low serotonin and high levels of aggressive behaviors (Valzelli, 1981a).

It is possible that diet may affect violent behavior in humans as well as animals. According to Mawson and Jacobs (1978), the murder rate is highest in those countries that consume the greatest amounts of corn. Corn contains very low amounts of tryptophan, the precursor to serotonin. That is, eating a lot of corn decreases serotonin synthesis (Lytle, Messing, Fisher, & Phebus,

1975). Needless to say, the relationship between corn in the diet and the murder rate could be explained in many other ways, including a relationship to poverty. This point certainly calls for thorough investigation before we draw any conclusions. In the meantime, it may be prudent for people with a history of violent behavior to be cautious about eating a great deal of corn or other foods low in tryptophan. Similar caution might be advisable about foods high in phenylalanine (such as NutraSweet), since phenylalanine competes with tryptophan for entry into the brain.

A number of studies have found that people with a history of violent behavior tend to have lower than normal serotonin turnover (Brown, Goodwin, Ballenger, Goyer, & Major, 1979; Yaryura-Tobias & Neziroglu, 1981). Serotonin turnover is significantly depressed in people who attempt suicide by violent means. Such people have low levels of 5-HIAA in their blood and urine, suggesting decreased release of serotonin (Brown, Ebert et al., 1982; Edman, Åsberg, Levander, & Schalling, 1986). They also have an *increase* in the number of serotonin receptors in the cerebral cortex; the increase in receptors is believed to be the brain's compensation for the decrease in serotonin release (Mann, Stanley, McBride, & McEwen, 1986).

Although we are still far from understanding how a decrease in serotonin release may lead to increased violent behavior, we may be able to make practical use of this relationship even now. Träskman, Åsberg, Bertilsson, & Sjöstrand (1981) examined 119 psychiatric patients in a mental hospital; of those with below-average serotonin turnover levels, 20 percent committed suicide within the following year. Perhaps a blood test may be developed to identify those mental patients or other people most at risk for attempting suicide; if so, they might be monitored especially carefully or given other types of treatment to prevent suicide.

FEAR AND ANXIETY

Fear and anxiety feel much the same. We distinguish between them on the basis of when they occur. Fear occurs in a limited situation, such as being out in a small boat in a hurricane. One can escape the fear by escaping the situation. Anxiety is a more long-lasting state that one cannot escape easily. For example, one can have anxiety about the future, anxiety about interactions with other people, or general "free-floating anxiety" that is not tied to any identifiable stimulus.

Fear serves a useful function; it steers us away from dangers. Mild anxiety may promote cautiousness. But beyond a certain point, anxiety ceases to serve a useful function and begins to interfere with normal activity. A great deal of clinical psychology is devoted to the reduction of anxiety.

Anxiety and fear probably share a similar physiological basis. Much progress has been made toward understanding that basis, partly from the study of drugs that decrease anxiety and partly from the study of people with an abnormal degree of anxiety.

Anxiety-Reducing Drugs

Decades ago, **barbiturates** were the drugs most widely used to combat anxiety. Although barbiturates are effective in reducing anxiety, they have two

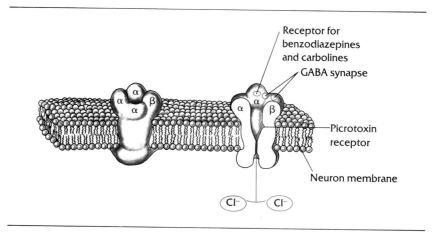

Figure 12-11. The GABA_A receptor complex. (Based on Guidotti et al., 1986.)

significant drawbacks: They are habit forming, and it is fairly easy to kill oneself with an overdose—either intentionally or accidentally—especially if they are combined with alcohol.

Another class of drugs, **benzodiazepines**, (BEN-zo-die-AZ-uh-peens), are currently much more widely used than barbiturates. Although benzodiazepines can be habit forming, too, they are less so than barbiturates. Moreover, a large dose is less likely to be fatal. Benzodiazepines such as diazepam (trade name Valium), chlordiazepoxide (Librium), and alprazolam (Xanax) are among the most widely used prescription drugs in the United States (Frazer & Winokur, 1977; Tallman, Paul, Skolnick, & Gallager, 1980). Benzodiazepines relieve anxiety, relax the muscles, induce sleep, and decrease the likelihood of convulsions. They are therefore used not only as tranquilizers but also as sleeping pills and as antiepileptic drugs.

How do they work? The simplest answer is that they facilitate transmission at GABA_A synapses. The brain has at least two kinds of receptors for the synaptic transmitter GABA: GABA_A and GABA_B receptors; benzodiazepines act only at the GABA_A sites. GABA is an inhibitory synaptic transmitter that apparently decreases anxiety, among other effects. When benzodiazepines facilitate GABA, they help to decrease anxiety.

That, however, is just the simplest answer. The GABA_A receptor is such a complicated assembly that it is no longer referred to simply as a receptor but as the **GABA_A receptor complex**, as shown in Figure 12-11. The heart of the GABA_A receptor complex is a chloride channel. When it is open, it permits chloride ions (Cl⁻) to cross the membrane into the neuron, hyperpolarizing the cell. (That is, the synapse is an inhibitory one.) Surrounding the chloride channel are four units, each of which contains one or more sites sensitive to GABA. Three of those four units also contain a benzodiazepine receptor. When a benzodiazepine molecule attaches to that receptor, even though it has no effect by itself on the chloride channel, it facilitates the GABA receptor. Exactly how it does so, we do not know; presumably it alters the shape of the receptor so that the GABA attaches more easily or binds more tightly (Macdonald, Weddle, & Gross, 1986). The net result is an increased flow of chloride ions across the membrane.

The GABA$_A$ receptor complex has at least two additional binding sites. One of those sites is actually inside the chloride channel itself. Certain drugs such as *picrotoxin* are capable of binding to that site; when they do so, they block the passage of chloride ions, regardless of what the GABA or benzodiazepine molecules are doing. The other binding site (not shown in Figure 12-11) is sensitive to barbiturates and to the metabolites of certain hormones (Majewska, Harrison, Schwartz, Barker, & Paul, 1986). Like the benzodiazepine receptor, the barbiturate receptor facilitates the binding of GABA to its own receptor.

Alcohol, a relaxant, also facilitates the binding of GABA and thereby facilitates the flow of chloride ions across the membrane. (See Digression 12-1.) Caffeine, which makes many people feel nervous, displaces benzodiazepines from their receptor and thereby impairs the flow of chloride (Dunwiddie, 1985).

When we talk about the "benzodiazepine receptor," we do not imply that benzodiazepines are the only chemicals that bind to it. Benzodiazepines are artificial substances; evolution developed these receptors long before chemists developed benzodiazepines. As we might expect, these receptors are sensitive to some chemicals naturally produced by the brain. One family of such chemicals is the **carbolines**. Several carbolines found in mammalian brains bind to the same receptors as benzodiazepines. Certain carbolines excite those receptors; others inhibit them. In addition, a brain protein known as **diazepam-binding inhibitor** (**DBI**) acts the opposite of diazepam and other benzodiazepines (Guidotti, Forchetti et al., 1983).

Diazepam-binding inhibitor and the carbolines function in nature to modify the sensitivity of the GABA synapse. We do not know yet what causes various of these chemicals to be present in different amounts at different times. We do know, though, that when certain carbolines activate their receptor the same way benzodiazepines do, anxiety decreases. When other carbolines or DBI affect the receptor in the opposite way, anxiety increases (Crawley et al., 1985; Insel, Ninan et al., 1984; Jensen, Petersen, Honoré, & Drejer, 1986).

The GABA$_A$ receptor complex is the first known case in which the sensitivity to a synaptic transmitter is modifiable by other chemicals, which attach to receptors adjacent to the primary receptor. Perhaps similar interactions will later be found at other synapses.

Panic Disorder

We may be able to learn more about the physiology of anxiety by studying clinical conditions associated with excess anxiety. One such condition is obsessive-compulsive disorder. (See Digression 12-2.) Another is **panic disorder**, a fairly common psychological disorder that afflicts about 1 percent of all adults (Robins et al., 1984). A person with panic disorder suffers occasional attacks of extreme fear, breathlessness, heart palpitations, fatigue, and dizziness.

Why do certain people and not others develop panic disorder? One possibility is that people prone to panic attacks have too much DBI or too much of the carbolines that impair GABA transmission. No direct evidence

12-1

The Relationship Between Alcohol and Tranquilizers

Ethyl alcohol (the kind of alcohol that people drink) has behavioral effects similar to those of benzodiazepine tranquilizers. It decreases anxiety and decreases the effects of punishment. Moreover, a combination of alcohol and tranquilizers produces a greater depression of body activities and brain functioning than either drug alone would. (A combination of alcohol and tranquilizers can be fatal.) Furthermore, alcohol, benzodiazepines, and barbiturates all exhibit the phenomenon of **cross-tolerance**: An individual who has used one of the drugs enough to develop a tolerance to it will show a partial tolerance to other depressant drugs as well.

We now know the reason behind these relationships: Alcohol promotes the flow of chloride ions through the $GABA_A$ receptor complex, just as tranquilizers do (Sudzak et al., 1986). Exactly how alcohol promotes the chloride flow is not known, although it is unlikely that alcohol directly attaches to any of the receptor sites. A more likely hypothesis is that alcohol alters the membrane structure around the GABA and benzodiazepine binding sites in some manner that makes their binding more effective.

Although this is not the only way that alcohol affects the brain, it is apparently the way in which alcohol exerts both its antianxiety effects and its intoxicating effects. Drugs that block the effects of alcohol on the $GABA_A$ receptor complex also block most of alcohol's effects on behavior. One particular experimental drug, known only as Ro15-4513, is particularly effective in this regard (Sudzak et al., 1986).

The company that discovered that drug, Hoffman-LaRoche, deliberated long and hard on whether it might have any medical value (Kolata, 1986). The drug is highly successful at sobering up animals that have been given large doses of alcohol (see photo); perhaps it could be used to help drunken humans sober up, too. Or perhaps it could be used in some way to help people who want to give up alcohol.

Eventually Hoffman-LaRoche decided the drug was likely to do more harm than good and should not be marketed. It would be risky to market a "sobering-up pill" for people to take after overindulging at a party; the pill might encourage drunkenness as well as driving after drinking, in a condition that might or might not be safe. Furthermore, alcoholics drink to get drunk; a pill that decreased their feeling of intoxication would probably lead them to drink even greater amounts, thus damaging their liver and other organs. (Ro15-4513 cancels the effects of alcohol on the brain but not on the rest of the body.)

Perhaps someone will find a practical use for this drug some day. For the time being, however, it is used only in experimental laboratories.

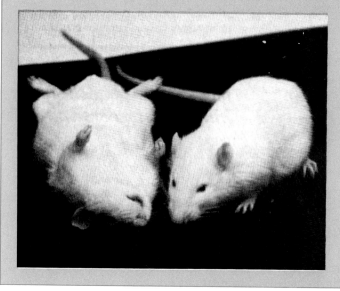

Two rats that were given the same amount of alcohol. The one on the right was later given the experimental drug Ro 15-4513, which sobered it up within 2 minutes. (Photo courtesy of Jules Asher.)

Although **obsessive-compulsive disorder** is uncommon in its full-blown form that requires the care of a mental health professional, it is more widespread in milder forms. *Obsessions* are nagging, intrusive thoughts. *Compulsions* are urges to perform repetitive acts such as hand washing or endlessly double-checking of everything one does (Pollak, 1979).

Although the causes of obsessive-compulsive disorder are not known in any detail, several facts point to a biological predisposition of some sort (Turner, Beidel, & Nathan, 1985). The disorder runs in families and is more common among people with type A blood—for reasons unknown. It also tends to run in the same families as Gilles de la Tourette's syndrome, which may be a different expression of the same underlying problem (Pauls, Towbin, Leckman, Zahner, & Cohen, 1986).

According to EEG measures, obsessive-compulsive people have excessive excitation in the temporal lobe, including the amygdala. They also have a number of sleep abnormalities, including frequent awakenings, a shortage of stage 4 sleep, and fewer rapid eye movements than normal during the REM periods of sleep (Insel, Gillin et al., 1982). Some with the disorder show signs of frontal lobe impairments (Behar et al., 1984).

Obsessive-compulsive disorder is generally treated with behavior modification or other forms of psychotherapy. In many cases it also responds well to a drug known as clomipramine, also known as chlorimipramine (Flament et al., 1985; Yaryura-Tobias, 1977). Clomipramine is a potent inhibitor of serotonin reuptake by the presynaptic neuron; that is, clomipramine prolongs the effects of serotonin at the synapse. That may not be the full explanation for its therapeutic success, however; certain other drugs that also block reuptake of serotonin have less clinical effectiveness.

is yet available on this point, although we do have indirect evidence from studies of depressed people (Barbaccia et al., 1986) and emotionally overresponsive rodents (Valzelli, 1981b). So far, all we can say is that the hypothesis is plausible.

A second possibility is that many people prone to panic disorder have excessive activity in the right hippocampal area (Reiman et al., 1986) and an overresponsive sympathetic nervous system. Such people have higher than normal heart rate and elevated levels of epinephrine (adrenalin) in their blood. Moreover, they respond to even moderate amounts of exercise with excessive autonomic arousal (Liebowitz et al., 1985; Nesse, Cameron, Curtis, McCann, & Huber-Smith, 1984). They show signs of having chronically high levels of norepinephrine, both at the synapses in the brain and circulating in the blood.

An excess of norepinephrine activity in the brain leads to a state of arousal and anxiety. Several drugs that increase the release of norepinephrine at synapses can produce anxiety even in normal people. The same doses produce even greater release of norepinephrine, and even greater anxiety, in people susceptible to panic attacks (Charney & Heninger, 1986; Charney, Heninger, & Breier, 1984).

Why do panic attack victims apparently have such high levels of norepinephrine activity? Part of the answer may have to do with physical fitness. A person in poor physical condition has shortness of breath and rapid heart rate after moderate exercise or even after a stressful emotional experience (Hull, Young, & Zeigler, 1984). Similarly, mild stress or mildly strenuous activity, which would cause only a little autonomic arousal in most people, may trigger a panic attack in susceptible people. To avoid such attacks, many people with panic disorder refrain from exercise, thus impairing their physical fitness even further.

Once people have had a few panic attacks, they start worrying about the panic attacks themselves. They actually develop anxiety about anxiety. Many of them deal with this anxiety by **hyperventilating** (breathing more often or more deeply than they need to). The chronic hyperventilation lowers the levels of carbon dioxide and phosphates in their blood, which in turn causes their bodies to respond strongly to a sudden increase in carbon dioxide (Gorman et al., 1986; Woods et al., 1986). In other words, many people with panic disorder aggravate their own problems by worrying about them and hyperventilating in response to the worry.

Several types of therapy are common for panic disorder. First, many people with panic disorder take tranquilizers. Not only are the tranquilizers effective in reducing anxiety, but having them available "just in case" provides reassurance. Second, psychotherapy is helpful, particularly in helping panic attack sufferers to break the cycle of panic attacks leading to worry and hyperventilation that in turn lead to still greater panic attacks. Third, a controlled plan of exercise may lead to improved body condition and thereby lessen the autonomic response to mild stressors (Ledwidge, 1980).

What do we learn about anxiety in general from studying victims of panic disorder? We learn that many of the symptoms of anxiety are due to autonomic arousal; also that anxiety is related to increased norepinephrine activity as well as decreased GABA activity. These two transmitters are presumably not independent; it could be, for example, that GABA inhibits the effects of norepinephrine synapses.

PLEASURE AND REINFORCEMENT

So far in this chapter we have discussed aggressive behavior and anxiety. It is now time to deal with more pleasant emotions.

Electrical Stimulation of the Brain and Pleasure in Nonhuman Animals

The brain mechanisms of pleasure and reinforcement were discovered by accident. Two young scientists, James Olds and Peter Milner (1954), were investigating whether rats would respond to electrical stimulation of the brain as a punishment. To their surprise, a rat that had been stimulated in certain areas would sit up, look around, and sniff. In an inspired guess, Olds supposed that the rat had enjoyed the stimulation and was "looking around for more." Olds and Milner then set up a lever that a rat could press to deliver electrical stimulation to its own brain. Rats pressed the lever to stimulate certain parts of their limbic system as often as 2,000 times per hour—in certain cases, hour after hour until the rat collapsed from exhaustion (Olds, 1958a). In similar experiments, monkeys pressed a lever as often as 8,000 times per hour (Olds, 1962). Follow-up experiments indicated that the electricity was not simply stimulating involuntary movements; all indications were that the animals regarded the stimulation as pleasant and that they worked for it in much the same way that they might work for food or other natural reinforcers. Animals will press levers to stimulate areas that extend over about one-third of the brain, certain areas much more vigorously than others. They will also work to turn off stimulation in about 5 percent of the brain.

A note on terminology: Many psychologists object to the use of such terms as *pleasure* when talking about animals, because such terms refer to private experiences that cannot be observed by the investigator. Technically, the most we can say is this: The animal is acting as we might expect it to act if it were undergoing an experience that, if we had it, we would describe by the term *pleasure*. Although this chapter will use the term *pleasure* for sake of convenience, you should bear in mind that we do not know what the animal is experiencing.

Why is electrical stimulation of the brain pleasant or reinforcing? Presumably the stimulation taps into circuits responsible for eating, sexual behaviors, and other pleasant activities. Depending on the location of the electrode and the intensity of the stimulation, the animal may experience even more intense pleasant sensations than it would with normal activities. In one experiment, rats in a T-maze could choose food by turning one direction or choose electrical stimulation of part of the limbic system by turning the other direction (Spies, 1965). Rats chose the brain stimulation on more than 80 percent of their trials, even though they had been kept on a near-starvation diet for 10 days. In another experiment, rats selected brain stimulation in preference to water and avoidance of shock to the feet (Valenstein & Beer, 1962). Still more impressive, four mother rats abandoned and ignored their newborn pups in order to press a lever for brain stimulation (Sonderegger, 1970). Ordinarily, a mother rat will stick with her young at all costs.

Electrical Stimulation of the Brain and Pleasure in Humans

Because the brain contains no pain receptors as such—in fact, no touch receptors of any kind—it is possible to conduct brain surgery in an awake patient after anesthetizing only the scalp. In certain cases it is desirable to do so, as we saw in Chapter 4. Furthermore, during the 1960s a few surgeons experimented with electrical stimulation of the human brain as a possible therapy for depression or severe pain.

From such medical studies we have learned about the subjective experience of brain stimulation in a way that animal studies cannot reveal. One 36-year-old epileptic woman received electrical stimulation in the right temporal lobe of her cortex. She reported a pleasant, tingling sensation on the left side of her body. She giggled, said that she enjoyed the sensation very much, and began flirting with the therapist (Delgado, 1969a). Electrical stimulation in the temporal lobe of an 11-year-old boy led him to say, "Hey! You can keep me here longer when you give me these; I like those." After more stimulations of the same point, he expressed a desire to become a girl and to marry the (male) therapist (Delgado & Hamlin, 1960; Higgins, Mahl, Delgado, & Hamlin, 1956).

On the other hand, a few patients pressed buttons to stimulate their brains electrically yet described the experience as not altogether pleasant.

One patient described the result of self-stimulation of the brain as "almost orgasm." He continued pressing, hoping to produce the orgasm. The result, however, was only prolonged frustration (Heath, 1963).

Pharmacology of the Reinforcement Systems of the Brain

Although an animal will work to self-stimulate a number of points in the brain, these points are largely concentrated along a few pathways (Gallistel, Gomita, Yadin, & Campbell, 1985). Because these pathways are believed to use only a limited number of synaptic transmitters, reinforcement (reward) itself may depend on only a few transmitters.

Many of the areas that mediate reinforcement are rich in catecholamines (the synaptic transmitters dopamine, norepinephrine, and epinephrine). The effects of several drugs are consistent with the hypothesis that catecholamines are important for reinforcement (Stein, 1968). Drugs known to increase the release of catecholamines or to prolong their effectiveness at the synapses also increase self-stimulation of the brain. Conversely, drugs that deplete the stores of catecholamines in the brain decrease self-stimulation.

On the other hand, several studies cast doubt on the exact role that catecholamines play. By varying the intensity and other electrical parameters of electrical brain stimulation, it is possible to determine a great deal about the properties of the neurons that an animal works to self-stimulate. Careful studies of these neurons have found refractory periods, conduction velocities, and other properties that do not match what we know about catecholamine neurons (Gallistel, Shizgal, & Yeomans, 1981). That is, for an animal to press a lever to self-stimulate its neurons, the electrode must be in a region rich in catecholamine neurons, and those neurons must be active, but the electrode apparently does not need to stimulate the catecholamine neurons themselves.

It may be that self-stimulation activates endorphin synapses. Endorphin synapses are known to activate certain dopamine-containing neurons that contribute to reward (Wise & Bozarth, 1984). Drug studies point to endorphin synapses as an important site of reinforcement. Animals will work for heroin and other opiates that stimulate endorphin synapses, and the reinforcing effects of these drugs depend on activity in the brain, not effects in the periphery (Vaccarino, Pettit, Bloom, & Koob, 1985).

SUMMARY

1. Many emotional stimuli increase the activity of the sympathetic nervous system. Removal of such a stimulus increases activity of the parasympathetic nervous system as a rebound effect. (p. 323)

2. A given event may produce either a great deal of sympathetic nervous system arousal, a little, or none at all, depending on how the individual interprets the event. (p. 324)

3. Ulcers and possibly also voodoo death result from excessive activity of the parasympathetic nervous system as a rebound after excessive sympathetic activation. (pp. 324–326)

4. Although the development of biofeedback techniques was inspired by animal experiments that later proved to be unreplicable, they can be helpful in a few settings. (p. 329)

5. According to the James-Lange theory, autonomic arousal and other body activities come before emotions; an emotion is a label for activity that has already begun. (p. 330)

6. According to the Cannon-Bard theory, autonomic arousal and emotional experiences are caused independently by a given stimulus. (p. 330)

7. The brain area most important for emotional be-

haviors is the limbic system, a circuit that includes the amygdala, the hypothalamus, parts of the cerebral cortex, and several other structures. (p. 331)
8. Aggressive behavior in animals serves the functions of territorial defense, defense of mates, and self-defense. (p. 334)
9. Damage to the amygdala of animals can lead to a decrease in aggressive behavior and a decrease in social rank, partly because of misinterpretation of social stimuli. (pp. 335–336)
10. Irritation of the amygdala, such as irritation caused by an epileptic seizure, leads to outbursts of violent behavior in certain individuals. (p. 337)
11. A decrease in the release and turnover of serotonin in the brain is associated with an increase in aggressive behavior. (p. 339)
12. Both drugs and diets that decrease the synthesis or release of serotonin increase violent behavior in animals and perhaps in humans too, although the evidence for humans is less extensive. (p. 340)
13. Decreased turnover of serotonin has been reported in the brains of mental patients who later committed suicide. (p. 341)

14. Benzodiazepine tranquilizers decrease anxiety by attaching to a receptor next to the $GABA_A$ synapse on the $GABA_A$ receptor complex. (p. 342)
15. The benzodiazepine receptor is also sensitive to certain naturally occurring chemicals in the brain, including carbolines, that modify the sensitivity of the $GABA_A$ synapse. (p. 343)
16. Alcohol also relieves anxiety by increasing the sensitivity of the $GABA_A$ synapse. (p. 344)
17. Panic disorder is a clinical condition marked by attacks of anxiety; people with panic disorder have overresponsive sympathetic nervous systems. (p. 343)
18. Animals will work to deliver an electrical stimulation to certain areas of their brains, presumably areas responsible for natural reinforcements and pleasure. (p. 346)
19. The reinforcement areas of the brain are generally rich in catecholamines, although the contribution of catecholamine neurons to reinforcement and pleasure may prove to be indirect. (p. 348)

REVIEW QUESTIONS

1. What happens to autonomic nervous system arousal just after removal of a stimulus that excited sympathetic nervous system arousal? (p. 323)
2. Why is it difficult to estimate someone's stress level just by counting recent potentially stressful experiences? (p. 324)
3. If periods of stress alternate with periods of rest, when are ulcers most likely to form? Why? (p. 326)
4. What activity of the autonomic nervous system may be responsible for certain cases of sudden death, as in voodoo death? (p. 326)
5. Distinguish among these theories of emotions: The James-Lange theory, Schachter and Singer's modification of that theory, and the Cannon-Bard theory. (pp. 329–331)
6. What is the evidence, pro and con, concerning the James-Lange theory? (p. 330)
7. What structures compose the limbic system? What function is that system believed to serve? (p. 331)
8. What are the effects of damage to the amygdala in animals? (p. 336)

9. What behavioral effects sometimes occur in people with temporal lobe epilepsy? (p. 337)
10. What evidence links aggressive behavior with a decrease in serotonin turnover? (p. 339)
11. What dietary habits may alter the likelihood of aggressive behavior? (p. 340)
12. How may it be possible to identify which people are most likely to commit suicide? (p. 341)
13. Describe the $GABA_A$ complex. How do benzodiazepines affect it? (p. 342)
14. Biologically, how do people with panic attacks differ from other people? (p. 343)
15. In what way may people with panic attacks aggravate their own problem? (p. 346)
16. What are possible therapies for panic disorder? (p. 346)
17. How was it discovered that distinct areas of the brain are responsible for pleasure and reinforcement? (p. 346)
18. Which synaptic transmitters are believed to be critical for reinforcement? (p. 348)

THOUGHT QUESTIONS

1. Suppose someone has just gone through a highly stressful experience and is now at risk for developing ulcers. What kind of drug might be helpful in preventing the ulcers? Would it be best to use a drug that increases or decreases activity of the sympathetic sys-

tem? One that increases or decreases activity of the parasympathetic system?
2. According to one interpretation of why electrical stimulation of the brain is rewarding, stimulation of different brain areas produces experiences corre-

sponding to different natural reinforcements. That is, stimulation in one area might produce sexual sensations and stimulation in another area might produce food or drink sensations. How might one test this hypothesis? (For two examples of tests—which came to opposite conclusions—see Olds, 1958b, and Frutiger, 1986.)

TERMS TO REMEMBER

biofeedback (p. 329)
James-Lange theory (p. 329)
Cannon-Bard theory (p. 330)
limbic system (p. 331)
sham rage (p. 331)
amygdala (p. 334)
rabies (p. 336)
psychosurgery (p. 339)
5-HIAA (p. 339)
PCPA (p. 339)

barbiturates (p. 341)
benzodiazepines (p. 342)
GABA$_A$ receptor complex (p. 342)
carbolines (p. 343)
diazepam-binding inhibitor (DBI) (p. 343)
panic disorder (p. 343)
cross-tolerance (p. 344)
obsessive-compulsive disorder (p. 345)
hyperventilation (p. 346)

SUGGESTIONS FOR FURTHER READING

Izard, C. E., Kagan, J., & Zajonc, R. B. (Eds.) (1984). *Emotions, cognition, and behavior.* Cambridge, England: Cambridge University. A collection of articles on emotion, including some on nonbiological aspects.

Valzelli, L. (1981). *Psychobiology of aggression and violence.* New York: Raven. A thorough, scholarly review of emotional behavior in general and aggressive behavior in particular.

The Biology of Learning and Memory

CHAPTER 13

MAIN IDEAS

1. Understanding the physiology of learning requires answering two questions: What changes take place in a single cell during learning, and how do a number of changed cells work together to produce adaptive behavior?

2. Learning depends on widespread changes throughout much of the brain, although different areas may contribute in different ways and specific areas may be critical for learning in a given instance.

3. An individual neuron may change in several ways during learning; it may increase its release of transmitter, for example, or it may have increased responsiveness to stimulation.

4. Learning depends on increased synthesis of proteins in certain neurons and on facilitated transmission at certain synapses.

5. People suffering from damage to the hippocampus, Korsakoff's syndrome, or Alzheimer's disease have great trouble storing memories of specific experiences, although they can still learn new skills and recall general information previously learned.

6. Damage to the hippocampus, amygdala, or prefrontal cortex impairs memory of specific events, including memory of what one has just done.

Suppose I type a short program into my computer:

```
10 HOME
20 FOR A=1 TO 100
30 PRINT A^[0.5]
40 NEXT A
```

I can now leave the computer, come back later, and type "RUN." Provided that the power has not been interrupted, the computer will print out a list of the square roots of the integers 1 to 100. How does the computer remember what to do?

That question is really two questions, which call for two kinds of answers. The first question is, how does the computer store a representation of the keys I type? Somehow, my hitting those keys leads to a physical change in some tiny silicon chips inside the computer. To explain how that happens, we would need to understand the physics of the silicon chip.

But explaining how a silicon chip stores information does not tell us how the computer as a whole works. To explain how the computer is able to run my program, we would have to answer a second question: How does the computer put together the information stored in numerous silicon chips to make its response? In other words, we would have to understand the wiring diagram.

Similarly, when we try to explain how a person remembers to stop at a stop sign or to show up for work at 8 A.M., we are really facing two questions. One is, how does a pattern of sensory information set up a lasting change in the input-output properties of one or more neurons in the nervous system? That question concerns the biophysics of the neuron. The second question is, after the properties of certain neurons have changed, how does the nervous system as a whole produce the appropriate behavior? That question concerns the wiring diagram.

In this chapter we shall deal first with how sensory information can change the properties of individual neurons. Second, we shall consider what we know about the wiring diagram: how various areas of the nervous system work together to produce learned behaviors.

LASHLEY'S SEARCH FOR THE ENGRAM

Karl Lashley (see BioSketch 13-1) made the first serious attempt to analyze how experience can change the properties of neurons. He set out to test the hypothesis that learning represents a new connection that forms between one part of the brain and another.

According to Ivan Pavlov, who discovered **classical conditioning**, learning consists of transferring a reflex from one stimulus to another. Initially an *unconditioned stimulus (US)*, such as food, elicits an *unconditioned response (UR)*, such as salivating. If the person or animal is repeatedly presented with some other stimulus (one that does not normally elicit the response) just

BIOSKETCH
13-1

Karl S. Lashley (1890–1958)

Karl S. Lashley received his bachelor's degree from the University of West Virginia, his M.S. from the University of Pittsburgh, and his Ph.D. in zoology from Johns Hopkins in 1914, where he studied with H. S. Jennings and J. B. Watson, one of the founders of behaviorism.

Different scientists contribute in different ways. The usual way of achieving scientific fame is by proposing a new theory or by discovering new evidence for someone else's theory. Karl Lashley, however, is best remembered for demonstrating the inadequacies of certain theories that were widely accepted in his time.

For example, it had been widely believed that learning and memory depended on the growth of new connections between two points in the brain. Lashley's extensive series of experiments demonstrated that no knife cut or small lesion anywhere in the brain would destroy a specific memory. Although Lashley did not offer a detailed theory of how memory *is* organized in the brain, he made it difficult to believe that a memory depends on one small area of the cortex.

Lashley also played a small but important part in the origins of American sex research. His adviser in graduate school, John B. Watson, conducted some unpublished research on sexual behavior, using himself and a female graduate student as the subjects. That episode led to Watson's divorce and to his losing his job at Johns Hopkins. Watson, nevertheless, convinced Lashley that sexual behavior was worthy of serious research. Lashley took surveys of the sexual behavior of as many people as he could find who would discuss it with him. Although he never published his results, he happened to discuss his project with a young biologist, Alfred Kinsey, who took the idea and made a career of surveying people's sexual behavior (McConnell, 1979).

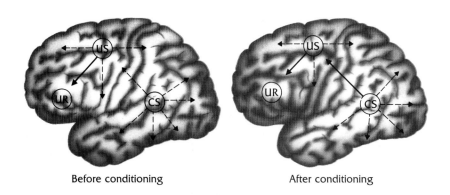

Before conditioning   After conditioning

Figure 13-1. Pavlov's view of the physiology of learning.

prior to the US, the new stimulus comes to elicit that response. In this case the new stimulus is called the *conditioned stimulus (CS)*, and the learned response is called the *conditioned response (CR)*. Pavlov believed that pairing the CS with the US caused the growth of a new or strengthened connection between a CS center in the brain and a US center in the brain. (See Figure 13-1.) Because of that connection, presentation of the CS directly excites the US center.

That theory was merely Pavlov's inference; neither he nor anyone else had observed the growth of any connections in the brain. Lashley set out to test Pavlov's theory. He said he was searching for the **engram**—the physical representation of learning. (An axon connecting a CS center to a US center would be one example of an engram.)

Lashley reasoned that if learning depended on connections between a CS center and a US center, as Pavlov asserted, then a knife cut somewhere in the brain should interrupt that connection and abolish the learned response. He therefore trained rats on a variety of mazes and a brightness discrimination task and then made one or more deep cuts in the rats' cerebral cortexes (Lashley, 1929, 1950). For each rat, he made a cut in a different location. To his surprise, no cut or combination of cuts seemed to impair a rat's memory. It was possible, of course, that Lashley had managed to spray cuts all over the rats' cortexes without ever hitting the one critical connection. The more likely explanation, however, was that learning does not depend on connections across the cortex.

Lashley further demonstrated that learning in rats is not simply a matter of connecting one sensory stimulus to one motor response. A rat that has learned to approach a white cross on a black card will also approach a black cross on a white card. A rat that has learned to walk through a maze will limp, hobble, or roll through the maze if its ability to walk is impaired. Evidently, what the rat learns is more abstract than a simple stimulus-response connection.

Lashley's Attempt to Localize Learning in the Cerebral Cortex

Lashley further considered whether any portion of the cerebral cortex is more important than others for learning. He trained rats on mazes before or after he removed large portions of their cortex. An average intact rat required about twenty passages through the maze before it could traverse it without error ten times in a row. Lashley's brain-damaged rats needed more trials to reach that criterion. The amount of retardation depended more on the amount of brain damage than on the location of the damage. In other words, according to Lashley, a memory does not depend on a single location in the cortex. Lashley (1929) suggested two basic principles of brain organization:

1. **Mass action.** The cortex works together as a whole; the more brain the better. For certain complex tasks, that principle holds for humans as well as for rats. For example, soldiers who survived bullet wounds to the head during the Vietnam War showed a decrease in overall IQ score. Their deterioration on the IQ tests depended on the overall amount of brain damage (Grafman, Salazar, Weingartner, Vance, & Amin, 1986).

2. **Equipotentiality.** The various parts of the cortex contribute to behavioral processes almost equally, at least for complex behaviors. No one part of the cortex is more specialized for learning than other parts.

A more recent study, using an imaginative design, has demonstrated that Lashley's principle of equipotentiality is partly but not entirely correct (John, Tang, Brill, Young, & Ono, 1986). The investigators trained a split-brain cat to approach a visual stimulus for food. Then they tested the effects

DIGRESSION
13-1
Brain Cells as a Tape Recorder for Memory?

Wilder Penfield (1955; Penfield & Perot, 1963) made a claim at the opposite extreme from Lashley's principle of equipotentiality. He suggested that each neuron in the temporal cortex of the brain stores a particular memory, which can be retrieved by the proper stimulation.

Penfield sometimes performed brain surgery for severe epilepsy on awake patients who had only scalp anesthesia. When he applied a brief, weak electrical stimulus to part of the brain, the patient could describe the experience the stimulation evoked. Stimulation of the temporal cortex often evoked vivid descriptions:

"I feel as though I were in the bathroom at school."

"I see myself at the corner of Jacob and Washington in South Bend, Indiana."

"I remember myself at the railroad station in Vanceburg, Kentucky; it is winter and the wind is blowing outside, and I am waiting for a train."

Repeat stimulation at a single point often elicited the same response. Stimulation of neighboring areas elicited different responses. Because certain episodes were experiences that the patient had not thought about for a long time, Penfield argued that the cortex served as a kind of video tape recorder of all experience.

We have serious reason to doubt Penfields's conclusion, however. First, the results he reported have not been successfully demonstrated in non-epileptic patients. Second, and more seriously, the brain stimulation only rarely gave rise to a memory of a single event. More often it elicited vague sights and sounds, or repeated experiences such as "seeing a bed" or "hearing a choir sing 'White Christmas.'" Almost never did it elicit memories of doing anything—just seeing and hearing. Also, a number of the elicited reports were of events the person had never experienced, such as being chased by a robber or seeing Christ descend from the sky.

In short, it may be more accurate to say that the stimulation produces dreamlike experiences than to say that it turns on a video tape of the person's memories.

of the relevant stimulus on one hemisphere and an irrelevant stimulus on the other hemisphere. They injected a radioactively labeled chemical similar to glucose to find out which parts of the cortex were most active on each side. Any area that was equally active on both sides was presumably responding to the visual and other stimuli, regardless of their learned meaning, whereas any area that was more active on the side exposed to the relevant stimuli must be participating in the learned reaction. Although the relevant stimulus increased activity in much of the brain, it did not increase it in all areas equally. Certain parts of the cerebral cortex, the hippocampus, the cerebellum, and other areas were activated more than others. Evidently, a learned response requires the participation of many neurons but not all. (For the extreme opposite point of view on localization of memories, see Digression 13-1.)

Lashley's Hidden Assumptions

Any study begins with certain assumptions, some of them apparently so obvious that the investigators may not have been aware that they were assumptions. Lashley's results were of limited generality because of two assumptions that he made. One was that the cerebral cortex is the site of learning. As we shall see later in this chapter, however, certain subcortical structures are critical for learning, and the principle of equipotentiality cer-

BIOSKETCH
13-2

John
Garcia

An important
and surprising
discovery, once it has been accepted by a field, is honored and
respected. At the moment of its
first report, however, it is sometimes greeted with skepticism.
John Garcia has been responsible
for several discoveries that have
gone through the sequence
from initial skepticism to widespread respect within a fairly
short time.

Born in 1917, the second of
six sons of a Hispanic immigrant
family living north of San Francisco, John Garcia studied first at
Santa Rosa Junior College, then
at the University of California at
Berkeley. He left graduate

school at Berkeley in 1951 to
work in a research laboratory of
the Defense Department, studying the effects of x-rays on animals. In that capacity he
discovered that rats can actively
avoid x-rays, previously believed
to be completely imperceptible
stimuli. His x-ray research led
him to a belated return to graduate school at Berkeley, where he
finally received his Ph.D. in 1965.
He then conducted his pioneering studies on learned associations between taste and illness,
known variously as taste-aver-
sion learning, conditioned taste
avoidance, and bait shyness.

Garcia balanced out his unusually long trek through graduate school with an unusually
rapid rise through academic
ranks, receiving the Warren
Medal from the Society of Experimental Psychologists in 1978
and the American Psychological
Association's prestigious Award

for Distinguished Scientific Contributions in 1979. He has served
as a professor at UCLA since
1973 and was elected to the
National Academy of Science in
1983.

Several of Garcia's pioneering
papers were at first rejected by a
number of psychology journals
because of minor procedural
criticisms. Garcia (1981) says he
felt like Don Quixote, who explained his attack on the Spanish
windmills by saying, "The same
evil influence . . . would like us to
believe that its monstrous lack-
eys are mere grinders of corn in
order to rob us of the glory of
exposing their true malignant
nature." Garcia goes on to remark, "Some researchers feel the
same way about journal editors
and their consultants." Nevertheless, Garcia excuses journal
editors on the grounds that they
are merely suffering from *neophobia*—the fear of the new.

tainly does not apply to these structures: The effect of subcortical brain
damage on learning depends on the exact location of the damage (Thompson, 1969, 1978).

Lashley's other assumption seemed so obvious at the time that he probably gave it little thought: He assumed that learning is pretty much the same
from one situation to another. If so, the conclusions he drew from maze
learning in rats would hold for the learning of anything, by any species. But
maze learning is in fact a complex task that requires the use of many senses;
it is likely to differ from tasks that use only one sense. Furthermore, we now
know that the learning of motor skills (such as how to shoot a basketball) is
different from the learning of factual information, and that the memory of
general principles (such as the rules of basketball) is different from the memory of a specific event (such as the outcome of a particular basketball game).

Moreover, learning about tastes and foods is different from learning
about other stimuli in several ways, as discovered by John Garcia (see Bio-
Sketch 13-2). An animal that tastes an unfamiliar food and later gets sick,
even from a cause other than the food, learns an avoidance of that taste. It
learns the avoidance in a single trial, even if the taste is separated from the
food by minutes or hours (Garcia, Ervin, & Koelling, 1966; Rozin & Kalat,
1971). Furthermore, it associates illness with food more readily than with

lights, sounds, or the location where it was when it got ill. It also associates food with illness more than with shock (Garcia & Koelling, 1966). Because associating food with illness is special in these regards, its physiology must be studied separately from that of other learning (Ashe & Nachman, 1980).

Localized Traces of Learning

If we change our focus to studies of subcortical structures instead of the cerebral cortex and to studies of a different, possibly simpler form of learning than mazes, we may find that learning depends on a small, well-defined area of the brain. Richard F. Thompson (1986) and his colleagues have studied one type of classical conditioning in rabbits. They paired a tone (CS) with an airpuff (US) to the cornea. At first, rabbits blinked to the airpuff but not to the tone; after repeated pairings, they blinked to the tone as well. That is, classical conditioning took place. At various points in this procedure the investigators recorded the activity from various brain cells. They found changes in cells in the hippocampus and in one nucleus of the cerebellum, the *lateral interpositus* nucleus. They further found that damage to the lateral interpositus nucleus caused a permanent loss of the conditioned response (McCormick & Thompson, 1984; Woodruf-Pak, Lavond, & Thompson, 1985). Apparently, at least in certain circumstances, learning depends on a small part of the nervous system.

SINGLE-CELL MECHANISMS OF LEARNING

What did Lashley's results tell us about the engram, or about the single-cell basis of learning? First, his findings indicated that at least certain kinds of learning are likely to be diffuse, not limited to a single neuron or a single connection. Second, they suggested that researchers need to look elsewhere to discover how a single cell changes during learning—perhaps to invertebrates, which have a simpler nervous system.

During learning, some change must take place in one or more neurons of the brain. That change might take many possible forms—the growth of a new axon, new connections among neurons, increased or decreased release of a synaptic transmitter, increased or decreased sensitivity to a transmitter, a change in the spontaneous activity of a neuron, and so forth. The mechanisms are probably not the same for all instances of learning. The best way to approach the topic is first to find out what mechanisms *can* work for certain instances of learning—presumably those mechanisms that are easiest to study. Answering that question may later make it easier to discover which mechanisms actually work in any particular instance.

Learning in *Aplysia*

Invertebrates have certain advantages for the study of the single-cell basis of learning because they have a simpler nervous system than vertebrates (see Digression 13-2). A particularly popular animal is *Aplysia*, a marine invertebrate related to the common slug (see Color Plate 27). *Aplysia* has fewer neurons than any vertebrate, and many of its neurons are large enough to be studied easily. Moreover, because the anatomy of its nervous system is practically the same from one individual to another, investigators can study the

DIGRESSION

13-2

Learning in Decapitated Cockroaches (?!)

Many investigators have sought to demonstrate learning in animals with as little nervous system as possible, in hope that the physiological basis for learning would be easier to discover in a small nervous system. Horridge (1962) took this idea to the extreme by apparently demonstrating learning in decapitated cockroaches.

Horridge cut the connections between a cockroach's head and the rest of its body. Then he suspended the cockroach so that its legs dangled just above a water surface. An electrical circuit was arranged as shown in the accompanying figure, such that the roach's leg would get a shock whenever it touched the water. For each experimental roach, a control roach got a leg shock whenever the first roach did. That is, the experimental and control roaches got shocks at the same time, but the shocks were correlated with leg position only for the experimental group. (This kind of experiment is known as a "yoked-control" design.)

Over a period of 5 to 10 minutes, the experimental group "learned" a response of tucking the leg under the body or (in other experiments) extending it straight to the side to avoid shocks. Roaches in the control group did not, on the average, change their leg position during the training period. Thus, the changed response apparently qualifies as learning and not as some accidental by-product of the shocks.

Similar results have been reported for frogs (Horn & Horn, 1969), rats (Buerger & Fennessy, 1971), and cats (Patterson, Cegavske, & Thompson, 1973) that have had their spinal cords disconnected from the brain. In cockroaches, learning has been reported even after the ganglion attached to the shocked leg has been detached from all other ganglia (Eisenstein & Cohen, 1965). However, in nearly all experiments the animals learn slowly and individuals vary greatly in their responses. These variations limit the usefulness of this preparation for studies of the single-cell basis of learning.

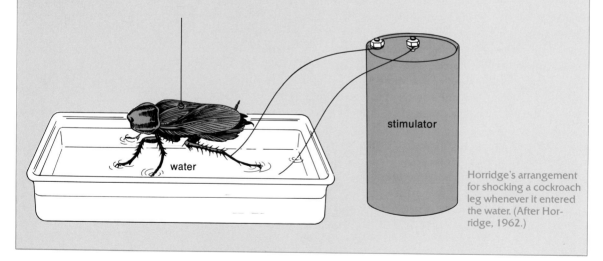

Horridge's arrangement for shocking a cockroach leg whenever it entered the water. (After Horridge, 1962.)

same neuron in different aplysias. For example, after an experimenter identifies the properties of the *R2* cell in one aplysia, other experimenters can find the same cell in their own animals and can carry the studies further or relate that neuron to other identified neurons. We could hardly imagine doing the same with a vertebrate.

We do not know, of course, whether the single-cell basis of learning is the same for *Aplysia* as it is for vertebrates. The *Aplysia* studies are a way of identifying a mechanism and studying how it works in detail. Once we

BIOSKETCH

13-3

Eric R. Kandel

Born in Vienna, Eric Kandel came to the United States in 1939. He received a bachelor's degree from Harvard and an M.D. from the New York University Medical School. He is director of the Center for Neurobiology and Behavior at the Columbia University College of Physicians and Surgeons.

Because of the difficulties he encountered in his early experiments on the mammalian hippocampus, Kandel switched to studies on *Aplysia*, which has larger neurons and connections

that can be precisely specified. When he began his *Aplysia* studies in the early 1960s, many students of behavior were skeptical that studies in a mollusc would prove relevant to mammals. Kandel reasoned, however, that since the evolution of many other biological functions has been conservative, the same was probably true of the mechanisms of learning. Moreover, the neurons and synapses of humans resemble those of molluscs on the cellular level.

Kandel found that *Aplysia* is capable of habituation, sensitization, and classical conditioning. The studies of Kandel and his colleagues have provided the first compelling evidence that learning results in functional and structural changes of specific neurons and their connections.

Kandel believes that a broad, multidisciplinary approach provides the key to much of the future progress in neurobiology: "... the questions posed by mentation are formidable, and we have only begun to explore them. Although elementary aspects of mental processes such as learning in invertebrates can be analyzed in terms of specific molecules in specific neurons, we still know little about comparable processes in higher animals and even less about higher mental activities. I have suggested that there is an elementary molecular alphabet of mentation that can be combined to yield the words and sentences, indeed paragraphs and whole volumes, of progressively more complex mental processes."

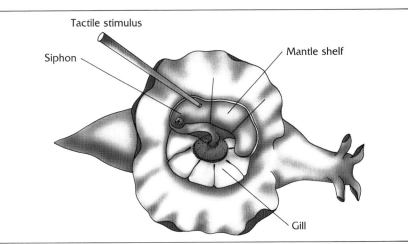

Tactile stimulus

Siphon

Mantle shelf

Gill

Figure 13-2. Stimulation of an aplysia's mantle or siphon causes a retraction, or withdrawal response. The relevant sensory and motor neurons inside the animal can be identified and studied.

understand the mechanism in *Aplysia* or any other invertebrate, we can study vertebrates to see whether they have the same mechanism. (This same strategy has proved successful in studies of the action potential and other properties of the neuron.)

If someone touches the siphon, mantle, or gill of an aplysia, the animal makes a vigorous withdrawal movement (Figure 13-2). Eric Kandel (see BioSketch 13-3) and other investigators have traced the neural path from the touch receptors through various identifiable interneurons to the motor neurons that direct the withdrawal response. The withdrawal response is subject to three learning-related phenomena:

1. Repetitive weak touch at any point leads to a decline of the withdrawal response (*habituation*).

2. A strong stimulus leads to a prolonged facilitation of the withdrawal response, even to stimuli at other locations on the body (*sensitization*).

3. Pairing a weaker stimulus with a stronger stimulus increases the later effectiveness of the weaker stimulus (*classical conditioning*).

Habituation.   **Habituation** is a decrease in response to a stimulus that is presented repeatedly and that is accompanied by no change in other stimuli. That is, the animal learns to ignore irrelevant stimuli. Habituation can be demonstrated in an aplysia by repeatedly stimulating its gills with a brief jet of seawater. At first it withdraws the gills, but after many repetitions it stops responding.

Several possible mechanisms of habituation can be eliminated. First, muscle fatigue can be ruled out because, even after habituation has occurred, direct stimulation of the motor neuron produces a full-sized muscle contraction (Kupfermann, Castellucci, Pinsker, & Kandel, 1970). Second, habituation does not depend on a change in the firing rate of the sensory neuron. After repeated stimulation of the sensory neuron, the neuron still gives a full, normal response to stimulation; it merely fails to excite the motor neuron as much as before (Kupfermann et al., 1970). Third, the decrease in response by the motor neuron is not due to an increase in inhibitory impulses from somewhere other than the sensory neuron. Even when the inhibitory input is carefully held constant by drugs, habituation of the motor neuron still occurs (Castellucci, Pinsker, Kupfermann, & Kandel, 1970).

By process of elimination, we are left with the conclusion that habituation in *Aplysia* depends on a change in the synapse between the sensory neuron and the motor neuron (Figure 13-3). To determine the nature of that change, Castellucci and Kandel (1974) measured the EPSPs (see Chapter 3) in the motor neuron during habituation. As habituation proceeded, the average size of the EPSP decreased, but each EPSP was still an integral multiple of the quantum of membrane response (as described in Chapter 3), which is presumably based on a quantum of transmitter release. From this evidence, Castellucci and Kandel inferred that habituation takes place by a decrease in release of transmitter by the presynaptic cell. Bailey and Chen (1983) later confirmed that the presynaptic cell has fewer synaptic vesicles as a result of habituation.

Sensitization.   After a strong electrical shock or any other intense stimulus, a person undergoes **sensitization**, becoming overresponsive to mild stimuli. Similarly, a strong noxious stimulus almost anywhere on *Aplysia's* surface can increase later withdrawal responses to a touch on the siphon, mantle, or gill. The sensitization may last as briefly as a few seconds or as long as days, depending on the intensity and repetition of the sensitizing stimulus.

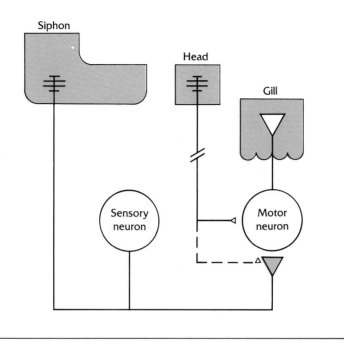

Figure 13-3. Habituation of the gill-withdrawal reflex in *Aplysia* apparently depends on decreased transmission at the synapse between the sensory neuron and the motor neuron. Stimulation at other locations, such as the head, can temporarily re-excite a habituated synapse. (After Castellucci, Pinsker, Kupfermann, & Kandel, 1970.)

As in the case of habituation, sensitization can be traced to a change in the number of quanta of transmitter released at two synapses, the one between the sensory neuron and an interneuron, and one between the sensory neuron and the motor neuron. (See Figure 13-4.) The mechanism of that change is now known in some detail (Kandel & Schwartz, 1982).

Strong stimulation (of the head, tail, or elsewhere) excites a facilitating interneuron, which has been described in enough detail that it can be identified in any aplysia. The facilitating interneuron has presynaptic synapses that are known to release serotonin onto the synapses of the sensory neurons. Serotonin interacts with a receptor in the sensory neuron to produce **cyclic AMP** within the cell. An enzyme dependent on cyclic AMP is thereby activated, which blocks potassium channels in the membrane. As you will recall from Chapter 2, potassium flows out of the cell during the second half of an action potential; the exit of potassium restores the neuron to its usual polarization. When the cyclic AMP-dependent enzyme blocks the potassium channels, the net effect is to prolong the action potential and therefore to prolong the release of transmitter by the presynaptic cell.

If the sensitizing stimulus is repeated, the prolonged elevation of cyclic AMP in the sensory neuron leads to the production of a new protein responsible for long-term sensitization. Long-term sensitization, unlike the short-term variety, can be prevented by drugs that block protein synthesis.

Classical Conditioning. Ordinarily, an aplysia responds weakly or not at all to a mild touch on the siphon; it responds vigorously to an electrical stimulation of the tail. If the mild touch on the siphon is repeatedly paired

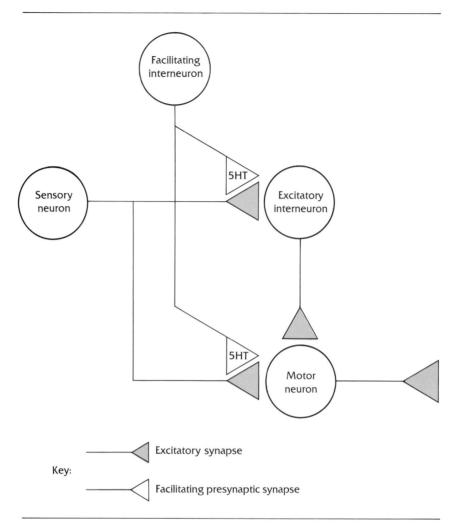

Key:

Figure 13-4. Sensitization of the withdrawal response in *Aplysia* depends on the release of serotonin (5HT) at presynaptic synapses. (After Kandel & Schwartz, 1982.)

with the electrical stimulation of the tail, the animal gradually develops a conditioned response of vigorous withdrawal to the siphon touch.

The mechanism of classical conditioning probably resembles that of sensitization, except that it is more specific. The electrical stimulation of the tail stimulates neurons that facilitate the release of transmitter from the sensory neuron that responds to the siphon (Kandel & Schwartz, 1982). Hawkins and Kandel (1984) suggest that learning depends on combinations of a few elementary mechanisms, including those identified for habituation and sensitization.

Learning in *Hermissenda*

Another series of experiments have been conducted on *Hermissenda*, a marine snail (see Color Plate 28). Ordinarily, *Hermissenda* crawls toward a light source. The approach response can be decreased by presenting a light and then subjecting the animal to rotation. The approach response is de-

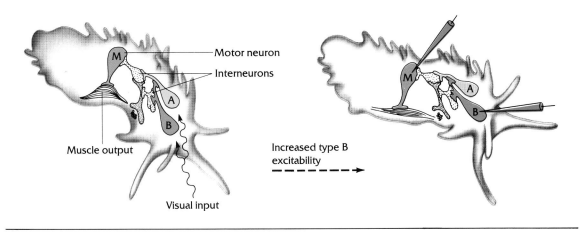

Motor neuron
Interneurons
Muscle output
Visual input
Increased type B excitability

Figure 13-5. Connections in *Hermissenda* controlling response to light. Photoreceptor B inhibits photoreceptor A, which promotes crawling toward light. An increased activity by B decreases the response of A; the result is decreased approach to the light. (Based on Alkon, 1984.)

creased only if the light and rotation are presented together, not if the animal experiences the two at different times. For that reason the change in response qualifies as learning (Lederhendler, Gart, & Alkon, 1986).

Hermissenda has two kinds of photoreceptor cell in its eye, called A and B (Figure 13-5). Type B inhibits type A; type A excites other neurons that eventually lead to movement of the animal toward the light. Thus, type A promotes crawling toward light, while type B inhibits the approach. When the animal learns a decreased approach to light, type B cells increase their response. An increased amount of calcium enters the type B cells; the calcium enhances a phosphorylation reaction of proteins, which in turn closes the potassium gates in the membrane. As in the *Aplysia* example, a decrease in potassium flow means a prolongation of the action potential (Alkon, 1984; Goh, Lederhendler, & Alkon, 1985).

Note, however, the distinction between the mechanism found in *Hermissenda* and the mechanism found in *Aplysia*. In *Aplysia*, both habituation and sensitization of gill withdrawal depend on a change in the release of transmitter by a presynaptic cell. In *Hermissenda*, learned decrease of the approach to light depends on a change in the membrane properties of a receptor cell. The difference is probably not due to the difference in species but to a difference between learning one response and learning another. It may be that all species have multiple mechanisms of learning, some of them presynaptic and others postsynaptic.

Long-Term Potentiation in the Mammalian Hippocampus

Despite the difficulties of studying single-cell mechanisms in the mammalian nervous system, one procedure has proved useful for identifying possible mechanisms of learning. A burst of many stimuli to certain neurons of the hippocampus within less than 1 second changes the properties of those neurons for a period of weeks. During that period, stimulation via the synaptic transmitter glutamate produces a greater response than usual. That increase in response is known as **long-term potentiation**, abbreviated **LTP**. Although the route from LTP to learned behavior is not yet known, LTP does offer us an opportunity to study how a pattern of input can change the properties of mammalian neurons.

The burst of stimulation to the hippocampus increases the concentration of calcium in the dendrites of the postsynaptic neuron. The increased level of calcium activates a protein known as **calpain**, which breaks a network of molecules normally found in the dendrites. With that network broken, the dendrites change their shape and expose additional glutamate receptors. Because of the additional receptors, the cell becomes more sensitive to the excitatory transmitter glutamate (Akers, Lovinger, Colley, Linden, & Routtenberg, 1986; Baudry & Lynch, 1980; Lynch & Baudry, 1984). This mechanism is found not only in the hippocampus but in cells throughout the forebrain.

Long-term potentiation is sensitive to the presence of certain chemicals. Elevated levels of calcium or the synaptic transmitter norepinephrine in the hippocampus facilitate LTP. Low levels of calcium can block LTP; so can high levels of magnesium (which competes with calcium) (Hopkins & Johnston, 1984; Kessler, Baudry, Cummins, Way, & Lynch, 1986).

Summary of Single-Cell Mechanisms

Although this section has been somewhat complex, the main points can be summarized briefly: Learning is often associated with changes distributed over large areas of the nervous system. Lashley first demonstrated that principle in the case of maze learning. In certain cases, however, such as eyelid conditioning in rabbits, the critical changes are localized to a small brain area. No matter how much of the brain participates, learning always requires changes within individual cells. Studies of two mollusc species and of long-term potentiation of the mammalian hippocampus have identified several mechanisms by which neurons may change their properties. The action potential may be prolonged in either the presynaptic or the postsynaptic cell, or the postsynaptic cell may increase its number of synaptic receptors. Many combinations of these and other mechanisms may be responsible for the variety of behavioral changes we see in learning.

THE BIOCHEMISTRY OF LEARNING AND MEMORY

Studies of the single-cell basis of learning have attributed learning to increases in calcium within neurons, decreases in potassium flow, increased numbers of certain synaptic receptors, and other chemical changes. Such findings suggest that impaired learning might be due to chemical deficiencies in the brain and that certain drugs might impair or improve learning. Research on the biochemistry of learning has followed a number of routes.

RNA and Proteins as Memory
Code Molecules: Controversial Research

Loosely speaking, heredity is a kind of memory, passed from one generation to the next. We know that heredity is based on the DNA molecule, which serves as a template for the formation of RNA molecules, which in turn determine the structure of protein molecules (see Appendix). Clearly, DNA,

RNA, and protein can code enormous amounts of information. Might they code individual memories as well?

Several investigators, especially in the 1960s and early 1970s, took the position that each memory is coded as a specific molecule, probably RNA or protein. The boldest test of that hypothesis was an attempt to transfer memories chemically from one individual to another. McConnell (1962) reported that when planaria (flatworms) cannibalized other planaria that had been classically conditioned to respond to a light, they apparently "remembered" what the cannibalized planaria had learned. (At least they learned the response faster than planaria generally do.)

Inspired by that report, Babich, Jacobson, Bubash, and Jacobson (1965) trained rats to approach a clicking sound for food. After the rats were well trained, the experimenters ground up the rats' brains, extracted RNA, and injected it into some untrained rats. When the recipient rats were placed in the training apparatus, they learned to approach the clicking sound faster than rats in the control group.

That report led to a sudden flurry of experiments on the transfer of training by brain extracts. After rats were trained on a task, an extract of RNA or protein from their brains was injected into untrained rats. A second group of recipients got brain extracts from untrained rats. The result—sometimes—was that the rats that received brain extracts from the trained group showed apparent memory of the task while those that received extracts from an untrained group did not (Fjerdingstad, 1973).

The results were undependable, however. About half of all studies obtained statistically significant, positive results (Dyal, 1971), but the results were never consistent, even within a single laboratory (L. T. Smith, 1975). By the mid-1970s most investigators had given up on this line of research as a dead end (Gaito, 1976). Those who continued to believe that transfer by brain extracts was possible were unable to get grants approved to continue their research. The research area slipped rapidly into obscurity, although a few studies continued to be reported from time to time (e.g., Holt & Miller, 1983; Oden, Clohisy, & Francois, 1982).

Few scientific fields meet the fate this one did. Transfer of training by brain extracts was abandoned because most investigators decided that such transfer is not possible. Other investigators are still not so sure. Perhaps our science is ignoring an elusive but important phenomenon. But unreplicable research is like an unprofitable gold mine: Eventually one must give up and try something else, even at the risk that a little more persistence might have paid off.

Protein Synthesis and Memory

Studies of the single-cell basis of learning have pointed to protein synthesis as a necessary step in any long-term change in a neuron. Furthermore, drugs that inhibit protein synthesis impair the long-term storage of memory, although they do not impair short-term retention (Davis & Squire, 1984). The greater the inhibition of synthesis, the greater the retardation of learning (Bennett, Rosenzweig, & Flood, 1979). The effects do vary, however, from one task to another. For example, in one experiment anisomycin, a drug that inhibits protein synthesis, blocked a rat's memory of the location of a shock but did not block memory of which odor to approach for food (Stäubli, Faraday, & Lynch, 1985).

How does protein synthesis contribute to learning and memory? One hypothesis is that protein synthesis modifies the properties of neurons to store information. Another hypothesis is that it is necessary only for keeping the brain healthy in general. To evaluate these two hypotheses, Davis, Rosenzweig, Bennett, & Squire (1980) tested the effects of anisomycin on learning. They gave one group of rats a large dose 5 hours before training and a second group a small dose 20 minutes before training. At the time of training, the rats that had received the smaller but more recent dose had the greater impairment of protein synthesis and the greater impairment in learning, even though the group that received the larger, less recent dose were still suffering greater side effects, including diarrhea, inactivity, and watery eyes. It appears, therefore, that the inhibition of protein synthesis impairs learning directly, not just by making the animal sick.

Drugs and Hormones That Facilitate Memory

Several drugs and hormones have shown potential for improving people's memory. Research on this topic is motivated largely by a desire to help senile people or others with memory impairments.

Cyclic AMP is a chemical found in many neurons, especially in conjunction with synaptic receptors sensitive to norepinephrine and dopamine. It is known as a **second messenger** because, after it is released by certain synaptic transmitters, it sets in motion a great many activities within the cell. Cyclic AMP is important for learning in many situations (Chute, Villiger, & Kirton, 1981). The enzyme *phosphodiesterase*, also found normally in the neuron, breaks down cyclic AMP. The drug **papaverine** inhibits phosphodiesterase and thereby increases the activity of cyclic AMP. Papaverine has shown some success in helping both normal young people and senile older people learn material better and recall it better later (Chute, 1980). It does not, however, help people to retrieve old, forgotten materials.

The adrenal hormone **ACTH** and the pituitary hormone **vasopressin** have improved the performance of rats on a number of learning tasks (Edelstein, 1981; Martinez, Jensen, & McGaugh, 1981; Messing & Sparber, 1985). Vasopressin also enhances the memory performance of senile people (Delwaide, Devoitille, & Ylieff, 1980). In a study with rats, long-term use of vasopressin partially prevented the deterioration of memory that usually occurs in old age (Meck & Church, 1985). How these hormones work is not known, however. It is possible that they improve performance by changing emotions or activity levels rather than learning itself (van Haaren, van Zanten, & van de Poll, 1986).

Piracetam and **aniracetam** are experimental drugs that enhance memory, especially in older animals and in animals whose memory has been impaired by electroconvulsive drugs or other treatments (Gamzu, 1985; Valzelli, Bernasconi, & Sala, 1980). Again, how these drugs work is not yet known.

Table 13-1. Deutsch's Predictions for Experiments on Acetylcholine and Memory

Drug	Biochemical effect	Predicted effect on weak memory	Predicted effect on strong memory
Scopolamine	Blocks acetylcholine synapses	Weaken	Weaken, but perhaps not noticeably
Physostigmine or DFP	Blocks the enzyme acetylcholinesterase, thereby prolonging the effect of acetylcholine	Strengthen	Weaken via synaptic block

Acetylcholine Synapses and Memory

Ultimately, the outcome of increased protein synthesis, hormonal stimulation, or whatever must be either a change in the resting activity of certain neurons or a change in the responsiveness at certain synapses. Much evidence points to acetylcholine synapses as one of the important sites of learning.

Animal Studies.   Deutsch (1973) reasoned that if learning depends on an increase in response at acetylcholine synapses, then drugs that increase or decrease activity at those synapses should facilitate or inhibit learned performance. He predicted that scopolamine, which blocks acetylcholine synapses, should impair memories, especially memories that were weak already. His predictions were more complex for **physostigmine** and **DFP** (diisopropylfluorophosphate): After acetylcholine stimulates its synaptic receptors, the enzyme **acetylcholinesterase** breaks it down into inactive fragments. Because physostigmine and DFP block the effects of acetylcholinesterase, they prolong the effects of the synaptic transmitter acetylcholine. Deutsch predicted that these drugs should strengthen weak memories. When a memory is strong, however, the acetylcholine activity is presumably high already, so a still further increase may cause **synaptic block**, a cessation of response due to overstimulation. (For example, physostigmine is beneficial to patients with myasthenia gravis, who have a deficit of acetylcholine transmission, but giving the same dose to a normal person can cause temporary paralysis.) Consequently, Deutsch predicted that physostigmine would impair strong memories. Table 13-1 summarizes these predictions.

The results supported Deutsch's predictions. After he trained rats on a simple maze, he tested some rats after a 7-day delay and others after an 18-day delay. In the absence of drugs, the rats' memory was strong after the 7-day delay and weak after the 18-day delay. Scopolamine weakened performance slightly after either delay. DFP greatly interfered with a strong memory (7-day delay) but improved a weak memory (18-day delay).

A number of later studies have confirmed the importance of acetylcholine synapses in learning. Chemically induced damage to acetylcholine neurons impairs learning and memory (Sandberg, Sanberg, Hanin, Fisher, & Coyle, 1984). Scopolamine impairs memory and physostigmine enhances memory on a variety of tasks (e.g., Aigner & Mishkin, 1986; Murray & Fibiger, 1986).

Human Studies. Several lines of evidence suggest a relationship between acetylcholine and human memory. People suffering from Alzheimer's disease (discussed later in this chapter) suffer memory dysfunctions and a decline in acetylcholine content of the brain. In normal aging, some memory impairment is common; the degree of memory loss correlates with a decline in brain acetylcholine levels (Bartus, Dean, Beer, & Lippa, 1982; Davies, 1985).

In several experiments, young adult volunteers have received injections of scopolamine. While under the influence of the drug, they show clear deficiencies on a variety of memory tasks. Their performance resembles that of senile people in several ways, although it does not match that of Alzheimer's patients (Beatty, Butters, & Janowsky, 1986; Drachman & Leavitt, 1974).

Given these results, the question arises, would it be possible to improve human memory by using physostigmine, DFP, or similar drugs? Several studies have found that physostigmine does improve memory, especially that of older people and others with poor memories (Davis et al., 1978; Sitaram, Weingartner, & Gillin, 1978). Unfortunately, the required doses produce prominent, unwelcome side effects such as restlessness, sweating, diarrhea, and excessive salivation (Bartus et al., 1982). The side effects of DFP are even more troublesome. Such drug treatments are therefore not clinically useful.

Another approach has been to try to increase the production of acetylcholine in the brain by providing dietary precursors, such as choline and lecithin. In a number of studies, these substances have been given to senile or brain-damaged people with serious memory failures. Unfortunately, they apparently produce no significant benefits (Bartus, Dean, Pontecorvo, & Flicker, 1985). It may be that senility and other memory failures are associated with such a massive depletion of acetylcholine synapses that a slight increase in the availability of the transmitter is ineffective.

Although dietary enrichment does not reverse a loss of memory that has already taken place, long-term enrichment may prevent such a loss. In one study, mice that were given a high-choline diet over a 4 1/2-month period had better than normal memory in old age (Bartus, Dean, Goas, & Lippa, 1980).

Other Synapses and Memory

In old age it is common to suffer a loss of norepinephrine, serotonin, and dopamine as well as acetylcholine (Wong et al., 1984). Damage limited to the norepinephrine and dopamine input to the prefrontal cortex of monkeys produces learning deficits that resemble those of non-brain-damaged old monkeys. Clonidine, a drug that stimulates the norepinephrine receptors, reverses these deficits (Arnsten & Goldman-Rakic, 1985a). Similarly, drugs that enhance the activity of neurons that release norepinephrine improve memory performance of aged mice (Zornetzer, 1985). Evidently, norepinephrine and dopamine play an important part in memory, as well as acetylcholine.

THE DISTINCTION BETWEEN SHORT-TERM AND LONG-TERM MEMORY

The physiology of memory encompasses two questions: How does experience change the properties of one or more neurons, and how do the changed neurons work together to produce adaptive behavior? So far we have dealt with the first question; we turn now to the second.

Why Hebb Distinguished Short-Term From Long-Term Memory

A basic problem for any theory of the physiology of memory is that memories may form rapidly yet remain permanently. Donald Hebb (1949) puzzled about what structural change in the brain could occur rapidly enough to account for the immediacy of memory and yet remain stable for a lifetime, once the change had taken place. He concluded that nothing could be both that changeable and that stable. Today, that reasoning is less obvious. We can almost instantaneously store information on an audio tape, a video tape, or a computer disk, and if the stored information is protected from strong magnetic fields and other damage, it can last indefinitely. Still, in the 1940s Hebb thought it unlikely that anything in the brain could store information rapidly but permanently. He proposed therefore that we have two kinds of memory, **short-term memory** and **long-term memory**.

A short-term memory might be represented by a rapid-forming, temporary process, such as a *reverberating circuit* of neuronal activity in the brain, with a self-exciting loop of neurons. If the reverberating circuit maintained its activity long enough, it could enable the brain to make some chemical or structural change that would store the memory permanently, even after activity in the circuit had stopped. The transfer of a short-term memory into long-term storage is referred to as **consolidation**.

Behavioral Differences Between Short-Term and Long-Term Memory

Hebb's theory implied that recent, short-term memories might differ from memories stored in the past. Behaviorally, we can observe a number of differences between old and recent memories. First, much of the information we store temporarily—telephone numbers, for example—is unavailable to memory later. Second, short-term memory has a limited capacity. A normal adult can repeat a list of about seven words immediately after hearing them but generally fails on a list much longer than seven (Miller, 1956). Long-term memory, on the other hand, has a large limit, not easily measured. When you form a new memory, you do not have to discard an old memory to make room for it.

Note, however, that these behavioral distinctions do not necessarily imply that short-term memory and long-term memory are entirely different, stored in different ways. It is possible to imagine a continuum between memories that are superficially, temporarily stored and memories that are processed more deeply and are readily recalled later (Craik & Lockhart, 1972).

Attempts to Disrupt the Transfer from Short-Term to Long-Term Memory

Hebb's theory also implied that a certain period of time is required to consolidate short-term memory into long-term memory. Anything that disrupts brain activity during that consolidation period would prevent long-term recall of the information. This idea is borne out by the fact that in humans, head injury that leads to loss of consciousness blots out memories of events just prior to the trauma (Crovitz, Horn, & Daniel, 1983).

To examine consolidation in more detail, we turn to animal studies. In a typical experiment, a rat is placed on a wooden platform above a metal floor. When it steps down to the floor, it gets a shock to its feet. A day later, placed again on the platform, the rat will stay for 5 minutes or more, unlike control rats that received no foot shock. (This is an example of *passive-avoidance learning*.) Another group of rats gets the same foot shock on the training day but is given an electroconvulsive shock (ECS) through the skull a second or two after the foot shock. When placed on the platform on a later day, the rats that have received ECS step down as quickly as they did the first time. They act as if they have forgotten both the foot shock and the ECS. The results are similar after several other treatments that interrupt consciousness and blood supply to the brain.

The standard interpretation of these findings has been that the experience of the foot shock is still in short-term memory at the time of the ECS; therefore, the electrical disruption caused by the ECS destroys the short-term memory trace before it has a chance to be consolidated into long-term memory. In support of this interpretation, numerous experiments have found that a delay between the shock and the ECS decreases the **amnesia** (memory loss) produced by ECS. Presumably, as time passes the short-term memory of foot shock is consolidated into a long-term storage that is less vulnerable to disruption by ECS.

This interpretation, though appealing, does not fit the data. One difficulty is that the effect of a delay varies greatly from one experiment to another. That is, in one experiment it may take only seconds for a memory to become consolidated and protected from disruption by ECS; in another experiment, it may take minutes, hours, or even days (Squire & Spanis, 1984). In humans, ECS (which is sometimes used as a therapy for severe depression) sometimes impairs memories more than a year old (Squire & Cohen, 1979).

A second, more serious difficulty is that ECS does not completely destroy the memory of a foot shock. In rat experiments, a brief "reminder," such as a foot shock in an unfamiliar apparatus, can revive a memory that had apparently been erased by ECS (e.g., Miller & Springer, 1972). Furthermore, when people suffer amnesia based on ECS or head trauma, the lost memories sometimes return after a delay or under the influence of tranquilizers (Whitty & Zangwill, 1977).

A third difficulty, theoretically the most significant, is that under certain circumstances ECS can interfere with both long-term and short-term memories. In several experiments, rats were trained on a task, given a few days' delay, and then given a stimulus similar to the training trials, followed by ECS. The ECS produced amnesia for the training, even though that training should have been well established in long-term memory (e.g., Lewis, Bregman, & Mahan, 1972; Robbins & Meyer, 1970; Schneider & Sherman, 1968). Apparently ECS interferes with memories that are *active* at the time of the ECS, regardless of whether they were formed recently or long ago (Lewis, 1979).

What can we conclude from these results? Because ECS can impair long-term memories as well as short-term ones, it must impair memory by doing something other than blocking the transfer from short-term memory to long-term. Furthermore, although memories do get consolidated into a more durable, less vulnerable form, they do so in a gradual manner over a long period of time, not necessarily in a matter of seconds or minutes.

INFERENCES FROM HUMAN AMNESIA

Even if we decide not to distinguish sharply between short-term and long-term memory, it remains the case that memories must be processed in some manner if they are to be available for recall later. We can learn something about that processing from studies of people suffering from amnesia.

H.M.

A man known to us by the initials H.M. has become one of the most famous cases in neurology (Milner, 1959; Penfield & Milner, 1958; Scoville & Milner, 1957). In 1953, H.M.'s epileptic seizures, which had proved unresponsive to all antiepileptic drugs, had become so frequent and incapacitating that he had to quit his job. As a desperation measure, neurosurgeons removed the hippocampus from both sides of his brain (see Figure 13-6), because the seizures seemed to be originating from that structure. They also removed several neighboring structures, including the amygdala. Although the surgeons did not know what to expect from the operation, they had acted on the belief that desperate cases call for desperate measures.

The results of the surgery were favorable in certain regards. The epileptic seizures indeed decreased in frequency and severity, and H.M. was able to take less of the antiepileptic medications. His personality and intellect remained the same; in fact, his IQ score increased slightly after the operation, presumably because of the decreased epileptic interference. However, he suffered severe amnesia. He experienced a moderate **retrograde amnesia** (loss of memories prior to a certain event, such as brain damage) and an extensive **anterograde amnesia** (inability to store new memories after a certain event). He could recall events that happened before the operation, although not so well as most people recall their past. He could still store new information briefly, but he had great difficulty storing it in such a way that he could recall it after his attention was distracted.

For example, after the operation he could not learn his way to the hospital bathroom. After reading a story, he was unable to describe what had happened in it. He could read a single magazine over and over without any indication of familiarity or any loss of interest. He lived with his parents,

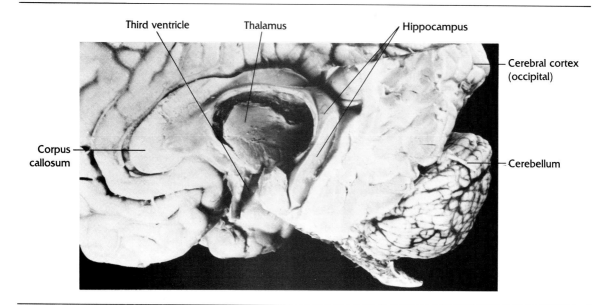

Third ventricle   Thalamus   Hippocampus

Cerebral cortex
(occipital)

Corpus
callosum

Cerebellum

Figure 13-6. View of part of the hippocampus, which curves into the interior of each hemisphere. (Photo courtesy of Dr. Dana Copeland.)

and when they moved to a new address, he had great difficulty finding his way home or locating anything within the house. After living there for eight years, he had finally memorized the floor plan and could find his way from one room to another; however, he still could not find his way home from a distance of more than two blocks (Milner, Corkin, & Teuber, 1968).

In one test of H.M.'s memory, Milner (1959) asked him to memorize the number "584." After a 15-minute delay without distractions, he was able to recall the number correctly. He explained how he did so. "It's easy. You just remember 8. You see, 5, 8, and 4 add to 17. You remember 8, subtract it from 17, and it leaves 9. Divide 9 in half and you get 5 and 4, and there you are, 584. Easy." A moment later, after H. M.'s attention had been shifted to another subject, he had forgotten both the number and the complicated line of thought he had associated with it.

In 1980, he moved to a nursing home. Four years later, he could not say where he lived or who cared for him. For several years after the operation, whenever he was asked his age and the date, he answered "27" and "1953," which were correct at the time of the operation. After a few years, he started guessing wildly, generally underestimating his age by 10 years or more, and misestimating the year by as much as 43 years (Corkin, 1984).

Although H.M. watches the news on television every night, he can recall only a few fragments of the events since 1953. On the other hand, he can learn new skills. He has learned a simple finger maze, he has learned to read material written in mirror fashion, and he has learned the correct solution to the puzzle shown in Figure 13-7 (Cohen, Eichenbaum, Deacedo, & Corkin, 1985). Although he has learned these skills, he does not remember learning them. In fact, he does not remember seeing the maze or the puzzle before. One way of describing H.M.'s defect is that he is normal on *knowing how* but greatly impaired on *knowing that*.

Figure 13-7. The Tower of Hanoi puzzle. The task is to transfer all the disks to another peg, moving just one at a time, without ever placing a larger disk on top of a smaller disk. Patient H.M. has learned to solve the problem, although he says he does not remember ever seeing it before.

The kind of surgery H.M. received will not be repeated. However, some people may experience similar damage to the hippocampus through a stroke or head injury. One patient suffered a stroke that destroyed one area of the hippocampus on both sides of the brain, with only slight damage outside the hippocampus. During the 5 years that he survived after the stroke, he, like H.M., had severe difficulty storing new memories, although he could still remember events that happened before the stroke (Zola-Morgan, Squire, & Amarai, 1986).

Korsakoff's Syndrome

Korsakoff's syndrome, also known as *Wernicke-Korsakoff syndrome*, is a type of brain damage caused by thiamine deficiency. Among the prominent characteristics of this syndrome are apathy, confusion, and memory impairment.

Ordinarily, the brain uses glucose as its main fuel. For the brain or any other organ to metabolize glucose, it needs thiamine (vitamin B_1). Prolonged thiamine deficiency leads to a loss or shrinkage of neurons throughout the brain, especially in the dorsomedial thalamus and the mamillary bodies (part of the hypothalamus) (Brierley, 1977; Victor, Adams, & Collins, 1971).

Such severe thiamine deficiency is almost unheard of except in severe alcoholics. Certain extreme alcoholics may go days or weeks at a time eating almost nothing and drinking only alcoholic beverages. In doing so, they become deficient in thiamine and other vitamins and minerals. If they get some thiamine soon enough, they avoid brain damage. The longer they remain thiamine deficient, the greater the brain damage. Certain hospitals, especially in large cities, report about one person with Korsakoff's syndrome per 1,000 hospital admissions. Most such patients must be confined to a mental hospital for the rest of their lives.

Consider an example: A 59-year-old man easily recalls details of his early life and of military experience as a young man, although he can recall almost no recent events. When an interviewer leaves the room after a long conversation and returns a few minutes later, the patient does not recognize the interviewer and does not remember having had a conversation. He does not recognize any doctors or nurses at the hospital, nor can he find his way around. He reads a newspaper repeatedly, showing the same surprise at the news items each time. When seated at the dinner table with an empty plate in front of him, he does not remember whether he has just finished eating or has not yet started (Barbizet, 1970).

Korsakoff's syndrome patients may have both retrograde and antero-grade amnesia. Some suffer a nearly complete loss of memory for their entire adult lives. The anterograde amnesia, characterized by slow learning, impulsive answering, and poor reconstruction of events, resembles that seen in patients with frontal lobe damage (Oscar-Berman, 1980; Squire, 1982). Although frontal lobe damage is not particularly characteristic of Korsakoff's patients, damage to the dorsomedial thalamus is; the dorsomedial thalamus is a nucleus that projects to the frontal lobe. Generally, the more severe a patient's anterograde amnesia—that is, the worse the patient's ability to learn new material—the worse the patient's memory for the recent past, up to 10 years before (Shimamura & Squire, 1986).

Although patients with Korsakoff's syndrome seem to remember almost nothing that happens to them, they often show some evidence of memory if they are tested indirectly. For example, they may be asked to read over a list of words, such as DEFEND, HELIUM, CONVEY, MODIFY, SINKER, BELFRY, and so on. Afterward, if they are asked to write as many words as they can remember from the list, they fail completely. In fact, they may reply, "What list?" But if they are given a list of partial words and asked to complete them (DEF---, HEL---, CON---, MOD---, SIN---, BEL---, and so on), they complete most of the words to match the words they read on the list, even though each of those words can be completed in several ways (Schacter, 1985). Evidently, some memory trace of the words is stored in the patients' brains, despite the fact that cues like "Remember that list?" fail to trigger the memories.

Alzheimer's Disease

Another cause of severe memory loss is **Alzheimer's disease,** a condition moderately common in old age that occasionally begins in middle age. The symptoms begin with minor forgetfulness and progress to more serious memory loss, confusion, depression, irritability, hallucinations, delusions, and inability to complete an action or a train of thought (Schneck, Reisberg, & Ferris, 1982; Sinex & Myers, 1982).

People with a moderate case of Alzheimer's disease may, like H.M. and Korsakoff's patients, successfully remember general principles and yet fail to remember the specifics of what is going on at the moment. For example, Schacter (1983) reported playing golf with an Alzheimer's patient who, although he remembered the rules and jargon of the game correctly, could not remember how many strokes he took on any hole. Five times he teed off, waited for the other player to tee off, and then teed off again, having forgotten his first shot. Even when he did remember not to tee off again, he could not remember where he had hit his ball. He could not say what label was on his ball, although when he picked up a ball he could recognize whether it was his.

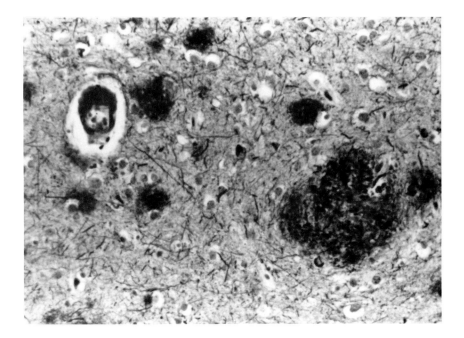

Figure 13-8. Microscopic photo of the cerebral cortex of an Alzheimer's patient, showing plaques (the small grayish spheres) and amyloid deposits (the larger dark areas). (From Rogers & Morrison, 1985.)

Also like H.M. and Korsakoff's patients, Alzheimer's patients can learn skills but not facts. In one study, Alzheimer's patients were unable to learn a list of words and were unable to learn to recognize new faces. They learned a motor skill about as well as normal people, however—the skill of maintaining contact between a hand-held pointer and a moving object (Eslinger & Damasio, 1986).

Alzheimer's disease is associated with degeneration of neurons that release acetylcholine (Mash, Flynn, & Potter, 1985) and to a lesser extent norepinephrine and other transmitters (Morrison, Rogers, Scherr, Benoit, & Bloom, 1985; Winblad, Hardy, Bäckman, & Nilsson, 1985). Cell damage is found in many brain areas, especially the cerebral cortex and the hippocampus (Hyman, van Hoesen, Damasio, & Barnes, 1984). Large numbers of tangles and *plaques* (formed from degenerating axons and dendrites) appear in the damaged areas, as shown in Figure 13-8 (Rogers & Morrison, 1985).

Alzheimer's disease runs in certain families. It also occurs in certain people who have no relatives with the disease. When it occurs in the absence of any hereditary tendency, one possible cause is a virus that takes effect very slowly and that damages the blood-brain barrier, allowing aluminum and other heavy ions to enter certain parts of the brain (Brown, Salazar, Gibbs, & Gajdusek, 1982; Wietgrefe et al., 1985; Wisniewski & Kozlowski, 1982). Although such a virus may be a factor, we have no solid evidence that Alzheimer's disease can be transmitted from one individual to another.

When Alzheimer's disease runs in a family, it is controlled by a dominant gene on chromosome number 21 (St. George-Hyslop et al., 1987). That linkage was first suspected because people with *Down's syndrome* (a type of mental retardation) invariably get Alzheimer's disease if they survive into middle age. Most cases of Down's syndrome are caused by having three copies of chromosome 21, as opposed to the usual two copies.

Chromosome 21 includes a gene that codes for a certain protein that is found in many tissues of the body. One fragment of that protein is found in abundance in the plaques that form in the brains of people with Alzheimer's disease and Down's syndrome (Goldgaber, Lerman, McBride, Saffiotti, & Gajdusek, 1987; Tanzi et al., 1987). Evidently the cause of these plaques is overproduction of this protein. People with Down's syndrome overproduce the protein because they have an extra copy of the gene for it. We do not know why people with Alzheimer's disease overproduce it; either they have an abnormal form of the gene or they have something else in their genes or environment that activates the gene excessively.

What Amnesic Patients Teach Us About Memory

Although H.M., Korsakoff's patients, and Alzheimer's patients have different underlying causes for their memory disorders, the resulting deficits have important points in common: Memory for events of the remote past is relatively intact, while memory for recent events is grossly impaired. Patients can learn skills better than they can learn facts, and they can remember general principles better than they can remember the specifics of what is happening at a given moment. Apparently, memory is of several types, and it is possible to impair a specific type without impairing others.

THE DISTINCTION BETWEEN REFERENCE MEMORY AND WORKING MEMORY

Although the distinction between short-term memory and long-term memory may be approximately valid, it may not be the most useful distinction we can draw in memory. A distinction that has gained popularity among many researchers is that between **reference memory** and **working memory**. Reference memory is memory for general principles, including both skills and facts that do not change from time to time. Working memory is memory for specific events, including memory for what has just happened.

To illustrate: Suppose your task is to name as many cities as possible in Texas. You could make two kinds of mistakes. One would be to say, "Dallas, Fort Worth, Houston, San Antonio, San Marcos, Waco, Albuquerque, Phoenix . . ." This is an error of reference memory. You have included Albuquerque and Phoenix, which are not cities in Texas. A different kind of mistake would be to say, "Dallas, Fort Worth, Houston, San Antonio, San Marcos, Austin, Fort Worth, San Antonio . . ." This is an error of working memory. Every city you have mentioned is in Texas, but you have lost track of which cities you already named.

Many tasks require both reference memory and working memory. A golfer needs to remember the rules of golf (reference) and where he or she has just hit the ball (working). To give a lecture, a psychology professor must remember the principles of psychology (reference) and what he or she has just said (working). To find your lost sunglasses, you must remember the layout of your house and the places where you generally leave your glasses

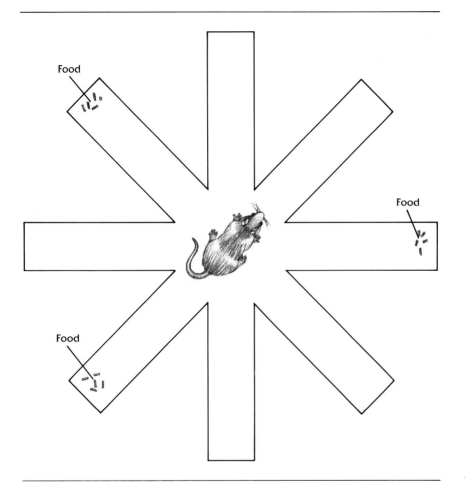

Figure 13-9. The radial eight-arm maze.

(reference), but you must also remember which places you have already checked (working).

H.M. and patients suffering from Korsakoff's syndrome or Alzheimer's disease are more impaired in their working memory than in their reference memory. Experiments on laboratory animals indicate that a system of the brain including the hippocampus, the amygdala, and their connections to other structures is particularly important for working memory.

Tests of Reference Memory and Working Memory in Animals

Two popular ways to test animals for their reference memory and working memory are the radial maze and the delayed nonmatching-to-sample test. Although these are certainly not the only tasks used, they illustrate the same points as a number of others.

The **radial maze** is illustrated in Figure 13-9. In a typical experiment, a rat is placed in the center of eight or more arms. A bit of food is present at the ends of certain arms—always the same arms. The rat stays in the maze until it has found all the food or until it has gone, say, 2 minutes without finding any more food. After enough training trials, a rat may learn to go down each of the correct arms once and only once and not to try any of the incorrect arms. A rat can make two kinds of mistakes: If it goes down one of the always-incorrect arms, it has made an error of reference memory. If it fails to try one of the correct arms, or if it tries one correct arm repeatedly, it has made an error of working memory (by apparently losing track of which arms it has tried). A normal rat makes only a few errors of either kind. Moreover, it does not solve the task by following any simple rule. For example, it does not take all the correct arms in a clockwise or counterclockwise order (Olton, Collison, & Werz, 1977).

A *matching-to-sample* task is one in which an animal sees an object and then gets a choice between two objects, from which it must choose the one that matches the first one it saw (the sample). In the more commonly used *nonmatching-to-sample* task, an animal first sees an object and then gets a choice between two objects, from which it must choose the one that is *different* from the first one. For example, it might first see a square object and then get a choice between a square and a triangle. To get a reward, it must touch the triangle. If the animal has to sit through a delay between seeing the first object and choosing between the pair of objects, the task is referred to as **delayed nonmatching-to-sample**. Any error on this task (after the animal has been trained) is considered an error of working memory, as the animal is presumed to have forgotten what it saw before the delay.

Matching-to-sample and nonmatching-to-sample tasks are best suited to an animal with good vision. For that reason, they are used more often with monkeys than with rats or other species. These tasks and the radial maze are commonly used to study the effects of brain damage on working memory in animals.

The Effects of Brain Damage on Working Memory

After the report of H.M.'s severe memory loss, many investigators examined the effects of hippocampal damage on learning and memory in animals. The deficits they found in the early experiments were generally small. Although these deficits may have been small for many reasons, one of the most likely is that the experiments dealt with the wrong kind of learning and memory. If the task is to approach a light for food or to press a lever when a buzzer sounds, hippocampal damage does not impair performance. We might regard such tasks either as skill learning or as establishing reference memories. In either case, they do not test working memory, which is the aspect of memory most impaired in H.M. and Korsakoff's and Alzheimer's patients.

Hippocampal damage produces major deficits in tests of working memory. On the radial maze, rats with damage to the hippocampus, or with damage to the axons that connect the hippocampus to other structures, make frequent errors of reentering certain arms without trying other correct arms at all. Nevertheless, they seldom make the mistake of entering an arm that has never been correct (Jarrard, Okaichi, Steward, & Goldschmidt, 1984; Olton & Papas, 1979; Olton, Walker, & Gage, 1978). In other words, their working memory is deficient but their reference memory is intact.

Monkeys with hippocampal damage make a number of errors on a delayed nonmatching-to-sample task. Their performance becomes a great deal worse if they have lesions to the amygdala as well as the hippocampus. The same monkeys perform almost normally on tests of reference memory, such as learning to approach one visual pattern and not another (Malamut, Saunders, & Mishkin, 1984; Zola-Morgan & Squire, 1986; Zola-Morgan, Squire, & Mishkin, 1982).

Can we arrive at any conclusions as to the role of the hippocampus in memory? Not exactly, although it does seem clear that it is most important for working memory. Moreover, experiments like those just described enable us to make some reasonable guesses about exactly what the hippocampus contributes:

1.   The hippocampus and related structures (including the amygdala) may be like a map of where memories are stored in the cerebral cortex— analogous to the card catalog of a library (Teyler & DiScenna, 1986).

2.   The hippocampus may select relevant cues and turn attention away from irrelevant cues (Winocur, 1982).

3.   The hippocampus may code information about space and time (Olton, Wible, & Shapiro, 1986) and the order in which various events occurred (Kesner, 1985). A good deal of memory is, of course, a record of changes over space and time.

The Hippocampus and Age Changes in Memory

Both infants and old individuals perform relatively poorly on the kinds of task impaired by damage to the hippocampus. For example, monkeys completely fail the nonmatching-to-sample task until age 4 months, and they do not reach adult levels of performance until age 2 years (Bachevalier & Mishkin, 1984). Presumably, the reason is that the hippocampus is slow to mature. This interpretation has implications for **infant amnesia**, a phenomenon that has long puzzled psychologists: People remember very few specific events that occurred during their first four or five years, even though children of that age learn a great many skills and general principles. That is, the memory impairments of young children resemble those of people and animals with damage to the hippocampus, perhaps because that structure is not yet fully mature (Moscovitch, 1985).

Many old people and aged animals have problems of slow learning and rapid forgetting, although one individual may differ sharply from another. Experiments with rats have explored the relationship between this memory decline and the hippocampus. In old age, a certain number of neurons die in parts of the hippocampus; the remaining neurons become less active and less subject to long-term potentiation (Barnes & McNaughton, 1985). The loss of neurons is hastened by exposure to high levels of corticosterone, a hormone released by the adrenal glands during periods of stress (Sapolsky, Krey, & McEwen, 1985). Corticosterone itself does not damage the neurons. Rather, it increases the metabolic activity of the cells and in the process makes them more vulnerable to damage by any toxic substances that may happen to be present (Sapolsky, 1985). In other words, corticosterone magnifies the damage to the brain caused by toxins and thereby accelerates the aging process in the brain.

Memory and the Frontal Lobes

The hippocampus and amygdala send part of their output to the prefrontal area of the cerebral cortex. Damage to the prefrontal cortex causes memory impairments similar to those noted after damage to the hippocampus and amygdala themselves. Monkeys with such damage fail on delayed nonmatching-to-sample tasks (Bachevalier & Mishkin, 1986). They also fail on a task similar to the radial maze, in which they have to find peanuts behind twenty-five doors by opening each door, without opening any door twice (Passingham, 1985b).

Humans with frontal lobe damage face similar difficulties. They are impaired on a *delayed alternation* task, in which they have to alternate between picking up an object on their left and picking it up on their right, with a delay between responses (Freedman & Oscar-Berman, 1986). Good performance on that task requires working memory for what one has just done.

People with prefrontal damage also have trouble remembering the order of events or planning the order of their own movements. Different cells in the intact prefrontal cortex are active prior to different movements (Sakurai & Sugimoto, 1986). Although these cells are not necessary for the movements themselves, they participate in planning the order of the movements.

In old age, the prefrontal cortex deteriorates as well as the hippocampus. Aged monkeys and monkeys with prefrontal damage perform poorly on many of the same tasks. The deficits in old age may be due in part to a declining number of dopamine and norepinephrine synapses in the prefrontal cortex (Arnsten & Goldman-Rakic, 1985a, 1985b).

As you have seen in this chapter, an investigator of the physiology of learning must deal with processes ranging from molecular changes to behavior. We cannot say simply that a particular drug or physiological change improves or impairs memory; we have to specify the type of memory it affects and the way it affects it. In the process, we stand to clarify our understanding not only of the physiology, but also of memory itself.

SUMMARY

1. Karl Lashley showed that learning does not depend on new connections across the cerebral cortex, because cuts through the cerebral cortex do not interrupt learned behaviors. (p. 354)

2. Lashley further demonstrated that maze learning by rats can be disrupted by damage to the cerebral cortex but that the disruption depends on the amount of damage more than on the location of the damage. (p. 354)

3. Different kinds of learning differ behaviorally, as well as in their physiology. (p. 356)

4. In certain instances, learning even in vertebrates

depends on changes in a small group of neurons. (pp. 357–364)

5. Habituation of the gill-withdrawal reflex in *Aplysia* depends on a mechanism that decreases the release of transmitter from a particular presynaptic neuron. (p. 360)

6. Sensitization of the gill-withdrawal reflex in *Aplysia* depends on the release of an enzyme that blocks potassium channels in a presynaptic neuron and thereby prolongs the release of transmitter from that neuron. (p. 361)

7. Learning a particular task by *Hermissenda*, an-

other marine mollusc, depends on a different mechanism from that in *Aplysia*. When *Hermissenda* learns not to crawl toward a light source, a particular receptor cell increases its activity. (p. 363)

8. Long-term potentiation in the mammalian hippocampus depends on an increased concentration of calcium in certain dendrites. The calcium activates a protein that changes the shape of the dendrites and thereby exposes additional glutamate receptors. (p. 364)

9. In certain cases, mammalian learning, like learning in *Aplysia* and *Hermissenda*, depends on changes in a small number of localized neurons. (pp. 357, 364)

10. Research on transfer of training by brain extracts was abandoned because the results were not replicable. (p. 365)

11. In many cases the long-term storage of memory requires the synthesis of proteins. (p. 366)

12. A few drugs and hormones facilitate memory, through a route of action that is not yet well understood. (p. 366)

13. In certain cases learning depends on an enhancement of transmission at synapses that use acetylcholine or other identified transmitters. (p. 367)

14. Drugs that alter those synapses may improve or impair memory, although no practical applications have yet been demonstrated for humans. (p. 368)

15. Donald Hebb distinguished between short-term and long-term memory largely because he could not imagine a structural change that occurs as fast as memory forms yet remains permanently afterward. (p. 369)

16. Although it is possible to disrupt the consolidation of long-term memories, the data suggest that consolidation is a gradual process over days, not something that corresponds to the behavioral distinction between immediate, short-term memory and all longer-term memories. (p. 370)

17. Although electroconvulsive shock disrupts active memories and impairs their later recall, it probably does so in a way other than preventing a transfer from short-term to long-term memory. (p. 370)

18. H.M., a patient with damage to the hippocampus, has severe trouble forming new memories of specific events, although he is unimpaired at learning skills. (p. 371)

19. Korsakoff's syndrome and Alzheimer's disease also impair the formation of new memories of specific events. People suffering from these diseases quickly lose track of what they have been doing. (pp. 373–375)

20. In animals, damage to the hippocampus and amygdala, or to the prefrontal cortex, impairs working memory more than reference memory; that is, it impairs recall of a specific signal or of the animal's last response but not recall of a consistent stimulus-response connection. (p. 377)

21. Infant amnesia may be due to slow maturation of the hippocampus; memory impairments in old age can be related to gradual loss of neurons and synapses in the hippocampus and prefrontal cortex. (pp. 379–380)

REVIEW QUESTIONS

1. How did Lashley test Pavlov's theory of the physiology of learning? (p. 354)

2. What two principles did Lashley propose as descriptions of how the cerebral cortex contributes to learning? (p. 354)

3. Which type of learning apparently depends just on small areas of the brain, and which are those areas? (p. 357)

4. What are the cellular mechanisms of habituation and sensitization in *Aplysia*? (p. 360)

5. How does the cellular basis of learning observed in *Hermissenda* differ from that found in *Aplysia*? (p. 363)

6. What changes in neurons are responsible for long-term potentiation in the mammalian hippocampus? (p. 364)

7. What happened to the research on transfer of training by brain extracts? (p. 365)

8. What is the evidence that an inhibition of protein synthesis impairs learning, and not just overall health? (p. 366)

9. Name some drugs and hormones that have been reported to facilitate memory. (p. 366)

10. What are the effects of scopolamine and physostigmine on memory? (p. 367)

11. Why was it supposed that choline and lecithin might improve memory? What was the result of research on that question? (p. 368)

12. What reasoning led Hebb to distinguish between short-term and long-term memory? (p. 369)

13. Why do the experiments on ECS fail to say anything definitive about the transfer from short-term to long-term memory? (p. 370)

14. What brain damage did H.M. suffer, and what effect did it have on his memory? (p. 371)

15. What type of learning and memory is unimpaired in H.M.? (p. 372)

16. What brain damage is found in Alzheimer's disease? (p. 374)

17. What are two possible causes of Alzheimer's disease? (p. 375)

18. In what ways are the memory deficits similar for H.M., Korsakoff's patients, and Alzheimer's patients? (p. 376)

19. What behavioral tests distinguish between reference memory and working memory? (p. 376)

20. What kinds of brain damage impair working memory? (p. 378)
21. Why are the effects of prefrontal cortex damage similar to those of damage to the hippocampus and amygdala? (p. 380)
22. What are several reasons why old people may have memory difficulties? (pp. 368, 379, 380)

THOUGHT QUESTIONS

1. Lashley sought to find the engram, the physiological representation of learning. In general terms, how would you recognize an engram if you saw one? That is, what would someone have to demonstrate before you could conclude that a particular change in the nervous system was really an engram?
2. In Castellucci and Kandel's (1974) experiment, habituation was attributed to a presynaptic change because the size of the quantum remained the same even though the size of the EPSP decreased. What conclusion, if any, could one draw if the size of the quantum decreased during habituation? Can you think of any other way to decide whether an alteration in EPSP size was due to presynaptic or postsynaptic changes?

TERMS TO REMEMBER

classical conditioning (p. 352)
engram (p. 354)
mass action (p. 354)
equipotentiality (p. 354)
habituation (p. 360)
sensitization (p. 360)
cyclic AMP (p. 361)
long-term potentiation (LTP) (p. 363)
calpain (p. 364)
second messenger (p. 366)
papaverine (p. 366)
ACTH (p. 366)
vasopressin (p. 366)
piracetam (p. 366)
aniracetam (p. 366)
physostigmine (p. 367)

DFP (p. 367)
acetylcholinesterase (p. 367)
synaptic block (p. 367)
short-term memory (p. 369)
long-term memory (p. 369)
consolidation (p. 369)
amnesia (p. 370)
retrograde amnesia (p. 371)
anterograde amnesia (p. 371)
Korsakoff's syndrome, (p. 373)
Alzheimer's disease (p. 374)
reference memory (p. 376)
working memory (p. 376)
radial maze (p. 377)
delayed nonmatching-to-sample (p. 378)
infant amnesia (p. 379)

SUGGESTIONS FOR FURTHER READING

Lynch, G., McGaugh, J. L., & Weinberger, N. M. (1984). *Neurobiology of learning and memory.* New York: Guilford. Collection of 34 chapters by prominent investigators, covering most aspects of current research.
Olton, D. S., Gamzu, E., & Corkin, S. (Eds.) (1985). *Memory dysfunctions. Annals of the New York Academy of Sciences,* whole vol. 444.
Squire, L. R. (1986). Mechanisms of memory. *Science, 232,* 1612–1619.
Thompson, R. F. (1986). The neurobiology of learning and memory. *Science, 233,* 941–947.

Recovery from Brain Damage

MAIN IDEAS

1. The human brain can be damaged by a sharp blow, an interruption of blood flow, or several other types of injury. Batteries of tests are available for estimating the location and extent of damage.

2. Although both humans and animals typically recover in part from brain damage, behavior is never as securely established as it would be if the brain had never been damaged. Behavior is likely to deteriorate again as a result of stress or fatigue, in old age, or after a period of inactivity or sleep.

3. Many mechanisms contribute to recovery from brain damage, including restoration of undamaged neurons to full activity, regrowth of axons, readjustment of surviving synapses, and behavioral adjustments.

4. The degree of recovery is sometimes better and sometimes worse if the damage occurs in infancy.

5. Several forms of therapy are available for helping people recover from brain damage.

An American soldier who suffered a wound in the left hemisphere of his brain during the Korean War was at first unable to speak at all. Three months later he was able to speak in short fragments. When he was shown a letterhead, "New York University College of Medicine," and asked to read it, all he could say was, "Doctors—little doctors." Eight years later, when someone asked him again to read the letterhead, he replied, "Is there a catch? It says 'New York University College of Medicine'" (Eidelberg & Stein, 1974).

Sometimes people recover substantially from brain damage, as in this soldier's case. Sometimes they do not. Why?

We would like to know how recovery occurs for both practical and theoretical reasons. On the practical side, we would like to understand the recovery process so that we can facilitate it. On the theoretical side, we would like to know how recovery occurs even though destroyed neurons cannot be replaced.

CAUSES OF HUMAN BRAIN DAMAGE

The human brain can incur damage in many ways. In young adults the most common cause is a sharp blow to the head, whether from a fall, an automobile or motorcycle accident, a violent assault, or other sources. It is estimated that about 8 million people each year receive head injuries in the United States, of whom 400,000 suffer a coma and probable brain damage (Peterson, 1980). Head injuries cause damage partly by subjecting the brain to rotational forces (see Digression 14-1).

In old age the most common source of brain damage is a **stroke**, also known as a **cerebrovascular accident**. In a stroke, a blood clot or other obstruction closes an artery, or an artery ruptures. In either case, the artery is no longer able to supply oxygen and nutrients to an area of the brain. The neurons deprived of oxygen die within a few minutes. Other neurons may die if a ruptured blood vessel floods them with excessive amounts of calcium. The damage may be limited to a fairly sharply defined region; neurons outside that region survive without permanent impairment. Figure 14-1 illustrates one brain immediately after a stroke, another brain of a person who survived long after a stroke, and the brain of a victim of a bullet wound.

Strokes are rare in young people and fairly common in old age. People in their 60s have about a 1 percent chance per year of having a stroke; the probability increases to about a 5 percent chance per year in people over 85. (Kurtzke, 1976). Stroke is one of the leading causes of death in the United States. Because strokes vary in their magnitude as well as in their location, a given stroke may be fatal or may produce effects so minor that they are hardly noticed. Certain old people suffer a large number of small strokes over a period of years.

In addition to closed head injuries and strokes, other sources of brain damage include tumors in the brain, certain bacteria and viruses, drugs and toxic substances, bullet wounds, and exposure of the head to radiation.

DIGRESSION

14-1

Why Don't Woodpeckers Give Themselves Concussions?

When a woodpecker strikes its bill against a tree, it repeatedly bangs its head against an unyielding object at a velocity of 600 to 700 cm per second (about 15 miles per hour). How does it escape brain injury?

May, Fuster, Haber, and Hirschman (1979) used slow-motion photography to observe the behavior of woodpeckers. They found that a woodpecker often makes a pair of quick, preliminary taps against the wood before a hard strike, much like a carpenter lining up a hammer with a nail. When it makes the hard strike, it does so in an almost perfectly straight line, keeping its neck rigid. The result is a near absence of rotational forces and whiplash. The fact that woodpeckers are so careful to avoid rotating their heads during impact is one line of evidence (among several others) that rotational forces are a major factor in traumatic brain injuries.

May and associates (1979) suggest several implications for football players, racecar drivers, and others who wear protective helmets. One implication is that the helmet would give more protection if it extended down to the shoulders, like the metal cases worn by medieval knights. The advice for nonhelmet wearers is: If you see a potential automobile accident or similar trauma on the way, tuck your chin to your chest and tighten your neck muscles.

Cerebral palsy is brain damage caused by complications during the birth process that interrupt blood flow to the brain. Huntington's disease and Korsakoff's syndrome cause gradual, diffuse damage to many brain areas. In this chapter we focus mainly on the outcome of strokes and other sudden, localized brain damage.

If it is known or suspected that a person has suffered brain damage, clinical neuropsychologists administer certain tests to determine the nature of the behavioral deficits. From past experience, they can use the results of these tests to infer the location of the damage in the brain. Of greater practical importance, they can use the results to plan a program of physical therapy, occupational therapy, or speech therapy to help the person regain control over the activities of daily living.

One battery of tests for brain damage is the **Halstead-Reitan test**. It consists of a series of measurements ranging from speed of finger tapping to comprehension of language, each of which is known to be sensitive to a particular type of brain damage. Other items on the test include placing blocks into the correct holes in a board with one's eyes closed, identifying whether two rhythms are the same or different, and connecting twenty-five numbered circles in order from 1 to 25 (Golden, 1981). The Halstead-Reitan test is a lengthy one, taking about 8 hours to complete.

Another examination is the **Luria-Nebraska neuropsychological battery**, pioneered by the Russian psychologist A. R. Luria and revised by researchers at the University of Nebraska (Golden, 1984). The test consists of 269 items divided into 14 scales. Here are a few examples of items:

- Touch your thumb to each of the other four fingers, one at a time.
- Count the number of tones in a musical sequence.
- Localize where you have been touched on the arm.
- Copy drawings of a circle, square, and triangle.

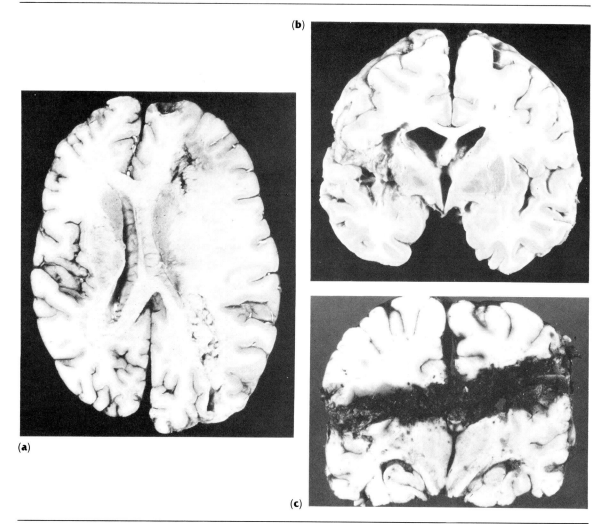

(b)

(a)

(c)

Figure 14-1. Three damaged human brains. (**a**) Brain of a person who died immediately after a stroke. Note the swelling on the right side. (**b**) Brain of a person who survived a long time after a stroke. Note the cavities on the left side, where large numbers of cells were lost. (**c**) Brain of person who suffered a gunshot wound and died immediately. (Photos courtesy of Dr. Dana Copeland.)

■ Memorize a list of seven words.
■ Tap a rhythm to copy one you have heard.

The Luria-Nebraska test is about as accurate as the Halstead-Reitan in identifying brain damage; it has the advantage that because most of its items are easier, it can be completed in about 2.5 hours (Golden, 1981).

The reason that both batteries include so many items is that a person may fail a given item for any of several reasons. Interpreting the result on one item requires comparing it with results on other items. For example, someone might fail to copy drawings of circles, squares, and triangles because of poor vision, poor coordination of the hand muscles, or inability to remember the instructions. To evaluate the results of this item, it helps to know whether the person has also failed other visual items, other hand coordination items, or all items in general.

AN EXAMPLE OF RECOVERY FROM DAMAGE: THE LATERAL HYPOTHALAMUS

A certain degree of recovery is common after many kinds of brain damage in both humans and other animals. For the sake of convenience, we focus here on one example that has been carefully studied: damage to the lateral hypothalamus. This example illustrates certain general principles of recovery. It also provides a mean of evaluating influences that might be responsible for recovery; we shall refer back to it during the discussion of mechanisms of recovery later in this chapter.

As discussed in Chapter 10, rats and other animals with damage to the lateral hypothalamus stop eating. They also become inactive, fail to groom themselves, and become unresponsive to sensory stimuli. They fail to respond normally to cold, sodium deficiency, low blood volume, and low blood glucose. As time passes, each of these symptoms gradually becomes less severe. A good deal of research has been done to describe the recovery and explore some of the processes responsible for it.

Stages of Recovery

Immediately after a lateral hypothalamic lesion, a rat ceases to eat or drink. If left to itself, it will starve to death in the presence of food. It is possible, however, to force-feed the rat by inserting liquid food into its stomach through a plastic tube slid down the rat's throat once or twice a day. In this manner, the rat can be kept alive for months; eventually, unless the damage is quite severe, the rat will begin to eat again. Close observation reveals that such rats progress through four stages of recovery over a period of weeks, from the initial, complete avoidance of food to the final stage of near normality (Teitelbaum & Epstein, 1962):

Stage 1 is the stage of **aphagia** (ay-FAY-juh, meaning "no eating") and **adipsia** (ay-DIP-see-uh, meaning "no drinking"). Not only does the rat ignore food, but if food is placed in or near its mouth, it turns away from it. It behaves toward all food the way a normal rat behaves toward bad-tasting food.

Stage 2 is the stage of **anorexia** (which means "no appetite," as in anorexia nervosa) and adipsia. Philip Teitelbaum discovered this stage by accident when he was a graduate student. While walking through the lab to check on his rats, he started eating a chocolate bar. To his surprise, many of the rats with lateral hypothalamic lesions, which had been ignoring the Lab Chow pellets in their cages, came to the front of their cages and started sniffing. On the hunch that the rats were sniffing out of interest in his chocolate bar, he offered them a bite and found that the rats—which would have starved to death in the presence of Lab Chow and water—eagerly nibbled at the candy bar. Rats at this stage of recovery will eat a little of any good-tasting food. (Rats' preferences in foods are similar to those of humans.) Rats at this stage do not eat enough to stay alive, however; the experimenter must continue to supplement their eating with force-feedings. The rats also continue to refrain from drinking water.

Stage 3 is characterized only by an avoidance of plain water. The rat no longer needs to be force-fed; it eats enough to survive, even if the food is not

Table 14-1.   Stages of Recovery from a Lesion in the Lateral Hypothalamus in Rats

Stage	Eating	Drinking
1. Aphagia and adipsia	None	None
2. Anorexia	Eats highly palatable foods in small amounts	Drinks water only if sweetened
3. Adipsia	Eats all normal foods, enough to maintain steady, low body weight	Drinks water only if sweetened
4. Almost normality	Eats all normal foods, enough to maintain steady, low body weight	Drinks even unsweetened water, but mostly to wash down dry food
5. Recovered rat under stressful conditions	Temporary return to one of earlier stages	Temporary return to one of earlier stages

particularly tasty. If the rat has access to sweetened drinks or to moist food, it can survive without help. But if the food is dry and the water is unsweetened, the rat gradually becomes dehydrated until it can no longer eat.

In stage 4, the final stage, the rat returns almost to normality. It eats and drinks (even water) enough to keep its body weight steady, though below normal. However, it seldom drinks between meals. It drinks a little water after every few bites to wash down its food (Epstein & Teitelbaum, 1964). Table 14-1 summarizes the stages of recovery.

As the rat regains its eating and drinking behaviors, it simultaneously recovers its activity levels and responsiveness to stimuli (Golani, Wolgin, & Teitelbaum, 1979). Shortly after the lesion, the rat is generally inactive. The first movements to return are side-to-side head movements, followed by backward and forward head movements. Over a period of weeks, both types of movements gradually spread to include the whole body. After both movements are well developed, the rat begins to add vertical movements. At first it pauses for long times between movements; as recovery proceeds, the pauses get shorter.

The recovering rat's responsiveness to stimuli also progresses through distinct stages. It responds first to vestibular stimuli and later to proprioceptive, tactile, and visual stimuli, in that order (Wolgin, Hein, & Teitelbaum, 1980).

An Alternative Interpretation of Recovery

When a rat resumes eating and drinking weeks after sustaining lateral hypothalamic damage, the apparent interpretation is that the rat has recovered certain behavioral capacities. An alternative interpretation is that the brain has not changed at all; it reacts differently only because the animals' weight has declined. According to this view (Keesey, Powley, & Kemnitz, 1976; Powley & Keesey, 1970), the main effect of the lateral hypothalamic lesion is that it makes the animal defend a lower *set point* for body weight (see Chapter 10). For example, a normal female rat may defend a set point of 300 g for body weight. In response to any fluctuation in her weight, she increases or decreases her intake until her weight returns to 300 g. After the lesion, her set point may be only, say, 220 g. She fails to eat for the first several weeks after the lesion only because something in her brain tells her she is overweight. She regains her appetite only after her weight has dropped.

In support of this clever interpretation, it has been found that a rat that is deprived of food for a few days before the lesion recovers faster than other rats with lesions (Balagura & Harrell, 1974; Powley & Keesey, 1970). Similarly, depriving a rat of water before the lesion causes it to recover its drinking faster than it would have otherwise (Schallert, 1982).

Is that the whole story behind recovery? Probably not. The weight-loss explanation does not explain how the rat gradually recovers its activity or its responsiveness to sensory stimuli. Some change must be taking place in the rat's brain, even if recovery does depend in part on a reduction of body weight.

The Precarious Nature of Recovery from Brain Damage

A person who has recovered from brain damage is never fully the same as a person who has never suffered brain damage. For analogy, someone with a sore foot may be able to walk just about normally under most conditions. The same person carrying a heavy load uphill, however, may slow down or stumble more than a person with healthy feet and may even have to quit altogether. Similarly, when people who have recovered from brain damage are behaving normally, they are already working up to capacity. Add even a mild interference, and their behavior deteriorates.

The Impairment of Recovered Behavior as a Result of Stress. Someone who loses the ability to speak after a stroke and then gradually regains it may lose it again, temporarily, after a couple of beers or at the end of a tiring day.

The behavior of brain-damaged rats also deteriorates under stress. For example, in a slightly cold room, both normal rats and rats recovered from lateral hypothalamic lesions react to the cold by increasing their food intake. (Eating and digesting food generates body heat.) If the room gets still colder, a normal rat eats still more, but the animal recovered from brain damage may fail to eat altogether, especially if only dry food and water are available (Snyder & Stricker, 1985).

Second example: A normal rat reacts to hypovolemia (decreased blood volume) by drinking and reacts to decreased blood glucose by eating. A rat recovered from lateral hypothalamic damage does neither. In fact, the rat temporarily acts the way it did just after the damage: It ignores food and water, it does not react to sensory stimuli, and it hardly moves (Stricker, Cooper, Marshall, & Zigmond, 1979).

For a third example, let us consider a different kind of brain damage. After damage to one side of the cerebral cortex, both humans and rats pay less attention to stimuli on the opposite side of the body. They may ignore stimuli on the opposite side altogether, at least at first. This reaction is known as **sensory neglect** (Figure 14-2). In milder cases or after partial recovery, they respond to stimuli on the side opposite the brain damage *if* those stimuli are presented alone. If a competing stimulus is present on the normal side of the body, they respond to that stimulus first. Human patients say that the

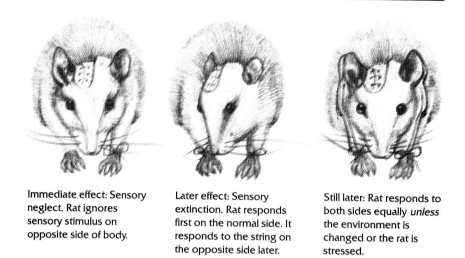

Immediate effect: Sensory neglect. Rat ignores sensory stimulus on opposite side of body.

Later effect: Sensory extinction. Rat responds first on the normal side. It responds to the string on the opposite side later.

Still later: Rat responds to both sides equally *unless* the environment is changed or the rat is stressed.

Figure 14-2. Behavior of a rat after unilateral cortical damage.

stimulus on the normal side feels stronger. This reaction is known as **sensory extinction.**

Eventually, both people and rats come to respond to stimuli on both sides equally. For example, a rat with strings attached to both forelimbs works equally hard at trying to remove one as the other. However, under mild stress or after a slight change in the environment, the rat loses its recovered behavior. If the experimenter even turns on the lights or opens the cage door, the rat temporarily goes back to paying more attention to the normal side (Schallert & Whishaw, 1984). Presumably, humans, too, would revert to sensory neglect or sensory extinction under conditions of stress or an altered environment. Again, the point is that the recovered behavior is disrupted by influence that would scarcely affect a normal individual.

The Loss of Recovered Behavior in Old Age.   A recovered rat deteriorates more than normal not only as a result of stress but also in old age. In rats as in humans, a certain number of neurons can be expected to die in old age. If the brain is initially intact, the loss of neurons may not impair behavior noticeably. A brain-damaged animal, however, cannot afford to lose any additional neurons. When a rat that has recovered from lateral hypothalamic damage reaches 2 years of age, which is old age for a rat, it begins to lose its recovered feeding and drinking behaviors and its responsiveness to sensory stimuli. Eventually the rat returns to a condition approximating its behavior just after the lesion (Schallert, 1983).

The same principle may hold for humans, Schallert (1983) speculates. For example, Parkinsons's disease may be the result of brain damage suffered early in life, probably not even noticed at the time if it was due to the gradual effects of toxins. When the person reaches old age, the loss of a small number of additional neurons leads to a great impairment of behavior.

Impairment After a Period of Inactivity.   Humans and other animals recovered from brain damage also differ from normals in their ability to mobilize their responses after a period of inactivity. A normal rat can return to vigorous activity, if necessary, almost as soon as it is aroused. A rat recovered from lateral hypothalamic damage, however, must go through a warm-up period after arousal from sleep or other inactivity. It begins with side-to-side movements, then makes forward and backward movements, and finally performs vertical movements (Golani, Wolgin, & Teitelbaum, 1979). The whole sequence may last as long as a few minutes. (Note that the movements emerged in this same order during the recovery process in the first few weeks after the brain damage.)

Infant rats also need a warm-up period. An 11-day-old rat, picked up and placed on a surface outside the nest, goes through a warm-up period similar to that of a rat recovered from brain damage (Golani, Bronchti, Moualem, & Teitelbaum, 1981). It would be interesting to examine whether young children, and perhaps old people, also need a warm-up period before they can respond at full capacity. The general point is that an individual with fewer than normal neurons----because of damage, immaturity, or aging---may need some extra time to arouse all available resources before engaging in normal activity.

POSSIBLE MECHANISMS OF RECOVERY FROM BRAIN DAMAGE

When the behavior of a human or any other mammal recovers, even slightly, from the effects of brain damage, it is a challenge to try to understand how the recovery took place. Unlike the skin, which can make new cells to replace any that are lost, the brain cannot recover by making new neurons.

A simple, popular assumption is that some other area of the brain takes over the functions of the damaged area. Only in a very limited sense is that likely to be correct. Someone who has injured one leg may learn to walk on the other leg and crutches. In a sense we may say that the healthy leg and the two arms have taken over the function of the damaged leg. Yet they are not doing anything that they could not have done before the injury. If we say that a healthy area of the brain takes over the function of a damaged area, we mean it in only this same sense. It does not reorganize its structure to mimic that of the damaged area; it does nothing that it could not have done before the injury.

To explain recovery from brain damage, then, we have two basic possibilities: Either structural changes occur in and around the area of the damage, or the person or animal learns to make more efficient use of abilities that were impaired but not destroyed. We shall discuss a number of mechanisms by which recovery might occur in at least certain instances.

Recovery by Removal of Toxins

After a lesion, one part of the behavioral deficit is due to the death of neurons, but another part is due to the spread of toxic materials from the dead cells into surrounding cells. Also, if the lesion is made with a metal

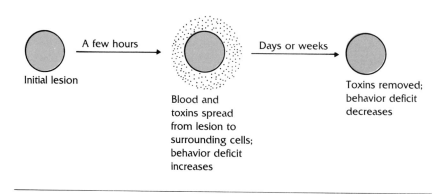

Figure 14-3. Possible mechanism for recovery from brain damage via removal of toxic materials surrounding the lesion.

anode, some metal ions leave the tip of the electrode and irritate surrounding, living neurons (Whishaw & Kolb, 1979; Whishaw & Robinson, 1974). The surrounding cells may suffer additionally from being deprived of their normal input from their now-destroyed neighbors. As time passes, the living but malfunctioning cells may recover their activity as glia remove some of the toxic materials and the bloodstream washes away some of the metal ions. As this happens, the malfunctioning cells return to normal activity, and part of the behavioral deficit disappears. Figure 14-3 illustrates this process.

One experiment offers direct support for this possibility. Van Sommers and Teitelbaum (1974) reasoned that the behavioral deficit immediately after a lesion should reflect the impairment of only those cells that were actually destroyed. As toxic materials from those cells spread to other cells, the behavioral deficit should grow.

Because experimenters ordinarily make lesions in the brains of animals that are deeply anesthetized, they cannot test the animal's behavior until it recovers from the anesthesia, at least hours later. Van Sommers and Teitelbaum made lesions in a way that enabled them to test a rat shortly after the lesion. First they implanted electrodes into the lateral hypothalamus on each side of the brain, under deep anesthesia, and cemented the electrodes to the skull, leaving just a tip of each electrode exposed. They allowed the rats to recover from the operation for 3 weeks, by which time the rats were behaving normally. Then, with the rats under very brief ether anesthesia, the experimenters attached wires to the electrodes and passed an electric current to make small lesions in the lateral hypothalamus.

The rats were offered food and water as soon as they awoke. A control group, treated with ether but not given a lesion, accepted the food and water at once and ate and drank again at regular times throughout the next 24 hours. The rats with the lesions immediately showed a moderate deficit in their eating and drinking that increased steadily over the next 4 to 8 hours. For example, one rat refused water and dry pellets 30 minutes after the lesion but accepted eggnog, Pablum, and moist chocolate chip cookies. An hour after the lesion, it accepted only the Pablum and cookies. Another hour later, it nibbled at the cookies but nothing else. Another 3 hours later, it ate nothing and drank nothing.

During the next week or so, each rat gradually recovered from the lesion. A possible explanation is that, just as the behavioral deficit increased while toxins spread out from the lesion, the behavior recovered while toxins gradually washed away.

Other Ways of Restoring the Surviving Neurons to Full Activity

After brain damage, the surviving neurons may fail to function normally for reasons besides the presence of toxic substances from the dead tissue. An alteration in blood flow is one such reason. For example, one group of stroke patients were examined via the rCBF method (see Chapter 4) to examine the blood flow to various parts of the brain. Shortly after the stroke, while they were unable to speak, blood flow to the speech areas of the left hemisphere was barely adequate to keep the neurons alive. Six months later, the arteries were delivering a great deal more blood to those areas and the patients had recovered much of their language abilities (Olsen, Bruhn, & Öberg, 1986). Presumably, the change in blood flow was responsible for at least part of the improvement in function by the speech areas.

Healthy neurons can deteriorate after brain damage for yet another reason: When a neuron is destroyed, other neurons that used to receive input from it are now cut off from one source of stimulation. At least temporarily, they function at less than normal capacity. For example, after a cut through the spinal cord, the neurons below the level of the cut become temporarily unresponsive to all stimulation. Even though these neurons continue to receive input from skin receptors that would ordinarily evoke a reflex, the neurons produce no output. The reason is that they have been cut off from the long axons descending from the brain and upper levels of the spinal cord, axons that kept the lower spinal neurons at a certain level of excitability. Days later, chemical changes in the lower spinal neurons compensate for the loss, and the excitability returns.

A similar process can occur in the brain. For example, cells in both the hypothalamus and the cerebral cortex contribute to the control of eating (Braun, 1975; Whishaw, Schallert, & Kolb, 1981). Because of connections between the two areas, damage to the lateral hypothalamus also suppresses activity in the relevant portions of the cerebral cortex (Kolb & Whishaw, 1977). Eventually, chemical changes within the cerebral cortex neurons restore their excitability and their ability to promote eating.

Recovery by the Regrowth of Axons

Although a destroyed neuron cannot be replaced, damaged axons do grow back under certain circumstances. A neuron of the peripheral nervous system has a cell body in the spinal cord and an axon that extends into the periphery. When such an axon is crushed, it degenerates back to the cell body. It then regenerates back toward the periphery at a rate of about 1 mm per day. If it is a myelinated axon, the Schwann cells (a type of glia cell found in the periphery) form a new myelin sheath. The regenerating axon follows the Schwann cells back to its original target, whether muscle, gland, or sensory receptor. If the axon was cut instead of crushed, the Schwann cells and myelin on the two sides of the cut cannot line up correctly, and a regenerating axon cannot follow a path back to its original target. Although each axon will grow back to *some* target, the result is only a partial recovery of sensation or muscle control.

Within the mammalian brain or spinal cord, a damaged axon degenerates but does not regenerate, or regenerates only briefly over an insignificant distance. That is why the paralysis caused by spinal cord injury is permanent. On the other hand, after a cut through the optic nerve or the spinal cord of certain species of fish, enough axons regenerate across the cut to restore fairly normal functioning, even though the connections are not the same as before (Bernstein & Gelderd, 1970; Rovainen, 1976; Scherer, 1986; Selzer, 1978). The question, therefore, is why damaged axons regenerate in the central and peripheral nervous systems of fish and in the peripheral nervous system of mammals, but not in the central nervous system of mammals.

If we find the answer, perhaps we can find some way to make such regeneration possible in mammals, including humans. So far, investigators have found at least three answers.

Scar Tissue.   One impairment to regeneration of axons in the mammalian central nervous system is that a thicker layer of scar tissue forms at the point of injury in mammals than forms in fish. If an artificial substitute scar tissue is implanted at the point of injury in a goldfish spinal cord and left in place for a month, the goldfish axons do not regenerate either (Bernstein & Bernstein, 1967, 1969).

Several attempts have been made to promote recovery in the mammalian spinal cord by trying to reduce the formation of scar tissue. In the 1950s and early 1960s, several investigators followed up on reports that a bacterial infection inhibits the growth of scar tissue, for unknown reasons. A number of animals were given daily injections of bacteria after spinal cord injury. Even when the bacteria slightly reduced the formation of scar tissue, however, very few axons regenerated across the cut, and most of those failed to make lasting synapses (McMasters, 1962; Scott & Clemente, 1955; Windle, Littrell, Smart, & Joralemon, 1956).

In the 1970s, experimenters in the Soviet Union reported that application of the enzymes trypsin and elastase to an injured spinal cord prevented the formation of scar tissue, enabled axons to grow across the cut, and enabled both rats and humans to regain control of the muscles below the cut (discussed by Pettegrew & Windle, 1976; Puchala & Windle, 1977). Unfortunately, experimenters outside the Soviet Union have been unable to replicate these findings (Guth, Bright, & Donati, 1978; Knowles & Berry, 1978; Kosel et al., 1979). Did the Soviet investigators misrepresent their results? Did they perhaps neglect to report a key element of their procedure? We do not know.

A Gap Between Two Ends of a Cut Spinal Cord.   During development, the bones of the spinal column continue to grow after the nervous tissue of the spinal cord has stopped (see Chapter 4). Consequently, the spinal cord is under a small amount of mechanical tension. When the spinal cord is cut, the lower half may pull away from the upper half, as shown in Figure 14-4

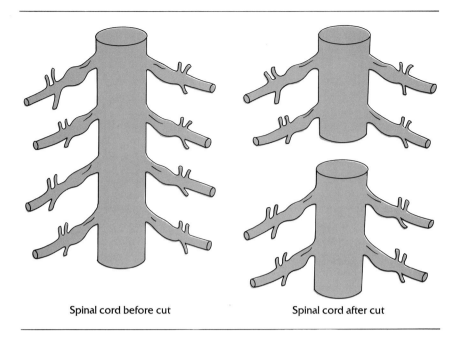

Spinal cord before cut   Spinal cord after cut

Figure 14-4. After a cut, the two halves of the spinal cord pull apart.

(Gearhart, Oster-Granite, & Guth, 1979). Thus, even if an axon regenerated it would have to traverse a substantial distance to reach the other half of the cord.

One way to deal with this difficulty is to construct a bridge made of peripheral nerve and to attach it to the two ends of a cut spinal cord, as David and Aguayo (1981) did with rats. Axons that entered the bridge did not have to cross scar tissue; furthermore, they had myelin sheaths to follow for guidance between the two ends of the cord. Axons in the bridge regenerated substantial distances, up to 30 mm, until they reached the other half of the cut spinal cord. When they did reach that point, however, the growth stopped.

One implication of these results is that axons in the central nervous system *can* regenerate over significant distances. Another implication is that simply getting across the cut is not enough.

Chemicals That Promote Regeneration.   The regeneration of an axon may depend on promotion by certain chemicals, produced either in the axon itself or by surrounding cells. Such chemicals may be present in fish and in the mammalian peripheral nervous system but absent in the mammalian central nervous system. In David and Aguayo's axon bridge experiment, axons in the mammalian central nervous system regenerated much more than normal because they grew through a bridge of peripheral nerve, which provided the chemical environment that promotes regeneration. Several other experiments have confirmed that CNS axons will regenerate along transplanted segment of peripheral nerve but not along a segment of transplanted axons from another part of the brain (Friedman & Aguayo, 1985; Schwab & Thoenen, 1985).

It may be possible to identify chemicals that increase regeneration. For example, a damaged peripheral nerve in a rat undergoes a tenfold increase in the synthesis and modification of proteins while it regenerates; a damaged optic nerve, which does not regenerate, does not increase its protein synthesis (Shyne-Athwal, Riccio, Chakraborty, & Ingoglia, 1986). A particular protein that has been found in high concentration in the developing neurons of infant rats accumulates in large quantities in regenerating peripheral axons; it does not accumulate in damaged axons of the central nervous system (Müller, Gebicke-Härter, Hangen, & Shooter, 1985). Although the function of this protein is not known, such a protein could easily play a necessary role in regeneration.

In fish, the nonneuronal cells that surround a damaged axon, in either the central or the peripheral nervous system, release chemicals that promote regrowth. One group of experimenters cut the optic nerves of fish and of rabbits. The optic nerve of the fish regenerated; that of the rabbits did not. Then they took a segment of regenerating fish nerve and placed it near an injured rabbit optic nerve. The fish tissues apparently released a chemical that promotes regeneration, as the optic nerve of the rabbit regenerated in part (Schwartz et al., 1985).

These results suggest that fish nerves regenerate more than mammalian nerves in the central nervous system because the fish axons themselves or the surrounding cells release chemicals that make regrowth possible. Perhaps if we can find ways to produce large amounts of that chemical, we may enable axons of the mammalian central nervous system to regenerate, too.

Activation of Previously Silent Synapses

The dendrites and soma of almost any neuron are thoroughly covered with synapses from a large number of other neurons. Some of these synapses are silent—the postsynaptic neuron does not respond to the transmitter. In some manner certain postsynaptic neurons select a pattern of synapses to which they will respond, based on the pattern of activity in those synapses. For example, as discussed in Chapter 7, a neuron in the visual cortex may select its synapses such that it will get input from one part of the left retina and a corresponding part of the right retina. Other synapses remain anatomically intact but ineffective.

If the synapses that ordinarily stimulate a given neuron are destroyed, certain of the previously silent synapses may become active. For example, in the primary somatosensory cortex of a monkey, one section is responsive to touch stimuli from the five fingers of one hand, as shown in Figure 14-5 (a). Although each set of neurons responds to synapses representing a given finger, it probably has silent synapses representing other, adjacent fingers. After finger 3 was amputated in an owl monkey, the neurons that had previously responded to it became inactive temporarily. As time passed, more and more of them became responsive to finger 2, finger 4, or part of the palm, until eventually the cortex had the pattern of responsiveness shown in Figure 14-5 (b) (Kaas, Merzenich, & Killackey, 1983; Merzenich et al., 1984).

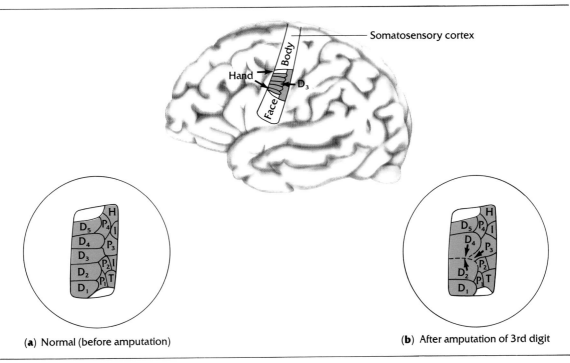

(a) Normal (before amputation)

(b) After amputation of 3rd digit

Such reorganization does not cause fingers 2 and 4 to feel like the lost finger. When humans lose a finger, they become more sensitive in the neighboring fingers, better able to localize a sensation on one of them.

The general point here is that the connections from the sensory receptors to the brain do not become permanently fixed. Synapses that were once silent may become functional when other synapses become inactive.

Figure 14-5. Changes in representation of the fingers in the somatosensory cortex of an owl monkey after amputation of the third digit. (Based on Kaas, Merzenich, & Killackey, 1983.)

Sprouting

After damage to one set of axons, the uninjured axons in the surrounding area may form new branches, or **collateral sprouts**, that attach to vacant synapses. (See Figure 14-6.) Gradually, over a period of months, the sprouts fill in most but not all of the vacated synapses (Matthews, Cotman, & Lynch, 1976). An axon sprouts to occupy such synapses only if its field of innervation previously overlapped that of the damaged axon (Cotman & Nieto-Sampedro, 1982; Finger & Stein, 1982). In certain cases axons may, however, sprout to make functional synapses at sites that previously responded to a different transmitter (Moore, 1974; Moore, Björklund, & Stenevi, 1971; Raisman, 1969; Raisman & Field, 1973). We must assume that the sprouted axons induce the postsynaptic cells to manufacture different synaptic receptors.

Sprouting is probably a normal condition, not one that occurs only in response to brain damage (Cotman & Nieto-Sampedro, 1984). Certain synapses are broken while new ones are made via sprouting; in time, some of these new ones may be broken and replaced themselves.

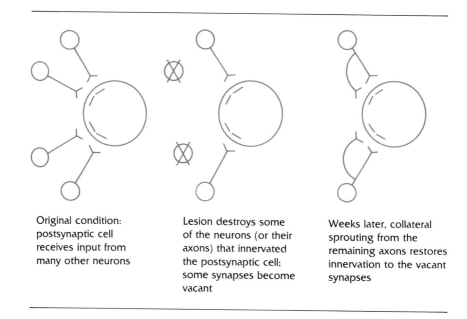

Original condition:
postsynaptic cell
receives input from
many other neurons

Lesion destroys some
of the neurons (or their
axons) that innervated
the postsynaptic cell;
some synapses become
vacant

Weeks later, collateral
sprouting from the
remaining axons restores
innervation to the vacant
synapses

Figure 14-6. Collateral sprouting.

Sprouting is likely to be useful in combating the effects of brain damage if the sprouting axon is similar to the damaged one; in that case, it provides a good substitute. In other cases, however, when an axon sprouts to occupy the synapses previously occupied by an unrelated axon, the usefulness of sprouting is more doubtful.

Evidence exists that sprouting is at least sometimes beneficial, although that evidence is largely indirect. For example, *gangliosides* are chemicals believed to enhance collateral sprouting, among other effects; gangliosides reduce the behavioral deficits caused by damage to the caudate nucleus (Sabel, Slavin, & Stein, 1984). For another example, it has been demonstrated that the time course of behavioral recovery after brain damage matches the time course of sprouting (Scheff & Cotman, 1977). In this experiment, connections from one side of the cerebral cortex to one side of the hippocampus were destroyed. Over the next 2 weeks, axons from the opposite side of the cerebral cortex formed collateral sprouts onto the hippocampus on the damaged side. The behaviors that were initially impaired after the lesion recovered over the same two weeks.

Denervation Supersensitivity

A postsynaptic cell that is deprived of synaptic input for a prolonged time increases its sensitivity to the synaptic transmitter. For example, a normal muscle cell responds to the synaptic transmitter acetylcholine only at the nerve-muscle junction. If the axon is cut, or if it is inactive for days, the muscle cell builds up additional receptors to acetylcholine both at the usual site and at more distant sites (Johns & Thesleff, 1961; Levitt-Gilmour & Salpeter, 1986). The same process occurs in neurons. An increased sensitivity to the synaptic transmitter as a result of decreased exposure to it is known as **denervation supersensitivity** (Glick, 1974).

Denervation supersensitivity can partially compensate for a loss of some of the axons that innervate a neuron. Suppose that 100 axons, all using the same transmitter, attach to neuron X. Suppose further that 50 of those axons are destroyed. One way to compensate for the loss is for the 50 surviving axons to sprout and occupy the vacant synapses. Another way is for the postsynaptic cell to increase the density of receptors at the 50 healthy synapses (Creese, Burt, & Snyder, 1977). Either method of compensation may work, in different cases. We can sometimes infer that the compensation has taken place in the postsynaptic neurons, presumably by denervation supersensitivity, because the metabolic rate of these cells increases while behavioral recovery takes place (Kozlowski & Marshall, 1981).

One study demonstrated that denervation supersensitivity contributes to recovery from lesions to the lateral hypothalamus. Zigmond and Stricker (1972, 1973) made lesions in the lateral hypothalamus of rats by injecting **6-OH-DA (6-hydroxy-dopamine)** into the lateral ventricles, from which it diffused into the lateral hypothalamus. (Because 6-OH-DA is chemically similar to dopamine and norepinephrine, the neurons that release these transmitters recognize 6-OH-DA as their own transmitter and absorb it. After entering the neurons, it is oxidized into toxic chemicals that kill the neurons. Note that it selectively kills neurons that use dopamine or norepinephrine as their transmitter. The injection of 6-OH-DA produces behavioral effects similar to other methods of damaging the lateral hypothalamus, and the animals recover through the same stages.)

After Zigmond and Stricker's animals had recovered behaviorally, their brains continued to show the same deficits in dopamine and norepinephrine that had been present shortly after the 6-OH-DA injections. That is, the rats had recovered without producing any greater quantities of the transmitters. That left two possibilities: Either the postsynaptic cells had become more sensitive to the remaining amounts of dopamine and norepinephrine, or the recovery had depended on some other transmitter altogether. Zigmond and Stricker resolved this issue by injecting small quantities of a drug that inhibits the synthesis of dopamine and norepinephrine. When the drug produced a great impairment of feeding, they knew that the recovered feeding still depended on those transmitters. In other words, the recovery must have depended on denervation supersensitivity.

Learned Adjustments in Behavior

Much of the recovery that takes place after brain damage is learned; it is a matter of making better use of abilities the person or animal already had on the day after the damage, rather than a matter of waiting for structural changes in the nervous system. For example, someone who has lost vision in all but the center of the visual field may at first fail to see a good bit of the environment. Later, the person moves his or her head back and forth to compensate for the loss in peripheral vision (Marshall, 1985).

A brain-damaged person or animal may also learn to make use of abilities that appear to be lost but actually are just impaired. For example, as discussed in Chapter 8, a monkey that receives no sensation from one arm does not use it in walking. It is clearly capable of using it, however, since if

Table 14-2.   Summary of Possible Mechanisms of Recovery from Brain Damage

1. Return to normal function by undamaged neurons
   By removal of toxins from the dead tissue
   By an increase in the blood supply
   By metabolic compensation for the decreased input

2. Regeneration of damaged axons
   (central and peripheral nervous systems of fish; peripheral
   nervous system only in mammals)

3. Changes at synapses in the brain
   Activation of previously silent synapses
   Sprouting
   Denervation supersensitivity

4. Learned adjustments in behavior

sensation is cut off from the other arm as well, the monkey makes use of both arms. When it has one normal arm and one with no sensation, the monkey apparently finds it easier to use the normal one than to use both.

Similarly, many victims of brain damage find it easier, especially at first, to struggle along without using some ability that has been partly impaired by the damage. Many of them are capable of doing more than they are doing, and more than they themselves realize they can do. Therapy for brain-damaged people sometimes focuses on showing them how much they are already capable of doing and encouraging them to practice those skills.

Table 14-2 summarizes the mechanisms we have discussed that may contribute to recovery from brain damage.

AGE AND OTHER FACTORS THAT INFLUENCE RECOVERY
If two individuals suffer the same brain damage, one of them may show more severe symptoms. In this section we consider some of the reasons why that is true.

Age at the Time of the Damage
According to the **Kennard principle**, named after Margaret Kennard, who first offered this generalization (Kennard, 1938), it is easier to recover from brain damage early in life than later in life. A child who suffers damage to the left hemisphere eventually gains or regains a greater ability to speak than an adult with similar damage. A child with damage limited to the sensory or motor cortex also shows greater gains than an adult with similar damage (Hécaen, Perenin, & Jeannerod, 1984).

The Kennard principle is no more than partly correct, however. Depending on the location of the damage and the behavioral deficits studied, the effects of early brain damage may be greater than, less than, or the same as the effects of adult brain damage (Stein, Finger, & Hart, 1983). For example, although damage limited to, say, the motor cortex of a young child may produce only a moderate impairment of motor control, it is likely to lead to other, more generalized difficulties not found after adult brain damage, such as slow learning and a low IQ score (Taylor, 1984).

Moreover, the effect of age on recovery from brain damage depends on the reason for the brain damage. Although children may recover better than adults from the destruction of a limited area of the brain, they recover less from infection, poor nutrition, inadequate oxygen, or exposure of the brain to alcohol or other drugs (O'Leary & Boll, 1984). Such factors disrupt the organization of developing neurons without killing them. The neurons may therefore make abnormal connections. The result is a generalized loss of sensory and motor functions and intelligence.

Why might the effects of infant brain damage be different from those of adult brain damage? We can identify several possible reasons.

Effects on Other, Still Developing Neurons.

In normal development, the immature brain produces a great many more neurons than will actually survive, and the immature neurons produce more synapses than will survive. As development proceeds, many of the extra neurons and extra connections are lost. If damage strikes during this early stage of development, the brain can react in ways that would be impossible later in life. When one set of neurons dies, a second set that might otherwise have perished may survive instead. Alternatively, when one set dies, a second set may die, too, if it depends on the first set as a source of input or as a primary target of output.

Both of those possibilities do occur, in fact. First, after complete removal of one hemisphere of a rat brain in infancy, the other hemisphere increases in thickness (Kolb, Sutherland, & Whishaw, 1983). No such increase occurs after removal of a hemisphere in adult rats. Evidently, neurons of each hemisphere compete with neurons of the other hemisphere for the chance to survive; if one hemisphere is damaged, a greater percentage of cells in the opposite hemisphere can survive.

Second, after removal of the anterior portion of the cortex in infant rats, the posterior portion of the cortex develops less than normal (Kolb & Holmes, 1983). Apparently neurons in the posterior cortex require an interaction with neurons in the anterior cortex in order to survive. The same is not true in adulthood. For that reason, damage to the anterior cortex produces *greater* effects on the behavior of infant rats than it does on the behavior of adults, even though damage to an entire hemisphere produces weaker effects.

Effects on Axons.

Damage to any structure in the adult brain destroys not only the neurons with cell bodies in that area but also neurons whose axons go into or through that structure. For that reason, brain damage in infancy may spare axons that would have been destroyed by similar damage in adulthood. If a structure is damaged early in infancy, before a certain set of axons have entered the area, those axons may grow around the area of damage and still reach their target (Bregman & Goldberger, 1982).

If a structure is damaged before the axons that ordinarily innervate it have reached it, those axons may innervate a neighboring structure. For example, suppose the superior colliculus has been damaged on the left side of the brain in an infant hamster, before the optic nerve has reached it. When these axons of the optic nerve eventually reach the damaged area, they cross to attach to the superior colliculus on the right side. (See Figure 14-7.) The hamsters then show some spatial orientation toward what they see in the

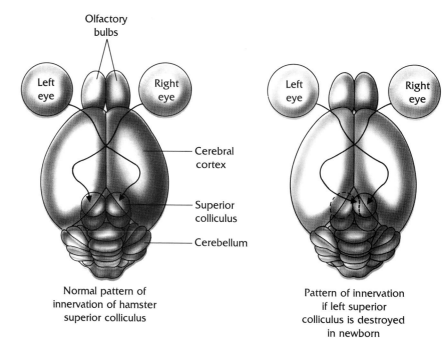

Olfactory
bulbs

Left
eye

Right
eye

Left
eye

Right
eye

Cerebral
cortex

Superior
colliculus

Cerebellum

Normal pattern of
innervation of hamster
superior colliculus

Pattern of innervation
if left superior
colliculus is destroyed
in newborn

Figure 14-7. If the superior colliculus is destroyed unilaterally in a newborn hamster, axons that normally innervate the damaged side go to the opposite superior colliculus. (Based on results in Schneider & Jhaveri, 1974.)

right visual field. Unfortunately, the hamsters orient in the wrong direction. That is, a hamster that sees something on the right turns to the left. It is as if the right superior colliculus interprets all the input it receives as coming from the left visual field as usual (Schneider & Jhaveri, 1974). Although this odd recovery may not do the animal any good, it provides an example of how early brain damage can lead to a different pattern of connections than adult damage—possibly better, possibly worse.

Effects on Sprouting and Denervation Supersensitivity.   Various types of brain damage elicit more vigorous collateral sprouting in young animals than in adults. After damage to one of the sources of input to the hippocampus, axons from the other sources sprout to fill the vacant synapses. The sprouting takes place more rapidly in young rats than in adults, and it results in the reinnervation of a higher percentage of the vacant synapses (Mc-Williams & Lynch, 1983, 1984).

After partial damage to dopamine pathways in the brain, many neurons increase their sensitivity to the remaining dopamine—that is, they display denervation supersensitivity. According to one study, aging mice (24 to 26 months old) failed to show denervation supersensitivity (Randall, Severson, & Finch, 1981). In a different study, however, 27- to 28-month-old rats showed just as much denervation supersensitivity as younger rats and just as much behavioral recovery after damage to axons containing dopamine (Marshall, Drew, & Neve, 1983). It may be that sprouting and denervation

Patricia S. Goldman-Rakic

Patricia Goldman-Rakic is a prominent contemporary investigator of the prefrontal cortex. Her early studies on the effects of damage to this brain area during infancy have pointed out some of the complexities of development, in contrast to earlier views that infant brain damage was simply "easier to recover from" or "harder to recover from" than adult damage.

After receiving a bachelor's degree from Vassar in 1959, she went to UCLA, where she received a Ph.D. in psychology in 1963. She then worked at the National Institutes of Mental Health until 1979, when she became a professor of neuroscience at the Yale School of Medicine.

She says that her goal is to understand what the prefrontal cortex does, because it is essential for those behavioral characteristics that are distinctively human. An understanding of the prefrontal cortex could lead to a neurology of cognition, comparable to the well-established neurologies of sensation, motor control, and homeostatic regulation.

Such a complex problem must be approached from many angles; Goldman-Rakic has conducted studies that range from anatomy to biochemistry to behavior. She was the first person to study the effects of prenatal brain lesions in monkeys. (That requires removing the monkey fetus, performing the surgery, returning the fetus to the mother's uterus, maintaining it until delivery, and then following the infant's behavioral development.) She devoted considerable energies to mapping the connections between the prefrontal cortex and other areas of the brain, and to mapping the distribution of synaptic transmitters throughout the entire monkey cerebral cortex. Previously, little had been known about the detailed structure of the prefrontal cortex and its connections with other structures. Goldman-Rakic demonstrated that the prefrontal cortex has a well-organized geometrical arrangement and that each part of it is connected in precise ways with such structures as the putamen and caudate nucleus. One of her findings was that the prefrontal cortex is organized in columns, similar to the columns found in the visual cortex (see Chapter 7).

Several of her studies of monkeys have clear relevance to human disorders. For example, she found that depletion of the dopamine, norepinephrine, and serotonin content of the prefrontal lobes leads to cognitive deficits in monkeys; also that restoration of those transmitters can reverse the cognitive losses. As we shall see in Chapter 16, schizophrenic patients suffer cognitive impairments that are apparently related to disorders at their dopamine synapses; studies on monkeys may enable us to advance our understanding of the relationship between dopamine and cognition.

Furthermore, Goldman-Rakic and her colleagues found that the norepinephrine and dopamine content of the prefrontal cortex decline naturally in aging monkeys, and that drugs that stimulate those synapses can reverse the memory losses of aging monkeys. These studies have led to clinical trials to determine whether such drugs can improve memory for aged people, including patients with Alzheimer's disease.

supersensitivity deteriorate in old age under some circumstances but not others.

Effects on Development of Other Structures.   Injury at an early age may damage a structure before it is mature enough to contribute to behavior. Patricia Goldman (see BioSketch 14-1) found that monkeys that had received injuries to the dorsolateral part of the prefrontal cortex in infancy showed only a moderate deficit on a delayed alternation task, in which they had to alternate between choosing an object on the left and choosing an object on the right. A year after the injury, they performed better than other monkeys that had received the same damage at a later age. When tested 2 years after the lesion, however, the monkeys that had received the damage in infancy did no better than the others (Goldman, 1971). The interpretation is that the dorsolateral prefrontal cortex does not mature until a monkey is about 2 years old. The monkeys tested at 1 year of age were unimpaired because this structure would not have been contributing much to behavior at that age anyway. The effects of the lesion were not seen until the age when the structure would normally have become mature.

In other cases the deficit caused by a lesion in one area may *decrease* when another area becomes mature. If infant monkeys receive damage to the orbital part of the prefrontal cortex, they show deficits at age 1 year on the delayed alternation task. By age 2 years, the behavior improves considerably. If the damage occurs at age 2 or later, however, the monkeys show no such improvement (Goldman, 1976; Miller, Goldman, & Rosvold, 1973). Early damage apparently leads other, later developing brain areas—probably including the dorsolateral prefrontal cortex—to change their organization in a way that compensates for the damage. By age 2, these other areas are already established in their normal functions and cannot reorganize in response to brain damage elsewhere.

Differences Between Slow-Onset and Rapid-Onset Lesions

After sudden damage to the motor cortex on both sides of its brain, a monkey suffers a total and permanent loss of fine movements. If, however, the damage occurs in several stages, with a couple of weeks to recover from one small brain injury before the next one takes place, the monkey may continue to walk and to carry on other activities even though the entire motor cortex is ultimately destroyed (Travis & Woolsey, 1956). Better recovery after a series of small lesions than after a sudden, large lesion is known as the **serial-lesion effect**.

The serial-lesion effect does not apply to all kinds of brain damage; sometimes a series of small lesions produces just as great an effect as one large lesion. When the serial-lesion effect does occur, two explanations are possible: (1) Gradual brain damage may allow for collateral sprouting or other structural changes that cannot occur after sudden, complete damage, or (2) gradual damage may enable the individual to learn new ways of coping and better ways to make use of the abilities spared by the lesion.

The Effects of Experiences Prior to the Damage

Once an animal has engaged in a given behavior, the representation of that behavior in the brain may change in ways that make it easier to elicit the same behavior again. The behavior may also become less vulnerable to the effects of brain damage. For example, if a rat with damage in its lateral hypothalamus becomes sodium deficient, it does not increase its salt preference the way a normal rat does. If a rat has had experience with sodium deficiency or with drinking salt water prior to such brain damage, however, it reacts normally to the sodium deficiency after the damage (Schulkin & Fluharty, 1985; Wolf, Schulkin, & Fluharty, 1983).

THERAPIES FOR BRAIN DAMAGE

After someone suffers brain damage, medical doctors and members of allied professions try to help the person recover. Although therapy at this time consists almost entirely of supervised practice of the impaired behaviors, direct intervention in the brain may become possible in the future.

Behavioral Interventions

You may fail to find a book in the library that you know the library used to have, either because the library has lost or misplaced the book or because it has lost the card that identifies the location of the book. Similarly, a brain-damaged person or animal may seem to have forgotten something or to have lost a particular skill either because it is indeed completely lost or because it "cannot be found."

In certain cases it can be demonstrated that an animal that seems to have lost some ability has not lost it completely. After damage to its visual cortex, a rat that has previously learned to approach a white card instead of a black card for food will now choose randomly between the two cards (Figure 14-8). Has the rat forgotten the discrimination completely? Evidently not, since it can relearn to approach the white card significantly more easily than it can learn to approach the black card (LeVere & Morlock, 1973). Apparently some trace of the original learning has remained after the brain damage.

LeVere (1975) proposed that such a lesion does not destroy the memory representation but merely impairs the rat's ability to find the memory. When the rat relearns the maze, it is going through a process of refinding or reaccessing the memory, which is very different from original learning. The reaccessing process is not impaired by a drug that inhibits protein synthesis and that greatly impedes the learning of new tasks (Davis & LeVere, 1979).

Similarly, humans who have suffered brain damage may have trouble finding or accessing certain skills and memories that they still have. Further, just as a monkey that has no sensation in one arm may try to get by without using it, a person who has an impairment of one sensory system may try to get by without using it (LeVere, 1980). The task of physical therapists, occupational therapists, and speech therapists is thus to prod brain-damaged patients to practice their impaired skills instead of ignoring them altogether.

In support of this view, LeVere and LeVere (1982) trained rats with visual cortex lesions on a brightness discrimination task, in which tactile stimuli were present as well. For one group of rats the tactile stimuli were redundant with the brightness cues; the rats could solve the problem by responding to either type of stimulus. This group solved the task rapidly but paid attention only to the tactile stimuli. If the tactile stimuli were removed, the rats responded randomly. For a second group of rats the tacile stimuli were irrelevant; they could solve the problem only on the basis of brightness. This group took much longer than normal rats to solve the problem; their attention to the tactile stimuli distracted them from the relevant visual cues. In short, rats with visual cortex lesions are capable of learning about visual stimuli, but they are unlikely to do so if other stimuli are available to which

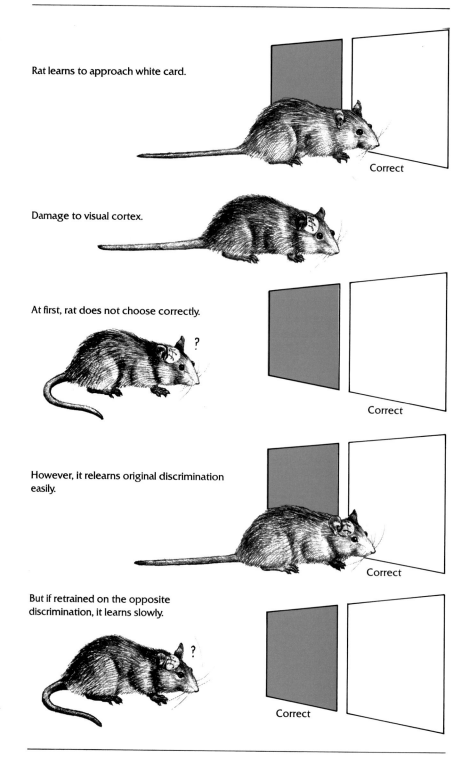

Rat learns to approach white card.

Correct

Damage to visual cortex.

At first, rat does not choose correctly.

?

Correct

However, it relearns original discrimination easily.

Correct

But if retrained on the opposite discrimination, it learns slowly.

?

Correct

Figure 14-8. Results of experiment by LeVere and Morlock (1973). Brain damage impairs retrieval of a memory but does not destroy it completely.

they can respond (Davis & LeVere, 1982). To help such rats, or to help humans with similar brain damage, it would be useful either to simplify the problem by removing distracting stimuli or to teach the individual to concentrate on the relevant stimuli.

The Prospects of Therapy by Brain Grafts

Therapy for brain damage concentrates on molding behavior, not on trying to induce structural changes. In the future it may be possible to use drugs to encourage or regulate collateral sprouting, denervation supersensitivity, and the like (Sabel, Slavin, & Stein, 1984). A more exotic possibility is to promote recovery by grafting brain tissue to replace dead neurons.

It is possible to graft brain tissue from one individual to another with little problem of tissue rejection. Perhaps because the blood-brain barrier protects the brain from foreign substances, the immune system is relatively inactive in the brain. The grafted brain tissue may not be functional, however. If a piece of brain is transplanted from one adult brain to another, its axons and dendrites make no contacts with the host brain. On the other hand, if neurons are transplanted from a fetal brain into the appropriate portion of an adult brain, the axons and dendrites do form synapses with the host brain. The difference is that fetal neurons are still growing and developing.

In a pioneering study, Perlow and colleagues (1979) injected the chemical 6-OH-DA to make lesions in the substantia nigra on one side of the brain in rats. (The substantia nigra is the part of the brain that is damaged in Parkinson's disease.) Each rat developed movement abnormalities resembling Parkinson's disease, although the abnormalities were limited to one side of the body. After the movement abnormalities had stabilized, the experimenters transplanted the substantia nigra from rat fetuses to locations where those cells would normally make synapses in the adult rat brains. The grafts survived in twenty-nine of the thirty rats that received them, making synapses in varying numbers. Four weeks after the grafts were implanted, most recipients showed a great deal of recovery of normal movement. Control animals that suffered the same brain damage without receiving the brain grafts showed little or no behavioral recovery.

Inspired by this report, a number of other investigators have tried transplanting fetal tissue to reverse the effects of many types of brain damage (Gash, Collier, & Sladek, 1985). An implant of hypothalamic neurons from one strain of rats to another alleviated genetically determined diabetes in the second strain (Gash, Sladek, & Sladek, 1980). Similarly, an implant of hypothalamic neurons from one strain of mice to another increased the gonadal growth of a strain that otherwise develops only small gonads (Krieger et al., 1982). Grafts of neurons rich in acetylcholine into the hippocampus improved the memory performances of aged rats (Gage, Björklund, Stenevi, Dunnett, & Kelly, 1984). In at least certain experiments of this type, the degree of behavioral recovery has depended on how many of the transplanted neurons survive (Deckel, Moran, Coyle, Sanberg, & Robinson, 1986). Many researchers refer to these studies as "Frankenstein research" or as science fiction come to life. Many also refer to it as the therapy of the future for human brain damage.

Could similar surgery relieve Parkinson's disease, Alzheimer's disease, or other human disorders? Maybe. Most research so far has dealt with rats and mice, although the few studies with monkeys suggest that the procedure will succeed with primates, too (Gash et al., 1985). To perform such surgery with humans raises not only scientific issues but also the ethical and political question of how to find donors.

One apparently obvious but probably unsatisfactory source is aborted human fetuses. The difficulty with using aborted fetuses extends beyond the controversial nature of abortion in general. Even in rats, fetal tissue is suitable for transplantation only for a brief period during development; after it is removed, it must be transplanted into the recipient brain rapidly or it will not survive. In short, human fetuses could be a suitable source for neural transplants only if the abortion were to take place at exactly the right time in the development of the fetus and if the tissue could be rushed almost instantaneously into transplantation surgery.

A second possibility is to transplant tissue from a fetal monkey into a human brain. Transplants from mouse brain to rat brain have succeeded (Björklund, Stenevi, Dunnett, & Gage, 1982; Daniloff, Wells, & Ellis, 1984). Perhaps transplants from monkey to human may succeed as well, although it is difficult to guess what the result would be.

A third possibility—the simplest, but limited in its potential application—is to transplant tissue from a person's own adrenal medulla into the brain. The adrenal medulla, part of the adrenal gland, is an elaboration and expansion of the sympathetic nervous system. Its cells produce and release epinephrine, norepinephrine, and dopamine. If such cells are transplanted into the brain, they continue to release those chemicals, which may substitute for the synaptic transmitters previously released by now-destroyed neurons. An operation of this type has been tried on human patients suffering from severe Parkinson's disease. Such patients lose a pathway of neurons that release dopamine. Parts of each patient's adrenal medulla was transplanted into his or her brain. The behavioral results include an immediate decrease in arm rigidity and an increase in movement, although the benefits for certain patients lasted only a period of weeks (Backlund et al., 1985). With improvements in technique, this method may become clinically useful.

SUMMARY

1. Strokes, rare in young people, are a common cause of brain damage in old age. A sudden blow to the head is a more common cause in young people. (p. 384)

2. The Halstead-Reitan and Luria-Nebraska tests are batteries of tests for assessing brain damage. Because performance on a given item may be impaired for many reasons, these batteries compare a person's performance across a variety of items. (pp. 385–386)

3. A rat with damage to the lateral hypothalamus initially fails to eat, drink, move, or respond to sen-

sory stimuli. If kept alive, it gradually recovers each of those behaviors to some degree. (p. 387)

4. The recovery of feeding by rats with lateral hypothalamic damage may be due in part to their losing weight. This explanation does not account for recovery of nonfeeding behaviors, however. (p. 388)

5. People and animals that have recovered from brain damage are more likely than normals to deteriorate under conditions of stress or in old age. (p. 389)

6. Animals that have recovered from brain damage may need a longer time than normal animals to warm

up after a period of inactivity, before engaging in normal behavior. (p. 391)

7. Immediately after brain damage, neurons surrounding the area of damage may be impaired by toxins that spread out from the area of damage. The neurons may recover as the toxins wash away. (pp. 391–392)

8. Neurons that survive after brain damage may also increase their functioning because of shifts in blood flow or because of chemical changes that compensate for the loss of input from the damaged neurons. (p. 393)

9. A cut axon may regenerate in the peripheral nervous system of a mammal and in either the central or peripheral nervous system of certain fish. Several explanations have been proposed for why cut axons do not regenerate in the mammalian central nervous system. (p. 393)

10. After brain damage, some of the synapses that had previously been silent in the brain may become active, causing certain neurons to respond to stimuli that had previously not activated them. (p. 396)

11. When one set of axons dies, neighboring axons may under certain conditions sprout new branches to innervate the vacant synapses. (p. 397)

12. If many of the axons innervating a given postsynaptic neuron die or become inactive, that neuron may increase its sensitivity to its remaining synaptic inputs. (p. 398)

13. Much of the recovery that takes place after brain damage does not require structural changes in the brain; it depends on learned changes in behavior to take advantage of the skills that remain, even if they are impaired. (p. 399)

14. Recovery from brain damage may be better or worse in infants, depending on a number of circumstances. (p. 401)

15. Recovery is sometimes better if the damage develops in several stages, instead of all at once, or if the damaged individual had certain experiences prior to the damage. (p. 404)

16. At present, therapy for brain damage consists mostly of helping the person practice the abilities that have been impaired but not destroyed. (p. 405)

17. Animal experiments suggest the possibility of transplanting brain grafts from fetal donors as a therapy for brain damage. (p. 407)

REVIEW QUESTIONS

1. What is a stroke? (p. 384)
2. Besides stroke, what are some other causes of human brain damage? (p. 384)
3. Why do the Halstead-Reitan and Luria-Nebraska tests assess a large number of separate behaviors? (p. 386)
4. Describe the four stages of recovery from damage to the lateral hypothalamus. (pp. 387–388)
5. In what ways is a person or animal that has recovered from brain damage different from one that has never suffered brain damage? (p. 389)
6. Describe three ways in which neurons that have survived brain damage might be temporarily impaired after the damage. (pp. 392–393)
7. Give three reasons why axons may fail to regenerate across a cut through the mammalian spinal cord. (pp. 394–395)
8. How may the functions of a part of the brain change when previously silent synapses become active? (p. 396)

9. What is the evidence that collateral sprouting sometimes aids in recovery from brain damage? (p. 398)
10. What is the evidence that denervation supersensitivity sometimes aids in recovery from brain damage? (p. 399)
11. Describe one example that shows that brain-damaged animals are sometimes capable of behaviors they do not spontaneously engage in. (p. 399)
12. Why might the effects of infant brain damage differ from those of adult brain damage? Give more than one reason, and evidence for each. (p. 401)
13. What are the usual methods and goals of therapy for people with brain damage? (p. 405)
14. What kind of donor must be used in brain graft experiments if the transplanted tissue is to survive and make connections? (p. 407)
15. If brain graft transplants are to be used in humans, what are the possible sources of brain tissue? (p. 408)

THOUGHT QUESTIONS

1. One group of rats is injected with a drug that inhibits the synthesis of dopamine and norepinephrine for 3 days. As a result, the rats eat little on those days. At the end of the 3 days, they and a second group of rats are given lesions to the lateral hypothalamus. The rats injected with the drug recover more rapidly from the lesion (Glick, 1974). What interpretation could you offer for these results? (Based on this chapter, it is possible to suggest more than one possible interpretation.)

2. If brain grafts could be made successfully from fetal monkeys to adult humans, what procedures should we go through to decide whether we *should* conduct such surgery?

TERMS TO REMEMBER

stroke (p. 384)
cerebrovascular accident (p. 384)
Halstead-Reitan test (p. 385)
Luria-Nebraska neuropsychological battery (p. 385)
aphagia (p. 387)
adipsia (p. 387)
anorexia (p. 387)

sensory neglect (p. 389)
sensory extinction (p. 390)
collateral sprouts (p. 397)
denervation supersensitivity (p. 398)
6-OH-DA (6-hydroxy-dopamine) (p. 399)
Kennard principle (p. 400)
serial-lesion effect (p. 404)

SUGGESTIONS FOR FURTHER READING

DeMille, A. (1981). *Reprieve: A memoir.* Garden City, NY: Doubleday. A stroke victim's own account of her stroke and recovery from it, with interpolated commentary by a neurologist, Fred Plum.

Freed, W. J., Medinaceli, L., & Wyatt, R. M. (1985). Promoting functional plasticity in the damaged nervous system. *Science, 227,* 1544–1552. A review article that focuses largely on the regeneration of nerves, in both the central and peripheral nervous systems.

Marshall, J. F. (1985). Neural plasticity and recovery of function after brain injury. *International Review of Neurobiology, 26,* 201–247. A general review of mechanisms of recovery.

Sladek, J. R., Jr., & Gash, D. M. (1984). *Neural transplants.* New York: Plenum. Discussion of the use of brain grafts.

Stein, D. G., Finger, S., & Hart, T. (1983). Brain damage and recovery: Problems and perspectives. *Behavioral and Neural Biology, 37,* 185–222.

Biology of Depression and Related Disorders

CHAPTER

15

MAIN IDEAS

1. Depression and mania are the product of a combination of numerous physiological and environmental influences.

2. Depression is associated with several biological abnormalities, ranging from hormonal deficiencies to relative inactivity by the left hemisphere of the brain.

3. Studies of antidepressant drugs indicate that depressed people have abnormalities of synaptic transmission at norepinephrine, dopamine, or serotonin synapses. The exact nature of these abnormalities is not yet clearly understood.

4. A number of biological treatments are effective against certain cases of depression, including drugs, electroconvulsive shock, changes in sleep patterns, exposure to bright light, and the use of lithium salts.

Why do people live in a particular city? Some were born there. Some chose the city because of some attraction. Others came because of a job offer, or because of a college or hospital or other institution that fits their needs. If the city has a prison, some people have been required to come there because of a criminal conviction. Although all these people have ended up in about the same place, the reasons they have for being there are quite diverse.

The same is true for many psychological conditions, including depression, a common disorder. Some people are depressed because of extremely unpleasant events that would have made anyone depressed. Others are depressed because of a chemical imbalance that developed gradually in their brains for genetic or hormonal reasons. Others may have had their depression triggered by poor dietary or sleeping habits. Still others have become depressed for a combination of reasons. In short, people reach the same final destination, depression, through many routes.

In this chapter we focus on the biological factors that affect mood and activity levels. Experiential factors undeniably play a major role as well. Although this chapter is limited to the biological factors, remember that we are discussing just one part of a complex story.

TYPES OF DEPRESSION

A depressed person feels fearful and gloomy, helpless and hopeless. Depressed people are generally inactive; when they do anything at all, it is unproductive, such as pacing back and forth, wringing their hands. They say they feel unhappy and their facial expressions indicate unhappiness.

Depressed people almost invariably have trouble sleeping. On the average, they take longer than most normal people to fall asleep. After sleeping not very restfully, they awaken earlier than they wanted and cannot get back to sleep. During the day they feel drowsy.

The opposite of depression is **mania**. An approximate synonym for mania is *uninhibited*. A manic person is characterized by restless activity, excitement, laughter, and a mostly happy mood. The manic person's speech rambles from one idea to another. Some of the ideas may be good ones; the problem is that the manic person does not distinguish between the good and the bad. He or she is also impulsive, investing money recklessly and engaging in aggressive or sexual behavior that a normal person would restrain. In extreme cases, manic people are dangerous to themselves and others. In mild cases, known as **hypomania**, people are energetic, likeable, and sometimes highly successful. The cycle of mania for one hospitalized person who experienced extremes in mania is presented in Figure 15-1.

Unipolar Versus Bipolar Disorder

Depression can occur as either a unipolar or a bipolar disorder. A **unipolar disorder** is one with only one pole, or extreme. That is, a person varies between normal mood and depression. A **bipolar disorder** is one with two

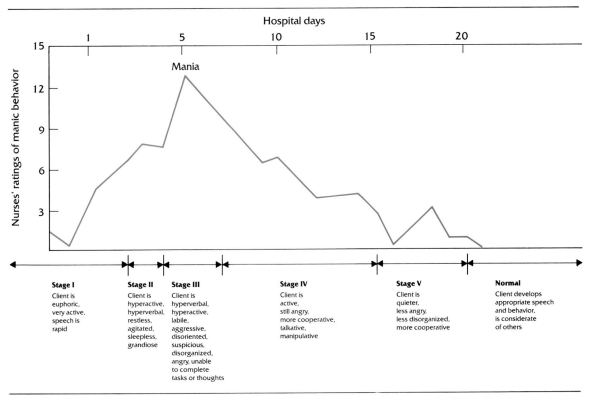

Figure 15-1. Stages of a manic episode of a hospitalized patient over a three-week period. (After Janosik and Davies, 1986.)

poles, mania and depression. Someone suffering from bipolar disorder varies between mania and depression, passing through a normal mood on the way. This condition is also known as **manic-depressive disorder**. Although hypomania may occur as a unipolar condition, indeed as a permanent personality characteristic, extreme mania is almost unheard of as a unipolar condition. That is, extreme mania occurs almost exclusively as a condition that alternates with depression.

A depressed person may become less depressed, gradually pass through normality and into a manic state, and then return toward normality and depression again. The entire cycle may last a year or more, or only a few days (Bunney, Murphy, Goodwin, & Borge, 1972). Not uncommonly, the cycle may follow such a regular rhythm that it is possible to predict far in advance whether a person will be manic or depressed on a given date (Richter, 1938, 1957b, 1957c).

The manic-depressive condition affects only about one person in 1,000 in the United States. The mean age of onset is the late 20s. Unipolar depression, on the other hand, is quite common. Almost everyone, of course, has at least brief and mild periods of depression. About 5 percent of all people suffer from a **major depression** at some time in their lives—that is, a depression so severe that it greatly interferes with normal living for a period of months or years (Robins et al., 1984). The mean age of onset for unipolar depression is about 40. Depression is diagnosed more frequently in women than in men (Murphy, Sobol, Neff, Olivier, & Leighton, 1984).

Endogenous Versus Reactive Depression

Both investigators and therapists have long drawn a distinction between endogenous and reactive types of depression. An **endogenous depression** is one that develops gradually because of internal, biological factors. A **reactive depression** is one that develops suddenly as a result of a painful event, such as the death of a loved one.

Although this distinction seems reasonable in principle, it is hard to apply in actual practice. Nearly all depressed patients report a large number of stressful events in their lives during the year prior to the onset of depression, although some report more than others (Cornell, Milden, & Shimp, 1985). In many cases, it is difficult for a therapist to judge whether the stresses a patient reports are sufficient for the condition to qualify as reactive.

For this reason, researchers have tried to devise a biochemical or behavioral test that would discriminate between the two conditions. One such test is the **dexamethasone suppression test**. In most normal people, the drug dexamethasone suppresses release of the adrenal hormone cortisol. In people with endogenous depression, dexamethasone does not suppress cortisol secretion (Feinberg & Carroll, 1984), presumably because of some abnormality in their hypothalamus, pituitary, or adrenal gland. Dexamethasone does suppress cortisol in most people with an apparently reactive depression—that is, those who have recently gone through a divorce or other stressful events, and those who have little social support (Zimmerman, Coryell, & Pfohl, 1986). This test does not distinguish between the two types of depression with high accuracy, however.

A second test is to examine sleep patterns. Generally, people with endogenous depression enter REM sleep within less than 45 minutes after falling asleep. Such rapid entry into REM sleep is rare in normal people when they go to sleep at their normal time, and in people with reactive depression. Those with endogenous depression may continue to enter REM sleep soon after falling asleep even after they have recovered from depression (Rush et al., 1986). Although the REM test, like the dexamethasone test, is subject to error, the results of the two tests can be combined to discriminate more accurately between endogenous depression and reactive depression (Feinberg & Carroll, 1984).

On the other hand, for many purposes it is not worth the bother to distinguish between endogenous and reactive depressions. First, it may well be that endogenous and reactive are two ends of a continuum and that most depressions are partly endogenous and partly reactive. Furthermore, most depressed patients respond about equally well to antidepressant drugs or to cognitively based psychotherapy (Berman, Miller, & Massman, 1985; Conte, Plutchik, Wild, & Karasu, 1986). Knowing whether someone's depression is endogenous or reactive does not enable anyone to predict very accurately whether the person will respond better to the drugs or to psychotherapy (Arana, Baldessarini, & Ornsteen, 1985; Keller et al., 1986). For analogy, the distinction between a fire set by an arsonist and a fire started by accident may be useful to the police and the insurance companies but not to the fire department. Similarly, the distinction between endogenous and reactive depression may be more useful to researchers than to therapists.

POSSIBLE BIOLOGICAL CAUSES OF DEPRESSION AND MANIC-DEPRESSIVE DISORDER

The causes of depression may differ from one person to another. Further, we need not assume even that a given individual becomes depressed for only one reason. A depression could easily result from a combination of several biological (endogenous) factors and several experiential (reactive) ones. We discuss here a few causes that are particularly likely or particularly worthy of further investigation.

Stressful Events

Stressful events activate the sympathetic nervous system, the reticular formation, and other parts of the nervous system, increasing the release of norepinephrine, dopamine, and certain other synaptic transmitters. Particularly intense stress may release these transmitters faster than they can be resynthesized. The result could easily be a decreased availability of the transmitters. The postsynaptic neurons might decrease their number of receptors to the transmitter in response to the great release of transmitters during the stress period. Alternatively, they might increase their number of transmitters in response to the later deficit of transmitter release. Although we admittedly do not know the net effect on the norepinephrine and dopamine synapses, it is likely that their activity changes in some way, perhaps in a long-lasting way. Because changes in these synapses are linked to depression (as we shall see later in this chapter), it is at least plausible that severe stress could trigger a bout of depression (Anisman & Zacharko, 1982).

One impediment to evaluating this hypothesis is the difficulty of measuring stress. The death of a loved one is an incapacitating stress for many people, yet for someone who has nursed a suffering relative through years of painful decline, the final moment of death may be a relief. Similarly, divorce, pregnancy, or the loss of a job may be highly stressful, nonstressful, or even a cause for celebration, depending on a multitude of circumstances. For this reason we must be cautious in interpreting studies that ask depressed patients and nondepressed people to report how many stressful experiences they have undergone recently.

A better way to construct a study of the effects of stress on depression is to examine people who have been exposed to undeniable stress and then to find out how many of them became depressed. One such study compared normal mothers to mothers of children with serious disabilities, on the assumption that caring for a handicapped child is a source of chronic stress. The mothers of handicapped children had no greater probability than the other women of becoming depressed, although if they did become depressed, their depression was in certain regards more severe (Breslau & Davis, 1986). In other words, in this study, stress aggravated depression, but it did not appear to be the primary cause of it.

Hormonal Changes

Several lines of evidence link depression to fluctuations in sex hormones, particularly in women. Of all women admitted to one psychiatric hospital for depression, 41 percent were admitted on the day before or the first day of menstruation (Abramowitz, Baker, & Fleischer, 1982). Certainly this does not mean that menstruation causes depression; it suggests that the hormonal changes preceding menstruation may slightly aggravate a preexisting depression, making it severe enough to require treatment.

Similarly, a certain amount of depression is common just after giving birth. A majority of women experience "the blues" for a day or two after delivery, because of pain, the inconvenience of hospital care, and other reasons. About 20 percent experience a **postpartum depression**—that is, a depression after giving birth—that is more serious and more long lasting than a mere case of the blues, although it is still well within their ability to cope. Finally, a rare woman, about one in a 1,000, enters a severe, major depression (Hopkins, Marcus, & Campbell, 1984). Even in these cases, however, it is doubtful that giving birth caused the depression, because a large number of such women will have one or more other episodes of major depression at other times in her life, independent of giving birth (Schöpf, Bryois, Jonquière, & Le, 1984). A reasonable interpretation is that giving birth can trigger an episode of depression in women who are already predisposed to depression.

Thyroid hormones may also play a role in depression. A majority of depressed and manic-depressive patients have at least mild deficiencies of thyroid hormone production (Lipton, Breese, Prange, Wilson, & Cooper, 1976; Fieve & Platman, 1969).

Genetics

Both depression and manic-depressive disorder run in families. About 10 to 20 percent of the parents, brothers, and sisters of depressed and manic-depressed patients suffer from these same disorders themselves (Smeraldi, Kidd, Negri, Heimbuch, & Melica, 1979; Weissman et al., 1984). Those who develop a major depression before age 30 are particularly likely to have depressed relatives (Weissman et al., 1986).

The fact that depressed people have depressed relatives tells us only that we cannot rule out genetics as a contributing factor. Stronger evidence for a genetic basis of depression is that adopted children who become depressed have, on the average, more depressed biological relatives than depressed adoptive relatives (Wender et al, 1986).

In one genetically isolated population, the Old Order Amish of Pennsylvania, a gene that predisposes to manic-depressive illness is located on chromosome 11. The evidence for this conclusion is relatives who resemble one another with regard to manic-depressive illness also resemble one another with regard to certain genes known to be on chromosome 11 (Egeland et al., 1987). Two other studies, however, one in the United States and one in Iceland, found no evidence linking manic-depressive disorder to chromosome 11 (Detera-Wadleigh et al., 1987; Hodgkinson et al., 1987). Appar-

Table 15-1.   Borna Disease Virus and Depression

	Tested positive for Borna virus	Total people tested
Depressed and manic-depressed	12	265
Nondepressed	0	105

ently manic-depressive illness is related to different genes in different populations, or to a gene that can lie in different locations for different people.

Still, genetics cannot be the whole story. It is possible for someone with no depressed relatives to become severely depressed or manic-depressive. It is also possible to be normal despite having close relatives, even an identical twin, with depression.

Viruses

Before 1985, hardly anyone had ever heard of Borna disease except for European veterinarians. **Borna disease** is a viral disease that infects the nervous systems of animals, mostly horses and sheep. It has been reported only in parts of Germany and Switzerland, although it is possible that unrecognized, unreported cases occur elsewhere. The effects of the virus vary from one species to another. One common effect is a spectacular change in behavior: The infected animal has a period of frantic activity followed by a period of inactivity.

Although no humans, either in Germany and Switzerland or elsewhere, were known to suffer from Borna disease, the question remained as to whether any humans might carry the virus. (Many viruses can be passed between humans and other species, even if the effects on humans are quite different from the effects on other species.) In 1985, one group of investigators reported the results of a blood test given to several hundred humans in the United States (Amsterdam et al., 1985). Twelve people tested positive for Borna disease virus. *All twelve were suffering from major depression or manic-depressive disorder*, mostly manic-depressive disorder. These twelve were a small percentage of the depressed people tested in the study; still, it is significant that *no* nondepressed people tested positive for the virus. (See Table 15-1.)

Here are some of the known characteristics of the Borna disease virus: (1) The virus attacks the nervous system, not other organs. (2) The virus has a long incubation period; that is, the symptoms do not begin until months or years after the infection. Because of the long incubation period, it is difficult to tell when a person or animal first acquired the virus or what transmits the virus from one individual to another. (It is interesting to note that the twelve people who were found to be infected with Borna disease had all spent extensive time with pets or farm animals.) (3) The virus spreads directly from one neuron to another, without going through the bloodstream. Although the body builds up antibodies to the virus, these antibodies are confined to the bloodstream and are therefore ineffective against the virus. (The same can be said for the AIDS virus.)

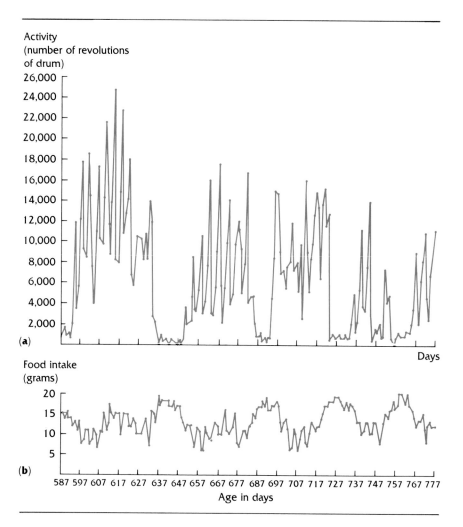

Figure 15-2. Record of (**a**) daily activity in running wheel and (**b**) food intake by a rat treated with the drug sulfamerazine. Notches on horizontal axis represent blocks of 10 days. (From Richter, 1957d.)

More research is clearly needed to determine whether the Borna virus or similar viruses cause certain cases of depression or manic-depressive disorder. At this point all we can say is that it is a highly interesting possibility.

ANIMAL MODELS OF DEPRESSION AND MANIC-DEPRESSIVE DISORDER

One way to test a hypothesis—or sometimes even to form a hypothesis—about the cause of some disorder is to see what will cause a similar disorder in animals. Curt Richter offered the first serious animal model of a major psychiatric disorder when he studied activity cycles in rats.

Richter kept rats in cages with running wheels; mechanical counters attached to the wheels recorded the number of wheel turns for each rat each day. During an extensive investigation of the variables that control a rat's running activity, Richter found that partial damage to the thyroid gland caused a rat to show unusual cycles of activity and inactivity (Richter, 1933a, 1955, 1957b, 1957c, 1957d; Richter, Jones, & Biswanger, 1959; Richter &

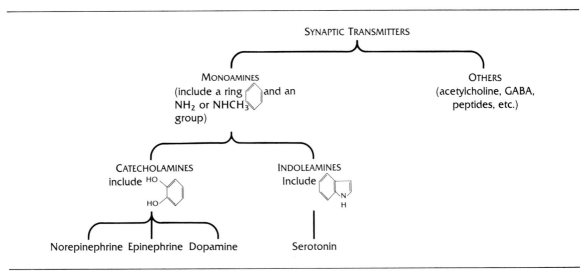

Figure 15-3. Classification of some synaptic transmitters.

Rice, 1956). Figure 15-2 shows the effects of chemically induced damage to the thyroid on the activity of one rat. Note that periods of 8 to 13 days of almost complete inactivity alternated with periods of high activity.

Richter got similar results after damage to the pituitary gland (Richter, 1933b), the parathyroid gland (Richter, Honeyman, & Hunter, 1940), or the ovaries (Richter, 1931, 1955). On the basis of such results, he proposed that the underlying cause of manic-depressive cycles may be an impairment somewhere in the endocrine system. Although his hypothesis received little attention at the time, it still remains a viable possibility.

A more influential animal model emerged in the early 1960s. Several investigators independently and almost simultaneously suggested that depression could be due to a deficiency of activity at catecholamine synapses (Garattini & Valzelli, 1960; MacLean, 1962; Stein, 1962). The clearest and most explicit of these models was offered by Larry Stein, who reported that antidepressant drugs increase rats' self-stimulation of the brain, apparently by increasing catecholamine activity. He inferred that depressed people have deficient stimulation of the reward areas of their brains because of low catecholamine activity. Later studies with animal models indicated that depletion of norepinephrine (one of the catecholamines—see Figure 15-3) could lead to inactivity and a lack of hunger and exploration; additional depletion of serotonin added an element of fearfulness (Ellison, 1977).

An additional animal model, more behavioral than physiological, is the **learned helplessness** model. An animal that receives a series of inescapable shocks on one day will act helpless in the face of escapable, avoidable shocks the following day (Maier, Seligman, & Solomon, 1969). Both the animal's general demeanor and its failure to engage in productive behavior resemble human depression. It is possible that certain cases of depression begin when someone fails repeatedly on an important task, particularly if the person attributes the failure to his or her own shortcomings, as opposed to something about the task or to some temporary interference with performance (Abramson, Seligman, & Teasdale, 1978).

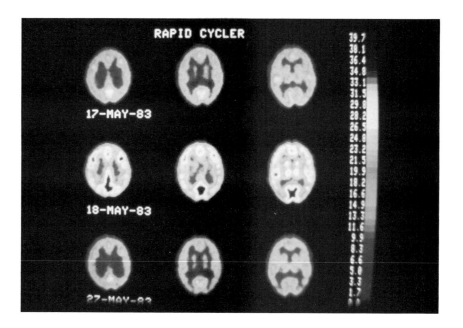

Figure 15-4. PET scans of the brain of a rapid cycling manic-depressive patient. (See Color Plate 23.) (From Baxter et al., 1985.)

ABNORMALITIES OF HEMISPHERIC DOMINANCE IN DEPRESSION

The rate of metabolism of glucose, a good indicator of overall brain activity, varies as a function of mania and depression, as shown in Figure 15-4 and Color Plate 23. During mania, activity is higher than normal. During depression, it is lower than normal, especially in the left frontal lobe (Baxter et al., 1985).

Several other lines of evidence suggest that the left hemisphere, especially the left frontal cortex, is relatively inactive in depressed people. In response to an arousing stimulus, they have less than the normal increase in electrical conduction of the skin on the right hand. When dealing with a cognitive problem, their eyes gaze to the left, not to the right as in most people (Lenhart & Katkin, 1986). The EEG shows more activation in the right hemisphere than in the left hemisphere. People with brain damage in the frontal lobes of the left hemisphere are generally depressed, or at least pessimistic. Those with damage in the right frontal cortex are either emotionally unresponsive or perhaps euphoric (Davidson, 1984).

One final peculiarity of depressed people, which probably relates in some way to the activities of the two hemispheres, although it is difficult to interpret: When people are asked to draw circles with the two hands simultaneously, most normal people draw one circle clockwise and one counterclockwise, but most depressed people draw both circles counterclockwise (Ulrich, Zeller, & Mühlbauer, 1983). (See Figure 15-5.)

MONOAMINES AND DEPRESSION

During the 1960s, a clear pattern emerged concerning antimanic and antidepressant drugs (Schildkraut & Kety, 1967): The drugs that are effective against mania decrease transmission at catecholamine synapses—by deplet-

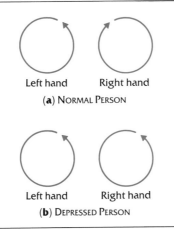

Left hand   Right hand

(**a**) NORMAL PERSON

Left hand   Right hand

(**b**) DEPRESSED PERSON

Figure 15-5. Typical way of drawing two circles simultaneously by (**a**) a normal person and (**b**) a depressed person. (Based on Ulrich, Zeller, & Mühlbauer, 1983.)

ing catecholamines from the brain, for example. Conversely, drugs that are effective against depression increase catecholamine stimulation. One group of antidepressant drugs, the **tricyclics**, operate by preventing the presynaptic neuron from reabsorbing catecholamines after releasing them; that is, they cause the catecholamines to remain longer in the synaptic cleft and to stimulate the postsynaptic cell for a longer time. Others, the **monoamine oxidase inhibitors** (**MAOIs**), block the enzyme **monoamine oxidase** (**MAO**), which metabolizes catecholamines and serotonin into inactive forms. When this enzyme is blocked, any catecholamines or serotonin released will remain longer than usual at the synapse without being inactivated; they will therefore stimulate the postsynaptic cell more than usual.

By the late 1960s, the biological basis for depression and mania appeared rather simple: Mania was due to an excess of catecholamines (norepinephrine, epinephrine, and dopamine) and serotonin; depression was due to a deficiency of these transmitters. Drugs that were effective against these disorders worked by diminishing or prolonging the effects of the transmitters.

Later evidence made this simple explanation unsatisfactory. First, direct measurements of norepinephrine and serotonin metabolites in the urine and CSF (cerebrospinal fluid) indicated enormous variations among depressed people (Åsberg, Thorén, Träskman, Bertilsson, & Ringberger, 1976; Roy, Pickar, Linnoila, & Potter, 1985; Schatzberg et al., 1982). Moreover, it was found that certain depressed people respond best to drugs that affect catecholamines more than serotonin, while others respond best to drugs that affect mostly serotonin (Gastpar, 1979). Evidently, depression can be related to any of several biochemical patterns in the brain. Further, it may be related to an improper proportion between one transmitter and another, not simply to an improper amount of a single transmitter.

A more serious difficulty is the time course of the effects of antidepressant drugs. Although the antidepressant drugs elevate catecholamine and serotonin concentrations at the synapses almost immediately, their effects on behavior develop gradually. Most patients must take the medication for 2 or 3 weeks before they experience the antidepressant effects. Obviously, the

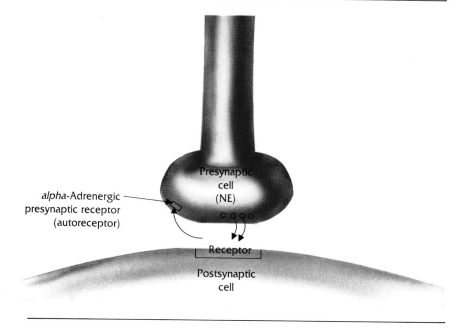

Figure 15-6. A norepineph-rine synapse with an auto-receptor.

effects of the drugs must be changing in some way over the course of 2 or more weeks as they take effect on behavior. But what is happening during those 2 or 3 weeks?

One possibility relates to denervation supersensitivity (Chapter 14). A prolonged period of low stimulation at a synapse leads to an increased receptor density. The opposite is also true: A prolonged increase in the release of a transmitter can lead to a decrease in receptor density. Because antidepressant drugs prolong the effects of catecholamines and serotonin at the synapses, we can expect a gradual decrease in the number of receptors for those transmitters.

One more complication: The brain includes more than one kind of receptor for each transmitter, and the different kinds of receptors differ from one another in their response to various drugs. In particular, many presyn-aptic endings have **autoreceptors**, receptors that respond to the transmitter released by the presynaptic neuron itself (Starke, 1981). Ordinarily, the au-toreceptors serve a negative feedback function. When the presynaptic cell releases its transmitter, some of it comes back to stimulate the autoreceptors, which then inhibit the cell from releasing more of the transmitter. (See Figure 15-6.)

Most antidepressant drugs, it turns out, decrease the sensitivity of the autoreceptors, at least at dopamine and norepinephrine synapses (Antelman, Chiodo, & DeGiovanni, 1982; Crews & Smith, 1978; Sulser, Gillespie, Mishra, & Manier, 1984). The consequence of the decreased sensitivity of autoreceptors is decreased inhibition of release of transmitter—that is, pro-longed release of transmitter. That, of course, leads to still further compen-sation by the postsynaptic cell, as it decreases its number of synaptic receptors. The antidepressant drugs thus produce competing effects: They increase the amount of synaptic transmitter available to the postsynaptic cell, and they decrease the sensitivity of the postsynaptic cell to that transmitter. It is believed that the second of these two effects is the dominant one. That is, the net effect of the antidepressant drugs is to decrease the stimulation of the postsynaptic cell (Dubocovich, 1984; Sulser et al., 1984).

That still leaves the question, what is the original biochemical state of the brain that led to depression? According to measurements of binding sites, a depressed person has greater than normal sensitivity of the autoreceptors, particularly at norepinephrine synapses (García-Sevilla, Guimón, García-Vallejo, & Fuster, 1986). Because increased sensitivity of autoreceptors leads to decreased release of transmitter from the presynaptic cell, an unmedicated depressed person has a deficient release of norepinephrine and probably other transmitters. Presumably, the postsynaptic cells produce extra synaptic receptors to compensate for the deficient release. All these abnormalities are reversed by antidepressant drugs.

Overall, the relationship between depression and synaptic transmission is complex. Moreover, views of this relationship have changed repeatedly since the 1960s. The final word has not been spoken; it may be some time before we have a complete picture of what happens at the synapses during depression.

OTHER BIOLOGICAL THERAPIES FOR DEPRESSION AND MANIC-DEPRESSIVE DISORDER

Antidepressant drugs are effective for about two-thirds of all seriously depressed patients. These drugs have unpleasant side effects, however, including dry mouth, blurred vision, and sometimes decreased sexual potency. It is dangerous to combine antidepressant drugs with alcohol. In short, although antidepressant drugs are beneficial to many people, they are not a perfect treatment. Several other biological treatments are beneficial under certain circumstances.

Electroconvulsive Shock Therapy

Electroconvulsive shock therapy (ECT) has had a stormy history (Fink, 1985). Its use originated with the observation that among certain people who suffer from both epilepsy and schizophrenia, an increase in the symptoms of one disorder is associated with a decrease in the symptoms of the other (Trimble & Thompson, 1986). In the 1930s, a Hungarian physician, Ladislas Meduna, intentionally induced a convulsive seizure in schizophrenic patients to see whether it would relieve the symptoms of schizophrenia. Soon other physicians throughout the world were doing the same, generally inducing the seizures by a large dose of insulin. Insulin shock is a dreadful experience, however, and very difficult to control. Ugo Cerletti, after years of experimentation with animals, developed a method of inducing seizures by an electric shock across the head (Cerletti & Bini, 1938). Electroconvulsive shock was quicker than insulin; more important, most patients awakened from it calmly and did not remember the shock.

Although ECT proved to be only occasionally beneficial in treating schizophrenia, psychiatrists began experimenting with it for other disorders.

They discovered that it did seem to help many people suffering from major depression. ECT became a common treatment for depression, even though its use for this disorder was based on no theory at all. It developed a bad reputation, however, because of overuse and misuse, especially during the 1950s. Certain patients were given ECT a hundred times or more, without their consent, even if it seemed to be doing them no good.

When antidepressant drugs became available in the late 1950s, the use of ECT declined rapidly. All states now have laws that permit the use of ECT only after a patient has given informed consent. Many states have imposed other laws, restricting the ages of people who can receive ECT, the disorders for which it can be used, and so forth (Winslade, Liston, Ross, & Weber, 1984).

Beginning in the 1970s, ECT has made a partial comeback, with many modifications. It is now used almost exclusively for major depression, with rare use in schizophrenia. It is generally limited to six to eight applications per patient, on alternate days. To reduce the intensity of side effects, the intensity of the shock is much lower than in earlier years. Patients are given muscle relaxants or anesthetics to minimize discomfort and the possibility of injury.

ECT is used primarily for three kinds of depressed patients (Scovern & Kilmann, 1980; Weiner, 1979). First, it is used for patients who have not responded to any of the antidepressant drugs; ECT produces good results in most such patients (Paul et al., 1981). Second, it is used for patients with suicidal tendencies. ECT is preferable to drugs for such patients simply because it takes effect in about a week, whereas antidepressant drugs usually take 2 to 3 weeks. Third, ECT has proved particularly effective for depressed patients who suffer from delusions.

Commissions in both the United States and Great Britain have concluded that ECT is both safe and effective (Fink, 1985). According to one extensive review of the literature, 80 percent of all severely depressed patients respond well to ECT, while only 64 percent respond well to tricyclic drugs and even fewer respond to MAOIs (Janicak et al., 1985). For most patients, ECT produces only minor side effects (Weiner, 1984), generally less serious than the side effects of antidepressant drugs. The benefits of ECT are not permanent, however; many patients will have a relapse of depression unless they are given drugs or other therapies to prevent it.

One disadvantage of ECT is that it causes a temporary state of confusion and both retrograde and anterograde amnesia in many patients (Summers, Robins, & Reich, 1979). Squire, Wetzel, and Slater (1979), using a variety of laboratory tests of memory, found that people had a demonstrable memory deficit for 1 to 6 months after ECT, although their complaints lasted several months longer. It is possible that subtle but real deficits last longer than the laboratory tests reveal. It is also possible that the memory deficits that patients experience early after ECT cause them to be more aware of the normal forgetfulness that all of us have.

It is possible to decrease the memory impairments by limiting the ECT to the right hemisphere of the brain. Given in that manner, ECT produces very little impairment of memory (Squire & Zouzounis, 1986). It can be just

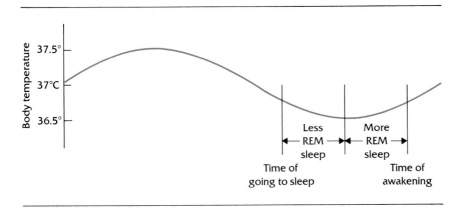

Figure 15-7. Body temperature of a normal person in relation to sleep and REM.

as effective as bilateral ECT for relieving depression *if* the right-side-only ECT is intense enough to induce a seizure (Horne, Pettinati, Sugerman, & Varga, 1985; Miller, Small, Milstein, Malloy, & Stout, 1981).

Half a century after the introduction of ECT, no one yet is sure how it relieves depression. We know that it does not act as a punishment, nor does it require an impairment of memory in order to be effective. It must induce a seizure, however. An application of ECT that produces a seizure affects the brain in many ways, such as increasing the release of hormones from the hypothalamus and pituitary (Fink, 1980). One of its effects that is particularly likely to be relevant is that it decreases receptor sensitivity at autoreceptors (Chiodo & Antelman, 1980). Another is that it leads to a decreased number of receptors to norepinephrine at postsynaptic cells (Kellar & Stockmeier, 1986; Lerer & Shapira, 1986). Both of these effects resemble those of antidepressant drugs.

Alterations of Sleep Patterns

Most depressed people, especially those middle-aged or older, experience sleep abnormalities that suggest a disorder of their biological rhythms. Recall from Chapter 9 that a normal person, going to sleep at the normal time, does not enter REM sleep until well over 45 minutes after falling asleep. The normal person has little REM sleep during the first half of the night's sleep and an increasing percentage in the second half. That trend is controlled by the time of day, not by how long the person has been asleep. If someone who usually goes to sleep at 11 P.M. waits until 3 A.M. to go to sleep, that person is likely to enter REM sleep rapidly and to have a large amount of REM sleep per hour.

One way to think of this is to examine the curve representing body temperature at different times of day and night in Figure 15-7. REM sleep occupies a small percentage of total sleep while body temperature is declining; it occupies a larger percentage while body temperature is rising (Czeisler, Weitzman, Moore-Ede, Zimmerman, & Knauer, 1980).

What this has to do with depression is that most depressed people, especially those with an endogenous depression, enter REM sleep within less than 45 minutes after going to bed at their normal time. The reason is that

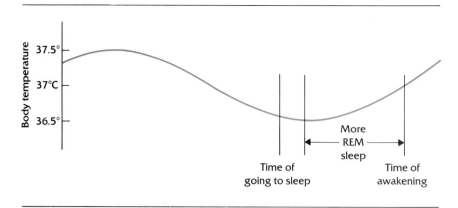

Figure 15-8. Body temperature of a depressed person in relation to sleep and REM.

their waking-sleeping rhythms are out of phase with their temperature rhythms. The depressed person's body temperature rises and falls several hours earlier than normal (Wirz-Justice, Groos, & Wehr, 1982). At the time the depressed person goes to sleep, body temperature may already be starting to rise, as shown in Figure 15-8. For that reason, REM sleep begins early and may occupy a great deal of sleep time throughout the night.

Several means of adjusting sleep habits can alleviate depression. One method that shows a great deal of promise is to have the person go to sleep earlier than usual, in phase with his or her temperature cycle. The person goes to sleep at, say, 6 P.M., when the temperature cycle is at about the point it is in nondepressed people at 11 P.M.; he or she sleeps 8 hours and awakens at 2 A.M. On each succeeding night the person goes to sleep half an hour later, until the bedtime reaches 11 P.M. or some other satisfactory point. In short, the therapists treat the depressed patient like someone who is having trouble adjusting to a change in time zones. The result is a relief from depression that lasts for at least months (Sack, Nurnberger, Rosenthal, Ashburn, & Wehr, 1985).

Another approach is to keep the person awake all night. Doing so produces a rapid relief from depression (Pflug, 1973). It is not known why this procedure is effective; furthermore, its benefits last only a day or two, and depressed patients frankly hate to go through this treatment. It is also possible to relieve depression by depriving the depressed person of REM sleep by awakening him or her whenever signs of REM appear (Vogel, Thompson, Thurmond, & Rivers, 1973). The benefits of REM deprivation last longer than those of total sleep deprivation, although they, too, fade over a period of days to weeks. Again, the mechanism of the effect is not known. For normal people, or even for people suffering from psychological disorders other than depression, sleep deprivation or REM deprivation makes mood worse, not better (Roy-Byrne, Uhde, & Post, 1986).

Bright Lights

One uncommon form of depression is known as **seasonal affective disorder,** conveniently abbreviated **SAD.** People who suffer from seasonal affective disorder become depressed, sometimes seriously depressed, every winter.

Most of them become at least slightly manic in the summer. The disorder is more common and more severe in regions closer to the poles. Patients have been reported who suffer depression every winter in their far northern homes but who experience no such depression if they spend the winter in, say, southern California (Pande, 1985; Rosenthal et al., 1984).

The underlying problem is apparently not the cold of winter but the darkness. Sunlight has antidepressant effects. Most people feel more cheerful on a sunny day than on a dark day. Some people, including most manic-depressive patients, are more sensitive than others to the mood-lifting effects of sunlight (Lewy et al., 1985). Certain of these people become depressed during the winter, when the sun rises late and sets early.

It is possible to relieve this type of depression by exposing the person to bright lights that extend the day. The person sits in front of bright lights (e.g., 2500 lux) for about 6 hours a day before the sun rises or after it sets. The lights, acting as an artificial sun, relieve seasonal affective disorder for people who follow this plan daily (Wehr et al., 1986). A similar period of exposure to dim lights has no effect on mood (Rosenthal et al., 1985).

Bright lights may help to relieve certain other kinds of depression besides seasonal affective disorder. Exposure to bright lights in the evening shifts the circadian rhythm of body temperature to a later time (Czeisler et al., 1986). Because it is typical for body temperature to rise and fall earlier in the day for depressed people than for nondepressed people (Figure 15-8), the effect of the bright lights is to adjust the body temperature rhythm back to normal.

Lithium

The most effective known therapy for manic-depressive illness, and for certain cases in which a person alternates on a regular basis between depression and normal mood, is the use of **lithium** salts. The effectiveness of lithium was discovered by accident. An Australian investigator, J. F. Cade, believing that uric acid would be therapeutically useful for treating mania and depression, mixed uric acid with a lithium salt to help it dissolve and then gave the mixed solution to patients. It was indeed helpful, although the uric acid had nothing to do with the benefits. Eventually investigators realized that the lithium was the effective agent.

Although lithium soon became a popular treatment for manic-depressive disorder in the Scandinavian countries, psychiatrists in the United States were slow to adopt it. One reason for this reluctance was that lithium is known to have toxic effects in larger doses. Another reason is that American drug companies were not eager to market lithium, because it is a chemical element and therefore not eligible for a patent.

Lithium levels out the mood of a manic-depressive patient. With continued use, it prevents a relapse into either mania or depression. The use of lithium must be regulated carefully, however. The therapeutic dose is not much less than the dose that begins to produce toxic effects. Also, lithium sometimes produces serious medical harm if it is combined ith ECT or with the drug haloperidol (Gottfried & Frankel, 1981; Small, Kellams, Milstein, & Small, 1980).

Because lithium is chemically similar to sodium, it may partly take the place of sodium in crossing the membrane and in various other body functions. It produces a great many effects on the brain, the blood, and other systems (Tosteson, 1981). How it relieves manic-depressive disorder is not known. Because it alleviates both mania and depression—opposite states—its effects cannot be explained simply in terms of increasing or decreasing the activity at a particular type of synapse. One way in which it may act is by stabilizing both dopamine and serotonin synapses, preventing alternations between increased and decreased receptor density (Pert, Rosenblatt, Sivit, Pert, & Bunney, 1978; Treiser et al., 1981). Another way in which it may act is by lengthening the circadian rhythms of temperature and sleep (Wirz-Justice et al., 1982).

ATTENTION-DEFICIT DISORDER

Before leaving this chapter, let us deal briefly with **attention-deficit disorder** (**ADD**), a disorder commonly reported in children. Behaviorally, this disorder has a few points of overlap with mania. At the synaptic level, it resembles depression and mania in being associated—probably—with an abnormality of activity at catecholamine synapses.

Symptoms

"A 6-year-old boy . . . restless and unable to concentrate on schoolwork . . . easily distracted . . . impulsive, undeterred by probable punishment . . . prone to outbursts of aggressive behavior . . . fails to live up to expectations in school . . . has wide mood swings." Have I just described a child with a serious problem, in need of professional help? Or is this a fairly typical 6-year-old boy, well within the normal range of variation? It could be either, depending on degree. If the restlessness and distractibility are extreme, the condition is referred to as *attention deficit disorder* (Solanto, 1984), also known by the terms *hyperactivity, hyperkinesis,* or the hopelessly vague term *minimal brain dysfunction.* The condition is usually identified in early childhood, about age 5 to 7, and is at least two or three times more common in boys than in girls. Although the symptoms—high activity level, distractibility, and impulsiveness—resemble those of mania, the children do not as a rule become manic adults, nor do they respond favorably to the same drugs.

Because attention deficit disorder is merely an exaggeration of common characteristics of young children, there is much room for disagreement on how to classify a child. The diagnosis is unusually sloppy and unreliable, even by comparison to other psychiatric diagnoses (Carey & McDevitt, 1980). Even when it is agreed that a problem exists, a great many underlying causes are possible. Children can become hyperactive, distractible, and impulsive because of problems such as inadequate sleep, allergies, family conflicts, head injuries, complications during prenatal development and birth, malnutrition, early exposure to toxins, viral infections, delayed brain maturation, or genetics (Leonard, 1979; Rutter, 1982).

Although half or more of all children with this disorder show some improvement when they reach adolescence, a large number have continuing problems, especially with impulse control (Gittelman, Mannuzza, Shenker,

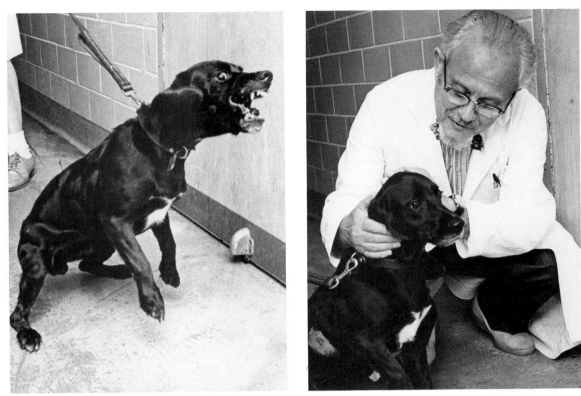

Figure 15-9. A vicious, hyperactive dog (left) that became very calm and tame after injections of amphetamine (right). (From Corson et al., 1973.)

& Bonagura, 1985; Hechtman & Weiss, 1983; Thorley, 1984). About 20 percent eventually get in trouble for delinquency or crime. Many also have problems of poor self-esteem and low academic achievement.

Treatment

The most common treatment for ADD is the use of stimulant drugs, such as amphetamine and methylphenidate (Ritalin), which stimulate the norepinephrine and dopamine synapses. The benefit of these drugs is paradoxical; they increase arousal and activity in normal adults, yet they seem to subdue children who have excess activity and arousal. A number of experiments attest to the effectiveness of stimulant drugs in treating ADD (e.g., Pelham, Bender, Caddell, Booth, & Moorer, 1985). In fact, they can calm hyperactive animals as well as children. (See Figure 15-9.) Nevertheless, we have much reason to regard the drugs as overprescribed. If a child with attention deficit disorder fails to respond to the drug, as a significant number do, many physicians continue increasing the dose until side effects begin to appear (Varley & Trupin, 1983). In other words, many of the children taking the largest doses are the ones getting the least benefit. In reaction against this overuse of drugs, many parents turn to a variety of other treatments, including some of doubtful usefulness (see Digression 15-1).

How do stimulant drugs help children with attention deficit disorder? We do not know. Presumably they act on catecholamine synapses in some way. Several investigators have proposed that the underlying problem

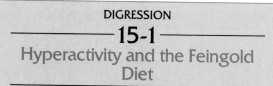

DIGRESSION

15-1

Hyperactivity and the Feingold Diet

In 1975, B. F. Feingold published a book titled *Why Your Child Is Hyperactive*, in which he argued that many cases of hyperactivity were due to, or at least aggravated by, artificial additives in the foods the children ate. He reported that hyperactivity could be alleviated by putting the children on a diet free from the artificial colorings and flavors found in most packaged foods.

Feingold's recommendations have been followed by the families of many hyperactive children in spite of the difficulty and expense of the diet. Well-controlled experimental investigations of the effects of this diet have, however, yielded mostly discouraging results.

One group of thirty-six hyperactive boys, ages 6 to 12, lived on a diet strictly controlled by the experimenters (Harley et al., 1978). Half the boys started on a Feingold diet and then shifted to a control diet for the second half of the experiment. The other boys started on the control diet and then shifted to the Feingold diet. The children, parents, and teachers did not know which diet any child was on at any time. To be certain that the children would stick to the diet, the experimenters supplied all meals to each child and his family at all times. They even provided the refreshments for all birthday parties that were given in the children's school classes.

The results provided only weak support for the Feingold diet. Of the thirty-six boys, only four were rated by both the parents and the teacher as "improved in behavior" while on the Feingold diet. However, in a similar study of ten preschool hyperactive boys ages 3 to 5, all ten mothers rated the child as better when he was on the Feingold diet than when he was on the control diet.

Mattes and Gittelman (1981) conducted a study with a similar experimental design, using only hyperactive children whose parents insisted that the Feingold diet (one free from artificial additives) had helped their children. The experimenters found no evidence that the diet had an effect on any of the eleven children. While a few experimenters have reported favorable results with the Feingold diet (Weiss, 1982), a consensus is growing that it is helpful to only a small minority of hyperactive children (probably 10 percent or fewer).

is deficient activity at catecholamine synapses; according to this view, amphetamine and methylphenidate act by increasing that activity (Shaywitz, Gordon, Klopper, Zelterman, & Irvine, 1979).

Although this view may prove to be correct, there are reasons to be skeptical that it is the whole story. First, measurements of autonomic nervous system activity indicate normal arousal levels in children with ADD (Hastings & Barkley, 1978; Rosenthal & Allen, 1978).

Second, amphetamine improves the attention span of normal children as well as those with ADD (Zahn, Rapoport, & Thompson, 1980). Apparently, children react differently to the drug than adults do. Since it helps children with normal brains, the fact that it helps children with ADD cannot be taken as evidence for any brain abnormality.

Third, amphetamine is known to have multiple effects in the brain, acting not only on norepinephrine and dopamine synapses but also on serotonin synapses and probably others. Drugs that act more selectively than amphetamine, altering only one transmitter, are less effective as therapy for attention deficit disorder (Zametkin, Rapoport, Murphy, Linnoila, & Ismond, 1985). Evidently, the benefits of amphetamine and other drugs depend on complex effects on several transmitters, and possibly on certain subsets of norepinephrine and dopamine synapses more than others.

SUMMARY

1.   A person with a unipolar disorder has periods of depression; someone with a bipolar disorder has periods of both depression and mania. (pp. 412–413)
2.   It is possible to use the dexamethasone suppression test and EEG measures of sleep to distinguish between endogenous and reactive depression. However, at present the distinction does not seem highly relevant to therapy. (p. 414)
3.   Intense stress may aggravate depression by provoking release of certain transmitters faster than they can be resynthesized. (p. 415)
4.   A large percentage of depressed people have abnormalities in their hormones, especially sex hormones and thyroid hormones. (p. 416)
5.   It is possible to have a hereditary predisposition toward depression. (p. 416)
6.   The Borna disease virus has been found in the blood of a small percentage of people suffering from depression or manic-depressive disorder; conceivably it or a similar virus may be responsible for certain cases of these disorders. (p. 417)
7.   Several animal models resemble depression. (p. 418)
8.   Studies of the effects of antidepressants on animals led to the initial hypothesis that depression and mania relate to abnormalities at the catecholamine synapses. (p. 419)
9.   Many depressed people have deficient activity in their left frontal cortex. (p. 420)
10.   The common antidepressants—tricyclic drugs and monoamine oxidase inhibitors—prolong the effects of catecholamines and serotonin at the synapses. (p. 421)
11.   Activities of several transmitters may be abnormal in depression, and the abnormality probably varies from one individual to another. (p. 421)
12.   Although antidepressant drugs alter synaptic activities rapidly, they do not alleviate depression until a person has taken the drugs for 2 weeks or more. (p. 421)
13.   The long-term effect of antidepressant drugs is apparently a net decrease in the stimulation of postsynaptic neurons responsive to catecholamines and serotonin. (p. 423)
14.   Electroconvulsive shock, now used under different conditions from those common in its early days, is effective against certain types of depression. (p. 424)
15.   Most depressed people have sleep troubles related to a shift of their circadian rhythms. Shifting their time of sleep or temporarily depriving them of sleep can relieve their depression. (p. 425)
16.   Certain people become depressed every winter; their depression can be relieved by bright light that extends the apparent daylight period. (p. 426)
17.   The most effective known therapy for manic-depressive disorder is lithium. (p. 427)
18.   Attention deficit disorder is an exaggeration of behavioral tendencies common in young children. (p. 428)
19.   The usual treatment for attention deficit disorder is the use of stimulant drugs. (p. 429)

REVIEW QUESTIONS

1.   Describe the symptoms of depression and of mania. (p. 412)
2.   What is the difference between a unipolar disorder and a bipolar disorder? (pp. 412–413)
3.   What tests have been devised to help distinguish between endogenous and reactive forms of depression? (p. 414)
4.   In what way is the distinction between endogenous and reactive depression not useful? (p. 414)
5.   Describe evidence indicating that stress and hormonal fluctuations trigger episodes of depression, even if they may not be the ultimate cause of depression. (pp. 415–416)
6.   What evidence links the Borna disease virus to certain cases of depression or manic-depressive illness? (p. 417)
7.   By what means do tricyclic drugs and MAOIs prolong the effects of catecholamines and serotonin at the synapses? (p. 421)
8.   In what way does the time course of antidepressant drugs argue against the simple hypothesis that depression is caused by a deficiency of such synaptic transmitters as dopamine, norepinephrine, and serotonin? (p. 421)
9.   What are the effects of antidepressant drugs on the autoreceptors at dopamine and norepinephrine synapses? (p. 422)
10.   How are the procedures for delivering ECT different today from what they were in the 1950s? (p. 424)
11.   For what kinds of depressed patients is ECT most likely to be used? (p. 424)
12.   What modification of the procedure for ECT reduces the impairment it causes in memory? (p. 424)
13.   What accounts for the fact that many depressed people enter REM sleep soon after falling asleep, while nondepressed people do not? (p. 425)

14.   What change in sleep habits sometimes relieves depression? (p. 426)
15.   What treatment is effective for seasonal affective disorder? (p. 427)
16.   What is the most common treatment for manic-depressive disorder, and why were American psychia-trists long reluctant to use this treatment? (p. 427)
17.   What are the symptoms of attention deficit disorder? (p. 428)
18.   Why is it difficult to draw conclusions from the fact that stimulant drugs alleviate the symptoms of attention deficit disorder in most cases? (pp. 429–430)

THOUGHT QUESTIONS

1.   Certain people suffer from what they describe as "post-Christmas depression." They claim that they feel depressed as a letdown after all the excitement of the holiday season. What other explanation could you offer?

2.   Depressed people apparently have impaired activity in the left hemisphere of the cerebral cortex. ECT applied only to the right hemisphere can relieve depression. How might you interpret this combination of results?

TERMS TO REMEMBER

mania (p. 412)
hypomania (p. 412)
unipolar disorder (p. 412)
bipolar disorder (p. 412)
manic-depressive disorder (p. 413)
major depression (p. 413)
endogenous depression (p. 414)
reactive depression (p. 414)
dexamethasone suppression test (p. 414)
postpartum depression (p. 416)

Borna disease (p. 417)
learned helplessness (p. 419)
tricyclics (p. 421)
monoamine oxidase inhibitors (MAOIs) (p. 421)
monoamine oxidase (MAO) (p. 421)
autoreceptors (p. 422)
electroconvulsive shock therapy (ECT) (p. 423)
seasonal affective disorder (SAD) (p. 426)
lithium (p. 427)
attention deficit disorder (ADD) (p. 428)

SUGGESTIONS FOR FURTHER READING

Galton, L. (1979). *You may not need a psychiatrist.* New York: Simon & Schuster. Discusses how vitamin deficiencies, sleep abnormalities, brain damage, and a variety of other problems can lead to depression and other disorders.

McNeal, E. T., & Cimbolic, P. (1986). Antidepressants and biochemical theories of depression. *Psychological Bulletin, 99,* 361–374. A good overview of evidence linking depression to abnormalities of transmission at the synapses.

Ross, D. M., & Ross, S. A. (1982). *Hyperactivity* (2nd ed.). New York: Wiley-Interscience. Overview of all aspects of research on hyperactive children.

Biology of Schizophrenia and Related Disorders

CHAPTER

16

MAIN IDEAS

1. Schizophrenia is a psychological disorder associated, in many cases, with gradual, minor brain damage.

2. Although the causes of schizophrenia are not fully understood, much evidence points to genetics as one major factor.

3. Drugs that relieve schizophrenia block dopamine synapses in the brain.

4. Autism is a rare childhood disorder that resembles schizophrenia in certain regards, although the underlying causes differ.

Until the late 1860s, people with aphasia were considered mentally ill. After it was discovered that aphasia is caused by localized brain damage, those patients were considered a problem for neurologists instead of psychiatrists. Similarly, after it was discovered that general paresis, a type of intellectual deterioration, was due to the third stage of syphilis infection (see Figure 16-1), people with this problem were classified as neurological instead of psychiatric patients. Apparently our concept of mental illness encompasses disorders of behavior not caused by neurological damage. As soon as we find a neurological basis for a disorder, it is no longer considered a mental illness.

Regardless of whether schizophrenia is considered a mental illness or a neurological disorder, it constitutes a serious disruption of normal behavior, apparently caused by dysfunction of several parts of the brain. In this chapter we shall consider the biological basis of schizophrenia and of a slightly similar condition in children, autism.

THE CHARACTERISTICS OF SCHIZOPHRENIA

Schizophrenia is a widespread disorder. Because of borderline cases and disagreements about diagnosis, it is difficult to state the exact incidence of the disorder. A common estimate is that 1 to 2 percent of the population will be afflicted with schizophrenia at one time or another during their lives (Robins et al., 1984). Schizophrenia occurs in all ethnic groups and in all parts of the world, although it is rare in the tropics. It is between ten and one hundred times more common in the United States and Europe than in most Third World countries (Torrey, 1986). Within the United States, it is more common in impoverished areas than in wealthy areas. It is about equally common in men and women, although it is generally diagnosed at an earlier age in men than in women (Lewine, 1981).

Schizophrenia is generally first diagnosed in people between the ages of 15 and 30, less commonly in people ages 30 to 45. Once a person has schizophrenia, however, the condition is likely to continue for years, perhaps for life.

Schizophrenia was originally known as *dementia praecox*, which is Latin for "deterioration of the mind at an early age." In 1911 Eugen Bleuler introduced the term *schizophrenia*, which has been the preferred term ever since.

The term is often misunderstood. Although schizophrenia is Greek for "split mind," it is *not* the same thing as *multiple personality*, a condition in which a person alternates between one personality and another. A schizophrenic person has only one personality. The split in the schizophrenic mind is between the emotional and intellectual sides of the person. That is, what the person expresses emotionally—or fails to express emotionally—is often at odds with what the person is saying.

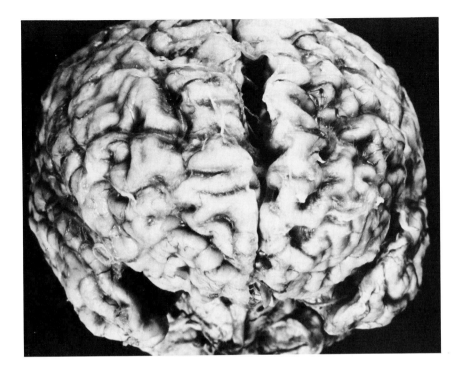

Figure 16-1. Brain of a person with general paresis (the final stage of syphilis). Note the shrinkage of gyri of the cerebral cortex. (Photo courtesy of Dr. Dana Copeland.)

Behavioral Symptoms

According to the American Psychiatric Association (1980), to be diagnosed as schizophrenic, a person must show: (1) deterioration of functioning in everyday life, and (2) hallucinations or delusions or thought disorder. **Hallucinations** are sensory experiences that do not correspond to reality. Many schizophrenics have auditory hallucinations, such as hearing voices. Very few have visual hallucinations, which are more characteristic of drug abuse. **Delusions** are beliefs that the rest of humanity regards as unfounded, such as the belief that one is persecuted, the belief that one's behavior is being controlled from outer space, or the belief that the headlines of the morning newspaper are a coded message intended only for oneself.

The most typical **thought disorder** of schizophrenia is a difficulty understanding and using abstract concepts. For example, a schizophrenic person has trouble understanding such proverbs as "When the cat is away, the mice will play," interpreting them literally. Schizophrenic people also show a lack of organizing purpose in their stream of thoughts and have loose associations among ideas, as in a dream. What they say is often difficult to understand. (See Digression 16-1.)

Hallucinations, delusions, and thought disorder are sometimes known as **positive symptoms** of schizophrenia because they represent the presence of certain behaviors. In contrast, **negative symptoms** represent the absence of certain behaviors: Many schizophrenics lack emotional expression, fail to interact socially with other people, and speak very little.

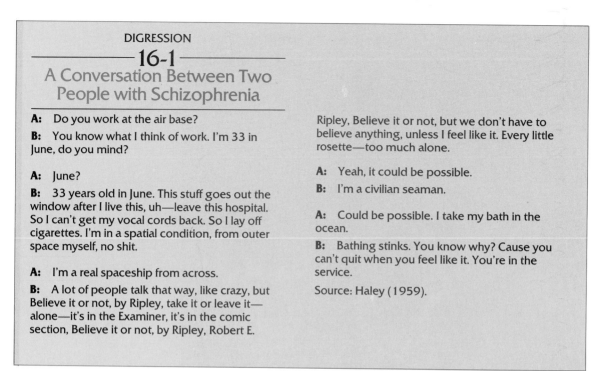

DIGRESSION

16-1

A Conversation Between Two People with Schizophrenia

A: Do you work at the air base?

B: You know what I think of work. I'm 33 in June, do you mind?

A: June?

B: 33 years old in June. This stuff goes out the window after I live this, uh—leave this hospital. So I can't get my vocal cords back. So I lay off cigarettes. I'm in a spatial condition, from outer space myself, no shit.

A: I'm a real spaceship from across.

B: A lot of people talk that way, like crazy, but Believe it or not, by Ripley, take it or leave it—alone—it's in the Examiner, it's in the comic section, Believe it or not, by Ripley, Robert E.

Ripley, Believe it or not, but we don't have to believe anything, unless I feel like it. Every little rosette—too much alone.

A: Yeah, it could be possible.

B: I'm a civilian seaman.

A: Could be possible. I take my bath in the ocean.

B: Bathing stinks. You know why? Cause you can't quit when you feel like it. You're in the service.

Source: Haley (1959).

Prior to the mid-1950s, when antischizophrenic drugs first became available, most schizophrenic people were confined to a mental hospital for life. Today, the outcome varies. About one-third of all people with schizophrenia manage to live a normal life, with the aid of drugs and outpatient treatment. About 10 percent enter a mental hospital once and then leave, never to return (Pokorny, 1978). The others are alternately in and out of mental hospitals all their lives. Because schizophrenia lasts so many years, its economic costs to society are almost as great as those of more common ailments, such as heart attacks (Andrews et al., 1985). The costs in terms of wasted years of human life are enormous.

Evidence of Brain Damage in Schizophrenia

Many but not all schizophrenic patients show signs of mild brain damage or atrophy, mostly in the cerebral cortex. In contrast, brain damage or atrophy is not typically found in patients suffering from depression, anxiety disorder, or other conditions classed as psychological disorders. The brain damage of schizophrenia is relatively mild, however, in comparison to the damage found in Alzheimer's disease and Huntington's disease.

Several lines of evidence point to brain damage in schizophrenia. First, examinations after death reveal that the brains of schizophrenics are overall about 6 percent lighter than the brains of other mental patients (Brown et al., 1986). The schizophrenic brains have fewer neurons in the cerebral cortex (Benes, Davidson, & Bird, 1986), the amygdala, and the hippocampus (Bogerts, Meertz, & Schönfeldt-Bausch, 1985). (See Figures 16-2 and 16-3.)

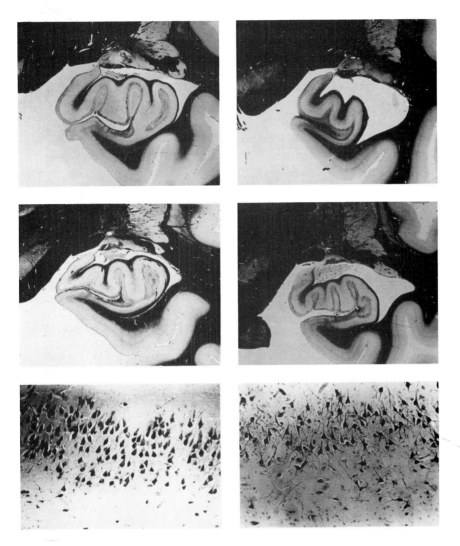

Figure 16-2. The hippocampus of two normal people (left) and two people with schizophrenia (right). (From Bogerts, Meertz, & Schönfeldt-Bausch, 1985; photos courtesy of B. Bogerts.)

Figure 16-3. Structure of the hippocampus in a normal person (left) and a person with schizophrenia (right). (Photos courtesy of Arnold Scheibel.)

In living people, it is possible to determine the size and activity of various structures through such techniques as PET scans, CAT scans, and regional cerebral blood flow (see Color Plates 25 and 26). The results indicate that most schizophrenics have larger than normal ventricles (DeLisi et al, 1986; Luchins, Lewine, & Meltzer, 1984). The ventricles are fluid-filled spaces; enlarged ventricles mean that less space is occupied by neurons. Schizophrenic people also have a smaller than normal frontal cortex and lower than average levels of metabolism in the temporal and frontal areas of the cortex—especially in the left frontal cortex (Andreasen et al., 1986; Farkas et al., 1984; Wolkin et al., 1985).

Furthermore, when healthy people engage in certain cognitive tasks, such as sorting cards according to complex rules, the rate of metabolic activity increases sharply in the dorsolateral part of their prefrontal cortex. Generally, the greater the increase in metabolic activity, the better their performance on the task. Schizophrenics fail to show such an enhancement in metabolic activity in their prefrontal cortex when they attempt these tasks (Berman, Zec, & Weinberger, 1986; Weinberger, Berman, & Zec, 1986). As you might expect, they perform the tasks poorly.

Here is a final line of evidence for damage to the frontal and temporal cortex of schizophrenic patients: When given tests that have been devised to measure brain damage (such as the Halstead-Reitan and Luria-Nebraska tests, discussed in Chapter 14), most schizophrenic patients perform poorly on the same tasks that are failed by patients who are known to have suffered damage to the frontal or temporal cortex (Kolb & Whishaw, 1983).

POSSIBLE CAUSES OF SCHIZOPHRENIA

The results just discussed indicate that something is causing brain damage—probably slow and gradual brain damage—in schizophrenic people. What might that something be?

Over the years, a great many hypotheses have been proposed and considered. A few examples: Schizophrenia may be due to the accumulation of copper or other heavy metal ions in the brain (Bowman & Lewis, 1982). The schizophrenic brain may produce certain chemicals such as bufotenine that can induce hallucinations (Kety, 1975; Potkin et al., 1979; Wyatt, Termini, & Davis, 1971). The schizophrenic brain may produce 6-hydroxydopamine, which would destroy norepinephrine synapses, lead to a loss of pleasure and motivated behavior, and sometimes produce movement impairments like those shown in Figure 16-4 (Stein & Wise, 1971).

Support for all of those hypotheses, as well as several others, has faded, although we are not in a position to rule them out altogether. Now let us consider several other possibilities in more detail.

Genetics

According to most studies, schizophrenia runs in families. That is, people with schizophrenia are more likely than others to have schizophrenic relatives (e.g., Baron, Gruen, Kane, & Asnis, 1985; Kendler, Gruenberg, & Tsuang, 1985), although the reported strength of that relationship varies from one study to another. Furthermore, even among the nonschizophrenic relatives of a schizophrenic patient, many are not fully normal. Many give indications of minor brain damage or dysfunction, just as the schizophrenic patients themselves do (Kinney, Woods, & Yurgelun-Todd, 1986; Marcus, Hans, Mednick, Schulsinger, & Michelsen, 1985).

Similarity within a family indicates only that genetics is a possible factor, however. Members of a family may resemble one another because of either genetics or similar environment. We must look further to distinguish between these two possibilities.

Twin Studies.   One line of evidence is a comparison of monozygotic (identical) twins and dizygotic (fraternal) twins. (See the Appendix for a review of genetics.) When one member of a pair of monozygotic twins is schizophrenic, the other twin has about a 50 percent probability of becoming schizophrenic also. Even those who do not become schizophrenic are likely to develop other serious disturbances, including borderline schizophrenia

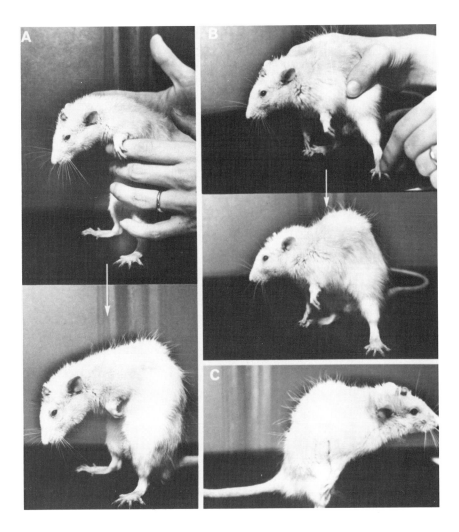

Figure 16-4. A rat showing catatonic behaviors after seven injections of 6-hydroxydopamine into the ventricles of the brain. The rat can be molded into some unnatural positions, which it maintains for at least several minutes. (From Stein & Wise, 1971.)

(Kendler & Robinette, 1983). On the other hand, if one of a pair of dizygotic twins is schizophrenic, the other twin has only about a 15 percent probability of schizophrenia (Kendler, 1983; McGuffin, Farmer, Gottesman, Murray, & Reveley, 1984). We say that the monozygotic twins have a 50 percent **concordance** for schizophrenia and that the dizygotic twins have a 15 percent concordance. Presumably, the monozygotic twins have a greater concordance because they share more genes in common. Furthermore, those twin pairs who mistakenly thought they were monozygotic (identical) but who were really dizygotic are less concordant for schizophrenia than those twin pairs who always thought they were dizygotic but who were really monozygotic (Kendler, 1983). That is, it makes more difference for a pair of twins to *be* monozygotic than to *think* they are monozygotic and to be treated as such.

Curiously, the concordance rate for schizophrenia between monozygotic twins is related to the concordance rate for handedness. Many but not all pairs of monozygotic twins are mirror images of one another: One is right-handed, the other is left-handed, and the two are mirror images in their physical appearance (Segal, 1984). Among pairs of monozygotic twins that are both right-handed, the schizophrenia concordance rate is 92 percent. That is, if one is schizophrenic, the other has a 92 percent probability of being schizophrenic, too. But among pairs in which one is right-handed and the other is left-handed, the concordance rate is only 25 percent (Boklage, 1977).

When a pair is discordant for schizophrenia, the nonschizophrenic twin has a high probability of bearing schizophrenic children (Nicol & Gottesman, 1983). Evidently, both twins have the gene or genes for schizophrenia, although some unidentified factor related to handedness causes the genetic effects to make themselves manifest in the behavior of one twin and not the other.

Adopted Children Who Become Schizophrenic.   A second line of evidence supporting a genetic basis for schizophrenia is an examination of adopted children who become schizophrenic. More of the biological relatives than the adoptive relatives of such children suffer from schizophrenia themselves (Kessler, 1980; Kety, Rosenthal, Wender, Schulsinger, & Jacobsen, 1975; Lowing, Mirsky, & Pereira, 1983). A child of a schizophrenic parent adopted by a normal couple is more likely to become schizophrenic than a child of normal parents adopted by a couple that includes one schizophrenic (Wender, Rosenthal, Kety, Schulsinger, & Welner, 1974). These data point to either genetics or prenatal environment as a determining factor in schizophrenia.

Finally, in rare cases an adopted child has a **paternal half-sibling** who was also adopted. Paternal half-siblings have the same father but different mothers; they are more closely related than cousins but less closely related than brother and sister. One study in Denmark found sixty-three adopted schizophrenics who had a paternal half-sibling adopted by another family. Eight of the sixty-three half-siblings were schizophrenic also—a concordance well above the approximately 1 percent prevalence of schizophrenia in the population. Note that because these children had different mothers, they did not share a common environment even before birth.

Limitations of the Genetic Explanation.   All these results leave little doubt that heredity is an important factor in schizophrenia. On the other hand, heredity cannot be the whole story. Occasionally someone with no known schizophrenic relatives becomes schizophrenic. Conversely, someone who has a monozygotic twin with schizophrenia may appear normal. These data do not fit a one-gene hypothesis, although they may fit a hypothesis of a major gene modified by many other genes and by environmental influences (Faraone & Tsuang, 1985).

Furthermore, if certain genes are responsible for schizophrenia, how did they get so common in the population? Evolution should select against such genes. Schizophrenic people have a higher than normal probability of dying young, from a wide variety of causes ranging from heart attacks to traffic accidents (Allebeck & Wistedt, 1986). They are less likely than other people to have children. Not only are many of them confined to mental hospitals, but most schizophrenics, especially male schizophrenics, have a lower than average sex drive and most of them are socially inept, socially unresponsive, and in general unlikely to attract partners. Even the nonschizophrenic relatives of schizophrenic patients have an increased likelihood of both psychological and medical problems. If indeed a small number of genes are responsible for this condition, it is puzzling to contemplate what maintains those genes against what appears to be a strong evolutionary pressure.

Stress as a Possible Trigger for Schizophrenia

It was once believed that schizophrenia was caused by the parents' behavior. The parents of certain schizophrenics were reported to give confusing "come here, go away" messages, for example. This hypothesis is now considered obsolete. The main reason for its downfall was the results of adoption studies. The probability of schizophrenia relates more to the genes provided by the biological parents than to the environment provided by the adopting parents. Furthermore, the time course of the disorder does not fit the hypothesis; schizophrenia is usually first diagnosed at ages 20 to 30, when the influence of the parents should be lessening.

Other types of experience may have something to do with the onset of schizophrenia, however. Stress in particular may aggravate the condition, even if it is not the original cause. Curt Richter (1956, 1958a, 1958b) offered an animal model of schizophrenia. He exposed rats to the highly stressful experience of swimming in turbulent water nonstop for 60 hours. The survivors held abnormal positions rigidly for long times and occasionally leaped suddenly, as if they were responding to a hallucinated sight or sound. Promising as this demonstration may have been, however, it was not pursued further.

In humans, surveys have indicated that people with schizophrenia are no more likely than other psychiatric patients—and only slightly more likely than normal, healthy people—to report stressful life events during the months just prior to their first diagnosis of schizophrenia (Rabkin, 1980). A reasonable hypothesis is that extreme stress may provoke a sudden onset of schizophrenia in very rare cases, which might not be evident in the group averages reviewed by Rabkin. In more cases, stress may accelerate a schizophrenic deterioration or trigger it to start earlier than it would have otherwise. In most cases, however, stressful life events are probably not responsible for the onset of schizophrenia.

A Virus?

One peculiarity sets schizophrenia apart from other psychological disorders: A greater percentage of schizophrenic people are born during the winter months than during any other season (Bradbury & Miller, 1985). No such tendency is found in the birth dates of people suffering from depression, alcoholism, or other psychological disturbances (Watson, Tilleskjor, Kucala, & Jacobs, 1984). The **season-of-birth effect** for schizophrenia is stronger in the northern parts of the United States than in the south; worldwide, the tendency disappears in the tropics. It is particularly pronounced for schizo-

16-2

Effects of the AIDS Virus on the Brain

Acquired immune deficiency syndrome (AIDS) is a fatal condition caused by a retrovirus, specifically one known as HTLV-III (human T-lymphotropic virus III). Unlike the influenza virus and other viruses that can be transmitted by casual contact between two people, the AIDS virus can be transmitted only if it enters the blood of the recipient. It enters the blood if one receives a blood transfusion from a person with the virus or if one takes an injection with a needle previously used by an infected person. The virus can also be transmitted along with the sperm during sex if the sex partner has a break in the skin where the virus can enter. It has spread widely among homosexuals. Among heterosexuals, men can transmit it to women more easily than women can transmit it to men.

Because the AIDS virus resembles a virus common in African monkeys, humans probably got the virus from those monkeys, perhaps as recently as the 1950s. From its point of origin it spread slowly at first, then more rapidly. The virus has an incubation period of 5 years or more. That is, a person may have the virus for years before showing any symptoms.

The virus most often infects T4 lymphocytes, cells that are important for the body's immune response (Gallo, 1987). With these cells inactivated, the body becomes more vulnerable to all infections; the person has no defense against any of the viruses and bacteria that it would otherwise fight off without any trouble.

The AIDS virus can cause brain damage in two ways. First, because the virus has weakened the body's immune system, the brain is vulnerable to infections, just as the other organs are. Various patients suffer from encephalitis, meningitis, bacterial infections, brain tumors, and hemorrhage of the blood vessels in the brain (Levy, Bredesen, & Rosenblum, 1985). Second, the virus itself enters the brain in many if not most patients, where it may be found in the spaces between cells, in glia cells, or in distinctive *multinucleated giant cells*, which are not found in people without the virus (Budka, 1986; Epstein et al., 1984). The damage caused by the virus may lead to intellectual deterioration or to psychotic symptoms.

---

phrenics who have no schizophrenic relatives. That is, a family with several close schizophrenic relatives has a fairly high probability that any given child will become schizophrenic, regardless of when that child is born. A family with no history of schizophrenia ordinarily has very little probability of having a child who will become schizophrenic, but that probability does increase if the child is born in the winter (Bradbury & Miller, 1985).

What might account for the season-of-birth effect? One possibility, though not the only one, is that being born at a certain time and place may increase a baby's probability of contracting an infection. Crow (1984; Crow & Done, 1986) has proposed the hypothesis that schizophrenia may be caused by a virus, specifically a retrovirus. A **retrovirus**, like other viruses, is composed of RNA. Unlike other viruses, it forms a DNA copy of itself that can be incorporated into the genes. Thus, although the virus is acquired, it can be passed on genetically to one's offspring. Leukemia and AIDS are two diseases believed to be caused by retroviruses. (See Digression 16-2.)

Crow further suggests that the retrovirus responsible for schizophrenia (if there is one) is acquired either at the moment of birth or during prenatal development. Such an assumption is necessary if the retrovirus hypothesis is to account for the season-of-birth effect. He further supposes that this virus, like the AIDS virus, takes years to show its effects.

The retrovirus hypothesis is at least consistent with a number of facts about schizophrenia: We can imagine that such a virus could cause gradual brain damage. A disease caused by a retrovirus may have a strong hereditary component yet occasionally appear in a family in which it never appeared before. The virus could continue to spread the gene even though evolution selected strongly against the gene. It is possible to imagine that such a virus might interact with the genes controlling handedness, such that monozygotic twins concordant for handedness would be concordant for schizophrenia also.

On the other hand, appealing though the hypothesis seems, it is not supported by any strong direct evidence so far. No one has isolated a virus in schizophrenic brains that is absent from normal brains. We have no evidence that the season-of-birth effect is particularly severe during winters with high levels of infectious diseases. No one has demonstrated that an injection of schizophrenic brain extract can cause a viral infection in, say, monkeys, although one preliminary report found that such an injection led to a long-term decrease in activity levels (Baker et al., 1983). Overall, we can regard the retrovirus hypothesis as no more than a fascinating speculation worthy of further investigation.

THE BIOCHEMISTRY OF SCHIZOPHRENIA

Whatever the actual cause of schizophrenia may be—genetics, stress, virus, whatever—it must act through changes in the structure and chemistry of the brain. Since the discovery of antischizophrenic drugs in the 1950s, a great deal of research has made it clear that schizophrenia is related to an abnormality related to the dopamine synapses of the brain. Still, the exact nature of that abnormality remains elusive.

Chemicals That Can Provoke a State Similar to Schizophrenia

The use of large doses of amphetamine, especially if repeated numerous times within a few days, can lead to **amphetamine psychosis,** a condition that includes hallucinations, delusions, and other symptoms similar to schizophrenia. Large doses of certain other drugs, including cocaine, LSD, and Antabuse, sometimes also induce a state similar to schizophrenia. The main differences between drug-induced psychosis and schizophrenia are that victims of the drug-induced states often report visual hallucinations, while schizophrenics seldom do, and that a drug-induced psychosis is generally temporary (Ellinwood, 1969; Sloviter, Damiano & Connor, 1980).

The drugs that can produce psychosis all increase the stimulation of dopamine synapses. For example, amphetamine, which chemically resembles dopamine (see Figure 16-5), increases the release of dopamine from the presynaptic endings.

Another drug that stimulates dopamine synapses is L-DOPA, which is often given as a treatment for Parkinson's disease (Chapter 8). Among the typical side effects reported for L-DOPA are delusions, such as delusions of persecution, and other behaviors that are also characteristic of schizophrenia (Gershon, Angrist, & Shopsin, 1977). When L-DOPA has been given to schizophrenic patients, it has aggravated their symptoms. In short, excessive stimulation of dopamine synapses can produce the symptoms of schizophrenia.

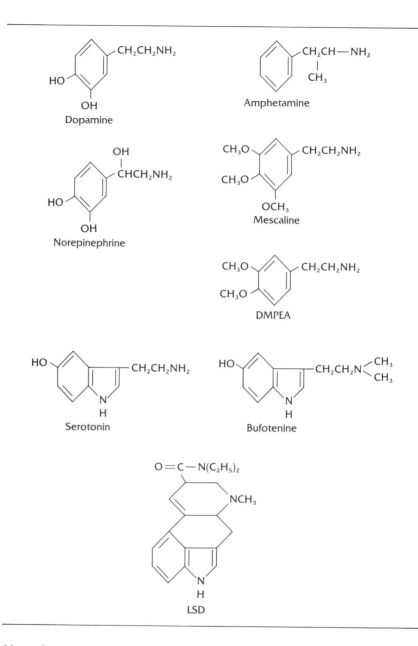

Figure 16-5. Chemical structures of three synaptic transmitters (left) and some chemicals that can induce hallucinations and (in large doses) a condition similar to schizophrenia.

Neuroleptics and the Dopamine Hypothesis of Schizophrenia

Probably the strongest link we have between dopamine synapses and schizophrenia comes from studies of drugs that alleviate schizophrenia. In the 1950s it was discovered that the drug **chlorpromazine** (trade name Thorazine) is an effective treatment for schizophrenia. Before the introduction of chlorpromazine, few schizophrenic patients who entered a mental hospital ever left. The introduction of chlorpromazine and related drugs made it possible to halt the course of the disease, especially if the drug treatment begins early enough. The drugs do not actually cure schizophrenia; rather,

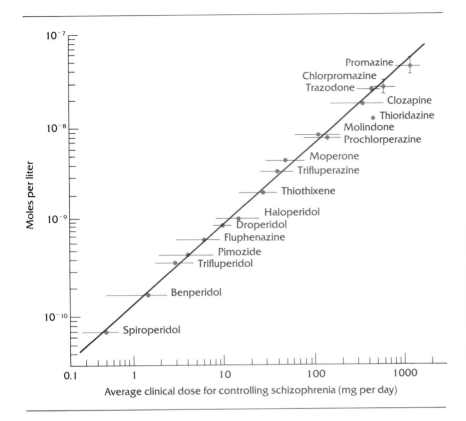

Figure 16-6. Antischizophrenic drugs. Drugs are arranged along the horizontal axis in terms of the average daily dose prescribed for schizophrenia. (Horizontal lines indicate ranges of dosage.) Along the vertical axis is a measurement of the amount of each drug required to achieve a certain degree of blockage of postsynaptic dopamine receptors. (From Seeman, Lee, Chau-Wong, & Wong, 1976.)

they control it, much the way insulin controls diabetes. A schizophrenic person must continue to take the drug on a regular basis—daily or monthly, depending on the drug—or the symptoms will gradually return (Davis, 1976).

If chlorpromazine were the only drug useful in treating schizophrenia, we would have no easy way to determine how it works, because its effects on brain chemistry are so numerous. The best way to determine how it works is to find what it has in common with other effective drugs.

A large number of antischizophrenic, or **neuroleptic drugs** have been found, most of which belong to two chemical families, the **phenothiazines**, which include chlorpromazine, and the **butyrophenones**, which include **haloperidol** (trade name Haldol). All these drugs have two properties in common: They block the postsynaptic dopamine receptors (Snyder, Banerjee, Yamamura, & Greenberg, 1974; van Praag, 1977) and they block the release of dopamine from the presynaptic neuron (Pickar et al., 1986; Seeman & Lee, 1975).

Figure 16-6 illustrates the relationship between the antischizophrenic effect of a drug and its ability to block postsynaptic dopamine receptors. For each drug, Seeman, Lee, Chau-Wong, and Wong (1976) determined the mean dose prescribed for schizophrenic patients (displayed along the horizontal axis). Presumably, drugs such as spiroperidol (at the lower left in the figure) are prescribed in the lowest doses because they are effective in these low doses; drugs such as chlorpromazine are prescribed in larger doses because such doses are necessary to achieve the desired effect. The investigators also determined what dose of each drug is necessary to block dopamine receptors (displayed along the vertical axis). As the figure shows, the more effective a given drug is for blocking dopamine receptors, the more effective it is for relieving schizophrenia. These results give rise to the **dopamine hypothesis of schizophrenia**. According to this hypothesis, schizophrenia is due to excess activity at dopamine synapses; neuroleptic drugs relieve schizophrenia by decreasing that activity.

Weaknesses of the Dopamine Hypothesis

If neuroleptic drugs alleviate schizophrenia by blocking dopamine synapses, it is natural to guess that people become schizophrenic because of an excess of dopamine activity. The evidence does not strongly support this hypothesis, however. Direct measurements of dopamine and its metabolites in the blood or in the CSF have sometimes indicated that schizophrenics have normal amounts, sometimes that they have slightly elevated amounts (Bacopoulous, Spokes, Bird, & Roth, 1979; Davis et al., 1985; Haracz, 1982; Rao, Gross, & Huber, 1984). In either case, the elevations are not impressive.

A more likely possibility is that schizophrenics may have increased numbers of dopamine receptors. Substantial increases in the number of receptors were reported in one study of schizophrenic brains after death (Seeman et al., 1984). Because nearly all those patients had been taking neuroleptic drugs, however, we do not know whether the high number of receptors was associated with the schizophrenia itself or whether it was a reaction to prolonged use of the drugs.

A further difficulty for the dopamine hypothesis is the time course for the effects of neuroleptic drugs. Although such drugs block dopamine receptors almost at once and reach their full effectiveness within a few days, their effects on behavior build up gradually over 2 or 3 weeks (Lipton & Nemeroff, 1978). Something must be going on within that time.

One possibility is that prolonged use of neuroleptic drugs decreases the number of spontaneously active dopamine neurons in what is known as the **mesolimbic system**, a set of neurons that project from the midbrain tegmentum to the limbic system (White & Wang, 1983). Another possibility is that the underlying problem in schizophrenia is not an excess of dopamine activity at all but a deficit of glutamate activity (Kornhuber, 1983). Glutamate is a synaptic transmitter released by axons extending from the cerebral cortex to the limbic system; dopamine synapses are known to inhibit the release of glutamate in that area. One study has reported that schizophrenics have only about half as much glutamate as normal in their brain (Kim & Kornhuber, 1982). If glutamate levels are low, one way to increase them would be to block the dopamine synapses that inhibit the glutamate synapses. The increase in glutamate activity might develop gradually over weeks. One attraction of the decreased-glutamate hypothesis is that it fits with the evidence of damage to the cerebral cortex.

Side Effects of Neuroleptic Drugs and the Search for Improved Drugs

Neuroleptic drugs produce some unpleasant side effects. Certain of these effects, such as impotence in males, develop quickly and cease as soon as the person stops taking the drug (Mitchell & Popkin, 1982). A more serious side effect is **tardive dyskinesia** (TAR-deev dis-kie-NEE-zee-uh), which develops gradually over years of drug use in many but not all people who take neuroleptics (Chouinard & Jones, 1980). Tardive dyskinesia is an impairment of voluntary movement that includes tremors and other involuntary movements. It is most likely to occur in those schizophrenics who have greater indications of minor brain damage and those who have been socially withdrawn for a long time (Wegner, Catalano, Gibralter, & Kane, 1985). These, incidentally, are the patients for whom the drugs are least likely to relieve their symptoms (Csernansky, Kaplan, & Hollister, 1985).

Tardive dyskinesia occurs as a result of denervation supersensitivity (Chapter 14). One of the results of a prolonged block of transmission at dopamine synapses is an increase in the number of receptors. After years of neuroleptic use, these receptors may become so numerous that the postsynaptic cell responds vigorously to even small amounts of dopamine. Because dopamine synapses in the basal ganglia stimulate movement—recall that damage to these synapses leads to Parkinson's disease—increased sensitivity in these synapses can cause bursts of involuntary movement, like that seen in tardive dyskinesia.

Once tardive dyskinesia emerges, it is apparently permanent. A patient who stops taking the drug does not experience a decrease in symptoms. In fact, without the drug, the dopamine receptors are no longer blocked and the symptoms of tardive dyskinesia grow *worse*. The only known way to combat tardive dyskinesia is to inhibit the dopamine synapses as much as possible by *increasing* the dosage of the neuroleptic drugs that had *caused* tardive dyskinesia! Naturally, in the long run the increased dosage leads to still greater denervation supersensitivity and greater tardive dyskinesia.

Given the difficulties of combating tardive dyskinesia after it starts, the best solution would be to prevent it from starting, by using different drugs. (See Digression 16-3.) Certain new drugs, referred to as *atypical antipsychotic drugs*, show much promise for alleviating schizophrenia without causing tardive dyskinesia. The brain has at least two types of dopamine receptors (Seeman & Grigoriadis, 1987) that are sensitive to different drugs. The neuroleptic drugs that produce tardive dyskinesia stimulate both the dopamine path from the substantia nigra to the basal ganglia, and the mesolimbic system (the path from the midbrain tegmentum to the limbic system). Apparently the mesolimbic system is the one that has the most to do with the symptoms of schizophrenia; the path to the basal ganglia is the one that is responsible for tardive dyskinesia. (See Figure 16-7.) The new, atypical antipsychotic drugs, such as clozapine and thioridazine, block dopamine activity in the mesolimbic system and thereby alleviate schizophrenia. Because they produce less effect on the dopamine receptors in the basal ganglia, they are less likely to produce tardive dyskinesia (White & Wang, 1983).

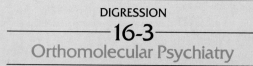

DIGRESSION
16-3
Orthomolecular Psychiatry

Brain functioning is known to be highly sensitive to a great many nutrients. A deficit of vitamins or excessive exposure to metallic ions such as lead, mercury, or cadmium can impair brain functioning and lead to psychotic behavior. In particular, certain symptoms of schizophrenia resemble those of vitamin deficiencies, especially those of niacin deficiency. (Niacin, or nicotinic acid, is one of the B vitamins.) In the words of Hoffer (1973), "If all the [niacin] were removed from our food, everyone would become psychotic within one year."

Niacin can alleviate the symptoms of schizophrenia in a number of cases. The improvement is slow, but it can be long-lasting (Osmond, 1973). Although most schizophrenics and other mental patients are not actually vitamin-deficient by usual standards, it is possible that they have a greater than normal need for certain vitamins because they have abnormalities of other aspects of body chemistry.

Orthomolecular psychiatry, a branch of psychiatry that emphasizes nutrition, has been defined by Pauling (1968) as "the treatment of mental disease by the provision of the optimum molecular environment for the mind, especially the optimum concentrations of substances normally present in the human body." Orthomolecular psychiatry is controversial. The exaggerated and poorly documented claims made by a few orthomolecular psychiatrists have aroused the hostility of other mental health professionals. Certain psychiatrists contend that the extra vitamin doses are usually of negligible value; others emphasize the lack of theoretical explanation for how the vitamins might affect schizophrenia or other conditions. Nevertheless, the role of vitamins and nutrition in mental illness is certainly worthy of serious research.

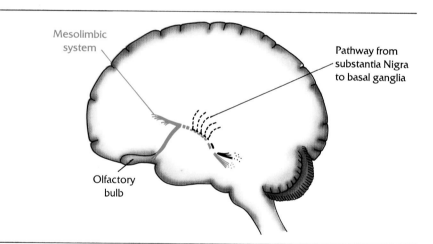

Figure 16-7. Two dopamine pathways. The mesolimbic system is apparently responsible for the symptoms of schizophrenia; the path to the basal ganglia is responsible for the tardive dyskinesia that sometimes results from use of neuroleptic drugs.

PROSPECTS FOR PREDICTION OR EARLY DIAGNOSIS OF SCHIZOPHRENIA

Suppose you are a psychiatrist. You have a patient who you believe may be in the early stages of schizophrenia. Do you start the patient on neuroleptic drugs? If you do and the patient does not have schizophrenia, you do no good and you run the risk of causing tardive dyskinesia and other side effects. On the other hand, if the patient is suffering from schizophrenia, the longer you wait before starting the drugs, the more deteriorated the patient will become and the less chance the he or she will have of recovery.

Now suppose you are a mental health researcher. You would like to follow some people during the early stages of schizophrenia to determine how their behavior changes and whether certain kinds of early intervention can prevent later deterioration.

In either case, it would be important to identify accurately which people are on their way to becoming schizophrenic and to do so as early as possible. Several kinds of studies have attempted to determine what distinguishes people who are likely to become schizophrenic.

The Behavior of Children at Risk for Schizophrenia

One way to study the characteristics of people who will later become schizophrenic is to collect voluminous data on children or adolescents and then to conduct a follow-up study when they reach the age of 40, to determine which of them became schizophrenic and which did not. This kind of study faces two practical difficulties: It necessarily requires about 30 years to complete, and it requires an enormous sample of children or adolescents, since only about 1 or 2 percent will become schizophrenic. In spite of these difficulties, one such study has been conducted (Hartmann et al., 1984). It started with extensive interviews of 1,000 teenage boys. Many years later, after all the boys had passed the age of 40, investigators reexamined them. The 24 boys who eventually became schizophrenic had been different from other boys in several regards during their teenage years: They had unusual levels of anxiety, difficulty in interpersonal relationships, a lack of ambition, a fear of trying anything new, and a negative attitude toward school. Most of them felt no affection for their fathers, and most played little or no role in group activities. They reported a lack of pleasure and a lack of a "sense of self continuing over time." We may regard these as characteristics of boys who are more likely than others to develop schizophrenia.

It is possible to simplify such a study, at the expense of losing part of the accuracy. An experimenter may compare a large number of children of schizophrenic mothers to children of other mothers. We can safely assume that a larger percentage of the children of schizophrenic mothers will eventually become schizophrenic themselves, though certainly not all of them will. Anything that is more common among these children than among children of normal mothers is presumably a characteristic of children *at risk* for schizophrenia.

Two such studies found that (1) children at risk for schizophrenia are relatively passive as babies, with a short attention span; (2) in school they make few friends and they often disrupt class (Parnas, Schulsinger, Schulsinger, Mednick, & Teasdale, 1982); and (3) they have mild degrees of the same thought disorders found in adult schizophrenics (Arboleda & Holzman, 1985).

Biological Markers of Schizophrenia

Another approach to early diagnosis of schizophrenia is to identify biological markers—that is, biological characteristics that are found in schizophrenics, including both young, never-medicated schizophrenics and schizophrenics whose behavior has been restored to normal by neuroleptic drugs. For example, early-onset REM periods are a biological marker for depression (Chapter 15). If we could identify any such markers for schizophrenia, we might be able to use them to help diagnose someone whose behavior has not yet deteriorated badly. Two possible markers are a disturbance of long-term concentration and certain abnormalities of EEG recordings (Kornhuber, 1983).

Another possible marker that seems particularly promising is an impairment of smooth pursuit eye movements. There are two kinds of eye movements, saccadic movements and pursuit movements. A **saccadic eye movement** is a sudden shift from one target to another. When you read this page, your eyes jump from one fixation point to another by a saccadic movement. A **pursuit eye movement** is a movement that follows a moving target, as when you watch another person walk by. A majority of schizophrenics have deficits in their pursuit eye movements; either the eyes stop moving while the target continues, or the eyes make a saccadic movement that takes them off the target. They have such difficulties both when their symptoms are severe and after drugs have relieved them. Schizophrenics with greater thought disorders tend to have greater impairments of their pursuit eye movements (Solomon, Holzman, Levin, & Gale, 1987). Almost half of their close relatives also have dysfunctions of pursuit eye movements (Holzman, 1985). Furthermore, college students with the least accurate pursuit eye movements have the greatest incidence of *schizotypal personality*, a mild personality disorder related to schizophrenia (Siever, Coursey, Alterman, Buchsbaum, & Murphy, 1984). All these results support the hypothesis that impaired pursuit eye movements may be a marker indicating vulnerability to schizophrenia.

INFANTILE AUTISM

Infantile autism is a rare condition, affecting about one child in 2,500. It resembles schizophrenia in certain regards, although the underlying causes are different. Like other kinds of abnormal behavior, autism comes in all degrees, from mild to severe. In full-blown cases the following behaviors are characteristic (Creak, 1961; Kanner, 1943; Ornitz & Ritvo, 1976):

Figure 16-8. An autistic boy with two stereotyped behaviors—pulling on his ears and biting his hand. His right hand is covered with welts and calluses.

1. *Social isolation.* The autistic child largely ignores other people, shows little attachment to parents or other relatives, and retreats into a world of his or her own.

2. *Stereotyped behaviors.* An autistic child rocks back and forth, bites the hands, stares at something, rotates an object, or engages in other repetitive behaviors for long, uninterrupted time periods. Each autistic child has his or her own repertoire of preferred stereotyped behaviors. (See Figure 16-8.)

3. *Resistance to any change in routine.* The child establishes strong habits and becomes upset if the routine is changed.

4. *Abnormal responses to sensory stimuli.* The autistic child may ignore visual stimuli and sounds, especially speech sounds, sometimes to such an extent that others assume the child is deaf. At other times the child may show an excessive startle reaction to a mild stimulus.

5. *Insensitivity to pain.* At least some of the time, autistic children fail to react to cuts, burns, extreme hot or cold, and other pain.

Table 16-1.   Distinctions Between Schizophrenia and Autism

Characteristics	Schizophrenia	Autism
Usual age at first diagnosis	15–30 years	A few months to 3 years
Sex ratio	Equal numbers of males and females	Mostly males
Genetics	Clear genetic tendency	Uncertain; usually does not appear in same family with other autistics or schizophrenics
Response to neuroleptic drugs	Symptoms generally reduced	Little effect other than sedation

6. *Inappropriate emotional expressions.* Autistic children have sudden bouts of fear and crying for no obvious reason; at other times they display utter fearlessness and unprovoked laughter. Their emotions seem to spring from spontaneous internal sources rather than from any event.

7. *Disturbances of movement.* Certain autistic children may be hyperactive or inactive for prolonged periods.

8. *Poor use of speech.* Some autistic children never speak. A larger number learn the names of many common objects and develop good pronunciation but seldom use language to ask for anything or to enhance social relationships. Although they often repeat what they hear, they seldom initiate a conversation. Autistic children do not resemble deaf children or children with brain damage in the left hemisphere, however (Fein, Humes, Kaplan, Lucci, & Waterhouse, 1984). Although autistic children use language poorly, language impairment does not appear to be the root of their problems.

9. *Specific, limited intellectual abnormalities.* Many autistic children do well, even unusually well, on certain intellectual tasks but very poorly on others. The exact pattern of impairment varies from one case to another. It is difficult to estimate their overall intelligence because they often fail to follow the instructions for a standard IQ test.

Autism has often been compared to schizophrenia because social isolation is a prominent characteristic of both. The two conditions differ in many regards, however. (See Table 16-1.) It is rare that an autistic child becomes a schizophrenic adult, although a few cases have been reported (Petty, Ornitz, Michelman, & Zimmerman, 1984).

Autistic children have clear signs of neurological impairment even at the time of birth (Gillberg & Gillberg, 1983). Abnormal behaviors are usually noticed at an early age, perhaps even within the first 6 months, and always (by definition) by age 3 years. Parents remark that their autistic child was an unresponsive infant who showed no emotional attachment. The baby did not orient to adult faces or speech and did not "mold" to the parent's body when held.

Biological Abnormalities in Autistic Children

It is easy to demonstrate a wide variety of biological abnormalities in autistic children. The variety of problems is as much a curse as a blessing to biological investigators. Although it is easy to argue that autistic children are bio-logically abnormal, it is difficult to specify which of the many abnormalities might actually be responsible for the autistic behaviors and which are just secondary manifestations of some more primary disorder.

Autistic children give no indication of gross brain atrophy, damage, or malformation (Creasey et al., 1986). They do, however, have a high inci-dence of regional asymmetries of cerebral metabolic rate (Rumsey et al., 1985). That is, they may have a very high metabolic rate in one brain area and a very low rate in another. Many autistic children suffer from a variety of other miscellaneous abnormalities, including deficient response to vestibular sensation (Ornitz, Atwell, Kaplan, & Westlake, 1985), EEG ab-normalities, irregular waking-sleeping cycles, presence of potentially hallu-cinogenic chemicals in their blood, and many minor physical anomalies. One striking and puzzling characteristic, which no theory to date has even at-tempted to explain, is that most autistic children are unusually good looking. Also surprising is the report that many autistic children huddle around radia-tors or other heat sources in a room at normal temperature, as if they feel cold (Jeddi, 1970). Moreover, many parents have reported that whenever their autistic children have a fever, they behave almost normally, with better than usual communication with other people and attention to their sur-roundings (Sullivan, 1980).

Possible Causes of Autism

Autism, like most other psychological disorders, is probably the product of several causes. At this time, the most likely factors are biological.

Parental behavior.   The early accounts of autistic children described their parents as well-educated, upper-middle-class, intellectual people who offered little display of emotion (Kanner, 1943). Certain theorists suggested that the parents' lack of emotional warmth actually caused the children to become autistic. Virtually all authorities now dismiss this hypothesis for a number of reasons. One is that later studies have failed to confirm the sup-posed overrepresentation of autism in intellectual or upper-middle-class families (Koegel, Schreibman, O'Neill, & Burke, 1983; Tsai, Stewart, & August, 1981). Second, providing a great deal of extra warmth and love does not alleviate autism significantly. Third, the brothers and sisters of autistic children are normal in the great majority of cases. If the parents were bad enough to make one child reject social contact so completely and to act so strangely, one would expect the other children in the family to be a bit odd as well. The fact that they are not is a strong argument against the bad-parent theory.

Genetics.   Considering how early the condition develops, it is natural to look for indications of a genetic basis. Twin studies do support a heredi-tary contribution. It is not easy to find many autistic children who have twins, considering how rare autism is and how few people have twins. The most extensive study examined forty pairs of twins that included at least one autistic child. Of twenty-three monozygotic pairs, twenty-two were concordant for autism; of seventeen dizygotic pairs, four were concordant (Ritvo, Freeman, Mason-Brothers, Mo, & Ritvo, 1985). Family studies indicate, however, that autism is unlikely to depend on a single gene. In certain cases a given family has two or three autistic children (Ritvo, Spence, Freeman, Mason-Brothers, Mo, & Marazita, 1985). Overall, however, only about 2 percent of the brothers and sisters of autistic children are themselves autistic.

One possible way to reconcile the high concordance in identical twins to the much lower concordance in brothers and sisters is to assume that autism depends on a large number of genes, many of which must be present to produce the condition. Tsai, Stewart, and August (1981) further suggest that the greater frequency of autism in males than in females could mean that females need a greater "dose" of the abnormal genes than males to become autistic. Indeed, they found that female autistic chidren have more EEG abnormalities, more movement disturbances, worse bladder and bowel control, and more evidence of brain dysfunction than equally autistic males.

One interesting development in genetic research on autism is the discovery that a large number of autistic children have a **fragile X chromosome**. That is, they have a weak spot on an X chromosome where it is vulnerable to breaking under certain conditions. The fragile X syndrome has also been noted in many mentally retarded people and in the relatives of autistic and mentally retarded children (August & Lockhart, 1984; Gillberg, Wahlström, & Hagberg, 1984). An explanation in terms of a fragile X chromosome would help to make sense of the disproportionate number of boys with autism: Girls have a second X chromosome that can compete with the effects of a defective one.

Endorphins.   One characteristic of autistic children is that they sometimes fail to react to painful stimuli. One of the most reliable ways to decrease sensitivity to pain is an injection of morphine or other opiate drugs. Consider some other symptoms of morphine intoxication (Desmond & Wilson, 1975; Glass, Evans, & Rajegowda, 1975; Ream, Robinson, Richter, Hegge, & Holloway, 1975): (1) social withdrawal, (2) repetitive and sometimes stereotyped behaviors, (3) ignoring most sensory stimuli but hallucinating others, (4) sedation under most circumstances but sometimes a driven hyperactivity, and (5) happiness and fearlessness. During withdrawal from morphine, the symptoms include restlessness, fear and anxiety, crying, and a jumpy overresponsiveness to stimulation. In short, a person who alternately took morphine injections and then went through the withdrawal process would show many of the same behaviors as autism.

Children who are born to narcotic-addicted mothers suffer a great many effects on their brain development and behavior (Householder, Hatcher, Burns, & Chasnoff, 1982). A few of these effects resemble the behavior of autistic children: The children of addicts have delayed learning and language development, and they are less responsive to their caregivers in infancy.

Obviously, autistic children are not themselves morphine addicts, and few of their mothers were narcotics users. If opiate synapses relate to autism, they must do so via some less direct route.

The brain uses one category of synaptic transmitters, called endorphins (including enkephalins), that have effects similar to those of morphine. If for some unknown reason a child's brain sometimes produced excessive amounts of endorphins and at other times produced smaller amounts, the behavioral effect might resemble that of a person who occasionally took morphine and thus might also resemble the behavior of autistic children (Kalat, 1978; Panksepp, Herman, & Vilberg, 1978).

Panksepp and his colleagues attempted to test this hypothesis through animal models. They isolated puppies and infant guinea pigs from their mothers and found **separation distress**, characterized by whimpering, crying, and motor agitation. Small doses of morphine greatly reduced the separation distress of these infants. In a sense, the drugs produced social indifference. On the other hand, drugs that blocked the endorphin synapses increased separation distress (Herman & Panksepp, 1978; Panksepp, Herman, Vilberg, Bishop, & DeEskinazi, 1980). In other words, animal morphine intoxication is a good model of at least the social-isolation aspect of autism.

Do autistic children in fact have some anomaly in their endorphins? One study measured endorphin levels in the CSF of autistic children and normal children. Of twenty autistic children, eleven had higher endorphin levels than the highest of the eight normal children (Gillberg, Terenius, & Lönnerholm, 1985). Although these results are only a first step, they do suggest that endorphins may play a significant role in autism.

Therapies for Autism

Autistic children generally show little improvement over time, with or without any of the currently common treatments. Special education, generally making use of behavior modification, can help autistic children make progress toward self-management and other useful skills (Rincover, Cook, Peoples, & Packard, 1979). The progress is limited, however; few of these children ever enter the mainstream of normal life.

None of the drug therapies that have been tried so far have proved to be reliably helpful. Chlorpromazine, amphetamine, Ritalin, Valium, and several other drugs seem to do as much harm as good. Possibly encouraging results have been reported for large doses of a combination of vitamins and minerals, including vitamin B_6 and magnesium. Over a period of days to months, some of the autistic chidren treated with this **megavitamin therapy** approach use more words, sleep better, are less irritable, show more interest in learning, and sometimes display less self-mutilating behavior (Lelord, Muh, Barthelemy, Martineau, & Garreau, 1981; Rimland, Callaway, & Dreyfus, 1978). The improvement does not amount to a cure, however, even in those who respond best.

SUMMARY

1. The positive symptoms of schizophrenia are hallucinations, delusions, and thought disorder. The negative symptoms are the absence of emotional expression, social interactions, and speech. (p. 435)

2. According to the results of autopsies, PET scans, CAT scans, and rCBF studies, many schizophrenic patients have a moderate amount of atrophy of the cerebral cortex, especially the frontal lobes. (p. 437)

3. Studies of twins and adopted children indicate that schizophrenia has a genetic basis. (p. 438)

4. Monozygotic twins who are concordant for handedness are generally also concordant for schizophrenia. (p. 439)
5. Genetics cannot be the whole story, because a person with no schizophrenic relatives can become schizophrenic, and because it is hard to imagine how a gene with such detrimental effects could become so widespread. (p. 440)
6. More schizophrenic patients were born during the winter months than during other seasons. (p. 441)
7. Some investigators have speculated that a retrovirus could be responsible for schizophrenia, although the supporting evidence is not strong. (p. 442)
8. Large doses of amphetamine and certain other chemicals can induce a temporary state that resembles schizophrenia. (p. 443)
9. Neuroleptics, the drugs that relieve schizophrenia, block dopamine synapses and block the release of dopamine. (p. 445)
10. Because neuroleptics affect dopamine synapses much faster than they change behavior, it is clear that they must set in motion certain other changes in the brain that develop more slowly. (p. 446)
11. Neuroleptic drugs induce tardive dyskinesia as a side effect in certain patients. Because tardive dyskinesia is apparently irreversible after it begins, researchers and physicians try to find ways to prevent it. (p. 447)
12. Children at risk for schizophrenia have mild thought disorders, poor social interactions, a lack of pleasure, and other behavioral abnormalities. (p. 449)
13. Impairment of pursuit eye movements may prove to be a biological marker that indicates vulnerability to schizophrenia. (p. 450)
14. Infantile autism, a rare condition that begins in early childhood, is characterized by social isolation, stereotyped behaviors, insensitivity to pain, and other behaviors. It resembles schizophrenia in certain regards, although the underlying causes are almost certainly different. (p. 450)
15. Autistic children differ from normal children in many biological regards; it is not known which of these differences relates most directly to the causes of autism. (p. 452)
16. Monozygotic twins are almost always concordant for autism; however, most brothers and sisters of autistic children are normal. Autism may have a genetic basis, but if so, it cannot be a simple effect of a single gene. (p. 452)
17. Certain symptoms of autism suggest a possible disorder of endorphin synapses. (p. 453)

REVIEW QUESTIONS

1. What are the symptoms of schizophrenia? (p. 435)
2. What evidence of brain damage is found in many schizophrenic patients? (p. 436)
3. What is the evidence for a genetic basis of schizophrenia? (p. 438)
4. Is stress a likely cause of schizophrenia? (p. 441)
5. What is a retrovirus, and why have certain investigators speculated that a retrovirus may be responsible for schizophrenia? (p. 442)
6. How can one tell the difference between schizophrenia and amphetamine psychosis? (p. 443)
7. What synaptic effects do neuroleptic drugs have? (p. 445)
8. What are the weaknesses of the dopamine hypothesis of schizophrenia? (p. 446)
9. What modifications or alternatives to the dopamine hypothesis might overcome its weaknesses? (p. 446)
10. What causes tardive dyskinesia? (p. 447)
11. What makes it possible for certain drugs to alleviate schizophrenia without a high probability of causing tardive dyskinesia? (p. 447)
12. For what reasons might it be helpful to diagnose schizophrenia at an earlier age than is currently possible? (p. 448)
13. What behaviors are characteristic of children at risk for schizophrenia? (p. 449)
14. What is apparently a biological marker indicating vulnerability to schizophrenia? (p. 449)
15. What are the symptoms of infantile autism? (pp. 450–451)
16. List some biological abnormalities of autistic children. (p. 452)
17. What are the pros and cons of the evidence for a genetic basis for autism? (p. 453)
18. Why might one suspect a link between endorphins and autism? (p. 453)
19. What treatment is generally used for autistic children, and what are its effects? (p. 454)

THOUGHT QUESTIONS

1. Schizophrenics are reported to have fewer dreams than other people and to have some PGO spikes during wakefulness. (See Chapter 9 to review PGO spikes.) Speculate on what this might mean in relation to the causes of schizophrenia.
2. According to available evidence, the concordance rate for autism is higher for dizygotic twins than for brother and sister, even though the genetic similarity is no greater for one relationship than the other. What possible explanation might you offer?

_____ TERMS TO REMEMBER _____

schizophrenia (p. 434)
hallucinations (p. 435)
delusions (p. 435)
thought disorder (p. 435)
positive symptoms (p. 435)
negative symptoms (p. 435)
concordance (p. 439)
paternal half-sibling (p. 440)
season-of-birth effect (p. 441)
retrovirus (p. 442)
amphetamine psychosis (p. 443)
chlorpromazine (p. 444)
neuroleptic drugs (p. 445)

phenothiazines (p. 445)
butyrophenones (p. 445)
haloperidol (p. 445)
dopamine hypothesis of schizophrenia (p. 446)
mesolimbic system (p. 446)
tardive dyskinesia (p. 447)
orthomolecular psychiatry (p. 448)
saccadic eye movement (p. 450)
pursuit eye movement (p. 450)
infantile autism (p. 450)
fragile X chromosome (p. 453)
separation distress (p. 454)
megavitamin therapy (p. 454)

_____ SUGGESTIONS FOR FURTHER READING _____

Fann, W. E., Karacan, I., Pokorny, A., & Williams, R. L. (Eds.). (1978). *Phenomenology and treatment of schizophrenia*. New York: Spectrum. Includes chapters on the behavior as well as the biology of schizophrenia.

Namba, N., & Kaiya, H. (Eds.) (1982). *Psychobiology of schizophrenia*. Oxford: Pergamon. A collection of articles covering research on the biology of schizophrenia.

Rutter, M., & Schopler, E. (1978). *Autism*. New York: Plenum.

Appendix: Genetics and Evolution

MAIN IDEAS

1. The expression of a given gene depends on the environment and on interactions with other genes.

2. Genes are located on chromosomes, which are composed of the chemical DNA. DNA chains determine the structure of RNA chains, which in turn determine the structure of proteins.

3. It is difficult to measure the contribution of heredity to the variations in human behavior, although several methods are in common use.

4. Although it is often difficult to determine exactly how a species has evolved from its ancestors, the basic process of evolution through natural selection is a logical necessity.

This appendix is not intended to be comprehensive. It presents only those aspects of genetics and evolution that one needs to know in order to deal with biological psychology. Readers with a strong previous background should just skim over the parts familiar to them.

MENDELIAN GENETICS

Prior to the work of Gregor Mendel, a late-nineteenth-century monk, it was believed that inheritance was a blending process, in which the properties of the sperm and the egg simply mixed, much as one might mix red paint and yellow paint.

Mendel demonstrated that there are **genes**, or hereditary materials, that maintain their structural identity from one generation to another and do not blend with one another. Suppose, as in one of Mendel's experiments, we breed a pea plant with brown seeds and one with white seeds. (Most plants reproduce sexually just as animals do.) All the offspring of this cross have brown seeds. Now we breed two of these offspring with each other. In the next generation, about three-fourths have brown seeds and one-fourth have white seeds. Thus, although the second generation had only brown seeds, the genes for white seeds have not been lost.

To account for results like these, Mendel assumed that inheritance depends on structural particles (later called genes) that come in pairs. In the example of the pea plants, one parent has two genes for brown seeds, which we could represent as *AA*. The other parent has two genes for white seeds, which we could designate *aa*. (Each parent also has millions of other genes controlling a wide variety of characteristics.) During reproduction, each parent contributes one of each pair of genes. Therefore, the first parent contributes an *A* gene (for brown seeds) and the second parent contributes an *a* gene (for white seeds). The offspring therefore have an *Aa* gene combination. In this case the gene for brown seeds, *A*, is **dominant** over the gene for white seeds, *a*, which is **recessive**. If an individual has one of each gene, it shows the trait corresponding to the dominant gene.

Although all members of the second generation produce brown seeds, they carry both an *A* and an *a* gene. Therefore, during reproduction, each individual can contribute either gene to offspring. If both parents contribute an *a* gene, they can produce a white-seed offspring, even though both parents have brown seeds. (On the other hand, if both parents produce only white seeds, none of their offspring can produce brown seeds. Do you see why?)

An *Aa* individual contributes an *A* gene to 50 percent of its offspring and an *a* gene to the other 50 percent. Therefore, an *Aa* and *Aa* mating produces 25 percent *AA* offspring, 50 percent *Aa*, and 25 percent *aa*. (See Figure A-1.)

Many human traits depend on a single gene that follows these simple Mendelian ratios. Examples include eye color (brown dominant, blue recessive), ability to taste the chemical phenylthiocarbamide (ability to taste dom-

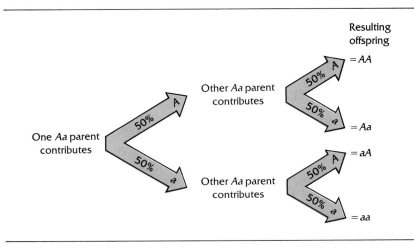

Figure A-1. Results of an *Aa* and *Aa* mating.

inant, inability recessive), and ability to curl one's tongue lengthwise (ability dominant, inability recessive).

An individual who has two genes identical for some trait (either *AA* or *aa*) is said to be **homozygous** for that gene. One who has different genes (*Aa*) is **heterozygous**.

In many cases, neither gene is dominant over the other; the heterozygous individual is then intermediate between the two homozygous conditions. In the preceding example, if neither gene were dominant, the *Aa* individuals might produce light brown seeds. A cross between two *Aa* individuals would then yield about 25 percent brown-seed individuals (*AA*), 50 percent light brown (*Aa*), and 25 percent white (*aa*).

Many characteristics depend on more than one gene pair. Suppose, for example, that the length of some kind of worm depends on two gene pairs. Genes *B* and *C* are dominant genes for long body; genes *b* and *c* are recessive for short body. If we cross a long worm with *BBCC* **genotype** (gene pattern) and a short worm with *bbcc* genotype, the first worm contributes a *B* and a *C*; the second contributes a *b* and a *c*. Therefore, the offspring will have a *BbCc* genotype and will have long bodies.

Now, let us cross a *BbCc* with another *BbCc*. Assume that the *B* and *C* genes arrange themselves independently of each other. That is, if a parent contributes a *B* gene, it could also contribute either a *C* or a *c*; it has an equal chance of contributing any of the combinations *BC*, *Bc*, *bC*, and *bc*. The same goes for the other parent. Thus, the possibilities for offspring are as shown in Figure A-2.

In nine of the sixteen possibilities, the offspring has at least one *B* gene and at least one *C* gene. Since *B* and *C* are dominant genes, all these offspring are long. Only one of the possible offspring types has both a *bb* and a *cc* combination; only the individuals of this type are short. The other six possibilities have at least one dominant gene at either the *B* or the *C* locus, and two recessive genes at the other (e.g., *Bbcc* or *bbCC*); these worms are intermediate in length between the two original types.

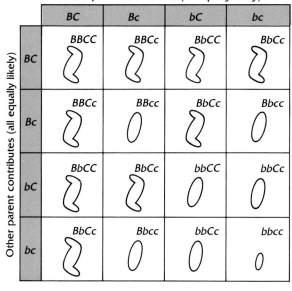

One parent contributes (all equally likely)

	BC	Bc	bC	bc
BC	BBCC	BBCc	BbCC	BbCc
Bc	BBCc	BBcc	BbCc	Bbcc
bC	BbCC	BbCc	bbCC	bbCc
bc	BbCc	Bbcc	bbCc	bbcc

Other parent contributes (all equally likely)

Figure A-2. Results of a *BbCc* (long) and *BbCc* (long) cross.

Things can get more complicated. Perhaps *B* makes more of a difference than *C*, so that a *Bbcc* worm is longer than a *bbCc*. Or perhaps more than two gene pairs contribute to body length (or any other characteristic). Furthermore, the effects of a gene may depend on the environment or on what other genes the individual has.

Chromosome Linkage

Up to this point we have dealt with genes that are inherited independently of one another. Genes can be physically linked so that someone who inherits one gene is likely to inherit a second one, too.

Genes are located on strands called **chromosomes**. Each chromosome participates in reproduction independently of the others, and each species has a certain number of chromosomes (twenty-three pairs in humans, four pairs in fruit flies). Thus, if an individual has a *BbCc* genotype, and if the *B* and *C* genes are on different chromosomes, its contribution of a *B* or *b* gene has nothing to do with whether it contributes a *C* or a *c*. But suppose they are on the same chromosome. If one chromosome has the *BC* combination and the other has *bc*, then an individual who contributes a *B* gene will probably also contribute a *C*.

The exception to this statement comes about as a result of a process known as **crossing over**. During reproduction, a pair of chromosomes may break apart and reconnect such that part of one chromosome attaches to the other part of the second chromosome. If one chromosome has the *BC* combination and the other chromosome has the *bc* combination, crossing over between the *B* locus and the *C* locus leaves new chromosomes with the combinations *Bc* and *bC*. The closer the *B* locus is to the *C* locus, the less often crossing over will occur between them.

The phenomenon of crossing over can be used to determine the location of a particular gene on the chromosomes. For example, human chromosome number 4 has a marker known as "G8," which is visible on the chromosome although no one knows what contribution it makes to heredity. The G8 marker has four identifiable forms. The gene for Huntington's disease (see Chapter 8) is believed to lie close to the G8 marker. When a parent and child both have Huntington's disease, about 98 percent of the time they have the same form of the G8 marker (Gusella et al., 1984). That is, the gene for Huntington's disease and the G8 marker lie so close together on the chromosome that crossing over occurs between them on only 2 percent of all matings.

Sex-Linked and Sex-Limited Genes

Each individual has a certain number of chromosomes. All but one pair are known as autosomal chromosomes; all genes located on these chromosomes are referred to as **autosomal genes**. The other two chromosomes are the sex chromosomes; genes located on them are known as **sex-linked genes**.

In mammals, the two sex chromosomes are designated **X** and **Y**. (Unlike the symbols *A, B,* and *C* introduced for the purpose of illustrating gene pairs, X and Y are standard symbols for sex chromosomes used by all geneticists.) A female mammal has two X chromosomes; a male has an X and a Y. During reproduction, the female necessarily contributes an X chromosome, and the male contributes either an X or a Y. If he contributes an X, the offspring will be female; if he contributes a Y, the offspring will be male. (Birds are different. Male birds have two sex chromosomes alike, designated ZZ; the female has two different sex chromosomes, designated ZW.)

The Y chromosome is small and carries few if any genes other than the gene that causes the individual to develop as a male instead of a female. The X chromosome, however, carries a large number of genes. Thus, when biologists speak of sex-linked genes, they ordinarily mean X-linked genes.

Characteristics controlled by sex-linked genes occur more often in one sex than in the other. If a gene is a sex-linked dominant, the characteristic it controls occurs more often in females than in males, because females, with two X chromosomes, have twice the chance males have of getting the sex-linked gene. (Manic-depressive illness, described in Chapter 15, occurs more often in women than in men. Some evidence suggests that it is determined in part by a sex-linked dominant gene.)

A characteristic that is controlled by a sex-linked recessive gene, on the other hand, produces its effects only if the dominant gene is not present. Thus, for a female to show the effects of a sex-linked recessive, she would have to have two such genes. A male, however, has only one X chromosome; thus, if he has an X-linked recessive gene, he cannot have a dominant gene to overrule it. Color blindness is an example of a condition controlled by a sex-linked recessive gene in humans. Most color-blind people are male. For a female to be color-blind, she would have to have a color-blind father and a mother with at least one gene for color blindness. Other examples of sex-linked recessive genes are those for hemophilia ("bleeder's disease") and albinism.

Distinct from sex-linked genes are the **sex-limited genes**. A sex-limited gene has an effect in one sex only, or at least it has a much stronger effect in one sex than the other. For instance, genes control the amount of chest hair in men, breast size in women, the amount of crowing in roosters, and the rate of egg production in hens. Such genes need not be on the sex chromosomes; both sexes have the genes, but the genes exert their effects only under the influence of sex hormones.

Sources of Variation

If the reproduction process always produced offspring that were exact copies of the parents, evolution would not be possible. One source of variation is **recombination**. The effects of a gene depend on what other genes are present. An offspring, in receiving some genes from one parent and some from the other, may have a new combination of genes that together yield characteristics not found in either parent.

Another source of variation is a **mutation**, or change in a single gene. For instance, during the reproductive process, a gene for brown eyes might spontaneously mutate into a gene for blue eyes. Mutation of a given gene is a rare event, but because each of us has millions of genes, mutations provide a constant source of variation.

A mutation is a random event; that is, it is not guided by the needs of the organism. A mutation is analogous to having an untrained person add, remove, or distort something on the blueprints for your new house. The likely result is to make the house less desirable than it would have been, perhaps even to make it collapse; only on rare occasions would the random change improve the house.

A third source of variation—almost always disadvantageous—is for one parent to contribute something other than exactly one copy of each chromosome. Occasionally one parent contributes two or zero copies of a given chromosome. For example, if one human parent contributes two copies of chromosome 21, the child has a total of three copies, counting the one obtained from the other parent. The consequence is **Down's syndrome**, a genetic disorder characterized by mental retardation. An extra or absent sex chromosome can cause the XXY pattern, the XXX pattern, or the XO pattern, all of which cause sterility and various abnormalities of appearance.

Penetrance

When we refer to, say, "a gene for brown eyes," we mean that the gene makes a difference between having brown eyes and some other color of eyes *under the usual environmental conditions*. Some genes have observable effects only if the individual experiences a certain climate, a particular pattern of light and darkness, a specific diet, a given social setting, or some other environmental condition. A gene may also have effects that emerge only in individuals who have certain other genes. A gene that affects some individuals but not others is said to have partial **penetrance**. That is, its effects "penetrate" into observable characteristics only under certain conditions.

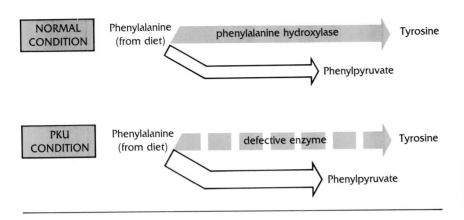

Figure A-3. Conversion of phenylalanine in normal individuals and those with phenylketonuria (PKU).

Because of the phenomenon of partial penetrance, it is sometimes possible to reduce the undesirable effects of a gene by changing the environment. One clear example is a condition known as **phenylketonuria** (FEE-nil-kee-tone-YOO-ree-uh), or **PKU**. PKU is caused by a gene that prevents the body from metabolizing **phenylalanine**, an amino acid found in a variety of foods. Normally, some phenylalanine is incorporated into proteins and most of the rest is converted in the liver to another important amino acid, tyrosine (Figure A-3). A small amount of phenylalanine is converted to other products, including **phenylpyruvate**. Children with PKU lack the enzyme that converts phenylalanine to tyrosine (Kaufman, 1975). As a result, such children accumulate excessive levels of both phenylalanine and phenylpyruvate, which lead to structural malformations of the brain and thus to mental retardation.

Physicians can determine whether a newborn baby has PKU by measuring the levels of phenylalanine or phenylpyruvate in the blood or urine. This test is routinely performed on all babies born in the United States, unless the parents object. If the level is excessively high, indicating PKU, the condition can be controlled by diet. The child is put on a strict, rather difficult diet containing very low levels of phenylalanine. If the parents enforce this diet conscientiously, the child's brain can develop nearly normally and he or she will escape mental retardation. The diet is particularly important while the brain is still developing, over the first 10 years or so. After a child reaches maturity, it is no longer necessary to stick closely to the diet. (The exception to this rule is that a pregnant woman with PKU should return to the diet during pregnancy and nursing. Even if her baby is normal, the baby's enzymes cannot handle the enormous levels of phenylalanine that accumulate in the mother's bloodstream on a normal diet.)

In short, the gene for PKU causes mental retardation if the child has a normal diet, but an altered diet can minimize the effects of the gene.

THE BIOCHEMISTRY OF GENETICS

A chromosome is actually a double chain of the chemical deoxyribonucleic acid, or **DNA**. Each chain of DNA is composed of four bases in varying orders—guanine, cytosine, adenine, and thymine—attached to a skeleton

Figure A-4. A strand of RNA forms by pairing the complementary base to each base in the DNA.

RNA strand G–C–U–A–C–A–G–U–U

DNA strand C–G–A–T–G–T–C–A–A

made of phosphate and a sugar, deoxyribose. All the genetic information is determined by the order of these four bases along the chromosome. A gene is a small portion of the DNA molecule consisting of a sequence of bases.

A chain of DNA serves as a **template**, or model, for the synthesis of **RNA** (ribonucleic acid) molecules. RNA is a single chain composed of a sequence of bases—guanine, cytosine, adenine, and uracil—attached to a skeleton made of phosphate and the sugar ribose. The RNA bases are arranged in a manner complementary to those of DNA: Where a DNA chain has guanine, the RNA chain has cytosine; similarly, DNA's cytosine, adenine, and thymine pair up with RNA's guanine, uracil, and adenine, respectively, as shown in Figure A-4.

After being synthesized from the DNA template, RNA molecules disperse to various places in the cell. Different kinds of RNA serve different functions. One kind, tRNA (transfer RNA), transports amino acids to the ribosomes of the cell. Another kind, mRNA (messenger RNA), serves as a template for the formation of proteins. An mRNA chain determines the structure of a protein by a code: Each sequence of three RNA bases codes for one amino acid. For instance, the RNA sequence guanine-cytosine-guanine codes for the amino acid arginine. The order of RNA bases determines the order of the protein's amino acids, as shown in Figure A-5.

The proteins then determine the development and properties of the organism. Some proteins form part of the structure of the body; others serve as **enzymes**, or biological catalysts that regulate chemical reactions in the body.

The classical sequence of DNA producing RNA is reversed by **retroviruses**. Viruses are composed of RNA. Like any other kind of RNA, they serve as templates for the formation of proteins. One of the proteins produced by a retrovirus, however, causes the formation of a new segment of DNA complementary to the RNA. If that segment of DNA becomes incorporated into one of the chromosomes, it will continue producing more of the retrovirus, in the standard DNA-to-RNA direction. The retrovirus DNA may even be inherited by the next generation. A retrovirus is therefore extremely difficult to attack medically.

Before the mid-1980s, retroviruses were considered an obscure and esoteric subject of little interest to psychologists. Evidence then arose that the AIDS virus is a retrovirus and that retroviruses may also be linked to schizophrenia and possibly other disorders (see Chapter 16).

MEASURING THE CONTRIBUTIONS OF HEREDITY AND ENVIRONMENT IN HUMANS

It is often theoretically important to distinguish between the contributions of heredity and environment in the development of behavior. Sometimes

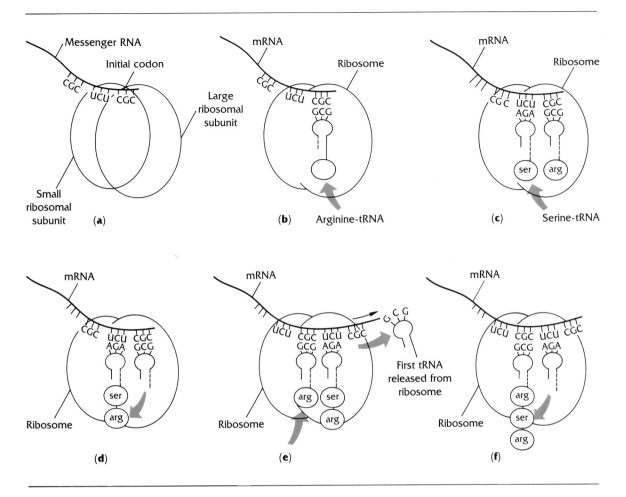

Figure A-5. Proteins, made of amino acids, are built according to plans carried on molecules of mRNA. Each triplet of RNA bases is a code for one amino acid. Transfer RNA brings the amino acids; messenger RNA joins them in a specific order.

people phrase the question in the form, "Which is more important for such-and-so behavior, heredity or environment?" The question is meaningless in that form, although we can rephrase it in a meaningful way. To see what is wrong with the phrasing of the question, consider two analogies:

1.   Why does your computer do the things it does? Is it because of the computer's hardware or its software? (You see at once that the question is meaningless. Everything the computer does depends on both its hardware and its software.)

2.   Which is more important for the area of a rectangle, its height or its width? (Again, the question is meaningless; neither height nor width contributes anything independently of the other.)

Now let us rephrase these questions:

■ Why does your computer do some tricks differently from my computer? Is it because the two computers have different hardware, or because you are running different software?

Figure A-6. It is pointless to ask whether the area of a rectangle depends more on height or width, but it is possible to ask (and to determine) whether the differences in area for a given group of rectangles depend more on differences in height or in width. The same is true for the roles of heredity and environment in determining behavior.

■ The rectangles in Figure A-6 differ in area. Is that *difference* in area due mostly to differences in height or to differences in width?

Similarly, the proper way to phrase the heredity-environment question is: This group differs from that group in such-and-so behavior; do they differ because of differences in their heredity or because of differences in their environment? This question may be difficult to answer in practice, but at least it makes sense in principle. Note that the answer will depend not only on which behavior we examine but also which groups we compare. For the rectangles in Figure A-6, the differences in area depend mostly on differences in width; for some other set of rectangles, the answer might be different. Similarly, the differences in behavior between red lizards and green lizards might be mostly due to genetic differences, while the differences between green lizards and blue lizards might be due mostly to environmental differences. We have to examine each case separately.

The standard measurement of the contributions of heredity and environment is **heritability**. Heritability is a mathematical construct designed to measure how closely the variations in some characteristic correlate with differences in heredity as opposed to differences in environment. Heritability can vary from zero to 1.0. A heritability of zero means that none of the observed variations are due to differences in heredity; a heritability of 1.0 means that all the observed differences are due to differences in heredity.

Types of Evidence Regarding Human Heritability

It is difficult to get adequate data about heritability in humans. Investigators have no control over who mates with whom or what environment their children grow up in. The time between one generation and another is long, and we are often uncertain which aspects of the environment are critical.

In many cases the goal of research is merely to determine whether heredity contributes at all to the differences in behavior. The following are types of evidence that can be used in studies of the heritability of human behavior, beginning with the *least* convincing and working up from there.

Does the Similarity in Behavior Between Individuals Correspond to Their Degree of Genetic Relationship?   If we designate the genetic relationship between a person and himself or herself as 1.0, then other relationships are as follows:

Relationship	Degree of Relationship
Identical twin	1.0
Fraternal twin	0.5
Brother or sister	0.5
Father, mother, son, daughter	0.5
Grandparent, grandchild	0.25
Uncle, aunt, nephew, niece	0.25
Half-brother, half-sister	0.25
First cousin	0.125
Second cousin	0.0625
Unrelated person	0.0

(These figures assume that people mate randomly rather than choosing genetically similar individuals as mates. Because that assumption is false for humans, the correct numerical coefficients should be somewhat higher.)

If some variation in behavior depends partly on genetics, then the closer the genetic relationship between people, the greater should be the similarity in their behavior. For example, identical twins should resemble each other more than siblings, who should resemble each other more than cousins, and so on.

When this is *not* true—if identical twins resemble each other no more than two unrelated people, for example—we may confidently reject genetics as a significant reason for the variation in behavior. On the other hand, this type of information is never strong evidence *in favor* of a genetic explanation. Identical twins share more of their environment in common than brother and sister, who in turn share more than cousins. Thus, strong similarity between closely related people does not distinguish between genetic and environmental explanations.

Is the Similarity Greater Between Identical Twins Than Between Fraternal Twins?   Fraternal, or nonidentical, twins are also known as **dizygotic** ("two-egg") twins. Although they are born at the same time, they are no more closely related genetically than brother and sister. Identical twins, also known as **monozygotic** ("one-egg") twins, begin as a single fertilized egg; they have identical genetics.

A pair of twins of either kind grow up sharing a common environment. Identical twins, however, share more genetics in common. Therefore, if some behavior shows greater similarity between identical twins than between fraternal twins, we can suspect that this added similarity reflects a genetic influence.

This kind of evidence does not support a firm conclusion, however. Identical twins are more likely to be treated alike than fraternal twins by their families and by other people. Thus, identical twins have greater environmental similarity than fraternal twins as well as greater genetic similarity.

Do Twins Reared in Separate Environments Resemble Each Other?
Occasionally twins are adopted by different families. If we examine a large

number of twin pairs who were reared in separate adoptive homes and find that some behavior shows marked similarity within most pairs, one likely interpretation is that the genetic simlarity is responsible for the behavioral similarity. Two other interpretations are possible: One is that pairs of twins have been adopted by similar families, providing similar environments. (This is in fact a reasonable possibility. Adoption agencies do not place children at random.) The other is that something in the **prenatal** (before-birth) environment had a strong influence on development.

Does the Behavior of an Adopted Child More Closely Resemble That of the Genetic Relatives or of the Adopted Relatives? If a child is adopted at an early age, the people who provide the child's environment are different from those who provided the genes. In some cases it can be demonstrated that a child's probability of developing some behavior corresponds more closely to the incidence of that behavior among the genetic relatives than to its incidence among the adopted relatives. The most likely interpretation then would be a genetic influence on the behavior or an influence by the prenatal environment.

Although evidence of this type can be fairly strong, it is not without its complications (Kamin, 1974). For example, most adoption agencies try to place a child in an adoptive family that resembles the child's biological family. In some cases a child may come to resemble his or her biological family because of environmental influences provided by the adoptive family.

Do Adopted Paternal Half-Siblings Resemble Each Other? A sibling is a brother or sister. Half-siblings have one parent in common but not the other. **Paternal half-siblings** have the same father but different mothers.

Occasionally two paternal half-siblings are adopted at early ages by different families—generally because the same man has fathered illegitimate children by more than one mother. Such children have been reared in different environments and did not even share a common prenatal environment, because they had different mothers. Therefore, any strong resemblance between adopted paternal half-siblings is almost certainly due to genetics.

Evidence of this type is potentially about as convincing as any evidence we can get about human heritability. The only problem is that such evidence is scarce. Adopted paternal half-siblings are not easy to locate.

EVOLUTION

Evolution is a change in the gene frequencies for a population. It is important to distinguish two questions concerning evolution: How *did* species evolve, and how *do* species evolve? To ask how species did evolve is to ask what evolved from what. To answer this question, biologists have to reconstruct a history based on fossils and other kinds of evidence. Their inferences are always subject to revision if new evidence becomes available.

How species *do* evolve is a question of how the process works, and to a large extent we could establish the process of evolution as a logical necessity, even if we had no fossil evidence at all, using the following argument:

The study of genetics has established that offspring generally resemble their parents. We also know, however, that mutations and recombinations lead to a steady supply of new variations within the population and that these new variations are themselves passed on to later generations. If individuals with some genetic variation have an advantage, in the sense that they reproduce more often and more successfully, then their genes will become more common in the population; that is, evolution will occur.

This general principle has long been familiar to animal and plant breeders as **artificial selection**. By selectively breeding only the most productive egg-laying chickens, or the dogs that are the best at herding sheep, breeders can develop a new strain of chickens or dogs with a high degree of the desired characteristic. Darwin's (1859) theory of evolution merely extended this idea, saying that nature acts like a selective breeder. If individuals with a particular new gene combination are more successful than others in finding food, or escaping enemies, or attracting mates, or protecting their offspring, the result will be a gradual increase in the frequency of that gene combination, just as surely as if some breeder had been selecting for that gene.

SUMMARY

1. In a normal environment, every individual with a dominant gene will show its effects. The effects of a recessive gene are fully expressed only if no dominant gene is present. (p. 458)
2. If two genes are on the same chromosome, someone who inherits one of those genes is likely to inherit the other as well. (p. 460)
3. Because sex-linked genes are on the X chromosome, sex-linked recessive genes show their effects more in males than in females, whereas sex-linked dominant genes show their effects more frequently in females. Although a sex-limited gene may be on any chromosome, its effects occur only in one sex. (p. 461)

4. A gene is said to have partial penetrance if its effects depend on variations in the environment. (p. 462)
5. Chromosomes are composed of the molecule DNA, which makes RNA copies of itself that, in turn, determine the formation of proteins. (pp. 463–464)
6. It is difficult to estimate the heritability of most significant human behaviors because the available evidence is subject to alternative explanations. (p. 466)
7. Although it is difficult to be certain about which species evolved from which and how, the fundamental process of evolution is a logical necessity. (p. 468)

REVIEW QUESTIONS

1. Distinguish between dominant and recessive, homozygous and heterozygous. (pp. 458–459)
2. How can a researcher determine the approximate location of a given gene on human chromosomes? (p. 461)
3. Why do sex-linked dominant genes show their effects more in women than in men? (p. 461)
4. Why do sex-linked recessive genes show their effects mostly in men? (p. 461)
5. What is a sex-limited gene? (p. 462)
6. What is a mutation? (p. 462)
7. Describe an example of a gene whose effects can

be modified or eliminated by a change in the environment. (p. 463)
8. What are chromosomes composed of? (pp. 463–464)
9. What is the route by which DNA controls the production of proteins? (p. 464)
10. How does a retrovirus reproduce? (p. 464)
11. What is the best way to phrase the heredity-environment question? (p. 466)
12. Describe the strengths and weaknesses of the various lines of evidence used to determine the role of heredity in the development of human behavior. (pp. 466–468)

_____ THOUGHT QUESTION _____

1. How is it possible to study the evolution of behavior? Behavior leaves no fossils, with the exception of occasional footprints. (Hint: How might one study the evolution of the heart, kidney, or other internal organs, which also leave few fossils?)

_____ TERMS TO REMEMBER _____

genes (p. 458)
dominant gene (p. 458)
recessive gene (p. 458)
homozygous (p. 459)
heterozygous (p. 459)
genotype (p. 459)
chromosomes (p. 460)
crossing over (p. 460)
autosomal gene (p. 461)
sex-linked gene (p. 461)
X chromosome (p. 461)
Y chromosome (p. 461)
sex-limited genes (p. 462)
recombination (p. 462)
mutation (p. 462)
Down's syndrome (p. 462)

penetrance (p. 462)
phenylketonuria (PKU) (p. 463)
phelylalanine (p. 463)
phenylpyruvate (p. 463)
DNA (p. 463)
template (p. 464)
RNA (p. 464)
enzymes (p. 464)
retroviruses (p. 464)
heritability (p. 466)
dizygotic (p. 467)
monozygotic (p. 467)
prenatal (p. 468)
paternal half-siblings (p. 468)
evolution (p. 468)
artificial selection (p. 469)

Glossary

Note: This glossary includes many terms that are not used in the text, including a number of drugs. It is intended for reference not only while you are reading the text but also while you are reading journal articles or technical books. For additional terms not listed here, try a medical dictionary. See also the index.

a-   prefix meaning lack of, absence of

abasia   inability to walk

ablation   removal of a structure

absolute refractory period   the period of time after an action potential when a point along the axon membrane is incapable of generating another action potential

acetaldehyde   a poisonous substance that occurs as a breakdown product of the metabolism of ethyl alcohol

acetaldehyde dehydrogenase   an enzyme that converts acetaldehyde to acetic acid

acetic acid   a chemical that (in low concentrations) is a source of energy for the body

acetylcholine (ACh)   a synaptic transmitter

acetylcholinesterase (AChE)   an enzyme that breaks acetylcholine into acetate and choline

ACh   acetylcholine

AChE   acetylcholinesterase

across-fiber pattern theory   theory that a sensation such as taste or smell is coded as a pattern of activity across many fibers rather than as a level of activity in any one fiber

ACTH   adrenocorticotropic hormone, a hormone released by the anterior pituitary

action potential   an all-or-none depolarization of a neuron, produced by stimulation beyond the threshold

activating effect   a temporary effect of a hormone on behavior or anatomy, occurring only while the hormone is present

activation-synthesis hypothesis   the hypothesis that the brain synthesizes dreams from spontaneous brain activity occurring during sleep

active sleep   *See* REM sleep

activity cycles   *See* circadian rhythm

acute   of sudden onset and brief duration

ADD   attention deficit disorder

adenohypophysis   the anterior pituitary

adenosine   a naturally occurring substance within the brain that stimulates the formation of cyclic AMP within certain neurons

adipsia   lack of drinking

adrenalin   *See* epinephrine

AF64A   drug that destroys synapses that use acetylcholine as their synaptic transmitter

affect   (as a noun) emotion

affective attack   an attack showing apparent emotion, directed at a target (opposite of a sham attack)

affective psychosis   major depression or manic-depressive illness

afferent neuron   a neuron that carries information toward a structure

agenesis   failure to develop

ageusia   a deficient sense of taste

agnosia   loss of knowledge, loss of ability to recognize something

agonist   something that stimulates a receptor; opposite of antagonist

agraphesthesia   the inability to recognize figures written on the skin

akinetic   not moving

aldosterone   an adrenal hormone that reduces the excretion of salts by the kidney

alexia   the inability to read

all-or-none law   law stating that the amplitude of an action potential is independent of the strength of the stimulus that excited it

alpha-feto-protein   a protein, found in the fetus of certain mammalian species, that binds estrogens

alpha-methyl-para-tyrosine (AMPT)   a drug that inhibits the conversion of tyrosine to L-DOPA and thereby decreases the production of both norepinephrine and dopamine

alpha waves   rhythm of 8 to 12 brain waves per second, generally associated with relaxation

altruism   acting to help another individual, without expecting direct benefit to oneself

Alzheimer's disease or dementia   a disease of old age, marked by gradual damage to the brain and gradual loss of memory and other psychological abilities

amacrine cell   one type of neuron found in the vertebrate eye

amblyopia ex anopsia   poor vision that results from prolonged disuse of an eye

amiloride   a drug that blocks the passage of sodium ions through a membrane

amnesia   loss of memory

amphetamine   a drug that stimulates the release of norepinephrine and dopamine from the presynaptic cell

amphetamine psychosis   a condition similar to schizophrenia, induced by a large dose of amphetamine

AMPT   alpha-methyl-para-tyrosine

amygdala   a brain area located within the temporal lobe of the cerebral cortex

amyotrophic lateral sclerosis   a disease that leads to paralysis, due to loss of motor neurons in the spinal cord and loss of input to spinal cord from brain; also called Lou Gehrig's disease

amytal   a drug that can be used either to tranquilize or to anesthetize the brain, depending on dose; because of its ability to relax inhibitions, amytal has been used as the controversial "truth serum"

analgesia   relief from pain

androgen insensitivity   a condition in which someone has a normal androgen level but does not respond to it

androgens   a group of hormones, including testosterone, found in greater amounts in males than in females

anesthetic   blocking all sensations from an area of the body

angiotensin   a hormone that constricts blood vessels

aniracetam   an experimental drug believed to enhance memory

anisomycin   a drug that inhibits protein synthesis

anomia   the inability to recall the names of objects

anorexia   loss of appetite

anorexia nervosa   a condition in which a person refuses to eat adequately

anosmia   lack of smell sensation

anosognosia   the inability to recognize that one has a certain disease or defect

anoxia   lack of oxygen

Antabuse   a drug that causes illness if one also consumes alcohol; used to help people quit an alcohol habit (generic name: disulfiram)

antagonist   something that counteracts the activity of something else

antagonist (drug)   a drug that blocks the effect of a synaptic transmitter or of another drug

antagonistic muscles   muscles that move a limb in opposite ways (e.g., extensor and flexor)

anterior   toward the front end

anterior commissure   a set of axons connecting the two cerebral hemispheres; smaller than the corpus callosum

anterior pituitary   an endocrine gland located at the base of the brain that releases growth hormone, prolactin, follicle-stimulating hormone, luteinizing hormone, adrenocorticotropic hormone, and thyroid-stimulating hormone

anterograde amnesia   loss of memory from some point in time onward, such as from the onset of a disease (contrast retrograde amnesia)

antidromic transmission   propagation of an action potential toward the axon hillock from a more peripheral point on the axon; opposite of orthodromic

anxiolytic   reducing anxiety

apex   one end of the cochlea, farthest from the point where the stirrup meets the cochlea

aphagia   lack of eating

aphasia   lack of language abilities

apomorphine   a drug that stimulates dopamine receptors

apraxia   lack of the ability to organize movements purposefully

arachnoid   one of the membranes that cover the brain and spinal cord

ARAS   ascending reticular activating system

archistriatum   the amygdala

arcuate fasciculus   a band of fibers that communicate between Broca's area and Wernicke's area

area 17   *See* striate cortex

area 18   *See* parastriate cortex

arecoline   a drug that inhibits the action of the enzyme acetylcholinesterase and thereby prolongs the effects of acetylcholine at its synapses

artificial selection   a change in the gene pool of a population by a breeder's selection of desired individuals for mating purposes

ascending reticular activating system   a diffuse system of neurons heavily interconnected with one another, extending from the medulla into the forebrain

aspartate   an amino acid, believed to be a synaptic transmitter

astasia the inability to stand

astereognosis the inability to recognize objects by touch

astigmatism blurring of vision for either horizontal or vertical lines but not both, because of an asymmetry of the eyeball

astroglia a large star-shaped glial cell, believed to remove waste products from the brain

ataxia failure of muscular coordination

attention deficit disorder a childhood condition characterized by restlessness and distractibility

atrophy deterioration

atropine a drug that blocks the acetylcholine receptors that muscarine excites

aura a distinctive sensation that occurs just before an epileptic attack

autism a behavior abnormality with early childhood onset, characterized by deficit of social contact

autoceptor autoreceptor

automatism a nonreflexive yet unconscious movement

autonomic nervous system a set of neurons that regulate functioning of the internal organs

autoreceptor a presynaptic receptor that responds to the transmitter released by the presynaptic cell itself

autosomal gene a gene on any of the chromosomes other than the sex chromosomes (X and Y)

axon a long fiber carrying impulses from the cell body of a neuron toward other cells

axon hillock the swelling of the soma from which an axon originates

8-azaguanine a drug that inhibits protein synthesis

Babinski reflex a reflexive flexion of the big toe when the sole of the foot is stimulated

baclofen a drug that stimulates $GABA_B$ synapses

ballistic movement movement that proceeds as a single organized unit that cannot be redirected once it begins

barbiturates a class of drugs used as anticonvulsants, sedatives, and tranquilizers

baroreceptor a receptor that detects blood pressure

basal ganglia a set of subcortical forebrain structures including the caudate nucleus, putamen, and globus pallidus

basal metabolism the rate of metabolic activity when the body is at rest

base (of tympanic membrane) one end of the cochlea, adjacent to the stirrup

basilar membrane the floor of the scala media, within the inner ear

belladonna a preparation containing atropine, used to block the parasympathetic nervous system and other acetylcholine synapses

Bell-Magendie Law the observation that the dorsal roots of the spinal cord carry sensory information and that the ventral roots carry motor information toward the muscles and glands

benzodiazepines a class of drugs used as tranquilizers

beta blocker a drug that impedes transmission at certain "beta" norepinephrine synapses

beta carboline a family of naturally occurring chemicals that increase or decrease the responsiveness of GABA synapses

beta endorphin *See* endorphins

beta rhythm fast, low-amplitude EEG activity

bicuculline a drug that blocks $GABA_A$ synapses

bifurcate to split into two parts

binocular using two eyes

biofeedback the attempt to control internal processes by providing sensory feedback or reward for the desired changes

biogenic amines chemicals containing an amine ($-NH_2$) group that are active in the brain, including catecholamines and indoleamines

biological clock an internal mechanism for controlling behaviors that reoccur on a regular time schedule, such as sleep or migration

biopsy removal and microscopic examination of body tissues for purpose of diagnosis

bipolar cell a neuron with two nearly equal processes extending from the cell body

bipolar disorder a psychological disorder characterized by alternation between depression and mania

blindsight the ability to localize visual stimuli in an area of the retina in which one reports blindness

blind spot an area on the retina lacking in rods and cones

blood-brain barrier a mechanism that prevents some chemicals from passing between the bloodstream and the brain

Borna disease a viral disease that causes behavioral changes in several animal species

botulin toxin a chemical that blocks the release of acetylcholine

bradykinesia movements slower than normal

brainstem the hindbrain, midbrain, and posterior central structures of the forebrain

bregma a point on the skull where the frontal and parietal bones join

bretylium tosylate a drug that facilitates the passage of sodium ions through a membrane

Broca's area an area in the left frontal lobe critical for the production of speech

bufotenine a hallucinogenic chemical

bulbar pertaining to the medulla of the brain

bulimia occasional episodes of overeating

butyrophenones a family of drugs that block dopamine receptors, often used in the treatment of schizophrenia

caffeine a stimulant that acts by antagonizing the ability of adenosine to increase the formation of cyclic AMP

callosal pertaining to the corpus callosum

calpain a protein that breaks a network of molecules normally found in the dendrites

cAMP cyclic AMP

Cannon-Bard theory the theory that autonomic changes occur simultaneously with emotions but that neither one causes the other

cannula a thin tube used for delivering chemicals

capsaicin the chemical responsible for the hot taste of jalapeños and other hot peppers; it can also stimulate neurons and (in high concentrations) kill them

carbachol a drug that excites acetylcholine receptors

carbidopa a drug that prevents the conversion of L-DOPA into dopamine outside the central nervous system

carbolines a family of chemicals found in the brain that bind to the same receptors as benzodiazepines

cardiac muscle the muscle of the heart

carotid an artery of the head

castration removal of the gonads

cataplexy a state of immobility and rigidity

catatonia stereotyped behavior, especially prolonged fixed positions

catecholamines compounds such as dopamine, norepinephrine, and epinephrine that contain both catechol and an amine ($-NH_2$)

cation a positively charged ion

CAT scan a method of mapping the areas of relative activity and inactivity in the brain

caudal toward the rear of an animal, away from the head (opposite of rostral)

caudate nucleus one of the components of the basal ganglia

CCK cholecystokinin

cell a unit of the body, surrounded by a membrane

cell body the part of the neuron that contains the nucleus (also called soma, perikaryon)

central canal a fluid-filled channel in the center of the spinal cord

central nervous system (CNS) the brain and the spinal cord

central sulcus a large groove in the surface of the primate cerebral cortex, separating frontal from parietal cortex

centrifugal carrying impulses away from a given structure

centripetal carrying impulses toward a given structure

cerebellar cortex the outer covering of the cerebellum

cerebellum a large, highly convoluted structure in the hindbrain

cerebral cortex the outer layer of the mammalian forebrain

cerebrospinal fluid (CSF) fluid similar to blood serum, found in the ventricles of the brain and in the central canal of the spinal cord

cerebrovascular pertaining to the blood supply to the head

cerebrovascular accident interruption of the blood supply to part of the brain

cerveau isolé a preparation in which the forebrain and midbrain are separated from the medulla and spinal cord

cervical the nerves that enter or leave the spinal cord in the neck

chlordiazepoxide one of the benzodiazepine tranquilizers (trade name: Librium)

chlorimipramine a drug that prolongs the effects of serotonin at the synapse by inhibiting the reuptake of serotonin by the presynaptic cell

chlorpromazine a drug with many effects, including blocking transmission at dopamine synapses

cholecystokinin (CCK) a duodenal hormone that inhibits emptying of the stomach; also found in the brain

cholinergic pertaining to the synaptic transmitter acetylcholine

chorea a behavioral condition characterized by involuntary jerky movements

choreiform rapid repetitive movement resembling dance (note that the root *chore-* is also the basis of the word *choreograph*)

chromosome a strand of DNA, bearing the genes

chronic gradual onset, long duration

circadian rhythm the occurrence of a body process that repeats on a cycle of approximately 24 hours

classical conditioning the process of establishing a conditioned response by pairing a conditioned stimulus with an unconditioned stimulus

clonic having a spasmic alternation of rigidity and relaxation

clonidine a drug that stimulates norepinephrine presynaptic receptors (which inhibit the release of norepinephrine into the synapse)

clozapine a dibenzodiazepine drug that produces antischizophrenic effects with less risk of tardive dyskinesia than many other drugs

CNS central nervous system

cocaine a stimulant drug that stimulates the release of norepinephrine and dopamine from the presynaptic cell

coccygeal spinal cord the most posterior segment of the spinal cord

cochlea a structure in the inner ear, containing auditory receptors

coding a correspondence between some aspect of a physical stimulus and some aspect of the nervous system's activity

cogwheel rigidity a series of jerks in a limb when it is pulled

collateral sprouts branches of an axon that may form to provide innervation to a structure that has lost its input

color constancy the ability to perceive the same colors in a scene, even after the color of the lighting (or of one's glasses) has changed

comatose being in a state of unconsciousness from which one cannot be aroused even by strong stimulation

commissurotomy cutting of the corpus callosum or other connections between the two halves of the cerebral cortex

complex cell a cell in the visual cortex with a receptive field that cannot be mapped on a point-by-point basis

complex partial seizure a series of minor seizures causing confusion and loss of contact with the environment for 1 to 2 minutes; another term for psychomotor seizures

compulsion a forced, driven behavior

computerized axial tomography *See* CAT scan

COMT catechol-o-methyl-transferase, an enzyme that metabolizes catecholamines

concentration gradient difference in concentration of a solute across some distance

concordance similarity (a pair of twins is said to be concordant for a trait if both of them have the trait or if neither has the trait)

conduction aphasia difficulty in repeating what others say and in carrying on a conversation

conductive deafness a hearing impairment that occurs because the bones of the middle ear do not transmit sound waves properly

cone one of the two types of receptor in the retina

congenital present from birth

conjugate vision movement or focus of the eyes together

consolidation gradual establishment or strengthening of a memory

contralateral on the opposite side of the body

convergence (in evolution) similarity in related or unrelated species due to similar evolutionary pressures acting on different ancestral characters

convergence (of the eyes) movement of the axes of the two eyes toward one another

coronal plane a plane through the head or body perpendicular to the direction of locomotion and parallel to the direction of standing legs

corpus callosum the large set of axons that connects the two hemispheres of the cerebral cortex

cortex an outer covering

cortical pertaining to the cerebral cortex

cortical spreading depression a technique for temporarily inactivating one hemisphere of the cerebral cortex by applying concentrated KCl to its surface

corticospinal fluid fluid similar to blood serum, found in the ventricles of the brain and in the central canal of the spinal cord

corticospinal pathways the nerve pathways from the cerebral cortex to the spinal cord

cortisol a hormone released by the adrenal cortex

cranial nerves the set of nerves controlling sensory and motor information of the head, connecting to nuclei in the medulla, pons, midbrain, or forebrain

Creutzfeldt-Jacob disease an inherited, usually fatal disease that leads to progressive damage to the cerebral cortex, basal ganglia, and spinal cord in middle age or old age

critical period a time early in development during which some event (such as the presence of a hormone) has a long-lasting effect

crossing over the exchange of parts between two chromosomes during replication

cross-tolerance tolerance to one drug caused by previous exposure to another drug

CSF cerebrospinal fluid

curare a drug that blocks acetylcholine receptors on skeletal muscles

Cushing's disease condition caused by adrenal-gland tumor, often leading to emotional instability

cyclic AMP a "second messenger" that acts within a cell in response to a synaptic transmitter or hormone

cytoplasm material inside the membrane of a cell, other than the nucleus

D sleep REM sleep

DA dopamine

Dale's Law the statement that all branches of a neuron's axon release the same synaptic transmitter

DBH dopamine-beta-hydroxylase

DBI diazepam-binding inhibitor

deafferented limb   a limb in which the afferent connections have been destroyed

decerebrate   lacking a cerebrum (forebrain), or having the cerebrum cut off from communication with the rest of the nervous system

delayed nonmatching-to-sample   a task in which the subject first sees one object and later sees the same and a different object and has to select the different one

delusion   a false, unfounded belief

dementia   general deterioration of intellectual functioning

dementia praecox   schizophrenia

dendrites   the numerous tapering and widely branching fibers that convey information toward the cell body of a neuron

dendritic spines   small bulges along a dendrite

denervation supersensitivity   an increased sensitivity of a neuron or muscle cell as a result of prolonged lack of stimulation

2-deoxyglucose   a chemical similar to glucose taken up by brain cells but not metabolized by them

depolarization   a reduction in the electrical gradient across a membrane

dermatome   the area of skin connected to a particular spinal nerve

desynchronized   not occurring at the same time

desynchronized EEG   a pattern of EEG recordings indicating that neurons are becoming active out of phase with one another

desynchronized sleep   See REM sleep

dexamethasone suppression test   a test of whether the drug dexamethasone suppresses the release of cortisol

dextral   right-handed

DFP   diisopropylfluorophosphate, a drug that inhibits the enzyme acetylcholinesterase

2-DG   2-deoxyglucose

5,7-DHT   5,7-dihydroxytryptamine

diagnosis   the act of identifying a disease; discriminating one disease from another

diazepam   a benzodiazepine tranquilizer (trade name: Valium)

diazepam-binding inhibitor (DBI)   a naturally occurring brain chemical that binds to the same receptors as the benzodiazepine tranquilizers, blocking their behavioral effects

dichotic listening task   a task in which a person is presented with different messages in the two ears and is tested for which one is heard or remembered better (a test of hemispheric dominance)

diencephalon   the posterior part of the forebrain, including the thalamus and hypothalamus

5,7-dihydroxytryptamine   a drug that destroys synaptic terminals that release serotonin

Dilantin   an antiepileptic drug

diplopia   perception of two images of one object

discordant   dissimilar (a pair of twins is said to be discordant for a trait if one of them has the trait and the other does not)

distention   filling up, applying pressure from inside

disulfiram   a drug that binds with and inactivates enzymes that contain copper, including the enzyme that converts acetaldehyde to acetic acid and the one that converts dopamine to norepinephrine; see also Antabuse

dizygotic   fraternal (nonidentical) twins

DMPEA   dimethoxyphenylethylamine, a hallucinogenic drug

DNA   deoxyribonucleic acid, the chemical that composes the chromosomes

dominant gene   a gene that exerts noticeable effects even in an individual who has only one copy of the gene per cell

domperidone   a drug that blocks dopamine activity in the periphery but not in the central nervous system

DOPA   See L-DOPA

dopamine   a catecholamine synaptic transmitter; also released by the hypothalamus as a hormone

dopamine hypothesis of schizophrenia   the hypothesis that excessive activity at dopamine synapses is responsible for schizophrenia

dopamine-beta-hydroxylase (DBH)   an enzyme that converts dopamine into norepinephrine

dorsal   toward the back, away from the stomach side

dorsal root ganglion   a set of sensory neuron somas on the dorsal side of the spinal cord

dorsomedial nucleus of thalamus   a nucleus whose axons project mainly to the nonmotor areas of the frontal lobe of the cerebral cortex

Dostoyevskian epilepsy   epilepsy that sometimes produces episodes of euphoria

double dissociation of function   demonstration that one lesion impairs behavior A more than behavior B, while a second lesion impairs behavior B more than behavior A

Down's syndrome   a condition caused by having three strands of chromosome 21 per cell instead of two, resulting in mental retardation (also known as mongoloidism)

dualism   the philosophical position that mind and brain are fundamentally different and that each can exist independently of the other

duodenum   the first part of the small intestine, adjoining the stomach

dura mater   one of the membranes that cover the brain and spinal cord

dys-   prefix meaning impairment, dysfunction of

dyscalculia   impairment of the ability to make mathematical calculations

dyscontrol syndrome   a condition marked by outbursts of unprovoked violent behavior

dysdiadochokinesia   impairment of the ability to make rapid alternating movements such as clapping hands

dyslexia   impairment of reading ability

dysmnesia   impairment of memory

dysphasia   impairment of language

dysphoria   unhappy mood (opposite of euphoria)

dyspnea   impaired or labored breathing

echolocation   localization of objects by hearing echos of sound waves bounced off those objects

ECS   electroconvulsive shock

ECT   electroconvulsive shock therapy

edema   an excessive fluid build-up in the intercellular spaces of the body

EEG   electroencephalograph

effector   a muscle or gland

effector neuron   a neuron that conveys impulses to a muscle or gland

efferent neuron   a neuron that conveys impulses away from any structure under consideration

electrical gradient   a difference in electrical potential across some distance

electroconvulsive shock therapy (ECT)   a series of brief seizures induced by electrical shock to the head, sometimes used for reduction of depression

electroencephalograph (EEG)   a device that records the electrical activity of the brain via electrodes on the scalp

electrotonic conduction   conduction by the flow of electrical current

emergent property position   the philosophical view that mind emerges as a new property when neural tissue is organized in a particular way

encephale isolé   a preparation in which most of the brain is separated from the spinal cord

encephalitis   inflammation of the brain

encephalopathy   any degenerative disease of the brain

end bulb   a swelling at the end of an axon from which the synaptic transmitter is released

endocrine gland   a gland that releases hormones

endogenous   developing from within, as opposed to being a reaction to external events

endogenous circadian rhythm   a rhythm generated within the body that lasts about one year

endogenous circannual rhythm   a rhythm generated within the body that lasts about 24 hours

endogenous depression   a depression that originates within the body, not as a reaction to outside events

endoplasmic reticulum   a network of thin tubes within a cell

endorphins   a category of chemicals produced by the body that have effects similar to those of opiate drugs

engram   the physical representation of something that has been learned

enkephalin   one type of endorphin; a chemical believed to act as a synaptic transmitter

enuresis   bed-wetting

enzyme   any protein that catalyzes biological reactions

epilepsy   a disease characterized by abnormal rhythmic activity of the neurons in some area of the brain

epileptic focus   the point in the brain from which an epileptic seizure originates

epileptogenic   causing epileptic seizures

epinephrine   a hormone released by the adrenal gland; also a synaptic transmitter (also called adrenalin)

epiphenomenalism   the philosophical position that brain activity produces a mind, but only as an accidental by-product

epiphenomenon   something that occurs as an accidental by-product of something else

episodic dyscontrol syndrome   a condition marked by outbursts of unprovoked violent behavior

epithelial   pertaining to the skin

EPSP   excitatory postsynaptic potential

equipotentiality   the ability of all parts of the cerebral cortex to contribute equally to some function such as learning or memory

ergot   a product of a fungus that sometimes grows on grains

esophagus   the tube leading from the stomach to the mouth

esotropia   cross-eyedness

estradiol   a hormone released by the ovaries

estrogens   a category of hormones released by the ovaries

estrus   the period of sexual fertility and sexual receptivity in a female mammal

ethology   the study of the natural behavior of animals

etiology   causation

evoked potential   electrical activity recorded from the brain, usually via electrodes on the scalp, in response to sensory stimuli

evolution   a change in the gene pool of a population over generations

evolutionary explanation   an explanation of a characteristic in terms of its evolutionary history

evolutionary theory of sleep   the theory that the need to sleep evolved as a means of conserving energy during periods of relative inefficiency

excitatory postsynaptic potential (EPSP)   a brief depolarization of a membrane due to synaptic transmission

exogenous   caused by something outside the body

extend   to push away from the trunk of the body; e.g., to stretch out an arm or leg

extensor   a muscle that extends a limb

extracellular   outside the cells

extraocular   outside the eyes

extrapyramidal system   a system within the nervous system that controls certain aspects of movement, especially gross movements of the body as a whole, such as walking

Factor S   a small glycopeptide, apparently capable of inducing sleep

feedback   sensory information resulting from previous activities

fimbria   a band of axons along the medial surface of the hippocampus

final common path   the motor neuron, which participates in all types of movement

fissure   a fold in the side of the cortex

fistula   a tube into some part of the digestive system, allowing nutrients to be placed into the system or to be removed from it

flex   to draw an extremity such as an arm toward the trunk of the body

flexor   a muscle that flexes a limb

flurazepam   a long-acting benzodiazepine tranquilizer

focal   originating at a discrete point in the brain

focus   See epileptic focus

follicle-stimulating hormone (FSH)   a hormone released by the anterior pituitary that stimulates development of ova and sperm cells

forebrain   the most anterior part of the brain, including the cerebral cortex and other structures

fornix   a tract of axons connecting the hippocampus with the hypothalamus and other areas

Fourier analysis   a mathematical method of expressing any function as the sum of a series of sine functions

fovea   the center of the retina, where detailed vision is most acute

fragile X syndrome   a condition in which part of the X chromosome is susceptible to detaching

free nerve ending   a somatosensory receptor

free-running rhythm   a circadian or circannual rhythm that is not being periodically reset by light or other cues

frequency theory   the theory that pitch perception depends on differences in frequency of action potentials by auditory neurons

frontal lobe   one of the lobes of the cerebral cortex

frontal lobotomy   See prefrontal lobotomy

FSH   follicle-stimulating hormone

FTG neurons   neurons of the gigantocellular tegmental field

functional disorder   a mental disorder due to experiences, not biological disorder

fusaric acid   a drug that blocks the enzyme DBH

GABA   gamma-amino-butyric acid

GABA$_A$ receptor complex   a structure that includes a site that binds GABA as well as sites that bind other chemicals that modify the sensitivity of the GABA site

GABAergic   using GABA as a synaptic transmitter

galvanic skin response (GSR)   a change in the electrical conduction of the skin

gamma-amino-butyric acid (GABA)   a synaptic transmitter

ganglion (plural: ganglia)   a cluster of neuron cell bodies

ganglion cell   a neuron type within the eye

gate theory   the theory that excitation of certain non-pain axons can inhibit transmission of pain messages in the spinal cord

gegenhalten   increased muscle tension; resistance to passive movements of the limbs

gender identity   psychological identification with one sex or the other

gene   a physical particle that determines some aspect of inheritance

generator potential   a local depolarization or hyperpolarization of a neuron membrane, caused by stimulation of a receptor

genetic   under the control of differences in genes between one individual and another

geniculate   a part of the thalamus; the lateral geniculate is important for vision, while the medial geniculate is important for audition

genotype   the total collection of an individual's genes

gigantocellular tegmental field   an area of the pons with large cell bodies

Gilles de la Tourette's syndrome   a behavioral condition characterized by tics and other repetitive movements

glia   supportive cells in the brain that do not transmit synaptic information

glioma   tumorous growth of glia

globus pallidus   one of the components of the basal ganglia

glucagon   a hormone released by the pancreas

glucose   the most common sugar in the blood and the main fuel of neurons

glutamate   an amino acid found throughout the body; also used as a synaptic transmitter

glycine   an amino acid found throughout the body; also used as a synaptic transmitter

glycoside   a compound that contains a sugar

Golgi stain   a method of staining an entire neuron with silver salts

Golgi tendon organ   a receptor that responds to increases in muscle tension

graded potential   a depolarization of a neuron membrane less than the threshold for an action potential

grand mal   a form of epilepsy in which a person loses control of the muscles

graphesthesia   the ability to recognize figures drawn on the skin

gray matter   areas of the nervous system with a high density of cell bodies and dendrites, with few myelinated axons

GSR   galvanic skin response

gyrus   an outward bulge in the folds of the cerebral cortex

habituation   reduction of response to a repeated stimulus that does not predict any other stimuli

hair cell   a type of sensory receptor

hair follicle receptor   a receptor that responds to movements of a hair

hallucination   a sensory experience that does not correspond to events in the outside world

hallucinogen   a drug that induces hallucinations

haloperidol   a drug that blocks dopamine receptors

Halstead-Reitan battery   a set of behavioral tests designed to identify the type and extent of brain damage

hemi   prefix meaning half

hemianopsia   blindness in the left or right visual field

hemiballismus   violent motor restlessness in half of the body

hemicholinium   a drug that blocks the reuptake of acetate and choline into the presynaptic cells that release acetylcholine

hemiparesis   muscular weakness in half of the body

hemiplegia   paralysis of the muscles on one side of the body

hemisphere   either the left or the right half of the brain

hepatic   pertaining to the liver

heritability   a correlation coefficient, ranging from zero to one, indicating the degree to which variations in some characteristic depend on variations in heredity for a given population

hermaphrodite   an individual with sexual anatomy resembling both male and female or intermediate between the two

heroin   a drug that stimulates the receptors that normally respond to endorphins

Hertz (Hz)   cycles per second

heterozygous   having two unlike genes for a given trait

hexamethonium   a drug that blocks the ion pores controlled by the acetylcholine receptor without attaching to the receptor itself

5-HIAA   5-hydroxy-indole-acetic acid

hillock   *See* axon hillock

hindbrain   the most posterior part of the brain, including the medulla, pons, and cerebellum

hippocampus   a large forebrain structure situated between the thalamus and cortex

histamine   a chemical with many functions in the body, including that of synaptic transmitter

histology   the study of tissues

histopathology   abnormality of tissues

homeostasis   the tendency to maintain some variable, such as temperature, within a fixed range

homeostatic drive   a behavior directed toward maintaining homeostasis

homeothermic   maintaining nearly constant body temperature over a wide range of environmental temperatures

homologous   having two identical genes for a given trait

homovanillic acid (HVA)   a metabolite of dopamine

homozygous   having two identical genes for a given characteristic

horizontal cell   one of the neuron types of the retina

horizontal plane   a plane through the body parallel to the ground

hormone   a chemical released into the blood that affects other parts of the body

horseradish peroxidase   a chemical that is absorbed by axon terminals and transported to the cell body; useful as a means of anatomically tracing the origin of a given axon

5-HT   5-hydroxytryptamine (serotonin)

5-HTP   5-hydroxytryptophan

Huntington's disease   an inherited disorder characterized by tremor, movement disorder, and psychotic behavior (also called Huntington's chorea)

HVA   homovanillic acid

hydrocephalus   accumulation of excessive fluid in the head

6-hydroxy-dopamine (6-OH-DA)   a chemical that can destroy dopamine or norepinephrine synapses or both

5-hydroxy-indole-acetic acid (5-HIAA)   a metabolite of serotonin

5-hydroxytryptamine (5-HT)   serotonin

5-hydroxytryptophan (5-HTP)   a precursor in the synthesis of serotonin

hypalgesia   low sensitivity to pain

hyper-   prefix meaning higher than normal

hypercapnia   higher than normal levels of carbon dioxide in the blood

hypercomplex cell   a neuron type in the visual cortex that responds best to stimuli of a precisely limited type, anywhere in a large receptive field

hyperpolarization   an increase in the electrical gradient across a cell membrane

hyperreflexia   stronger than normal reflexes

hypertension   high blood pressure

hyperthermia   higher than normal body temperature

hyperventilation   excessive breathing

hypnagogic   hypnotic, or sleep-inducing

hypo-   prefix meaning lower than normal

hypocalcemia   lower than normal levels of calcium

hypoglycemia   lower than normal levels of glucose

hypomania   a mild degree of mania

hyponatremia   lower than normal levels of sodium

hypophysis   the pituitary gland

hyposomnia   lower than normal amounts of sleep

hypothalamus   a forebrain structure located just ventral to the thalamus

hypothermia   lower than normal body temperature

hypovolemia   lower than normal blood volume

hypovolemic thirst   thirst provoked by decreased blood volume

hypsarhythmia   an EEG abnormality sometimes observed in infants, characterized by random high-voltage slow waves and spikes from multiple foci

hysterectomy   surgical removal of the uterus

Hz   Hertz

iatrogenic   caused by a physician

ibotenic acid   a neurotoxin that destroys cell bodies of neurons in the area where it is applied without damaging fibers passing through

ictal   pertaining to an epileptic seizure

identity position   the philosophical position that mind and brain are two ways of talking about the same thing

ideomotor apraxia   the inability to perform certain acts voluntarily, although the same acts or similar ones can still be performed by habit in other situations

idiopathic   "self-originated," that is, of unknown origin

impulse   an action potential

incomplete penetrance   expression of a gene's effects to different degrees in different individuals

indoleamines   a set of chemical compounds including serotonin

infant amnesia   the inability to remember events that happened during one's infancy

infantile autism   a behavioral abnormality with early childhood onset, characterized by deficit of social contact

infarct   an area of tissue that dies because of impaired blood supply to it

inferior colliculus   a part of the auditory system located in the midbrain

inferior temporal cortex   a part of the temporal lobe of the cerebral cortex important for complex visual pattern perception

inhibitory postsynaptic potential (IPSP)   a brief hyperpolarization of a neuron's membrane due to synaptic transmission to that neuron

inner-ear deafness   permanent hearing impairment caused by damage to the cochlea, hair cells, or auditory nerve

insomnia   sleeplessness

insulin   a hormone that increases the conversion of glucose into stored fat and facilitates the transfer of glucose across the cell membrane

interactionism   the philosophical position that mind and brain interact with each other and influence each other

intermittent explosive disorder   a condition marked by outbursts of unprovoked violent behavior

interneuron   a neuron that receives synaptic input from other neurons and makes synaptic contact onto other neurons

intersex   an individual whose sexual anatomy is intermediate between male and female

intrathecal   into the space under the arachnoid membrane, one of the membranes that cover the brain and spinal cord

intrinsic neuron   a neuron whose dendrites and axons are all confined to the same brain structure as the cell body

invertebrate   an animal lacking a spinal cord

ion   an atom or bound group of atoms bearing an electrical charge

ionic synaptic effects   synaptic interactions based on changes in the permeability of the membrane to one or more types of ions

iproniazid   a drug that inhibits the enzyme monoamine oxidase

ipsilateral   on the same side of the body

IPSP   inhibitory postsynaptic potential

ischemic   suppression of blood flow to part of the body

isocortex   a portion of the cerebral cortex that contains six layers

James-Lange theory   the theory that physiological states cause emotions, not vice versa

jet lag   the disruption of biological rhythms as a result of crossing time zones

kainic acid   a chemical similar to glutamate that destroys cell bodies in contact with it but does not destroy passing axons

Kennard principle   the generalization that recovery from brain damage early in life is more complete than recovery from damage later in life

kinesthesia (kinesthetic sensation)   perception of the position and motion of the muscles

kin selection   selection for a genetic trait that benefits one's relatives

Kleine-Levin syndrome   a condition characterized by decreased activity and increased eating

Klinefelter's syndrome   a physical and behavioral condition associated with an XYY chromosome pattern

koniocortex   areas of the cerebral cortex with conspicuous granular layers

Korsakoff's syndrome   a condition including memory deficits and other disorders caused by thiamine deficiency; usually secondary to chronic alcoholism

Krause end bulb   one type of somatosensory receptor

labeled line theory   a theory of taste and smell sensation holding that each receptor is sensitive to a particular stimulus and that it has a direct line to the brain

lactate (as verb)   to secrete milk

lactate (as noun)   a breakdown product of starches formed in the muscles during exercise

lactation   production of milk

lactic acid   *See* lactate

lamina   a layer of cell bodies separated from other cell bodies by a layer of fibers

lateral   to the side

lateral fissure   one of the major fissures (or folds) on the side of the cortex

lateral geniculate   a nucleus of the thalamus; part of the visual system

lateral hypothalamus   an area of the hypothalamus in which damage impairs eating, drinking, and activity

lateral inhibition   inhibition of activity in one neuron by activity in a neighboring neuron

lateral preoptic area   a part of the hypothalamus important for osmotic thirst and maternal behavior

lateral ventricles   two large fluid-filled cavities, one in each hemisphere of the brain

law of specific nerve energies   the statement that any activity by a given neuron conveys the same kind of information, differing only in degree

L-DOPA   a chemical precursor of dopamine and other catecholamines

learned helplessness   decreased activity and learning as a result of a previous period of unreinforced responding

lecithin   a dietary precursor to acetylcholine

lenticular nucleus   the putamen and globus pallidus

lesion   damage to a structure

leu-enkephalin   *See* enkephalin

LH   lateral hypothalamus or luteinizing hormone

Librium   a benzodiazepine tranquilizer (chemical name: chlordiazepoxide)

lidocaine   a local anesthetic that acts by blocking sodium pores in the neural membrane

limbic system   a set of subcortical structures in the forebrain, including the hypothalamus, hippocampus, amygdala, olfactory bulb, septum, other small structures, and parts of the thalamus and cerebral cortex

lipids   fat molecules

lithium   an element whose salts are often used in the treatment of manic-depressive illness

lobectomy   removal of a lobe of the brain

lobotomy   *See* prefrontal lobotomy

local circuit   a cluster of small neurons exchanging information over very short distances, usually with graded potentials rather than action potentials

local neuron   a neuron whose axons and dendrites are confined to a small area, all within a given structure

locus coeruleus   a small structure in the hindbrain

longitudinal fissure   the long groove that separates the left hemisphere of the cerebral cortex from the right hemisphere

long-term memory   memory that continues to be stored after attention is distracted from the event

long-term potentiation (LTP)   an increased responsiveness of a neuron to a synaptic transmitter as a result of a brief burst of stimuli to that neuron

LSD   lysergic acid diethylamide, a hallucinogenic chemical that blocks serotonin synapses for about 4 hours and decreases the number of serotonin receptors for days; also affects dopamine synapses

LTP   long-term potentiation

L-tryptophan   an amino acid; a precursor in the synthesis of serotonin

lumbar puncture   removal of fluid from the lumbar area of the spinal cord

Luria-Nebraska neuropsychological battery   a set of items used to test for brain damage

luteinizing hormone (LH)   a hormone released by the anterior pituitary that (in females) promotes ovulation and secretion of estrogen

macropsia   disturbance of vision in which objects appear larger than they really are

maintenance insomnia   trouble staying asleep

major depression   a depression of great severity and duration

MAM   methylazoxymethanol acetate

mania   a condition of uninhibited activity; opposite of depression

manic-depressive disorder   a condition in which a person alternates between periods of mania and depression

MAO   monoamine oxidase

MAOI   monoamine oxidase inhibitor

marche à petit pas   a gait in which the person takes very short steps

mass action   the theory that neurons of the cerebral cortex operate as a unit for certain functions

materialism   the philosophical position that only the material world exists; minds do not exist independently

MBD   minimal brain dysfunction

medial   toward the midline

medial forebrain bundle   an axon tract that courses through the hypothalamus and makes contact diffusely in the forebrain

medial geniculate nucleus   a part of the auditory system located in the thalamus

medulla   a hindbrain structure just above the spinal cord

megavitamin therapy   treatment of autism or other disorders by giving large doses of vitamins

Meissner's corpuscles   receptors found in hairless parts of the skin that respond to sudden movement across the skin

melatonin   a hormone released by the pineal gland

membrane of a cell   the covering that surrounds a cell

meninges   the three membranes (dura, pia, and arachnoid) that cover the brain and spinal cord

meningioma   a tumor that grows along the meninges

meningitis   inflammation of the meninges

menstruation   sloughing of the uterine lining about every 28 days in nonpregnant women

mentalism   the philosophical position that the physical world exists only in one's mind

Merkel's disk   a receptor that reponds to pressure on the skin

mescaline   a hallucinogenic chemical

mesencephalon   the midbrain

mesolimbic system   a set of neurons in the tegmentum of the midbrain that send axons containing dopamine to the limbic system

metabolic synaptic effects   synaptic interactions that cause changes in the metabolic activity of the postsynaptic neuron, requiring changes in the proteins of the postsynaptic cell

metabolism   the chemical reactions that make energy available for use by the body

metamorphopsia   a disturbance of vision in which objects appear distorted in shape

met-enkephalin   *See* enkephalin

methadone   a drug sometimes given to opiate addicts as a less-disabling substitute for morphine or heroin; it stimulates the receptors that normally respond to endorphins

methylazoxymethanol acetate   drug that destroys neurons that are dividing or developing

methylphenidate   a stimulant drug

methysergide   a drug that blocks serotonin receptors

metoclopramide   a drug that blocks certain dopamine receptors, producing undesirable effects on the extrapyramidal system without producing significant antischizophrenic effects

MHPG   3-methoxy-5-hydroxyphenylethylene glycol, a metabolic breakdown product of norepinephrine

mianserin   an antidepressant drug that inhibits autoceptors to catecholamine synaptic transmitters

microcephaly   abnormal smallness of the head

microelectrode   a very thin electrode, generally made of glass and filled with an electrolyte solution

microglia   very small glia cells that remove waste materials from the brain

micrographia   a reduction in the size of one's handwriting

micropsia   a disturbance of vision in which objects appear smaller than they really are

midazolam   a short-acting benzodiazepine tranquilizer

midbrain   the middle part of the brain, including the superior and inferior colliculi

middle-ear deafness   a hearing impairment caused by impaired transmission of sounds through the bones of the middle ear

middle temporal cortex   a part of the temporal lobe of the cerebral cortex; part of the visual system

mind-brain problem   the philosophical question of how brain activity is related to mental experience

miniature end-plate potential   an EPSP in a muscle cell

minimal brain dysfunction or minimal brain disorder (MBD)   *See* attention deficit disorder

miracle berries   tropical fruits containing miraculin

miraculin   a protein that alters taste receptors in such a way that all acids taste sweet

mitochondrion (plural: mitochondria)   a structure within a cell that carries out chemical reactions that produce energy

molar   in chemistry, a measure of concentration of solutions; a one-molar concentration has a number of grams equal to the molecular weight of a compound dissolved in one liter of water solution

molindone   an antischizophrenic drug that acts by blocking dopamine postsynaptic receptors

monism   the philosophical position that only one kind of "substance" exists in the universe, which, according to various versions, may be either mental or material

monoamine   a chemical that includes one -NH$_2$ group; e.g., dopamine, epinephrine, norepinephrine, serotonin

monoamine oxidase (MAO)   an enzyme that converts catecholamines and serotonin into synaptically inactive forms

monoamine oxidase inhibitor (MAOI)   a drug that inhibits the enzyme monoamine oxidase

monocular   seeing with one eye

monosodium glutamate   a chemical that can kill neurons by overstimulating them

monozygotic   identical twins

Moro reflex   a startle reflex in infants in which the arms are thrown out as if to embrace someone

morphine   a drug that stimulates the receptors that normally respond to endorphins

morphology   the shape or structure of something

motor cortex   the part of the cerebral cortex that controls movement

motor neuron   a neuron that makes synaptic contact onto a muscle or gland

motor program   a fixed sequence of movements that occur as a single unit

multiple sclerosis   a disease characterized by hardening of parts of the brain or spinal cord, leading to weakness and incoordination

muricide   mouse killing

muscarine   a drug that excites some acetylcholine receptors but not others

muscimol   a drug that stimulates GABA receptors

muscle spindle   a receptor that responds to stretching of a muscle

mutation   a change in a gene during reproduction

mutism   failure to speak

myasthenia gravis   a disease that leads to increasing paralysis of muscles

myelin (or myelin sheath)   a fatty substance that surrounds and insulates axons

myelination   development of a myelin sheath

NA   noradrenalin

naloxone   a drug that blocks the effects of opiates and endorphins in the brain

narcolepsy   a condition characterized by sudden attacks of sleep

narcosis   stupor induced by a drug

natural selection   the mechanism of evolution through differences in rates of reproduction by individuals bearing different genes

Nauta method   a method of applying a dark stain to degenerating axons

NE   norepinephrine

negative symptoms   symptoms defined by the absence of certain behaviors, such as emotional expression and social interaction

neglect   *See* sensory neglect

neocortex   the most recently evolved portion of the cerebral cortex

neonatal   pertaining to newborns

neophobia   a fear of the new

neostigmine   a drug that blocks acetylcholinesterase, the enzyme that breaks down acetylcholine

neostriatum   the caudate nucleus and putamen

nerve deafness   deafness resulting from damage to the cochlea, hair cells, or auditory nerve

nerve growth factor   a chemical that stimulates growth of axons, especially of sympathetic nervous system axons

nerve impulse   *See* action potential

nerve-muscle junction   a special type of synapse in which an axon meets a muscle fiber

neuritic plaque   a patch that forms because of inflammation of a nerve

neuroanatomy   the anatomy of the nervous system

neuroembryology   the embryological development of the nervous system

neurofilament   a long threadlike structure found in axons

neuroglia   *See* glia

neurohypophysis   the posterior pituitary

neuroleptic drug   any antischizophrenic drug

neurological   pertaining to the medical study of the nervous system

neuromodulator   a chemical that alters the release of a synaptic transmitter or the sensitivity of the postsynaptic neuron

neuron   the basic cell of the nervous system

neuropil   a dense assortment of dendrites, other parts of neurons, and glia cells

neurotoxin   a chemical that damages neurons

neurotransmitter   *See* synaptic transmitter

niacin   one of the B vitamins

nicotine   a drug that stimulates certain acetylcholine receptors but not all

night terror   a sudden arousal from sleep accompanied by panic

Nissl stain   any of several methods for staining cell bodies violet

NMR   nuclear magnetic resonance

nocturnal   being awake at night and sleeping during the day

nocturnal myoclonus   a periodic involuntary movement of the legs and sometimes arms during sleep

nodes of Ranvier   the interruptions in a myelin sheath

non-REM sleep   sleep other than REM sleep

noradrenalin (NA)   norepinephrine

norepinephrine (NE)   a catecholamine synaptic transmitter, also released by the adrenal gland as a hormone

normetanephrine   a breakdown product of norepinephrine

nosology   the classification and naming of diseases

Novocaine   an anesthetic drug that acts by blocking the transport of sodium through the membrane

nuclear magnetic resonance (NMR)   a method of mapping the anatomy of a living brain

nucleus (plural: nuclei)   a cluster of neurons; also, the structure within a cell that contains the chromosomes

nucleus solitarius   an area in the medulla that receives input from taste receptors and from the digestive organs

nystagmus   involuntary rapid eye movements

obsession   a repetitive line of thinking

obsessive-compulsive disorder   a psychological disorder characterized by obsessions and compulsions

occipital lobe   one of the four lobes of the cerebral cortex

6-OH-DA   6-hydroxy-dopamine

olfaction   the sense of smell

olfactory bulb   a forebrain structure that receives most of its input from the olfactory cells

olfactory cell   a receptor for the sense of smell

oligodendrocyte   a type of glia cell with few branches

onset insomnia   trouble falling asleep

ontogeny   development within an individual

opiates   drugs derived from the seeds of opium poppies

opponent-process theory   the theory that we perceive color in terms of pairs of opposites: red-green and yellow-blue

opsin   protein bound to 11-*cis*-retinal to form the photopigments in the retina

optical illusions   visual patterns that are often seen as something other than what they are

optic chiasm   the point at which parts of the optic nerves cross to the opposite side of the brain

optic nerve   axons from the retina to the brain (also known as optic tract)

optokinetic   pertaining to eye movements

organizing effects   the long-lasting effects of a hormone that is present during a sensitive period early in life

orientation (of a bar of light)   the angle (such as vertical or horizontal) of a bar of light in the visual field

orthodromic transmission   propagation of an action potential in the normal direction, from the axon hillock toward the end bulbs (opposite of antidromic)

orthomolecular psychiatry   treatment of psychiatric problems by maintaining or establishing optimal levels of various chemicals in the body

oscillator   a mechanism producing a repetitive alternation between two actions

osmotic pressure   pressure exerted by the concentration of a solute in water solution toward other solutions separated from it by a semipermeable membrane

osmotic thirst   thirst induced by an elevated concentration of solutes in the body fluids

otolith   an organ responsible for vestibular sensation

ovaries   the organs that produce eggs

ovum (plural: ova)   an egg (the reproductive cell that contains more cytoplasm than the sperm)

oxytocin   a hormone from posterior pituitary that induces contractions of the uterus and release of milk

P300 wave   a positive wave on an EEG recording that occurs about 300 milliseconds after a stimulus

Pacinian corpuscle   a receptor that responds to displacement of the skin, including vibration

paleostriatum   the globus pallidus

pallidum   the globus pallidus

palsy   paralysis

panic disorder   a condition characterized by attacks of excess anxiety

panprotopsychic identism   a variant form of the identity position, according to which consciousness is present in a primitive, potential form in all matter

papaverine   a chemical related to opiates that inhibits the enzyme phosphodiesterase and thereby decreases the breakdown of cyclic AMP

Papez's theory of emotion   the theory that emotions depend on the limbic system in the brain

papillae   folds on the surface of the tongue containing taste buds

paradoxical   apparently self-contradictory

paradoxical sleep   a stage of sleep characterized by complete relaxation of the large muscles but high activity in the brain; REM sleep

parallelism (in philosophy)   the philosophical position that mind and brain exist separately and do not affect each other

parallelism (in evolution)   a similarity in related species due to similar evolutionary forces, not due to common ancestry

paralysis   the inability to move certain muscles

paraplegia   paralysis of the lower part of the body including both legs

parastriate cortex   an area of the cerebral cortex surrounding the striate, or primary visual cortex

parasympathetic ganglia   the clusters of cell bodies located close to various internal organs and innervated by nerves from the cranial and sacral parts of the spinal cord

parasympathetic nervous system   the system of nerves innervating the internal organs, tending to conserve energy

paresthesia   abnormal or distorted sensations

parietal lobe   one of the lobes of the cerebral cortex

parity   the number of times a mother has given birth

Parkinson's disease   a disease caused by gradual destruction of the substantia nigra in the brain, resulting in loss of voluntary movement

paroxysmal   pertaining to a sudden intensification of a disease or its symptoms

passive avoidance learning   learning to suppress a behavior that is followed by punishment

paternal half-siblings   individuals with the same father but different mothers

pathognomonic   characteristic of a disease; useful for diagnosis

pathology   the study of disease

pavor nocturnus   night terrors

PCPA   parachlorophenylalanine, a drug that interferes with the synthesis of serotonin

PEA   phenylethylamine, a hallucinogenic chemical that occurs naturally in the body

penetrance   the degree of expression of a gene

peptide   a compound of two or more amino acids

peptide hormone   a hormone composed of amino acids

peptide neurotransmitter   a synaptic transmitter composed of amino acids

perikaryon   the cell body of a neuron; the soma

perinatal   around the time of birth

peripheral nervous system   the nerves outside the brain and spinal cord

permeability   the ability of an ion to cross a membrane

perseveration   repetition of a given response to a stimulus

petit mal   a type of epilepsy that gives rise to a brief loss of consciousness with little motor activity

PET scan   positron-emission tomography, a method of mapping activity in a living brain by recording the emission of radioactivity from injected chemicals

peyote   a hallucinogenic chemical derived from mushrooms

PGO waves   repetitive action potentials that can be recorded successively in the pons, lateral geniculate, and occipital cortex

phantom limb   the sensation of a limb that has been amputated

pharmacological dose   a dose of a hormone or other chemical that exceeds the normal range that occurs in nature (compare with physiological dose)

phenothiazines   a class of drugs that block dopamine receptors; often used to combat schizophrenia

phenylalanine   an amino acid

phenylketonuria (PKU)   an inherited inability to metabolize phenylalanine, leading to mental retardation unless the afflicted person stays on a strict low-phenylalanine diet throughout childhood

phenylpyruvate   a breakdown product of phenylalanine

pheromone   a chemical released by one animal that affects the behavior of another member of the species

phosphodiesterase   a drug that breaks down cyclic AMP

phrenology   the nineteenth-century theory that personality types are related to bumps on the skull

phylogeny   the evolutionary origin of a species and its genetic relationship to other species

physiological dose   a dose of a hormone or other chemical that stays within the normal range that occurs in nature (compare with pharmacological dose)

physiological explanation   an explanation of a characteristic in terms of the body machinery that produces it

physiology   mechanisms of control of body functions

physostigmine   a drug that antagonizes the enzyme acetylcholinesterase

pia mater   one of the membranes that surround the brain and spinal cord

pica   the eating of nonfood substances, such as dirt

picrotoxin   a drug that blocks GABA synapses

pilocarpine   a drug that excites acetylcholine receptors

piloerection   erection of the hairs ("gooseflesh" in humans)

pineal gland   a hormone-releasing gland inside the brain

piracetam   a drug believed to enhance memory

pitch perception   the ability to distinguish one pitch of sound from another

pituitary gland   an endocrine gland whose secretions regulate the activity of many other hormonal glands

PKU   phenylketonuria

placebo   an inactive substance given as a substitute for an active drug, usually as a treatment for a control group in an experiment

place theory   the theory that pitch perception depends on which part of the inner ear has cells with the greatest activity level

Planaria   a flatworm

planum temporale   part of the primate temporal cortex

PMS   premenstrual syndrome

pneumoencephalography   the making of x-rays of the head after injecting air into the fluid spaces of the head

PNS   parasympathetic nervous system or peripheral nervous system

POA   the preoptic area

poikilothermic   maintaining the same body temperature as the surrounding environment

polarized   having an electrical gradient across a membrane

poliomyelitis   paralysis caused by a virus that attacks motor neurons in the spinal cord

polygenic   controlled by many genes

pons   a hindbrain structure, anterior to the medulla

positive symptoms   symptoms of schizophrenia defined by the presence of a behavior, such as hallucinations, delusions, and thought disorder

postcentral gyrus   the gyrus of the cerebral cortex just posterior to the central gyrus; a primary projection site for touch sensations

posterior   toward the rear

posterior parietal cortex   part of the parietal lobe of the cerebral cortex; important for attention to a visual object in preparation for a movement

posterior pituitary   an endocrine gland at the base of the brain that releases oxytocin and vasopressin

postictal   following an epileptic seizure

postmortem   examination after death

postpartum   after giving birth

postpartum depression   period of depression after giving birth

postrolandic   the sensory (especially touch) area of the brain

postsynaptic cell   the cell on the receiving end of a synapse

postsynaptic membrane   a specialized area of the membrane of a postsynaptic cell that is responsive to the synaptic transmitter

posture   position of body parts with respect to one another and to gravity

precentral gyrus   the gyrus of cerebral cortex just anterior to the central sulcus; a primary point of origin for axons of the pyramidal system of motor control

prefrontal cortex   the most anterior portion of the frontal lobe of the cerebral cortex

prefrontal lobotomy   surgical disconnection of the prefrontal cortex from the rest of the brain

premenstrual syndrome (PMS)   tension and discomfort reported by certain women during the day or days just before menstruation

premorbid   what someone's condition was prior to the onset of a disease

premotor cortex   an area of the cerebral cortex just anterior to the primary motor cortex that is active during the planning of a movement and during movements that must be integrated with sensory information

prenatal   prior to birth

preoptic area (POA)   a nucleus of the hypothalamus important for temperature regulation

prestriate cortex   *See* parastriate cortex

presymptomatic test   a test to predict the onset of a disease, conducted before any symptoms appear

presynaptic cell   a neuron on the releasing end of a synapse

presynaptic ending   a bulge at the end of an axon from which a synaptic transmitter is released

presynaptic inhibition   an effect on a presynaptic neuron that decreases its tendency to release its transmitter

presynaptic receptor   a receptor on a presynaptic ending, sensitive to a synaptic transmitter

primary motor cortex   an area of cerebral cortex just anterior to the central sulcus; a primary point of origin for axons of the pyramidal system of motor control

primates   an order of mammals including monkeys, apes, and humans

priming stimulus   a stimulus that increases the response to a later stimulus

proband   the individual who is the starting point for an investigation, especially a study of the relatives of a disordered individual

Procion yellow or Procion brown   a fluorescent stain that is injected into a neuron through a glass electrode that was used to record from the cell; used to mark the cell for later identification

progesterone   a hormone that prepares the uterus to receive a fertilized ovum

prognosis   prediction of the outcome of a disease

progressive disorder   a disorder that grows progressively more severe

projection   an extension of axons from one area to another

prolactin   a hormone released by the anterior pituitary that stimulates lactation in mammary glands

propagation of the action potential   regeneration of the action potential at one point after another along an axon

prophylactic preventing disease

proprioception the sensation of location of body parts

prosopagnosia an inability to recognize faces

prostaglandin E a chemical naturally found in the body that contracts smooth muscles and also acts on certain neurons to raise body temperature

pseudobulbar a condition similar to those originating in the medulla

pseudohermaphrodite an individual whose sexual anatomy is intermediate between male and female

psilocin a hallucinogenic chemical

psychomotor seizure a minor seizure causing confusion and loss of contact with the environment for 1 to 2 minutes

psychosomatic illness an illness whose onset or resistance to treatment is influenced by the individual's personality or experiences

psychosurgery surgery conducted to alter behavior

puberty the onset of sexual maturity

pulvinar a nucleus of the thalamus

pupil the opening in the eyeball through which light enters

Purkinje cell a cell found in the cerebellum

pursuit eye movement eye movements to maintain constant focus on a moving object

putamen one of the components of the basal ganglia

pyramidal neuron a neuron with a cell body shaped like a pyramid, generally having a long axon

pyramidal system a system originating mostly in the precentral and postcentral gyri whose axons cross in the pyramids of the medulla and extend to interneurons in the spinal cord; important for control of discrete movements

pyramids swellings in the medulla, where pyramidal system axons cross to the contralateral side

quadriplegia loss of sensation and muscle control in all four limbs

quantum the minimum amount of release of transmitter at a synapse

quazepam a long-acting benzodiazepine tranquilizer

quiet sleep non-REM sleep

quinolinic acid a chemical resembling glutamate that kills certain neurons by overstimulating them

rabies a viral disease of the nervous system

racemic a mixture of the D- and L- forms of a stereochemical

radial glia glia cells with long fibers that guide the migration of neurons and growth of their fibers during embryological development

radial maze an apparatus with straight arms leaving a start box at various angles; at least some of the arms lead to reinforcement

raphe system a system of neurons in the pons and medulla whose axons extend throughout much of the forebrain

rapid eye movement (REM) sleep stage of sleep characterized by rapid eye movements and dreaming (also called paradoxical sleep)

rCBF regional cerebral blood flow

reactive depression a depression that arises as a reaction to external events

reactive disorders disorders that originate as reactions to experiences

reception the absorption of physical energy

receptive field a set of receptors (such as visual receptors) that can affect the activity of a particular neuron

receptor neuron a cell that responds directly to light, sound, or other external stimuli

recessive gene a gene that exerts noticeable effects only in an individual who has two copies of the gene per cell

recombination a reassortment of genes during reproduction, sometimes leading to a characteristic not apparent in either parent

reference memory the memory of general principles and skills

reflex an automatic response to a stimulus

refractory period the time period following one action potential during which a neuron does not produce another action potential to the usually adequate stimulus

regional cerebral blood flow a method of estimating activity of different areas of the brain by dissolving radioactive xenon in the blood and measuring radioactivity from different brain areas

relative refractory period a period after an action potential during which the threshold for another action potential is elevated

releasing hormone a hormone from the hypothalamus that causes the anterior pituitary to release another hormone

remission relief from the symptoms of a disease

REM sleep rapid eye movement sleep

renin a hormone released by the kidney that leads to constriction of the blood vessels

repair and restoration theory of sleep the theory that the function of sleep is to allow recovery from the damage and exhaustion that occur during wakefulness

resection removal of a large portion of a structure in the body

reserpine a drug that causes depletion of norepinephrine, dopamine, and serotonin from their vesicles

resting potential   the electrical potential across a membrane when a neuron is at rest

reticular formation   a diffuse network of neurons in the medulla and higher brain areas, important for behavioral arousal

retina   the receptive area at the back surface of the eye, including the rods and cones

retinex theory   the theory that we perceive color through a combination of processes in the retina and in the cerebral cortex

retinoblastoma   a tumor of the glia cells in the retina

retrograde amnesia   loss of memory for events prior to some damage, such as the onset of a disease or a trauma

retrovirus   a virus made of RNA that makes a DNA copy of itself that can be incorporated into the chromosomes

rhinencephalon   a traditional term for certain structures of the forebrain that were once believed to be all active in olfactory perception; nearly synonymous with limbic system

rhombencephalon   the hindbrain

ribosomes   structures within cells where proteins are synthesized

Ritalin   trade name for methylphenidate, a stimulant drug sometimes used as a treatment for attention deficit disorder

RNA   ribonucleic acid, a chemical whose structure is determined by DNA and that in turn determines the structure of proteins

rod   one type of receptor found in the retina

Rolandic fissure   a deep groove in the cerebral cortex, also known as the central sulcus, which divides the frontal lobe from the parietal lobe

Ruffini ending   a receptor that responds to stretch of the skin

saccades or saccadic eye movement   a sudden movement of the eyes from one fixation point to another

SAD   seasonal affective disorder

sagittal plane   a plane through the body dividing left from right

salicylate or salicylic acid   aspirin

saltatory conduction   transmission of an impulse along a myelinated axon by jumping from one node to another

satiety   a feeling of fullness after a meal

schizophrenia   a mental illness characterized by deterioration and thought disorder or hallucinations or delusions

Schwann cell   a type of glia cell that forms myelin for axons in the peripheral nervous system

scintillating scotomata   areas of the retina in which one sees only sparks

sclerosing   hardening

SCN   suprachiasmatic nucleus

scopolamine   a drug that inhibits muscarinic acetylcholine synaptic transmission by competing with acetylcholine for receptor sites

scotoma (plural: scotomata)   an area of the retina in which one has impaired vision

scratch reflex   repetitive scratching induced by skin irritation

seasonal affective disorder (SAD)   depression that reoccurs every winter

season-of-birth effect   an increased probability of schizophrenia among people who were born during the winter months

second messenger   a chemical within a neuron, activated by a synaptic transmitter, that in turn initiates processes within the neuron

sedative   something that reduces activity and excitement

selective permeability   permitting certain chemicals but not others to cross a membrane

semicircular canals   three hair-lined canals oriented in three planes and sensitive to the direction of tilt of the head

semipermeable membrane   a membrane that permits only water and a few other molecules to cross

sensitive period in development   a time during early development when a chemical or experience has a long-lasting effect on later development

sensitization   an increase in response to stimuli because of previous exposure to one or more intense stimuli

sensory extinction   the tendency to respond first and more strongly to stimuli on the same side of the body as brain damage, as opposed to stimuli on the opposite side

sensory neglect   ignoring of stimuli on the side of the body opposite an area of brain damage

sensory neuron   a neuron that responds directly to a stimulus such as light, sound, or chemicals in the environment

separation distress   a disturbance felt after separation from one's mother or from other social contacts

septum   a limbic system structure located anterior and medial to the hippocampus

serial-lesion effect   the tendency for behavioral effects to be less after a series of small brain lesions than after a single lesion of the same total size

serotonin (5-HT)   a synaptic transmitter

serum   the liquid portion of the blood, free of cells

servomechanism   a mechanism that produces behaviors that are influenced by feedback from previous behaviors

set point   the level at which some variable, such as temperature, is generally maintained through a combination of physiological and behavioral activities

sex-limited gene   a gene whose effects are seen only in one sex, although members of both sexes may have the gene

sex-linked gene   a gene on either the X or the Y chromosome

sex role   social behaviors assumed by members of one sex or the other

sham-feeding   feeding that does not aid nutrition because the swallowed food is removed from the digestive system

sham lesion   a control procedure for an experiment, in which certain individuals go though all the procedures for producing a lesion except for the final passing of a current

sham rage   motor components of attack that are not directed against any target

short term memory   memory for an event that has just occurred

simple cell (of visual cortex)   a cell in the visual cortex with fixed excitatory and inhibitory regions of its receptive field

sine-wave grating   an alternation of light and dark over space following a sine wave function

sinistral   left-handed

skeletal muscle   the kind of muscle found in the limbs (also called striated muscle)

sleep apnea   a condition in which the individual has trouble breathing while sleeping

slow-wave sleep   stages of sleep with slow waves of synchronized brain activity

smooth muscle   the kind of muscle found in the internal organs

sodium amytal   *See* amytal

sodium-potassium pump   the process that transports sodium ions out of a cell while simultaneously transporting potassium ions in

soma   the cell body of a neuron

somatosensory cortex   the portion of the cerebral cortex that responds to touch and other body information

somatosensory system   all the touch sensations

somesthetic   somatosensory

somnambulism   sleepwalking

somnolence   sleepiness, drowsiness

spasm   sudden, violent, unpleasant involuntary contraction of muscles

spasticity   increased tension of muscles and increased resistance to stretching of them

spastic paralysis   lack of voluntary movements in part of the body due to interruption of fibers from the brain to the spinal cord

spatial summation   the summation of effects of activity from two or more synapses onto a single neuron

specific anosmia   an inability to smell a particular chemical

specific hunger   an increased preference for foods containing a specified vitamin, mineral, or other nutrient

sphenoidal   pertaining to the sphenoid bone at the base of the skull

spike   action potential

spinal cord   that part of the central nervous system found within the spinal column

spindle   *See* muscle spindle

spiroperidol   a drug that binds to dopamine receptors

splanchnic nerves   several nerves of the sympathetic nervous system

splenium   posterior part of the corpus callosum

spontaneous rate   the rate of action potentials produced by a neuron in the absence of synaptic input

sprouting   the branching of axons to fill synaptic spaces left vacant by the loss of other axons

state-dependent memory   memory that is better recalled under the same physiological conditions that were present during learning

status epilepticus   a series of repeated epileptic convulsions not separated by periods of normal consciousness

stereognosis   recognition of objects by the sense of touch

stereotaxic atlas   an atlas of the location of brain areas relative to external landmarks

stereotaxic (or stereotactic) instrument   a device for the precise placement of electrodes in the head

steroid hormones   hormones derived from cholestrol that exert their effects by attaching to the chromosomes and influencing expression of the genes

strabismus   a deviation of the eyes preventing binocular focus

striate cortex   the primary visual cortex, receiving its name from its striped appearance

striated muscle   the kind of muscle found in the limbs (also called skeletal muscle)

striatum   the caudate nucleus and putamen

stroke   an interruption of blood flow to part of the brain

strychnine   a drug that antagonizes synaptic activity of glycine

stupor partial unconsciousness or unresponsiveness

subacute between acute and chronic

subarachnoid space the space beneath the arachnoid membrane that surrounds the nervous system

subdural beneath the dura; a membrane that surrounds the nervous system

subfornical organ a brain structure adjoining the third ventricle

substance P a synaptic transmitter released by nerves that report pain

substantia nigra a midbrain area that gives rise to a dopamine-containing pathway

sulcus (plural: sulci) a groove in the surface of the brain

sulpiride drug that binds certain dopamine receptors; sometimes used as a treatment for schizophrenia

summation *See* spatial summation, temporal summation

superior colliculus a midbrain structure active in vision, visuomotor coordination, and other processes

superior olive a nucleus in the medulla, shaped somewhat like an olive, that receives input from both ears

superior temporal cortex a part of the temporal lobe of the cerebral cortex important for the visual perception of the movement of an object

supplementary motor cortex an area of the frontal lobe of the cerebral cortex active in the planning of movements and in integrating movements with perception

suprachiasmatic nucleus (SCN) a nucleus of the hypothalamus, located just above the optic chiasm; critical for control of circadian activity rhythms

SWS slow-wave sleep

Sydenham's chorea a condition producing rapid, jerky, involuntary movements

Sylvian fissure a large groove in the side of the cerebral cortex

sympathetic nervous system a system of nerves innervating the internal organs that prepare the body for vigorous activity

symptomatic resulting from a disease

synapse the point of communication between two neurons or between a neuron and a muscle

synaptic block cessation of firing of a postsynaptic cell due to an excess of synaptic transmitter at a synapse

synaptic cleft the space separating presynaptic from postsynaptic cell

synaptic transmitter a chemical released by a neuron at a synapse that affects the activity of a second cell

synchronized occurring at the same time

synchronized sleep sleep with a high prevalence of slow, large-amplitude EEG waves

syncope fainting; a sudden temporary loss of consciousness

synergistic effect a combined effect of two influences that is greater than the sum of the two influences acting separately

synesthesia a sensation of one type induced by stimulation of another type (for example, a hearing sensation induced by light)

synkinesis an unintentional movement accompanying a voluntary movement

tabes dorsalis the third stage of syphilis infection, causing psychotic symptoms

tachycardia excessively rapid heartbeat

tardive first occurring late in life

tardive dyskinesia tremors and other movement impairments that result from prolonged use of antischizophrenic drugs

taste buds structures on the tongue that contain taste receptors

tectum the roof of the midbrain

tegmentum the dorsal part of the midbrain

telencephalon the forebrain

template a model from which copies are made

temporal lobe one of the lobes of the cerebral cortex

temporal summation summation of effects of more than one synaptic input at different times

terminal button a swelling at the end of an axon from which synaptic transmitter is released

termination insomnia the tendency to awaken earlier than desired

testicular feminization feminine body development in a genetic male, caused by inability of testosterone to enter cells

testosterone a hormone released by the gonads, more in the male than in the female

thalamotomy a cutting away of parts of the thalamus

thalamus a structure in the center of the forebrain

theophylline a stimulant; acts by antagonizing the ability of phosphodiesterase to inactivate cyclic AMP

theta rhythm a rhythm of 4 to 7 cycles per second in subcortical brain activity

thiamine vitamin B_1, required for metabolism of glucose

thioridazine a phenothiazine derivative that produces antischizophrenic effects with less risk of tardive dyskinesia than many other drugs

Thorazine trade name for chlorpromazine, a drug commonly used in the treatment of schizophrenia and related conditions

thought disorder   an impairment in the use of abstractions or other thought processes

threshold   the degree of depolarization required for a neuron to produce an action potential

tonic   characterized by continuous tension

tract   a bundle of axons within the central nervous system

tranquilizers   drugs that decrease anxiety

transcutaneous electrical nerve stimulation   mild electrical stimulation applied to the skin to relieve pain

transduction   the transfer of energy from the absorbed physical stimulus to an electrochemical pattern in the neurons

transmitter   *See* synaptic transmitter

traveling wave   a wave in which the point of maximum displacement travels along the vibrating medium

tremor   involuntary trembling

TRH   thyrotropin releasing hormone, a hormone from the hypothalamus that causes the pituitary to release TSH, a hormone that stimulates the thyroid gland

triazolam   a short-acting benzodiazepine tranquilizer

trichromatic theory   the theory that we perceive color by the combination of activities from three types of receptors in the retina

tricyclic drugs   a group of drugs that block reuptake of norepinephrine, dopamine, and serotonin by the presynaptic neuron; often used for treatment of depression

trisomy 21   having three strands of chromosome 21 per cell, leading to Down's syndrome

tryptophan   an amino acid that serves as a precursor of serotonin

TSH   a hormone from the anterior pituitary gland that stimulates the thyroid gland

tubero-infundibular   a neural pathway connecting two parts of the hypothalamus, the medial preoptic area and the median eminence

Turner's syndrome   a genetic condition of anatomical females with an XO chromosome pattern

turnover   release and resynthesis of a transmitter

tympanic membrane   the eardrum

tyrosine   an amino acid that serves as the precursor to several synaptic transmitters

unipolar disorder   an affective condition including periods of depression but not mania

unit   a neuron or part of a neuron (something from which a single response can be recorded)

unmyelinated   lacking a myelin sheath

V2   the secondary visual area of the cerebral cortex (*See also* parastriate cortex)

vacuole   a small space or cavity

vagus nerve   the tenth cranial nerve, which sends branches to the stomach and several other internal organs

Valium   a benzodiazepine tranquilizer (chemical name: diazepam)

vascular   pertaining to the blood vessels

vasopressin   a posterior pituitary hormone that constricts blood vessels and increases water retention by the kidneys

ventral   toward the stomach side

ventricles   the four fluid-filled cavities in the brain

ventromedial hypothalamus (VMH)   one of the nuclei of the hypothalamus

vertebrates   all species with spinal cords

vertigo   a hallucination of moving or being moved

vesicle   a small enclosure within the presynaptic ending containing a high concentration of synaptic transmitter

vestibular organ   the organ in the inner ear that detects tilt of the head

vestibular sensation   the sense of orientation of the head with respect to gravity

visual cortex   the part of the cerebral cortex that receives the most direct input from the visual receptors

visual field   the part of the world that one sees

VMH   ventromedial hypothalamus

volley principle   the principle that a sound wave of a moderately high pitch may produce a volley of impulses by various fibers even if no individual fiber can produce impulses in synchrony with the sound waves

voltage-activated   a channel in a neural membrane that changes its openness to the passage of ions when the voltage across the membrane changes

Weigert stain   a stain that is absorbed by axon terminals and transported to the cell body; useful as a means of finding the cell bodies that gave rise to a given axon

Wernicke-Korsakoff syndrome   a neurological condition caused by thiamine deficiency, characterized by memory failure and other disorders (*See also* Korsakoff's syndrome)

Wernicke's area   an area of the temporal lobe in the human left cerebral cortex important for language comprehension

white matter   area of the nervous system consisting mostly of myelinated axons

Wilson's disease   a progressive degeneration of the basal ganglia of the brain

word-blindness   an inability to read words despite the ability to understand spoken language and the ability to see

word deafness   an inability to understand spoken language despite the abilities to read, to speak, and to hear

working memory   the memory of what one is doing, what one has just done, and what has just happened (compare with reference memory)

X chromosome   a chromosome of which female mammals have two and males have one

xenon   an inert gas

XO chromosome pattern   abnormal chromosome pattern found in certain infertile females

XXY chromosome pattern   abnormal chromosome pattern found in certain infertile males

Xylocaine   an anesthetic drug that acts by blocking the transport of sodium across the membrane

XYY chromosome pattern   abnormal chromosome pattern found in certain males

Y chromosome   a chromosome of which female mammals have none and males one

yohimbine   a drug that antagonizes alpha$_2$ adrenergic receptors, which are presynaptic receptors that inhibit the release of norepinephrine from the presynaptic cell

Young-Helmholtz theory   the theory that we perceive color by the combination of activities from three types of receptors in the retina

Zeitgeber (German for "time-giver")   a stimulus that resets an animal's circadian rhythm

References

Numbers in parentheses indicate the chapters in which a reference is cited.

Abraham, S.F., Baker, R.M., Blaine, E.H., Denton, D.A., & McKinley, M.J. (1975). Water drinking induced in sheep by angiotensin—A physiological effect? *Journal of Comparative and Physiological Psychology, 88,* 503–518. (10)

Abramowitz, E.S., Baker, A.H., & Fleischer, S.F. (1982). Onset of depressive psychiatric crises and the menstrual cycle. *American Journal of Psychiatry, 139,* 475–478. (15)

Abramson, L.Y., Seligman, M.E.P., & Teasdale, J.D. (1978). Learned helplessness in humans: Critique and reformulation. *Journal of Abnormal Psychology, 87,* 49–74. (15)

Adam, K. (1980). Sleep as a restorative process and a theory to explain why. *Progress in Brain Research, 53,* 289–305. (9)

Adams, D.B., Gold, A.R., & Burt, A.D. (1978). Rise in female-initiated sexual activity at ovulation and its suppression by oral contraceptives. *New England Journal of Medicine, 299,* 1145–1150. (11)

Adkins, E.K., & Adler, N.T. (1972). Hormonal control of behavior in the Japanese quail. *Journal of Comparative and Physiological Psychology, 81,* 27–36. (11)

Adkins, E.K., & Pniewski, E.E. (1978). Control of reproductive behavior by sex steroids in male quail. *Journal of Comparative and Physiological Psychology, 92,* 1169–1178. (11)

Aggleton, J.P., & Passingham, R.E. (1981). Syndrome produced by lesions of the amygdala in monkeys (*Macaca mulatta*). *Journal of Comparative and Physiological Psychology, 95,* 961–977. (12)

Aigner, T.G., & Mishkin, M. (1986). The effects of physostigmine and scopolamine on recognition memory in monkeys. *Behavioral and Neural Biology, 45,* 81–87. (13)

Akers, R.F., Lovinger, D.M., Colley, P.A., Linden, D.J., & Routtenberg, A. (1986). Translocation of protein kinase C activity may mediate hippocampal long-term potentiation. *Science, 231,* 587–589. (13)

Alberts, J.R. (1978). Huddling by rat pups: Group behavioral mechanisms of temperature regulation and energy conservation. *Journal of Comparative and Physiological Psychology, 92,* 231–245. (10)

Alexander, D., Ehrhardt, A.A., & Money, J. (1966). Defective figure drawing, geometric and human, in Turner's syndrome. *Journal of Nervous and Mental Disease, 142,* 161–167. (11)

Alexander, D., Walker, H.T., Jr., & Money, J. (1964). Studies in direction sense. *Archives of General Psychiatry, 10,* 337–339. (11)

Alkon, D.L. (1984). Calcium-mediated reduction of ionic currents: A biophysical memory trace. *Science, 226,* 1037–1045. (13)

Allebeck, P., & Wistedt, B. (1986). Mortality in schizophrenia. *Archives of General Psychiatry, 43,* 650–653. (16)

Allison, T., & Cicchetti, D.V. (1976). Sleep in mammals: Ecological and constitutional correlates. *Science, 194,* 732–734. (9)

Almli, C.R., Fisher, R.S., & Hill, D.L. (1979). Lateral hypothalamus destruction in infant rats produces consummatory deficits without sensory neglect or attenuated arousal. *Experimental Neurology, 66,* 146–157. (10)

Al-Rashid, R.A. (1971). Hypothalamic syndrome in acute childhood leukemia. *Clinical Pediatrics, 10,* 53–54. (10)

Altner, H. (1978). Physiology of taste. In R.F.Schmidt (Ed.), *Fundamentals of sensory physiology* (pp. 218–227). New York: Springer-Verlag. (6)

American Psychiatric Association. (1980). *Diagnostic and statistical manual of mental disorders* (3rd ed.) Washington, DC: American Psychiatric Association. (16)

Amoore, J.E. (1963). Stereochemical theory of olfaction. *Nature, 198,* 271–272. (6)

Amoore, J.E. (1967). Specific anosmia: A clue to the olfactory code. *Nature, 214,* 1095–1098. (6)

Amoore, J.E. (1977). Specific anosmia and the concept of primary odors. *Chemical Senses and Flavor, 2,* 267–281. (6)

Amsterdam, J.D., Winokur, A., Dyson, W., Herzog, S., Gonzalez, F., Rott, R., & Koprowski, H. (1985). Borna disease virus. *Archives of General Psychiatry, 42,* 1093–1096. (15)

Anders, J.J., Dorovini-Zis, K., & Brightman, M.W. (1980). Endothelial and astrocytic cell membranes in relation to the composition of cerebral extracellular fluid. In H.M. Eisenberg & R.L. Suddith (Eds.), *The cerebral microvasculature* (pp. 193–209). New York: Plenum. (2)

Andersen, R.A., Essick, G.K., & Siegel, R.M. (1985). Encoding of spatial location by posterior parietal neurons. *Science, 230,* 456–458. (4)

Anderson, W.J., & Altman, J. (1972). Retardation of cerebellar and motor development in rats by focal x-irradiation beginning at four days. *Physiology & Behavior, 8,* 57–67. (4)

Andreasen, N., Nasrallah, H.A., Dunn, V., Olson, S.C., Grove, W.M., Ehrhardt, J.C., Coffman, J.A., & Crossett, J.H.W. (1986). Structural abnormalities in the frontal system in schizophrenia. *Archives of General Psychiatry, 43,* 136–144. (16)

Andrews, G., Hall, W., Goldstein, G., Lapsley, H., Bartels, R., & Silove, D. (1985). The economic costs of schizophrenia. *Archives of General Psychiatry, 42,* 537–543. (16)

Anías, J., Holmgren, B., Urbá Holmgren, R., & Eguíbar, J.R. (1984). Circadian rhythm of yawning behavior. *Acta Neurobiologiae Experimentalis, 44,* 179–186. (9)

Anisman, H., & Zacharko, R.M. (1982). Depression: The predisposing influence of stress. The *Behavioral and Brain Sciences, 5,* 89–137. (15)

Antelman, S.M., Chiodo, L.A., & DeGiovanni, L.A. (1982). Antidepressants and dopamine autoreceptors: Implications for both a novel means of treating depression and understanding bipolar illness. *Advances in Biochemical Psychopharmacology, 31,* 121–132. (15)

Antin, J., Gibbs, J., Holt, J., Young, R.C., & Smith, G.P. (1975). Cholecystokinin elicits the complete behavioral sequence of satiety in rats. *Journal of Comparative and Physiological Psychology, 89,* 784–790. (10)

Antin, J., Gibbs, J., & Smith, G.P. (1978). Intestinal satiety requires pregastric food stimulation. *Physiology & Behavior, 20,* 67–70. (10)

Aram, D.M., & Ekelman, B.L. (1986). Spoken syntax in children with acquired unilateral hemispheric lesions. *Brain and Language, 27,* 75–100. (5)

Arana, G.W., Baldessarini, R.J., & Ornsteen, M. (1985). The dexamethasone suppression test for diagnosis and prognosis in psychiatry. *Archives of General Psychiatry, 42,* 1193–1204. (15)

Arboleda, C., & Holzman, P.S. (1985). Thought disorder in children at risk for psychosis. *Archives of General Psychiatry, 42,* 1004–1013. (16)

Arkin, A.M., Toth, M.F., Baker, J., & Hastey, J.M. (1970). The frequency of sleep talking in the laboratory among chronic sleep talkers and good dream recallers. *Journal of Nervous and Mental Disease, 151,* 369–374. (9)

Arnsten, A.F.T., & Goldman-Rakic, P.S. (1985a). Alpha-drenergic mechanisms in prefrontal cortex associated with cognitive decline in aged nonhuman primates. *Science, 230,* 1273–1276. (13)

Arnsten, A.F.T., & Goldman-Rakic, P.S. (1985b). Catecholamines and cognitive decline in aged nonhuman primates. *Annals of the New York Academy of Sciences, 444,* 218–234. (13)

Aronson, L.R., & Cooper, M.L. (1979). Amygdaloid hypersexuality in male cats re-examined. *Physiology & Behavior, 22,* 257–265. (12)

Arvidson, K., & Friberg, U. (1980). Human taste: Response and taste bud number in fungiform papillae. *Science, 209,* 807–808. (6)

Asanuma, H. (1981). The pyramidal tract. In V.B. Brooks (Ed.), *Handbook of physiology: Section 1: The nervous system, volume II. Motor control, part 1* (pp. 703–733). Bethesda, MD: American Physiological Society. (8)

Åsberg, M., Thorén, P., Träskman, L., Bertilsson, L., & Ringberger, V. (1976). "Serotonin depression"—a biochemical subgroup within the affective disorders? *Science, 191,* 478–480. (15)

Aschoff, J., Gerecke, U., & Wever, R. (1967). Desynchronization of human circadian rhythms. *Japanese Journal of Physiology, 17,* 450–457. (9)

Aschoff, J., & Wever, R. (1976). Human circadian rhythms: A multioscillatory system. *Federation Proceedings, 35,* 2326–2332. (9)

Aserinsky, E., & Kleitman, N. (1955). Two types of ocular motility occurring in sleep. *Journal of Applied Physiology, 8,* 1–10. (9)

Ashe, J.H., & Nachman, M. (1980). Neuronal mechanisms in taste aversion learning. *Progress in Psychobiology and Physiological Psychology, 9,* 233–262. (13)

Astic, L., Sastre, J.-P., & Brandon, A.-M. (1973). Étude polygraphique des etats de vigilance chez le foetus de cobaye. *Physiology & Behavior, 11,* 647–654. (9)

Attardi, D.G., & Sperry, R.W. (1963). Preferential selection of central pathways by degenerating optic fibers. *Experimental Neurology, 7,* 46–64. (5)

August, G.J., & Lockhart, L.H. (1984). Familial autism and the fragile-X chromosome. *Journal of Autism and Developmental Disorders, 14,* 197–204. (16)

Axelrod, J., & Reisine, T.D. (1984). Stress hormones: Their interaction and regulation. *Science, 224,* 452–459. (12)

Babich, F.R., Jacobson, A.L., Bubash, S., & Jacobson, A. (1965). Transfer of a response to naive rats by injection of ribonucleic acid extracted from trained rats. *Science, 149,* 656–657. (13)

Bachevalier, J., & Mishkin, M. (1984). An early and a late developing system for learning and retention in infant monkeys. *Behavioral Neuroscience, 98,* 770–778. (13)

Bachevalier, J., & Mishkin, M. (1986). Visual recognition impairment follows ventromedial but not dorsolateral prefrontal lesions in monkeys. *Behavioral Brain Research, 20,* 249–261. (13)

Backlund, E.-O., Granberg, P.-O., Hamberger, B., Sedvall, G., Seiger, A., & Olson, L. (1985). Transplantation of adrenal medullary tissue to striatum in Parkinsonism. In A. Björklund & U. Stenevi (Eds.), *Neural grafting in the mammalian CNS* (pp. 551–556). Amsterdam: Elsevier. (14)

Bacopoulos, N.C., Spokes, E.G., Bird, E.D., & Roth, R.H. (1979). Antipsychotic drug action in schizophrenic patients: Effect on cortical dopamine metabolism after long-term treatment. *Science, 205,* 1405–1407. (16)

Bahill, A.T., & LaRitz, T. (1984). Why can't batters keep their eyes on the ball? *American Scientist, 72,* 249–253. (8)

Bailey, C.H., & Chen, M. (1983). Morphological basis of long-term habituation and sensitization in *Aplysia. Science, 220,* 91–93. (13)

Baker, H.F., Ridley, R.M., Crow, T.J., Bloxham, C.A., Parry, R.P., & Tyrrell, D.A.J. (1983). An investigation of the effects of intracerebral injection in the marmoset of cytopathic cerebrospinal fluid from patients with schizophrenia or neurological disease. *Psychological Medicine, 13,* 499–511. (16)

Balagura, S., & Harrell, L.E. (1974). Lateral hypothalamic syndrome: Its modification by obesity and leanness. *Physiology & Behavior, 13,* 345–347. (14)

Balasubramaniam, V., & Kanaka, T.S. (1976). Hypothalamotomy in the management of aggressive behavior. In T.P. Morley (Ed.), *Current controversies in neurosurgery* (pp. 768–777). Philadelphia: Saunders. (12)

Ballard, P.A., Tetrud, J.W., & Langston, J.W. (1985). Permanent human parkinsonism due to 1-methyl-4phenyl-1,2,3,6-tetrahydropyridine (MPTP). *Neurology, 35,* 949–956. (8)

Banker, G.A. (1980). Trophic interactions between astroglial cells and hippocampal neurons in culture. *Science, 209,* 809–810. (2)

Banks, M.S., Aslin, R.N., & Letson, R.D. (1975). Sensitive period for the development of human binocular vision. *Science, 190,* 675–677. (7)

Barbaccia, M.L., Costa, E., Ferrero, P., Guidotti, A., Roy, A., Sunderland, T., Pickar, D., Paul, S.M., & Goodwin, F.K. (1986). Diazepam-binding inhibitor. *Archives of General Psychiatry, 43,* 1143–1147. (12)

Barbizet, J. (1970). *Human memory and its pathology.* San Francisco: W.H. Freeman. (13)

Bard, P. (1929). The central representation of the sympathetic system. *Archives of Neurology and Psychiatry, 22,* 230–246. (12)

Bard, P. (1934). On emotional expression after decortication with some remarks on certain theoretical views. *Psychological Review, 41*, 309–329. (12)

Bardach, J.E., & Villars, T. (1974). The chemical senses of fishes. In P.T. Grant & A.M. Mackie (Eds.), *Chemoreception in marine organisms* (pp. 49–104). New York: Academic. (6)

Bardin, C.W., & Catterall, J.F. (1981). Testosterone: A major determinant of extragenital sexual dimorphism. *Science, 211*, 1285–1294. (11)

Barnes, C.A., & McNaughton, B.L. (1985). An age comparison of the rates of acquisition and forgetting of spatial information in relation to long-term enhancement of hippocampal synapses. *Behavioral Neuroscience, 99*, 1040–1048. (13)

Baron, M., Gruen, R., Kane, J.M., & Asnis, L. (1985). Modern research criteria and the genetics of schizophrenia. *American Journal of Psychiatry, 142*, 697–701. (16)

Bartoshuk, L.M., Gentile, R.L., Moskowitz, H.R., & Meiselman, H.L. (1974). Sweet taste induced by miracle fruit (*Synsephalum dulcificum*). *Physiology & Behavior, 12*, 449–456. (6)

Bartoshuk, L.M., Lee, C.-H., & Scarpellino, R. (1972). Sweet taste of water induced by artichoke (*Cynara scolymus*). *Science, 178*, 988–990. (6)

Bartus, R.T., Dean, R.L. III, Beer, B., & Lippa, A.S. (1982). The cholinergic hypothesis of geriatric memory dysfunction. *Science, 217*, 408–417. (13)

Bartus, R.T., Dean, R.L., Goas, J.A., & Lippa, A.S. (1980). Age-related changes in passive avoidance retention: Modulation with dietary choline. *Science, 209*, 301–303. (13)

Bartus, R.T., Dean, R.L., Pontecorvo, M.J., & Flicker, C. (1985). The cholinergic hypothesis: A historical overview, current perspective, and future directions. *Annals of the New York Academy of Sciences, 444*, 332–358. (13)

Batini, C., Magni, F., Palestini, M., Rossi, G.F., & Zanchetti, A. (1959). Neural mechanisms underlying the enduring EEG and behavioral activation in the midpontine pretrigeminal cat. *Archives Italiennes de Biologie, 97*, 13–25. (9)

Batini, C., Moruzzi, G., Palestini, M., Rossi, G.F., & Zanchetti, A. (1958). Persistent patterns of wakefulness in the pretrigeminal midpontine preparation. *Science, 128*, 30–32. (9)

Batini, C., Moruzzi, G., Palestini, M., Rossi, G.F., & Zanchetti, A. (1959). Effects of complete pontine transections on the sleep-wakefulness rhythm: The midpontine pretrigeminal preparation. *Archives Italiennes de Biologie, 97*, 1–12. (9)

Batini, C., Palestini, M., Rossi, G.F., & Zanchetti, A. (1959). EEG activation patterns in the midpontine pretrigeminal cat following sensory deafferentation. *Archives Italiennes de Biologie, 97*, 26–32. (9)

Baudry, M., & Lynch, G. (1980). Hypothesis regarding the cellular mechanisms responsible for long-term synaptic potentiation in the hippocampus. *Experimental Neurology, 68*, 202–204. (13)

Baxter, L.R., Phelps, M.E., Mazziotta, J.C., Schwartz, J.M., Gerner, R.H., Selin, C.E., & Sumida, R.M. (1985). Cerebral metabolic rates for glucose in mood disorders. *Archives of General Psychiatry, 42*, 441–447. (15)

Bayer, S.A. (1985). Neuron production in the hippocampus and olfactory bulb of the adult rat brain: Addition or replacement? *Annals of the New York Academy of Sciences, 457*, 163–172. (2)

Beach, F.A. (1948). *Hormones and behavior.* New York: Paul B. Hoeber. (11)

Beach, F.A. (1967). Cerebral and hormonal control of reflexive mechanisms involved in copulatory behavior. *Physiological Reviews, 47*, 289–316. (11)

Beach, F.A. (1970). Hormonal effects on socio-sexual behavior in dogs. In M. Gibian & E.J. Plotz (Eds.), *Mammalian reproduction* (pp. 437–466). Berlin: Springer-Verlag. (11)

Beach, F.A. (1974a). Effects of gonadal hormones on urinary behavior in dogs. *Physiology & Behavior, 12*, 1005–1013. (11)

Beach, F.A. (l974b). Autobiography. In G.Lindzey (Ed.), *A history of psychology in autobiography*, Vol. 6 (pp. 31–58). Englewood Cliffs, N.J.: Prentice-Hall. (11)

Beach, F.A., Buehler, M.G., & Dunbar, I.F. (1982). Competitive behavior in male, female, and pseudohermaphroditic female dogs. *Journal of Comparative and Physiological Psychology, 96*, 855–874. (11)

Beal, M.F., Kowall, N.W., Ellison, D.W., Mazurek, M.F., Swartz, K.J., & Martin, J.B. (1986). Replication of the neurochemical characteristics of Huntington's disease by quinolinic acid. *Nature, 321*, 168–171. (8)

Bear, D.M. & Fedio, P. (1977). Quantitative analysis of interictal behavior in temporal lobe epilepsy. *Archives of Neurology, 34*, 454–467. (12)

Beatty, W.W., Butters, N., & Janowsky, D.S. (1986). Patterns of memory failure after scopolamine treatment: Implications for cholinergic hypotheses of dementia. *Behavioral and Neural Biology, 45*, 196–211. (13)

Bechara, A., & van der Kooy, D. (1985). Opposite motivational effects of endogenous opioids in brain and periphery. *Nature, 314*, 533–534. (6)

Begleiter, H., Porjesz, B., Bihari, B., & Kissin, B. (1984). Event-related brain potentials in boys at risk for alcoholism. *Science, 225*, 1493–1496. (10)

Behar, D., Rapoport, J.L., Berg, C.J., Denckla, M.B., Mann, L., Cox, C., Fedio, P., Zahn, T., & Wolfman, M.G. (1984). Computerized tomography and neuropsychological test measures in adolescents with obsessive-compulsive disorder. *American Journal of Psychiatry, 141*, 363–369. (12)

Békésy—See von Békésy

Bellugi, U., Poizner, H., & Klima, E.S. (1983). Brain organization for language: Clues from sign aphasia. *Human Neurobiology, 2*, 155–170. (5)

Benes, F.M., Davidson, J., & Bird, E.D. (1986). Quantitative cytoarchitectural studies of the cerebral cortex of schizophrenics. *Archives of General Psychiatry, 43*, 31–35. (16)

Bennett, E.L., Rosenzweig, M.R., & Flood, J.F. (1979). Role of neurotransmitters and protein synthesis in short- and long-term memory. In J. Obiols, C. Ballús, E. González Monclús, & J.Pujol (Eds.), *Biological Psychiatry Today* (pp. 211–219). Amsterdam: Elsevier/North Holland Biomedical Press. (13)

Berkowitz, L. (1983). Aversively stimulated aggression: Some parallels and differences in research with animals and humans. *American Psychologist, 38*, 1135–1144. (12)

Berlin, F.S., & Meinecke, C.F. (1981). Treatment of sex offenders with antiandrogenic medication: Conceptualization, review of treatment modalities, and preliminary findings. *American Journal of Psychiatry, 138,* 601–607. (11)

Berman, J.S., Miller, R.C., & Massman, P.J. (1985). Cognitive therapy versus systematic desensitization: Is one treatment superior? *Psychological Bulletin, 97,* 451–461. (15)

Berman, K.F., Zec, R.F., & Weinberger, D.R. (1986). Physiologic dysfunction of dorsolateral prefrontal cortex in schizophernia: II. Role of neuroleptic treatment, attention, and mental effort. *Archives of General Psychiatry, 43,* 126–135. (16)

Bernstein, J.J., & Bernstein, M.E. (1967). Effect of glialependymal scar and Teflon arrest on the regenerative capacity of goldfish spinal cord. *Experimental Neurology, 19,* 25–32. (14)

Bernstein, J.J., & Bernstein, M.E. (1969). Ultrastructure of normal regeneration and loss of regenerative capacity following Teflon blockage in goldfish spinal cord. *Experimental Neurology, 24,* 538–557. (14)

Bernstein, J.J., & Gelderd, J.B. (1970). Regeneration of the long spinal tracts in the goldfish. *Brain Research, 20,* 33–38. (14)

Bickford, R.G., Dodge, H.W., Jr., & Uihlein, A. (1960). Electrographic and behavioral effects related to depth stimulation in human patients. In E.R. Ramey & D.S. O'Doherty (Eds.), *Electrical stimulation in the unanesthetized brain* (pp. 248–261). New York: P.B.Hoeber. (1)

Birch, G.G., & Mylvaganam, A.R. (1976). Evidence for the proximity of sweet and bitter receptor sites. *Nature, 260,* 632–634. (6)

Bishop, G.H. (1959). The relation between nerve fiber size and sensory modality: Phylogenetic implications of the afferent innervation of cortex. *Journal of Nervous and Mental Disease, 128,* 89–114. (4)

Bisiach, E., & Luzzatti, C. (1978). Unilateral neglect of representational space. *Cortex, 14,* 129–133. (4)

Björklund, A., Stenevi, U., Dunnett, S.B., & Gage, F.H. (1982). Cross-species neural grafting in a rat model of Parkinson's disease. *Nature, 298,* 652–654. (14)

Black, I.B., Adler, J.E., Dreyfus, C.F., Jonakait, G.M., Katz, D.M., LaGamma, E.F., & Markey, K.M. (1984). Neurotransmitter plasticity at the molecular level. *Science, 225,* 1266–1270. (2)

Blakemore, C. (1974). Developmental factors in the formation of feature extracting neurons. In F.O. Schmitt & F.G. Worden (Eds.), *The neurosciences: Third study program* (pp. 105–113). Cambridge: MIT press. (7)

Blanchard, E.B., & Young, L.D. (1973). Self-control of cardiac functioning: A promise as yet unfulfilled. *Psychological Bulletin, 79,* 145–163. (12)

Blanchard, E.B., & Young, L.D. (1974). Clinical applications of biofeedback training: A review of evidence. *Archives of General Psychiatry, 30,* 573–589. (12)

Blass, E.M. (1976). (Ed.), *The psychobiology of Curt Richter.* Baltimore: York Press. (12)

Blass, E.M., & Epstein, A.N. (1971). A lateral preoptic osmosensitive zone for thirst in the rat. *Journal of Comparative and Physiological Psychology, 76,* 378–394. (10)

Blass, E.M., & Hall, W.G. (1976). Drinking termination: Interactions among hydrational orogastric, and behavioral controls in rats. *Psychological Review, 83,* 356–374. (10)

Blass, E.M., & Teicher, H.M. (1980). Suckling. *Science, 210,* 15–22. (10)

Bleuler, E. (1950). *Dementia praecox; or the group of schizophrenias.* New York: International Universities Press. Translation from the German edition published in 1911. (16)

Bliss, J., edited by D.J. Cohen & D.X. Freedman. (1980). Sensory experiences of Gilles de la Tourette syndrome. *Archives of General Psychiatry, 37,* 1343–1347. (3)

Blumstein, S.E., Katz, B., Goodglass, H., Shrier, R., & Dworetsky, B. (1985). The effects of slowed speech on auditory comprehension in aphasia. *Brain and Language, 24,* 246–265. (5)

Boder, E. (1973). Developmental dyslexia: A diagnostic approach based on three atypical reading-spelling patterns. *Developmental Medicine and Child Neurology, 15,* 663–687. (5)

Bogardus, C., Lillioja, S., Ravussin, E., Abbott, W., Zawadzki, J.K., Young, A., Knowler, W.C., Jacobowitz, R., & Moll, P.P. (1986). Familial dependence of the resting metabolic rate. *New England Journal of Medicine, 315,* 96–100. (10)

Bogerts, B., Meertz, E., & Schönfeldt-Bausch, R. (1985). Basal ganglia and limbic system pathology in schizophrenia. *Archives of General Psychiatry, 42,* 784–791. (16)

Boklage, C.E. (1977). Schizophrenia, brain asymmetry development, and twinning: Cellular relationship with etiological and possibly prognostic implications. *Biological Psychiatry, 12,* 19–35. (16)

Borbély, A.A. (1982). Circadian and sleep-dependent processes in sleep regulation. In J. Aschoff, S. Daan, & G.A. Groos (Eds.), *Vertebrate circadian rhythms* (pp. 237–242). Berlin: Springer-Verlag. (9)

Borod, J.C., Koff, E., Perlman Lorch, M., & Nicholas, M. (1986). The expression and perception of facial emotion in brain-damaged patients. *Neuropsychologia, 24,* 169–180. (5)

Bowman, M.B., & Lewis, M.S. (1982). The copper hypothesis of schizophrenia: A review. *Neuroscience & Biobehavioral Reviews, 6,* 321–328. (16)

Bradbury, M. (1979). Why a blood-brain barrier? *Trends in Neurosciences, 2,* 36–38. (2)

Bradbury, T.N., & Miller, G.A. (1985). Season of birth in schizophrenia: A review of evidence, methodology, and etiology. *Psychological Bulletin, 98,* 569–594. (16)

Brady, J.V., Porter, R.W., Conrad, D.G., & Mason, J.W. (1958). Avoidance behavior and the development of gastroduodenal ulcers. *Journal of the Experimental Analysis of Behavior, 1,* 69–72. (12)

Brain, P.F. (1979). Steroidal influences on aggressiveness. In J. Obiols, C. Ballús, E. González Monclús, & J. Pujol (Eds.), *Biological Psychiatry Today* (pp. 1204–1208). Amsterdam: Elsevier/North Holland Biomedical Press. (11)

Brauman, H., & Gregoire, F. (1979). Hormonal abnormalities in anorexia nervosa (AN). In J. Obiols, C. Ballús, E. González Monclús, & J. Pujol (Eds.), *Biological Psychiatry Today* (pp. 602–608). Amsterdam: Elsevier/North Holland Biomedical Press. (10)

Braun, J.J. (1975). Neocortex and feeding behavior in the rat. *Journal of Comparative and Physiological Psychology, 89,* 507–522. (14)

Braus, H. (1960). *Anatomie des Menschen, 3.Band: Periphere Leistungsbahnen II. Centrales Nervensystem, Sinnesorgane.* 2.Auflage. Berlin: Springer-Verlag. (4)

Bregman, B.S., & Goldberger, M.E. (1982). Anatomical plasticity and sparing of function after spinal cord damage in neonatal cats. *Science, 217,* 553–555. (14)

Breslau, N., & Davis, G.C. (1986). Chronic stress and major depression. *Archives of General Psychiatry, 43,* 309–314. (15)

Bridgeman, B., & Staggs, D. (1982). Plasticity in human blindsight. *Vision Research, 22,* 1199–1203. (7)

Bridges, R.S. (1975). Long-term effects of pregnancy and parturition upon maternal responsiveness in the rat. *Physiology & Behavior, 14,* 245–249. (11)

Bridges, R.S., DiBiase, R., Loundes, D.D., & Doherty, P.C. (1985). Prolactin stimulation of maternal behavior in female rats. *Science, 227,* 782–784. (11)

Brierley, J.B. (1977). The neuropathology of amnesic states. In C.W.M. Whitty & O.L. Zangwill (Eds.), *Amnesia,* 2nd ed. (pp. 199–223). New York: Appleton-Century-Crofts. (13)

Broderick, P.A., Bridger, W.H. (1984). A comparative study of the effect of L-tryptophan and its acetylated derivative N-acetyl-L-tryptophan on rat muricidal behavior. *Biological Psychiatry, 19,* 89–94. (12)

Bronson, F.H. (1974). Pheromonal influences on reproductive activities in rodents. In M.C. Birch (Ed.), *Pheromones* (pp. 344–365). Amsterdam: North Holland Publishing Co. (6)

Brooks, D.C., & Bizzi, E. (1963). Brain stem electrical activity during deep sleep. *Archives Italiennes de Biologie, 101,* 648–665. (9)

Brooks, V.B. (1984). Cerebellar functions in motor control. *Human Neurobiology, 2,* 251–260. (8)

Brown, G.L., Ebert, M.H., Goyer, P.F., Jimerson, D.C., Klein, W.J., Bunney, W.E., & Goodwin, F.K. (1982). Aggression, suicide, and serotonin: Relationships of CSF amine metabolites. *American Journal of Psychiatry, 139,* 741–746. (12)

Brown, G.L., Goodwin, F.K., Ballenger, J.C., Goyer, P.F., & Major, L.F. (1979). Aggression in humans correlates with cerebrospinal fluid amine metabolites. *Psychiatry Research, 1,* 131–139. (12)

Brown, J.W. (1972). *Aphasia, apraxia, and agnosia.* Springfield, IL: Charles C Thomas. (8)

Brown, P., Salazar, A.M., Gibbs, C.J., Jr., & Gajdusek, D.C. (1982). Alzheimer's disease and transmissible virus dementia (Creutzfeldt-Jakob disease). *Annals of the New York Academy of Sciences, 396,* 131–143. (13)

Brown, R., Colter, N., Corsellis, N., Crow, T.J., Frith, C., Jagoe, R., Johnstone, E.C., & Marsh, L. (1986). Postmortem evidence of structural brain changes in schizophrenia. *Archives of General Psychiatry, 43,* 36–42. (16)

Brown, R.E. (1986). Paternal behavior in the male Long-Evans rat (*Rattus norvegicus*). *Journal of Comparative Psychology, 100,* 162–172. (11)

Bruce, C., Desimone, R., & Gross, C.G. (1981). Visual properties of neurons in a polysensory area in superior temporal sulcus of the macaque. *Journal of Neurophysiology, 46,* 369–384. (7)

Brügger, M. (1943). Fresstrieb als hypothalamisches Symptom. *Helvetica Physiologica et Pharmacologica Acta, 1,* 183–198. (10)

Bruun, R.D. (1984). Gilles de la Tourette's syndrome: An overview of clinical experience. *Journal of the American Academy of Child Psychiatry, 23,* 126–133. (3)

Bryan, A.L. (1963). The essential basis for human culture. *Current Anthropology, 4,* 297–306. (5)

Budka, H. (1986). Multinucleated giant cells in brain: A hallmark of the acquired immune deficiency syndrome (AIDS). *Acta Neuropathologica, 69,* 253–258. (16)

Buerger, A.A., & Fennessy, A. (1971). Long-term alteration of leg position due to shock avoidance by spinal rats. *Experimental Neurology, 30,* 195–211. (13)

Buell, S.J., & Coleman, P.D. (1981). Quantitative evidence for selective dendritic growth in normal human aging but not in senile dementia. *Brain Research, 214,* 23–41. (2)

Buggy, J., Fisher, A.E., Hoffman, W.E., Johnson, A.K., & Phillips, M.I. (1975). Ventricular obstruction: Effect on drinking induced by intracranial injection of angiotensin. *Science, 190,* 72–74. (10)

Buisseret, P., & Imbert, M. (1976). Visual cortical cells: Their developmental properties in normal and dark reared kittens. *Journal of Physiology, 255,* 511–525. (7)

Bullock, T.H. (1979). Evolving concepts of local integrative operations in neurons. In F.O. Schmitt & F.G. Worden (Eds.), *The Neurosciences: Fourth study program* (pp. 43–49). Cambridge, MA: MIT. (2)

Bunney, W.E., Jr., Murphy, D.L., Goodwin, F.K., & Borge, G.F. (1972). The "switch process" in manic-depressive illness. *Archives of General Psychiatry, 27,* 295–302. (15)

Calford, M.B., Graydon, M.L., Huerta, M.F., Kaas, J.H., & Pettigrew, J.D. (1985). A variant of the mammalian somatotopic map in a bat. *Nature, 313,* 477–479. (4)

Calne, D.B., Langston, J.W., Martin, W.R.W., Stoessl, A.J., Ruth, T.J., Adam, M.J., Pate, B.D., & Schulzer, M. (1985). Positron emission tomography after MPTP: Observations relating to the cause of Parkinson's disease. *Nature, 317,* 246–248. (8)

Camel, J.E., Withers, G.S., & Greenough, W.T. (1986). Persistence of visual cortex dendritic alterations induced by postweaning exposure to a "superenriched" environment in rats. *Behavioral Neuroscience, 100,* 810–813. (2)

Campbell, S.S., & Tobler, I. (1984). Animal sleep: A review of sleep duration across phylogeny. *Neuroscience & Biobehavioral Reviews, 8,* 269–300. (9)

Campion, J., Latto, R., & Smith, Y.M. (1983). Is blindsight an effect of scattered light, spared cortex, and near-threshold vision? *The Behavioral and Brain Sciences, 6,* 423–486. (7)

Cannon, W.B. (1927). The James-Lange theory of emotion. *American Journal of Psychology, 39,* 106–124. (12)

Cannon, W.B. (1929). Organization for physiological homeostasis. *Physiological Reviews, 9,* 399–431. (10)

Cannon, W.B. (1942). "Voodoo" death. *American Anthropologist, 44,* 169–181. (12)

Cannon, W.B. (1945). *The way of an investigator.* New York: Norton. (10)

Caplan, P.J., & Kinsbourne, M. (1976). Baby drops the rattle: Asymmetry of duration of grasp by infants. *Child Development, 47,* 532–534. (5)

Caporael, L.R. (1976). Ergotism: the Satan loosed in Salem? *Science, 192,* 21–26. (3)

Cappannari, S.C., Rau, B., Abram, W.S., & Buchanan, D.C. (1975). Voodoo in the general hospital. *Journal of the American Medical Association, 232,* 938–940. (12)

Capranica, R.R., & Frishkopf, L.S. (1966). Responses of auditory units in the medulla of the cricket frog. *Journal of the Acoustical Society of America, 40,* 1263. (6)

Capranica, R.R., Frishkopf, L.S., & Nevo, E. (1973). Encoding of geographic dialects in the auditory system of the cricket frog. *Science, 182,* 1272–1275. (6)

Carey, W.B., & McDevitt, S.C. (1980). Minimal brain dysfunction and hyperkinesis: A clinical viewpoint. *American Journal of Diseases of Children, 134,* 926–929. (15)

Carpenter, G.A., & Grossberg, S. (1984). A neural theory of circadian rhythms: Aschoff's rule in diurnal and nocturnal mammals. *American Journal of Physiology, 247,* R1067-R1082. (9)

Carroll, P.T., & Aspry, J.-A.M. (1980). Subcellular origin of cholinergic transmitter release from mouse brain. *Science, 210,* 641–642. (3)

Casagrande, V.A., Harting, J.K., Hall, W.C., Diamond, I.T., & Martin, G.F. (1972). Superior colliculus of the tree shrew: A structural and functional division into superficial and deep layers. *Science, 177,* 444–447. (7)

Castellucci, V.F., & Kandel, E.R. (1974). A quantal analysis of the synaptic depression underlying habituation of the gill-withdrawal reflex in *Aplysia. Proceedings of the National Academy of Sciences, U.S.A., 71,* 5004–5008. (13)

Castellucci, V., Pinsker, H., Kupfermann, I., & Kandel, E. (1970). Neuronal mechanisms of habituation and dishabituation of the gill-withdrawal reflex in *Aplysia. Science, 167,* 1745–1748. (13)

Catterall, W. A. (1984). The molecular basis of neuronal excitability. *Science, 223,* 653–661. (2)

Cerletti, U. & Bini, L. (1938). L'Elettroshock. *Archivio Generale di Neurologia e Psichiatria e Psicoanalisi, 19,* 266–268. (15)

Cespuglio, R., Laurent, J.P., & Jouvet, M. (1975). Étude des relations entre l'activité ponto-géniculo-occipitale (PGO) et la motricité oculaire chez le chat sous reserpine. *Brain Research, 83,* 319–335. (9)

Chandra, V., Bharucha, N.E., & Schoenberg, B.S. (1984). Mortality data for the US for deaths due to and related to twenty neurologic diseases. *Neuroepidemiology, 3,* 149–168. (8)

Changeux, J.-P., Devillers-Thiéry, A., & Chemouilli, P. (1984). Acetylcholine receptor: An allosteric protein. *Science, 225,* 1335–1345. (3)

Charney, D.S., & Heninger, G.R. (1986). Abnormal regulation of noradrenergic function in panic disorder. *Archives of General Psychiatry, 43,* 1042–1054. (12)

Charney, D.S., Heninger, G.R., & Breier, A. (1984). Noradrenergic function in panic anxiety. *Archives of General Psychiatry, 41,* 751–763. (12)

Chase, M.H. (1983). Synaptic mechanisms and circuitry involved in motoneuron control during sleep. *International Review of Neurobiology, 24,* 213–258. (9)

Chase, T.N., Wexler, N.S., & Barbeau, A. (1979). *Advances in neurology, vol. 23: Huntington's disease.* New York: Raven. (8)

Chiodo, L.A., & Antelman, S.M. (1980). Electroconvulsive shock: Progressive dopamine autoreceptor subsensitivity independent of repeated treatment. *Science, 210,* 799–801. (15)

Chouinard, G., & Jones, B.D. (1980). Neuroleptic-induced supersensitivity psychosis: Clinical and pharmacological characteristics. *American Journal of Psychiatry, 137,* 16–21. (16)

Chugani, H.T., & Phelps, M.E. (1986). Maturational changes in cerebral function in infants determined by 1DG positron emission tomography. *Science, 231,* 840–843. (4)

Chute, D.L. (1980). Phosphodiesterase inhibition and memory facilitation. *Clinical Neuropsychology, 2,* 72–74. (13)

Chute, D.L., Villiger, J.W., & Kirton, N.F. (1981). Testing cyclic AMP mediation of memory: Reversal of alpha-methyl-para-tyrosine-induced amnesia. *Psychopharmacology, 74,* 129–131. (13)

Cirignotta, F., Todesco, C.V., & Lugaresi, E. (1980). Temporal lobe epilepsy with ecstatic seizures (so-called Dostoevsky epilepsy). *Epilepsia, 21,* 705–710. (12)

Clemens, L.G., Gladue, B.A., & Coniglio, L.P. (1978). Prenatal endogenous androgenic influences on masculine sexual behavior and genital morphology in male and female rats. *Hormones and Behavior, 10,* 40–53. (11)

Cohen, N.J., Eichenbaum, H., Deacedo, B.S., & Corkin, S. (1985). Different memory systems underlying acquisition of procedural and declarative knowledge. *Annals of the New York Academy of Sciences, 444,* 54–71. (13)

Coile, D.C., & Miller, N.E. (1984). How radical animal activists try to mislead humane people. *American Psychologist, 39,* 700–701. (1)

Comings, D.E., & Comings, B.G. (1984). Tourette's syndrome and attention deficit disorder with hyperactivity: Are they genetically related? *Journal of the American Academy of Child Psychiatry, 23,* 138–146. (3)

Conte, H.R., Plutchik, R., Wild, K.V., & Karasu, T.B. (1986). Combined psychotherapy and pharmacotherapy for depression. *Archives of General Psychiatry, 43,* 471–479. (15)

Coons, E.E., Levak, M., & Miller, N.E. (1965). Lateral hypothalamus: Learning of food-seeking response motivated by electrical stimulation. *Science, 150,* 1320–1321. (1)

Coren, S., & Porac, C. (1977). Fifty centuries of right-handedness: The historical record. *Science, 198,* 631–632. (5)

Corkin, S. (1984). Lasting consequences of bilateral medial temporal lobectomy: Clinical course and experimental findings in H.M. *Seminars in Neurology, 4,* 249–259. (13)

Cornell, D.G., Milden, R.S., & Shimp, S. (1985). Stressful life events associated with endogenous depression. *Journal of Nervous and Mental Disease, 173,* 470–476. (15)

Corso, J.F. (1973). Hearing. In B.B. Wolman (Ed.), *Handbook of general psychology* (pp. 348–381). Englewood Cliffs, NJ: Prentice-Hall. (6)

Corso, J.F. (1985). Communication, presbycusis, and technological aids. In H.K. Ulatowska (Ed.), *The aging brain: Communication in the elderly* (pp. 33–51). San Diego, CA: College Hill. (6)

Corson, S.A., Corson, E.O., Kirilcuk, V., Kirilcuk, J., Knopp, W., & Arnold, L.E. (1973). Differential effects of amphetamines on clinically relevant dog models of hyperkinesis and stereotypy: Relevance to Huntington's chorea. In A. Barbeau, T.N. Chase, & G.W. Paulson (Eds.), *Advances in neurology, vol.1: Huntington's chorea 1872–1972* (pp. 681–697). New York: Raven. (15)

Coss, R.G., Brandon, J.G., & Globus, A. (1980). Changes in morphology of dendritic spines on honeybee calycal interneurons associated with cumulative nursing and foraging experiences. *Brain Research, 192,* 49–59. (2)

Coss, R.G., & Globus, A. (1979). Social experience affects the development of dendritic spines and branches on tectal interneurons in the Jewel fish. *Developmental Psychobiology, 12,* 347–358. (2)

Cotman, C.W., & Nieto-Sampedro, M. (1982). Brain function, synapse renewal, and plasticity. *Annual Review of Psychology, 33,* 371–401. (14)

Cotman, C.W., & Nieto-Sampedro, M. (1984). Cell biology of synaptic plasticity. *Science, 225,* 1287–1294. (14)

Cowan, J.D. (1983). Testing the escape hypotheses: Alcohol helps users to forget their feelings. *Journal of Nervous and Mental Disease, 171,* 40–48. (10)

Cowan, W.M., Fawcett, J.W., O'Leary, D.D.M., & Stanfield, B.B. (1984). Regressive events in neurogenesis. *Science, 225,* 1258–1265. (4)

Craik, F.I.M., & Lockhart, R.S. (1972). Levels of processing: A framework for memory research. *Journal of Verbal Learning and Verbal Behavior, 11,* 671–684. (13)

Crawley, J.N., Ninan, P.T., Pickar, D., Chrousos, G.P., Linnoila, M., Skolnick, P., & Paul, S.M. (1985). Neuropharmacological antagonism of the β-carboline-induced "anxiety" response in rhesus monkeys. *Journal of Neuroscience, 5,* 477–485. (12)

Crawshaw, L.I., Moffitt, B.P., Lemons, D.E., & Downey, J.A. (1981). The evolutionary development of vertebrate thermoregulation. *American Scientist, 69,* 543–550. (10)

Creak, M. (1961). Schizophrenic syndrome in childhood. *British Medical Journal, 2,* 889–890. (16)

Creasey, H., Rumsey, J.M., Schwartz, M., Duara, R., Rapoport, J.L., & Rapoport, S.I. (1986). Brain morphometry in autistic men as measured by volumetric computed tomography. *Archives of Neurology, 43,* 669–672. (16)

Creese, I., Burt, D.R., & Snyder, S.H. (1977). Dopamine receptor binding enhancement accompanies lesion-induced behavioral supersensitivity. *Science, 197,* 596–598. (14)

Crews, F., & Smith, C.B. (1978). Presynaptic alpha-receptor subsensitivity after long-term antidepressant treatment. *Science, 202,* 322–324. (15)

Crisp, A.H., Hsu, L.K.G., Harding, B., & Hartshorn, J. (1980). Clinical features of anorexia nervosa. *Journal of Psychosomatic Research, 24,* 179–191. (10)

Crisp, A.H., Palmer, R.L., & Kalucy, R.S. (1976). How common is anorexia nervosa? A prevalence study. *British Journal of Psychiatry, 128,* 549–554. (10)

Crovitz, H.F., Horn, R.W., & Daniel, W.F. (1983). Inter-relationships among retrograde amnesia, post-traumatic amnesia, and time since head injury: A retrospective study. *Cortex, 19,* 407–412. (13)

Crow, T.J. (1984). A re-evaluation of the viral hypothesis: Is psychosis the result of retroviral integration at a site close to the cerebral dominance gene? *British Journal of Psychiatry, 145,* 243–253. (16)

Crow, T.J., & Done, D.J. (1986). A retrovirus/transposon hypothesis of psychosis. In C. Shagass, R.C. Josiassen, W.H. Bridger, K.J. Weiss, D. Stoff, & G.M. Simpson (Eds.), *Biological Psychiatry 1985* (pp. 1083–1085). New York: Elsevier. (16)

Csernansky, J.G., Kaplan, J., & Hollister, L.E. (1985). Problems in classification of schizophrenics as neuroleptic responders and nonresponders. *Journal of Nervous and Mental Disease, 173,* 325–331. (16)

Curry, J.J. III, & Heim, L.M. (1966). Brain myelination after neonatal administration of oestradiol. *Nature, 209,* 915–916. (11)

Cynader, M., Leporé, F., & Guillemot, J.-P. (1981). Inter-hemispheric competition during postnatal development. *Nature, 290,* 139–140. (7)

Czaja, J.A., & Bielert, C. (1975). Female rhesus sexual behavior and distance to a male partner: Relation to stage of the menstrual cycle. *Archives of Sexual Behavior, 4,* 583–597. (11)

Czeisler, C.A., Allan, J.S., Strogatz, S.H., Ronda, J.M., Sánchez, R., Ríos, C.D., Freitag, W.O., Richardson, G.S., & Kronauer, R.E. (1986). Bright light resets the human circadian pacemaker independent of the timing of the sleep-wake cycle. *Science, 233,* 667–671. (15)

Czeisler, C.A., Weitzman, E.D., Moore-Ede, M.C., Zimmerman, J.C., & Knauer, R.S. (1980). Human sleep: Its duration and organization depend on its circadian phase. *Science, 210,* 1264–1267. (15)

Dabrowska, B., Harmata, W., Lenkiewicz, Z., Schiffer, Z., & Wojtusiak, R.J. (1981). Colour perception in cows. *Behavioural Processes, 6,* 1–10. (6)

Dakof, G.A., & Mendelsohn, G.A. (1986). Parkinson's disease: The psychological aspects of a chronic illness. *Psychological Bulletin, 99,* 375–387. (8)

Dalhouse, A.D., Langford, H.G., Walsh, D., & Barnes, T. (1986). Angiotensin and salt appetite: Physiological amounts of angiotensin given peripherally increase salt appetite in the rat. *Behavioral Neuroscience, 100,* 597–602. (10)

Dalton, K. (1968). Ante-natal progesterone and intelligence. *British Journal of Psychiatry, 114,* 1377–1382. (11)

Damasio, A. (1979). The frontal lobes. In K.M. Heilman & E. Valenstein (Eds.), *Clinical neuropsychology* (pp. 360–412). New York: Oxford University. (4)

Damasio, A.R., & Geschwind, N. (1984). The neural basis of language. *Annual Review of Neuroscience, 7,* 127–147. (5)

Damasio, H., & Damasio, A.R. (1980). The anatomical basis of conduction aphasia. *Brain, 103,* 337–350. (5)

Daniloff, J.K., Wells, J., & Ellis, J. (1984). Cross-species septal transplants: Recovery of choline acetyltransferase activity. *Brain Research, 324,* 151–154. (14)

Darley, S.A., & Katz, I. (1973). Heart rate changes in children as a function of test versus game instructions and test anxiety. *Child Development, 44,* 784–789. (12)

Darwin, C. (1859). *The origin of species.* Reprinted by various publishers. (A)

Dascombe, M.J. (1986). The pharmacology of fever. *Progress in Neurobiology, 25*, 327–373. (10)

David, S., & Aguayo, A.J. (1981). Axonal elongation into peripheral nervous system "bridges" after central nervous system injury in adult rats. *Science, 214*, 931–933. (14)

Davidson, J.M., Camargo, C.A., & Smith, E.R. (1979). Effects of androgen on sexual behavior in hypogonadal men. *Journal of Clinical Endocrinology and Metabolism, 48*, 955–958. (11)

Davidson, R.J. (1984). Affect, cognition, and hemispheric specialization. In C.E. Izard, J. Kagan, & R.B. Zajonc (Eds.), *Emotions, cognition, & behavior* (pp. 320–365). Cambridge, England: Cambridge University. (15)

Davies, P. (1985). A critical review of the role of the cholinergic system in human memory and cognition. *Annals of the New York Academy of Sciences, 444*, 212–217. (13)

Davis, H.P., Rosenzweig, M.R., Bennett, E.L., & Squire, L.R. (1980). Inhibition of cerebral protein synthesis: Dissociation of nonspecific effects and amnesic effects. *Behavioral and Neural Biology, 28*, 99–104. (13)

Davis, H.P., & Squire, L.R. (1984). Protein synthesis and memory: A review. *Psychological Bulletin, 96*, 518–559. (13)

Davis, J.D., Wirtshafter, D., Asin, K.E., & Brief, D. (1981). Sustained intracerebroventricular infusion of brain fuels reduces body weight and food intake in rats. *Science, 212*, 81–83. (10)

Davis, J.M. (1976). Recent developments in the drug treatment of schizophrenia. *American Journal of Psychiatry, 133*, 208–214. (16)

Davis, K.L., Davidson, M., Mohs, R.C., Kendler, K.S., Davis, B.M., Johns, C.A., DeNigris, Y., & Horvath, T.B. (1985). Plasma homovanillic acid concentration and the severity of schizophrenic illness. *Science, 227*, 1601–1602. (16)

Davis, K.L., Mohs, R.C., Tinklenberg, J.R., Pfefferbaum, A., Hollister, L.E., & Kopell, B.S. (1978). Physostigmine: Improvement of long-term memory processes in normal humans. *Science, 201*, 272–274. (13)

Davis, N., & LeVere, T.E. (1979). Recovery of function after brain damage: Different processes and the facilitation of one. *Physiological Psychology, 7*, 233–240. (14)

Davis, N., & LeVere, T.E. (1982). Recovery of function after brain damage: The question of individual behaviors or functionality. *Experimental Neurology, 75*, 68–78. (14)

Deckel, A.W., Moran, T.H., Coyle, J.T., Sanberg, P.R., & Robinson, R.G. (1986). Anatomical predictors of behavioral recovery following fetal striatal transplants. *Brain Research, 365*, 249–258. (14)

DeCoursey, P. (1960). Phase control of activity in a rodent. *Cold Spring Harbor symposia on quantitative biology, 25*, 49–55. (9)

Delgado, J.M.R. (1963). Cerebral heterostimulation in a monkey colony.

Delgado, J.M.R. (1963). Cerebral heterostimulation in a monkey colony. *Science, 141*, 161–163. (1)

Delgado, J.M.R. (1969a). *Physical control of the mind.* New York: Harper & Row. (1, 12)

Delgado, J.M.R. (1969b). Offensive-defensive behaviour in free monkeys and chimpanzees induced by radio stimulation of the brain. In S. Garattini & E.B. Sigg (Eds.), *Aggressive behaviour* (pp. 109–119). New York: Wiley Interscience. (12)

Delgado, J.M.R. (1981). Neuronal constellations in aggressive behavior. In L. Valzelli & L. Morgese (Eds.), *Aggression and violence: A psychobiological and clinical approach* (pp. 82–98). Milan, Italy: Edizioni Saint Vincent. (12)

Delgado, J.M.R., & Hamlin, H. (1960). Spontaneous and evoked electrical seizures in animals and in humans. In E.R. Ramey & D.S. O'Doherty (Eds.), *Electrical studies on the unanesthetized brain* (pp. 133–158). New York: P.B. Hoeber. (12)

DeLisi, L.E., Goldin, L.R., Hamovit, J.R., Maxwell, E., Kurtz, D., & Gershon, E.S. (1986). A family study of the association of increased ventricular size with schizophrenia. *Archives of General Psychiatry, 43*, 148–153. (16)

DeLong, M.R., Alexander, G.E., Georgopoulos, A.P., Crutcher, M.D., Mitchell, S.J., & Richardson, R.T. (1984). Role of basal ganglia in limb movements. *Human Neurobiology, 2*, 235–244. (8)

Delwaide, P.J., Devoitille, J.M., & Ylieff, M. (1980). Acute effect of drugs upon memory of patients with senile dementia. *Acta Psychiatrica Belgica, 80*, 748–754. (13)

Dement, W. (1960). The effect of dream deprivation. *Science, 131*, 1705–1707. (9)

Dement, W. (1972). *Some must watch while some must sleep.* San Francisco: W.H. Freeman. (9)

Dement, W., Ferguson, J., Cohen, H., & Barchas, J. (1969). Non-chemical methods and data using a biochemical model: The REM quanta. In A.J. Mandell & M.P. Mandell (Eds.), *Psychochemical research in man* (pp. 275–325). New York: Academic. (9)

Dement, W., & Kleitman, N. (1957a). Cyclic variations in EEG during sleep and their relation to eye movements, body motility, and dreaming. *Electroencephalography and Clinical Neurophysiology, 9*, 673–690. (9)

Dement, W., & Kleitman, N. (1957b). The relation of eye movements during sleep to dream activity: An objective method for the study of dreaming. *Journal of Experimental Psychology, 53*, 339–346. (8)

Dement, W., & Wolpert, E.A. (1958). The relation of eye movements, body motility, and external stimuli to dream content. *Journal of Experimental Psychology, 55*, 543–553. (9)

Desiderato, O., MacKinnon, J.R., & Hissom, H. (1974). Development of gastric ulcers in rats following stress termination. *Journal of Comparative and Physiological Psychology, 87*, 208–214. (12)

Desimone, J.A., Heck, G.L., Mierson, S., & Desimone, S.K. (1984). The active ion transport properties of canine lingual epithelia in vitro. *Journal of General Physiology, 83*, 633–656. (6)

Desimone, R., Albright, T.D., Gross, C.G., & Bruce, C. (1984). Stimulus-selective properties of inferior temporal neurons in the macaque. *Journal of Neuroscience, 4*, 2051–2062. (7)

Desimone, R., & Gross, C.G. (1979). Visual areas in the temporal cortex of the macaque. *Brain Research, 178*, 363–380. (7)

Desimone, R., Schein, S.J., Moran, J., & Ungerleider, L.G. (1985). Contour, color and shape analysis beyond the striate cortex. *Vision Research, 25*, 441–452. (7)

Désir, D., van Cauter, E., Fang, V.S., Martino, E., Jadot, C., Spire, J.-P., Noël, P., Refetoff, S., Copinschi, G., & Golstein, J. (1981). Effects of "jet lag" on hormonal patterns. I. Procedure variations in total plasma proteins, and disruption of adrenocorticotropin-cortisol periodicity. *Journal of Clinical Endocrinology and Metabolism, 52,* 628–641. (9)

Desmond, M.M., & Wilson, G.S. (1975). Neonatal abstinence syndrome: Recognition and diagnosis. *Addictive Diseases, 2,* 113–121. (16)

Detera-Wadleigh, S.D., Berrettini, W.H., Goldin, L.R., Boorman, D., Anderson, S., & Gershon, E.S. (1987). Close linkage of c-Harvey-ras-1 and the insulin gene to affective disorder is ruled out in three North American pedigress. *Nature, 325,* 806–808. (15)

Deutsch, J.A. (1964). Behavioral measurement of the neural refractory period and its application to intracranial self-stimulation. *Journal of Comparative and Physiological Psychology, 58,* 1–9. (2)

Deutsch, J.A. (1973). The cholinergic synapse and the site of memory. In J.A. Deutsch (Ed.), *The physiological basis of memory* (pp. 59–76). New York: Academic. (13)

Deutsch, J.A. (1983). Dietary control and the stomach. *Progress in Neurobiology, 20,* 313–332. (10)

Deutsch, J.A., & Ahn, S.J. (1986). The splanchnic nerve and food intake regulation. *Behavioral and Neural Biology, 45,* 43–47. (10)

Deutsch, J.A., Young, W.G., & Kalogeris, T.J. (1978). The stomach signals satiety. *Science, 201,* 165–167. (10)

DeValois, R.L., Albrecht, D.G., & Thorell, L.G. (1982). Spatial frequency selectivity of cells in macaque visual cortex. *Vision Research, 22,* 545–559. (7)

DeValois, R.L., & Jacobs, G.H. (1968). Primate color vision. *Science, 162,* 533–540. (6)

Devinsky, O. (1983). Neuroanatomy of Gilles de la Tourette's syndrome. *Archives of Neurology, 40,* 508–514. (3)

Diamond, I.T. (1979). The subdivisions of neocortex: A proposal to revise the traditional view of sensory, motor, and association areas. *Progress in Psychobiology and Physiological Psychology, 8,* 1–43. (4)

Diamond, I.T. (1983). Parallel pathways in the auditory, visual, and somatic systems. In G. Macchi, A. Rustioni, & R. Spreafico (Eds.), *Somatosensory integration in the thalamus* (pp. 251–272). Amsterdam: Elsevier. (4)

Diamond, M., Llacuna, A., & Wong, C.L. (1973). Sex behavior after neonatal progesterone, testosterone, estrogen, or antiandrogens. *Hormones and Behavior, 4,* 73–88. (11)

Diamond, M.C., Johnson, R.E., & Ehlert, J. (1979). A comparison of cortical thickness in male and female rats—normal and gonadectomized, young and adult. *Behavioral and Neural Biology, 26,* 485–491. (11)

Dichgans, J. (1984). Clinical symptoms of cerebellar dysfunction and their topodiagnostic significance. *Human Neurobiology, 2,* 269–279. (8)

Dimond, S.J. (1979). Symmetry and asymmetry in the vertebrate brain. In D.A. Oakley & H.C. Plotkin (Eds.), *Brain, behaviour, and evolution* (pp. 189–218). London: Methuen. (5)

Dinarello, C.A., & Wolff, S.M. (1982). Molecular basis of fever in humans. *American Journal of Medicine, 72,* 799–819. (10)

Dörner, G. (1967). Tierexperimentelle Untersuchungen zur Frage einer hormonellen Pathogenese der Homosexualität. *Acta Biologica et Medica Germanica, 19,* 569–584. (11)

Dörner, G. (1974). Sex-hormone-dependent brain differentiation and sexual functions. In G. Dörner (Ed.), *Endocrinology of sex* (pp. 30–37). Leipzig: J.A. Barth. (11)

Dörner, G., & Hinz, G. (1975). Androgen-dependent brain differentiation and life span. *Endokrinologie, 65,* 378–380. (11)

Dörner, G., Rohde, W., & Krell, L. (1972). Auslösung eines positiven Östrogenfeedback-Effekt bei homosexuellen Männern. *Endokrinologie, 60,* 297–301. (11)

Dowling, J.E., & Boycott, B.B. (1966). Organization of the primate retina. *Proceedings of the Royal Society of London,* B, *166,* 80–111. (7)

Drachman, D.A., & Leavitt, J. (1974). Human memory and the cholinergic system. *Archives of Neurology, 30,* 113–121. (13)

Drachman, D.B. (1978). Myasthenia gravis. *New England Journal of Medicine, 298,* 136–142, 186–193. (8)

Drachman, D.B., Adams, R.N., & Josifer, L.F. (1982). Functional activities of autoantibodies to acetylcholine receptors and the clinical severity of myasthenia gravis. *New England Journal of Medicine, 307,* 769–775. (8)

Drager, U.C., & Hubel, D.H. (1975). Physiology of visual cells in mouse superior colliculus and correlation with somatosensory and auditory input. *Nature, 253,* 203–204. (7)

Dreyfus-Brisac, C. (1970). Ontogenesis of sleep in human prematures after 32 weeks of conceptional age. *Developmental Psychobiology, 3,* 91–121. (9)

Dubocovich, M.L. (1984). Presynaptic alpha-adrenoceptors in the central nervous system. *Annals of the New York Academy of Sciences, 430,* 7–25. (3, 15)

Duggan, J.P., & Booth, D.A. (1986). Obesity, overeating, and rapid gastric emptying in rats with ventromedial hypothalamic lesions. *Science, 231,* 609–611. (10)

Dunlap, J.L., Zadina, J.E., & Gougis, G. (1978). Prenatal stress interacts with prepubertal social isolation to reduce male copulatory behavior. *Physiology and Behavior, 21,* 873–875. (11)

Dunwiddie, T.V. (1985). The physiological role of adenosine in the central nervous system. *International Journal of Neurobiology, 27,* 63–139. (12)

Duvoisin, R.C., Eldridge, R., Williams, A., Nutt, J., & Calne, D. (1981). Twin study of Parkinson disease. *Neurology, 1981, 31,* 77–80. (8)

Dworkin, B.R., & Miller, N.E. (1986). Failure to replicate visceral learning in the acute curarized rat preparation. *Behavioral Neuroscience, 100,* 299–314. (12)

Dyal, J.A. (1971). Transfer of behavioral bias: Reality and specificity. In E.J. Fjerdingstad (Ed.), *Chemical transfer of learned information* (pp. 219–263). New York: American Elsevier. (13)

Dykes, R.W., Sur, M., Merzenich, M.M., Kaas, J.H., & Nelson, R.J. (1981). Regional segregation of neurons responding to quickly adapting, slowly adapting, deep and Pacinian receptors within thalamic ventroposterior lateral and ventroposterior inferior nuclei in the squirrel monkey (*Saimiri sciureus*). *Neuroscience, 6,* 1687–1692. (6)

Eaton, G.G., & Resko, J.A. (1974). Ovarian hormones and sexual behavior in *Macaca nemestrina*. *Journal of Comparative and Physiological Psychology, 86,* 919–925. (11)

Eccles, J.C. (1964). *The physiology of synapses.* Berlin: Springer-Verlag. (3)

Edelstein, E.L. (1981). Vasopressins and other neuropeptides as CNS mental modulators: A review. *Israel Journal of Psychiatry & Related Sciences, 18,* 229–236. (13)

Edman, G., Åsberg, M., Levander, S., & Schalling, D. (1986). Skin conductance habituation and cerebrospinal fluid 5-hydroxyindoleacetic acid in suicidal patients. *Archives of General Psychiatry, 43,* 586–592. (12)

Egeland, J.A., Gerhard, D.S., Pauls, D.L., Sussex, J.N., Kidd, K.K., Allen, C.R., Hostetter, A.M., & Housman, D.E. (1987). Bipolar affective disorders linked to DNA markers on chromosome 11. *Nature, 325,* 783–787. (15)

Ehman, G.K., Albert, D.J., & Jamieson, J.L. (1971). Injections into the duodenum and the induction of satiety in the rat. *Canadian Journal of Psychology, 25,* 147–166. (10)

Ehret, C.F., Potter, V.R., & Dobra, K.W. (1975). Chronotypic action of theophylline and of pentobarbital as circadian Zeitgebers in the rat. *Science, 188,* 1212–1215. (9)

Ehrhardt, A.A., & Money, J. (1967). Progestin-induced hermaphroditism: IQ and psychosexual identity in a study of ten girls. *Journal of Sex Research, 3,* 83–100. (11)

Ehrlichmann, H., & Weinberger, A. (1978). Lateral eye movements and hemispheric asymmetry: A critical review. *Psychological Bulletin, 85,* 1080–1101. (5)

Eidelberg, E., & Stein, D.G. (1974). Functional recovery after lesions of the nervous system. *Neurosciences Research Program Bulletin, 12,* 191–303. (14)

Eisenberg, E. (1981). Toward an understanding of reproductive function in anorexia nervosa. *Fertility and Sterility, 36,* 543–550. (10)

Eisenstein, E.M., & Cohen, M.J. (1965). Learning in an isolated prothoracic insect ganglion. *Animal Behaviour, 13,* 104–108. (13)

Ekman, P., Levenson, R.W., & Friesen, W.V. (1983). Autonomic nervous system activity distinguishes among emotions. *Science, 221,* 1208–1210. (12)

Ellinwood, E.H., Jr. (1969). Amphetamine psychosis: A multi-dimensional process. *Seminars in Psychiatry, 1,* 208–226. (16)

Elliott, T.R. (1905). The action of adrenalin. *Journal of Physiology* (London), *32,* 401–467. (3)

Ellison, G.D. (1977). Animal models of psychopathology: The low-norepinephrine and low-serotonin rat. *American Psychologist, 32,* 1036–1045. (15)

Elwood, R.W. (1985). Inhibition of infanticide and onset of paternal care in male mice (*Mus musculus*). *Journal of Comparative Psychology, 99,* 457–467. (11)

Epstein, A.N. (1983). The neuropsychology of drinking behavior. In E. Satinoff & P. Teitelbaum (Eds.), *Handbook of behavioral neurobiology, 6: Motivation* (pp. 367–423). New York: Plenum. (10)

Epstein, A.N., & Teitelbaum, P. (1964). Severe and persistent deficits in thirst produced by lateral hypothalamic damage. In W.J. Wayner (Ed.), *Thirst—Proceedings of the first international symposium on thirst in the regulation of body water* (pp. 395–410). New York: Pergamon. (14)

Epstein, L.G., Sharer, L.R., Cho, E.S., Myenhofer, M., Navia, B., & Price, R.W. (1984). HTLV-III/LAV-like retrovirus particles in the brains of patients with AIDS encephalopathy. *AIDS Research, 1,* 447–454. (16)

Erickson, C., & Lehrman, D. (1964). Effect of castration of male ring doves upon ovarian activity of females. *Journal of Comparative and Physiological Psychology, 58,* 164–166. (11)

Erickson, C.J., & Zenone, P.G. (1976). Courtship differences in male ring doves: Avoidance of cuckoldry? *Science, 192,* 1353–1354. (11)

Erickson, R.P. (1963). Sensory neural patterns and gustation. In Y. Zotterman (Ed.), *Olfaction and taste* (pp. 205–213). Oxford: Pergamon. (6)

Eslinger, P.J., & Damasio, A.R. (1986). Preserved motor learning in Alzheimer's disease: Implications for anatomy and behavior. *Journal of Neuroscience, 6,* 3006–3009. (13)

Essman, W.B., & Essman, E.J. (1986). Drug effects and receptor changes in aggressive behavior. In C. Shagass, R.C. Josiassen, W.H. Bridger, K.J. Weiss, D. Stoff, & G.M. Simpson (Eds.), *Biological Psychiatry 1985* (pp. 663–665). New York: Elsevier. (12)

Evarts, E.V. (1979). Brain mechanisms of movement. *Scientific American, 241* (3), 164–179. (8)

Faglioni, P., & Basso, A. (1985). Historical perspectives on neuroanatomical correlates of limb apraxia. In E.A. Roy (Ed.), *Neuropsychological studies of apraxia and related disorders* (pp. 3–44). Amsterdam: North Holland. (8)

Faraone, S.V., & Tsuang, M.T. (1985). Quantitative models of the genetic transmission of schizophrenia. *Psychological Bulletin, 98,* 41–66. (16)

Farkas, T., Wolf, A.P., Jaeger, J., Brodie, J.D., Christman, D.R., & Fowler, J.S. (1984). Regional brain glucose metabolism in chronic schizophrenia. *Archives of General Psychiatry, 41,* 293–300. (16)

Feder, H.H. (1981). Estrous cyclicity in mammals. In N.T. Adler (Ed.), *Neuroendocrinology of reproduction* (pp. 279–348). New York: Plenum. (11)

Fein, D., Humes, M., Kaplan, E., Lucci, D., & Waterhouse, L. (1984). The question of left hemisphere dysfunction in infantile autism. *Psychological Bulletin, 95,* 258–281. (16)

Feinberg, M., & Carroll, B.J. (1984). Biological markers for endogenous depression in series and parallel. *Biological Psychiatry, 19,* 3–11. (15)

Feingold, B.F. (1975). *Why your child is hyperactive.* New York: Random House. (15)

Fentress, J.C. (1973). Development of grooming in mice with amputated forelimbs. *Science, 179,* 704–705. (8)

Ferguson, N.B.L., & Keesey, R.E. (1975). Effect of a quinine-adulterated diet upon body weight maintenance in male rats with ventromedial hypothalamic lesions. *Journal of Comparative and Physiological Psychology, 89,* 478–488. (10)

Fieve, R.R., & Platman, S.R. (1969). Follow-up studies of lithium and thyroid function in manic-depressive illness. *American Journal of Psychiatry, 125,* 1443–1445. (15)

Finger, S., & Stein, D.G. (1982). *Brain damage and recovery.* New York: Academic. (14)

Fink, M. (1980). A neuroendocrine theory of convulsive therapy. *Trends in Neurosciences, 3,* 25–27. (15)

Fink, M. (1985). Convulsive therapy: Fifty years of progress. *Convulsive Therapy, 1,* 204–216. (15)

Fitzsimons, J.T. (1961). Drinking by nephrectomized rats injected with various substances. *Journal of Physiology, 155,* 563–579. (10)

Fitzsimons, J.T. (1971). The hormonal control of water and sodium appetite. In L. Martini & W.F. Ganong (Eds.), *Frontiers in neuroendocrinology, 1971* (pp. 103–128). New York: Oxford University. (10)

Fitzsimons, J.T. (1973). Some historical perspectives in the physiology of thirst. In A.N. Epstein, H.R. Kissileff, & E. Stellar (Eds.), The *neurophysiology of thirst* (pp. 3–33). Washington, DC: Winston. (10)

Fjerdingstad, E.J. (1973). Transfer of learning in rodents and fish. In W.B. Essman & S. Nakajima (Eds.), *Current biochemical approaches to learning and memory* (pp. 73–98). Flushing, NY: Spectrum. (13)

Flament, M.F., Rapoport, J.L., Berg, C.J., Sceery, W., Kilts, C., Mellström, B., & Linnoila, M. (1985). Clomipramine treatment of childhood obsessive-compulsive disorder. *Archives of General Psychiatry, 42,* 977–983. (12)

Fluharty, S.J., & Epstein, A.N. (1983). Sodium appetite elicited by intracerebroventricular infusion of angiotensin II in the rat: II. Synergistic interaction with systemic mineralocorticoids. *Behavioral Neuroscience, 97,* 746–758. (10)

Flynn, J.P. (1973). Patterning mechanisms, patterned reflexes, and attack behavior in cats. *Nebraska Symposium on Motivation 1972,* 125–153. (12)

Flynn, J.P., Edwards, S.B., & Bandler, R.J., Jr. (1971). Changes in sensory and motor systems during centrally elicited attack. *Behavioral Science, 16,* 1–19. (12)

Folkard, S., Hume, K.I., Minors, D.S., Waterhouse, J.M., & Watson, F.L. (1985). Independence of the circadian rhythm in alertness from the sleep/wake cycle. *Nature, 313,* 678–679. (9)

Folstein, S.E., Phillips, J.A. III, Meyers, D.A., Chase, G.A., Abbott, M.H., Franz, M.L., Waber, P.G., Kazazian, H.H., Jr., Conneally, P.M., Hobbs, W., Tanzi, R., Faryniarz, A., Gibbons, K., & Gusella, J. (1985). Huntington's disease: Two families with differing clinical features show linkage to the G8 probe. *Science, 229,* 776–779. (8)

Foltz, E.L., & Millett, F.E. (1964). Experimental psychosomatic disease states in monkeys. I. Peptic ulcer— "executive monkeys." *Journal of Surgical Research, 4,* 445–453. (12)

Foulkes, D. (1967). Nonrapid eye movement mentation. *Experimental Neurology,* supplement 4, 28–38. (9)

Frazer, A., & Winokur, A. (1977). Therapeutic and pharmacological aspects of psychotropic drugs. In A. Frazer & A. Winokur (Eds.), *Biological bases of psychiatric disorders* (pp. 151–177). New York: Spectrum. (12)

Freedman, M., & Oscar-Berman, M. (1986). Bilateral frontal lobe disease and selective delayed response deficits in humans. *Behavioral Neuroscience, 100,* 337–342. (13)

Frese, M., & Harwich, C. (1984). Shiftwork and the length and quality of sleep. *Journal of Occupational Medicine, 26,* 561–566. (9)

Friedlander, W.J. (1986). Who was "the father of bromide treatment of epilepsy"? *Archives of Neurology, 43,* 505–507. (3)

Friedman, B., & Aguayo, A.J. (1985). Injured neurons in the olfactory bulb of the adult rat grow axons along grafts of peripheral nerve. *Journal of Neuroscience, 5,* 1616–1625. (14)

Friedman, M.I., & Stricker, E.M. (1976). The physiological psychology of hunger: A physiological perspective. *Psychological Review, 83,* 409–431. (10)

Fritsch, G, & Hitzig, E. (1870). Über die elektrische Erregbarkeit des Grosshirns. *Archiv fur Anatomie Physiologie und Wissenschaftliche Medicin,* 300–332. (1)

Frutiger, S.A. (1986). Changes in self-stimulation at stimulation-bound eating and drinking sites in the lateral hypothalamus during food or water deprivation, glucoprivation, and intracellular or extracellular dehydration. *Behavioral Neuroscience, 100,* 221–229. (12)

Fukuda, Y., Hsiao, C.-F., & Watanabe, M. (1985). Morphological correlates of Y, X, and W type ganglion cells in the cat's retina. *Vision Research, 25,* 319–327. (7)

Fuller, C.A., Lydic, R., Sulzman, F.M., Albers, H.E., Tepper, B., & Moore-Ede, M.C. (1981). Circadian rhythm of body temperature persists after suprachiasmatic lesions in the squirrel monkey. *American Journal of Physiology, 241,* R385–R391. (9)

Fuller, R.K., & Roth, H.P. (1979). Disulfiram for the treatment of alcoholism: An evaluation in 128 men. *Annals of Internal Medicine, 90,* 901–904. (10)

Gage, F.H., Björklund, A., Stenevi, U., Dunnett, S.B., & Kelly, P.A.T. (1984). Intrahippocampal septal grafts ameliorate learning impairments in aged rats. *Science, 225,* 533–536. (14)

Gaito, J. (1976). Molecular psychobiology of memory: Its appearance, contributions, and decline. *Physiological Psychology, 4,* 476–484. (13)

Galaburda, A.M. (1985). Norman Geschwind 1926–1984. *Neuropsychologia, 23,* 297–304. (5)

Galin, D., Johnstone, J., Nakell, L., & Herron, J. (1979). Development of the capacity for tactile information transfer between hemispheres in normal children. *Science, 204,* 1330–1332. (5)

Gallistel, C.R. (1980). *The organization of action: A new synthesis.* Hillsdale, NJ: Erlbaum. (8)

Gallistel, C.R. (1981). Bell, Magendie, and the proposals to restrict the use of animals in neurobehavioral research. *American Psychologist, 36,* 357–360. (1, 4)

Gallistel, C.R., Gomita, Y., Yadin, E., & Campbell, K.A. (1985). Forebrain origins and terminations of the medial forebrain bundle metabolically activated by rewarding stimulation or by reward-blocking doses of pimozide. *Journal of Neuroscience, 5,* 1246–1261. (12)

Gallistel, C.R., Shizgal, P., & Yeomans, J.S. (1981). A portrait of the substrate for self-stimulation. *Psychological Review, 88,* 228–273. (12)

Gallo, R.C. (January 1987). The AIDS virus. *Scientific American, 256* (1), 46–56. (16)

Gallup, G.G., Jr., & Suarez, S.D. (1980). On the use of animals in psychological research. *Psychological Record, 30,* 211–218. (1)

Gallup, G.G., Jr., & Suarez, S.D. (1985). Alternatives to the use of animals in psychological research. *American Psychologist, 40,* 1104–1111. (1)

Gamse, R., Leeman, S.E., Holzer, P., & Lembeck, F. (1981). Differential effects of capsaicin on the content of somatostatin, substance P, and neurotensin in the nervous system of the rat. *Naunyn-Schmiedeberg's Archives of Pharmacology, 317,* 140–148. (6)

Gamzu, E. (1985). Animal behavioral models in the discovery of compounds to treat memory dysfunction. *Annals of the New York Academy of Sciences, 444,* 370–393. (13)

Garattini, S., & Valzelli, L. (1960). Sulla valutazione farmacologica delle sostanze antidepressive. In *Le sindromi depressive* (pp. 7–30.) (15)

Garcia, J. (1981). Tilting at the paper mills of Academe. *American psychologist, 36,* 149–158. (13)

Garcia, J., Ervin, F.R., & Koelling, R.A. (1966). Learning with prolonged delay of reinforcement. *Psychonomic Science, 5,* 121–122. (13)

Garcia, J., & Koelling, R.A. (1966). Relation of cue to consequence in avoidance learning. *Psychonomic Science, 4,* 123–124. (13)

García-Sevilla, J.A., Guimón, J., García-Vallejo, P., & Fuster, M.J. (1986). Biochemical and functional evidence of supersensitive platelet alpha$_2$-adrenoceptors in major affective disorder. *Archives of General Psychiatry, 43,* 51–57. (15)

Gardner, B.T., & Gardner, R.A. (1975). Evidence for sentence constituents in the early utterances of child and chimpanzee. *Journal of Experimental Psychology: General, 104,* 244–267. (5)

Gardner, H., & Zurif, E. (1975). *Bee* but not *be*: Oral reading of single words in aphasia and alexia. *Neuropsychologia, 13,* 181–190. (5)

Gardner, H., Zurif, E.B., Berry, T., & Baker, E. (1976). Visual communication in aphasia. *Neuropsychologia, 14,* 275–292. (5)

Gardner, R.A., & Gardner, B.T. (1969). Teaching sign language to a chimpanzee. *Science, 165,* 664–672. (5)

Gash, D.M., Collier, T.J., & Sladek, J.R., Jr. (1985). Neural transplantation: A review of recent developments and potential applications to the aged brain. *Neurobiology of Aging, 6,* 131–150. (14)

Gash, D.M., Notter, M.F.D., Dick, L.B., Kraus, A.L., Okawara, S.H., Wechkin, S.W., & Joynt, R.J. (1985). Cholinergic neurons transplanted into the neocortex and hippocampus of primates: Studies on African green monkeys. In A. Björklund & U. Stenevi (Eds.), *Neural grafting in the mammalian CNS* (pp. 595–603). Amsterdam: Elsevier. (14)

Gash, D., Sladek, J.R., Jr., & Sladek, C.D. (1980). Functional development of grafted vasopressin neurons. *Science, 210,* 1367–1369. (14)

Gastpar, M. (1979). L-HTP and the serotonin hypothesis, their meaning for treatment of depression. In J. Obiols, C. Ballús, E. González Monclús, & J. Pujol (Eds.), *Biological psychiatry today* (pp. 535–540). Amsterdam: Elsevier/North Holland Biomedical. (15)

Gazzaniga, M.S., LeDoux, J.E., & Wilson, D.H. (1977). Language, praxis, and the right hemisphere: Clues to some mechanisms of consciousness. *Neurology, 27,* 1144–1147. (5)

Gearhart, J., Oster-Granite, M.L., & Guth, L. (1979). Histological changes after transection of the spinal cord of fetal and neonatal mice. *Experimental Neurology, 66,* 1–15. (14)

Geliebter, A., Westreich, S., Hashim, S.A., & Gage, D. (1987). Gastric balloon reduces food intake and body weight in obese rats. *Physiology & Behavior, 39,* 399–402. (10)

Gershon, S., Angrist, B., & Shopsin, B. (1977). Pharmacological agents as tools in psychiatric research. In E.S. Gershon, R.H. Belmaker, S.S. Kety, & M. Rosenbaum (Eds.), *The impact of biology on modern psychiatry* (pp. 65–93). New York: Spectrum. (16)

Geschwind, N. (1965). Disconnexion syndromes in animals and man. *Brain, 88,* 237–294, 585–644. (5)

Geschwind, N. (1970). The organization of language and the brain. *Science, 170,* 940–944. (5)

Geschwind, N. (1972). Language and the brain. *Scientific American, 226* (4), 76–83. (5)

Geschwind, N. (1975). The apraxias: Neural mechanisms of disorders of learned movements. *American Scientist, 63,* 188–195. (5, 8)

Geschwind, N., & Galaburda, A.M. (1985). Cerebral lateralization: Biological mechanisms, associations, and pathology: I. A hypothesis and a program for research. *Archives of Neurology, 42,* 428–459. (5)

Geschwind, N., & Levitsky, W. (1968). Human brain: left-right asymmetries in temporal speech region. *Science, 161,* 186–187. (5)

Geschwind, N., Quadfasel, F.A., & Segarra, J.M. (1968). Isolation of the speech area. *Neuropsychologia, 6,* 327–340. (5)

Getchell, T.V., Margolis, F.L., & Getchell, M.L. (1985). Perireceptor and receptor events in vertebrate olfaction. *Progress in Neurobiology, 23,* 317–345. (6)

Gibbs, F.P. (1983). Temperature dependence of the hamster circadian pacemaker. *American Journal of Physiology, 244,* R607–R610. (9)

Gibbs, J., Young, R.C., & Smith, G.P. (1973). Cholecystokinin decreases food intake in rats. *Journal of Comparative and Physiological Psychology, 84,* 488–495. (10)

Gillberg, C., & Gillberg, I.C. (1983). Infantile autism: A total population study of reduced optimality in the pre-, peri-, and neonatal period. *Journal of Autism and Developmental Disorders, 13,* 153–166. (16)

Gillberg, C., Terenius, L., & Lönnerholm, G. (1985). Endorphin activity in childhood psychosis. *Archives of General Psychiatry, 42,* 780–783. (16)

Gillberg, C., Wahlström, J., & Hagberg, B. (1984). Infantile autism and Rett's syndrome: Common chromosomal denominator? *The Lancet, 2* (8411), 1094–1095. (16)

Giraudat, J., & Changeux, J.-P. (1981). The acetylcholine receptor. In J.W. Lamble (Ed.), *Towards understanding receptors* (pp. 34–43). Amsterdam: Elsevier/North Holland Biomedical. (3)

Gittelman, R., Mannuzza, S., Shenker, R., & Bonagura, N. (1985). Hyperactive boys almost grown up. *Archives of General Psychiatry, 42,* 937–947. (15)

Gjedde, A. (1984). Blood-brain transfer of galactose in experimental galactosemia, with special reference to the competitive interaction between galactose and glucose. *Journal of Neurochemistry, 43*, 1654–1662. (2)

Gladue, B.A., Green, R., & Hellman, R.E. (1984). Neuroendocrine response to estrogen and sexual orientation. *Science, 225*, 1496–1499. (11)

Glaser, R., Rice, J., Speicher, C.E., Stout, J.C., & Kiecolt-Glaser, J.K. (1986). Stress depresses interferon production by leukocytes concomitant with a decrease in natural killer cell activity. *Behavioral Neuroscience, 100*, 675–678. (12)

Glass, A.V., Gazzaniga, M.S., & Premack, D. (1973). Artificial language training in global aphasics. *Neuropsychologia, 11*, 95–103. (5)

Glass, L., Evans, H.E., & Rajegowda, B.K. (1975). Neonatal narcotic withdrawal. In R.W. Richter (Ed.), *Medical aspects of drug abuse* (pp. 124–133). Hagerstown, MD: Harper & Row. (16)

Glenn, L.L., & Dement, W.C. (1985). Membrane potential and input resistance in alpha motoneurons of hindlimb extensors during isolated and clustered episodes of phasic events in REM sleep. *Brain Research, 339*, 79–86. (9)

Glick, S.D. (1974). Changes in drug sensitivity and mechanisms of functional recovery following brain damage. In D.G. Stein, J.J. Rosen, & N. Butters (Eds.), *Plasticity and recovery of function in the central nervous system* (pp. 339–372). New York: Academic. (14)

Goh, Y., Lederhendler, I., & Alkon, D.L. (1985). Input and output changes of an identified neural pathway are correlated with associative learning in *Hermissenda. Journal of Neuroscience, 5*, 536–543. (13)

Golani, I., Bronchti, G., Moualem, D., & Teitelbaum, P. (1981). "Warm-up" along dimensions of movement in the ontogeny of exploration in rats and other infant mammals. *Proceedings of the National Academy of Sciences, U.S.A., 78*, 7226–7229. (14)

Golani, I., Wolgin, D.L., & Teitelbaum, P. (1979). A proposed natural geometry of recovery from akinesia in the lateral hypothalamic rat. *Brain Research, 164*, 237–267. (14)

Gold, P.W., Gwirtsman, H., Avgerinos, P.C., Nieman, L.K., Gallucci, W.T., Kaye, W., Jimerson, D., Ebert, M., Rittmaster, R., Loriaux, D.L., & Chrousos, G.P. (1986). Abnormal hypothalamic-pituitary-adrenal function in anorexia nervosa. *New England Journal of Medicine, 314*, 1335–1342. (10)

Golden, C.J. (1981). *Diagnosis and rehabilitation in clinical neuropsychology*, 2nd ed. Springfield, IL: Charles C Thomas. (14)

Golden, C.J. (1984). Rehabilitation and the Luria-Nebraska neuropsychological battery. In B.A. Edelstein & E.T. Couture (Eds.), *Behavioral assessment and rehabilitation of the traumatically brain-damaged* (pp. 83–120). New York: Plenum. (14)

Goldgaber, D., Lerman, M.I., McBride, O.W., Saffiotti, U., & Gajdusek, D.C. (1987). Characterization and chromosomal localization of a cDNA encoding brain amyloid of Alzheimer's disease. *Science, 235*, 877–880. (13)

Goldman, B.D. (1981). Puberty. In N.T. Adler (Ed.), *Neuroendocrinology of reproduction* (pp. 229–239). New York: Plenum. (11)

Goldman, M.S. (1983). Cognitive impairment in chronic alcoholics: Some cause for optimism. *American Psychologist, 38*, 1045–1054. (10)

Goldman, P.S. (1971). Functional development of the prefrontal cortex in early life and the problem of neuronal plasticity. *Experimental Neurology, 32*, 366–387. (14)

Goldman, P.S. (1976). The role of experience in recovery of function following orbital prefrontal lesions in infant monkeys. *Neuropsychologia, 14*, 401–412. (14)

Goldstein, A. (1980). Thrills in response to music and other stimuli. *Physiological Psychology, 8*, 126–129. (6)

Goldstein, M. (1974). Brain research and violent behavior. *Archives of Neurology, 30*, 1–35. (11, 12)

Gonzalez, M.F., & Deutsch, J.A. (1981). Vagotomy abolishes cues of satiety produced by gastric distension. *Science, 212*, 1283–1284. (10)

Gorman, J.M., Cohen, B.S., Liebowitz, M.R., Fyer, A.J., Ross, D., Davies, S.O., & Klein, D.F. (1986). Blood gas changes and hypophosphatemia in lactate-induced panic. *Archives of General Psychiatry, 43*, 1067–1071. (12)

Gorski, R.A. (1980). Sexual differentiation of the brain. In D.T. Krieger & J.C. Hughes (Eds.), *Neuroendocrinology* (pp. 215–222). Sunderland, MA: Sinauer. (11)

Gorski, R.A. (1985). The 13th J.A.F. Stevenson memorial lecture. Sexual differentiation of the brain: Possible mechanisms and implications. *Canadian Journal of Physiology and Pharmacoloy, 63*, 577–594. (11)

Gottfried, S., & Frankel, M. (1981). New data on lithium and haloperidol incompatibility. *American Journal of Psychiatry, 138*, 818–821. (15)

Grafman, J., Salazar, A., Weingartner, H., Vance, S., & Amin, D. (1986). The relationship of brain-tissue loss volume and lesion location to cognitive deficit. *Journal of Neuroscience, 6*, 301–307. (13)

Graziadei, P.P.C., & deHan, R.S. (1973). Neuronal regeneration in frog olfactory system. *Journal of Cell Biology, 59*, 525–530. (2)

Graziadei, P.P.C., & Monti Graziadei, G.A. (1985). Neurogenesis and plasticity of the olfactory sensory neurons. *Annals of the New York Academy of Sciences, 457*, 127–142. (2)

Green, D.J., & Gillette, R. (1982). Circadian rhythm of firing rate recorded from single cells in the rat suprachiasmatic brain slice. *Brain Research, 245*, 198–200. (9)

Greenblatt, S.H. (1973). Alexia without agraphia or hemianopsia: Anatomical analysis of an autopsied case. *Brain, 96*, 307–316. (5)

Greenough, W.T. (1975). Experiential modification of the developing brain. *American Scientist, 63*, 37–46. (2)

Griffin, D.R., Webster, F.A., & Michael, C.R. (1960). The echolocation of flying insects by bats. *Animal Behaviour, 8*, 141–154. (1, 6)

Gross, C.G., Bruce, C.J., Desimone, R., Fleming, J., & Gattass, R. (1981). Cortical visual areas of the temporal lobe: Three areas in the macaque. In C.N. Woolsey (Ed.), *Cortical sensory organization: Multiple visual areas* (pp. 187–216). Clifton, NJ: Humana. (7)

Grossman, M., Carey, S., Zurif, E., & Diller, L. (1986). Proper and common nouns: Form class judgments in Broca's aphasia. *Brain and Language, 28*, 114–125. (5)

Grossman, S.P. (1964a). Behavioral effects of direct chemical stimulation of central nervous system structures. *International Journal of Neuropharmacology, 3,* 45–58. (3)

Grossman, S.P. (1964b). Some neurochemical aspects of the central regulation of thirst. In M.J. Wayner (Ed.), *Thirst* (pp. 487–514). New York: Pergamon. (3)

Grossman, S.P., Dacey, D., Halaris, A.E., Collier, T., & Routtenberg, A. (1978). Aphagia and adipsia after preferential destruction of nerve cell bodies in hypothalamus. *Science, 202,* 537–539. (10)

Guidotti, A., Ferrero, P., Fujimoto, M., Santi, R.M., & Costa, E. (1986). Studies on endogenous ligands (endocoids) for the benzodiazepine/beta carboline binding sites. *Advances in Biochemical Pharmacology, 41,* 137–148. (12)

Guidotti, A., Forchetti, C.M., Corda, M.G., Konkel, D., Bennett, C.D., & Costa, E. (1983). Isolation, characterization, and purification to homogeneity of an endogenous polypeptide with agonistic action on benzodiazepine receptors. *Proceedings of the National Academy of Sciences, U.S.A., 80,* 3531–3535. (12)

Guillery, R.W. (1972). Binocular competition in the control of geniculate cell growth. *Journal of Comparative Neurology, 144,* 117–130. (7)

Gulick, W.L. (1971). *Hearing: physiology and psychophysics.* New York: Oxford University. (6)

Gur, R.E., Gur, R.C., Sussman, N.M., O'Connor, M.J., & Vey, M.M. (1984). Hemispheric control of the writing hand: The effect of callosotomy in a left-hander. *Neurology, 34,* 904–908. (5)

Gusella, J.F., Tanzi, R.E., Anderson, M.A., Hobbs, W., Gibbons, K., Raschtchian, R., Gilliam, T.C., Wallace, M.R., Wexler, N.S., & Conneally, P.M. (1984). DNA markers for nervous system diseases. *Science, 225,* 1320–1326. (A)

Gusella, J.F., Wexler, N.S., Conneally, P.M., Naylor, S.L., Anderson, M.A., Tanzi, R.E., Watkins, P.C., Ottina, K., Wallace, M.R., Sakachi, A.Y., Young, A.B., Shoulson, I., Bonilla, E., & Martin, J.B. (1983). A polymorphic DNA marker genetically linked to Huntington's disease. *Nature, 306,* 234–238. (8)

Guth, L., Bright, D., & Donati, E.J. (1978). Functional deficits and anatomical alterations after high cervical spinal hemisection in the rat. *Experimental Neurology, 58,* 511–520. (14)

Guyton, A.C. (1974). *Function of the human body.* (4th ed.). Philadelphia: Saunders. (2)

Gwinner, E. (1986). Circannual rhythms in the control of avian rhythms. *Advances in the Study of Behavior, 16,* 191–228. (9)

Haley, J. (1959). An interactional description of schizophrenia. *Psychiatry, 22,* 321–332. (16)

Hamilton, J.B., Hamilton, R.S., & Mestler, G.E. (1969). Duration of life and causes of death in domestic cats: Influence of sex, gonadectomy, and inbreeding. *Journal of Gerontology, 24,* 427–437. (11)

Hamilton, J.B., & Mestler, G.E. (1969). Mortality and survival: Comparison of eunuchs with intact men and women in a mentally retarded population. Journal of Gerontology, 24, 395–411. (11)

Haracz, J.L. (1982). The dopamine hypothesis: An overview of studies with schizophrenic patients. *Schizophrenia Bulletin, 8,* 438–469. (16)

Harley, J.P., Ray, R.S., Tomasi, L. Eichman, P.L., Matthews, C.G., Chun, R., Cleeland, C.S., & Traisman, E. (1978). Hyperkinesis and food additives: Testing the Feingold hypothesis. *Pediatrics, 61,* 818–828. (15)

Harrison, J.M., & Irving, R. (1966). Visual and nonvisual auditory systems in mammals. *Science, 154,* 738–743. (4)

Hartline, H.K. (1949). Inhibition of activity of visual receptors by illuminating nearby retinal areas in the Limulus eye. *Federation Proceedings, 8,* 69. (7)

Hartmann, E. (1973). *The functions of sleep.* New Haven: Yale University. (9)

Hartmann, E. (1983). Two case reports: Night terrors with sleepwalking—A potentially lethal disorder. *Journal of Nervous and Mental Disease, 171,* 503–505. (9)

Hartmann, E., Chung, R., Draskoczy, P.R., & Schildkraut, J.J. (1971). Effects of 6-hydroxydopamine on sleep in the rat. *Nature, 233,* 425–427. (9)

Hartmann, E., Milofsky, E., Vaillant, G., Oldfield, M., Falke, R., & Ducey, C. (1984). Vulnerability to schizophrenia. *Archives of General Psychiatry, 41,* 1050–1056. (16)

Hastings, J.E., & Barkley, R.A. (1978). A review of psychophysiological research with hyperkinetic children. *Journal of Abnormal Child Psychology, 6,* 413–447. (15)

Hauri, P. (1979). What can insomniacs teach us about the functions of sleep? In R. Drucker-Colín, M. Shkurovich, & M.B. Sterman (Eds.), *The functions of sleep* (pp. 251–271). New York: Academic. (9)

Hawkins, R.A., & Biebuyck, J.F. (1979). Ketone bodies are selectively used by individual brain regions. *Science, 205,* 325–327. (2)

Hawkins, R.D., & Kandel, E.R. (1984). Is there a cell-biological alphabet for simple forms of learning? *Psychological Review, 91,* 375–391. (13)

Hawkins, R.D., Roll, P.L., Puerto, A., & Yeomans, J.S. (1983). Refractory periods of neurons mediating stimulation-elicited eating and brain stimulation reward: Interval scale measurement and tests of a model of neural integration. *Behavioral Neuroscience, 97,* 416–432. (2)

Heath, R.G. (1963). Electrical self-stimulation of the brain in man. *American Journal of Psychiatry, 120,* 571–577. (1, 12)

Heath, R. G. (1964). Pleasure response of human subjects to direct stimulation of the brain: Physiologic and psychodynamic considerations. In R.G. Heath (Ed.), *Role of pleasure in behavior* (pp. 219–243). New York: Harper. (1)

Heathcote, R.D., & Sargent, P.B. (1985). Loss of supernumerary axons during neuronal morphogenesis. *Journal of Neuroscience, 5,* 1940–1946. (2)

Hebb, D.O. (1949). *Organization of behavior.* New York: Wiley. (13)

Hécaen, H., & Kremin, H. (1976). Neurolinguistic research on reading disorders resulting from left hemisphere lesions: Aphasic and "pure" alexias. In H. Whitaker & H.A. Whitaker (Eds.) *Studies in neurolinguistics, Vol. 2* (pp. 269–329). New York: Academic. (5)

Hécaen, H., Perenin, M.T., & Jeannerod, M. (1984). The effects of cortical lesions in children: Language and visual functions. In C.R. Almli & S. Finger (Eds.), *Early brain damage* (pp. 277–298). Orlando, FL: Academic. (14)

Hechtman, L., & Weiss, G. (1983). Long-term outcome of hyperactive children. *American Journal of Orthopsychiatry, 53*, 532–541. (15)

Heffner, H.E., & Heffner, R.S. (1984). Temporal lobe lesions and perception of species-specific vocalizations by macaques. *Science, 226*, 75–76. (5)

Heffner, R.S., & Heffner, H.E. (1982). Hearing in the elephant (*Elephas maximus*): Absolute sensitivity, frequency discrimination, and sound localization. *Journal of Comparative and Physiological Psychology, 96*, 926–944. (6)

Helm-Estabrooks, N., & Ramsberger, G. (1986). Treatment of agrammatism in long-term Broca's aphasia. *British Journal of Disorders of Communication, 21*, 39–45. (5)

Henley, K., & Morrison, A.R. (1974). A re-evaluation of the effects of lesions of the pontine tegmentum and locus coeruleus on phenomena of paradoxical sleep in the cat. *Acta Neurobiologiae Experimentalis, 34*, 215–232. (9)

Hennig, R., & Lømo, T. (1985). Firing patterns of motor units in normal rats. *Nature, 314*, 164–166. (8)

Herman, B.H., & Panksepp, J. (1978). Effects of morphine and naloxone on separation distress and approach attachment: Evidence for opiate mediation of social affect. *Pharmacology, Biochemistry & Behavior, 9*, 213–220. (16)

Herrero, S. (1985). *Bear attacks: Their causes and avoidance.* Piscataway, NJ: Winchester. (6, 10)

Hess, W.R. (1944). Das Schlafsyndrom als Folge dienzephaler Reizung. *Helvetica Physiologica Acta, 2*, 305–344. (1)

Hesselbrock, M.N., Meyer, R.E., & Keener, J.J. (1985). Psychopathology in hospitalized alcoholics. *Archives of General Psychiatry, 42*, 1050–1055. (10)

Hicks, R.E. (1975). Intrahemispheric response competition between vocal and unimanual performance in normal adult human males. *Journal of Comparative and Physiological Psychology, 89*, 50–60. (5)

Higgins, J.W., Mahl, G.F., Delgado, J.M.R., & Hamlin, H. (1956). Behavioral changes during intracerebral electrical stimulation. *Archives of neurology and psychiatry, 76*, 399–419. (12)

Hikosaka, O., & Wurtz, R.H. (1986). Saccadic eye movements following injection of lidocaine into the superior colliculus. *Experimental Brain Research, 61*, 531–539. (7)

Hines, M. (1982). Prenatal gonadal hormones and sex differences in human behavior. *Psychological Bulletin, 92*, 56–80. (11)

Hines, M., Davis, F.C., Coquelin, A., Goy, R.W., & Gorski, R.A. (1985). Sexually dimorphic regions in the medial preoptic area and the bed nucleus of the stria terminalis of the guinea pig brain: A description and an investigation of their relationship to gonadal steroids in adulthood. *Journal of Neuroscience, 5*, 40–47. (11)

Hobson, J.A. (1977). The reciprocal interaction model of sleep cycle control: Implications for PGO wave generation and dream amnesia. In R.R. Drucker-Colín & J.L. McGaugh (Eds.), *Neurobiology of sleep and memory* (pp. 159–183). New York: Academic. (9)

Hobson, J.A., & McCarley, R.W. (1977). The brain as a dream state generator: An activation-synthesis hypothesis of the dream process. *American Journal of Psychiatry, 134*, 1335–1348. (9)

Hobson, J.A., McCarley, R.W., & Wyzinski, P.W. (1975). Sleep cycle oscillation: Reciprocal discharge by two brainstem neuronal groups. *Science, 189*, 55–58. (9)

Hodgkinson, S., Sherrington, R., Gurling, H. Marchbanks, R., Reeders, S., Mallet, J., McInnis, M., Petursson, H., & Brynjolfsson, J. (1987). Molecular genetic evidence for heterogeneity in manic depression. *Nature, 325*, 805–806. (15)

Hoffer, A. (1973). Mechanism of action of nicotinic acid and nicotinamide in the treatment of schizophrenia. In D. Hawkins & L. Pauling (Eds.), *Orthomolecular psychiatry* (pp. 202–262). San Francisco: W.H. Freeman. (16)

Hogan, J.A. (1980). Homeostasis and behaviour. In F.M. Toates & T.R. Halliday (Eds.), *Analysis of motivational processes* (pp. 3–21). London: Academic. (10)

Holst—see von Holst

Holt, G.L., & Miller, B.E. (1983). Interanimal task transfer as a function of dosage of brain and liver RNA injections. *Bulletin of the Psychonomic Society, 21*, 47–50. (13)

Holt, J., Antin, J., Gibbs, J., Young, R.C., & Smith, G.P. (1974). Cholecystokinin does not produce bait shyness in rats. *Physiology & Behavior, 12*, 497–498. (10)

Holtzman, J.D., & Gazzaniga, M.S. (1985). Enhanced dual task performance following corpus commissurotomy in humans. *Neuropsychologia, 23*, 315–321. (5)

Holzman, P.S. (1985). Eye movement dysfunctions and psychosis. *International Review of Neurobiology, 27*, 179–205. (16)

Hommer, D.W., Palkovits, M., Crawley, J.N., Paul, S.M., & Skirboll, L.R. (1985). Cholecystokinin-induced excitation in the substantia nigra: Evidence for peripheral and central components. *Journal of Neuroscience, 5*, 1387–1392. (10)

Hopkins, J., Marcus, M., & Campbell, S.B. (1984). Postpartum depression: A critical review. *Psychological Bulletin, 95*, 498–515. (15)

Hopkins, W.F., & Johnston, D. (1984). Frequency-dependent noradrenergic modulation of long-term potentiation in the hippocampus. *Science, 226*, 350–351. (13)

Horn, A.L.D., & Horn, G. (1969). Modification of leg flexion in response to repeated stimulation in a spinal amphibian (*Xenopus mullerei*). *Animal Behaviour, 17*, 618–623. (13)

Horne, J.A., & Minard, A. (1985). Sleep and sleepiness following a behaviourally "active" day. *Ergonomics, 28*, 567–575. (9)

Horne, R.L., Pettinati, H.M., Sugerman, A., & Varga, E. (1985). Comparing bilateral to unilateral electroconvulsive therapy in a randomized study with EEG monitoring. *Archives of General Psychiatry, 42*, 1087–1092. (15)

Horowitz, G.P., & Whitney, G. (1975). Alcohol-induced conditioned aversion: Genotype specificity in mice (*Mus musculus*). *Journal of Comparative and Physiological Psychology, 89*, 340–346. (10)

Horridge, G.A. (1962). Learning of leg position by the ventral nerve cord in headless insects. *Proceedings of the Royal Society of London, B, 157*, 33–52. (13)

Householder, J., Hatcher, R., Burns, W., & Chasnoff, I. (1982). Infants born to narcotic-addicted mothers. *Psychological Bulletin, 92*, 453–468. (16)

Hsu, L.K.G. (1986). The treatment of anorexia nervosa. *American Journal of Psychiatry, 143*, 573–581. (10)

Hubel, D.H., & Wiesel, T.N. (1959). Receptive fields of single neurons in the cat's striate cortex. *Journal of Physiology, 148,* 574–591. (7)

Hubel, D.H., & Wiesel, T.N. (1961). Integrative action in the cat's lateral geniculate body. *Journal of Physiology, 155,* 385–398. (7)

Hubel, D.H., & Wiesel, T.N. (1963). Receptive fields of cells in striate cortex of very young, visually inexperienced kittens. *Journal of Neurophysiology, 26,* 944–1002. (7)

Hubel, D.H., & Wiesel, T.N. (1977). Functional architecture of macaque monkey visual cortex. *Proceedings of the Royal Society of London,* B, *198,* 1–59. (7)

Hudspeth, A.J. (1985). The cellular basis of hearing: The biophysics of hair cells. *Science, 230,* 745–752. (6)

Hull, E.M., Nishita, J.K., Bitran, D., & Dalterio, S. (1984). Perinatal dopamine-related drugs demasculinize rats. *Science, 224,* 1011–1013. (11)

Hull, E.M., Young, S.H., & Zeigler, M.G. (1984). Aerobic fitness affects cardiovascular and catecholamine responses to stressors. *Psychophysiology, 21,* 353–360. (12)

Hurvich, L.M., & Jameson, D. (1957). An opponent-process theory of color vision. *Psychological Review, 64,* 384–404. (6)

Hyman, B.T., van Hoesen, G.W., Damasio, A.R., & Barnes, C.L. (1984). Alzheimer's disease: Cell-specific pathology isolates the hippocampal formation. *Science, 225,* 1168–1170. (13)

Hyvärinen, J., Hyvärinen, L., & Linnankoski, I. (1981). Modification of parietal association cortex and functional blindness after binocular deprivation in young monkeys. *Experimental Brain Research, 42,* 1–8. (7)

Iggo, A., & Andres, K.H. (1982). Morphology of cutaneous receptors. *Annual Review of Neuroscience, 5,* 1–31. (6)

Imperato-McGinley, J., Guerrero, L., Gautier, T., & Peterson, R.E. (1974). Steroid 5 alpha-reductase deficiency in man: An inherited form of male pseudohermaphroditism. *Science, 186,* 1213–1215. (11)

Innocenti, G.M. (1980). The primary visual pathway through the corpus callosum: Morphological and functional aspects in the cat. *Archives Italiennes de Biologie, 118,* 124–188. (5)

Innocenti, G.M., & Caminiti, R. (1980). Postnatal shaping of callosal connections from sensory areas. *Experimental Brain Research, 38,* 381–394. (5)

Innocenti, G.M., Frost, D.O., & Illes, J. (1985). Maturation of visual callosal connections in visually deprived kittens: A challenging critical period. *Journal of Neuroscience, 5,* 255–267. (5)

Inoué, S., Uchizono, K., & Nagasaki, H. (1982). Endogenous sleep-promoting factors. *Trends in neurosciences, 5,* 218–220. (9)

Inouye, S.T., & Kawamura, H. (1979). Persistence of circadian rhythmicity in a mammalian hypothalamic "island" containing the suprachiasmatic nucleus. *Proceedings of the National Academy of Sciences, U.S.A., 76,* 5962–5966. (9)

Insel, T.R., Gillin, J.C., Moore, A., Mendelson, W.B., Loewenstein, R.J., & Murphy, D.L. (1982). The sleep of patients with obsessive-compulsive disorder. *Archives of General Psychiatry, 39,* 1372–1377. (12)

Insel, T.R., Ninan, P.T., Aloi, J., Jimerson, D.C., Skolnick, P., & Paul, S.M. (1984). Benzodiazepine receptor-mediated model of anxiety. *Archives of General Psychiatry, 41,* 741–750. (12)

Irwin, P. (1985). Greater brain response of left-handers to drugs. *Neuropsychologia, 23,* 61–67. (5)

Ivy, G.O., & Killackey, H.P. (1981). The ontogeny of the distribution of callosal projection neurons in the rat parietal cortex. *Journal of Comparative Neurology, 195,* 367–389. (5)

Jacobs, B.L., & Trulson, M.E. (1979). Mechanisms of action of LSD.

Jacobs, B.L., & Trulson, M.E. (1979). Mechanisms of action of LSD. *American Scientist, 67,* 396–404. (3)

Jancsó, G., Kiraly, E., & Jancsó-Gábor, A. (1977). Pharmacologically induced selective degeneration of chemosensitive primary sensory neurones. *Nature, 270,* 741–743. (6)

Janicak, P.G., Davis, J.M., Gibbons, R.D., Ericksen, S., Chang, S., & Gallagher, P. (1985). Efficacy of ECT: A meta-analysis. *American Journal of Psychiatry, 142,* 297–302. (15)

Janosik, E.H., & Davies, J.L. (1986). *Psychiatric mental health nursing.* Boston: Jones & Bartlett. (15)

Jarrard, L.E., Okaichi, H., Steward, O., & Goldschmidt, R.B. (1984). On the role of hippocampal connections in the performance of place and cue tasks: Comparisons with damage to hippocampus. *Behavioral Neuroscience, 98,* 946–954. (13)

Jeddi, E. (1970). Confort du contact et thermoregulation comportementale. *Physiology & Behavior, 5,* 1487–1493. (16)

Jeeves, M.A. (1984). Functional and neuronal plasticity: The evidence from callosal agenesis. In C.R. Almli & S. Finger (Eds.), *Early brain damage* (pp. 233–252). Orlando, FL: Academic. (5)

Jensen, L.H., Petersen, E.N., Honoré, T., & Drejer, J. (1986). Bidirectional modulation of GABA function by β-carbolines. *Advances in Biochemical Pharmacology, 41,* 79–89. (12)

Jerison, H.J. (1985). Animal intelligence as encephalization. *Philosophical Transactions of the Royal Society of London,* B, *308,* 21–35. (4)

John, E.R., Tang, Y., Brill, A.B., Young, R., & Ono, K. (1986). Double-labeled metabolic maps of memory. *Science, 233,* 1167–1175. (13)

Johns, T.R., & Thesleff, S. (1961). Effects of motor inactivation on the chemical sensitivity of skeletal muscle. *Acta Physiologica Scandinavica, 51,* 136–141. (14)

Johnson, A.K., Mann, J.F.E., Rascher, W., Johnson, J.K., & Ganten, D. (1981). Plasma angiotensin II concentrations and experimentally induced thirst. *American Journal of Physiology, 240,* R229–R234. (10)

Johnson, C., Stuckey, M., & Mitchell, J. (1983). Psychopharmacological treatment of anorexia nervosa and bulimia: Review and synthesis. *Journal of Nervous and Mental Disease, 171,* 524–534. (10)

Johnson, L.C. (1969). Physiological and psychological changes following total sleep deprivation. In A. Kales (Ed.), *Sleep: Physiology & Pathology* (pp. 206–220). Philadelphia: Lippincott. (9)

Johnson, W.G., & Wildman, H.E. (1983). Influence of external and covert food stimuli on insulin secretion in obese and normal subjects. *Behavioral Neuroscience, 97,* 1025–1028. (10)

Jones, B.E., Harper, S.T., & Halaris, A.E. (1977). Effects of locus coeruleus lesions upon cerebral monoamine content, sleep-wakefulness states and the response to amphetamine in the cat. *Brain Research, 124,* 473–496. (9)

Jones, H.S., & Oswald, I. (1968). Two cases of healthy insomnia. *Electroencephalography and Clinical Neurophysiology, 24,* 378–380. (9)

Jones, R.K. (1966). Observations on stammering after localized cerebral injury. *Journal of Neurology, Neurosurgery, and Psychiatry, 29,* 192–195. (5)

Jordan, H.A. (1969). Voluntary intragastric feeding. *Journal of Comparative and Physiological Psychology, 68,* 498–506. (10)

Jouvet, M. (1960). Telencephalic and rhombencephalic sleep in the cat. In G.E.W. Wolstenholme & M. O'Connor (Eds.), *CIBA Foundation symposium on the nature of sleep* (pp. 188–208). Boston: Little, Brown. (9)

Jouvet, M., & Delorme, F. (1965). Locus coeruleus et sommeil paradoxal. *Comptes Rendus des Séances de la Société de Biologie, 159,* 895–899. (9)

Jouvet, M., & Renault, J. (1966). Insomnie persistante apres lesions des noyaux du raphe chez le chat. *Comptes Rendus des Séances de la Société de Biologie, 160,* 1461–1465. (9)

Jouvet-Mounier, D., Astic, L., & Lacote, D. (1969). Ontogenesis of the states of sleep in rat, cat, and guinea pig during the first postnatal month. *Developmental Psychobiology, 2,* 216–239. (9)

Juhler, M., Barry, D.I., Offner, H., Konat, G., Klinken, L., & Paulson, O.B. (1984). Blood-brain and blood-spinal cord barrier permeability during the course of experimental allergic encephalomyelitis in the rat. *Brain Research, 302,* 347–355. (2)

Kaas, J.H. (1983). What, if anything, is SI? Organization of first somatosensory area of cortex. *Physiological Reviews, 63,* 206–231. (6)

Kaas, J.H., Merzenich, M.M., & Killackey, H.P. (1983). The reorganization of somatosensory cortex following peripheral nerve damage in adult and developing mammals. *Annual Review of Neuroscience, 6,* 325–356. (14)

Kaas, J.H., Nelson, R.J., Sur, M., Lin, C.-S., & Merzenich, M.M. (1979). Multiple representations of the body within the primary somatosensory cortex of primates. *Science, 204,* 521–523. (4)

Kalat, J.W. (1978). Letter to the editor: Speculations on similarities between autism and opiate addiction. *Journal of Autism and Childhood Schizophrenia, 8,* 477–479. (16)

Kales, A., & Kales, J.D. (1984). *Evaluation and treatment of insomnia.* New York: Oxford. (9)

Kales, A., Scharf, M.B., & Kales, J.D. (1978). Rebound insomnia: A new clinical syndrome. *Science, 201,* 1039–1041. (9)

Kales, A., Soldatos, C.R., Bixler, E.O., & Kales, J.D. (1983). Early morning insomnia with rapidly eliminated benzodiazepines. *Science, 220,* 95–97. (9)

Kamin, L.J. (1974). *The science and politics of IQ.* New York: Wiley. (A)

Kandel, E.R., & Schwartz, J.H. (1982). Molecular biology of learning: Modulation of transmitter release. *Science, 218,* 433–443. (13)

Kanner, L. (1943). Autistic disturbances of affective contact. *Nervous Child, 2,* 217–250. (16)

Kaplan, M.S. (1985). Formation and turnover of neurons in young and senescent animals: An electromicroscropic and morphometric analysis. *Annals of the New York Academy of Sciences, 457,* 173–192. (2)

Kaufman, S. (1975). Hepatic phenylalanine hydroxylase and PKU. In N.A. Buchwald & M.A.B. Brazier (Eds.), *Brain mechanisms in mental retardation* (pp. 445–458). New York: Academic. (A)

Keesey, R.E., Powley, T.L., & Kemnitz, J.W. (1976). Prolonging lateral hypothalamic anorexia by tube-feeding. *Physiology & Behavior, 17,* 367–371. (14)

Kellar, K.J., & Stockmeier, C.A. (1986). Effects of electroconvulsive shock and serotonin axon lesions on beta-adrenergic and serotonin$_2$ receptors in rat brain. *Annals of the New York Academy of Sciences, 462,* 76–90. (15)

Keller, M.B., Lavori, P.W., Klerman, G.L., Andreasen, N.C., Endicott, J., Coryell, W., Fawcett, J., Rice, J.P., & Hirschfeld, R.M.A. (1986). Low levels and lack of predictors of somatotherapy and psychotherapy received by depressed patients. *Archives of General Psychiatry, 43,* 458–466. (15)

Kellerman, H. (1981). *Sleep disorders: Insomnia and narcolepsy.* New York: Brunner/Mazel. (9)

Kemper, T.L. (1984). Asymmetrical lesions in dyslexia. In N. Geschwind & A.M. Galaburda (Eds.), *Cerebral dominance* (pp. 75–89). Cambridge, MA: Harvard. (5)

Kendler, K.S. (1983). Overview: A current perspective on twin studies of schizophrenia. *American Journal of Psychiatry, 140,* 1413–1425. (16)

Kendler, K.S., Gruenberg, A.M., & Tsuang, M.T. (1985). Psychiatric illness in first-degree relatives of schizophrenic and surgical control patients. *Archives of General Psychiatry, 42,* 770–779. (16)

Kendler, K.S., & Robinette, C.D. (1983). Schizophrenia in the National Academy of Sciences–National Research Council twin registry—A 16-year update. *American Journal of Psychiatry, 140,* 1551–1563. (16)

Kennard, M.A. (1938). Reorganization of motor function in the cerebral cortex of monkeys deprived of motor and premotor areas in infancy. *Journal of Neurophysiology, 1,* 477–496. (14)

Kerr, N.H., Foulkes, D., & Jurkovic, G.J. (1978). Reported absence of visual dream imagery in a normally sighted subject with Turner's syndrome. *Journal of Mental Imagery, 2,* 247–264. (11)

Kesner, R.P. (1985). Correspondence between humans and animals in coding of temporal attributes: Role of hippocampus and prefrontal cortex. *Annals of the New York Academy of Sciences, 444,* 122–136. (13)

Kessler, M., Baudry, M., Cummins, J.T., Way, S., & Lynch, G. (1986). Induction of glutamate binding sites in hippocampal membranes by transient exposure to high concentrations of glutamate or glutamate analogs. *Journal of Neuroscience, 6,* 355–363. (13)

Kessler, S. (1980). The genetics of schizophrenia: A review. *Schizophrenia Bulletin, 6,* 404–416. (16)

Kety, S.S. (1975). Progress toward an understanding of the biological substrates of schizophrenia. In R.R. Fieve, D. Rosenthal, & H. Brill (Eds.), *Genetic research in psychiatry* (pp. 15–26). Baltimore, MD: Johns Hopkins University. (16)

Kety, S.S., Rosenthal, D., Wender, P.H., Schulsinger, F., & Jacobsen, B. (1975). Mental illness in the biological and adoptive families of adopted individuals who have become schizophrenic. In R.R. Fieve, D. Rosenthal, & H. Brill (Eds.), *Genetic research in psychiatry* (pp. 147–165). Baltimore, MD: Johns Hopkins University. (16)

Kiefer, S.W., Leach, L.R., & Braun, J.J. (1984). Taste agnosia following gustatory neocortex ablation: Dissociation from odor and generality across taste qualities. *Behavioral Neuroscience, 98,* 590–608. (6)

Killackey, H.P., & Chalupa, L.M. (1986). Ontogenetic change in the distribution of callosal projection neurons in the postcentral gyrus of the fetal rhesus monkey. *Journal of Comparative Neurology, 244,* 331–348. (5)

Killeffer, F.A., & Stern, W.E. (1970). Chronic effects of hypothalamic injury. *Archives of Neurology, 22,* 419–429. (10)

Kim, J.S., & Kornhuber, H.H. (1982). The glutamate theory in schizophrenia: Clinical and experimental evidence. In N. Namba & H. Kaiya (Eds.), *Psychobiology of schizophrenia* (pp. 221–234). Oxford: Pergamon. (16)

Kimura, D. (1973a). Manual activity during speaking—I. Right handers. *Neuropsychologia, 11,* 45–50. (5)

Kimura, D. (1973b). Manual activity during speaking—II. Left handers. *Neuropsychologia, 11,* 51–55. (5)

King, B.M., Smith, R.L., & Frohman, L.A. (1984). Hyperinsulinemia in rats with ventromedial hypothalamic lesions: Role of hyperphagia. *Behavioral Neuroscience, 98,* 152–155. (10)

Kinney, D.K., Woods, B.T., & Yurgelun-Todd, D. (1986). Neurologic abnormalities in schizophrenic patients and their families. *Archives f General Psychiatry, 43,* 665–668. (16)

Kinsbourne, M. (1972). Eye and head turning indicates cerebral lateralization. *Science, 176,* 539–541. (5)

Kinsbourne, M., & McMurray, J. (1975). The effect of cerebral dominance on time sharing between speaking and tapping by preschool children. *Child Development, 46,* 240–242. (5)

Klawans, H.L., Goetz, C.G., Paulson, G.W., & Barbeau, A. (1980). Levodopa and presymptomatic detection of Huntington's disease—eight-year follow-up. *New England Journal of Medicine, 302,* 1090. (8)

Kleitman, N. (1963). *Sleep and wakefulness* (revised and enlarged edition). Chicago: University of Chicago. (9)

Klerman, G.L. (1975). Relationships between preclinical testing and therapeutic evaluation of antidepressant drugs: The importance of new animal models for theory and practice. In A. Sudilovsky, S. Gershon, & B. Beer (Eds.), *Predictability in psychopharmacology* (pp. 159–178). New York: Raven. (3)

Kluger, M.J. (1978). The evolution and adaptive value of fever. *American Scientist, 66,* 38–43. (10)

Kluger, M.J., & Rothenburg, B.A. (1979). Fever and reduced iron: Their interaction as a host defense response to bacterial infection. *Science, 203,* 374–376. (10)

Kluger, M.J., & Vaughn, L.K. (1978). Fever and survival in rabbits infected with *Pasteurella multocida. Journal of Physiology, 282,* 243–251. (10)

Knowles, J.F., & Berry, M. (1978). Effect of enzyme treatment of central nervous system lesions in the rat. *Experimental Neurology, 59,* 450–454. (14)

Knudsen, E.I., & Konishi, M. (1978). Space and frequency are represented separately in the auditory midbrain of the owl. *Journal of Neurophysiology, 41,* 870–884. (6)

Kodama, J., Fukushima, M., & Sakata, T. (1978). Impaired taste discrimination against quinine following chronic administration of theophylline in rats. *Physiology & Behavior, 20,* 151–155. (6)

Koegel, R.L., Schreibman, L., O'Neill, R.E., & Burke, J.C. (1983). The personality and family-interaction characteristics of parents of autistic children. *Journal of Consulting & Clinical Psychology, 51,* 683–692. (16)

Koella, W.P. (1984). The organization and regulation of sleep: A review of the experimental evidence and a novel integrated model of the organizing and regulating apparatus. *Experientia, 40,* 309–338. (9)

Kolata, G. (1986). New drug counters alcohol intoxication. *Science, 234,* 1198–1199. (12)

Kolata, G. (1987). Clinical trials planned for new AIDS drug. *Science, 235,* 1138–1139. (6)

Kolb, B., & Holmes, C. (1983). Neonatal motor cortex lesions in the rat: Absence of sparing of motor behaviors and impaired spatial learning concurrent with abnormal cerebral morphogenesis. *Behavioral Neuroscience, 97,* 697–709. (14)

Kolb, B., Sutherland, R.J., & Whishaw, I.Q. (1983). Abnormalities in cortical and subcortical morphology after neonatal neocortical lesions in rats. *Experimental Neurology, 79,* 223–244. (14)

Kolb, B., & Taylor, L. (1981). Affective behavior in patients with localized cortical excisions: Role of lesion site and side. *Science, 214,* 89–90. (5)

Kolb, B., & Whishaw, I.Q. (1977). Effects of brain lesions and atropine on hippocampal and neocortical electroencephalograms in the rat. *Experimental Neurology, 56,* 1–22. (14)

Kolb, B., & Whishaw, I.Q. (1983). Performance of schizophrenic patients on tests sensitive to left or right frontal, temporal, or parietal function in neurological patients. *Journal of Nervous and Mental Disease, 171,* 435–443. (16)

Komisaruk, B.R., Adler, N.T., & Hutchison, J. (1972). Genital sensory field: Enlargement by estrogen treatment in female rats. *Science, 178,* 1295–1298. (11)

Komisaruk, B.R., & Wallman, J. (1977). Antinociceptive effects of vaginal stimulation in rats: Neurophysiological and behavioral studies. *Brain Research, 137,* 85–107. (6)

Komisaruk, B.R., & Whipple, B. (1986). Vaginal stimulation-produced analgesia in rats and women. *Annals of the New York Academy of Sciences, 467,* 30–39. (6)

Konishi, M., & Akutagawa, E. (1985). Neuronal growth, atrophy and death in a sexually dimorphic song nucleus in the zebra finch brain. *Nature, 315,* 145–147. (11)

Kornhuber, H.H. (1971). Motor functions of cerebellum and basal ganglia. *Kybernetik, 8,* 157–162. (8)

Kornhuber, H.H. (1974). Cerebral cortex, cerebellum, and basal ganglia: An introduction to their motor functions. In F.O. Schmitt & F.G. Worden (Eds.), *The neurosciences: Third study program* (pp. 267–280). Cambridge, MA: MIT. (8)

Kornhuber, H.H. (1983). Chemistry, physiology and neuropsychology of schizophrenia: Towards an earlier diagnosis of schizophrenia I. *Archiv für Psychiatrie und Nervenkrankheiten, 233,* 415–422. (16)

Kosel, K.C., Wilkinson, J.M., Jew, J., Itaya, S.K., Beckwith, K., & Williams, T.H. (1979). Enzyme therapy and spinal cord regeneration: A fluorescence microscopic evaluation. *Experimental Neurology, 64,* 365–374. (14)

Kostowski, W., Giacalone, E., Garattini, S., & Valzelli, L. (1969). Electrical stimulation of midbrain raphe: Biochemical, behavioral, and bioelectrical effects. *European Journal of Pharmacology, 7,* 170–175. (9)

Kozlowski, M.R., & Marshall, J.F. (1981). Plasticity of neostriatal metabolic activity and behavioral recovery from nigrostriatal injury. *Experimental Neurology, 74,* 318–323. (14)

Kraly, F.S. (1984). Physiology of drinking elicited by eating. *Psychological Review, 91,* 478–490. (10)

Krantz, D.S., & Manuck, S.B. (1984). Acute psychophysiologic reactivity and risk of cardiovascular disease: A review and methodological critique. *Psychological Bulletin, 96,* 435–464. (12)

Kreuz, L.E., & Rose, R.M. (1972). Assessment of aggressive behavior and plasma testosterone in a young criminal population. *Psychosomatic Medicine, 34,* 321–332. (11)

Krieger, D.T. (1983). Brain peptides: What, where, and why? *Science, 222,* 975–985. (3)

Krieger, D.T., Perlow, M.J., Gibson, M.J., Davies, T.F., Zimmerman, E.A., Ferin, M., & Charlton, H.M. (1982). Brain grafts reverse hypogonadism of gonadotropin releasing hormone deficiency. *Nature, 298,* 468–471. (14)

Krnjević, K., & Reinhardt, W. (1979). Choline excites cortical neurons. *Science, 206,* 1321–1323. (3)

Krueger, J.M., Pappenheimer, J.R., & Karnovsky, M.L. (1982). The composition of sleep-promoting factor isolated from human urine. *Journal of Biological Chemistry, 257,* 1664–1669. (9)

Kuffler, S.W. (1953). Discharge patterns and functional organization of the mammalian retina. *Journal of Neurophysiology, 16,* 37–68. (7)

Kupfermann, I., Castellucci, V., Pinsker, H., & Kandel, E. (1970). Neuronal correlates of habituation and dishabituation of the gill withdrawal reflex in *Aplysia. Science, 167,* 1743–1745. (13)

Kurata, K., & Tanji, J. (1986). Premotor cortex neurons in macaques: Activity before distal and proximal forelimb movements. *Journal of Neuroscience, 6,* 403–411. (8)

Kurtzke, J.R. (1976). An introduction to the epidemiology of cerebrovascular disease. In F. Scheinberg (Ed.), *Cerebrovascular diseases* (pp. 239–253). New York: Raven. (14)

Laguzzi, R.F., & Adrien, J. (1980). Inversion de l'insomnie produite par la para-chlorophenylalanine chez le rat. *Archives Italiennes de Biologie, 118,* 109–123. (9)

Laing, D.G. (1984). The effect of environmental odours on the sense of smell. In N.W. Bond (Ed.), *Animal models in psychopathology* (pp. 59–98). North Ryde, N.S.W.: Academic Press Australia. (6)

Lamb, M.E. (1975). Physiological mechanisms in the control of maternal behavior in rats: A review. *Psychological Review, 82,* 104–119. (11)

LaMotte, C.C., & Collins, W.F. (1982). Physiological anatomy of pain. In J.R. Youmans (Ed.), *Neurological surgery* 2nd ed., Vol. 6 (pp. 3461–3479). Philadelphia: Saunders. (6)

Lance, J.W., & McLeod, J.G. (1975). *A physiological approach to clinical neurology* (2nd ed.). London: Butterworth. (8)

Land, E.H., Hubel, D.H., Livingstone, M.S., Perry, S.H., & Burns, M.M. (1983). Colour-generating interactions across the corpus callosum. *Nature, 303,* 616–618. (6)

Land, E.H., & McCann, J.J. (1971). Lightness and retinex theory. *Journal of the Optical Society of America, 61,* 1–11. (6)

Landrigan, P.J., Powell, K.E., James, L.M., & Taylor, P.R. (1983). Paraquat and marijuana: Epidemiologic risk assessment. *American Journal of Public Health, 73,* 784–788. (8)

Lansdell, H. (1969). Verbal and nonverbal factors in right-hemisphere speech: Relation to early neurological history. *Journal of Comparative and Physiological Psychology, 69,* 734–738. (5)

Lashley, K.S. (1929). *Brain mechanisms and intelligence.* Chicago: University of Chicago. (4, 13)

Lashley, K.S. (1950). In search of the engram. *Symposia of the Society for Experimental Biology, 4,* 454–482. (13)

Lashley, K.S. (1951). The problem of serial order in behavior. In L.A. Jeffress (Ed.), *Cerebral mechanisms in behavior* (pp. 112–146). New York: Wiley. (8)

Lashley, K.S., & McCarthy, D.A. (1926). The survival of the maze habit after cerebellar injuries. *Journal of Comparative Psychology, 6,* 423–433. (8)

Lasiter, P.S., Deems, D.A., & Glanzman, D.L. (1985). Thalamocortical relations in taste aversion learning: I. Involvement of gustatory thalamocortical projections in taste aversion learning. *Behavioral Neuroscience, 99,* 454–476. (6)

Laurent, J.-P., Cespuglio, R., & Jouvet, M. (1974). Délimitation des voies ascendantes de l'activité ponto-géniculo-occipitale chez le chat. *Brain Research, 65,* 29–52. (9)

Lederhendler, I.I., Gart, S., & Alkon, D.L. (1986). Classical conditioning of *Hermissenda*: Origin of a new response. *Journal of Neuroscience, 6,* 1325–1331. (13)

Ledwidge, B. (1980). Run for your mind: Aerobic exercise as a means of alleviating anxiety and depression. *Canadian Journal of Behavioral Science, 12,* 126–140. (12)

Lehrman, D.S. (1964). The reproductive behavior of ring doves. *Scientific American, 211* (5), 48–54. (11)

Leiner, H.C., Leiner, A.L., & Dow, R.S. (1986). Does the cerebellum contribute to mental skills? *Behavioral Neuroscience, 100,* 443–454. (8)

Lelord, G., Muh, J.P., Barthelemy, C., Martineau, J., & Garreau, B. (1981). Effects of pyridoxine and magnesium on autistic symptoms—initial observations. *Journal of Autism and Developmental Disorders, 11,* 219–230. (16)

LeMagnen, J. (1967). Habits and food intake. In *Handbook of physiology*, Section 6, Vol. 1, *The alimentary canal* (pp. 11–30). Bethesda, MD: American Physiological Society, 1967. (10)

LeMagnen, J. (1981). The metabolic basis of dual periodicity of feeding in rats. *The Behavioral and Brain Sciences, 4,* 561–607. (10)

Lenhart, R.E., & Katkin, E.S. (1986). Psychophysiological evidence for cerebral laterality effects in a high-risk sample of students with subsyndromal bipolar depressive disorder. *American Journal of Psychiatry, 143,* 602–607. (15)

Lentz, T.L., Burrage, T.G., Smith, A.L., Crick, J., & Tignor, G.H. (1981). Is the acetylcholine receptor a rabies virus receptor? *Science, 215,* 182–184. (12)

Leonard, B.E. (1979). Pharmacological and biochemical aspects of hyperkinetic disorders. *Neuropharmacology, 18,* 923–929. (15)

Lerer, B., & Shapira, B. (1986). Neurochemical mechanisms of mood stabilization. *Annals of the New York Academy of Sciences, 462,* 367–375. (15)

Lesse, S. (1984). Psychosurgery. *American Journal of Psychotherapy, 38,* 224–228. (4)

Lester, L.S., & Fanselow, M.S. (1985). Exposure to a cat produces opioid analgesia in rats. *Behavioral Neuroscience, 99,* 756–759. (6)

Lettvin, J.Y., Maturana, H.R., McCulloch, W.S., & Pitts, W.H. (1959). What the frog's eye tells the frog's brain. *Proceedings of the Institute of Radio Engineers, 47,* 1940–1951. (6)

LeVere, N.D., & LeVere, T.E. (1982). Recovery of function after brain damage: Support for the compensation theory of the behavioral deficit. *Physiological Psychology, 10,* 165–174. (14)

LeVere, T.E. (1975). Neural stability, sparing and behavioral recovery following brain damage. *Psychological Review, 82,* 344–358. (14)

LeVere, T.E. (1980). Recovery of function after brain damage: A theory of the behavioral deficit. *Physiological Psychology, 8,* 297–308. (14)

LeVere, T.E., & Morlock, G.W. (1973). Nature of visual recovery following posterior neodecortication in the hooded rat. *Journal of Comparative and Physiological Psychology, 83,* 62–67. (14)

Levine, D.N., Warach, J.D., Benowitz, L., & Calvanio, R. (1986). Left spatial neglect: Effects of lesion size and premorbid brain atrophy on severity and recovery following right cerebral infarction. *Neurology, 36,* 362–366. (4)

Levine, J.S., & MacNichol, E.F., Jr. (1982). Color vision in fishes. *Scientific American, 246* (2), 140–149. (6)

Levitt, R.A. (1975). *Psychopharmacology.* Washington, DC: Hemisphere. (3)

Levitt-Gilmour, T.A., & Salpeter, M.M. (1986). Gradient of extrajunctional acetylcholine receptors early after denervation of mammalian muscle. *Journal of Neuroscience, 6,* 1606–1612. (14)

Levy, J. (1976). Lateral dominance and aesthetic preference. *Neuropsychologia, 14,* 431–445. (5)

Levy, J. (1982). Handwriting posture and cerebral organization: How are they related? *Psychological Bulletin, 91,* 589–608. (5)

Levy, J. (1984). A review, analysis, and some new data on hand-posture distributions in left-handers. *Brain and Cognition, 3,* 105–127. (5)

Levy, J., & Kueck, L. (1986). A right hemispatial field advantage on a verbal free-vision task. *Brain and Language, 27,* 24–37. (5)

Levy, J., & Nagylaki, T. (1972). A model for the genetics of handedness. *Genetics, 72,* 117–128. (5)

Levy, J., Nebes, R.D., & Sperry, R.W. (1971). Expressive language in the surgically separated minor hemisphere. *Cortex, 7,* 49–58. (5)

Levy, J., & Reid, M. (1976). Variations in writing posture and cerebral organization. *Science, 194,* 337–339. (5)

Levy, J., & Reid, M. (1978). Variations in cerebral organization as a function of handedness, hand posture in writing, and sex. *Journal of Experimental Psychology: General, 107,* 119–144. (5)

Levy, J., & Wagner, N. (1984). Handwriting posture, visuomotor integration, and lateralized reaction-time parameters. *Human Neurobiology, 3,* 157–161. (5)

Levy, R.M., Bredesen, D.E., & Rosenblum, M.L. (1985). Neurological manifestations of the acquired immunodeficiency syndrome (AIDS): Experience at UCSF and review of the literature. *Journal of Neurosurgery, 62,* 475–495. (16)

Levy-Agresti, J., & Sperry, R.W. (1968). Differential perceptual capacities in major and minor hemispheres. *Proceedings of the National Academy of Sciences (U.S.A.), 61,* 1151. (5)

Lewine, R.R.J. (1981). Sex differences in schizophrenia: Timing or subtypes? *Psychological Bulletin, 90,* 432–444. (16)

Lewis, D.J. (1979). Psychobiology of active and inactive memory. *Psychological Bulletin, 86,* 1054–1083. (13)

Lewis, D.J., Bregman, N.J., & Mahan, J.J., Jr. (1972). Cue-dependent amnesia in rats. *Journal of Comparative and Physiological Psychology, 81,* 243–247. (13)

Lewis, V.G., Money, J., & Epstein, R. (1968). Concordance of verbal and nonverbal ability in the adrenogenital syndrome. *Johns Hopkins Medical Journal, 122,* 192–195. (11)

Lewy, A.J., Nurnberger, J.I., Jr., Wehr, T.A., Pack, D., Becker, L.E., Powell, R.-L., Newsome, D.A. (1985). Supersensitivity to light: Possible trait marker for manic-depressive illness. *American Journal of Psychiatry, 142,* 725–727. (15)

Liebeskind, J.C., & Paul, L.A. (1977). Psychological and physiological mechanisms of pain. *Annual Review of Psychology, 28,* 41–60. (6)

Liebowitz, M.R., Gorman, J.M., Fyer, A.J., Levitt, M., Dillon, D., Levy, G., Appleby, I.L., Anderson, S., Palij, M., Davies, S.O., & Klein, D.F. (1985). Lactate provocation of panic attacks: II. Biochemical and physiological findings. *Archives of General Psychiatry, 42,* 709–719. (12)

Lindberg, N.O., Coburn, C., & Stricker, E.M. (1984). Increased feeding by rats after subdiabetogenic streptozotocin treatment: A role for insulin in satiety. *Behavioral Neuroscience, 98,* 138–145. (10)

Lindsay, P.H., & Norman, D.A. (1972). *Human information processing.* New York: Academic. (6)

Lindstrom, J. (1979). Autoimmune response to acetylcholine receptors in myasthenia gravis and its animal model. *Advances in Immunology, 27,* 1–50. (8)

Lipton, M.A., Breese, G.R., Prange, A.J., Jr., Wilson, I.C., & Cooper, B.R. (1976). Behavioral effects of hypothalamic polypeptide hormones in animals and man. In E.J. Sachar (Ed.), *Hormones, behavior, and psychopathology* (pp. 15–29). New York: Raven. (15)

Lipton, M.A., & Nemeroff, C.B. (1978). An overview of the biogenic amine hypothesis of schizophrenia. In W.E. Fann, I. Karacan, A. Pokorny, & R.L. Williams (Eds.), *Phenomenology and treatment of schizophrenia* (pp. 431–453). New York: Spectrum. (16)

Loewenstein, W.R. (August, 1960). Biological transducers. *Scientific American, 203* (2), 98–108. (6)

Loewi, O. (1960). An autobiographic sketch. *Perspectives in Biology, 4,* 3–25. (3)

Lowe, J., & Carroll, D. (1985). The effects of spinal injury on the intensity of emotional experience. *British Journal of Clinical Psychology, 24,* 135–136. (12)

Lowing, P.A., Mirsky, A.F., & Pereira, R. (1983). The inheritance of schizophrenia spectrum disorders: A reanalysis of the Danish adoptee study plan. *American Journal of Psychiatry, 140,* 1167–1171. (16)

Luchins, D.J., Lewine, R.R.J., & Meltzer, H.Y. (1984). Lateral ventricular size, psychopathology, and medication response in the psychoses. *Biological Psychiatry, 19,* 29–44. (16)

Ludlow, C.L., Rosenberg, J., Fair, C., Buck, D., Schesselman, S., & Salazar, A. (1986). Brain lesions associated with nonfluent aphasia fifteen years following penetrating head injury. *Brain, 109,* 55–80. (5)

Lyman, C.P., O'Brien, R.C., Greene, G.C., & Papafrangos, E.D. (1981). Hibernation and longevity in the Turkish hamster *Mesocricetus brandti. Science, 212,* 668–670. (9)

Lynch, G., & Baudry, M. (1984). The biochemistry of memory: A new and specific hypothesis. *Science, 224,* 1057–1063. (13)

Lynch, J.A., & Aserinsky, E. (1986). Developmental changes of oculomotor characteristics in infants when awake and in the "active state of sleep." *Behavioural Brain Research, 20,* 175–183. (9)

Lynch, J.C. (1980). The functional organization of posterior parietal association cortex. *The Behavioral and Brain Sciences, 3,* 485–534. (4)

Lytle, L.D., Messing, R.B., Fisher, L., & Phebus, L. (1975). Effects of long-term corn consumption on brain serotonin and the response to electric shock. *Science, 190,* 692–694. (12)

Maccoby, E.E., & Jacklin, C.N. (1974). *The psychology of sex differences.* Stanford, CA: Stanford University. (11)

Macdonald, R.L., Weddle, M.G., & Gross, R.A. (1986). Benzodiazepine, β-carboline, and barbiturate actions on GABA responses. *Advances in Biochemical Psychopharmacology, 41,* 67–78. (12)

MacFarlane, J.G., Cleghorn, J.M., & Brown, G.M. (1985a). Melatonin and core temperature rhythms in chronic insomnia. In G.M. Brown & S.D. Wainwright (Eds.), *The pineal gland: Endocrine aspects* (pp. 301–306). New York: Pergamon. (9)

MacFarlane, J.G., Cleghorn, J.M., & Brown, G.M. (September, 1985b). *Circadian rhythms in chronic insomnia.* Paper presented at the IVth World Congress of Biological Psychiatry, Philadelphia. (9)

MacLean, P.D. (1949). Psychosomatic disease and the "visceral brain": Recent developments bearing on the Papez theory of emotion. *Psychosomatic Medicine, 11,* 338–353. (12)

MacLean, P.D. (1954). Studies on limbic system ("visceral brain") and their bearing on psychosomatic problems. In E. D. Wittkower & R. A. Cleghorn (Eds.), *Recent developments in psychosomatic medicine* (pp. 101–125). Philadelphia: Lippincott. (12)

MacLean, P.D. (1958). Contrasting functions of limbic and neocortical systems of the brain and their relevance to psychophysiological aspects of medicine. *American Journal of Medicine, 25,* 611–626. (12)

MacLean, P.D. (1962). II Neurophysiologie. In *Monoamines et systeme nerveux central* (p. 269–276). Geneva: Georg a Cie, 1962. (15)

MacLean, P.D. (1970). The limbic brain in relation to the psychoses. In P. Black (Ed.), *Physiological correlates of emotion* (pp.129–146). New York: Academic. (4, 12)

MacLean, P.D. (1977). The triune brain in conflict. *Psychotherapy and Psychosomatics, 28,* 207–220. (4)

MacLusky, N.J., & Naftolin, F. (1981). Sexual differentiation of the central nervous system. *Science, 211,* 1294–1303. (11)

MacLusky, N.J., Naftolin, F., & Goldman-Rakic, P.S. (1986). Estrogen formation and binding in the cerebral cortex of the developing rhesus monkey. *Proceedings of the National Academy of Sciences, U.S.A., 83,* 513–516. (11)

MacPhail, E.M. (1985). Vertebrate intelligence: The null hypothesis. *Philosophical Transactions of the Royal Society of London,* B, *308,* 37–51. (4)

Maffei, L., & Fiorentini, A. (1973). The visual cortex as a spatial frequency analyser. *Vision Research, 13,* 1255–1267. (7)

Maier, S.F., Seligman, M.E.P., & Solomon, R.L. (1969). Pavlovian fear conditioning and learned helplessness: Effects on escape and avoidance behavior of (a) the CS-US contingency and (b) the independence of the US and voluntary responding. In B.A. Campbell & R.M. Church (Eds.), *Punishment and aversive behavior* (pp. 299–342). New York: Appleton-Century-Crofts. (15)

Maier, S.F., Sherman, J.E., Lewis, J.W., Terman, G.W., & Liebeskind, J.C. (1983). The opioid/nonopioid nature of stress-induced analgesia and learned helplessness. *Journal of Experimental Psychology: Animal Behavior Processes, 9,* 80–90. (6)

Majewska, M.D., Harrison, N.L., Schwartz, R.D., Barker, J.L., & Paul, S.M. (1986). Steroid hormone metabolites are barbiturate-like modulators of the GABA receptors. *Science, 232,* 1004–1007. (12)

Malamut, B.L., Saunders, R.C., & Mishkin, M. (1984). Monkeys with combined amygdalo-hippocampal lesions succeed in object discrimination learning despite 24-hour intertrial intervals. *Behavioral Neuroscience, 98,* 759–769. (13)

Malcuit, G. (1973). Cardiac responses in aversive situation with and without avoidance possibility. *Psychophysiology, 10,* 295–306. (12)

Maletzky, B.M. (1973). The episodic dyscontrol syndrome. *Diseases of the Nervous System, 34*, 178–185. (12)

Mangiapane, M.L., & Simpson, J.B. (1980). Subfornical organ: Forebrain site of pressor and dipsogenic action of angiotensin II. *American Journal of Physiology, 239*, R382–R389. (10)

Mangiapane, M.L., Thrasher, T.N., Keil, L.C., Simpson, J.B., & Ganong, W.F. (1983). Deficits in drinking and vasopressin secretion after lesions of the nucleus medianus. *Neuroendocrinology, 37*, 73–77. (10)

Mann, J.J., Stanley, M., McBride, A., & McEwen, B.S. (1986). Increased serotonin₂ and β-adrenergic receptor binding in the frontal cortices of suicide victims. *Archives of General Psychiatry, 43*, 954–959. (12)

Marcus, J., Hans, S.L., Mednick, S.A., Schulsinger, F., & Michelsen, N. (1985). Neurological dysfunctioning in offspring of schizophrenics in Israel and Denmark. *Archives of General Psychiatry, 42*, 753–761. (16)

Mark, V.H., & Ervin, F.R. (1970). *Violence and the brain.* New York: Harper & Row. (12)

Marsden, C.D. (1984). Motor disorders in basal ganglia disease. *Human Neurobiology, 2*, 245–250. (8)

Marshall, J.F. (1985). Neural plasticity and recovery of function after brain injury. *International Review of Neurobiology, 26*, 201–247. (14)

Marshall, J.F., Drew, M.C., & Neve, K.A. (1983). Recovery of function after mesotelencephalic dopaminergic injury in senescence. *Brain Research, 259*, 249–260. (14)

Marshall, J.F., & Teitelbaum, P. (1974). Further analysis of sensory inattention following lateral hypothalamic damage in rats. *Journal of Comparative and Physiological Psychology, 86*, 375–395. (10)

Marshall, W.A., & Tanner, J.M. (1986). Puberty. In F. Falkner & J.M. Tanner (Ed.), *Human growth* 2nd ed., Vol. 2: Postnatal growth, neurobiology (pp. 171–224). New York: Plenum. (11)

Martin, A.R. (1977). Junctional transmission. II. Presynaptic mechanisms. In E.R. Kandel (Ed.), *Handbook of physiology* (Section 1, Vol. 1, Part 1) (pp. 329–355). Bethesda, MD: American Physiological Society. (3)

Martin, R.C., & Blossom-Stach, C. (1986). Evidence of syntactic deficits in a fluent aphasic. *Brain and Language, 28*, 196–234. (5)

Martinez, J.L., Jr., Jensen, R.A., & McGaugh, J.L. (1981). Attenuation of experimentally induced amnesia. *Progress in Neurobiology, 16*, 155–186. (13)

Martinez-Vargas, M.C., & Erickson, C.J. (1973). Some social and hormonal determinants of nest-building behaviour in the ring dove (*Streptopelia risoria*). *Behaviour, 45*, 12–37. (11)

Mash, D.C., Flynn, D.D., & Potter, L.T. (1985). Loss of M2 muscarine receptors in the cerebral cortex in Alzheimer's disease and experimental cholinergic denervation. *Science, 228*, 1115–1117. (13)

Mason, S.T., & Fibiger, H.C. (1979). On the specificity of kainic acid. *Science, 204*, 1339–1341. (4)

Masters, W.M., Moffat, A.J.M., & Simmons, J.A. (1985). Sonar tracking of horizontally moving targets by the big brown bat *Eptesicus fuscus. Science, 228*, 1331–1333. (1)

Masterton, R.B. (1974). Adaptation for sound localization in the ear and brainstem of mammals. *Federation Proceedings, 33*, 1904–1910. (6)

Matheis, M., & Förster, C. (1980). Zur psychosexuellen Entwicklung von Mädchen mit adrenogenitalem Syndrom. *Zeitschrift für Kinder- und Jugend-Psychiatrie, 8*, 5–17. (11)

Matossian, M.K. (1982). Ergot and the Salem witchcraft affair. *American Scientist, 70*, 355–357. (3)

Mattes, J.A., & Gittelman, R. (1981). Effects of artificial food colorings in children with hyperactive symptoms: A critical review and results of a controlled study. *Archives of General Psychiatry, 38*, 714–718. (15)

Matthews, D.A., Cotman, C., & Lynch, G. (1976). An electron microscopic study of lesion-induced synaptogenesis in the dentate gyrus of the adult rat. II. Reappearance of morphologically normal synaptic contacts. *Brain Research, 115*, 23–41. (14)

Mawson, A.R., & Jacobs, K.W. (1978). Corn, tryptophan, and homicide. *Journal of Orthomolecular Psychiatry, 7*, 227–230. (12)

May, P.R.A., Fuster, J.M., Haber, J., & Hirschman, A. (1979). Woodpecker drilling behavior: An endorsement of the rotational theory of impact brain injury. *Archives of Neurology, 36*, 370–373. (14)

Mayer, A.D., & Rosenblatt, J.S. (1979). Hormonal influences during the ontogeny of maternal behavior in female rats. *Journal of Comparative and Physiological Psychology, 93*, 879–898. (11)

Mayer, J. (1953). Glucostatic mechanism of regulation of food intake. *New England Journal of Medicine, 249*, 13–16. (10)

Mayer, W., & Scherer, I. (1975). Phase shifting effect of caffeine in the circadian rhythm of *Phaseolus coccineus* L. *Zeitschrift fur Naturforschung, C, 30*, 855–856. (9)

McCarley, R.W., & Hobson, J.A. (1975). Neuronal excitability modulation over the sleep cycle: A structural and mathematical model. *Science, 189*, 58–60. (9)

McCarley, R.W., & Hobson, J.A. (1977). The neurobiological origins of psychoanalytic dream theory. *American Journal of Psychiatry, 134*, 1211–1221. (9)

McCarley, R.W., & Hoffman, E. (1981). REM sleep, dreams, and the activation-synthesis hypothesis. *American Journal of Psychiatry, 138*, 904–912. (9)

McConnell, J.V. (1962). Memory transfer through cannibalism in planarians. *Journal of Neuropsychiatry, 3* (Supplement 1), 42–48. (13)

McConnell, J.V. (1979). Worms and things. *Journal of Biological Psychology, 21*, 1. (13)

McCormick, D.A., & Thompson, R.F. (1984). Cerebellum: Essential involvement in the classically conditioned eyelid response. *Science, 223*, 296–299. (13)

McGuffin, P., Farmer, A.E., Gottesman, I.I., Murray, R.M., & Reveley, A.M. (1984). Twin concordance for operationally defined schizophrenia. *Archives of General Psychiatry, 41*, 541–545. (16)

McGuigan, F.J. (1984). Progressive relaxation: Origins, principles, and clinical applications. In R.L. Woolfolk & P.M. Lehrer (Eds.), *Principles and practice of stress management* (pp. 12–42). New York: Guilford. (12)

McHugh, P.R., & Moran, T.H. (1985). The stomach: A conception of its dynamic role in satiety. *Progress in*

Psychobiology and Physiological Psychology, 11, 197–232. (10)

McLean, S., Skirboll, L.R., & Pert, C.B. (1985). Comparison of substance P and enkephalin distribution in rat brain: An overview using radioimmunocytochemistry. *Neuroscience, 14,* 837–852. (6)

McMasters, R.E. (1962). Regeneration of the spinal cord in the rat: Effects of Piromen and ACTH upon the regenerative capacity. *Journal of Comparative Neurology, 119,* 113–121. (14)

McMinn, M.R. (1984). Mechanisms of energy balance in obesity. *Behavioral Neuroscience, 98,* 375–393. (10)

McWilliams, J.R., & Lynch, G. (1983). Rate of synaptic replacement in denervated rat hippocampus declines precipitously from the juvenile period to adulthood. *Science, 221,* 572–574. (14)

McWilliams, J.R., & Lynch, G. (1984). Synaptic density and axonal sprouting in rat hippocampus: Stability in adulthood and decline in late adulthood. *Brain Research, 294,* 152–156. (14)

Meck, W.H., & Church, R.M. (1985). Arginine vasopressin inoculates against age-related changes in temporal memory. *Annals of the New York Academy of Sciences, 444,* 453–456. (13)

Meddis, R. (1979). The evolution and function of sleep. In D.A. Oakley & H.C. Plotkin (Eds.), *Brain, behaviour and evolution* (pp. 99–125). London: Methuen. (9)

Meddis, R., Pearson, A.J.D., & Langford, G. (1973). An extreme case of healthy insomnia. *EEG and Clinical Neurophysiology, 35,* 213–214. (9)

Meisel, R.L., Dohanich, G.P., & Ward, I.L. (1979). Effects of prenatal stress on avoidance acquisition, open-field performance and lordotic behavior in male rats. *Physiology & Behavior, 22,* 527–530. (11)

Meisel, R.L, & Ward, I.L. (1981). Fetal female rats are masculinized by male littermates located caudally in the uterus. *Science, 213,* 239–242. (11)

Melzack, R., & Wall, P.D. (1965). Pain mechanisms: A new theory. *Science, 150,* 971–979. (6)

Merton, P.A. (1972). How we control the contraction of our muscles. *Scientific American, 226* (5), 30–37. (8)

Merzenich, M.M., Nelson, R.J., Stryker, M.P., Cynader, M.S., Schoppman, A., & Zook, J.M. (1984). Somatosensory cortical map changes following digit amputation in adult monkeys. *Journal of Comparative Neurology, 224,* 591–605. (14)

Messing, R.B., & Sparber, S.B. (1985). Greater task difficulty amplifies the facilitatory effect of des-glycinamide arginine vasopressin on appetitively motivated learning. *Behavioral Neuroscience, 99,* 1114–1119. (13)

Miczek, K.A., Thompson, M.L., & Shuster, L. (1986). Analgesia following defeat in an aggressive enounter: Development of tolerance and changes in opioid receptors. *Annals of the New York Academy of Sciences, 467,* 14–29. (6)

Miles, F.A., & Evarts, E.V. (1979). Concepts of motor organization. *Annual Review of Psychology, 30,* 327–362. (8)

Miles, L.E.M., Raynal, D.M., & Wilson, M.A. (1977). Blind man living in normal society has circadian rhythms of 24.9 hours. *Science, 198,* 421–423. (9)

Miller, E.A., Goldman, P.S., & Rosvold, H.E. (1973). Delayed recovery of function following orbital prefrontal lesions in infant monkeys. *Science, 182,* 304–306. (14)

Miller, G.A. (1956). The magical number seven, plus or minus two: Some limits on our capacity for processing information. *Psychological Review, 63,* 81–97. (13)

Miller, K.W. (1985). The nature of the site of general anesthesia. *International Review of Neurobiology, 27,* 1–61. (2)

Miller, M.J., Small, I.F., Milstein, V., Malloy, F., & Stout, J.R. (1981). Electrode placement and cognitive change with ECT: Male and female response. *American Journal of Psychiatry, 138,* 384–386. (15)

Miller, N.E. (1969). Learning of visceral and glandular responses. *Science, 163,* 434–445. (12)

Miller, N.E. (1985). The value of behavioral research on animals. *American Psychologist, 40,* 423–440. (1)

Miller, N.E., Bailey, C.J., & Stevenson, J.A.F. (1950). Decreased "hunger" but increased food intake resulting from hypothalamic lesions. *Science, 112,* 256–259. (10)

Miller, R.R., & Springer, A.D. (1972). Induced recovery of memory in rats following electroconvulsive shock. *Physiology & Behavior, 8,* 645–651. (13)

Milner, B. (1959). The memory defect in bilateral hippocampal lesions. *Psychiatric Research Reports, 11,* 43–58. (13)

Milner, B., Corkin, S., & Teuber, H.-L. (1968). Further analysis of the hippocampal amnesic syndrome: 1ear follow-up study of H.M. *Neuropsychologia, 6,* 215–234. (13)

Milner, E. (1976). CNS maturation and language acquisition. In H. Whitaker & H.A. Whitaker (Eds.), *Studies in neurolinguistics,* Vol. 1 (pp. 31–102). New York: Academic. (5)

Miselis, R.R., Shapiro, R.E., & Hand, P.J. (1979). Subfornical organ efferents to neural systems for control of body water. *Science, 205,* 1022–1025. (10)

Mitchell, D.E. (1980). The influence of early visual experience on visual perception. In C.S. Harris (Ed.), *Visual coding and adaptability* (pp. 1–50). Hillsdale, NJ: Erlbaum. (7)

Mitchell, J.E., & Popkin, M.K. (1982). Antipsychotic drug therapy and sexual dysfunction in men. *American Journal of Psychiatry, 139,* 633–637. (16)

Mohr, J.P., Weiss, G.H., Caveness, W.F., Dillon, J.D., Kistler, J.P., Meirowsky, A.M., & Rish, B.L. (1980). Language and motor disorders after penetrating head injury in Viet Nam. *Neurology, 30,* 1273–1279. (5)

Moltz, H., Lubin, M., Leon, M., & Numan, M. (1970). Hormonal induction of maternal behavior in the ovariectomized nulliparous rat. *Physiology & Behavior, 5,* 1373–1377. (11)

Money, J. (1967). Sexual problems of the chronically ill. In C.W. Wahl (Ed.), *Sexual problems: Diagnosis and treatment in medical practice* (pp. 266–287). New York: Free Press. (8)

Money, J. (1970). Matched pairs of hermaphrodites: Behavioral biology of sexual differentiation from chromosomes to gender identity. *Engineering and Science (Cal. Tech.), 33,* 34–39. (11)

Money, J., & Ehrhardt, A.A. (1968). Prenatal hormonal exposure: Possible effects on behaviour in man. In R.P. Michael (Ed.), *Endocrinology and human behaviour* (pp. 32–48). London: Oxford University. (11)

Money, J., & Ehrhardt, A.A. (1972). *Man & woman, boy & girl*. Baltimore, MD: Johns Hopkins University. (11)

Money, J., & Lewis, V. (1966). IQ, genetics and accelerated growth: Adrenogenital syndrome. *Bulletin of the Johns Hopkins Hospital, 118*, 365–373. (11)

Money, J., & Lewis, V. (1982). Homosexual/heterosexual status in boys at puberty: Idiopathic adolescent gynecomastia and congenital virilizing adrenocorticism compared. *Psychoneuroendocrinology, 7*, 339–346. (11)

Money, J., & Schwartz, M. (1978). Biosocial determinants of gender identity differentiation and development. In J.B. Hutchison (Ed.), *Biological determinants of sexual behaviour* (pp. 765–784). Chichester, England: John Wiley. (11)

Money, J., Schwartz, M., & Lewis, V.G. (1984). Adult erotosexual status and fetal hormonal masculinization and demasculinization: 46,XX congenital virilizing adrenal hyperplasia and 46,XY androgen-insensitivity syndrome compared. *Psychoneuroendocrinology, 9*, 405–414. (11)

Money, J., Wiedeking, C., Walker, P.A., & Gain, D. (1976). Combined antiandrogenic and counseling program for treatment of 46,XY and 47,XYY sex offenders. In E.J. Sachar (Ed.), *Hormones, behavior, and psychopathology* (pp. 105–120). New York: Raven. (11)

Moore, B.O., & Deutsch, J.A. (1985). An antiemetic is antidotal to the satiety effects of cholecystokinin. *Nature, 315*, 321–322. (10)

Moore, R.Y. (1974). Central regeneration and recovery of function: The problem of collateral reinnervation. In D.G. Stein, J.J. Rosen, & N. Butters (Eds.), *Plasticity and recovery of function in the central nervous system* (pp. 111–128). New York: Academic. (14)

Moore, R.Y., Björklund, A., & Stenevi, U. (1971). Plastic changes in the adrenergic innervation of the rat septal area in response to denervation. *Brain Research, 33*, 13–35. (14)

Moore-Ede, M.C., Czeisler, C.A., & Richardson, G.S. (1983a). Circadian timekeeping in health and disease. *New England Journal of Medicine, 309*, 469–476. (9)

Moore-Ede, M.C., Czeisler, C.A., & Richardson, G.S. (1983b). Circadian timekeeping in health and disease. Part 2. Clinical implications of circadian rhythmicity. *New England Journal of Medicine, 309*, 530–536. (9)

Morgane, P.J. (1981). Serotonin: Twenty-five years later. *Psychopharmacology Bulletin, 17*, 13–17. (9)

Morgane, P.J., & Stern, W.C. (1974). Chemical anatomy of brain circuits in relation to sleep and wakefulness. In E.D. Weitzman (Ed.), *Advances in sleep research (Vol. 1)* (pp. 1–131). Flushing, NY: Spectrum. (9)

Morley, J.E., Bartness, T.J., Gosnell, B.A., & Levine, A.S. (1985). Peptidergic regulation of feeding. *International Review of Neurobiology, 27*, 207–298. (10)

Morrison, J.H., Rogers, J., Scherr, S., Benoit, R., & Bloom, F.E. (1985). Somatostatin immunoreactivity in neuritic plaques of Alzheimer's patients. *Nature, 314*, 90–92. (13)

Morrow, L., Ratcliff, G., & Johnston, C.S. (1986). Externalising spatial knowledge in patients with right hemispheric lesions. *Cognitive Neuropsychology, 2*, 265–273. (5)

Moruzzi, G., & Magoun, H.W. (1949). Brain stem reticular formation and activation of the EEG. *Electroencephalography and clinical neurophysiology, 1*, 455–473. (9)

Moscovitch, M. (1985). Memory from infancy to old age: Implications for theories of normal and pathological memory. *Annals of the New York Academy of Sciences, 444*, 78–96. (13)

Moulton, D.G. (1976). Spatial patterning of response to odors in the peripheral olfactory system. *Physiological Reviews, 56*, 578–593. (6)

Mountcastle, V.B., Lynch, J.C., Georgopoulos, A., Sakata, H., & Acuna, C. (1975). Posterior parietal association cortex of the monkey: Command functions for operations within extrapersonal space. *Journal of Neurophysiology, 38*, 871–908. (7)

Moyer, K.E. (1974). Sex differences in aggression. In R.C. Friedman, R.M. Richart, & R.L. VandeWiele (Eds.), *Sex differences in behavior* (pp. 335–372). New York: Wiley. (11)

Müller, H.W., Gebicke-Härter, P.J., Hangen, D.H., & Shooter, E.M. (1985). A specific 37,000 Dalton protein that accumulates in regenerating but not in nonregenerating mammalian nerves. *Science, 228*, 499–501. (14)

Murphy, J.M., Sobol, A.M., Neff, R.K., Olivier, D.C., & Leighton, A.H. (1984). Stability of prevalence. *Archives of General Psychiatry, 41*, 990–997. (15)

Murphy, M.G., & O'Leary, J.L. (1973). Hanging and climbing functions in raccoon and sloth after total cerebellectomy. *Archives of Neurology, 28*, 111–117. (8)

Murray, C.L., & Fibiger, H.C. (1986). Pilocarpine and physostigmine attenuate spatial memory impairments produced by lesions of the nucleus basalis magnocellularis. *Behavioral Neuroscience, 100*, 23–32. (13)

Nabekura, J. Oomura, Y., Minami, T., Mizuno, Y., & Fukuda, A. (1986). Mechanism of the rapid effect of 17–β-estradiol on medial amygdala neurons. *Science, 233*, 226–228. (11)

Nachman, M. (1962). Taste preferences for sodium salts by adrenalectomized rats. *Journal of Comparative and Physiological Psychology, 55*, 1124–1129. (10)

Narabayashi, H. (1972). Stereotaxic amygdalotomy. In B.E. Eleftheriou (Ed.), *The neurobiology of the amygdala* (pp. 459–483). New York: Plenum. (12)

Nebes, R.D. (1974). Hemispheric specialization in commissurotomized man. *Psychological Bulletin, 81*, 1–14. (5)

Neitz, J., & Jacobs, G.H. (1986). Reexamination of spectral mechanisms in the rat (*Rattus norvegicus*). *Journal of Comparative Psychology, 100*, 21–29. (6)

Nelson, D.O., & Prosser, C.L. (1981). Intracellular recordings from thermosensitive preoptic neurons. *Science, 213*, 787–789. (10)

Nesse, R.M., Cameron, O.G., Curtis, G.C., McCann, D.S., & Huber-Smith, M.J. (1984). Adrenergic function in patients with panic anxiety. *Archives of General Psychiatry, 41*, 771–776. (12)

Netter, F.H. (1983). *CIBA Collection of Medical Illustrations, Vol. 1, Nervous System*. New York: CIBA. (11)

Neziroglu, F. (1979). Behavioral and organic aspects of aggression. In J. Obiols, C. Ballús, E. González Monclús, & J.Pujol (Eds.), *Biological psychiatry today* (pp. 1215–1222). Amsterdam: Elsevier/North Holland Biomedical. (12)

Niakan, E., Harati, Y., & Rolak, L.A. (1986). Immunosuppressive drug therapy in myasthenia gravis. *Archives of Neurology, 43,* 155–156. (8)

Nicol, S.E., & Gottesman, !.I. (1983). Clues to the genetics and neurobiology of schizophrenia. *American Scientist, 71,* 398–404. (13)

Nielsen, J. (1969). Klinefelter's syndrome and the XYY syndrome. *Acta Psychiatrica Scandinavica, 45* (Supplement 209), 1–353. (11)

Nordeen, E.J., Nordeen, K.W., Sengelaub, D.R., & Arnold, A.P. (1985). Androgens prevent normally occurring cell death in a sexually dimorphic spinal nucleus. *Science, 229,* 671–673. (11)

Northcutt, R.G. (1985). Central nervous system phylogeny: Evaluation of hypotheses. *Fortschritte der Zoologie, 30,* 497–505. (4)

Nottebohm, F. (1970). Ontogeny of bird song. *Science, 167,* 950–956. (5)

Nottebohm, F. (1985). Neuronal replacement in adulthood. *Annals of the New York Academy of Sciences, 457,* 143–161. (2)

O'Brien, D.P., Chesire, R.M., & Teitelbaum, P. (1985). Vestibular versus tail-pinch activation in cats with lateral hypothalamic lesions. *Physiology & Behavior, 34,* 811–814. (10)

Oden, B.G., Clohisy, D.J., & Francois, G.R. (1982). Interanimal transfer of learned behavior through injections of brain RNA. *Psychological Record, 32,* 281–290. (13)

O'Donohue, T.L., Millington, W.R., Handelmann, G.E., Contreras, P.C., & Chronwall, B.M. (1985). On the 50th anniversary of Dale's law: Multiple neurotransmitter neurons. *Trends in Pharmacological Sciences, 6,* 305–308. (3)

Olds, J. (1958a). Satiation effects in self-stimulation of the brain. *Journal of Comparative and Physiological Psychology, 51,* 675–678. (12)

Olds, J. (1958b). Effects of hunger and male sex hormone on self-stimulation of the brain. *Journal of Comparative and Physiological Psychology, 51,* 320–324. (12)

Olds, J. (1962). Hypothalamic substrates of reward. *Physiological Reviews, 42,* 554–604. (12)

Olds, J., & Milner, P. (1954). Positive reinforcement produced by electrical stimulation of the septal area and other regions of the rat brain. *Journal of Comparative and Physiological Psychology, 47,* 419–428. (12)

O'Leary, D.S., & Boll, T.J. (1984). Neuropsychological correlates of early generalized brain dysfunction in children. In C.R. Almli & S. Finger (Eds.), *Early brain damage* (pp. 215–229). Orlando, FL: Academic. (14)

Olsen, T.S., Bruhn, P., & Öberg, R.G.E. (1986). Cortical hypoperfusion as a possible cause of "subcortical aphasia." *Brain, 109,* 393–410. (5, 14)

Olton, D.S., Collison, C., & Werz, M.A. (1977). Spatial memory and radial arm maze performance of rats. *Learning and Motivation, 8,* 289–314. (13)

Olton, D.S., & Papas, B.C. (1979). Spatial memory and hippocampal function. *Neuropsychologia, 17,* 669–682. (13)

Olton, D.S., Walker, J.A., & Gage, F.H. (1978). Hippocampal connections and spatial discrimination. *Brain Research, 139,* 295–308. (13)

Olton, D.S., Wible, C.G., & Shapiro, M.L. (1986). Mnemonic theories of hippocampal function. *Behavioral Neuroscience, 100,* 852–855. (13)

O'Malley, S.S., & Maisto, S.A. (1985). Effects of family drinking history and expectancies on responses to alcohol in men. *Journal of Studies on Alcohol, 46,* 289–297. (10)

Orlosky, M.J. (1982). The Kleine-Levin syndrome: A review. *Psychosomatics, 23,* 609–621. (10)

Ornitz, E.M., Atwell, C.W., Kaplan, A.R., & Westlake, J.R. (1985). Brain-stem dysfunction in autism. *Archives of General Psychiatry, 42,* 1018–1025. (16)

Ornitz, E.M., & Ritvo, E.R. (1976). Medical assessment. In E.R. Ritvo (Ed.), *Autism* (pp. 7–23). New York: Spectrum. (16)

Oscar-Berman, M. (1980). Neuropsychological consequences of long-term chronic alcoholism. *American Scientist, 68,* 410–419. (13)

Osmond, H. (1973). The background to the niacin treatment. In D. Hawkins & L. Pauling (Eds.), *Orthomolecular psychiatry* (pp. 194–201). San Francisco: W.H. Freeman. (16)

Ostrin, R.K., & Schwartz, M.F. (1986). Reconstructing from a degraded trace: A study of sentence repetition in agrammatism. *Brain and Language, 28,* 328–345. (5)

Owen, D.R. (1972). The 47,XYY male: A review. *Psychological Bulletin, 78,* 209–233. (11)

Palay, S.L., & Chan-Palay, V. (1977). General morphology of neurons and neuroglia. In J.M. Brookhart & V.M. Mountcastle (Eds.), *Handbook of physiology, Section 1: The nervous system* (Vol.1, Part 1) (pp. 5–37). Bethesda, MD: American Physiological Society. (2)

Pande, A.C. (1985). Light-induced hypomania. *American Journal of Psychiatry, 142,* 1126. (15)

Panksepp, J. (1973). The ventromedial hypothalamus and metabolic adjustments of feeding behavior. *Behavioral Biology, 9,* 65–75. (10)

Panksepp, J., Herman, B., & Vilberg, T. (1978). An opiate excess model of childhood autism. *Neuroscience Abstracts, 4* (Abstract 1601), 500. (16)

Panksepp, J., Herman, B.H., Vilberg, T., Bishop, P., & DeEskinazi, F.G. (1980). Endogenous opioids and social behavior. *Neuroscience and Biobehavioral Reviews, 4,* 473–487. (16)

Papez, J.W. (1937). A proposed mechanism of emotion. *Archives of Neurology and Psychiatry, 38,* 725–743. (12)

Pappas, C.T.E., Diamond, M.C., & Johnson, R.E. (1979). Morphological changes in the cerebral cortex of rats with altered levels of ovarian hormones. *Behavioral and Neural Biology, 26,* 298–310. (11)

Parker, D.E. (1980). The vestibular apparatus. *Scientific American, 243* (5), 118–135. (6)

Parker, G.H. (1922). *Smell, taste, and allied senses in the vertebrates.* Philadelphia: Lippincott. (6)

Parlee, M.B. (1983). Menstrual rhythms in sensory processes: A review of fluctuations in vision, olfaction, audition, taste, and touch. *Psychological Bulletin, 93,* 539–548. (11)

Parnas, J., Schulsinger, F., Schulsinger, H., Mednick, S.A., & Teasdale, T.W. (1982). Behavioral precursors of schizophrenia spectrum. *Archives of General Psychiatry, 39,* 658–664. (16)

Passingham, R.E. (1985). Memory of monkeys (*Macaca mulatta*) with lesions in prefrontal cortex. *Behavioral Neuroscience, 99,* 3–21. (13)

Paton, J.A., O'Loughlin, B.E., & Nottebohm, F. (1985). Cells born in adult canary forebrain are local interneurons. *Journal of Neuroscience, 5,* 3088–3093. (2)

Patterson, M.M., Cegavske, C.G., & Thompson, R.F. (1973). Effects of a classical conditioning paradigm on hind-limb flexor nerve response in immobilized spinal cats. *Journal of Comparative and Physiological Psychology, 84,* 88–97. (13)

Paul, S.M., Extein, I., Calil, H.M., Potter, W.Z., Chodoff, P., & Goodwin, F.K. (1981). Use of ECT with treatment-resistant depressed patients at the National Institute of Mental Health. *American Journal of Psychiatry, 138,* 486–489. (15)

Pauling, L. (1968). Orthomolecular psychiatry. *Science, 160,* 265–271. (16)

Pauls, D.L., Kruger, S.D., Leckman, J.F., Cohen, D.J., & Kidd, K.K. (1984). The risk of Tourette's syndrome and chronic multiple tics among relatives of Tourette's syndrome patients obtained by direct interview. *Journal of the American Academy of Child Psychiatry, 23,* 134–137. (3)

Pauls, D.L., Towbin, K.E., Leckman, J.F., Zahner, G.E.P., & Cohen, D.J. (1986). Gilles de la Tourette's syndrome and obsessive-compulsive disorder. *Archives of General Psychiatry, 43,* 1180–1182. (12)

Peachey, J.E., & Naranjo, C.A. (1983). The use of disulfiram and other alcohol-sensitizing drugs in the treatment of alcoholism. *Research Advances in Alcohol and Drug Problems, 7,* 397–431. (10)

Pearson, K.G. (1979). Local neurons and local interactions in the nervous system of invertebrates. In F.O. Schmitt & F.G. Worden (Eds.), *The Neurosciences: Fourth study program* (pp. 145–157). Cambridge, MA: MIT Press. (2)

Peck, J.W., & Novin, D. (1971). Evidence that osmoreceptors mediating drinking in rabbits are in the lateral preoptic area. *Journal of Comparative and Physiological Psychology, 74,* 134–147. (10)

Pedersen, C.A., Ascher, J.A., Monroe, Y.L., & Prange, A.J., Jr. (1982). Oxytocin induces maternal behavior in virgin female rats. *Science, 216,* 648–650. (11)

Pelham, W.E., Bender, M.E., Caddell, J., Booth, S., & Moorer, S.H. (1985). Methylphenidate and children with attention deficit disorder. *Archives of General Psychiatry, 42,* 948–952. (15)

Pellegrino, L.J., & Cushman, A.J. (1967). *A stereotaxic atlas of the rat brain.* New York: Appleton-Century-Crofts. (4)

Pellis, S.M., Chen, Y.-C., & Teitelbaum, P. (1985). Fractionation of the cataleptic bracing response in rats. *Physiology & Behavior, 34,* 815–823. (8)

Penfield, W. (1955). The permanent record of the stream of consciousness. *Acta Psychologica, 11,* 47–69. (13)

Penfield, W., & Milner, B. (1958). Memory deficit produced by bilateral lesions in the hippocampal zone. *Archives of Neurology and Psychiatry, 79,* 475–497. (13)

Penfield, W., & Perot, P. (1963). The brain's record of auditory and visual experience. *Brain, 86,* 595–696. (13)

Penfield, W., & Rasmussen, T. (1950). *The cerebral cortex of man.* New York: Macmillan. (4)

Penfield, W., & Roberts, L. (1959). *Speech and brain mechanisms.* Princeton, NJ: Princeton University. (1)

Perenin, M.T., & Jeannerod, M. (1978). Visual function within the hemianopic field following early cerebral hemidecortication in man—I. Spatial localization. *Neuropsychologia, 16,* 1–13. (7)

Perlow, M.J., Freed, W.J., Hoffer, B.J., Seiger, A., Olson, L., & Wyatt, R.J. (1979). Brain grafts reduce motor abnormalities produced by destruction of nigrostriatal dopamine system. *Science, 204,* 643–647. (14)

Persky, H., Smith, K.D., & Basu, G.K. (1971). Relation of psychologic measures of aggression and hostility to testosterone production in man. *Psychosomatic Medicine, 33,* 265–277. (11)

Pert, A., Rosenblatt, J.E., Sivit, C., Pert, C.B., & Bunney, W.E., Jr. (1978). Long-term treatment with lithium prevents the development of dopamine receptor supersensitivity. *Science, 201,* 171–173. (15)

Pescovitz, O.H., Cutler, G.B., Jr., & Loriaux, D.L. (1985). Precocious puberty. *Neuroendocrine Perspectives, 4,* 73–93. (11)

Peterson, G.C. (1980). Organic mental disorders associated with brain trauma. In H.I. Kaplan, A.M. Freedman, & B.J. Sadlock (Eds.), *Comprehensive textbook of psychiatry,* 3rd ed., Vol. 2 (pp. 1422–1437). Baltimore, MD: Williams & Wilkins. (14)

Pettegrew, R.K., & Windle, W.F. (1976). Factors in recovery from spinal cord injury. *Experimental Neurology, 53,* 815–829. (14)

Petty, L.K., Ornitz, E.M., Michelman, J.D., & Zimmerman, E.G. (1984). Autistic children who become schizophrenic. *Archives of General Psychiatry, 41,* 129–135. (16)

Pfaffmann, C., Frank, M., & Norgren, R. (1979). Neural mechanisms and behavioral aspects of taste. *Annual Review of Psychology, 30,* 283–325. (6)

Pfaffmann, C., Norgren, R., & Grill, H. (1977). Sensory affect and motivation. *Annals of the New York Academy of Sciences, 290,* 18–34. (6)

Pflug, B. (1973). Therapeutic aspects of sleep deprivation. In W.P. Koella & P. Levin (Eds.), *Sleep: Physiology, biochemistry, psychology, pharmacology, clinical implications* (pp. 185–191). Basel: Karger. (15)

Phoenix, C.H., Slob, A.K., & Goy, R.W. (1973). Effects of castration and replacement therapy on sexual behavior of adult male rhesuses. *Journal of Comparative and Physiological Psychology, 84,* 472–481. (11)

Pickar, D., Labarca, R., Doran, A.R., Wolkowitz, O.M., Roy, A., Breier, A., Linnoila, M., & Paul, S.M. (1986). Longitudinal measurement of plasma homovanillic acid levels in schizophrenic patients. *Archives of General Psychiatry, 43,* 669–676. (16)

Pierrot-Deseilligny, C., Gray, F., & Brunet, P. (1986). Infarcts of both inferior parietal lobules with impairment of visually guided eye movements, peripheral visual inattention and optic ataxia. *Brain, 109,* 81–97. (7)

Pillard, R.C., & Weinrich, J.D. (1986). Evidence of familial nature of male homosexuality. *Archives of General Psychiatry, 43,* 808–812. (11)

Pincus, J.H. (1980). Can violence be a manifestation of epilepsy? *Neurology, 30,* 304–307. (12)

Pinel, J.P.J., Treit, D., & Rovner, L.I. (1977). Temporal lobe aggression in rats. *Science, 197,* 1088–1089. (12)

Pinsky, S.D., & McAdam, D.W. (1980). Electroencephalographic and dichotic indices of cerebral laterality in stutterers. *Brain and Language, 11,* 374–397. (5)

Pirozzolo, F.J. (1979). *The neuropsychology of developmental reading disorders.* New York: Praeger. (5)

Pi-Sunyer, X., Kissileff, H.R., Thornton, J., & Smith, G.P. (1982). C-terminal octapeptide of cholecystokinin decreases food intake in obese men. *Physiology & Behavior, 29,* 627–630. (10)

Plapinger, L., & McEwen, B.S. (1978). Gonadal steroid-brain interactions in sexual differentiation. In J.B. Hutchison (Ed.), *Biological determinants of sexual behavior* (pp. 153–218). Chichester, England: Wiley. (11)

Pokorny, A.D. (1978). The course and progress of schizophrenia. In W.E. Fann, I. Karacan, A.D. Pokorny, & R.L. Williams (Eds.), *Phenomenology and treatment of schizoprenia* (pp. 21–37). New York: Spectrum. (16)

Pollak, J.M. (1979). Obsessive-compulsive personality: A review. *Psychological Bulletin, 86,* 225–241. (12)

Pomeranz, B., & Chung, S.H. (1970). Dendritic-tree anatomy codes form-vision physiology in tadpole retina. *Science, 170,* 983–984. (4)

Potkin, S.G., Karoum, F., Chuang, L.-W., Cannon-Spoor, H.E., Phillips, I., & Wyatt, R.J. (1979). Phenylethylamine in paranoid chronic schizophrenia. *Science, 206,* 470–471. (16)

Powley, T.L., & Keesey, R.E. (1970). Relationship of body weight to the lateral hypothalamic feeding syndrome. *Journal of Comparative and Physiological Psychology, 70,* 25–36. (14)

Preilowski, B. (1975). Bilateral motor interaction: Perceptual-motor performance of partial and complete split-brain patients. In K.J. Zülch, O. Creutzfeldt, & G.C. Galbraith (Eds.), *Cerebral localization* (pp. 115–132). New York: Springer Verlag. (5)

Premack, A.J. (1976). *Why chimps can read.* New York: Harper & Row. (5)

Premack, A.J., & Premack, D. (1972). Teaching language to an ape. *Scientific American, 227* (4), 92–99. (5)

Premack, D. (1970). A functional analysis of language. *Journal of the Experimental Analysis of Behavior, 14,* 107–125. (5)

Price, R.A., Kidd, K.K., Cohen, D.J., Pauls, D.L., & Leckman, J.F. (1985). A twin study of Tourette syndrome. *Archives of General Psychiatry, 42,* 815–820. (3)

Pritchard, T.C., Hamilton, R.B., Morse, J.R., & Norgren, R. (1986). Projections of thalamic gustatory and lingual areas in the monkey, *Macaca fascicularis. Journal of Comparative Neurology, 244,* 213–228. (6)

Prosser, R., Kittrell, E.M.W., & Satinoff, E. (1984). Circadian body temperature rhythms in rats with suprachiasmatic nuclear lesions. In J.R.S. Hales (Ed.), *Thermal physiology* (pp. 67–70). New York: Raven. (9)

Provine, R.R. (1979). "Wing-flapping" develops in wingless chicks. *Behavioral and Neural Biology, 27,* 233–237. (8)

Provine, R.R. (1981). Wing-flapping develops in chickens made flightless by feather mutations. *Developmental Psychobiology, 14,* 481–486. (8)

Provine, R.R. (1984). Wing-flapping during development and evolution. *American Scientist, 72,* 448–455. (8)

Provine, R.R. (1986). Yawning as a stereotyped action pattern and releasing stimulus. *Ethology, 72,* 109–122. (8)

Provine, R.R., & Westerman, J.A. (1979). Crossing the midline: Limits of early eye-hand behavior. *Child Development, 50,* 437–441. (5)

Puchala, E., & Windle, W.F. (1977). The possibility of structural and functional restitution after spinal cord injury: A review. *Experimental Neurology, 55,* 1–42. (14)

Pujol, J.F., Buguet, A., Froment, J.L., Jones, B., & Jouvet, M. (1971). The central metabolism of serotonin in the cat during insomnia: A neurophysiological and biochemical study after administration of p-chlorophenylalanine or destruction of the raphe system. *Brain Research, 29,* 195–212. (9)

Pumariega, A.J., Edwards, P., & Michell, C.B. (1984). Anorexia nervosa in black adolescents. *Journal of the American Academy of Child Psychiatry, 23,* 111–114. (10)

Purves, D., & Hadley, R.D. (1985). Changes in the dendritic branching of adult mammalian neurones revealed by repeated imaging *in situ. Nature, 315,* 404–406. (2)

Purves, D., & Lichtman, J.W. (1985). Geometrical differences among homologous neurons in mammals. *Science, 228,* 298–302. (2)

Quadagno, D.M., Briscoe, R., & Quadagno, J.S. (1977). Effect of perinatal gonadal hormones on selected nonsexual behavior patterns: A critical assessment of the non-human and human literature. *Psychological Bulletin, 84,* 62–80. (11)

Quinn, P.T. (1972). Stuttering: Cerebral dominance and the dichotic word test. *Medical Journal of Australia, 2,* 639–643. (5)

Rabkin, J.G. (1980). Stressful life events and schizophrenia: A review of the research literature. *Psychological Bulletin, 87,* 408–425. (16)

Raisman, G. (1969). Neuronal plasticity in the septal nuclei of the adult rat. *Brain Research, 14,* 25–48. (14)

Raisman, G., & Field, P.M. (1973). A quantitative investigation of the development of collateral reinnervation after partial deafferentation of the septal nuclei. *Brain Research, 50,* 241–264. (14)

Rakic, P. (1985). DNA synthesis and cell division in the adult primate brain. *Annals of the New York Academy of Sciences, 457,* 193–211. (2)

Rakic, P., Bourgeois, J.-P., Eckenhoff, M.F., Zecevic, N., & Goldman-Rakic, P.S. (1986). Concurrent overproduction of synapses in diverse regions of the primate cerebral cortex. *Science, 232,* 232–235. (4)

Ramón y Cajal, S. (1937). Recollections of my life. *Memoirs of the American Philosophical Society, 8,* parts 1 and 2. (2)

Randall, P.K., Severson, J.A., & Finch, C.E. (1981). Aging and the regulation of striatal dopaminergic mechanisms in mice. *Journal of Pharmacology and Experimental Therapeutics, 219,* 695–700. (14)

Ranson, S.W., & Clark, S.L. (1959). *The anatomy of the nervous system,* 10th ed. Philadelphia: Saunders. (4)

Rao, M.L., Gross, G., & Huber, G. (1984). Altered interrelationship of dopamine, prolactin, thyrotropin and thyroid hormone in schizophrenic patients. *European Archives of Psychiatry and Neurological Sciences, 234,* 8–12. (16)

Ream, N.W., Robinson, M.G., Richter, R.W., Hegge, F.W., & Holloway, H.C. (1975). Opiate dependence and acute abstinence. In R.W. Richter (Ed.), *Medical aspects of drug abuse* (pp. 81–123). Hagerstown, MD: Harper & Row. (16)

Rechtschaffen, A., Gilliland, M.A., Bergmann, B.M., & Winter, J.B. (1983). Physiological correlates of prolonged sleep deprivation in rats. *Science, 221,* 182–184. (9)

Reeves, A.G., & Plum, F. (1969). Hyperphagia, rage, and dementia accompanying a ventromedial hypothalamic neoplasm. *Archives of Neurology, 20,* 616–624. (10)

Refinetti, R., & Carlisle, H.J. (1986a). Complementary nature of heat production and heat intake during behavioral thermoregulation in the rat. *Behavioral and Neural Biology, 46,* 64–70. (10)

Refinetti, R., & Carlisle, H.J. (1986b). Effects of anterior and posterior hypothalamic temperature changes on thermoregulation in the rat. *Physiology & Behavior, 36,* 1099–1103. (10)

Reiman, E.M., Raichle, M.E., Robins, E., Butler, F.K., Herscovitch, P., Fox, P., & Perlmutter, J. (1986). The application of positron emission tomography to the study of panic disorder. *American Journal of Psychiatry, 143,* 469–477. (12)

Reinisch, J.M. (1981). Prenatal exposure to synthetic progestins increases potential for aggression in humans. *Science, 211,* 1171–1173. (11)

Reisenzein, R. (1983). The Schachter theory of emotion: Two decades later. *Psychological Bulletin, 94,* 239–264. (12)

Rémillard, G.M., Andermann, F., Testa, G.F., Gloor, P., Aubé, M., Martin, J.B., Feindel, W., Guberman, A., & Simpson, C. (1983). Sexual ictal manifestations predominate in women with temporal lobe epilepsy: A finding suggesting sexual dimorphism in the human brain. *Neurology, 33,* 323–330. (12)

Rensch, B. (1964). Memory and concepts of higher animals. *Proceedings of the Zoological Society of Calcutta, 17,* 207–221. (4)

Rensch, B. (1971). Probleme der Gedachtnisspuren. *Rheinisch-Westfälische Akademie der Wissenschaften, 211,* 7–67. (4)

Rensch, B. (1973). *Gedachtnis Begriffsbildung und Planhandlungen bei Tieren.* Berlin: Verlag Paul Parey. (4)

Rensch, B., & Dücker, G. (1963). Haptisches Lern- und Unterscheidungs-Vermögen bei einem Waschbären. *Zeitschrift für Tierpsychologie, 20,* 608–615. (4)

Rettig, R., Ganten, D., & Johnson, A.K. (1981). Isoproterenol-induced thirst: Renal and extrarenal mechanisms. *American Journal of Physiology, 241,* R152–R157. (10)

Reynolds, C.F., Black, R.S., Coble, P., Holzer, B., & Kupfer, D.J. (1980). Similarities in EEG findings for Kleine-Levin syndrome and unipolar depression. *American Journal of Psychiatry, 137,* 116–118. (10)

Richter, C.P. (1922). A behavioristic study of the activity of the rat. *Comparative Psychology Monographs, 1,* 1–55. (9)

Richter, C.P. (1931). A biological approach to manic-depressive insanity. *Association for Research in Nervous and Mental Disease, 11,* 611. (15)

Richter, C.P. (1933a). The role played by the thyroid gland in the production of gross body activity. *Endocrinology, 17,* 73–87. (15)

Richter, C.P. (1933b). Cyclical phenomena produced in rats by section of the pituitary stalk and their possible relation to pseudopregnancy. *American Journal of Physiology, 106,* 80–90. (15)

Richter, C.P. (1936). Increased salt appetite in adrenalectomized rats. *American Journal of Physiology, 115,* 155–161. (10)

Richter, C.P. (1938). Two-day cycles of alternating good and bad behavior in psychotic patients. *Archives of Neurology and Psychiatry, 39,* 587–598. (15)

Richter, C.P. (1950). Taste and solubility of toxic compounds in poisoning of rats and humans. *Journal of Comparative and Physiological Psychology, 43,* 358–374. (6)

Richter, C.P. (1955). Experimental production of cycles in behaviour and physiology in animals. *Acta Medica Scandinavica, 152* (Supplement 307), 36–37. (15)

Richter, C.P. (1956). Ovulation cycles and stress. In C.A. Villee (Ed.), *Gestation—Transactions of the third conference* (pp. 53–70). New York: Josiah Macy, Jr. Foundation. (16)

Richter, C.P. (1957a). On the phenomenon of sudden death in animals and man. *Psychosomatic Medicine, 19,* 191–198. (12)

Richter, C.P. (1957b). Behavior and metabolic cycles in animals and man. In P.H. Hoch & J. Zubin (Eds.), *Experimental psychopathology* (pp. 34–54). New York: Grune & Stratton. (15)

Richter, C.P. (1957c). Hormones and rhythms in man and animals. In G.Pincus (Ed.), *Recent progress in hormone research (Vol. 13)* (pp. 105–159). New York: Academic. (15)

Richter, C.P. (1957d). Abnormal but regular cycles in behaviour and metabolism in rats and catatonic-schizophrenics. *Second International Congress for Psychiatry,* 4th report, 326–327. (15)

Richter, C.P. (1958a). Neurological basis of responses to stress. In G.E.W. Wolstenholme & C.M. O'Connor (Eds.), *CIBA foundation symposium on the neurological basis of behaviour* (pp. 204–217). Boston: Little, Brown. (16)

Richter, C.P. (1958b). Abnormal but regular cycles in behavior and metabolism in rats and catatonic-schizophrenics. In M. Reiss (Ed.), *Psychoendocrinology* (pp. 168–181). New York: Grune & Stratton. (16)

Richter, C.P. (1965). Sleep and activity: Their relation to the 24-hour clock. *Association for Research in Nervous and Mental Disease, 45,* 8–29. (9)

Richter, C.P. (1967). Psychopathology of periodic behavior in animals and man. In J. Zubin & H.F. Hunt (Eds.), *Comparative psychopathology* (pp. 205–227). New York: Grune & Stratton. (9)

Richter, C.P. (1970). Blood-clock barrier: Its penetration by heavy water. *Proceedings of the National Academy of Sciences, 66,* 244. (9)

Richter, C.P. (1975). Deep hypothermia and its effect on the 24-hour clock of rats and hamsters. *Johns Hopkins Medical Journal, 136,* 1–10. (9)

Richter, C.P., Honeyman, W., & Hunter, H. (1940). Behavior and mood cycles apparently related to parathyroid deficiency. *Journal of Neurology and Psychiatry, 3,* 19–25. (15)

Richter, C.P., Jones, G.S., & Biswanger, L. (1959). Periodic phenomena and the thyroid. *Archives of Neurology and Psychiatry, 81,* 233–255. (15)

Richter, C.P., & Langworthy, O.R. (1933). The quill mechanism of the porcupine. *Journal für Psychologie und Neurologie, 45,* 143–153. (4)

Richter, C.P., & Rice, K.K. (1956). Experimental production in rats of abnormal cycles in behavior and metabolism. *Journal of Nervous and Mental Disease, 124,* 393–395. (15)

Riley, J.N., & Walker, D.W. (1978). Morphological alterations in hippocampus after long-term alcohol consumption in mice. *Science, 201,* 646–648. (2)

Rimland, B., Callaway, E., & Dreyfus, P. (1978). The effect of high doses of vitamin B_6 on autistic children: A double-blind crossover study. *American Journal of Psychiatry, 135,* 472–475. (16)

Rincover, A., Cook, R., Peoples, A., & Packard, D. (1979). Sensory extinction and sensory reinforcement principles for programming multiple adaptive behavior change. *Journal of Applied Behavior Analysis, 12,* 221–233. (16)

Rinn, W.E. (1984). The neuropsychology of facial expression: A review of the neurological and psychological mechanisms for producing facial expressions. *Psychological Bulletin, 95,* 52–77. (5, 8)

Riska, B., & Atchley, W.R. (1985). Genetics of growth predict patterns of brain-size evolution. *Science, 229,* 668–671. (4)

Ritvo, E.R., Freeman, B.J., Mason-Brothers, A., Mo, A., & Ritvo, A.M. (1985). Concordance for the syndrome of autism in 40 pairs of afflicted twins. *American Journal of Psychiatry, 142,* 74–77. (16)

Ritvo, E.R., Spence, M.A., Freeman, B.J., Mason-Brothers, A., Mo, A., & Marazita, M.L. (1985). Evidence for autosomal recessive inheritance in 46 families with multiple incidences of autism. *American Journal of Psychiatry, 142,* 187–192. (16)

Robbins, M.J., & Meyer, D.R. (1970). Motivational control of retrograde amnesia. *Journal of Experimental Psychology, 84,* 220–225. (13)

Robins, L.N., Helzer, J.E., Weissman, M.M., Orvaschel, H., Gruenberg, E., Burke, J.D., Jr., & Regier, D.A. (1984). Lifetime prevalence of specific psychiatric disorders in three sites. *Archives of General Psychiatry, 41,* 949–958. (12, 15, 16)

Roeder, K.D. (1967). *Nerve cells and insect behavior.* Cambridge, MA: Harvard University. (1)

Roffwarg, H.P., Dement, W.C., Muzio, J.N., & Fisher, C. (1962). Dream imagery: Relationship to rapid eye movements of sleep. *Archives of General Psychiatry, 7,* 235–258. (9)

Rogers, J., & Morrison, J.H. (1985). Quantitative morphology and regional and laminar distributions of senile plaques in Alzheimer's disease. *Journal of Neuroscience, 5,* 2801–2808. (13)

Roland, P.E. (1984). Organization of motor control by the normal human brain. *Human Neurobiology, 2,* 205–216. (8)

Rolls, E.T., Murzi, E., Yaxley, S., Thorpe, S.J., & Simpson, S.J. (1986). Sensory-specific satiety: Food-specific reduction in responsiveness of ventral forebrain neurons after feeding in the monkey. *Brain Research, 368,* 79–86. (6)

Rome, L.C., Loughna, P.T., & Goldspink, G. (1984). Muscle fiber activity in carp as a function of swimming speed and muscle temperature. *American Journal of Psychiatry, 247,* R272–R279. (8)

Rose, J.E., Brugge, J.F., Anderson, D.J., & Hind, J.E. (1967). Phase-locked response to low-frequency tones in single auditory nerve fibers of the squirrel monkey. *Journal of Neurophysiology, 30,* 769–793. (6)

Rose, J.E., & Woolsey, C.N. (1949). Organization of the mammalian thalamus and its relationships to the cerebral cortex. *Electroencephalography and Clinical Neurophysiology, 1,* 391–404. (4)

Rosenblatt, J.S. (1967). Nonhormonal basis of maternal behavior in the rat. *Science, 156,* 1512–1514. (11)

Rosenblatt, J.S. (1970). Views on the onset and maintenance of maternal behavior in the rat. In L.R. Aronson, E. Tobach, D.S. Lehrman, & J.S. Rosenblatt (Eds.), *Development and evolution of behavior* (pp. 489–515). San Francisco: Freeman. (11)

Rosenfield, D.B., & Goodglass, H. (1980). Dichotic testing of cerebral dominance in stutterers. *Brain and Language, 11,* 170–180. (5)

Rosenthal, R.H., & Allen, T.W. (1978). An examination of attention, arousal, and learning dysfunctions of hyperkinetic children. *Psychological Bulletin, 85,* 689–715. (15)

Rosenthal, N.E., Sack, D.A., Carpenter, C.J., Parry, B.L., Mendelson, W.B., & Wehr, T.A. (1985). Antidepressant effects of light in seasonal affective disorder. *American Journal of Psychiatry, 142,* 163–170. (15)

Rosenthal, N.E., Sack, D.A., Gillin, C.J., Lewy, A.J., Goodwin, F.K., Davenport, Y., Mueller, P.S., Newsome, D.A., & Wehr, T.A. (1984). Seasonal affective disorder. *Archives of General Psychiatry, 41,* 72–80. (15)

Ross, E.D. (1980). Left medial parietal lobe and receptive language functions: Mixed transcortical aphasia after left anterior cerebral artery infarction. *Neurology, 30,* 144–151. (5)

Rosvold, H.E., Mirsky, A.F., & Pribram, K.H. (1954). Influence of amygdalectomy on social behavior in monkeys. *Journal of Comparative and Physiological Psychology, 47,* 173–178. (12)

Roth, R.H. (1984). CNS dopamine autoreceptors: Distribution, pharmacology, and function. *Annals of the New York Academy of Sciences, 430,* 27–53. (3)

Rothman, S.M. (1985). The neurotoxicity of excitatory amino acids is produced by passive chloride influx. *Journal of Neuroscience, 5,* 1483–1489. (4)

Rovainen, C.M. (1976). Regeneration of Müller and Mauthner axons after spinal transection in larval lampreys. *Journal of Comparative Neurology, 168,* 545–554. (14)

Rowland, C.V., Jr. (Ed.), (1970). *Anorexia and obesity.* Boston: Little, Brown. (10)

Rowland, L.P. (1981). Spinal cord III: Clinical syndromes. In E.R. Kandel & J.H. Schwartz (Eds.), *Principles of neural science* (pp. 305–311). New York: Elsevier/North Holland. (4)

Rowland, N. (1980). Drinking behavior: Physiological, neurological, and environmental factors. In T.M. Toates & T.R. Halliday (Eds.), *Analysis of motivational processes* (pp. 39–59). London: Academic. (10)

Rowland, N., & Flamm, C. (1977). Quinine drinking: More regulatory puzzles. *Physiology & Behavior, 18,* 1165–1170. (10)

Roy, A., Pickar, D., Linnoila, M., & Potter, W.Z. (1985). Plasma norepinephrine level in affective disorder. *Archives of General Psychiatry, 42,* 1181–1185. (15)

Roy-Byrne, P.P., Uhde, T.W., & Post, R.M. (1986). Effects of one night's sleep deprivation on mood and behavior in panic disorder. *Archives of General Psychiatry, 43,* 895–899. (15)

Rozin, P. (1965). Temperature independence of an arbitrary temporal discrimination in the goldfish. *Science, 149,* 561–563. (9)

Rozin, P. (1968). The use of poikilothermy in the analysis of behavior. In D. Ingle (Ed.), *The central nervous system and fish behavior* (pp. 181–192). Chicago: University of Chicago. (9)

Rozin, P., & Kalat, J.W. (1971). Specific hungers and poison avoidance as adaptive specializations of learning. *Psychological Review, 78,* 459–486. (10, 13)

Rozin, P., Poritsky, S., & Sotsky, R. (1971). American children with reading problems can easily learn to read English represented by Chinese characters. *Science, 171,* 1264–1267. (5)

Rumsey, J.M., Duara, R., Grady, C., Rapoport, J.L., Margolin, R.A., Rapoport, S.I., & Cutler, N.R. (1985). Brain metabolism in autism. *Archives of General Psychiatry, 42,* 448–455. (16)

Rusak, B., & Zucker, I. (1979). Neural regulation of circadian rhythms. *Physiological Reviews, 59,* 449–526. (9)

Rush, A.J., Erman, M.K., Giles, D.E., Schlesser, M.A., Carpenter, G., Vasavada, N., & Roffwarg, H.P. (1986). Polysomnographic findings in recently drug-free and clinically remitted depressed patients. *Archives of General Psychiatry, 43,* 878–884. (15)

Russell, M.J., Switz, G.M., & Thompson, K. (1980). Olfactory influences on the human menstrual cycle. *Pharmacology, Biochemistry, and Behavior, 13,* 737–738. (6)

Rutter, M. (1982). Syndromes attributed to "minimal brain dysfunction" in childhood. *American Journal of Psychiatry, 139,* 21–33. (15)

Sabel, B.A., Slavin, M.D., & Stein, D.G. (1984). G_{M1} ganglioside treatment facilitates behavioral recovery from bilateral brain damage. *Science, 225,* 340–342. (14)

Sack, D.A., Nurnberger, J., Rosenthal, N.E., Ashburn, E., & Wehr, T.A. (1985). Potentiation of antidepressant medications by phase advance of the sleep-wake cycle. *American Journal of Psychiatry, 142,* 606–608. (15)

Sackeim, H.A., Gur, R.C., & Saucy, M.C. (1978). Emotions are expressed more intensely on the left side of the face. *Science, 202,* 434–436. (5)

Saito, H., Yukie, M., Tanaka, K., Hikosaka, K., Fukada, Y., & Iwai, E. (1986). Integration of direction signals of image motion in the superior temporal sulcus of the macaque monkey. *Journal of Neuroscience, 6,* 145–157. (7)

Sakata, H., Shibutani, H., Kawano, K., & Harrington, T.L. (1985). Neural mechanisms of space vision in the parietal association cortex of the monkey. *Vision Research, 25,* 453–463. (7)

Sakurai, Y., & Sugimoto, S. (1986). Multiple unit activity of prefrontal cortex and dorsomedial thalamus during delayed go/no-go alternation in the rat. *Behavioural Brain Research, 20,* 295–301. (13)

Salthouse, T.A. (February, 1984). The skill of typing. *Scientific American, 250* (2), 128–135. (8)

Sanberg, P.R. (1976). "Neural capacity" in *Mimosa pudica*: A review. *Journal of Behavioral Biology, 17,* 435–452. (8)

Sanberg, P.R., & Coyle, J.T. (1984). Scientific approaches to Huntington's disease. *CRC Critical Reviews in Clinical Neurobiology, 1,* 1–44. (8)

Sanberg, P.R., & Johnston, G.A. (1981). Glutamate and Huntington's disease. *Medical Journal of Australia, 2,* 460–465. (8)

Sanberg, P.R., Pevsner, J., Autuono, P.G., & Coyle, J.T. (1985). Fetal methylazoxymethanol acetate-induced lesions cause reductions in dopamine receptor-mediated catalepsy and stereotypy. *Neuropharmacology, 24,* 1057–1062. (4)

Sandberg, K., Sanberg, P.R., & Coyle, J.T. (1984). Effects of intrastriatal injections of the cholinergic neurotoxin AF64A on spontaneous nocturnal locomotor behavior in the rat. *Brain Research, 299,* 339–343. (4)

Sandberg, K., Sanberg, P.R., Hanin, I., Fisher, A., & Coyle, J.T. (1984). Cholinergic lesion of the striatum impairs acquisition and retention of a passive avoidance response. *Behavioral Neuroscience, 98,* 162–165. (13)

Sandhu, S., Cook, P., Diamond, M.C. (1986). Rat cerebral cortical estrogen receptors: Male-female, right-left. *Experimental Neurology, 92,* 186–196. (11)

Sapolsky, R.M. (1985). A mechanism for glucocorticoid toxicity in the hippocampus: Increased neuronal vulnerability to metabolic insults. *Journal of Neuroscience, 5,* 1228–1232. (13)

Sapolsky, R.M., Krey, L.C., & McEwen, B.S. (1985). Prolonged glucocorticoid exposure reduces hippocampal neuron number: Implications for aging. *Journal of Neuroscience, 5,* 1222–1227. (13)

Sarnat, H.B., & Netsky, M.G. (1981). *Evolution of the nervous system* (2nd ed.). New York: Oxford University. (4)

Sastre, J.-P., Sakai, K., & Jouvet, M. (1979). Persistance du sommeil paradoxal chez le chat après destruction de l'aire gigantocellulaire du tegmentum pontique par l'acide kaïnique. *Comptes Rendus des Séances de l'Académie des Sciences, Série D, 289,* 959–964. (9)

Satinoff, E. (1983). A reevaluation of the concept of the homeostatic organization of temperature regulation. In E. Satinoff & P. Teitelbaum (Eds.), *Handbook of behavioral neurobiology, Vol. 6: Motivation* (pp. 443–472). New York: Plenum. (10)

Satinoff, E., Liran, J., & Clapman, R. (1982). Aberrations of circadian body temperature rhythms in rats with medial preoptic lesions. *American Journal of Physiology, 242,* R352–R357. (10)

Satinoff, E., McEwen, G.N., Jr., & Williams, B.A. (1976). Behavioral fever in newborn rabbits. *Science, 193,* 1139–1140. (10)

Satinoff, E., & Rutstein, J. (1970). Behavioral thermoregulation in rats with anterior hypothalamic lesions. *Journal of Comparative and Physiological Psychology, 71,* 77–82. (10)

Satinoff, E., Valentino, D., & Teitelbaum, P. (1976). Thermoregulatory cold-defense deficits in rats with preoptic/anterior hypothalamic lesions. *Brain Research Bulletin, 1,* 553–565. (10)

Satz, P. (1979). A test of some models of hemispheric speech organization in the left- and right-handed. *Science, 203,* 1131–1133. (5)

Savage-Rumbaugh, S., McDonald, K., Sevcik, R.A., Hopkins, W.D., & Rubert, E. (1986). Spontaneous symbol acquisition and communicative use by pygmy chimpanzees (*Pan paniscus*). *Journal of Experimental Psychology: General, 115,* 211–235. (5)

Savage-Rumbaugh, E.S., Rumbaugh, D.M., & Boysen, S. (1978). Symbolic communication between two chimpanzees (*Pan troglodytes*). *Science, 201,* 641–644. (5)

Scalia, F., & Winans, S.S. (1976). New perspectives on the morphology of the olfactory system: Olfactory and vomeronasal pathways in mammals. In R.L. Doty (Ed.), *Mammalian olfaction, reproductive processes and behavior* (pp. 7–28). New York: Academic. (6)

Schacter, D.L. (1983). Amnesia observed: Remembering and forgetting in a natural environment. *Journal of Abnormal Psychology, 92,* 236–242. (13)

Schacter, D.L. (1985). Priming of old and new knowledge in amnesic patients and normal subjects. *Annals of the New York Academy of Sciences, 444,* 41–53. (13)

Schachter, S., & Singer, J.E. (1962). Cognitive, social and physiological determinants of emotional state. *Psychological Review, 69,* 379–399. (12)

Schall, J.D., Vitek, D.J., & Leventhal, A.G. (1986). Retinal constraints on orientation specificity in cat visual cortex. *Journal of Neuroscience, 6,* 823–836. (7)

Schallert, T. (1982). Adipsia produced by lateral hypothalamic lesions: Facilitation of recovery by preoperative restriction of water intake. *Journal of Comparative and Physiological Psychology, 96,* 604–614. (14)

Schallert, T. (1983). Sensorimotor impairment and recovery of function in brain-damaged rats: Reappearance of symptoms during old age. *Behavioral Neuroscience, 97,* 159–164. (14)

Schallert, T., DeRyck, M., & Teitelbaum, P. (1980). Atropine stereotypy as a behavioral trap: A movement subsystem and electroencephalographic analysis. *Journal of Comparative and Physiological Psychology, 94,* 1–24. (8)

Schallert, T., & Whishaw, I.Q. (1984). Bilateral cutaneous stimulation of the somatosensory system in hemidecorticate rats. *Behavioral Neuroscience, 98,* 518–540. (14)

Schatzberg, A.F., Orsulak, P.J., Rosenbaum, A.H., Maruta, T., Kruger, E.R., Cole, J.O., & Schildkraut, J.J. (1982). Toward a biochemical classification of depressive disorders. V. Heterogeneity of unipolar depressions. *American Journal of Psychiatry, 139,* 471–475. (15)

Scheff, S.W., & Cotman, C.W. (1977). Recovery of spontaneous alternation following lesions of the entorhinal cortex in adult rats: Possible correlation to axon sprouting. *Behavioral Biology, 21,* 286–293. (14)

Scheibel, A.B. (1984). A dendritic correlate of human speech. In N. Geschwind & A.M. Galaburda (Eds.), *Cerebral Dominance* (pp. 43–52). Cambridge, MA: Harvard. (4)

Scheibel, M.E., & Scheibel, A.B. (1963). Some structure-functional correlates of development in young cats. *Electroencephalography and Clinical Neurophysiology, 15* (Supplement 24), 235–246. (4)

Scheller, R.H., Kaldany, R.-R., Kreiner, T., Mahon, A.C., Nambu, J.R., Schaefer, M., & Taussig, R. (1984). Neuropeptides: Mediators of behavior in *Aplysia. Science, 225,* 1300–1308. (3)

Schenk, L., & Bear, D. (1981). Multiple personality and related dissociative phenomena in patients with temporal lobe epilepsy. *American Journal of Psychiatry, 138,* 1311–1316. (12)

Scherer, S.S. (1986). Reinnervation of the extraocular muscles in goldfish is nonselective. *Journal of Neuroscience, 6,* 764–773. (14)

Schiffman, S.S. (1983). Taste and smell in disease. *New England Journal of Medicine, 308,* 1275–1279 and 1337–1343. (6)

Schiffman, S.S., Diaz, C., & Beeker, T.G. (1986). Caffeine intensifies taste of certain sweeteners: Role of adenosine receptor. *Pharmacology, Biochemistry & Behavior, 24,* 429–432. (6)

Schiffman, S.S., & Erickson, R.P. (1971). A psychophysical model for gustatory quality. *Physiology & Behavior, 7,* 617–633. (6)

Schiffman, S.S., & Erickson, R.P. (1980). The issue of primary tastes versus a taste continuum. *Neuroscience & Biobehavioral Reviews, 4,* 109–117. (6)

Schiffman, S.S., Lockhead, E., & Maes, F.W. (1983). Amiloride reduces the taste intensity of Na$^+$ and Li$^+$ salts and sweeteners. *Proceedings of the National Academy of Sciences, U.S.A., 80,* 6136–6140. (6)

Schiffman, S.S., McElroy, A.E., & Erickson, R.P. (1980). The range of taste quality of sodium salts. *Physiology & Behavior, 24,* 217–224. (6)

Schiffman, S.S., Moss, J., & Erickson, R.P. (1976). Thresholds of food odors in the elderly. *Experimental Aging Research, 2,* 389–398. (6)

Schiffman, S., & Pasternak, M. (1979). Decreased discriminaion of food odors in the elderly. *Journal of Gerontology, 34,* 73–79. (6)

Schiffman, S.S., Reilly, D.A., & Clark, T.B. III. (1979). Qualitative differences among sweeteners. *Physiology & Behavior, 23,* 1–9. (6)

Schiffman, S.S., Simon, S.A., Gill, J.M., & Beeker, T.G. (1986). Bretylium tosylate enhances salt taste. *Physiology & Behavior, 36,* 1129–1137. (6)

Schildkraut, J.J., & Kety, S.S. (1967). Biogenic amines and emotion. *Science, 156,* 21–30. (15)

Schiller, F. (1979). *Paul Broca.* Berkeley: University of California. (5)

Schneck, M.K., Reisberg, B., & Ferris, S.H. (1982). An overview of current concepts of Alzheimer's disease. *American Journal of Psychiatry, 139,* 165–173. (13)

Schneider, A.M., & Sherman, W. (1968). Amnesia: A function of the temporal relation of footshock to electroconvulsive shock. *Science, 159,* 219–221. (13)

Schneider, B.A., Trehub, S.E., Morrongiello, B.A., & Thorpe, L.A. (1986). Auditory sensitivity in preschool children. *Journal of the Acoustical Society of America, 79,* 447–452. (6)

Schneider, G.E. (1969). Two visual systems. *Science, 163,* 895–902. (7)

Schneider, G.E., & Jhaveri, S.R. (1974). Neuroanatomical correlates of spared or altered function after brain lesions in the newborn hamster. In D.G. Stein, J.J. Rosen, & N. Butters (Eds.), *Plasticity and recovery of function in the central nervous system* (pp. 65–109). New York: Academic. (14)

Schneider-Helmert, D., & Spinweber, C.L. (1986). Evaluation of L-tryptophan for treatment of insomnia: A review. *Psychopharmacology, 89,* 1–7. (9)

Schöpf, J., Bryois, C., Jonquière, M., & Le, P.K. (1984). On the nosology of severe psychiatric post-partum disorders. *European Archives of Psychiatry and Neurological Sciences, 234,* 54–63. (15)

Schramm, M., & Selinger, Z. (1984). Message transmission: Receptor controlled adenylate cyclase system. *Science, 225,* 1350–1356. (3)

Schreiner, L., & Kling, A. (1953). Behavioral changes following rhinencephalic injury in cat. *Journal of Neurophysiology, 16,* 643–659. (12)

Schuckit, M.A. (1984). Subjective responses to alcohol in sons of alcoholics and control subjects. *Archives of General Psychiatry, 41,* 879–884. (10)

Schulkin, J., & Fluharty, S.J. (1985). Further studies on salt appetite following lateral hypothalamic lesions: Effects of preoperative alimentary experiences. *Behavioral Neuroscience, 99,* 929–935. (14)

Schwab, M.E., & Thoenen, H. (1985). Dissociated neurons regenerate into sciatic but not optic nerve explants in culture irrespective of neurotrophic factors. *Journal of Neuroscience, 5,* 2415–2423. (14)

Schwabe, A.D. (moderator). (1981). Anorexia nervosa. *Annals of Internal Medicine, 94,* 371–381. (10)

Schwartz, D.M., & Thompson, M.G. (1981). Do anorectics get well? Current research and future needs. *American Journal of Psychiatry, 138,* 319–323. (10)

Schwartz, M., Belkin, M., Harel, A., Solomon, A., Lavie, V., Hadani, M., Rachailovich, I., & Stein-Izsak, C. (1985). Regenerating fish optic nerves and a regeneration-like response in injured optic nerves of adult rabbits. *Science, 228,* 600–603. (14)

Scott, D., Jr., & Clemente, C.D. (1955). Regeneration of spinal cord fibers in the cat. *Journal of Comparative Neurology, 102,* 633–669. (14)

Scott, T.R., & Chang, F.-C. T. (1984). The state of gustatory neural coding. *Chemical Senses, 8,* 297–314. (6)

Scott, T.R., & Perrotto, R.S. (1980). Intensity coding in pontine taste area: Gustatory information is processed similarly throughout rat's brain stem. *Journal of Neurophysiology, 44,* 739–750. (6)

Scott, T.R., Yaxley, S., Sienkiewicz, Z.J., & Rolls, E.T. (1986). Gustatory responses in the nucleus tractus solitarius of the alert cynomolgus monkey. *Journal of Neurophysiology, 55,* 182–200. (6)

Scovern, A.W., & Kilmann, P.R. (1980). Status of electroconvulsive therapy: Review of the outcome literature. *Psychological Bulletin, 87,* 260–303. (11)

Scoville, W.B., & Milner, B. (1957). Loss of recent memory after bilateral hippocampal lesions. *Journal of Neurology, Neurosurgery, and Psychiatry, 20,* 11–21. (13)

Seeman, P., & Grigoriadis, D. (1987). Dopamine receptors in brain and periphery. *Neurochemistry International, 10,* 1–25. (16)

Seeman, P., & Lee, T. (1975). Antipsychotic drugs: Direct correlation between clinical potency and presynaptic action on dopamine neurons. *Science, 188,* 1217–1219. (16)

Seeman, P., Lee, T., Chau-Wong, M., & Wong, K. (1976). Antipsychotic drug doses and neuroleptic/dopamine receptors. *Nature, 261,* 717–719. (16)

Seeman, P., Ulpian, C., Bergeron, C., Riederer, P., Jellinger, K., Gabriel, E., Reynolds, G.P., & Tourtellotte, W.W. (1984). Bimodal distribution of dopamine receptor densities in brains of schizophrenics. *Science, 225,* 728–731. (16)

Segal, N. (1984). Asymmetries in monozygotic twins. *American Journal of Psychiatry, 141,* 1638. (16)

Selemon, L.D., & Goldman-Rakic, P.S. (1985). Longitudinal topography and interdigitation of corticostriatal projections in the rhesus monkey. *Journal of Neuroscience, 5,* 776–794. (8)

Selzer, M.E. (1978). Mechanisms of functional recovery and regeneration after spinal cord transection in larval sea lamprey. *Journal of Physiology, 277,* 395–408. (14)

Sergent, J. (1986). Subcortical coordination of hemisphere activity in commissurotomized patients. *Brain, 109,* 357–369. (5)

Shapiro, B.E., & Danly, M. (1985). The role of the right hemisphere in the control of speech prosody in propositional and affective contexts. *Brain and Language, 25,* 19–36. (5)

Shapiro, C.M., Bortz, R., Mitchell, D., Bartel, P., & Jooste, P. (1981). Slow-wave sleep: A recovery period after exercise. *Science, 214,* 1253–1254. (9)

Shavit, Y., Terman, G.W., Martin, F.C., Lewis, J.W., Liebeskind, J.C., & Gale, R.P. (1985). Stress, opioid peptides, the immune system, and cancer. *Journal of Immunology, 135,* 834S–837S. (6)

Shaywitz, B.A., Gordon, J.W., Klopper, J.H., Zelterman, D.A., & Irvine, J. (1979). Ontogenesis of spontaneous activity and habituation of activity in the rat pup. *Developmental Psychobiology, 12,* 359–367. (15)

Shepherd, G.M. (1983). *Neurobiology.* New York: Oxford. (3)

Sherman, S.M., & Spear, P.D. (1982). Organization of visual pathways in normal and visually deprived cats. *Physiological Reviews, 62,* 738–855. (7)

Sherrington, C.S. (1906). *The integrative action of the nervous system.* New York: Charles Scribner's Sons. (2nd ed. New Haven, CT: Yale University press, 1947.) (3)

Shields, S.A. (1983). Development of autonomic nervous system responsivity in children: A review of the literature. *International Journal of Behavioral Development, 6,* 291–319. (12)

Shimamura, A.P., & Squire, L.R. (1986). Korsakoff's syndrome: A study of the relation between anterograde amnesia and remote memory impairment. *Behavioral Neuroscience, 100,* 165–170. (13)

Shiromani, P.J., Siegel, J.M., Tomaszewski, K.S., & McGinty, D.J. (1986). Alterations in blood pressure and REM sleep after pontine carbachol microinfusion. *Experimental Neurology, 91,* 285–292. (9)

Shutts, D. (1982). *Lobotomy: Resort to the knife*. New York: Van Nostrand Reinhold. (4)

Shyne-Athwal, S., Riccio, R.V., Chakraborty, G., & Ingoglia, N.A. (1986). Protein modification by amino acid addition is increased in crushed sciatic but not optic nerves. *Science, 231,* 603–605. (14)

Sidman, R.L., Green, M.C., & Appel, S.H. (1965). *Catalog of the neurological mutants of the mouse*. Cambridge, MA: Harvard University. (4)

Sidtis, J.J., Volpe, B.T., Holtzman, J.D., Wilson, D.H., & Gazzaniga, M.S. (1981). Cognitive interaction after staged callosal section: Evidence for transfer of semantic activation. *Science, 212,* 344–346. (5)

Siegel, J.M., McGinty, D.J., & Breedlove, S.M. (1977). Sleep and waking activity of pontine gigantocellular field neurons. *Experimental Neurology, 56,* 553–573. (9)

Siegel, J.M., Wheeler, R.L., & McGinty, D.J. (1979). Activity of medullary reticular formation neurons in the unrestrained cat during waking and sleep. *Brain Research, 179,* 49–60. (9)

Siegelman, M. (1974). Parental background of male homosexuals and heterosexuals. *Archives of Sexual Behavior, 3,* 3–18. (11)

Siever, L.J., Coursey, R.D., Alterman, I.S., Buchsbaum, M.S., & Murphy, D.L. (1984). Impaired smooth pursuit eye movement: Vulnerability marker for schizotypal personality disorder in a normal volunteer population. *American Journal of Psychiatry, 141,* 1560–1566. (16)

Simmons, J.A., Wever, E.G., & Pylka, J.M. (1971). Periodical cicada: Sound production and hearing. *Science, 171,* 212–213. (6)

Simpson, J.L. (1976). *Disorders of sexual differentiation*. New York: Academic. (11)

Simson, E.L., Gold, R.M., Standish, L.J., & Pellett, P.L. (1977). Axon-sparing brain lesioning technique: The use of monosodium-L-glutamate and other amino acids. *Science, 198,* 515–517. (4)

Sinex, F.M., & Myers, R.H. (1982). Alzheimer's disease, Down's syndrome, and aging: The genetic approach. *Annals of the New York Academy of Sciences, 396,* 3–13. (13)

Sitaram, N., Weingartner, H., & Gillin, J.C. (1978). Human serial learning: Enhancement with arecholine and choline and impairment with scopolamine. *Science, 201,* 274–276. (13)

Sklar, L.S., & Anisman, H. (1981). Stress and cancer. *Psychological Bulletin, 89,* 369–406. (12)

Skok, V.I. (1986). Channel-blocking mechanism ensures specific blockade of synaptic transmission. *Neuroscience, 17,* 1–9. (3)

Sloviter, R.S., Damiano, B.P., & Connor, J.D. (1980). Relative potency of amphetamine isomers in causing the serotonin behavioral syndrome in rats. *Biological Psychiatry, 15,* 789–796. (16)

Small, J.G., Kellams, J.J., Milstein, V., & Small, I.F. (1980). Complications with electroconvulsive treatment combined with lithium. *Biological Psychiatry, 15,* 103–112. (15)

Smeraldi, E., Kidd, K.K., Negri, F., Heimbuch, R., & Melica, A.M. (1979). Genetic studies of affective disorders. In J. Obiols, C. Ballús, E. González Monclús, & J.Pujol (Eds.), *Biological psychiatry today* (pp. 60–65). Amsterdam: Elsevier/North Holland Biomedical. (15)

Smith, D.V., VanBuskirk, R.L., Travers, J.B., & Bieber, S.L. (1983a). Gustatory neuron types in hamster brain stem. *Journal of Neurophysiology, 50,* 522–540. (6)

Smith, D.V., VanBuskirk, R.L., Travers, J.B., & Bieber, S.L. (1983b). Coding of taste stimuli by hamster brain stem neurons. *Journal of Neurophysiology, 50,* 541–558. (6)

Smith, G.P., Jerome, C., Cushin, B.J., Eterno, R., & Simansky, K.J. (1981). Abdominal vagotomy blocks the satiety effect of cholecystokinin in the rat. *Science, 213,* 1036–1037. (10)

Smith, L.T. (1975). The interanimal transfer phenomenon: A review. *Psychological Bulletin, 81,* 1078–1095. (13)

Smythies, J.R. (1970). *Brain mechanisms and behaviour* (2nd ed.). New York: Academic. (12)

Snyder, G.L., & Stricker, E.M. (1985). Effects of lateral hypothalamic lesions on food intake of rats during exposure to cold. *Behavioral Neuroscience, 99,* 310–322. (14)

Snyder, S.H. (1984). Drug and neurotransmitter receptors in the brain. *Science, 224,* 22–31. (3)

Snyder, S.H., Banerjee, S.P., Yamamura, H.I., & Greenberg, D. (1974). Drugs, neurotransmitters, and schizophrenia. *Science, 184,* 1243–1253. (16)

Snyder, S.H., & D'Amato, R.J. (1986). MPTP: A neurotoxin relevant to the pathophysiology of Parkinson's disease. *Neurology, 36,* 250–258. (8)

Solanto, M.V. (1984). Neuropharmacological basis of stimulant drug action in attention deficit disorder with hyperactivity: A review and synthesis. *Psychological Bulletin, 95,* 387–409. (15)

Solomon, C.M., Holzman, P.S., Levin, S., & Gale, H.J. (1987). The association between eye-tracking dysfunctions and thought disorder in psychosis. *Archives of General Psychiatry, 44,* 31–35. (16)

Sonderegger, T.B. (1970). Intracranial stimulation and maternal behavior. *APA Convention Proceedings*, 78th meeting, 245–246. (12)

Sperry, R.W. (1952). Neurology and the mind-brain problem. *American Scientist, 40,* 291–312. (5)

Sperry, R.W. (1959). The growth of nerve circuits. *Scientific American, 201* (5), 68–75. (5)

Sperry, R.W. (1975). In search of psyche. In F.G. Worden, J.P. Swazey, & G. Adelman (Eds.), *The neurosciences: Paths of discovery* (pp. 424–434). Cambridge, MA: MIT. (5)

Spiegel, T.A. (1973). Caloric regulation of food intake in man. *Journal of Comparative and Physiological Psychology, 84,* 24–37. (10)

Spies, G. (1965). Food versus intra-cranial self-stimulation reinforcement in food-deprived rats. *Journal of Comparative and Physiological Psychology, 60,* 153–157. (12)

Spurzheim, J.G. (1908). *Phrenology* (rev. ed.). Philadelphia: Lippincott. (4)

Squire, L.R. (1982). The neuropsychology of human memory. *Annual Review of Neuroscience, 5,* 241–273. (13)

Squire, L.R., & Cohen, N. (1979). Memory and amnesia: Resistance to disruption develops for years after learning. *Behavioral and Neural Biology, 25,* 115–125. (13)

Squire, L.R., & Spanis, C.W. (1984). Long gradient of retrograde amnesia in mice: Continuity with the findings in humans. *Behavioral Neuroscience, 98,* 345–348. (13)

Squire, L.R., Wetzel, C.D., & Slater, P.C. (1979). Memory complaint after electroconvulsive therapy: Assessment with a new self-rating instrument. *Biological Psychiatry, 14,* 791–801. (15)

Squire, L.R., & Zouzounis, J.A. (1986). ECT and memory: Brief pulse versus sine wave. *American Journal of Psychiatry, 143,* 596–601. (15)

Staller, J., Buchanan, D., Singer, M., Lappin, J., & Webb, W. (1978). Alexia without agraphia: An experimental case study. *Brain and Language, 5,* 378–387. (5)

Starká, L., Sipová, I., & Hynie, J. (1975). Plasma testosterone in male transsexuals and homosexuals. *Journal of Sex Research, 11,* 134–138. (11)

Starke, K. (1981). Presynaptic receptors. *Annual Review of Pharmacology and Toxicology, 21,* 7–30. (3, 15)

Stäubli, U., Faraday, R., & Lynch, G. (1985). Pharmacological dissociation of memory: Anisomycin, a protein synthesis inhibitor, and leupeptin, a protease inhibitor, block different learning tasks. *Behavioral and Neural Biology, 43,* 287–297. (13)

Steffen, H., Heinrich, U., & Kratzer, W. (1978). Raumorientierungsstörung und Körperschemairritation bei Turner-Syndrom-Patienten. Ein Syndrom der rechtshemisphärischen Hirnreifungsverzögerung. *Zeitschrift für Kinder- und Jugendpsychiatrie, 6,* 131–141. (11)

Steger, R.W. (1976). Extrahypothalamic neural influences affecting the onset of puberty in the female. In E.S.E. Hafez & J.J. Peluso (Eds.), *Sexual maturity* (pp. 53–69). Ann Arbor, MI: Ann Arbor Science. (11)

Stein, D.G., Finger, S., & Hart, T. (1983). Brain damage and recovery: Problems and perspectives. *Behavioral and Neural Biology, 37,* 185–222. (14)

Stein, L. (1962). Effects and interactions of imipramine, chlorpromazine, reserpine, and amphetamine on self-stimulation: Possible neurophysiological basis of depression. In J. Wortis (Ed.), *Recent advances in biological psychiatry* (Vol. 4) (pp. 288–308). New York: Plenum. (15)

Stein, L. (1968). Chemistry of reward and punishment. In D.H. Efron (Ed.), *Psychopharmacology: A review of progress, 1957–1967* (pp. 105–123). Washington, DC: U.S. Government. (12)

Stein, L., & Wise, C.D. (1971). Possible etiology of schizophrenia: progressive damage to the noradrenergic reward system by 6-hydroxydopamine. *Science, 171,* 1032–1036. (16)

Stephens, J.H., & Shaffer, J.W. (1973). A controlled replication of the effectiveness of diphenylhydantoin in reducing irritability and anxiety in selected neurotic outpatients. *Journal of Clinical Pharmacology, 13,* 351–356. (12)

Stern, W.C., & Morgane, P.J. (1974). Theoretical view of REM sleep function: Maintenance of catecholamine systems in the central nervous system. *Behavioral Biology, 11,* 1–32. (9)

St. George-Hyslop, P.H., Tanzi, R.E., Polinsky, R.J., Haines, J.L., Nee, L., Watkins, P.C., Myers, R.H., Feldman, R.G., Pollen, D., Drachman, D., Growdon, J., Bruni, A., Foncin, J. F., Salmon, D., Frommelt, P., Amaducci, L., Sorbi, S., Piacentini, S., Stewart, G.D., Hobbs, W.J., Conneally, M., & Gusella, J.F. (1987). The genetic defect causing familial Alzheimer's disease maps on chromosome 21. *Science, 235,* 885–890. (13)

Stockman, E.R., Callaghan, R.S., Gallagher, C.A., & Baum, M.J. (1986). Sexual differentiation of play behavior in the ferret. *Behavioral Neuroscience, 100,* 563–568. (11)

Straus, E., & Yalow, R.S. (1978). Cholecystokinin in the brains of obese and nonobese mice. *Science, 203,* 68–69. (10)

Stricker, E.M. (1969). Osmoregulation and volume regulation in rats: Inhibition of hypovolemic thirst by water. *American Journal of Physiology, 217,* 98–105. (10)

Stricker, E.M. (1976). Drinking by rats after lateral hypothalamic lesions: A new look at the lateral hypothalamic syndrome. *Journal of Comparative and Physiological Psychology, 90,* 127–143. (10)

Stricker, E.M. (1977). The renin-angiotensin system and thirst: A reevaluation. II. Drinking elicited in rats by caval ligation or isoproterenol. *Journal of Comparative and Physiological Psychology, 91,* 1220–1231. (10)

Stricker, E.M. (1983). Thirst and sodium appetite after colloid treatment in rats: Role of the renin-angiotensin-aldosterone system. *Behavioral Neuroscience, 97,* 725–737. (10)

Stricker, E.M., & Andersen, A.E. (1980). The lateral hypothalamic syndrome: Comparison with the syndrome of anorexia nervosa. *Life Sciences, 26,* 1927–1934. (10)

Stricker, E.M., Bradshaw, W.G., & McDonald, R.H., Jr. (1976). The renin-angiotensin system and thirst: A reevaluation. *Science, 194,* 1169–1171. (10)

Stricker, E.M., & Coburn, P.C. (1978). Osmoregulatory thirst in rats after lateral preoptic lesions. *Journal of Comparative and Physiological Psychology, 92,* 350–361. (10)

Stricker, E.M., Cooper, P.H., Marshall, J.F., & Zigmond, M.J. (1979). Acute homeostatic imbalances reinstate sensorimotor dysfunctions in rats with lateral hypothalamic lesions. *Journal of Comparative and Physiological Psychology, 93,* 512–521. (14)

Stricker, E.M., & Macarthur, J.P. (1974). Physiological bases for different effects of extravascular colloid treatments on water and NaCl solution drinking by rats. *Physiology & Behavior, 13,* 389–394. (10)

Stricker, E.M., Rowland, N., Saller, C.F., & Friedman, M.I. (1977). Homeostasis during hypoglycemia: Central control of adrenal secretion and peripheral control of feeding. *Science, 196,* 79–81. (10)

Stricker, E.M., Swerdloff, A.F., & Zigmond, M.J. (1978). Intrahypothalamic injections of kainic acid produce feeding and drinking deficits in rats. *Brain Research, 158,* 470–473. (10)

Stryker, M.P., Sherk, H., Leventhal, A.G., & Hirsch, H.V.B. (1978). Physiological consequences for the cat's visual cortex of effectively restricting early visual experience with oriented contours. *Journal of Neurophysiology, 41,* 896–909. (7)

Stunkard, A.J., Sørensen, T.I.A., Hanis, C., Teasdale, T.W., Chakraborty, R., Schull, W.J., & Schulsinger, F. (1986). An adoption study of human obesity. *New England Journal of Medicine, 314,* 193–198. (10)

Stuss, D.T., & Benson, D.F. (1984). Neuropsychological studies of the frontal lobes. *Psychological Bulletin, 95,* 3–28. (4)

Sudzak, P.D., Glowa, J.R., Crawley, J.N., Schwartz, R.D., Skolnick, P., & Paul, S.M. (1986). A selective imidazobenzodiazepine antagonist of ethanol in the rat. *Science, 234,* 1243–1247. (12)

Sullivan, R.C. (1980). Why do autistic children . . .? *Journal of Autism and Developmental Disorders, 10,* 231–241. (16)

Sulser, F., Gillespie, D.D., Mishra, R., & Manier, D.H. (1984). Desensitization by antidepressants of central norepinephrine receptor systems coupled to adenylate cyclase. *Annals of the New York Academy of Sciences, 430,* 91–101. (15)

Summers, W.K., Robins, E., & Reich, T. (1979). The natural history of acute organic mental syndrome after bilateral electroconvulsive therapy. *Biological Psychiatry, 14,* 905–912. (15)

Sussman, H.M., & MacNeilage, P.F. (1975). Hemispheric specialization for speech production and perception in stutterers. *Neuropsychologia, 13,* 19–26. (5)

Swaab, D.F., & Fliers, E. (1985). A sexually dimorphic nucleus in the human brain. *Science, 228,* 1112–1115. (11)

Swan, H., & Schatte, C. (1977). Antimetabolic extract from the brain of the hibernating ground squirrel *Citellus tridecemlineatus. Science, 195,* 84–85. (9)

Swash, M. (1972). Released involuntary laughter after temporal lobe infarction. *Journal of Neurology, Neurosurgery, and Psychiatry, 35,* 108–113. (12)

Szechtman, H., Ornstein, K., Teitelbaum, P., & Golani, I. (1985). The morphogenesis of stereotyped behavior induced by the dopamine receptor agonist apomorphine in the laboratory rat. *Neuroscience, 14,* 783–798. (8)

Szentágothai, J. (1983). Modular architectonic principle of neural centers. *Reviews of Physiology Biochemistry and Pharmacology, 98,* 11–61. (2)

Szymusiak, R., DeMory, A., Kittrell, M.W., & Satinoff, E. (1985). Diurnal changes in thermoregulatory behavior in rats with medial preoptic lesions. *American Journal of Physiology, 249,* R219–R227. (10)

Takeuchi, A. (1977). Junctional transmission: I. Postsynaptic mechanisms. In E.R. Kandel (Ed.), *Handbook of physiology* Section 1: Neurophysiology, Vol. 1, Cellular biology of neurons, Pt. 1 (pp. 295–327). Bethesda, MD: American Physiological Society. (3)

Tallman, J.F., Paul, S.M., Skolnick, P., & Gallager, D.W. (1980). Receptors for the age of anxiety: Pharmacology of the benzodiazepines. *Science, 207,* 274–281. (12)

Tan, T.-L., Kales, J.D., Kales, A., Soldatos, C.R., & Bixler, E.O. (1984). Biopsychobehavioral correlates of insomnia, IV: Diagnosis based on DSM-III. *American Journal of Psychiatry, 141,* 357–362. (9)

Tanabe, T., Iino, M., & Takagi, S.F. (1975). Discrimination of odors in olfactory bulb, pyriform-amygdaloid areas, and orbitofrontal cortex of the monkey. *Journal of Neurophysiology, 38,* 1284–1296. (6)

Tanzi, R.E., Gusella, J.F., Watkins, P.C., Bruns, G.A.P., St George-Hyslop, P., Van Keuren, M.L., Patterson, D., Pagan, S., Kurnit, D.M., & Neve, R. L. (1987). Amyloid beta protein gene: cDNA, mRNA distribution, and genetic linkage near the Alzheimer locus. *Science, 235,* 880–884. (13)

Tasker, R.R. (1976). Somatotopographic representation in the human thalamus, midbrain, and spinal cord. In T.P. Morley (Ed.), *Current controversies in neurosurgery* (pp. 485–495). Philadelphia: Saunders. (6)

Taub, E., & Berman, A.J. (1968). Movement and learning in the absence of sensory feedback. In S.J. Freedman (Ed.), *The neuropsychology of spatially oriented behavior* (pp. 173–192). Homewood, IL: Dorsey. (8)

Taylor, H.G. (1984). Early brain injury and cognitive development. In C.R. Almli & S. Finger (Eds.), *Early brain damage* (pp. 325–345). Orlando, FL: Academic. (14)

Teitelbaum, P. (1955). Sensory control of hypothalamic hyperphagia. *Journal of Comparative and Physiological Psychology, 48,* 156–163. (10)

Teitelbaum, P. (1957). Random and food-directed activity in hyperphagic and normal rats. *Journal of Comparative and Physiological Psychology, 1957, 50,* 486–490. (10)

Teitelbaum, P., & Epstein, A.N. (1962). The lateral hypothalamic syndrome. *Psychological Review, 69,* 74–90. (14)

Terman, G.W., & Liebeskind, J.C. (1986). Relation of stress-induced analgesia to stimulation-produced analgesia. *Annals of the New York Academy of Sciences, 467,* 300–308. (6)

Terrace, H.S., Petitto, L.A., Sanders, R.J., & Bever, T.G. (1979). Can an ape create a sentence? *Science, 206,* 891–902. (5)

Teyler, T.J., & DiScenna, P. (1986). The hippocampal memory indexing theory. *Behavioral Neuroscience, 100,* 147–154. (13)

Thomas, R.K. (1980). Evolution of intelligence: An approach to its assessment. *Brain Behavior and Evolution, 17,* 454–472. (4)

Thompson, D.A., & Campbell, R.G. (1977). Hunger in humans induced by 2-deoxy-D-glucose: Glucoprivic control of taste preference and food intake. *Science, 198,* 1065–1068. (10)

Thompson, J.K., Jarvie, G.J., Lahey, B.B., & Cureton, K.J. (1982). Exercise and obesity: Etiology, physiology, and intervention. *Psychological Bulletin, 91,* 55–79. (10)

Thompson, R. (1969). Localization of the "visual memory system" in the white rat. *Journal of Comparative and Physiological Psychology Monograph,* (Pt. 2), 1–29. (13)

Thompson, R. (1978). Localization of a "passive avoidance memory system" in the white rat. *Physiological Psychology, 6,* 263–274. (13)

Thompson, R.F. (1986). The neurobiology of learning and memory. *Science, 233,* 941–947. (13)

Thorley, G. (1984). Review of follow-up and follow-back studies of childhood hyperactivity. *Psychological Bulletin, 96,* 116–132. (15)

Tinbergen, N. (1973). The search for animal roots of human behavior. In N. Tinbergen, *The animal in its world,* Vol. 2 (pp. 161–174). Cambridge, MA: Harvard University. (1)

Tippin, J., & Henn, F.A. (1982). Modified leukotomy in the treatment of intractable obsessional neurosis. *American Journal of Psychiatry, 139,* 1601–1603. (4)

Tomkins, S. (1980). Affect as amplification: Some modifications in theory. In R. Plutchik & H. Kellerman (Eds.), *Emotion: Theory, research, and experience,* Vol. 1 (pp. 141–164). New York: Academic. (12)

Tootell, R.B., Silverman, M.S., & DeValois, R.L. (1981). Spatial frequency columns in primary visual cortex. *Science, 214,* 813–815. (7)

Toran-Allerand, C.D. (1976). Sex steroids and the development of the newborn mouse hypothalamus and preoptic area *in vitro:* Implications for sexual differentiation. *Brain Research, 106,* 407–412. (11)

Tordoff, M.G., Novin, D., & Russek, M. (1982). Effects of hepatic denervation on the anorexic response to epinephrine, amphetamine, and lithium chloride: A behavioral identification of glucostatic afferents. *Journal of Comparative and Physiological Psychology, 96,* 361–375. (10)

Torrey, E.F. (1986). Geographic variations in schizophrenia. In C. Shagass, R.C. Josiassen, W.H. Bridger, K.J. Weiss, D. Stoff, & G.M. Simpson (Ed.), *Biological Psychiatry 1985* (pp. 1080–1082). New York: Elsevier. (16)

Tosteson, D.C. (April 1981). Lithium and mania. *Scientific American, 244* (4), 164–174. (15)

Träskman, L., Åsberg, M., Bertilsson, L., & Sjöstrand, L. (1981). Monoamine metabolites in CSF and suicidal behavior. *Archives of General Psychiatry, 38,* 631–636. (12)

Travers, S.P., Pfaffmann, C., & Norgren, R. (1986). Convergence of lingual and palatal gustatory neural activity in the nucleus of the solitary tract. *Brain Research, 365,* 305–320. (6)

Traverse, J., & Latto, R. (1986). Impairments in route negotiation through a maze after dorsolateral frontal, inferior parietal or premotor lesions in cynomolgus monkeys. *Behavioural Brain Research, 20,* 203–215. (4)

Travis, A.M., & Woolsey, C.N. (1956). Motor performance of monkeys after bilateral partial and total cerebral decortications. *American Journal of Physical Medicine, 35,* 273–310. (14)

Treiser, S.L., Cascio, C.S., O'Donohue, T.L., Thoa, N.B., Jacobowitz, D.M., & Kellar, K.J. (1981). Lithium increases serotonin release and decreases serotonin receptors in the hippocampus. *Science, 213,* 1529–1532. (15)

Trevarthen, C. (1974). Cerebral embryology and the split brain. In M. Kinsbourne & W.L. Smith (Eds.), *Hemispheric disconnection and cerebral function* (pp. 208–236). Springfield, IL: Charles C Thomas. (5)

Trimble, M.R., & Thompson, P.J. (1986). Neuropsychological and behavioral sequelae of spontaneous seizures. *Annals of the New York Academy of Sciences, 462,* 284–292. (15)

Trivers, R.L. (1972). Parental investment and sexual selection. In B. Campbell (Ed.), *Sexual selection and the descent of man, 1871–1971* (pp. 136–179). Chicago: Aldine. (1)

Tsai, L., Stewart, M.A., & August, G. (1981). Implication of sex differences in the familial transmission of infantile autism. *Journal of Autism and Developmental Disorders, 11,* 165–173. (16)

Tucker, D.M. (1981). Lateral brain function, emotion, and conceptualization. *Psychological Bulletin, 89,* 19–46. (5)

Tunks, E.R., & Dermer, S.W. (1977). Carbamezepine in the dyscontrol syndrome associated with limbic system dysfunction. *Journal of Nervous and Mental Disease, 164,* 56–63. (12)

Turek, F.W. (1985). Circadian neural rhythms in mammals. *Annual Review of Physiology, 47,* 49–64. (9)

Turek, F.W., & Losee-Olson, S. (1986). A benzodiazepine used in the treatment of insomnia phase-shifts the mammalian circadian clock. *Nature, 321,* 167–168. (9)

Turner, S.M., Beidel, D.C., & Nathan, R.S. (1985). Biological factors in obsessive-compulsive disorders. *Psychological Disorders, 97,* 430–450. (12)

Udry, J.R., & Morris, N.M. (1968). Distribution of coitus in the menstrual cycle. *Nature, 220,* 593–596. (11)

Ulrich, G., Zeller, G., & Mühlbauer, H.-D. (1983). Studien zum Lateralitätsverhalten stationär behandelter endogen Depressiver. *Archiv für Psychiatrie und Nervenkrankheiten, 233,* 457–469. (15)

Ungerleider, L.G., & Pribram, K.H. (1977). Inferotemporal versus combined pulvinar-prestriate lesions in the rhesus monkey: Effects on color, object, and pattern discrimination. *Neuropsychologia, 15,* 481–498. (7)

Uphouse, L. (1980). Reevaluation of mechanisms that mediate brain differences between enriched and impoverished animals. *Psychological Bulletin, 88,* 215–232. (2)

Vaccarino, F.J., Pettit, H.O., Bloom, F.E., & Koob, G.F. (1985). Effects of intracerebroventricular administration of methyl naloxonium chloride on heroin self-administration in the rat. *Pharmacology Biochemistry & Behavior, 23,* 495–498. (12)

Vaillant, G.E., & Milofsky, E.S. (1982). The etiology of alcoholism. *American Psychologist, 37,* 494–503. (10)

Valenstein, E.S., & Beer, B. (1962). Reinforcing brain stimulation in competition with water reward and shock avoidance. *Science, 137,* 1052–1054. (12)

Valenstein, E.S., Cox, V.C., & Kakolewski, J.W. (1970). Reexamination of the role of the hypothalamus in motivation. *Psychological Review, 77,* 16–31. (1)

Valvo, A. (1971). *Sight restoration after long-term blindness.* New York: American Foundation for the Blind. (7)

Valzelli, L. (1973). The "isolation syndrome" in mice. *Psychopharmacologia, 31,* 305–320. (12)

Valzelli, L. (1980). *An approach to neuroanatomical and neurochemical psychophysiology.* Torino, Italy: C.G.Edizioni Medico Scientifiche. (3)

Valzelli, L. (1981a). Aggression and violence: A biological essay of the distinction. In L. Valzelli & L. Morgese (Eds.), *Aggression and violence* (pp. 39–60). Milano, Italy: Edizioni Saint Vincent. (12)

Valzelli, L. (1981b). Modulazione emotiva degli effetti delle benzodiazepine. In P. Fresia & R. Vertua (Eds.), *Nuove benzodiazepine: Aspetti strutturali, farmacodinamici e farmacocinetici* (pp. 53–65). Trieste: Istituto di Farmacologia e farmacognosia. (12)

Valzelli, L., & Bernasconi, S. (1979). Aggressiveness by isolation and brain serotonin turnover changes in different strains of mice. *Neuropsychobiology, 5,* 129–135. (12)

Valzelli, L., Bernasconi, S., & Dalessandro, M. (1983). Time-courses of P-CPA-induced depletion of brain serotonin and muricidal aggression in the rat. *Pharmacological Research Communications, 15,* 387–395. (12)

Valzelli, L., Bernasconi, S., & Garattini, S. (1981). p-Chlorophenylalanine-induced muricidal aggression in male and female laboratory rats. *Neuropsychobiology, 7,* 315–320. (12)

Valzelli, L., Bernasconi, S., & Sala, A. (1980). Piracetam activity may differ according to the age of the recipient mouse. *International Pharmacopsychiatry, 15,* 150–156. (13)

Valzelli, L., & Garattini, S. (1972). Biochemical and behavioural changes induced by isolation in rats. *Neuropharmacology, 11,* 17–22. (12)

Van den Aardweg, G.J. (1984). Parents of homosexuals—not guilty? Interpretation of childhood psychological data. *American Journal of Psychiatry, 38,* 180–189. (11)

Vanderweele, D.A., Novin, D., Rezek, M., & Sanderson, J.D. (1974). Duodenal or hepatic-portal glucose perfusion: Evidence for duodenally based satiety. *Physiology & Behavior, 12,* 467–473. (10)

van Essen, D.C., Newsome, W.T., & Bixby, J.L. (1982). The pattern of interhemispheric connections and its relationship to extrastriate visual areas in the macaque monkey. *Journal of Neuroscience, 2,* 265–283. (7)

van Haaren, F., van Zanten, S., & van de Poll, N.E. (1986). Vasopressin disrupts radial-maze performance in rats. *Behavioral and Neural Biology, 45,* 350–357. (13)

van Praag, H.M. (1977). The significance of the cerebral dopamine metabolism in the pathogenesis and treatment of psychotic disorders. In E.S. Gershon, R.H. Belmaker, S.S. Kety, & M. Rosenbaum (Eds.), *The impact of biology on modern psychiatry* (pp. 1–26). New York: Plenum. (16)

van Sommers, P., & Teitelbaum, P. (1974). Spread of damage produced by electrolytic lesions in the hypothalamus. *Journal of Comparative and Physiological Psychology, 86,* 288–299. (14)

Van Valen, L. (1974). Brain size and intelligence in man. *American Journal of Physical Anthropology, 40,* 417–423. (4)

Van Zoeren, J.G., & Stricker, E.M. (1977). Effects of preoptic, lateral hypothalamic, or dopamine-depleting lesions on behavioral thermoregulation in rats exposed to the cold. *Journal of Comparative and Physiological Psychology, 91,* 989–999. (10)

Varley, C.K., & Trupin, E.W. (1983). Double-blind assessment of stimulant medication for attention deficit disorder: A model for clinical application. *American Journal of Orthopsychiatry, 53,* 542–547. (15)

Varon, S.S., & Somjen, G.G. (1979). Neuron-glia interactions. *Neurosciences Research Program Bulletin, 17,* 1–239. (2)

Verbalis, J.G., McCann, M.J., McHale, C.M., & Stricker, E.M. (1986). Oxytocin secretion in response to cholecystokinin and food: Differentiation of nausea from satiety. *Science, 232,* 1417–1419. (10)

Victor, M., Adams, R.D., & Collins, G.H. (1971). *The Wernicke-Korsakoff syndrome.* Philadelphia: F.A. Davis. (13)

Vogel, G.W., Thompson, F.C., Jr., Thurmond, A., & Rivers, B. (1973). The effect of REM deprivation on depression. In W.P. Koella & P. Levin (Eds.), *Sleep: Physiology, biochemistry, psychology, pharmacology, clinical implications* (pp. 191–195). Basel: Karger. (15)

vom Saal, F.S., Grant, W.M., McMullen, C.W., & Laves, K.S. (1983). High fetal estrogen concentrations: Correlation with increased adult sexual activity and decreased aggression in male mice. *Science, 220,* 1306–1309. (11)

von Békésy, G. (1956). Current status of theories of hearing. *Science, 123,* 779–783. (6)

von Békésy, G. (1957). The ear. *Scientific American, 197* (2), 66–78. (6)

von Holst, E., & von St. Paul, U. (1960). Vom Wirkungsgefüge der Triebe. *Naturwissenschaften, 47,* 409–422. (1)

Wada, J., & Rasmussen, T. (1960). Intracarotid injection of sodium amytal for the lateralization of cerebral speech dominance. *Journal of Neurosurgery, 17,* 266–282. (4)

Wald, G. (1968). Molecular basis of visual excitation. *Science, 162,* 230–239. (6)

Wallesch, C.-W., Henriksen, L., Kornhuber, H.-H., & Paulson, O.B. (1985). Observations on regional cerebral blood flow in cortical and subcortical structures during language production in normal man. *Brain and Language, 25,* 224–233. (5)

Wallman, J., & Pettigrew, J.D. (1985). Conjugate and disjunctive saccades in two avian species with contrasting oculomotor strategies. *Journal of Neuroscience, 5,* 1418–1428. (6)

Ward, I.L. (1972). Prenatal stress feminizes and demasculinizes the behavior of males. *Science, 175,* 82–84. (11)

Ward, I.L. (1977). Exogenous androgen activates female behavior in noncopulating, prenatally stressed male rats. *Journal of Comparative and Physiological Psychology, 91,* 465–471. (11)

Ward, I.L., & Reed, J. (1985). Prenatal stress and prepubertal social rearing conditions interact to determine sexual behavior in male rats. *Behavioral Neuroscience, 99,* 301–309. (11)

Ward, I.L., & Weisz, J. (1980). Maternal stress alters plasma testosterone in fetal males. *Science, 207,* 328–329. (11)

Watkins, L.R., & Mayer, D.J. (1982). Organization of endogenous opiate and nonopiate pain control systems. *Science, 216,* 1185–1192. (6)

Watson, C.G., Tilleskjor, C., Kucala, T., & Jacobs, L. (1984). The birth seasonality effect in nonschizophrenic psychiatric patients. *Journal of Clinical Psychology, 40,* 884–888. (16)

Webb, W.B. (1974). Sleep as an adaptive response. *Perceptual and Motor Skills, 38,* 1023–1027. (9)

Wegner, J.T., Catalano, F., Gibralter, J., & Kane, J.M. (1985). Schizophrenics with tardive dyskinesia. *Archives of General Psychiatry, 42,* 860–865. (16)

Wehr, T.A., Jacobsen, F.M., Sack, D.A., Arendt, J., Tamarkin, L., & Rosenthal, N.E. (1986). Phototherapy of seasonal affective disorder. *Archives of General Psychiatry, 43,* 870–875. (15)

Weinberger, D.R., Berman, K.F., & Zec, R.F. (1986). Physiologic dysfunction of dorsolateral prefrontal cortex in schizophrenia. I. Regional cerebral blood flow evidence. *Archives of General Psychiatry, 43,* 114–124. (16)

Weiner, R.D. (1979). The psychiatric use of electrically induced seizures. *American Journal of Psychiatry, 136,* 1507–1517. (15)

Weiner, R.D. (1984). Does electroconvulsive therapy cause brain damage? *The Behavioral and Brain Sciences, 7,* 1–53. (15)

Weingarten, H.P., Chang, P.K., & Jarvie, K.R. (1983). Reactivity of normal and VMH-lesion rats to quinine-adulterated foods: Negative evidence for negative finickiness. *Behavioral Neuroscience, 97,* 221–233. (10)

Weiskrantz, L., Warrington, E.K., Sanders, M.D., & Marshall, J. (1974). Visual capacity in the hemianopic field following a restricted occipital ablation. *Brain, 97,* 709–728. (7)

Weiss, B. (1982). Food additives and environmental chemicals as sources of childhood behavior disorders. *Journal of the American Academy of Child Psychiatry, 21,* 144–152. (15)

Weiss, J.M. (1968). Effects of coping responses on stress. *Journal of Comparative and Physiological Psychology*, 65, 251–260. (12)

Weiss, J.M. (1971a). Effects of coping behavior in different warning signal conditions on stress pathology in rats. *Journal of Comparative and Physiological Psychology*, 77, 1–13. (12)

Weiss, J.M. (1971b). Effects of punishing the coping response (conflict) on stress pathology in rats. *Journal of Comparative and Physiological Psychology*, 77, 14–21. (12)

Weiss, P. (1941). Self-differentiation of the basic patterns of coordination. *Comparative Psychology Monographs*, 17 (4). (8)

Weissman, M.M., Gershon, E.S., Kidd, K.K., Prusoff, B.A., Leckman, J.F., Dibble, E., Hamovit, J., Thompson, D., Pauls, D.L., & Guroff, J.J. (1984). Psychiatric disorders in the relatives of probands with affective disorders. *Archives of General Psychiatry*, 41, 13–21. (15)

Weissman, M.M., Merikangas, K.R., Wickramaratne, P., Kidd, K.K., Prusoff, B.A., Leckman, J.F., & Pauls, D.L. (1986). Understanding the clinical heterogeneity of major depression using family data. *Archives of General Psychiatry*, 43, 430–434. (15)

Weisz, J., Brown, B.L., & Ward, I.L. (1982). Maternal stress decreases steroid aromatase activity in brains of male and female rat fetuses. *Neuroendocrinology*, 35, 374–379. (11)

Weitzman, E.D. (1981). Sleep and its disorders. *Annual Review of Neurosciences*, 4, 381–417. (9)

Weitzman, E.D., Czeisler, C.A., Coleman, R.M., Spielman, A.J., Zimmerman, J.C., & Dement, W. (1981). Delayed sleep phase syndrome. *Archives of General Psychiatry*, 38, 737–746. (9)

Wender, P.H., Kety, S.S., Rosenthal, D., Schulsinger, F., Ortmann, J., & Lunde, I. (1986). Psychiatric disorders in the biological and adoptive families of adopted individuals with affective disorders. *Archives of General Psychiatry*, 43, 923–929. (15)

Wender, P.H., Rosenthal, D., Kety, S.S., Schulsinger, F., & Welner, J. (1974). Crossfostering: A research strategy for clarifying the role of genetic and experiential factors in the etiology of schizophrenia. *Archives of General Psychiatry*, 30, 121–128. (16)

West, J.R., Hodges, C.A., & Black, A.C., Jr. (1981). Prenatal exposure to ethanol alters the organization of hippocampal mossy fibers in rats. *Science*, 211, 957–959. (2)

Whishaw, I.Q., & Kolb, B. (1979). Neocortical and hippocampal EEG in rats during lateral hypothalamic lesion-induced hyperkinesia: Relations to behavior and effects of atropine. *Physiology & Behavior*, 22, 1107–1113. (14)

Whishaw, I.Q., & Robinson, T.E. (1974). Comparison of anodal and cathodal lesions and metal deposition in eliciting postoperative locomotion in the rat. *Physiology & Behavior*, 13, 539–551. (14)

Whishaw, I.Q., Schallert, T., & Kolb, B. (1981). An analysis of feeding and sensorimotor abilities of rats after decortication. *Journal of Comparative and Physiological Psychology*, 95, 85–103. (14)

Whitaker, H. (1976). A case of the isolation of the language function. In H. Whitaker & H.A. Whitaker (Eds.), *Studies in neurolinguistics* (Vol. 2) (pp. 1–58). New York: Academic. (5)

White, F.J., & Wang, R.Y. (1983). Differential effects of classical and atypical antipsychotic drugs on A9 and A10 dopamine neurons. *Science*, 221, 1054–1057. (16)

Whitty, C.W.M., & Zangwill, O.L. (1977). Traumatic amnesia. In C.W.M. Whitty & O.L. Zangwill (Eds.), *Amnesia* (2nd ed.) (pp. 118–135). London: Butterworths. (13)

Wiesel, T.N. (1982). Postnatal development of the visual cortex and the influence of environment. *Nature*, 299, 583–591. (7)

Wiesel, T.N., & Hubel, D.H. (1963a). Effects of visual deprivation on morphology and physiology of cells in the cat's lateral geniculate body. *Journal of Neurophysiology*, 26, 978–993. (7)

Wiesel, T.N., & Hubel, D.H. (1963b). Single-cell responses in striate cortex of kittens deprived of vision in one eye. *Journal of Neurophysiology*, 26, 1003–1017. (7)

Wiesel, T.N., & Hubel, D.H. (1965). Comparison of the effects of unilateral and bilateral eye closure on cortical unit responses in kittens. *Journal of Neurophysiology*, 28, 1029–1040. (7)

Wiesendanger, M. (1984). Pyramidal tract function and the clinical "pyramidal syndrome." *Human Neurobiology*, 2, 227–234. (8)

Wietgrefe, S., Zupancic, M., Haase, A., Chesebro, B., Race, R., Frey, W. II, Rustan, T., & Friedman, R.L. (1985). Cloning of a gene whose expression is increased in scrapie and in senile plaques in human brain. *Science*, 230, 1177–1179. (13)

Wild, H.M., Butler, S.R., Carden, D., & Kulikowski, J.J. (1985). Primate cortical area V4 important for colour constancy but not wavelength discrimination. *Nature*, 313, 133–135. (6)

Wilson, D.S. (1975). A theory of group selection. *Proceedings of the National Academy of Sciences, U.S.A.*, 72, 143–146. (1)

Wilson, J.D., George, F.W., & Griffin, J.E. (1981). The hormonal control of sexual development. *Science*, 211, 1278–1284. (11)

Winblad, B., Hardy, J., Bäckman, L., & Nilsson, L.-G. (1985). Memory function and brain biochemistry in normal aging and in senile dementia. *Annals of the New York Academy of Sciences*, 444, 255–268. (13)

Windle, W.F., Littrell, J.L., Smart, J.O., & Joralemon, J. (1956). Regeneration in the cord of spinal monkeys. *Neurology*, 6, 420–428. (14)

Winfree, A.T. (1983). Impact of a circadian clock on the timing of human sleep. *American Journal of Physiology*, 245, R497–R504. (9)

Winocur, G. (1982). Radial-arm-maze behavior by rats with dorsal hippocampal lesions: Effects of cuing. *Journal of Comparative and Physiological Psychology*, 96, 155–169. (13)

Winslade, W.J., Liston, E.H., Ross, J.W., & Weber, K.D. (1984). Medical, judicial, and statutory regulation of ECT in the United States. *American Journal of Psychiatry*, 141, 1349–1355. (15)

Wintrob, R.M. (1973). The influence of others: Witchcraft and rootwork as explanations of behavior disturbances. *Journal of Nervous and Mental Disease*, 156, 318–326. (12)

Wirz-Justice, A., Groos, G.A., & Wehr, T.A. (1982). The neuropharmacology of circadian timekeeping in mammals. In J. Aschoff, S. Daan, & G.A. Groos (Eds.), *Vertebrate circadian rhythms* (pp. 183–193). Berlin: Springer-Verlag. (15)

Wise, R.A., & Bozarth, M.A. (1984). Brain reward circuitry: Four circuit elements "wired" in apparent series. *Brain Research Bulletin, 12,* 203–208. (12)

Wishart, T.B., & Walls, E.K. (1975). Water intoxication death following hypothalamic lesions in the rat. *Physiology & Behavior, 15,* 377–379. (10)

Wisniewski, H.M., & Kozlowski, P.B. (1982). Evidence for blood-brain barrier changes in senile dementia of the Alzheimer type (SDAT). *Annals of the New York Academy of Sciences, 396,* 119–129. (13)

Witelson, S.F. (1977). Developmental dyslexia: Two right hemispheres and none left. *Science, 195,* 309–311. (5)

Witelson, S.F. (1985). The brain connection: The corpus callosum is larger in left-handers. *Science, 229,* 665–668. (5)

Witelson, S.F., & Pallie, W. (1973). Left hemisphere specialization for language in the newborn: Neuroanatomical evidence of asymmetry. *Brain, 96,* 641–646. (5)

Witkin, H.A., Mednick, S.A., Schulsinger, F., Bakkestrom, E., Christiansen, K.O., Goodenough, D.R., Hirschhorn, K., Lundesteen, C., Owen, D.R., Philip, J., Rubin, D.B., & Stocking, M. (1976). Criminality in XYY and XXY men. *Science, 193,* 547–555. (11)

Wolf, G., Schulkin, J., & Fluharty, J.J. (1983). Recovery of salt appetite after lateral hypothalamic lesions: Effects of preoperative salt drive and salt intake experiences. *Behavioral Neuroscience, 97,* 506–511. (14)

Wolgin, D.L., Cytawa, J., & Teitelbaum, P. (1976). The role of activation in the regulation of food intake. In D. Novin, W. Wyrwicka, & G. Bray (Eds.), *Hunger: Basic mechanisms and clinical implications* (pp. 179–191). New York: Raven. (9)

Wolgin, D.L., Hein, A., & Teitelbaum, P. (1980). Recovery of forelimb placing after lateral hypothalamic lesions in the cat: Parallels and contrasts with development. *Journal of Comparative and Physiological Psychology, 94,* 795–807. (14)

Wolkin, A., Jaeger, J., Brodie, J.D., Wolf, A.P., Fowler, J., Rotrosen, J., Gomez-Mont, F., & Cancro, R. (1985). Persistence of cerebral metabolic abnormalities in chronic schizophrenia as determined by positron emission tomography. *American Journal of Psychiatry, 142,* 564–571. (16)

Wong, D.F., Wagner, H.N., Jr., Dannals, R.F., Links, J.M., Frost, J.J., Ravert, H.T., Wilson, A.A., Rosenbaum, A.E., Gjedde, A., Douglass, K.H., Petronis, J.D., Folstein, M.F., Toung, J.K.T., Burns, H.D., & Kuhar, M.J. (1984). Effects of age on dopamine and serotonin receptors measured by positron tomography in the living human brain. *Science, 226,* 1393–1396. (13)

Woodruf-Pak, D.S., Lavond, D.G., & Thompson, R.F. (1985). Trace conditioning: Abolished by cerebellar nuclear lesions but not lateral cerebellar cortex aspirations. *Brain Research, 348,* 249–260. (13)

Woods, S.W., Charney, D.S., Loke, J., Goodman, W.K., Redmond, D.E., Jr., & Heninger, G.R. (1986). Carbon dioxide sensitivity in panic anxiety. *Archives of General Psychiatry, 43,* 900–909. (12)

Wooley, O.W., Wooley, S.C., & Dunham, R.B. (1972). Can calories be perceived and do they affect hunger in obese and nonobese humans? *Journal of Comparative and Physiological Psychology, 80,* 250–258. (10)

Woolsey, C.N. (1981). *Cortical sensory organization, Vol. 2: Multiple visual areas.* Clifton, NJ: Humana. (7)

Woolston, D.C., & Erickson, R.P. (1979). Concept of neuron types in gustation in the rat. *Journal of Neurophysiology, 42,* 1390–1409. (6)

Wurtman, J.J. (1985). Neurotransmitter control of carbohydrate consumption. *Annals of the New York Academy of Sciences, 443,* 145–151. (3)

Wurtman, R.J. (1982). Nutrients that modify brain function. *Scientific American, 246* (4), 50–59. (3)

Wurtman, R.J. (1983). Behavioural effects of nutrients. *Lancet, 1* (8334), 1145–1147. (3)

Wurtman, R.J., Hefti, F., & Melamed, E. (1981). Precursor control of neurotransmitter synthesis. *Pharmacological Reviews, 32,* 315–335. (3)

Wurtz, R.H., & Albano, J.E. (1980). Visual-motor function of the primate superior colliculus. *Annual Review of Neuroscience, 3,* 189–226. (7)

Wyatt, R.J., Termini, B.A., & Davis, J. (1971). Biochemical and sleep studies of schizophrenia: A review of the literature 1960–1970: Part I. Biochemical studies. *Schizophrenia Bulletin, 4,* 10–66. (16)

Yamamoto, T. (1984). Taste responses of cortical neurons. *Progress in Neurobiology, 23,* 273–315. (6)

Yamamoto, T., Yuyama, N., Kato, T., & Kawamura, Y. (1985). Gustatory responses of cortical neurons in rats. II. Information processing of taste quality. *Journal of Neuroscience, 53,* 1356–1369. (6)

Yarsh, T.L., Farb, D.H., Leeman, S.E., & Jessell, T.M. (1979). Intrathecal capsaicin depletes substance P in the rat spinal cord and produces prolonged thermal analgesia. *Science, 206,* 481–483. (6)

Yaryura-Tobias, J.A. (1977). Obsessive-compulsive disorders: A serotoninergic hypothesis. *Journal of Orthomolecular Psychiatry, 6,* 317–326. (12)

Yaryura-Tobias, J.A., & Neziroglu, F.A. (1981). Aggressive behavior, clinical interfaces. In L. Valzelli & L. Morgese (Eds.), *Aggression and violence: A psycho/biological and clinical approach* (pp. 195–210). Milano, Italy: Edizioni Saint Vincent. (12)

Yau, K.-W., Matthews, G., & Baylor, D.A. (1979). Thermal activation of the visual transduction mechanism in retinal rods. *Nature, 279,* 806–807. (6)

Yaxley, S., Rolls, E.T., Sienkiewicz, Z.J., & Scott, T.R. (1985). Satiety does not affect gustatory activity in the nucleus of the solitary tract of the alert monkey. *Brain Research, 347,* 85–93. (6)

Yeni-Komshian, G.H., & Benson, D.A. (1976). Anatomical study of cerebral asymmetry in the temporal lobe of humans, chimpanzees, and rhesus monkeys. *Science, 192,* 387–389. (5)

Yost, W.A., & Nielsen, D.W. (1977). *Fundamentals of hearing.* New York: Holt, Rinehart, & Winston. (6)

Young, W.C., Goy, R.W., & Phoenix, C.H. (1964). Hormones and sexual behavior. Science, 143, 212–218. (11)

Zagrodzka, J., & Fonberg, E. (1979). Alimentary instrumental responses and neurological reflexes in amygdalar cats. *Acta Neurobiologiae Experimentalis, 39,* 143–156. (12)

Zahn, T.P., Rapoport, J.L., & Thompson, C.L. (1980). Autonomic and behavioral effects of dextroamphetamine and placebo in normal and hyperactive prepubertal boys. *Journal of Abnormal Child Psychology, 8,* 145–160. (15)

Zametkin, A., Rapoport, J.L., Murphy, D.L., Linnoila, M., & Ismond, D. (1985). Treatment of hyperactive children with monoamine oxidase inhibitors. I. Clinical efficacy. *Archives of General Psychiatry, 42,* 962–966. (15)

Zarrow, M.X., Gandelman, R., & Denenberg, V.H. (1971). Prolactin: Is it an essential hormone for maternal behavior in the mammal? *Hormones and Behavior, 2,* 343–354. (11)

Zeigler, H.P., Jacquin, M.F., & Miller, M.G. (1985). Trigeminal orosensation and ingestive behavior in the rat. *Progress in Psychobiology and Physiological Psychology, 11,* 63–196. (10)

Zeki, S. (1980). The representation of colours in the cerebral cortex. *Nature, 284,* 412–418. (6)

Zeki, S. (1983). Colour coding in the cerebral cortex: The responses of wavelength-selective and colour-coded cells in monkey visual cortex to changes in wavelength composition. *Neuroscience, 9,* 767–781. (6)

Żernicki, B., Gandolfo, G., Glin, L., & Gottesmann, C. (1984). Cerveau isolé and pretrigeminal rats. *Acta Neurobiologiae Experimentalis, 44,* 159–177. (9)

Zigmond, M.J., & Stricker, E.M. (1972). Deficits in feeding behavior after intraventricular injection of 6-hydroxydopamine in rats. *Science, 177,* 1211–1214. (14)

Zigmond, M.J., & Stricker, E.M. (1973). Recovery of feeding and drinking by rats after intraventricular 6-hydroxydopamine or lateral hypothalamic lesions. *Science, 182,* 717–719. (14)

Zihl, J. (1980). "Blindsight": Improvement of visually guided eye movements by systematic practice in patients with cerebral blindness. *Neuropsychologia, 18,* 71–77. (7)

Zimmerman, M., Coryell, W., & Pfohl, B. (1986). The validity of the dexamethasone suppression test as a marker for endogenous depression. *Archives of General Psychiatry, 43,* 347–355. (15)

Zimmerman, M.B., Blaine, E.H., & Stricker, E.M. (1981). Water intake in hypovolemic sheep: Effects of crushing the left atrial appendage. *Science, 211,* 489–491. (10)

Zola-Morgan, S., & Squire, L.R. (1986). Memory impairment in monkeys following lesions limited to the hippocampus. *Behavioral Neuroscience, 100,* 155–160. (13)

Zola-Morgan, S., Squire, L.R., & Amarai, D.G. (1986). Human amnesia and the medial temporal region: Enduring memory impairment following a bilateral lesion limited to field CA1 of the hippocampus. *Journal of Neuroscience, 6,* 2950–2967. (13)

Zola-Morgan, S., Squire, L.R., & Mishkin, M. (1982). The neuroanatomy of amnesia: Amygdala-hippocampus versus temporal stem. *Science, 218,* 1337–1339. (13)

Zornetzer, S.F. (1985). Catecholamine system involvement in age-related memory dysfunction. *Annals of the New York Academy of Sciences, 444,* 242–254. (13)

Zucker, R.S., & Landò, L. (1986). Mechanism of transmitter release: Voltage hypothesis and calcium hypothesis. *Science, 231,* 574–579. (3)

Zurif, E.B. (1980). Language mechanisms: A neuropsychological perspective. *American Scientist, 68,* 305–311. (5)

Zussman, L., Zussman, S., Sunley, R., & Bjornson, E. (1981). Sexual response after hysterectomy-oophorectomy: Recent studies and reconsideration of psychogenesis. *American Journal of Obstetrics and Gynecology, 140,* 725–729. (11)

Zwislocki, J.J. (1981). Sound analysis in the ear: A history of discoveries. *American Scientist, 69,* 184–192. (6)

Subject Index

Name Index

U

Uchizono, K., 259
Udry, J.R., 307
Uhde, T.W., 426
Uihlein, A., 11
Ulpian, C. *See* Seeman, P.
Ulrich, G., 420, 421
Ungerleider, L.G., 196
Uphouse, L., 32
Urbá Holmgren, R., 238

V

Vaccarino, F.J., 348
Vaillant, G.E., 289, 292, 449
Valenstein, E.S., 9, 20, 347
Valentino, D., 268
Valvo, A., 201
Valzelli, L., 57, 257, 339, 340, 345, 350, 366, 419
VanBuskirk, R.L., 175, 176
Vance, S., 354
van Cauter, E. *See* Désir, D.
Van den Aardweg, G.J., 315
van de Poll, N.E., 366
van der Kooy, D., 177
Vanderweele, D.A., 279
van Essen, D.C., 190
van Haaren, F., 366
van Hoesen, G.W., 375
Van Keuren, M.L. *See* Tanzi, R.E.
van Praag, H.M., 445
van Sommers, P., 392
Van Valen, L., 74
van Zanten, S., 366
Van Zoeren, J.G., 270
Varga, E., 425
Varley, C.K., 429
Varon, S.S., 29
Vasavada, N. *See* Rush, A.J.
Vaughn, L.K., 271
Verbalis, J.G., 280
Vey, M.M., 129
Victor, M., 373
Vilberg, T., 454
Villars, T., 170
Villiger, J.W., 366
Vitek, D.J., 191
Vogel, G.W., 426
Volpe, B.T., 140
vom Saal, F.S., 310
von Békésy, G., 157, 161
von Helmholtz, H., 151, 159
von Holst, E., 9
von St. Paul, U., 9

W

Waber, P.G. *See* Folstein, S.E.
Wada, J., 107

Wagner, H.N., Jr. *See* Wong, D.F.
Wagner, N., 129, 130
Wahlström, J., 453
Wald, G., 150, 152
Walker, D.W., 33
Walker, H.T., Jr., 318
Walker, J.A., 378
Walker, P.A., 307
Wall, P.D., 177
Wallace, M.R. *See* Gusella, J.F.
Wallesch, C.-W., 134
Wallman, J., 149, 178
Walls, E.K., 285
Walsh, D., 275
Wang, R.Y., 446, 447
Warach, J.D., 99
Ward, I.L., 310, 315, 316
Warrington, E.K., 199
Watanabe, M., 190
Waterhouse, J.M., 237
Waterhouse, L., 451
Watkins, L.R., 178
Watkins, P.C. *See* Gusella, J.F.; St. George-Hyslop, P.H.; Tanzi, R.E.
Watson, C.G., 441
Watson, F.L., 237
Watson, J.B., 327, 353
Way, S., 364
Webb, W., 140
Webb, W.B., 244
Weber, K.D., 424
Webster, F.A., 3, 145
Wechkin, S.W. *See* Gash, D.M.
Weddle, M.G., 342
Wegner, J.T., 447
Wehr, T.A., 426, 427. *See also* Lewy, A.J.; Rosenthal, N.E.
Weinberger, A., 122
Weinberger, D.R., 438
Weinberger, N.M., 382
Weiner, R.D., 424
Weingarten, H.P., 286
Weingartner, H., 354, 368
Weinrich, J.D., 315
Weiskrantz, L., 199
Weiss, B., 430
Weiss, G.H., 429. *See also* Mohr, P.
Weiss, J.M., 326
Weiss, P., 213
Weissman, M.M., 416. *See also* Robins, L.N.
Weisz, J., 315
Weitzman, E.D., 238, 240, 260–262, 425
Wells, J., 408
Welner, J., 440
Wender, P.H., 416, 440
Wernicke, C., 135, 138
Werz, M.A., 378

West, J.R., 33
Westerman, J.A., 126
Westlake, J.R., 452
Westreich, S., 279
Wetzel, C.D., 424
Wever, E.G., 145
Wever, R., 238
Wexler, N.S., 224, 225. *See also* Gusella, J.F.
Wheeler, R.L., 258
Whipple, B., 178
Whishaw, I.Q., 390, 392, 393, 401, 438
Whitaker, H., 140
White, F.J., 446, 447
Whitney, G., 228
Whitty, C.W.M., 370
Wible, C.G., 379
Wickham, M.G., 149
Wickramaratne, P. *See* Weissman, M.M.
Wiedeking, C., 307
Wiesel, T.N., 117, 190–193, 196, 200, 201, 205
Wiesendanger, M., 227
Wietgrefe, S., 375
Wild, H.M., 154
Wild, K.V., 414
Wildman, H.E., 281
Wilkinson, J.M. *See* Kosel, K.C.
Williams, A., 222
Williams, B.A., 270
Williams, R.L., 456
Williams, T.H. *See* Kosel, K.C.
Wilson, A.A. *See* Wong, D.F.
Wilson, D.H., 119, 140
Wilson, D.S., 15
Wilson, G.S., 453
Wilson, I.C., 416
Wilson, J.D., 300
Wilson, M.A., 236
Winans, S.S., 167
Winblad, B., 375
Windle, W.F., 394
Winfree, A.T., 239
Winocur, G., 379
Winokur, A., 342. *See also* Amsterdam, J.D.
Winslade, W.J., 424
Winter, J.B., 243
Wintrob, R.M., 326
Wirtshafter, D., 280
Wirz-Justice, A., 426, 428
Wise, C.D., 438, 439
Wise, R.A., 348
Wishart, T.B., 285
Wisniewski, H.M., 375
Wistedt, B., 440
Witelson, S.F., 125, 127, 128